Criminal Law and Procedure for Legal Professionals

John P. Feldmeier, J.D., Ph.D.
Wright State University

Frank Schmalleger, Ph.D.
*Distinguished Professor Emeritus,
The University of North Carolina at Pembroke*

Prentice Hall
Boston   Columbus   Indianapolis   New York   San Francisco   Upper Saddle River
Amsterdam   Cape Town   Dubai   London   Madrid   Milan   Munich   Paris   Montreal   Toronto
Delhi   Mexico City   Sao Paulo   Sydney   Hong Kong   Seoul   Singapore   Taipei   Tokyo

Editor in Chief: Vernon Anthony
Acquisitions Editor: Gary Bauer
Editorial Assistant: Tanika Henderson
Director of Marketing: David Gesell
Senior Marketing Manager: Leigh Ann Sims
Senior Marketing Assistant: Les Roberts
Project Manager: Holly Shufeldt
Senior Art Director: Jayne Conte
Manager, Rights and Permissions: Karen Sanatar
Cover Art: Alamy
Full-Service Project Management and Composition: Integra Software Services Pvt. Ltd.
Printer/Binder: RR Donnelley
Cover Printer: RR Donnelley
Text Font: Minion

Credits and acknowledgments borrowed from other sources and reproduced, with permission, in this textbook appear on appropriate page within text (or on page 582).

Library of Congress Cataloging-in-Publication Data

Feldmeier, John P. (John Phillip)
  Criminal law and procedure for legal professionals / John P. Feldmeier, Frank Schmalleger.
    p. cm.
  Includes bibliographical references and index.
  ISBN-13: 978-0-13-802116-0
  ISBN-10: 0-13-802116-3
  1. Criminal law—United States—Outlines, syllabi, etc.   2. Criminal procedure—United States—Outlines, syllabi, etc.   3. Criminal justice, Administration of—United States—Outlines, syllabi, etc.   I. Schmalleger, Frank.   II. Title.
  KF9219.85.F45 2012
  345.73—dc22

                                                          2010054534

10 9 8 7 6 5 4

Prentice Hall
is an imprint of

www.pearsonhighered.com

ISBN 10:   0-13-802116-3
ISBN 13: 978-0-13-802116-0

Dedication

To Emma and Jack, may you never have a personal need for the materials in this book.
John Feldmeier

For Willow
Frank Schmalleger

Contents

CHAPTER 3   Criminal Liability and the Essence of Crime   59

CHAPTER 10   Pretrial Procedures: Discovery, Motions, the Exclusionary Rule, and Plea Bargaining   353

CHAPTER 13   Rights to a Fair Trial: Due Process, Speedy Trial, Juries, Counsel, and Double Jeopardy   468

CHAPTER 14   Postconviction Procedures: Motions, Sentences, Appeals, and Habeas Corpus   510

Preface

This textbook brings together John Feldmeier, a criminal defense attorney and associate professor, and Frank Schmalleger, an acclaimed professor and scholar who has published dozens of textbooks and numerous scholarly articles exploring the highly dynamic world of crime, courts, and the criminally accused, to produce a textbook on criminal law and procedure that is designed for undergraduate and graduate students who are studying to become legal professionals.

In this book, the authors seek to bridge the gap between the theoretical presentations of criminal law and procedure and the practical realities of working in the field. The goal of this book is to help students build a solid knowledge base and the analytical and functional skills they will need to enter the legal field as paralegals, legal assistants, court administrators, and criminal justice professionals, as well as to prepare students for law school.

For many readers, this book will be their first formal introduction to criminal law and procedure. As a result, the text provides readers with a thorough, yet readable, introduction to the essential legal terms, doctrines, cases, and procedures that govern American criminal justice systems. But recognizing that many readers of the text are expecting, or at least hoping, to become criminal justice professionals, the book also illustrates many of the day-to-day realities of working in the field.

For example, a criminal law and procedure book would not be complete without a discussion of the "exclusionary rule" used to assess the legal pedigree of criminal evidence. This legal standard, along with relevant cases, terms, and doctrines, is, of course, thoroughly discussed in the text. But the book also requires students to move beyond the theoretical and into the practical realities of the exclusionary rule by providing actual motions to suppress, so that students can assess how the rule is actually used in legal pleadings. By examining these real-life materials, students can appreciate the realities of situations in which criminal justice professionals regularly find themselves.

This is just one of many opportunities the book provides in an effort to engage students in hypothetical (or even, real-pathetical) cases, requiring them to apply and interact with the book's material. At the end of each chapter, students are given analytical exercises, research projects, and writing assignments. Many of these items are derived from the actual experiences of real legal professionals in criminal cases, with numerous insights and examples of what legal professionals really do on a day-to-day basis. In addition, the book contains many sections that offer practical insights and daily realities of working in the criminal justice profession. Each chapter also contains excerpts from court opinions, including many of the landmark rulings by the U.S. Supreme Court.

The book covers each of the basic stages of the criminal justice system, from the initial investigation of a crime to the punishment and appellate phases. At each step, the book encourages the reader to appreciate that criminal law and procedure are dynamic processes that are implemented by a range of individuals, who may possess different and often competing values. The book approaches criminal law and procedure from the perspective that words and doctrines do not define themselves and that the values and attitudes of individuals (judges, lawyers, probation officers, and so on) are often the source of meaning within the criminal justice system. In other words, the book appreciates that criminal law and procedure are very much a part of a social and political process and that professionals within the system often have different and competing values and priorities. To be successful, a legal professional must not only understand the basic elements and procedures of the criminal justice system, but also appreciate the different ways other professionals can interpret and value these elements and procedures.

The book is written in a conversational tone, using language and style that is comfortable for most students. The book provides students with visual learning tools, such as sample documents (motions, warrants, pleadings, and sentencing guidelines), excerpts of landmark court cases, and charts outlining the essential steps in reviewing a criminal case. Students will be invited to review materials and scenarios from actual cases and to make assessments and perform tasks that are regularly performed by those working in the criminal justice profession.

Chapter Topics and Organization

This book is divided into two parts. Part One addresses the basic construction of criminal law. Chapters 1–7 address the nature of criminal law, how criminal statutes are written, the elements of some of the most frequently prosecuted crimes, and the essentials of the most common defenses presented in criminal cases. Part Two examines the processes of criminal cases, looking at the stages, constitutional protections, and basic tasks faced by legal professionals involved in moving cases through the criminal justice system. Chapters 8–14 identify legal standards for criminal procedure, the exclusionary rule, searches and seizures, interrogations, the rights of the accused at trial, and the procedures for appellate and postconviction review.

The first chapter introduces students to the nature, history, and purpose of criminal law by examining the distinguishing features of criminal statutes and explaining how they differ from other types of legal proceedings. In this chapter, students learn about the roots of natural law, positive law, and common law. The chapter also addresses the basic purpose of law, the history of the American legal tradition, and the unique features of criminal law. In addition, criminal law is compared to other methods of regulating human behavior, including morals, ethics, and civil law.

Chapter 2 examines the systems, sources, and semantics of criminal law. This chapter will introduce students to the importance of federalism and separated powers to criminal statutes. Students will also learn about the roles of judges, juries, prosecutors, defense attorneys, law enforcement, paralegals, and other legal professionals in the criminal justice system, and how they shape the meaning of law. This chapter also outlines and explains the different methods used to interpret and apply criminal statutes.

Chapter 3 discusses the fundamental elements of criminal statutes and the core nature of criminal liability. The chapter reviews the concepts of *mens rea*, *actus reus*, strict liability, and inchoate offenses. The chapter also examines the standards of evidentiary proof, the elements of causation and harm, and the theory of conspiracy and accomplice liability.

Chapter 4 introduces the elements of crimes involving harm to persons. This chapter reviews criminal liability standards for homicide, assault and battery, sexual offenses, and other personal crimes. The chapter also explains the different levels or degrees of these criminal offenses and how legal professionals go about proving or disproving their requisite elements.

Chapter 5 addresses crimes against property. In this chapter, students learn about such offenses as theft, burglary, robbery, arson, and identity theft. The chapter also explores the very dynamic world of computer-related or "cyber" crime.

Chapter 6 reviews the most common criminal statutes used to promote public morality and the administration of justice. This chapter looks at the criminal offenses of prostitution, gambling, and nudity. The chapter also examines offenses involving public intoxication, disorderly conduct, and curfew violations.

Chapter 7 addresses the most common defenses and justifications available to defendants facing criminal charges. This chapter looks at theories and realities of using self-defense, duress, entrapment, insanity, and other claims as methods to avoid criminal liability. Included in this section are examples of contemporary and creative defenses attempted by defendants.

Chapter 8 explores the legal fundamentals of criminal procedure by discussing the legal hierarchy in the American criminal justice system, as well as the multiple sources, layers, and branches for criminal procedures. This chapter gives an overview of the American federal system and how it impacts the process of criminal procedure. It also provides details on constitutional, statutory, and administrative standards that impact how criminal cases are handled.

Chapter 9 examines the different ways that criminal cases are initiated. Recognizing that a criminal case can begin in many different ways—investigation, grand jury hearing, arrest, criminal complaint—the chapter stresses the reality that there is no one-size-fits-all beginning to a criminal case. Students learn the basics about the intake process, grand juries, indictments, and writing/reviewing criminal complaints.

Chapter 10 discusses the many procedures that can be used during the pretrial stage of a criminal case. Appreciating that most criminal cases never go to trial, this chapter takes up the most likely reality for criminal justice professionals—that the case will be disposed of prior to a trial. Students examine the exclusionary rule, motions to suppress, and the elements of plea negotiations. This chapter also introduces students to the discovery process before criminal trials, where evidence is acquired and, at times, shared between the parties. Because the success of a criminal case largely depends on the nature and extent of evidence, this chapter emphasizes the importance of the discovery phases of criminal proceedings.

Chapter 11 takes up the subject of searches and seizures. In this chapter, students learn how to approach situations where law enforcement takes evidence from defendants and seeks to use it during a criminal trial. The chapter discusses how courts determine whether a search and seizure is reasonable and otherwise satisfies the requirements of the Fourth Amendment. The chapter also reviews search warrant applications, search warrants, and warrantless searches.

Chapter 12 analyzes the constitutional and practical challenges that come with confessions and other pretrial incriminating evidence sought by prosecutors and offered by defendants. Starting with the Fifth Amendment protection against compulsory self-incrimination, this chapter reviews the constitutional limitations on interrogating or otherwise interfacing with criminal suspects and defendants. In this chapter, students are introduced to the well-known *Miranda* warnings, learn about the stages of the criminal process where these warnings apply, and are exposed to the limitations and exceptions to the constitutional protection against self-incrimination.

Chapter 13 reviews the fundamental issues and procedures of a criminal trial. In this chapter, students will learn about the procedural issues that come with preparing a criminal case for trial. This includes discussions of jury selection, the right to counsel, preparing jury instructions, and the constitutional parameters for a fair and effective trial. This chapter also addresses jury and prosecutorial misconduct, ineffective assistance of counsel, confrontation clause matters, and issues associated with double jeopardy.

Finally, Chapter 14 examines the procedural and legal issues facing professionals after a defendant is convicted. This chapter addresses sentencing hearings, the appellate process, and other postconviction proceedings, including habeas corpus petitions. The chapter also presents examples of a motion to withdraw a plea, motion for judgment of acquittal, and a motion for new trial. Students will learn about the United States Sentencing Guidelines, appellate brief writing, the appellate standards used to review trial court proceedings, and habeas corpus petitions.

Text Features

Throughout the text, the term **legal professionals** is used to refer to a variety of individuals who might be involved with criminal cases. This term is intended to be inclusive in nature, encompassing the many roles that students might eventually play in the criminal justice system, including paralegals, legal assistants, legal secretaries, probation officers, and students preparing for law school.

The text is **flexible in its design**, allowing for use in combined courses on criminal law and criminal procedure or separate classes on each topic.

The book's **writing style** and language are intended to challenge but not overwhelm students. When legal terms are used, they are defined. And there are many examples provided throughout each chapter. In addition, **key terms** are cited and defined in the margins of the text and a running **glossary** is included at the end of each chapter. These tools further reinforce the understanding of legal concepts and doctrines.

Excerpts of criminal cases are also placed within each chapter. While each case has been well edited, we have been careful to retain the material needed to accomplish our pedagogical objectives, which include reinforcing the black letter law presented in our narrative, developing analytical skills, and exposing students to judicial writing. To remain true to our flexibility objective, we have designed the text so the cases may be omitted without losing any black letter learning. For those who want access to full-length opinions, the book provides links to many opinions on its companion website. But these abbreviated cases also provide briefing opportunities for those students who want to engage in this traditional practice used for legal research and writing projects. And at the end of each excerpt, the authors provide questions for students to initiate discussion and ponder future application of the standards and concepts found within the court's ruling.

Illustrations, charts, pleadings, and photos appear throughout the text. At times, the doctrines and tests used by courts to interpret and apply principles of criminal law and procedure can seem dense, confusing, and even contradictory, especially for those who are just learning about them. Within each chapter, the book provides organizational charts, directional diagrams, photos, sample pleadings, and other visual aids to help students understand complex topics and to provide an analytical framework to address future situations in criminal law and procedure.

In the Field is a special feature designed to make students aware that criminal law and procedure is more than a set of abstract and theoretical concepts. Throughout each chapter, the book offers practical insights and advice regarding working on criminal cases. These features help introduce students to the realities of criminal practice and the role some of the theories, cases, and concepts play in day-to-day cases.

Ethical Principles is a segment within each chapter that highlights a particular ethical rule or ethical consideration for legal assistants, paralegals, and other legal professionals. These principles are taken from the ethical canons and rules offered by the American Bar Association, the American Alliance of Paralegals, the National Federation of Paralegal Associations, Inc., and the National Association of Legal Assistants. Then at the end of each chapter, students are asked to consider and apply the featured ethics rule or standard to a factual scenario in which they may find themselves as a legal professional.

Law Line is another feature running throughout the book that connects students to primary sources—statutes, cases, and other texts—that illustrate core concepts of criminal law and procedure. Within each chapter, there are multiple references to the text's companion website, where students can go and find full-length cases, criminal statutes, constitutional provisions, and other materials that highlight the realities of working in the criminal justice profession.

Each chapter contains a **Summary** section that outlines the main concepts and doctrines found within text of the chapter. This section allows students to assess whether they have captured the primary points and principles after reading the full-length materials.

Questions for Discussion also appear at the end of each chapter. These require students to provide a short answer or explanation to basic questions involving the core concepts, doctrines, and cases addressed within the chapter. There are also more reflective questions that ask the student to consider the implication of concepts and cases for future cases.

Appendices include the United States Constitution, and directions for researching and briefing legal materials.

Developing Your Legal Analysis Skills

This section at the end of each chapter provides students with real-life exercises and assignments that reflect the work of legal professionals in criminal law and procedure. These might include preparing a legal memorandum, outlining the courtroom rules for a given jurisdiction, or locating a client within the Bureau of Prisons. Students are then asked to complete the assignments within the parameters of the instructions given by a hypothetical supervisor within an office setting. These assignments require students to apply key legal and procedural principles to tangible situations, using the knowledge gained from the chapter.

There are four types of assignments provided in this feature. The first is called **The Law Where You Live**, which contains assignments asking students to locate and apply the standards of criminal law and procedure within their own state or local jurisdiction. This section allows students to tailor their general understanding of criminal law and procedure to their home courts. The second area of assignments is called **Inside the Federal Courts**. This section provides assignments based on federal standards, rules, and requirements. It is designed to allow students to appreciate the fundamental differences of legal practice in the federal system. The third type of assignment is called **Cyber Sources**, which asks students to use electronic research methods and resources to complete a task that might be assigned to a legal professional in the criminal justice field. And finally, there is an assignment on **Ethics and Professionalism** that requires the students to apply the ethical principles for legal professionals, which are outlined in the chapter or otherwise referenced in the text, to a hypothetical situation in a criminal justice setting.

Resources for Students

Companion Website
Students can access a variety of study aids at www.prenhall.com/Schmalleger including **Law Line**, featuring up-to-date and full-length cases and many other supplemental materials that allow the text to grow with the ever-changing dynamics of criminal justice, along with chapter-specific resources including self-grading test-prep quizzes.

Resources for Instructors

Instructor's Manual

The Instructor's Manual includes content outlines for classroom discussion, teaching suggestions, and answers to end-of-chapter questions from the text.

Test Generator

The test bank is arranged by chapter, containing a variety of question formats such as true/false, multiple choice, completion, short answer, and essay.

PowerPoint Lecture Presentation

A PowerPoint presentation, organized by chapter, outlines and summarizes the major points covered, and corresponds to the organization of the text.

To access the Instructor's Manual, Test Generator, and PowerPoint Lecture Presentation package online, instructors need to request an instructor access code. Go to **www.pearsonhighered.com/irc**, where you can register for an instructor access code. Within forty-eight hours of registering you will receive a confirming e-mail including an instructor access code. Once you have received your code, locate your text in the online catalog and click on the Instructor Resources button on the left side of the catalog product page. Select a supplement and a log-in page will appear. Once you have logged in, you can access instructor material for all Pearson Prentice Hall textbooks.

CourseConnect Criminal Law Online Courses

Looking for robust online course content to reinforce and enhance your student learning? We have the solution: CourseConnect! CourseConnect courses contain customizable modules of content mapped to major learning outcomes. Each learning objective contains interactive tutorials, rich media, discussion questions, MP3 downloadable lectures, assessments, and interactive activities that address different learning styles. CourseConnect courses follow a consistent 21-step instructional design process, yet each course is developed individually by instructional designers and instructors who have taught the course online. Test questions, created by assessment professionals, were developed at all levels of Blooms Taxonomy. When you buy a CourseConnect course, you purchase a complete package that provides you with detailed documentation you can use for your accreditation reviews. CourseConnect courses can be delivered in any commercial platform such as WebCT, BlackBoard, Angel, Moodle, or eCollege platforms. For more information contact your representative or call 800-635-1579.

Acknowledgments

The authors would like to thank the following reviewers for their contributions to this work:

Laura Alfano, Virginia College Online
Carol Brady, Milwaukee Area Technical College
Robert M. Donley, Central Pennsylvania College
Claudine Rigaud Dulaney, Anthem Education Group
Arin Miller, Keiser University
Annalinda Ragazzo, Bryant & Stratton College
Charles R. Splawn, Horry-Georgetown Technical College
John Torraco, State College of Florida
Cathy Underwood, Pulaski Technical College
Laurie Wicker, Brookline

We also appreciate the efforts made by our Pearson Education team, including executive editor Gary Bauer, development editor Linda Cupp.

About the Authors

Frank Schmalleger, Ph.D., is Distinguished Professor Emeritus at the University of North Carolina at Pembroke. Dr. Schmalleger holds degrees from the University of Notre Dame and Ohio State University, having earned both a master's (1970) and doctorate (1974) from Ohio State University, with a special emphasis in criminology. From 1976 to 1994, he taught criminal justice courses at the University of North Carolina at Pembroke. For the last sixteen of those years, he chaired the university's Department of Sociology, Social Work, and Criminal Justice. He was named Professor Emeritus in 2001.

As an adjunct professor with Webster University in St. Louis, Missouri, Schmalleger helped develop the university's graduate program in security administration and loss prevention. He taught courses in that curriculum for more than a decade. Schmalleger has also taught in the New School for Social Research's online graduate program, helping to build the world's first electronic classrooms in support of distance learning through computer telecommunications. Frank Schmalleger is the author of numerous articles and many books, including the widely used *Criminal Justice Today* (Prentice Hall, 2011); *Criminology Today* (Prentice Hall, 2012); *Criminal Justice: A Brief Introduction* (Prentice Hall, 2012). See his website at www.schmalleger.com.

John P. Feldmeier, J.D., Ph.D., is an Associate Professor of Political Science at Wright State University in Dayton, Ohio, where he teaches courses in criminal justice, constitutional law, and legal ethics. He is also an attorney, serving "Of Counsel" with the Cincinnati, Ohio, law firm of Sirkin, Kinsely & Nazzarine LLP. He earned his bachelor's degree in political science from Ohio Dominican College, J.D. from Capital University Law School, and M.A. and Ph.D. in political science from Miami University. During his legal career, he has handled many cases involving important criminal justice issues, including one that reached the United States Supreme Court. He is the coauthor of the book *Constitutional Values* and has published several articles on public law and criminal justice topics. He currently resides in Cincinnati, Ohio, with his wife, Melissa, and his children, Emma and Jack.

chapter **one**

THE POWER OF CRIMINAL LAW

Law is the art of the good and the fair.
—Ulpian, Roman judge (circa A.D. 200)

Disgrace does not consist in the punishment, but in the crime.
—Vittorio Alfieri (Antigone, II, 2)

The law is that which protects everybody who can afford a good lawyer.
—Anonymous

LEARNING OBJECTIVES

After reading this chapter, you should be able to

- Identify the historical and cultural roots of criminal law in Western society.

- Trace the development of criminal law in the United States.

- Appreciate the role of common law in the modern criminal justice system.

- Explain the differences between procedural and substantive criminal law.

- Identify the different types of law and the purposes they serve.

- Understand the primary differences between civil and criminal law.

- Explain the differences between morals, ethics, law, and criminal law.

INTRODUCTION

What fascinates so many people about criminal cases? Is it the mystery of an unsolved homicide or other crime? Is it morbid curiosity about people engaging in antisocial behavior? Or is it just that the producers of popular television programs like *CSI* and *Law and Order* are very good storytellers? Perhaps these factors contribute to some of the modern-day interest in criminal justice. But overall, much of the public's interest stems largely from the fact that criminal cases involve law in its most critical and powerful form.

Unlike many other forms of law—domestic relations, personal injury, bankruptcy, property law, and so on—criminal law involves the full power of government being waged against individuals or entities, imposing a threat that these targeted parties might lose their liberty (or in some cases, even their life) as a result of the government's legal action. Certainly, in noncriminal cases, most parties probably believe that their case is of the utmost importance to them. And in many of these cases, parties may stand to lose a substantial amount of money, influence, or other resources. But in most criminal cases, the stakes are even higher, with the possibility that individuals actually could lose their freedom at the hands of the government. This dynamic—which pits the full power of government against the freedom of individuals—further fuels the high drama and substantial interest in criminal cases.

WHAT DOES LAW HAVE TO DO WITH IT?

rule of law
the belief that an orderly society must be governed by established principles and known standards that are uniformly and fairly applied; also known as "the supremacy of law"

law
an authoritative method by which people are committed to one another through societal enforcement of standards for human behavior; comes from the Latin root *lex* or *legare*, which means "to bind"

Law Line 1-1
The Rule of Law

The ***rule of law***, which is sometimes referred to as "the supremacy of law," involves the belief that an orderly society must be governed by established principles and known standards that are applied uniformly and fairly to all of its members. In fact, the word ***law*** comes from the Latin root *lex* or *legare*, which means "to bind." The notion is that law binds individuals together and allows them to coexist, even though their individual needs and desires may be very different. Similarly, *Black's Law Dictionary,* an authoritative source of legal terminology, defines law as follows: "that which is laid down, ordained, or established . . . a body of rules of action or conduct prescribed by controlling authority, and having binding *legal* force."[1] Under the rule of law no one is above the law, and those who enforce the law must abide by it.

One illustration of law as a "binding agent" is the payment of taxes. From a purely selfish standpoint, it makes very little sense for individuals to pay taxes. Why would rational people voluntarily give their own money to the government? Tax laws, however, are premised on the theory that the good of the whole community (the common good) is better served when individuals financially support public services. In this sense, these laws have the effect of binding self-interested individuals together by making them collectively responsible for the well-being of the community.

Max Weber (1864–1920), an eminent sociologist of the early twentieth century, said that the primary purpose of law is to regulate the flow of human interaction.[2] Without laws of some sort modern society probably could not exist, and social organization would be unable to rise above the level found in primitive societies (where mores and norms are the primary regulatory forces). Laws make for predictability in human events by using the authority of government to ensure that socially agreed-on standards of behavior will be followed and enforced. They allow people to plan their lives by guaranteeing a relative degree of safety to well-intentioned individuals, while constraining the behavior of those who would unfairly victimize others. Laws provide a stable foundation for individuals wishing to join together in a legitimate undertaking by enforcing rights over the control and ownership of property. They also provide for individual freedoms and personal safety by sanctioning the conduct of anyone who violates the legitimate expectations of others. Thus the first, and most significant, purpose of the law can be simply stated: laws support social order.

The rule of law has been called "the greatest political achievement of our culture,"[3] for without it few other human achievements—especially those that require the efforts of a large number of people working together—would be possible. The American Bar Association (ABA) defines the rule of law to include the following:[4]

- Freedom from private lawlessness provided by the legal system of a politically organized society
- A relatively high degree of objectivity in the formulation of legal norms and a like degree of evenhandedness in their application
- Legal ideas and juristic devices for the attainment of individual and group objectives within the bounds of ordered liberty
- Substantive and procedural limitations on governmental power in the interest of the individual for the enforcement of which there are appropriate legal institutions and machinery.

To many people, a society without laws is unthinkable. Were such a society to exist, it likely would be ruled by individuals and groups powerful enough to usurp control over others. The personal whims of the powerful would rule, and less powerful persons would live in constant fear of attack. The closest we have come in modern times to lawlessness can be seen in war-torn regions of the world. The wholesale looting of homes and businesses, and the frequent terrorist attacks on civilians in Iraq, Afghanistan, and other regions in recent years provide a glimpse of what can happen when the rule of law breaks down.

Law Line 1-2
Excerpts from Blackstone's
Commentaries

IN THE FIELD

Legal professionals should understand that legal work is connected to a much larger social system, where the law serves a greater purpose than just furthering individual interests or resolving isolated disputes. Certainly, the legal system is used to further the needs and wants of individuals. But the law itself is designed to be a neutral body of rules against which disputes will be resolved. As a result, working with the law requires legal professionals to use standards that are external to themselves. Instead of saying, "I want the charges to be dismissed" or "those charges should be dismissed," legal professionals should say, "pursuant to code section 4235.01, the charges must be dismissed" or "the case of *State v. Jones* dictates that the charges be dismissed." The use of objective standards to call for authoritative action is the essence of ***legal analysis***. Essentially, this involves taking an established rule, principle, or court opinion and applying it to a given set of factual circumstances. For individuals who are accustomed to simply declaring things to be right, wrong, good, or bad, learning to address disputes through legal analysis can be particularly challenging. But by being mindful of the larger purpose of law, legal professionals can more readily learn to use and apply external sources of right and wrong to address the individual needs of their employers and clients.

legal analysis
the use of objective standards
found in legal sources to review
and resolve disputes

HISTORICAL ROOTS

Criminal laws in the United States have been shaped by a number of cultural, historical, and philosophical influences. Early on, the theory of natural law influenced the content of many criminal laws and served as the basis for claims of certain individual rights and liberties. In addition, legal traditions found in ancient law and civil law societies, which stressed the importance of the written word as the basis of law, fostered the use of constitutions, statutes, and contracts to facilitate legal action. And finally, the English common law tradition, which relied on judicial decision making and local customs to resolve disputes, instilled the practice of judicial precedent and the role of courts in interpreting law. The combination of these movements in both culture and thought form much of the basis for criminal laws in the United States today.

Natural Law

natural law theory
a theory of law maintaining that law is not created by human beings, but rather originates from the natural order of things

Natural law is a theory about the source of law that some have asserted to justify certain forms of American law. In general, **natural law theory** maintains that just laws are not created by human beings, but rather originate from the natural order of things. Notions of natural law date back to Greek philosophers such as Aristotle (384 B.C.–322 B.C.), who claimed that, by observing the natural order of things, individuals could understand how to live together without doing harm to one another. According to Aristotle and other natural law theorists, inherent legal truths are found in the properties of nature, and individuals can discover these truths and adopt human-made laws that conform to them. For example, some natural law theorists would argue that human acts of suicide or bestiality violate the laws of nature and therefore should be prohibited by criminal laws made and enforced by humans. Under natural law theory, the wrongness of these acts does not depend on a written statute or law; rather these acts are inherently wrong because they violate the principles of nature. In the end, natural law relies on the belief in an unwritten code of morality found in nature to justify and otherwise support certain forms of human law.

natural rights
a theory based in natural law holding that individuals naturally possess certain freedoms that may not be encroached upon by other individuals or governments

One philosophical outgrowth of natural law is the theory of **natural rights**. This theory holds that individuals naturally possess certain freedoms that may not be encroached upon by other individuals or governments. For example, the theologian Thomas Aquinas (1225–74) wrote in his *Summa Theologica* that any man-made law that contradicts natural law is corrupt in the eyes of God.[5] Similarly, in the Declaration of Independence, Thomas Jefferson cited the "laws of nature" as support for his assertion "that all men are created equal, that they are endowed by their Creator with certain unalienable rights, that among these are life, liberty and the pursuit of happiness." These "self-evident" truths of which Jefferson spoke were based on his notion of the natural rights of human beings.

crimes against nature
a label used by natural law theorists to describe certain actions that are believed to violate the laws of nature

For many years in American jurisprudence, natural law or the laws of nature were cited by legislators and judges to support the creation and enforcement of some criminal laws. In some venues, human acts such as sodomy, interracial marriage, extramarital sex, and homosexuality were labeled **crimes against nature** and punished by criminal sanctions. In these settings, the government did not need to justify the legitimacy of its criminal prohibitions by showing that the targeted acts created tangible harm. Instead, it claimed that these acts went against the laws of nature, so the acts were deemed inherently harmful.

Today, courts often find theories of natural law insufficient to justify governmental action, particularly criminal prosecution. But vestiges of this theory are still found in some cases. For example, in *Lawrence v. Texas* (2003),[6] the United States Supreme Court struck down a Texas law that criminalized same-sex sodomy. The Court found that the law unconstitutionally infringed on a person's right of privacy. In a failed attempt to support the Texas law, several organizations filed *amicus curiae* (friend of the court) briefs with the Court, citing theories of natural law in defense of the Texas statute. Some groups actually cited Aristotle; others called marriage "a pre-legal moral reality"; and still others urged the Court to "accept and affirm the natural world." In each of these legal arguments, the groups relied upon theories of natural law in an attempt to justify the state's ban on same-sex sodomy. See LawLine 1-3. In recent years, some organizations have presented similar natural law claims in courts and legislative arenas in an effort to justify bans on same-sex marriage.

Law Line 1-3
Amicus Curiae Briefs Filed in *Lawrence v. Texas* (2003)

Some legal professionals also cite natural law as a reason to support human rights and other legal protections for individuals. In disputes involving issues such as the rights of "enemy combatants" held by the United States at Guantanamo Bay or the rights of undocumented aliens residing in the United States, natural law has been asserted as a basis for affording legal protections to individuals based purely on the fact that the persons involved are human beings. In this context, natural rights theorists identify with Thomas Jefferson's assertion of "inalienable rights" and claim that individuals have inherent rights within the "laws of nature" and are entitled to certain liberties regardless of whether they are citizens or legal residents of the United States. For some, individual rights should not depend on any written constitution, statute, or contract, but rather should be based on life itself.[7] In short, in these contexts, natural rights proponents maintain that there are certain fundamental privileges that are universal in their application and that are afforded individuals simply as human beings.

Positive Law

The theory of natural law is often contrasted with **legal positivism** or **positive law**, which asserts that law is a human creation maintained and enforced by government. For positivists, the source of law is people, not nature. The word *positivism* comes from the Latin word *positus*, which means to posit, postulate, or firmly affix the meaning of something. Positive law maintains that the only legitimate sources of law are those written rules, regulations, and principles that have been expressly enacted, adopted, or recognized by a governmental entity or political institution, including administrative, executive, legislative, and judicial bodies.

In criminal law, legal positivism is reinforced by the doctrine of *nullum crimen sine lege*, also known as the **principle of legality**. This doctrine holds that "there is no crime, if there is no statute." In contrast to natural law, positive law maintains that the viability of law depends on human documentation and promulgation of rules. For positivists, because law is a human construct, it is tangible and changeable. The roots of legal positivism are found in many ancient laws and Roman civil law traditions.

Ancient Laws

The development of criminal codes can be traced to the Code of Hammurabi, an ancient set of laws inscribed on a stone pillar near the ancient city of Susa around the year 1750 B.C. The **Hammurabi Code**, named after the Babylonian King Hammurabi (1792–1750 B.C.), specified a number of property rights and crimes and associated punishments. Hammurabi's laws spoke to issues of ownership, theft, sexual relationships, and interpersonal violence. Although the Hammurabi

legal positivism or **positive law**
also known as positive law; a theory of law asserting that the source of law is people, not nature, and is found in the written word; dervived from the Latin word *positus*, which means to posit, postulate, or firmly affix the meaning of something

principle of legality
a doctrine of legal positivism maintaining that, if a criminal law is not written down, then there can be no crime; expressed in the common law doctrine of *nullum crimen sine lege*

Hammurabi Code
a code of law named after the Babylonian King Hammurabi (1792–1750 B.C.); specified a number of property rights and crimes and associated punishments; regarded as one of the first examples of legal positivism

Code specified a variety of corporal punishments, even death, for named offenses, its major contribution was that it standardized the practice of justice in Babylonian society by lending predictability to punishments. Before the code, captured offenders often faced the most barbarous and capricious of punishments, frequently at the hands of revenge-seeking victims, no matter how minor their offenses had been. But as some have observed, "the Hammurabi Code, with its emphasis on retribution, amounted to a brilliant advance in penal philosophy mainly because it represented an attempt to keep cruelty within bounds."[8] The force of the laws found in the Hammurabi Code was derived from the fact that they were "written in stone" and promulgated for all to see.

Civil Law Codes

Like the Hammurabi Code, the legitimacy of much of Roman law was also based on its written form, tangible properties, and empirical accessibility by the people. Roman law was derived from the Twelve Tables, which were written about 450 B.C. The Tables, a collection of basic rules related to family, religious, and economic life, appear to have been based on common and fair practices generally accepted among early tribes that existed prior to the establishment of the Roman republic. Roman law was codified by order of Emperor Justinian I, who ruled the Byzantine Empire between 527 and 565 A.D. In its complete form, the **Justinian Code** or **Corpus Juris Civilis** (CJC), consisted of three lengthy legal documents: (1) the Institutes, (2) the Digest, and (3) the code itself.

Justinian's Code distinguished between two major legal categories—public laws and private laws. Public laws dealt with the organization of the Roman state, its senate, and governmental offices. Private law concerned itself with contracts, personal possessions, the legal status of various types of persons (citizens, free

Law Line 1-4
The Code of Hammurabi

Justinian Code or *Corpus Juris Civilis*
a form of Roman law that was codified by Emperor Justinian I; consists of three documents, (1) the Institutes, (2) the Digest, and (3) the code itself; regarded as an early example of legal positivism

Codified laws from the Code of Hammurabi, from Code of the Hammurabi, black basalt, 18th century b.c. Mesopotamian, from Susa, Iran.

persons, slaves, freedmen, guardians, husbands and wives, and so forth) and injuries to citizens. The CJC was abandoned and lost for several centuries. But it was found in the eleventh century and thereafter influenced the development of civil codes throughout Europe, including the Napoleonic and German codes. Indeed, Napoleon transplanted his code throughout the territories he conquered.

Today, many nations fall into the civil law tradition, including France, Italy, Spain, Germany, and Franco-Africa, Franco–South America, and Franco–Central America. Canon law—the law of the Catholic Church—was also influential in the development of the civil law tradition.

Law Line 1-5
Legal Codes

Common Law

While the civil law tradition spread through much of Europe and the world, it was not transplanted to England, where a separate legal tradition developed. This is called **common law**. Common law is a system of law based on judges deciding cases or disputes over time. Unlike the civil law tradition, which is legislative in nature, common law is developed by judges on a case-by-case basis. Traditionally, in common law courts, judges looked to local customs and practices to identify the law that would govern a dispute. As a result, common law is regarded as the traditional standards for resolving disputes that have been adopted by judges within a given region. As some have observed, "[c]ommon law involved the transformation of community rules into a national legal system."[9]

Unlike civil law traditions, which are based on the written codes or statutes of legislative bodies, common law is based on judicial interpretations or judge-made law. The common law tradition generally allows for change. As local practices and customs evolved, these changes would incrementally be recognized by judges and added to the body of law for the given jurisdiction. In this regard, the legitimacy of common law is derived from the practices of a community.

Under common law systems, when a court decides and reports its decision concerning a particular case, the case becomes part of the body of law and can be used later in cases involving similar matters. A case that already has been decided is called **precedent**. The process of using a precedent (prior case) to resolve a current dispute is known as **stare decisis**, which means "let the decision stand." Together, the doctrines of precedent and *stare decisis* reinforce the principle that similar cases should be resolved with similar standards of law.

common law
a legal tradition born in England that relies on judges deciding cases based on local custom or tradition; serves as the basis for American legal reliance on judicial opinions, precedent, and the doctrine of *stare decisis*

Law Line 1-6
Common Law

precedent
a case or judicial ruling that has already been decided

stare decisis
a common law doctrine that relies on precedent (prior cases) to resolve a current dispute; means "let the decision stand"

Common Law in America

Early English immigrants to America carried common law traditions with them. The American frontier provided an especially fertile ground for the acceptance of common law principles. For example, the scarcity of churches and infrequent visits by traveling ministers prompted many territories to recognize common law marriages. Similarly, the lack of formal legal authorities led to informal recognition that a meeting of minds (and a person's word) constituted a valid contract in most areas of human endeavor. But by the late 1800s, however, common law principles were giving way across America to written civil and penal codes.

Today, much of modern American law is codified in large volumes of statutes and ordinances enacted by legislative bodies at the federal, state, and local levels. Nevertheless, common law traditions and practices remain an integral part of jurisprudence in the United States. Today's primary lawmakers are legislatures, but judges, precedent, and common law doctrines continue to play a significant role in the creation and development of the law. Judges still recognize and adopt doctrines, principles, and theories of common law to resolve many legal disputes.

Attorneys and judges regularly cite case precedents as legal authority in their cases. And where the wording of legislative statutes is ambiguous, judges still bear the responsibility of interpreting and applying the law through their interpretation of both statutes and precedent. The opinions written to decide these cases further add to the body of common law that can be and is used as precedent.

For example, many courts often follow the common law **rule of lenity** with ambiguous criminal statutes. The rule of lenity maintains that, when interpreting vague words within a criminal law, courts should give defendants, rather than the government, the benefit of the doubt as to the statute's meaning. In *United States v. Santos* (2008),[10] the Supreme Court applied the rule of lenity to interpret the federal money laundering statute. In *Santos*, the defendant, who served as a runner in an illegal lottery scheme, received a salary for his work from the lottery operators. Based on the receipt of this salary, he was charged with violating a federal money laundering provision that prohibited using the "proceeds" of criminal activities. But the federal statute did not indicate whether the term "proceeds" meant "profits" from an illegal operation or whether it also included any "receipts" from the operation, such as the defendant's salary. The Court held that the rule of lenity required the statute to be interpreted in favor of the defendant, and therefore required the government to show that the defendant's salary came from the "profits" of the operation. The rule of lenity is one of many common law doctrines that are still used today by judges in criminal cases. See Table 1-1.

In addition, legislators often rely upon common law principles and practices when they draft statutes or ordinances. In many cases, statutes are simply codifications of the common law. For example, to understand what a legislature meant when it referred to malice aforethought, a judge would have to determine if the body simply codified the common law principle. If so, then the judge would turn to common law decisions to understand the meaning of the term. In the end, given the extent the legal profession relies on case precedent, some have claimed that common law is still the major source of modern American law.

Deference to the Legislature

Despite the importance of common law in American jurisprudence, it is important to realize that courts still give a substantial amount of deference to the written and legislative law (civil tradition). As a result, legislative statutes generally trump common law statutes where there is a conflict between the two. For example, the Florida Criminal Code states, "[t]he common law of England in relation to crimes, except so far as the same relates to the modes and degrees of punishment, shall be of full force in this state where there is no existing provision by statute on the subject."[11] Similarly, Arizona law reads, "[t]he common law only so far as it is consistent with and adapted to the natural and physical conditions of this state and the necessities of the people thereof, and not repugnant to or inconsistent with the Constitution of the United States or the constitution or laws of this state, or established customs of the people of this state, is adopted and shall be the rule of decision in all courts of this state."[12] While Florida, Arizona, and other states have passed legislation officially institutionalizing common law principles, all states today, with the exception of Louisiana, which employs a modified civil law system, are regarded as **common law states**.

Occasionally, individuals are arrested and tried under common law when appropriate statutory provisions are not in place. In 1996, for example, euthanasia advocate Dr. Jack Kevorkian was arrested and tried in Michigan on charges of violating the state's common law against suicide. After Kevorkian was acquitted,

rule of lenity
a common law rule maintaining that, when interpreting vague words within a criminal law, courts should give defendants, rather than the government, the benefit of the doubt as to the statute's meaning

TABLE 1-1 **Examples of Common Law Doctrines Still Used Today**

Castle Doctrine

A legal principle holding that a person's home should be treated as his castle, thereby bestowing certain rights and privileges upon the homeowner when acting inside the home. In some criminal cases, this doctrine allows homeowners to engage in self-defense of themselves or their homes rather than retreat from the home, even where it may be safe to do so.

Eiusdem generis ("of the same kind")

A rule that helps to clarify the meaning of a word found within a group of words. In criminal statutes, the principle is that where "general words follow enumerations of particular classes of persons or things, the general words shall be construed as applicable only to persons or things of the same general nature or kind as those enumerated."

Expressio unius est exclusio alterius ("the inclusion of one is the exclusion of all others")

A doctrine holding that when a legislative body includes specific items within a statute, the assumption is that it intends to exclude all other terms. At times, this doctrine can be used to limit the scope of criminal statutes.

Forfeiture by Wrongdoing

A principle holding that a person cannot benefit in a legal dispute by virtue of having committed a criminal act. The theory is that the person forfeits his or her claims by engaging in the wrongful act. For example, a person who intentionally kills her spouse cannot inherit property under the spouse's will.

Ignorantia juris non excusat ("ignorance of the law is no excuse")

A theory applied to defendants who attempt to claim that they were not aware of the criminal prohibitions they are accused of violating. Today, courts enforce this theory by holding that persons are presumed to know the law, thereby limiting the use of mistake of law as a viable criminal defense.

In pari materia ("upon the same matter or subject")

A doctrine maintaining that, when a statute is ambiguous, its meaning may be determined in light of other statutes on the same subject matter. This can be used to interpret criminal statutes.

Rule of Lenity

A rule maintaining that, when there are ambiguous terms found in a criminal statute, the court should interpret these terms in a light that is favorable to the defendant.

Sovereign Immunity

A theory maintaining that the state or sovereign ruler cannot engage in criminal wrongdoing and, therefore, is immune from civil liability or criminal culpability. Today, this doctrine is used to exempt some public officials from civil suits and other legal actions. But in some cases, the doctrine has limited application and often will not be applied to public officials sued in their personal or individual capacity.

Stare Decisis ("let the decision stand")

A judicial maxim that prior decisions ought to be maintained and respected, as opposed to being reversed. The notion is that respecting precedent (prior decisions) provides stability and predictability in the legal system.

---

jury foreman Dean Gauthier told reporters, "[w]e felt there was a lack of evidence regarding the interpretation of the common law."[13] In 1999, however, after Michigan enacted statutory legislation outlawing physician-assisted suicide, Kevorkian was convicted of a number of crimes and sentenced to ten to twenty-five years in prison. Evidence against Kevorkian came largely from a videotape aired on CBS's *60 Minutes,* showing the doctor giving a lethal injection to fifty-two-year-old Thomas Youk, who suffered from Lou Gehrig's disease.

In the end, many of the roots of American law are grounded in both the civil law and common law traditions. Together, the formal written pronouncements

FIGURE 1-1 **Civil and Common Law Legal Traditions Compared**

The Civil Law Legal Tradition	**The Common Law Legal Tradition**
Where: France, Italy, Portugal, Spain, Franco-Africa,	Where: England, United States, Australia, New Zealand,
Latin America, Louisiana (limited)	Belize, Canada, Anglo-Africa
Judges play minimal role in development of law	Judges play major role in development of law
Periodic, sometimes abrupt, legislative change	More evolutionary change through judicial decisions with occasional legislative change
Rational and forward thinking	More likely to change in response to current conditions

found in constitutions, statutes, and regulations are used in combination with the judicial interpretations, court precedents, and common law principles to form a legal system that is both fixed and flexible. Figure 1-1 compares these two legal traditions.

IN THE FIELD

As a legal professional, you should be aware that the theories, terms, and effect of civil codes and common law may impact the way in which your statutory laws are interpreted and applied. Certainly, the written standards found in constitutional provisions and criminal laws are the starting point for any legal analysis. But where these formal words do not provide clear-cut answers and applications for a given case, the use of precedent and/or common law principles may prove helpful. In these situations, judges may find the historic background of a written law or cases interpreting it to be instructive on the matter. In addition, the precedent and common law background of a statutory provision may also give you insight and understanding into the meaning of the statutory language and help you better assess the legal position of your client or employer. Do not assume that, simply because common law traditions and court precedents may appear old and outdated, they no longer have any relevance to modern-day jurisprudence. They may prove highly valuable to the most contemporary of criminal cases because they offer insight into how words and phrases in statutes should be interpreted and applied.

Law Line 1-7
Pound's "Jural Postulates"

THE PURPOSE OF CRIMINAL LAW

As stated in the opening of this chapter, criminal law is one brand of law or, put another way, one way among many of binding individuals within a society to one another. The word *criminal* can be traced to the Latin word *crîmen*, which means "charge, guilt accusation." In many forms of noncriminal cases—civil (see below), probate, patent, and so on—the law allows persons to be held responsible for their actions or inactions. For example, in a typical car accident, civil laws allow an injured driver to recover damages from and otherwise hold accountable the negligent driver who caused the injuries. In this sense, the law treats negligent drivers as *liable* or *responsible* for their harmful conduct. See Civil Law Distinguished (below).

But in criminal law, there is a deeper accounting that occurs. When the government brings criminal charges against defendants, it is not just seeking to hold those persons responsible or liable for the harm they caused. The government is not just looking for restitution or a fair resolution to a dispute. Instead, the government is seeking to have defendants declared *blameworthy* or *culpable* for their conduct. This is essentially the notion of a guilty verdict, as opposed to a verdict imposing liability. The distinction between being held *responsible* (liable) and being *blamed* (culpable or guilty) can be subtle, but it is a primary difference between criminal law and other forms of law. ***Responsibility*** or ***liability*** involves holding persons accountable for harmful behavior, without necessarily blaming them for their conduct. A responsible party will be ordered to compensate the harmed parties for their injuries. ***Blame*** or ***culpability***, however, involves publicly criticizing and punishing a person for wrongdoing—a public shaming of sorts. Thus, in addition to correcting the harm caused (in the form of restitution), a convicted (blameworthy) defendant in a criminal case will also be declared guilty and dealt with punitively.

Accordingly, for legal professionals, ***criminal law*** can be understood as that body of rules and regulations imposed by government that defines and specifies punishments (punitive measures) for offenses of a public nature, or for wrongs committed against the state or society. Be aware that criminal law is also called ***penal law*** and is usually embodied in the penal codes of various jurisdictions. Criminal law defines what conduct is criminal, and violations of the criminal law are referred to as ***crimes***.

Criminal laws serve many functions. They attempt to "make society safe for its members, and to punish and rehabilitate those who commit offenses."[14] They seek to deter potential offenders through examples of punishments applied to those found guilty of crimes. They "declare public disapproval of an offender's conduct by means of public trial and conviction."[15] And they serve as a register of the values of lawmakers who enact the laws. As you begin to review specific criminal laws in this text and in future cases, always be mindful of the larger purposes that the law is supposed to serve. Appreciate these larger interests and objectives and learn to question whether the law you are reviewing, as it is being applied to particular facts in a case, is actually fulfilling its larger purpose.

Categories of Criminal Law

Interestingly, the only crime mentioned in the Constitution is ***treason***, which is the act of a citizen to overthrow, substantially undermine, or make war against his or her own nation or country. To the founders of the United States, this was the highest crime an individual could commit. Beyond this constitutional category of crime, it is up to legislators to identify and classify criminal laws. This is done in a number of ways.

Felonies, Misdemeanors, and Infractions. Legislators typically distinguish crimes based on the severity or seriousness of harm that results from a person's conduct and the amount of punishment a legislative body wishes to assign to a particular criminal act. In this regard, legislators typically identify a criminal offense as being either a felony, misdemeanor, or infraction.[16] These categories are usually based on the degree of potential punishment assigned to the criminal offense.

In general, ***felonies*** are treated as serious crimes for which at least a year in prison is a possible punishment. The Texas Penal Code, for example, defines a felony as "an offense so designated by law or punishable by death or confinement

---

responsibility or **liability**
accountability for harmful behavior without necessarily being punished or blamed for one's conduct

blame or **culpability**
public criticism and punishment for a person's wrongdoing; a public shaming of sorts

criminal law
body of rules and regulations imposed by government that defines and specifies punishments (punitive measures) for offenses of a public nature, or for wrongs committed against the state or society

penal law
another term for criminal law, usually found in the penal codes of various jurisdictions

crime
a violation of a criminal law; also known as a criminal offense

---

Law Line 1-8
Criminal Law

---

treason
the act of a citizen to overthrow, substantially undermine, or make war against his or her own nation or country

felony
a serious crime for which at least a year in prison is a possible punishment

misdemeanor
a less serious criminal offense, generally punishable by less than a year of incarceration

infraction
a minor criminal offense, which is generally punishable by only a monetary sanction; often considered a "ticketable offense"

minor misdemeanor or *petty offense*
generally a minor criminal offense punishable by a monetary sanction

in a penitentiary." Other state codes provide similar definitions, such as the California Penal Code, which defines a felony as "a crime which is punishable with death or by imprisonment in the state prison."

Misdemeanors, which are regarded as less serious offenses, generally are punishable by less than a year of incarceration. A misdemeanor, according to the Texas Code, "means an offense so designated by law or punishable by fine, by confinement in jail, or by both fine and confinement in jail." In California, the law reads: "Except in cases where a different punishment is prescribed by any law of this state, every offense declared to be a misdemeanor is punishable by imprisonment in the county jail not exceeding six months, or by fine not exceeding one thousand dollars ($1,000), or by both."

Some jurisdictions also use classifications referred to as *infractions, minor misdemeanors*, or *petty offenses* to identify minor offenses. In some areas, these crimes are considered "ticketable offenses" to indicate that such minor crimes usually result in the issuance of citations, which are often payable through the mail. For example, in California, "[a]n infraction is not punishable by imprisonment." In many other jurisdictions, a minor misdemeanor or infraction is punishable by only a monetary fine. In these cases, no matter how bad or egregious the defendant's behavior was in committing the offense, the worst punishment that can be imposed is a monetary sanction. See Figure 1-2.

Inchoate Offenses. Another distinction used to identify crimes is the extent to which the criminal act is completed and the level of intended harm fulfilled. Some criminal acts are entirely executed and the intended harm is fully achieved. For example, a theft offense is completed after a person takes the property

FIGURE 1-2 **Common Punishments for Criminal Acts**

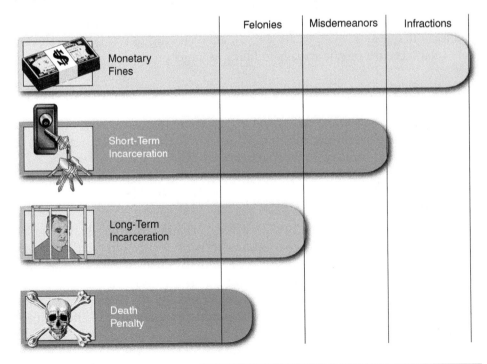

belonging to another person and does not intend to return it. In some instances, criminal acts are not completely fulfilled, but instead remain in the planning or attempt stage. For example, a thief who intended to steal another person's property might be caught while trying to break into the victim's home. In this case, the person did not achieve the desired ends of obtaining the victim's property, but still engaged in action that was criminal in nature. These types of incomplete or partial criminal acts are called **inchoate offenses**. The term *inchoate* means partial or unfinished. Inchoate offenses include such crimes as conspiracy, solicitation, or attempt. Inchoate crimes are discussed in greater detail in Chapter 3.

Mala in se or *Mala prohibita.* Some criminal justice theorists and academics classify crimes based on a characterization of the underlying nature of a person's actions. For some scholars, criminal acts can be either *mala in se* or *mala prohibita*. **Mala in se** crimes are regarded as acts that are wrong in and of themselves. Consistent with the theory of natural law (discussed above), some criminal justice professionals view certain human acts to be inherently evil or immoral. In some cases, these acts are called natural crimes or acts against conscience.[17] For some theorists, acts of murder, rape, or incest are deemed *mala in se* crimes because they are almost universally condemned and would be criminal even if strictures against such behaviors were not specified in the written criminal law.[18]

Mala prohibita crimes are regarded as acts that are criminal simply because a law prohibits them. In other words, *mala prohibita* offenses are treated as products of human construction and are considered "wrongs" only because there is a written law prohibiting certain actions. Consistent with the tradition of legal positivism or positive law (discussed above), this classification of crime is based on the notion that, without a statute specifically proscribing them, *mala prohibita* offenses might *not* be regarded as wrong by a large number of people. *Mala prohibita* offenses might include the category of "victimless crimes," such as prostitution, drug use, and gambling, in which a clear-cut victim is difficult to identify, and whose commission rarely leads to complaints from the parties directly involved in the offense.

In reality, however, within the American criminal justice system, an act or omission cannot be treated as a crime unless it is properly enacted and placed into law, most often in the form of a criminal statute. An act might be viewed as inherently wrong or evil. But if it is not proscribed by law, it is not a criminal act. Thus, for all practical purposes, within the criminal justice system, *all* crimes come in the form of *mala prohibita*.

Subject Matter Classifications. Criminal laws can also be organized based on the subject matter of the crime. This traditional method of classification generally involves organizing offenses into four categories: (1) property crimes, (2) personal crimes, (3) public order offenses, and (4) morals offenses. The distinction between property and personal crimes is of special importance in most state penal codes, and official reports on the incidence of crime, such as the Federal Bureau of Investigation's **Uniform Crime Reports** (UCR), are structured along such a division. The UCR is a database that accounts for the nature and amount of crime that occurs within the United States each year.

Crimes against property (discussed in Chapter 5) include burglary, larceny, arson, criminal mischief (vandalism), property damage, motor vehicle theft, passing bad checks, commission of fraud or forgery, and so on. **Personal crimes**, or offenses against persons (discussed in Chapter 4), include criminal homicide, kidnapping and false imprisonment, various forms of assault, and rape. Personal crimes are also

inchoate offense
a partial or unfinished crime, such as an attempt or conspiracy, which does not culminate in the complete commission of criminal harm

mala in se
crimes regarded as acts that are wrong in and of themselves

mala prohibita
crimes regarded as acts that are criminal simply because a law prohibits them

---

Law Line 1-9
Uniform Crime Reports

Uniform Crime Reports Crimes
a database maintained by the Federal Bureau of Investigation that accounts for the number and type of crimes committed each year

crimes against property
criminal offenses that involve property, including burglary, larceny, arson, criminal mischief (vandalism), property damage, and fraud

personal crimes
criminal offenses involving harm to persons; also known as offenses against persons; these include criminal homicide, kidnapping and false imprisonment, various forms of assault, and rape

public order offenses
criminal offenses that perpetrate harm on larger societal interests; sometimes called crimes against the public order; these include fighting, breach of peace, disorderly conduct, vagrancy, loitering, unlawful assembly, public intoxication, and illegal carrying of weapons

morality-based offenses
a category of unlawful conduct that was criminalized to protect the family and related social institutions; these include lewdness, indecency, prostitution, obscenity, sodomy, and other sex-related offenses

morals
principles, practices, or values held by individuals or small groups that are self-enforced or regulated through social rejection or approval

ethics
rules that govern more formal social settings or groups, including public or professional organizations, which are enforced by members within the group

termed "violent crimes." ***Public order offenses*** (discussed in Chapter 6) are sometimes called "crimes against the public order" and include offenses such as fighting, breach of peace, disorderly conduct, vagrancy, loitering, unlawful assembly, public intoxication, obstructing public passage, and (illegally) carrying weapons. Finally, ***morality-based offenses*** (discussed in Chapter 6) denote a category of unlawful conduct that was criminalized originally to protect the family and related social institutions. The "morals offense" category includes lewdness, indecency, sodomy, and other sex-related offenses, such as seduction, fornication, adultery, bigamy, pornography, obscenity, cohabitation, and prostitution.

Morals and Ethics Distinguished

Legal professionals must keep in mind that not all rules are laws, fewer still are criminal laws, and not all have "binding legal force." Some sociologists, for example, distinguish between ethics and morals. ***Morals*** are principles, practices, or values held by individuals or small groups that are self-enforced or regulated through social rejection or approval. These standards are often not written or codified, but rather developed through socialization. So, for example, in most social settings it is viewed as inappropriate to sneeze without covering your nose and mouth. Anyone who intentionally violates such a social expectation may be seen as inadequately socialized (others might call them "uncivilized"), offensive, and perhaps (if the violation is a serious one) even dangerous to an accepted way of life. Such behavior is normally sanctioned (punished) by way of self-regulation (people restrict themselves for fear of embarrassment) or through small group enforcement (negative reactions). Offenders against moral standards may find themselves ostracized or rejected through informal group rejection or the loss of reputation among peers.

Ethics, on the other hand, are typically regarded as rules that govern more formal social settings or groups, including public or professional organizations. Attorneys, physicians, journalists, and other professionals have ethical codes that are governed by the groups themselves. Indeed, most students have ethical obligations imposed by their schools through student codes of conduct. A breach of these codes may result in discipline by the group, including the possibility that a member might lose membership (license) to participate in group activities (practice law, medicine, or public service). Student ethics violations can also result in formal and serious sanctions, including reprimands, suspensions, or expulsions, imposed by the school the offending student attends.

Violations of both morals and ethics are forms of deviance and can properly be called deviant or antisocial behavior. Even so, few violations of social norms are illegal, and fewer still are crimes. Since laws have not been enacted against quite a large number of generally recognized taboos, it is possible for behavior to be contrary to accepted principles of social interaction and even immoral—but still legal. As you read through this book, it is important to remember that only human conduct that violates the criminal law can properly be called "criminal." While other forms of nonconformist behavior may be undesirable or even reprehensible, they are not crimes.[19] Accordingly, the distinguishing characteristic between a crime and other deviance is the presence of a public prohibition and the authority of the government to enforce the prohibition.

It is also important to keep in mind that, within any given situation, there may be multiple levels of sanctions for a person's conduct. Criminal defendants may initially come into the criminal justice system concerned about whether they

TABLE 1-2 **Methods of Controlling Human Behavior**

	Source	Form of Promulgation	Method of Enforcement
Morals	Cultural traditions, stories, customs, experiences	Individual or group-based attitudes about proper behavior	Social rejection or approval; reputation; self-restraint
Ethics	Group-negotiated standards for individuals in groups	Codes of conduct; professional ethics codes	Group-enforced sanctions, including reprimands, suspension, or removal
Law (general)	Government	Statutes, rules, orders, and rulings	Civil remedies issued by government in the form of damage awards or direct commands
Criminal Law	Government	Statutes, rules, orders, and rulings	Punitive sanctions issued by government, including fines, incarceration, and supervision

violated a criminal law and, if so, what punitive sanctions they might be facing. But in addition to these criminal concerns, there may also be moral, ethical, and other legal consequences for the defendants' alleged conduct.

For example, in recent years federal prosecutors have charged many physicians who operate "pain clinics" with drug-related offenses. The basic allegation in most of these cases is that the doctors are prescribing pain medication without conducting a legitimate and thorough exam, and thus, they are basically distributing drugs illegally. Of course, for most physicians charged criminally with drug-related offenses, the most immediate and serious concern will be the outcome of their criminal case. But even if the criminal matter is resolved without sanctions, there may be other implications and sanctions involved. Doctors charged with criminal acts usually face ethics charges before their state's medical board, which will determine—independent of the criminal case—whether the doctor's license should be suspended or removed. In fact, in some cases, physicians may escape criminal conviction altogether but then lose their license for violating the state's ethical standards for practicing medicine. Moreover, a doctor may also face additional noncriminal legal sanctions, if his or her actions violated other legal standards, such as zoning or tax laws. And of course, the allegations of misconduct may also bring moral consequences for physicians, including a tarnished professional reputation, loss of patients, and subtle or not-so-subtle rejection among friends and colleagues.

Overall, there are many ways to regulate human behavior. Criminal law is only one of them. To be an effective professional in the criminal justice system, you must be aware of the other dimensions of personal, social, professional, and legal sanctions that might be involved in a criminal case. Judges, attorneys, police officers, defendants, and other actors in the criminal justice system all have legal, ethical, and sometimes even moral obligations. Moreover, these obligations can sometimes compete with one another. These may be highly relevant to plea negotiations, assertion of rights, and ultimate decisions made by those involved in prosecuting, defending, and administering criminal cases.

Law Line 1-10
Criminal and Ethical Trouble for Kansas Physician

Within individual cases, legal professionals should try to become aware of the totality of obligations held by those involved. For some defendants, the legal sanctions threatened in their criminal case may be minor in comparison to the ethical or moral consequences facing them in their professional or personal associations. Attorneys, accountants, or doctors who are charged with a fairly minor criminal charge (petty theft, disorderly conduct, public intoxication, and the like) will typically only face a small fine, restitution, and/or probation as a likely punishment if convicted. Comparatively speaking, this is not a huge sanction. But the conviction or even the underlying factual accusation may have other implications, such as the loss or suspension of their professional license, the loss of their job, and/or rejection within family or other social settings. Such noncriminal consequences may impact the way the criminal case is handled, the strategies employed, and the ultimate form of resolution to the case.

LEGAL PROFESSIONALS AND THE PRACTICE OF LAW

National Federation of Paralegal Associations Model Code of Ethics and Professional Responsibility Rule 1.8

A PARALEGAL SHALL NOT ENGAGE IN THE UNAUTHORIZED PRACTICE OF LAW.

ETHICAL CONSIDERATION 1.8(A)

A paralegal shall comply with the applicable legal authority governing the unauthorized practice of law in the jurisdiction in which the paralegal practices.

Many jurisdictions do not provide a clear and comprehensive accounting of what activities constitute "the practice of law." But consider the standard for such activity established by Louisiana:

Louisiana Rules of Professional Conduct Rule 5.5 (e)(3)

For purposes of this Rule, the practice of law shall include the following activities:

i. holding oneself out as an attorney or lawyer authorized to practice law;

ii. rendering legal consultation or advice to a client;

iii. appearing on behalf of a client in any hearing or proceeding, or before any judicial officer, arbitrator, mediator, court, public agency, referee, magistrate, commissioner, hearing officer, or governmental body operating in an adjudicative capacity, including submission of pleadings, except as may otherwise be permitted by law;

iv. appearing as a representative of the client at a deposition or other discovery matter;

v. negotiating or transacting any matter for or on behalf of a client with third parties;

vi. otherwise engaging in activities defined by law or Supreme Court decision as constituting the practice of law.

Criminal Procedure Distinguished

While substantive criminal law defines what conduct is criminal, ***criminal procedure*** defines the processes that may be used by law enforcement, prosecutors, victims, and courts to investigate and adjudicate criminal cases. As discussed in Chapters 8–14, criminal procedure is broader than just process; it also includes the study of the Constitution's role in the process. For example, the Fourth Amendment's privilege against unreasonable searches and seizures, the Fifth Amendment's privilege against self-incrimination, and the Eighth Amendment's prohibition of cruel and unusual punishments are all criminal procedure topics.

In many ways, criminal law and criminal procedure are two different forms of controlling human behavior. Criminal law attempts to control individual harmful actions perpetrated against society by prohibiting certain forms of human behavior and imposing substantive consequences for such behavior. Criminal procedure, on the other hand, attempts to control harmful actions of law enforcement inflicted on criminal suspects and defendants by setting basic standards for treating individuals within the criminal justice system and imposing sanctions for violating these standards. In essence, while criminal law is a tool to police the behavior of the general public, criminal procedure is a method to "police" the police and other law enforcement officials.

criminal procedure
the processes used by law enforcement, prosecutors, victims, and courts to investigate and adjudicate criminal cases

Civil Law Distinguished

At this point, criminal law should be distinguished from civil law. Criminal law concerns the government's decision to prohibit and punish a person's conduct. ***Civil law***, which should not be equated with the Civil Law legal tradition (discussed above), governs relationships between private parties. Civil codes regulate private relationships of all sorts, including marriages, divorces, and many other forms of personal and business relationships, such as inheritance and adoption. Civil actions come in many varieties, including breach of contract, domestic, and tort. A ***tort*** is "the unlawful violation of a private legal right other than a mere breach of contract, express or implied. A tort may also be the violation of a public duty if, as a result of the violation, some special damage accrues to the individual."[20] An individual, business, or other legally recognized entity that commits a tort is called a ***tortfeasor***.

A tort may give rise to civil liability, under which the injured parties may sue the person or entity who caused the injury and ask that the offending party be ordered to pay damages directly to them. Civil law, however, is more concerned with assessing liability than it is with intent. Accidents, as in cases of airline or automobile crashes, may result in huge civil settlements, even though the defendant did not intend the crash to occur.

Parties to a civil suit are referred to as the plaintiff and the defendant and, as with criminal cases, the names of civil suits take the form *Named Plaintiff v. Named Defendant*. Unlike criminal cases, in which the state routinely prosecutes wrongdoers, most civil suits are brought by individuals. On occasion, however, the plaintiff in a civil suit may be the state or a government office or agency. For example, the state may bring a suit to revoke an attorney's right to practice law or a doctor's right to practice medicine. Similarly, the state may bring antitrust cases and initiate other types of civil action. In contrast to the criminal law, however, no civil action will be undertaken that is not initiated by the injured party.

Damage awards in civil cases, when they occur, may be both compensatory, in which the amount to be paid directly compensates the injured party for the amount of damage incurred, and punitive, in which the award serves to punish the

civil law
law that governs relationships between private parties; includes codes regulating marriages, divorces, and many other forms of personal and business relationships, such as inheritance and adoption

tort
the unlawful violation of a private legal right or the violation of a public duty

tortfeasor
a person who commits a tort

defendant for some especially wrongful or treacherous act. But in cases where punitive damages are awarded, they are not treated as forms of criminal punishment. Instead, they are deemed to be another form of civil liability, which is designed to remedy harm and deter future harmful conduct. In 1996, for example, thirty-seven-year-old Alex Hardy, an Alabama man who had been seriously injured when his Chevrolet Blazer flipped over, received a $150 million award from a civil jury.[21] One-third of the award, or $50 million, was in the form of compensatory damages intended to provide medical care for Hardy, who was left partially paralyzed. The other $100 million came in the form of punitive damages, with the jury accepting Hardy's claim that General Motors knew that the door latches on Blazers were defective and that the latches might allow the doors to open in crashes. Although Hardy had been thrown from his vehicle, GM claimed the door latches were safe and that Hardy had fallen asleep and was not wearing a seat belt at the time of the accident.

It is important to realize that the same conduct can be pursued as both a violation of criminal law and a breach of civil law. This is true even in cases where a criminal defendant is acquitted of criminal charges. Perhaps the most famous example of this is O. J. Simpson's legal matters involving the 1994 deaths of Simpson's ex-wife, Nicole Brown Simpson, and her friend, Ronald Goldman. In 1994, California prosecutors charged Simpson with murdering these two victims. For prosecutors, the objective of this criminal case was to hold Simpson culpable for the deaths of the victims and to allow the State of California to punish him for his harmful actions. But in 1995, in one of the most publicized criminal cases in American history, a California jury found O. J. Simpson not guilty of murdering Nicole Brown Simpson and Ronald Goldman.

This verdict, however, did not end Simpson's legal troubles. In 1995, family members of the deceased victims filed a civil suit against Simpson in a California court, alleging under theories of civil law that he caused the wrongful death of Nicole Brown Simpson and Ronald Goldman. The suit demanded monetary damages for Simpson's alleged actions. And in 1997, a California jury found Simpson liable for the deaths of Nicole Brown Simpson and Ronald Goldman and ordered Simpson to pay $33.5 million to the family of Ron Goldman and to Nicole Simpson's estate.[22] The verdict in the civil case did not result in any incarceration or other criminal punishment for Simpson. It was an award for damages based in civil law and was designed to compensate the victims' families for their loss.

Interestingly, in 2008, Simpson was convicted by a Las Vegas jury on twelve felony counts stemming from a gun- and theft-related confrontation in a hotel room in 2007. The convictions came thirteen years to the day after his 1995 acquittal in his California murder trial.[23]

Punitive v. Remedial Laws

The two cases involving O. J. Simpson offer perhaps the most notable example of the difference between criminal law and civil law. But in other legal contexts, the distinction between criminal law and civil law involves a more complex analysis. In some cases, legal professionals must closely examine the substance of laws to determine whether they seek to impose punitive sanctions or whether they are designed to simply administer a nonpunitive remedy to a particular problem. A ***punitive action*** happens when the government seeks to punish an individual for wrongdoing. This is the essence of what occurs in criminal cases. A ***remedial action*** is the response when government seeks to fix an identified problem or address a particular harm without actually inflicting punishment on someone. For example, if a

punitive action
governmental conduct designed to punish an individual for wrongdoing

remedial action
governmental conduct designed to fix an identified problem or address a particular harm without actually inflicting punishment

person destroys a public fire hydrant, the government may ask the person to pay for a replacement. Under most circumstances, this would not be considered a criminal case. At other times, however, the government may claim that its actions are remedial in nature and therefore do not create any criminal-like procedures or rights, but the substance of the government's actions may actually be quite punitive, thereby creating what amounts to a criminal case or context.

Take for example the enactment of sexual offender registration laws, often called Megan's laws or Adam Walsh acts. These laws generally prevent defendants who have been convicted of sexual offenses from living around schools, churches, and playgrounds, require them to register with local authorities as sexual offenders, and compel authorities to notify neighbors of the situation. Many of these laws have been challenged on the basis that they impose a second punishment for the same offense, thereby violating the double jeopardy clause of the Fifth Amendment or other double jeopardy protections found in state constitutions. Those challenging the registration laws assert that offenders have already been punished for their crime by virtue of their conviction and sentence, and that by imposing additional registration and notification requirements on the defendant the government is imposing a second form of punishment for the original offense. Prosecutors, however, claim that the registration laws are not punitive in nature, but rather simply impose administrative or remedial conditions for defendants to follow after being released from custody. Given the difference of opinion, the central question in cases challenging sexual offender registration law becomes: Are these laws punitive in nature, thereby constituting double jeopardy, or are they remedial in nature, and therefore permissible forms of administrative action?

Read the opinion in *Doe v. Alaska* (2008) (below), where a divided Alaska Supreme Court found that the state's sexual offender registration law imposed punitive sanctions on previously convicted sex offenders, and thus violated state constitutional standards against retroactive application of punishment (ex post facto laws). Pay particular attention to the standards used by the court to determine whether a law is punitive or remedial in nature. In many settings, legal professionals "brief" court opinions for themselves or their supervising attorneys. The process of ***briefing a case*** involves reading a court opinion and outlining the basic facts, issues, and rulings of the decision, so the case can be easily understood and used for legal research and writing. A recommended outline and instructions for briefing court opinions is found in Appendix A.

Law Line 1-11
Adam Walsh Act

briefing a case
reading a court opinion and outlining the basic facts, issues, and rulings of the decision, so the case can be easily understood and used for legal research and writing

IN THE FIELD

In the end, legal professionals should be mindful that criminal law and civil law are conceptually distinct in both function and process. As a result, individuals and entities can be held accountable under both types of law for the same instance of misbehavior without violating constitutional guarantees of double jeopardy. This can have profound constitutional, administrative, and practical consequences for many criminal defendants. Realize too that, oftentimes, the difference between a criminal law and civil law is not readily apparent, and thus legal professionals are encouraged to review the underlying facts of a criminal case in their totality and consider all possible consequences for the alleged conduct. In other words, for many criminal defendants, their criminal cases may be only the initial wave of legal proceedings and civil, administrative, and ethical consequences may follow.

CAPSTONE CASE *Doe v. State of Alaska,* 189 P.3d 999 (2008)

EASTAUGH, Justice.

"John Doe" was charged in 1985 with three counts of first-degree sexual abuse of a minor for molesting one of his daughters. Doe pleaded no contest to one count of first-degree sexual abuse of a minor, an unclassified felony, and to one count of second-degree sexual abuse of a minor, a class B felony. The superior court accepted his plea and sentenced him to twelve years of imprisonment with four suspended. Doe began serving his sentence in August 1985.

In December 1990 Doe completed serving the unsuspended portion of his sentence less a good-time reduction required by AS 33.20.010(a) and was released to mandatory parole and supervised probation. In September 1991 the Parole Board released Doe from mandatory parole nearly two years early, based on its determination that Doe had participated in rehabilitative counseling and posed little or no threat to the public. In 1995 Doe completed his period of probation.

In May 1994 the Alaska Legislature enacted the statute known as the Alaska Sex Offender Registration Act (ASORA). It became effective August 10, 1994, after Doe was convicted, sentenced, and released from prison, but before he completed his probation. ASORA requires sex offenders to register with the Alaska Department of Corrections, the Alaska State Troopers, or local police. It requires registrants to disclose their names, addresses, places of employment, date of birth, information about their conviction, all aliases used, driver's license numbers, information about the vehicles they have access to, any identifying physical features, anticipated address changes, and information about any psychological treatment received. . . .

[W] e asked the parties to submit supplemental briefs addressing whether as applied to Doe ASORA violates Alaska's prohibition against ex post facto laws.

Article I, section 15 of the Alaska Constitution, like article I, section 9 of the United States Constitution, provides that "[n]o . . . ex post facto law shall be passed." An ex post facto law is a law "passed after the occurrence of a fact or commission of an act, which retrospectively changes the legal consequences or relations of such fact or deed." . . . [T]he prohibition applies only to penal statutes; the critical question is therefore whether ASORA imposes additional punishment on individuals, like Doe, who committed their crimes before ASORA became effective. Federal courts use a two-part test to determine whether a statute imposes punishment. . . . We will refer to this test as the "intent-effects" test or the "multifactor effects" test. . . .

The intent-effects test would usually first require us to consider whether the Alaska Legislature, when it enacted ASORA, intended to enact a regulatory scheme that is civil and non-punitive. If the purpose was not punishment but regulation, the test would next require us to determine whether the effects of regulation are so punitive that we must nonetheless conclude that ASORA imposes punishment.

It is not necessary to address the first step of the test—whether the legislature intended ASORA to punish convicted sex offenders—because the second part of the test—whether ASORA's effects are punitive—resolves the dispute before us. Assuming without deciding that the legislature intended ASORA to be non-punitive, we therefore focus on the statute's effects to determine whether they are punitive.

In assessing a statute's effects, the Supreme Court indicated . . . seven factors [to consider:]. . . .

1. Affirmative disability or restraint

We first ask "[w]hether the sanction involves an affirmative disability or restraint." . . .

[We find] that ASORA "impose[s] significant affirmative obligations and a severe stigma on every person to whom [it] appl[ies]." First, ASORA compels affirmative post-discharge conduct (mandating registration, re-registration,

(continued)

disclosure of public and private information, and updating of that information) under threat of prosecution. The duties are significant and intrusive, because they compel offenders to contact law enforcement agencies and disclose information, some of which is otherwise private, most of it for public dissemination. . . .

[We also find] that ASORA "exposes registrants, through aggressive public notification of their crimes, to profound humiliation and community-wide ostracism." . . .

ASORA requires release of information that is in part not otherwise public or readily available. Moreover, the regulations authorize dissemination of most ASORA registration information "for any purpose, to any person." Taken in conjunction with the Alaska Public Records Act, ASORA's treatment of this information, confirmed by the regulations, seems to require that the information be publicly available. By federal law, it is disseminated statewide, indeed worldwide, on the state's website. . . . We also recognized in Doe A that several sex offenders had stated that they had lost their jobs, been forced to move from their residences, and received threats of violence following establishment of the registry, even though the facts of their convictions had always been a matter of public record. We therefore conclude that the harmful effects of ASORA stem not just from the conviction but from the registration, disclosure, and dissemination provisions. . . .

2. Sanctions that have historically been considered punishment

We next determine "whether [the statute's effects have] historically been regarded as a punishment." ASORA does not expressly impose sanctions that have been historically considered punishment. Because registration acts such as ASORA are "of fairly recent origin," courts addressing this issue have determined that there is no historical equivalent to these registration acts. [Instead] [t]he fact that ASORA's registration reporting provisions are comparable to supervised release or parole supports a conclusion that ASORA is punitive.

3. Finding of scienter

Third, we consider "whether [the statute] comes into play only on a finding of scienter." The obligations of ASORA are not imposed solely upon the finding of scienter. ASORA also applies to strict liability offenses, such as statutory rape, that the law deems sufficiently harmful to effectively assume scienter. But even though ASORA applies to a few strict liability offenses, it overwhelmingly applies to offenses that require a finding of scienter for conviction. The few exceptions do not imply a non-punitive effect, given the assumption of scienter for those exceptions and the fact that a reasonable-mistake-of-age defense is allowed in a charge of statutory rape. This factor therefore receives little weight in our analysis; it weakly implies a punitive effect.

4. The traditional aims of punishment

We next ask "whether [the statute's] operation will promote the traditional aims of punishment—retribution and deterrence." . . .

We assume for sake of discussion that a statute limiting registration requirements and public dissemination to the extent necessary to protect the public could have a deterrent effect that would be merely incidental to its non-punitive purpose. But ASORA's registration and unlimited public dissemination requirements provide a deterrent and retributive effect that goes beyond any non-punitive purpose and that essentially serves the traditional goals of punishment.

5. Application only to criminal behavior . . .

As the state concedes, ASORA applies only to those "convicted" of specified offenses. Defendants charged with sex offenses but who plead out to non-sex offenses such as coercion or simple assault do not have to register even though

(continued)

(continued)

they may have engaged in the same conduct as individuals who do have to register. Likewise, even convicted defendants whose convictions are overturned for reasons other than insufficiency of evidence of guilt do not have to register despite having engaged in the same conduct. . . .

Because it is the criminal conviction, and only the criminal conviction, that triggers obligations under ASORA, we conclude that this factor supports the conclusion that ASORA is punitive in effect.

6. Advancing a non-punitive interest

We next ask whether, in the words of the Supreme Court, "an alternative purpose to which [the statute] may rationally be connected is assignable for it." We translate this as an inquiry whether ASORA advances a legitimate, regulatory purpose. ASORA can rationally be viewed as advancing a non-punitive purpose. . . .

The Ninth Circuit stated that the state's non-punitive interest in public safety "unquestionably provides support, indeed, the principal support, for the view that the statute is not punitive for Ex Post Facto Clause purposes." The Supreme Court also stated that ASORA's rational connection to a non-punitive purpose was a "[m]ost significant" factor in its determination that ASORA is non-punitive in effect. We likewise conclude that ASORA advances a non-punitive interest.

7. Closeness of connection of means to the state's interest in public safety

It is significant that ASORA's scope is broad; it encompasses a wide array of crimes that vary greatly in severity. Moreover, ASORA provides no mechanism by which a registered sex offender can petition the state or a court for relief from the obligations of continued registration and disclosure. . . .

Although the non-punitive aims are undeniably legitimate and important, ASORA's registration and dissemination provisions have consequences to sex offenders that go beyond the state's interest in public safety; we must therefore conclude that the Alaska statute is excessive in relation to the state's interest in public safety.

8. ASORA's effect

Summing up the effects under the seven factors, we conclude that ASORA's effects are punitive, and convincingly outweigh the statute's non-punitive purposes and effect. . . .

Because ASORA compels (under threat of conviction) intrusive affirmative conduct, because this conduct is equivalent to that required by criminal judgments, because ASORA makes the disclosed information public and requires its broad dissemination without limitation, because ASORA applies only to those convicted of crime, and because ASORA neither meaningfully distinguishes between classes of sex offenses on the basis of risk nor gives offenders any opportunity to demonstrate their lack of risk, ASORA's effects are punitive. We therefore conclude that the statute violates Alaska's ex post facto clause.

WHAT DO *YOU* THINK?

1. Did the Alaska law impose punitive or remedial measures against sex offenders?

2. In general, do you find that sexual offender registration and notification statutes, like Alaska's, serve as second forms of punishment?

3. What might legislators do to keep communities safe without imposing retroactive or duplicative (double jeopardy) forms of punishment on offenders?

CHAPTER **SUMMARY**

- Law comes from the Latin root *lex* or *legare*, which means "to bind." Law is a body of rules of action or conduct prescribed by a controlling authority and having binding *legal* force, which is designed to bring (bind) people together.

- Laws in the United States have roots in a number of other legal traditions, including natural law, positive law, and common law.

- Natural law is a theory that maintains that legal "truths" are found in nature. This theory holds that there are certain crimes and legal rights that are natural and therefore should be recognized in the form of human-made law.

- Legal positivism is a theory of law that maintains the only legitimate form of law is that which is written down and promulgated to subjects. This theory stresses the importance of the written word and is used to justify the use of constitutions, statutes, and contracts to resolve legal disputes.

- The English common law relies on judges and local customs and practices to resolve cases. This tradition uses judicial opinions as the primary source of law. Also central to common law is the principle of *stare decisis,* which demands that judges recognize precedents, or earlier decisions, in their rulings.

- Criminal law is but one type of law. It can be distinguished from other forms of the law in that violations of the criminal law are considered to be offenses against the state, the community, and the public. Moreover, it is the power of the state that is brought to bear against criminal offenders when crimes are investigated, when suspected offenders are tried, and when those convicted of violating criminal statutes are punished.

- Criminal law defines crimes according to the nature of the proscribed conduct and distinguishes among crimes by degree of seriousness. Felonies are serious crimes for which offenders may be sentenced to lengthy prison terms or (for crimes such as murder) may be put to death. Misdemeanors are less serious offenses for which offenders may be fined, placed on probation, or sentenced to brief terms of incarceration. Infractions or minor misdemeanors are offenses punishable by only monetary sanctions.

- Two important forms of the criminal law are substantive and procedural. Substantive criminal law defines crimes and specifies punishments for violations of the law. Criminal procedural law specifies the methods to be used in enforcing substantive law.

- Another major category of the law is civil law. Civil laws regulate private relations among individuals, businesses, and other legal entities, such as corporations.

- All laws, including criminal and civil law, facilitate predictable social interaction and guarantee a relative degree of safety to members of society.

- In additional to criminal law, morals, ethics, and civil law are also used to regulate human behavior. Morals draw upon provincial customs and peer-group pressure to gain conformity. Ethics generally rely upon professional groups and group-based sanctions to generate compliance. And civil laws typically use the threat of monetary sanctions, including compensatory and punitive damages, to promote good behavior.

KEY **TERMS**

Blame
briefing a case
Civil law
common law
common law states
Corpus Juris Civilis
crimes
crimes against nature
Crimes against property
criminal law
criminal proce
culpability
dure
Ethics
felonies
Hammurabi Code

inchoate offenses
infractions
Justinian Code
law
legal positivism
liability
Mala in se
Mala prohibita
minor misdemeanors
Misdemeanors
morality-based offenses
Morals
natural law theory
natural rights
penal law
Personal crimes

petty offenses
positive law
precedent
principle of legality
Public order offenses
punitive action
remedial action
Responsibility
rule of law
rule of lenity
stare decisis
tort
tortfeasor
treason
Uniform Crime Reports

QUESTIONS FOR **DISCUSSION**

1. What is the "rule of law"? How does it differ from morals and ethics?

2. How has the theory of natural law been used to influence American jurisprudence?

3. What is the role of common law in modern criminal law? How do laws of criminal procedure differ from substantive criminal laws?

4. What influence has legal positivism had on law in the United States?

5. What are the differences between a felony, a misdemeanor, and a minor misdemeanor?

6. How is it possible that a person can be charged with a criminal offense and sued for civil damages based on the same act?

7. What is the difference between punitive law and a remedial law?

8. How has the distinction between criminal and civil law been relevant in the passage and implementation of sexual offender registration laws?

REFERENCES

1. Henry Campbell Black, Jacqueline M. Nolan-Haley, and Joseph R. Nolan, *Black's Law Dictionary*, 6th ed. (St. Paul, MN: West Publishing Company, 1990), p. 1026.

2. Max Rheinstein, ed., *Max Weber on Law in Economy and Society* (Cambridge, MA: Harvard University Press, 1954).

3. John S. Baker, Jr., Daniel H. Benson, Robert Force, and B. J. George, Jr., *Hall's Criminal Law: Cases and Materials*, 5th ed. (Charlottesville, VA: The Michie Company, 1993), p. 3.

4. American Bar Association Section of International and Comparative Law, *The Rule of Law in the United States* (Chicago, IL: American Bar Association, 1958).

5. Thomas Aquinas, *Summa Theologica* (Notre Dame, IN: University of Notre Dame Press, 1983).

6. 539 U.S. 558 (2003).

7. Louis Henkin, "Rights: Here and There," *Columbia Law Review* 81 (1981): 1582.

8. Marvin Wolfgang, *The Key Reporter* (Phi Beta Kappa) 52, no. 1.

9. Howard Abadinsky, *Law and Justice* (Chicago, IL: Nelson-Hall, 1988), p. 6.

10. 553 U.S. ___, 128 S. Ct. 2020 (2008).

11. Florida Criminal Code, Chapter 775, Section 1.

12. Arizona Revised Statutes, Title 1, Section 201.

13. Todd Nissen, "Suicide Advocate Kevorkian Acquitted for Third Time," *Reuters online*, May 14, 1996.

14. British Columbia Superior Courts home page, http://www.courts.gov.bc.ca/

15. A. Ashworth, "Punishment and Compensation: Victims and the State," *Oxford Journal of Legal Studies* 6 (1986): 89.

16. "Infractions" are not considered crimes under the Model Penal Code.

17. Clarence Ray Jeffery, "The Development of Crime in Early English Society," *Journal of Criminal Law, Criminology, and Police Science* 47 (1957): 647–66.

18. See, for example, James Q. Wilson, *The Moral Sense* (New York: Free Press, 1993).

19. Although they may be subject to civil, administrative, and other sanctions.

20. General Statutes of Georgia, 51–1–1.

21. Carrie Dowling, "Jury Awards $150 Million in Blazer Crash," *USA Today*, June 4, 1996, p. 3A.

22. Jane E. Allen, "Simpson Appeal Rejected," *USA Today*, April 29, 1997, p. 1A.

23. Steve Friess, "O. J. Simpson Found Guilty in Robbery Trial," *New York Times*, October 4, 2008, http://www.nytimes.com/2008/10/04/us/04simpson.html (accessed November 3, 2008).

APPENDIX
DEVELOPING YOUR LEGAL ANALYSIS

A. THE LAW WHERE YOU LIVE

Assume that Frances Justice, the general counsel for your school, has asked you to do some legal research for her. It seems that a few students at your institution have engaged in activities on campus that may be unethical or even criminal. Specifically, school authorities found Johnny Schlossed, an eighteen-year-old student, drinking alcohol in his dorm room. Authorities also apprehended Clare Joint, a thirty-year-old senior, after they saw her carrying marijuana into a classroom. In addition, school officials were notified that Ima Cheeter, a twenty-year-old junior who is married with two children, plagiarized the term paper she submitted to her English professor and was having an extramarital affair with another student.

The general counsel would like for you to prepare a legal memorandum (see format below) identifying all possible sanctions—legal, criminal, and ethical—that these students might face for their behavior. The school's attorney wants you to review the laws of your state and local jurisdictions, as well as the ethical standards for students at your school (most likely found in your Student Code of Conduct), and assess whether the students' actions are criminal, unethical, and/or just plain immoral. For example, what ethical consequences does your school impose for plagiarism? Could this conduct also be considered a form of criminal theft? In addition, the general counsel wants to know the possible penalties for any criminal or unethical behavior.

B. INSIDE THE FEDERAL COURTS

Assume that Sam Johnson, the elected county prosecutor for your local jurisdiction, has decided to run for Congress and has asked for your assistance on his campaign. Johnson has learned that you are studying criminal law and wants to use your newly acquired research skills. Specifically, as a part of his campaign platform, Johnson is thinking about proposing the repeal of federal laws that ban gambling and marijuana. Johnson has asked you to prepare a memorandum outlining the specifics of federal gambling and marijuana laws and assessing whether these laws should be repealed.

As a result, you are asked to identify and read the federal laws that restrict or prohibit gambling (found at the websites below) and assess whether these laws are consistent with the purposes of imposing criminal liability for certain forms of human behavior. Then, using the materials from this chapter, explain why you would maintain or repeal these laws.

Cornell University Law School Legal Information Institute

http://topics.law.cornell.edu/wex/gambling

National Gambling Impact Study Commission

http://govinfo.library.unt.edu/ngisc/reports/statutes.html

Next, review the federal laws criminalizing marijuana-related activities (found in the Controlled Substances Act (CSA) located at 21 U.S.C. § 811), as well as the information

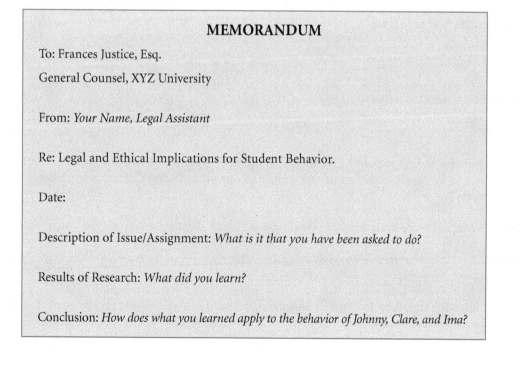

MEMORANDUM

To: Frances Justice, Esq.

General Counsel, XYZ University

From: *Your Name, Legal Assistant*

Re: Legal and Ethical Implications for Student Behavior.

Date:

Description of Issue/Assignment: *What is it that you have been asked to do?*

Results of Research: *What did you learn?*

Conclusion: *How does what you learned apply to the behavior of Johnny, Clare, and Ima?*

provided by groups who wish to relax the criminality of using the drug (see websites below). Using the purposes and standards for criminal law outlined in this chapter, address whether you would modify these laws to allow for a medical exception to the current law that would allow individuals to possess and use marijuana to treat serious medical conditions. Are there other exceptions or limitations to the current law that you would also make?

Americans for Safe Access

http://www.safeaccessnow.org/article.php?id=2638

National Organization for the Repeal of Marijuana Laws (NORML)

http://norml.org/index.cfm?group_id=4575

C. CYBER SOURCES

Assume that you are a legal professional within a law firm and that your supervising attorney has asked you to train Ima Novice, a newly hired legal assistant within the firm, on the various legal research tools used in criminal cases. Specifically, you are asked to compare the advantages and disadvantages of using electronic research methods (identified in Appendix A of this book, as well as any other electronic tools you find helpful), as opposed to those methods associated with more traditional legal research resources, such as bound materials.

Using classmates to play the role of Ima (your trainee), explain which resources you have found to be the most efficient, accurate, and user-friendly. As an illustration, use both online and hard-copy resources to locate the full-text opinion in *Doe v. Alaska,* 189 P.3d 999 (2008). Identify which method of research is most effective. Then, using the recommended format found below, as well as the "How to brief a case" feature located in Appendix A at the end of this book, demonstrate how to prepare a legal brief of the *Doe* case.

D. ETHICS AND PROFESSIONALISM

Assume that you are a legal assistant working with a local prosecutor's office. One of the assistant prosecutors in the office, Marty Miller, has been asked to give a presentation to a group of local police officers regarding the probable cause standard for obtaining search warrants. Mr. Miller asked you to create an electronic slide presentation for him on the subject and to otherwise outline his talk based on the standard principles and cases for probable cause and search warrants. You completed the task and Mr. Miller is very pleased with your work.

The presentation is scheduled for tomorrow, but Mr. Miller has just sent you an e-mail saying that he is very sick and will be unable to give the presentation as scheduled. Mr. Miller, however, does not want the police officers to miss out on the presentation and has asked if you would mind doing the presentation for him. You are quite comfortable sharing your materials and insights with the police group, but you are concerned about whether it would be ethically appropriate for you to deliver the talk, since it might be considered to be the practice of law. Review any ethical standards from your home state jurisdiction that might apply, as well as the ethical standards set forth in the following sources, and then draft an e-mail response to Mr. Miller regarding his request.

American Bar Association

http://www.abanet.org/legalservices/paralegals/downloads/modelguidelines.pdf

The American Alliance of Paralegals, Inc.

http://www.aapipara.org/Ethicalstandards.htm

National Federation of Paralegal Associations, Inc.

http://www.paralegals.org/displaycommon.cfm?an=1&subarticlenbr=133

National Association of Legal Assistants

http://www.nala.org/code.aspx

Doe v. Condon, 532 S.E.2d 879 (S.C. 2000)

CASE BRIEF

Case Title and Citation: *Doe v. Alaska 189 P.3d 999 (2008).*

Facts: *Provide the basic substantive and procedural history of the case.*

Issue(s): *Identify and state the legal question(s) addressed by the court. Typically, this section is phrased in the form of a question. For example, "Is Alaska's sexual offender registration law an unconstitutional ex post facto regulation under the Alaska Constitution?"*

Judgment: *Determine the decision and numeric vote of the court. How did the court answer the legal question(s)?*

Rationale: *Assess why the court reached the judgment. Explain the reasoning of the court's opinion. Typically, this should be the longest section of the brief.*

Concurring/Dissenting Opinions: Identify any concurring or dissenting opinions written by court members. Explain the rationale for these opinions.

chapter **two**

SYSTEMS, SOURCES, AND SEMANTICS OF CRIMINAL LAW

The language of law must not be foreign to the ears of those who are to obey it.

—Judge Learned Hand U.S. Court of Appeals for the Second Circuit (1924–61)

The United States is a nation of laws: badly written and randomly enforced.

—Frank Zappa American guitarist, record producer, and film director

LEARNING OBJECTIVES

After reading this chapter, you should be able to

- Identify the primary structures and characteristics of the American legal system.

- Appreciate the multiple layers and branches of government involved in the criminal justice system.

- Understand the importance and relevance of federalism in processing criminal cases.

- Discuss the impact of the separation of governmental powers in criminal cases.

- Explain the adversarial and accusatorial features of criminal justice.

- Identify the different sources of criminal law.

- Appreciate that the language of criminal laws must be interpreted and applied by actors within the criminal justice system.

- Identify and understand the different methods for interpreting the legal language found in criminal laws and constitutional provisions.

THE MODERN U.S. LEGAL SYSTEM

As outlined in Chapter 1, criminal law involves legal disputes in which the government seeks to impose punitive sanctions upon individuals and entities for allegedly harmful conduct. Given the necessary involvement of government in criminal cases, one of the first considerations for legal professionals is the nature and structure of government as it affects criminal cases.

As most people know, we do not have one source of government in the United States. The framers, having experienced abuses of consolidated power in the British monarchy, sought to avoid the concentration of power in a single entity. As a result, we do not have a unitary form of government, where all power is concentrated in the hands of one individual or source. Instead, governmental power has been spread out among different levels and different branches of authority. The division of power among layers of government is called *federalism*, with the federal, state, and local governments being the primary units. The division of power among branches of government is referred to as the *separation of powers*. In this arena, the legislative, executive, and judicial bodies at each layer of government constitute the primary units of authority. Together, the multiple levels and branches create many locations where criminal justice is conducted within the American political system. See Figure 2-1 (below).

The multiple layers and branches of authority in the American legal system illustrate that criminal law often is not a one-dimensional process. Activity that is viewed as legal at the federal level may be criminal at the state or local level—and vice versa. Similarly, what may be permitted by one branch of authority may be banned by another branch. As a result, in evaluating a person's criminal culpability, legal professionals must learn to assess cases in their totality, looking at the case from the vantage point of multiple layers and branches of governmental power.

federalism

the division of power among layers of government, with the federal, state, and local governments as the primary units of division.

separation of powers

the division of power among different branches of government, typically legislative, executive, and judicial bodies.

FIGURE 2-1 **Layers and Branches of Criminal Law in American Federalism**

Level/Branch	Legislative	Executive	Judicial
Federal	Congressional statutes	Attorney General U.S. Attorneys Federal law enforcement officers (FBI, DEA, ATF, etc.) Administrative rules	Court opinions from the U.S. Supreme Court, Courts of Appeals, and District Courts
State	State statutes	State attorneys general Local prosecutors State law enforcement officers Administrative rules	Court rulings from the state superior court, courts of appeals, and trial courts
Local	Codes or ordinances adopted by city, county, village, or other municipality	Local solicitor, prosecutor, or law director Local police or sheriffs Local agency rules	Court rulings by mayor's courts, municipal courts, or other local tribunals

Federalism

Federalism refers to a system of government that has both local and national elements. This is contrasted with unitary systems that have only one national or centralized government, although regional or local subunits may exist. The term *federal* comes from the Latin word *foedus*, which means compact or treaty. Consistent with this definition, a federal government, at least in the American experience, involves a compact (constitution) between a national government and a group of state governments. Accordingly, "[a] federal system of government is one in which two governments have jurisdiction over the inhabitants."[1]

In a federal form of government, a central government coexists with various state and local governments. In the American experience, the U.S. Constitution establishes the basic architecture for this relationship of power. This document provides organizational constructs for the national government and establishes bedrock principles for its powers. But it also has profound implications for state and local governments. The Constitution gives the national government jurisdiction over activities such as interstate and international commerce, foreign relations, warfare, immigration, bankruptcies, civil rights, and certain crimes committed on the high seas and against the "law of nations" (or international law). Individual states are prohibited from entering into treaties with foreign governments, from printing their own money, from granting titles of nobility (as is the central government), and various other things.

States, however, retain the power to make laws regulating or criminalizing activity within their boundaries. The general authority of the states to regulate for the health, safety, and welfare of their citizens is the police power. Among the states, there is considerable commonality among the criminal statutes because all state codes criminalize much of the same misconduct, such as murder, rape, robbery, assault and battery, burglary, and theft. Although statutory terminology may differ from state to state, and although particular crimes themselves may even be given different names, commonalities can be found among almost all of the states in terms of the types of behavior they define as criminal.

The **Model Penal Code** (MPC) represents one attempt to standardize American criminal law between jurisdictions. The MPC is a compilation of criminal codes drafted by legal experts that is offered as a model for legislative bodies to consider and perhaps adopt for their own criminal codes. State legislatures often consult and use the model codes found in the MPC when drafting legislation. This leads to substantial commonality among some state statutes. Portions of the MPC are found in Appendix C.

Practically speaking, American federalism has resulted in the creation of fifty state criminal codes, the creation of a separate U.S. criminal code, and numerous city and local ordinances detailing many types of violations. As a consequence, crimes can have different descriptions and associated penalties depending on the *jurisdiction* (the legal authority of a given location) that governs the alleged criminal conduct. In federalism, there are two primary forms of jurisdiction—exclusive and concurrent. **Exclusive jurisdiction** exists when only one government has the sole authority to prosecute a case. For example, a local government may have exclusive jurisdiction to prosecute jaywalking cases, whereas the federal government may have exclusive authority over cases involving treason, espionage, or counterfeiting crimes.

Concurrent jurisdiction exists when more than one government has authority to prosecute an alleged criminal act. In cases where both the federal and a state government have authority to charge a person with a crime based on the same

Model Penal Code (MPC)
a compilation of model criminal codes drafted by legal experts and offered as a model for legislative bodies to consider and perhaps adopt for their own criminal codes.

jurisdiction
the legal authority to address disputes within a given geographic location or subject matter.

exclusive jurisdiction
legal authority vested in one governmental body to the exclusion of all others; provides sole authority to prosecute a case.

concurrent jurisdiction
legal authority that is shared by more than one government; allows multiple governments to prosecute an alleged criminal act.

Escorted by U.S. Marshals, Atlanta Falcons quarterback Michael Vick (R) arrives at the federal courthouse for his arraignment in Richmond, Virginia on July 26, 2007. Later that year, Vick plead guilty to federal conspiracy and dogfighting charges and was sentenced to 23 months in federal prison. In November 2008, based on the same basic facts from the federal case, Vick plead guilty to state criminal charges in a Virginia state court and received a suspended criminal sentence. Vick served his federal term of incarceration and is now playing quarterback for the Philadelphia Eagles. Should federal laws have been used to prosecute a local dogfighting case? Why or why not?

Law Line 2-1
Michael Vick's Indictments

Supremacy Clause

a provision in Article VI of the U.S. Constitution that generally makes federal standards for criminal law and procedure superior to those standards at the state and local levels; ensures that federal standards serve as a minimum legal threshold for acceptable criminal practices, with which all levels and branches of authority must comply.

harmful conduct, each jurisdiction can initiate a criminal case without violating principles of double jeopardy. See Chapter 13. For example, in 2007, a federal court convicted and sentenced NFL quarterback Michael Vick for a federal conspiracy offense involving the bankrolling of a dogfighting operation in Newport News, Virginia. A few months later and based on the same general conduct, a Virginia grand jury indicted Vick on state charges of unlawfully torturing and killing dogs and promoting dogfights. Concurrent jurisdiction over criminal cases can also exist between two or more states where the criminal conduct occurred in or substantially affected multiple state jurisdictions.

Supremacy Clause.   In cases where both federal and state authorities have concurrent jurisdiction over a crime, but there is a conflict between the two laws, federal law usually will trump state law because of the Supremacy Clause of Article VI of the U.S. Constitution. This clause provides in relevant part:

> This Constitution, and the Laws of the United States which shall be made in Pursuance thereof; and all Treaties made, or which shall be made, under the Authority of the United States, shall be the supreme Law of the Land; and the Judges in every State shall be bound thereby, any Thing in the Constitution or Laws of any State to the Contrary notwithstanding.

The ***Supremacy Clause*** generally establishes federal standards for criminal procedure as the minimum threshold for acceptable practices, to which all levels and branches of authority must comply. Similarly, because local governments are essentially created or chartered by their home state, their legal authority must comply with state standards as well. In other words, under Article VI, there is an authoritative "pecking order" or food chain within the criminal justice system that is used to assure that criminal defendants and suspects are treated fairly. See Figure 2-2. In this pecking order, the U.S. Constitution is supreme with respect to all other forms of law, requiring that state and local authorities must provide at least the minimum level of protection set forth in the federal constitution. But

FIGURE 2-2 **The Legal Hierarchy in a Criminal Case**

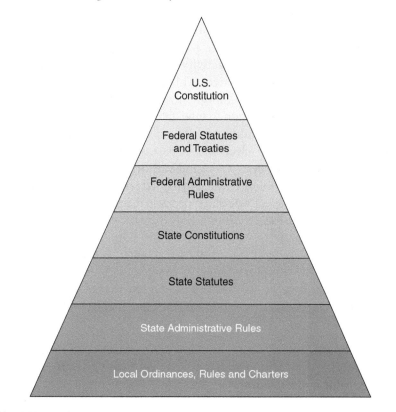

state constitutions are superior to local charters.[2] For example, a state statute governing search and seizure procedures cannot conflict with the standards established by the Fourth Amendment of the U.S. Constitution. Similarly, a local police practice for interrogating suspects cannot fall short of meeting Fourth Amendment requirements or state standards for such procedure.

The Supremacy Clause, however, does not authorize the federal government to regulate areas that belong exclusively to the states. The sovereignty of the states is preserved in the Tenth Amendment, which reads, "[t]he powers not delegated to the United States by the Constitution, nor prohibited by it to the states, are reserved to the states respectively, or to the people." This is sometimes called the states' rights provision because it essentially allows the states to exercise substantial police powers over those individuals within their jurisdiction. Most criminal laws at the state level are derived from the states' general *police powers*. Accordingly, the federal government may not assume general police powers and begin to punish thieves, robbers, rapists, and murderers whose crimes have no connection to federal constitutional authority.

The Constitution also protects several individual rights, with narrow exceptions, from governmental intrusion. For legal professionals, the challenge is determining which areas are (1) exclusive to state governments and thereby off-limits to federal regulation, (2) exclusive to federal authority and thus removed from state police power, and (3) subject to concurrent regulation by both federal and state authorities.

Expanding Federal Authority.   In recent decades, federal authorities have expanded their jurisdiction in criminal cases. This expansion has been facilitated by several constitutional provisions, most notably, the *Commerce Clause* of Article I,

police powers
the general power of states to make and enforce criminal laws within their geographic boundaries; derived in part from the Tenth Amendment.

Commerce Clause
provision in Article I, section 8 of the U.S. Constitution that allows Congress to regulate interstate commerce; used as constitutional authority for many federal criminal statutes.

interstate commerce
commerce that flows "among the several states," as opposed to exclusively within a given state.

affectation doctrine
a judicial doctrine interpreting the Commerce Clause; maintains that Congress has the authority to regulate interstate commerce and anything else that has a close and substantial relation to interstate commerce.

section 8 of the U.S. Constitution. This provision authorizes Congress to regulate *interstate commerce* (commerce "among the several states"). Over the years, courts and other authorities have interpreted the term *interstate commerce* to mean more than just goods and services traveling between and among the states. The courts have broadly referred to interstate commerce as "intercourse" of all types and have permitted Congress to regulate any activity—including purely local or intrastate activity—that affects interstate commerce. This is known as the *affectation doctrine* and it maintains that congressional authority includes the right to regulate all matters having a close and substantial relation to interstate commerce. See Figure 2-3.

The affectation doctrine would apply to a defendant who, without leaving his home, sends threatening mail—electronic or paper—to another person, seeking to extort money from the other person. Federal authorities likely could prosecute the defendant under federal fraud or extortion-related laws, even if it occurred exclusively within the boundaries of one state, because it involved the use of interstate commerce–the transmission of messages in the U.S. mail system or across the Internet.

In many cases, the federal authority to prosecute cases under the Commerce Clause can also override competing interests of the states. For example, in *Gonzales v. Raich* (2005),[3] the State of California passed a law protecting the use of marijuana for medical purposes. Under this law, the state had agreed not to prosecute

FIGURE 2-3 **The Affectation Doctrine: Can Congress Regulate Conduct under the Commerce Clause?**

The Affectation Doctrine

The Text of the Constitution's Commerce Clause reads: "Congress shall have power . . . To regulate commerce with foreign nations, and among the several states, and with the Indian tribes;"

The Supreme Court has interpreted the text of the Commerce Clause to mean that Congress can regulate any activity that substantially affects interstate commerce.

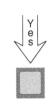

Locally Grown *Marijuana Gonzales v. Raich* (2005)

Using Internet to Commit Fraud

Local Acts of Arson or Rape *Jones v. U.S.* (2000) *U.S. v. Morrison* (2000)

individuals for growing or using marijuana if done for legitimate medical purposes. Federal authorities, however, continued to treat the cultivation of marijuana as a crime and refused to suspend the application of federal law in California. Angel Raich, who was using homegrown medical marijuana legally under California law, sued federal authorities seeking to halt the application of federal antimarijuana laws in California. The Supreme Court ruled against Raich, finding that the Commerce Clause authorized federal authorities to maintain criminal prohibitions against marijuana because the cultivation and use of the drug affected interstate commerce. Specifically, the Court found that "[g]iven the enforcement difficulties that attend distinguishing between marijuana cultivated locally and marijuana grown elsewhere, and concerns about diversion into illicit channels, we have no difficulty concluding that Congress had a rational basis for believing that failure to regulate the intrastate manufacture and possession of marijuana would leave a gaping hole in the [federal government's law]."

At times, it might seem like the affectation doctrine might allow Congress to regulate virtually every form of human behavior. But in recent years, the Supreme Court has placed some limitations on Congress's authority under the Commerce Clause. In 1995, the Court ruled in *United States* v. *Lopez*[4] that Congress had overstepped its authority to regulate interstate commerce in passing the 1990 Gun-Free School Zones Act. The legislation made it a crime to possess a firearm in a school zone. Federal authorities defended the act, arguing that, among other things, guns in schools have a negative impact on education, which in turn has an adverse effect on citizens' productivity. Authorities claimed that interstate commerce would be negatively affected by allowing guns to be carried in school zones. The Supreme Court, however, disagreed and invalidated the law, finding that the legislation exceeded Congress's authority to regulate commerce among the states.

Similarly, in *Jones v. United States* (2000),[5] the Supreme Court overturned the federal arson conviction of a man who had firebombed his cousin's home.[6] The defendant had been arrested and prosecuted under Section 844 of Title 18 of the United States Code, which makes it a federal crime to maliciously damage or

Angel Raich, left, of Oakland, Calif., and Diane Monson, right, from near Oroville, Calif., leave the U.S. Supreme Court in Washington, after the justices heard arguments on their medicinal use of marijuana, Monday, Nov. 29, 2004. Raich, who suffers from an inoperable brain tumor and scoliosis, and Monson, who has a degenerative spine disease, pleaded to the Court that they are law-abiding citizens who are seriously ill and need marijuana to survive the pain of their health problems. In *Gonzales v. Raich* (2005), the Supreme Court ruled that federal authorities can prosecute individuals under federal drug laws, even where state law allows for the medicinal use of marijuana. Should individuals using marijuana for medical purposes under state law be threatened with federal prosecution?

destroy, by means of fire or an explosive, any building used in interstate or foreign commerce or in any activity affecting interstate or foreign commerce. The Court found that this particular instance of arson could not be prosecuted under the law because the residence was not *used* in interstate or foreign commerce. The Court rejected the government's argument that the Indiana residence involved in this case was constantly used in at least three activities affecting commerce: (1) it was "used" as collateral to obtain and secure a mortgage from an Oklahoma lender, who, in turn, "used" it as security for the loan; (2) it was "used" to obtain from a Wisconsin insurer a casualty insurance policy, which safeguarded the interests of the home-owner and the mortgagee; and (3) it was "used" to receive natural gas from sources outside Indiana.

And in *United States v. Morrison* (2000),[7] the Supreme Court invalidated the federal Violence Against Women Act of 1994, which provided victims of gender crimes a civil cause of action against their perpetrators. *Morrison* involved a woman who sought civil damages under federal law against defendants who allegedly raped her. The Court, however, found that, because rape is "not, in any sense of the phrase, economic activity," Congress lacked authority to regulate it under the Commerce Clause. The Court concluded that the "Constitution requires a distinction between what is truly national and what is truly local . . . . The regulation and punishment of intrastate violence that is not directed at instrumentalities, channels, or goods involved in interstate commerce has always been the province of the states."

The *Lopez, Jones,* and *Morrison* rulings illustrate that there are some constitutional limitations on federal authority in the arena of criminal law. But the Court's decision in *Raich* and the general application of the affectation doctrine demonstrate that the power of the federal government to regulate individuals' behavior through criminal law is still quite substantial. Accordingly, legal professionals should be aware of Congress's expansive power to pass criminal laws under the Commerce Clause, while also being mindful that there might be some legal limitations on this authority. In these latter cases, constitutional challenges to federal criminal statutes might be raised under the Commerce Clause.

Federal Question Doctrine.   Invariably, even in state criminal cases, you will hear someone say, "I'm going to take my case all the way to the United States Supreme Court." The question is, how could the U.S. Supreme Court—the highest court in the federal judiciary—have jurisdiction in a matter that originated at the state level? The short answer is that, under Article III of the U.S. Constitution, federal courts, including the Supreme Court, may have jurisdiction to review state cases when a federal question has been properly raised in the matter. Article III provides in part:

> The judicial power [of the United States] shall extend to all cases, in law and equity, arising under this Constitution, the laws of the United States, and treaties made, or which shall be made, under their authority;—to all cases affecting ambassadors, other public ministers and consuls;—to all cases of admiralty and maritime jurisdiction;—to controversies to which the United States shall be a party;—to controversies between two or more states;—between a state and citizens of another state;—between citizens of different states;—between citizens of the same state claiming lands under grants of different states, and between a state, or the citizens thereof, and foreign states, citizens or subjects.

federal question
a legal issue that relates to the U.S. Constitution, a federal treaty, statute, administrative action, or some other federal legal standards; necessary in order to have jurisdiction in federal courts.

This provision, along within corresponding federal statutes, authorizes federal courts to review matters involving a ***federal question***, which is a legal issue that relates to the U.S. Constitution, a federal treaty, statute, administrative action, or some other federal legal standards.

Typically, federal judicial review of state criminal cases occurs in two scenarios. First, some parties in state cases seek review by the U.S. Supreme Court after they have exhausted all of their direct appeals through the state court system. They do this by asking the Court for a ***writ of certiorari***, which is an order "calling a case up" from a federal or state court. In most areas of the law, the Supreme Court has discretion to hear a case, and thus must issue a writ of certiorari before a case will have jurisdiction before the Court. The second scenario occurs after a defendant has exhausted all direct appeals and postconviction appeals in the state system and then seeks a federal ***writ of habeas corpus***, which is a court order to release a person who is being held in violation of his or her civil rights. As discussed in Chapter 14, some state inmates initiate a federal request for a writ of habeas corpus by filing a petition in the federal district court for the jurisdiction in which they are being detained. See Figure 2-4.

In both scenarios, petitioners seeking federal judicial review of state-initiated criminal cases must demonstrate that the case involves a substantial federal question. For example, if a local police officer engages in an unreasonable search of a person's car, there would be a federal question as to whether the officer's actions violated the Fourth Amendment. Even though the officer's actions were purely local in nature, they could nonetheless involve a federal question because there are federal standards (Fourth and Fourteenth Amendments) that apply to state and local searches. Thus, it is important for legal professionals to raise any and all legal standards—federal, state, and local—that might apply in a given case. If there are legal standards at the federal, state, and local levels for searches and seizures, interrogations, arrests, or any other conduct related to a case, you should identify all of

writ of certiorari
"to call the thing up"; an order from the U.S. Supreme Court demanding that a case at a lower federal court or a state court be sent up to the Supreme Court; mechanism by which most cases reach the U.S. Supreme Court.

writ of habeas corpus
a court order to release a person who is being held in custody in violation of his or her civil rights.

FIGURE 2-4 **Federal Court Review of State Criminal Cases**

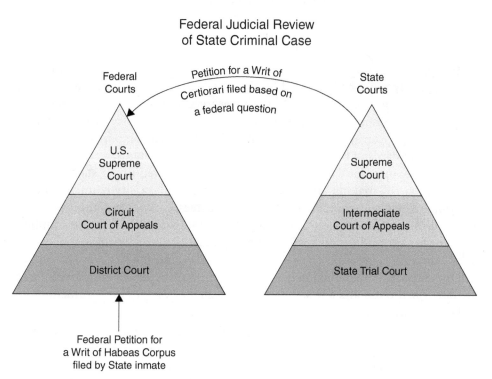

them at the inception of the case. In fact, in many areas, federal questions might be deemed to be waived by federal and state courts if they are not raised initially and consistently throughout the state and federal judicial process.

Overall, the federal question doctrine allows an expanded judicial review of state cases where federal issues are present. Cases that normally might end at the state appellate process might live to fight another day, perhaps even in a case accepted by the U.S. Supreme Court, if a federal question is present. As a result, it is incumbent on legal professionals involved in state and local criminal cases to recognize the companion federal standards present in some state and local cases and to identify these standards early in the process.

Separation of Powers

Just as federalism's vertical division of authority creates multiple sources for criminal law and enforcement power, so too does the horizontal separation of powers between the branches of government. The U.S. government, as well as the state and local governments, are generally divided into three branches, legislative, executive, and judicial. Within each branch, actors are vested with various degrees of authority to create, enforce, or interpret legal standards for criminal cases.

Legislative.   Article I of the Constitution established a bicameral (two-chambered) Congress. The two chambers of Congress—the House of Representatives and the Senate—together constitute the primary lawmaking body at the federal level. Within this authority, Congress declares what acts are criminal, defines the criminal process and the authorities of the governmental players (police, corrections, judges), and establishes the punishments for each crime. These measures are enacted in the form of statutes. To become law, they normally must be passed by majority vote within each chamber and approved by the president. If the president vetoes proposed legislation, Congress can override this veto if two-thirds of the members within each chamber vote to do so. To be enforceable, legislative statutes cannot violate provisions or principles of the U.S. Constitution.

States also have their own legislative bodies, of various names, that enact criminal laws. All states, except Nebraska, have two legislative chambers that must jointly approve legislation. These laws, often passed in the form of statutes or codes, typically must be approved by the state's governor to become effective, unless the state's legislature overrides the governor's veto. Once enacted, these laws apply to conduct committed in or involving the state's territorial jurisdiction. Within the American system of federalism, state laws must comport with the constitutional standards of both the federal and state governments.

Likewise, most local governments are also empowered under state law with limited penal rulemaking authority as well. As a result, a city council, county commission, village council, or township trustees can, within the authority delegated to them under state law, also pass local measures that impose criminal sanctions for harmful conduct within the local jurisdiction. These criminal provisions—sometimes referred to as ordinances, codes, and the like—must comply with the standards established in the U.S. Constitution, as well as the provisions of the state constitution and any standards established by the local government in its charter or other governing document.

Executive.   At the federal level, Article II of the Constitution vests executive authority in the president. This power makes the president the chief law enforcement officer of the United States. As such, the president is responsible for ensuring that all laws passed by Congress are enforced and that those who violate these laws are held accountable. In terms of prosecuting criminal violations, the **Department of Justice** (DOJ) serves as the primary prosecutorial authority at the federal level. This agency is directed by the **Attorney General** (AG), who is appointed by the president. In this role, the attorney general is regarded as the primary prosecutor for the federal government.

Within the DOJ, there are also **U.S. Attorneys** (USA), who serve as the lead prosecutor within one of ninety-four districts into which the federal judicial system is divided. The president appoints a U.S. Attorney for each district to direct the day-to-day affairs and prosecutions within the district. Within each U.S. Attorney's office, there are several **Assistant U.S. Attorneys** (AUSA) who work as prosecutors within the U.S. Attorney's office of a given federal judicial district. Most criminal cases at the federal level are directly prosecuted by AUSAs. Beyond the DOJ, there are many other federal law enforcement agencies, including Federal Bureau of Investigation (FBI), Drug Enforcement Agency (DEA), Secret Service, Homeland Security, Immigration and Customs, Transportation Security Administration, and others that are responsible for investigating and prosecuting crime.

In addition to having the power to investigate and prosecute crime, the president, operating through administrative agencies, also has the authority to enact regulations that have criminal implications. Under Articles I and II of the Constitution, Congress has delegated substantial authority to presidents to "execute" laws through the adoption of rules and regulations by administrative agencies. Any such delegation of authority by Congress must be accompanied by guidance, or in legal terms, an **intelligible principle**. Under the intelligible principle doctrine, Congress must provide clear and understandable directions and parameters for agencies to follow when adopting regulations.[8] When Congress supplies such principles, courts have held the delegation of such "quasi-legislative" functions to be constitutionally permissible. As a result, many administrative agencies within the executive branch can pass rules and regulations that impact criminal cases. For example, the Environmental Protection Agency may set limits on the amount of pollutants that can be emitted into the air. The violation of these administrative regulations may trigger a criminal investigation and/or prosecution.

At the state level, the governor is often regarded as the state's chief executor of the law, having been vested with constitutional authority to properly execute the laws of the state. But in terms of prosecution, states typically empower their attorney general with the lead authority to go after crime. Most **state attorneys general** are elected at large by state voters, but a few states allow the governor or legislative branch to appoint a person to this position. Within each state attorney general's office, there are many assistants who handle individual cases. In addition, states generally also allow **local prosecutors** to enforce the law through criminal prosecutions. In many states, prosecutors (often referred to as county prosecutors or district attorneys), who are either elected or appointed, serve as the primary enforcer of the state's law within a given local jurisdiction. Within each county prosecutor or district attorney's office, there are also several assistant prosecutors who administer cases within individual courtrooms. Many states also allow municipal governments to prosecute criminal violations of local ordinances or crime within a local jurisdiction. Prosecutors at the municipal level can be called **solicitors** or local prosecutors.

In addition to prosecutors, state and local governments have multiple agencies and departments that investigate criminal activity. These units include state attorney general investigators, state and local police departments, and administrative agencies. Overall, there are more than 20,000 law enforcement agencies in state and local government that are responsible for the investigation and prosecution of more than 90 percent of all crime in the United States.

Department of Justice (DOJ)
the primary prosecutorial authority and law enforcement agency at the federal level; led by the U.S. Attorney General.

Attorney General (AG)
the head of the U.S. Department of Justice; appointed by the president and serves as the lead prosecutor for the federal government.

U.S. Attorney (USA)
the lead prosecutor within a given federal district; appointed by the president.

Assistant U.S. Attorneys (AUSA)
prosecutors within the U.S. Attorney's office of a particular federal judicial district; serve as the primary trial attorneys for the government in criminal cases.

Law Line 2-2
The Department of Justice

intelligible principle
a judicial doctrine that allows Congress to delegate its legislative authority to executive agencies and officials, as long as intelligent and defined instructions are provided by Congress; allows presidents to "execute" laws through the adoption of rules and regulations by administrative agencies.

state attorney general
the lead prosecuting authority in most states; elected at large by voters in most states, but appointed by the governor or legislative branch in a few states.

local prosecutor
chief law enforcement officer in a particular local jurisdiction of a state; referred to as county prosecutor or district attorney in many states.

Judicial. At the federal level, Article III of the Constitution provides judicial power to the Supreme Court and such inferior courts that Congress chooses to create. Among other things, this judicial power vests the federal courts with the authority to adjudicate criminal cases prosecuted by the government. Today, there is a large system of federal courts composed primarily of **district courts** (trial courts), **circuit courts** (courts of appeals), and the **Supreme Court.**

There are ninety-four federal judicial districts, including at least one district in each state, the District of Columbia, and Puerto Rico. Within each district, there can be multiple courtrooms and judges. At the appellate level, there are thirteen circuit courts, organized into twelve regional circuits, which hear appeals from the district courts located within their geographic circuit, plus a Federal Circuit Court of Appeals, which has nationwide jurisdiction to hear appeals in specialized cases. The highest form of judicial authority in the United States is the U.S. Supreme Court. The Supreme Court has discretionary jurisdiction over nearly all cases where its review is sought. And generally speaking, the Court typically hears only about 1 percent of the cases that are appealed to it.

Each state also has a judicial system. Most states have a three-tier court structure, including a trial court layer, an intermediate court of appeals, and a supreme court. While the names for these courts can vary, the basic structure parallels that of the federal judicial system. A few states have a two-tiered system consisting of a trial court and a supreme court. Apart from this general structure, the organization of state courts and their personnel are determined by the laws that created the court system and by the court's own rules.

At both the federal and state levels, courts are responsible for administering justice, both civil and criminal. In criminal cases, trial courts are where criminal cases are filed, warrants are issued, juries are empaneled, witnesses and evidence are introduced, verdicts are rendered, and sentences are imposed. Trial courts hear and resolve legal disputes, oversee specific dimensions of the investigatory process, oversee the prosecution of cases once filed (and occasionally before charges are filed), and act as guardians of governmental architecture and civil liberties. The primary function of trial courts is to make factual determinations based on the available and admissible evidence and resolve disputes based on these facts and the relevant legal standards.

In addition, all judicial systems—both federal and state—also have at least one appellate court. These courts, which typically function in the form of three-judge panels, do not involve juries or other trial-like procedures. Instead, a panel of judges reviews the procedures of the trial court to determine whether there was reversible error. Advocates appearing before appellate courts typically submit written arguments to the court and, in many cases, will later appear before the court and present an oral argument. The court of appeals will then issue a ruling in the form of a written opinion. See Chapter 14 for more regarding the appellate process.

In addition, most state judicial systems have a second tier of appellate review, which is typically a supreme court consisting of multiple justices. While the first tier of appellate courts is usually organized geographically by districts throughout the state, the state supreme courts are generally a single court that occupies the highest judicial authority among the state's courts.

The primary power of courts is **judicial review**, which is the authority to review acts of government for their constitutionality and, where inconsistent with the Constitution, declare the acts null and void. This authority includes the ability to negate criminal laws, the actions of law enforcement officers, and the erroneous judgments of courts. Although this authority is not explicitly stated in the

---

District courts

trial courts in the federal judiciary; courts where most federal criminal cases are initiated.

Circuit courts

intermediate courts of appeals in the federal judiciary; hear most appeals from criminal cases decided by district courts.

Supreme Court

the only court required by Article III of the U.S. Constitution; the final arbiter of law regarding federal questions; hears appeals from lower federal courts and from state cases involving a federal question.

Law Line 2-3
The Federal Judiciary

judicial review

the authority of courts to review acts of government for their constitutionality and, where inconsistent with the Constitution, declare the acts null and void.

Constitution, the Supreme Court has claimed this authority ever since the landmark case of *Marbury v. Madison* (1803).[9] In that ruling, Chief Justice John Marshall asserted, "[i]t is emphatically the province and duty of the judicial department to say what the law is. Those who apply the rule to particular cases, must of necessity expound and interpret that rule. If two laws conflict with each other, the courts must decide on the operation of each."[10] Judicial review has been significant in criminal law. Through it, the Supreme Court and lower courts have reviewed, modified, and/or invalidated many state and federal legal standards applied in criminal cases.[11]

IN THE FIELD

Legal professionals should resist the temptation to employ a "one-size-fits-all" approach to criminal cases. The fact that there are multiple layers and branches of government involved in the creation, enforcement, and resolution of criminal standards means that legal professionals must be familiar with many different sets of rules and procedures. In many cases, these standards overlap or coexist with one another. In some state cases, federal standards may apply, and in some federal cases, state procedures may be relevant. The important thing to remember is that you must carefully review the rules and standards for the court in which your particular case is pending. Do not assume that the procedures and rules for one jurisdiction or court apply to all others.

AN ADVERSARIAL AND ACCUSATORIAL SYSTEM

Like other common law nations, the United States employs an adversarial and accusatorial system. An *adversarial system* is based on a competition between at least two parties. In most criminal cases, this involves a pitting of prosecutor against criminal defendant. An *accusatorial system* involves one party making an accusation (claim) about another party, thereby placing the accused party in a defensive position. In criminal cases, this typically involves the prosecutor filing an indictment or criminal complaint against a person, who thereby becomes labeled "the defendant." Criminal justice systems based on an adversarial and accusatorial process can be analogized to a dual between two parties, resulting in a winner and a loser.

This is unlike the dynamic in an inquisitorial system, which operates more like an ongoing inquiry, with both the prosecution and defense working together to find "the truth" of a particular dispute (Figure 2-5). In many inquisitorial

adversarial system
a justice system based on a competition between at least two parties; in most criminal cases, this involves a pitting of prosecutor against a criminal defendant.

accusatorial system
a justice system involving one party making an accusation (claim) about another party, thereby placing the accused party in a defensive position; in criminal cases, this typically involves the prosecutor filing an indictment or criminal complaint against a person, who thereby becomes labeled "the defendant."

FIGURE 2-5 **The Inquisitorial System versus the Adversarial System**

Inquisitorial System	**Adversarial System**
One continuous investigation/trial overseen by judge	Investigation overseen by police and separate judicial phase initiated by prosecutor with minimal judicial involvement in early stages
Judges play active role throughout process	Judges are more passive and attorneys play more active role
Truth is sought through investigation	Truth is sought through competition between prosecution and defense
Process is less formal than in an adversarial system	Process, especially once charges are filed, is highly formal and technical

systems, a magistrate leads the investigation and the transition from investigation to trial is seamless.

Accusatorial systems are punctuated by processes. Although exceptions can be found, such as when they seek warrants, police in the United States conduct their investigations with little judicial oversight. Then, the situation changes when the arrest occurs. A new player, the public prosecutor, enters the contest. In most cases, so too does defense counsel. From this point forward, the defense and prosecution are adversaries. The accusatorial process assumes that truth is best found by having competing forces searching, analyzing, and ultimately presenting their facts and theories. The judge plays a more passive role in the adversarial system than in the inquisitorial, largely acting as umpire between the parties and in a general oversight role. The accusatorial nature of the U.S. system refers to the balance that is struck between defendant and the government. The entire process is designed to protect the accused. The ultimate goal is to protect the civil liberties of all by protecting the rights of the accused.

Within this system, the government bears the burden of proof. It files the criminal charge against the defendant and has the responsibility of proving the defendant's guilt. The defense, on the other hand, has no obligation to prove innocence. In fact, defendants do not have to present any evidence at trial whatsoever. They may sit silent, call no witnesses, and present no facts. Nonetheless, defendants sometimes choose to present a defense, such as an alibi or an alternative theory of who committed the crime.

In any case, the prosecutors' ***burden of proof*** requires them to prove guilt beyond a **reasonable doubt**. Although the ***reasonable doubt standard*** is intertwined with the burden of proof requirement, the difference between the two is important (Figure 2-6). One is an *obligation* imposed on the prosecution; the other is a *criterion* that must be met if a conviction is to be obtained. In *In re Winship* (1970),[12] the Supreme Court held that "[t]he reasonable-doubt standard plays a vital role in the American scheme of criminal procedure . . . . The standard provides concrete substance for the presumption of innocence—that bedrock 'axiomatic and elementary' principle whose 'enforcement lies at the foundation of the administration of our criminal law.'" The Court went on to say, "[i]t is critical that the moral force of the criminal law not be diluted by a standard of proof that leaves people in doubt [about] whether innocent men are being condemned."[13] The Court, however, has not precisely defined "reasonable doubt." Instead, the Court has largely left it to the trial courts to communicate the essence of the concept to juries. Jury

burden of proof
a responsibility requiring a party to demonstrate the factual and legal liability or culpability of another party based on an identified level of evidentiary certainty.

reasonable doubt standard
the standard for the burden of proof in a criminal case, requiring the prosecutor to demonstrate with a high degree of evidentiary certainty that a defendant committed a criminal act.

FIGURE 2-6 **Standards of Proof Compared**

Standard	Defined	When Used
Beyond a reasonable doubt	High or moral certainty, but not 100% confidence	For convictions in criminal cases
Clear and convincing evidence	Greater than preponderance of evidence but less than beyond a reasonable doubt	To decide some select issues in criminal and quasi-criminal cases
Preponderance of evidence	Greater than 50% probability	For verdicts in civil cases

instructions regarding beyond a reasonable doubt are discussed in greater detail in Chapter 13.

In contrast to criminal cases, where the reasonable doubt standard prevails, a lesser standard of proof is needed in civil cases. A finding for the plaintiff in a civil case requires only the determination that a ***preponderance of the evidence*** shows that the defendant should be held accountable. A preponderance of the evidence can mean a probability of just over 50 percent that the defendant did what is claimed. Following the criterion of the preponderance of the evidence, a judge or jury can find for the plaintiff if they conclude that it is more likely than not that the allegations against the defendant are true.

A third standard of proof requires ***clear and convincing evidence***. Generally, this falls somewhere between beyond a reasonable doubt and preponderance of the evidence. Clear and convincing evidence establishes the reasonable certainty of a claim. The clear and convincing evidence standard requires less than proof beyond a reasonable doubt but more than a preponderance of the evidence. Oklahoma jury instructions on clear and convincing evidence, for example, read as follows: "[b]y requiring proof by clear and convincing evidence, I mean that you must be persuaded, considering all the evidence in the case, that each of these elements is highly probable and free from serious doubt."[14] Clear and convincing evidence is applied to specific issues in criminal cases. For example, some jurisdictions require defendants to prove insanity by clear and convincing evidence.

In the end, in a criminal case, the government is the accuser and shoulders a high burden of proof—beyond a reasonable doubt. The accused enjoys a presumption of innocence, freedom from self-incrimination, the right to a jury trial in most cases, the right to counsel (including free counsel, if indigent), the right to be free from unreasonable searches and seizures, and a host of other protections. The breach of some of these rights by the government can lead to dismissal of charges or to lesser remedies.

preponderance of the evidence
the standard for the burden of proof in some civil cases and some administrative hearings related to criminal cases, whereby a party must prove a claim by showing that it is more likely true than not; the lowest standard for a burden of proof.

clear and convincing evidence
a standard of proof used in some civil cases and in some administrative matters involving criminal cases; falls somewhere between the standards of proof beyond a reasonable doubt and preponderance of the evidence.

Law Line 2-4
Ethics for Legal Professionals

IN THE FIELD

The adversarial and accusatorial nature of the criminal justice system presents many challenges for legal professionals. Most people are used to participating in competitive environments, where winning is the primary objective. But for legal professionals working on criminal cases, the pursuit of client or employer interests must always be done within the parameters of the larger goals and objectives of the criminal justice system. Most jurisdictions have established rules and standards for the professional and ethical conduct of judges, attorneys, paralegals, and law enforcement officers. See Law Line 2-4. These rules and standards serve as the basis for the profession by maintaining minimum requirements for membership and participation within the field. And so while criminal cases themselves may create highly competitive venues for adversarial behavior, all work performed within this arena must conform to the underlying rules of the game. In short, the competitive nature of criminal cases can foster intense emotions and considerable temptations to win at all costs. But to be a true professional within the field, legal professionals must learn to balance these visceral feelings and competitive urges with sound and ethical judgments.

SOURCES OF CRIMINAL LAW

For most legal professionals, the primary source for criminal laws will be the statutes, codes, and ordinances passed by federal, state, and local legislative bodies. But legal standards established by federal and state constitutions, as well as those found in common law or in the Model Penal Code may also have real implications for criminal cases.

Statutes, Codes, and Ordinances

United States Code
body of federal statutes, including criminal laws, passed by Congress.

Law Line 2-5
United States Code

---

statutes
laws passed by legislative bodies at the federal and state levels; also known as codes in some states.

statutes or codes
the form of law used to organize a state's legislative enactments

Consistent with the doctrine of *nullum crimen sine lege* ("there is no crime if there is no statute"), most of today's criminal laws come in the form of legislative acts. These acts passed by federal, state, and local legislative bodies impose punitive sanctions for harmful conduct. At the federal level, criminal laws are called statutes. At the state level, these laws are referred to as statutes, codes, or revised codes. Criminal statutes are commonly organized by topic, such as homicide, theft, and computer crimes.

Federal criminal laws are found in the **United States Code**, which is the compilation of all federal laws passed by Congress. You will often see the Code abbreviated as "U.S.C." or "U.S.C.A." The latter set of initials refers to United States Code Annotated, which is an edited version of federal law that provides sources and explanatory material, including case references, to help readers understand the meaning of the statutory language. Citations of federal statutes usually contain the title of the code book in which the law is found and the precise section of the law. For example, the citation "18 U.S.C. § 3771(e)" refers the reader to Title 18 of the United States Code, section 3771(e). In that section, federal law defines the term *victim* for criminal cases. See Law Line 2-5.

At the state level, the sources for criminal law can vary. But typically, states use a body of **statutes or codes** to organize their laws. For example, the laws passed by the Louisiana legislature are compiled is a set of books called the Louisiana Statutes Annotated (abbreviated "LSA"). Some states have completed major revisions of their statutes and refer to their bodies of law as ***revised codes***. For example, in Ohio, most criminal laws are found in the Ohio Revised Code (often abbreviated as O.R.C. or just R.C.). Most codifications of law are organized by titles, chapters, and/or sections. See Law Line 2-6.

Local governments, which are subset forms of state government, typically organize their legal standards in the form of ***ordinances*** or resolutions, which must also provide at least the minimum level of protection as that found in superior forms of law. Local governments—counties, cities, townships, and villages—are often empowered by state law to define and punish crimes, usually misdemeanors and other petty offenses. Local laws are commonly known as ordinances. These measures read very much the same as statutes but are produced by local legislative authorities, such as city councils, county commissions, or township trustees. See Law Line 2-7.

revised code
the body of legislative laws in some states; indicates that the original body of statutes was revised at a particular time.

Law Line 2-6
State Statutes

ordinances
legislation enacted at the local level of some states.

Law Line 2-7
Local Ordinance Codes

Administrative Regulations

Another source of criminal law is administrative regulations, which are typically enacted by executive or administrative agencies at all levels of government. Properly enacted administrative regulations have the full authority of legislation and can be penal in nature, resulting in incarceration, fines, and other punishments.[15]

Executive or independent agencies also can create ***administrative rules*** that outline relevant procedures for criminal cases. These measures must satisfy not only the relevant constitutional standards applicable to the agency, but also any statutory requirements imposed by the legislative body that initially created the agency or whose laws are controlling against the agency. In other words, the rules imposed by administrative agencies are at the lowest level of the legal hierarchy in the American federal system. At the federal level, administrative rules are generally found in the ***Federal Register***, which is the official daily publication for rules, proposed rules, and notices of federal agencies and organizations, as well as executive orders and other presidential documents. See Law Line 2-8.

U.S. governmental agencies and commissions make rules that are semilegislative or semijudicial in character. The Federal Trade Commission (FTC), Internal Revenue Service (IRS), and Environmental Protection Agency (EPA) are examples of administrative agencies that make such rules. These agencies formulate rules, investigate violations, and impose sanctions. They enforce rules relating to a variety of crimes, including securities fraud, income tax evasion, selling contaminated food, and dumping toxic waste.

administrative rules
the legal standards adopted by executive officials and agencies; also known as administrative regulations.

Federal Register
the official daily publication for rules, proposed rules, and notices of federal agencies and organizations, as well as executive orders and other presidential documents.

Law Line 2-8
Administrative Rules

Constitutions

Constitutions are the highest form of law within a given jurisdiction. In the political realm, a constitution is an agreement between a governing body (an institution of government) and those parties it seeks to govern (the people). Typically, a constitution outlines the duties and powers of a government, as well as any rights or protections held by individuals. Among the three primary constitutional sources (federal, state, and local), there is a basic hierarchy or "chain of command." And so, for example, if police in Cincinnati, Ohio, charge a person with violating a city criminal ordinance, there may be at least three potential constitutional sources for criminal procedure—the U.S. Constitution, the Ohio Constitution, and the Charter for the City of Cincinnati. See Law Line 2-9.

Criminal laws are affected by constitutional law. The highest form of law in America is the U.S. Constitution. Technically speaking, the Constitution may not

constitution
the highest form of law within a given jurisdiction; an agreement between a governing body (an institution of government) and those parties it seeks to govern (the people).

Law Line 2-9
State Constitutions

be viewed as a source of specific laws or criminal prohibitions, although Article III, section 3 defines treason as a crime. But it does provide limitations on governmental police powers, including some restrictions on the power to prosecute crime. Specifically, the Constitution sets limits on the nature and extent of criminal law that the government can enact. And it guards personal liberties by restricting undue government interference in the lives of individuals and by ensuring personal privacy. See Chapter 8.

The Constitution can be seen as the sole piece of legislation by which all other laws and legislation are judged acceptable (constitutional) or unacceptable (unconstitutional). For example, the Constitution enshrines the notion that persons should only be held accountable for the acts they do (or do not do, i.e., omissions), rather than for what they think or believe. As a result, if a state legislature were to enact a law prohibiting thoughts of a seditious or carnal nature, such a law would likely be overturned should it ever come before the U.S. Supreme Court, which serves as our nation's constitutional interpreter.

Constitutional provisions determine the nature of criminal law by setting limits on just what can be criminalized or made illegal. Generally speaking, constitutional requirements hold that criminal laws can only be enacted where there is a compelling public need to regulate conduct. The U.S. Supreme Court has held that "to justify the exercise of police power the public interest must require the interference, and the measures adopted must be reasonably necessary for the accomplishment of the purpose."[16]

As will be addressed throughout this book, the Constitution also demands that anyone accused of criminal activity be accorded due process. Similarly, the Constitution helps ensure that accused persons are provided with the opportunity to offer a well-crafted defense. The Constitution imposes a number of specific requirements and restrictions on both the state and federal governments, and it protects individual rights in the area of criminal law. In addition to the federal Constitution, each state has its own constitution. Within these constitutions, states may not reduce the rights found in the U.S. Constitution, but they can enhance or add to them, either through their state constitutions or by statute. Most of the restrictions, requirements, protections, and rights inherent in the Constitution are addressed in the form of criminal procedures, and as such are discussed in Chapters 8–14.

Common Law

As addressed in Chapter 1, the common law, both historical and newly developed, continues to be important in the development of American law. Specifically, through interpretation, courts mold the law and contribute to the uniformity and predictability of the law. The reliance on court opinions as sources of criminal law is based on the doctrine of *stare decisis*. The extent to which a court should follow precedent is a perennial question. Should a lower court follow a higher court's decision that is over one hundred years old and was premised on social or economic circumstances that have changed? Should the Supreme Court be bound by its own precedent if the composition of the Court has changed significantly?

case law
legal opinions written by a court.

statutory law
law written by a legislature.

The Supreme Court has ruled that "[s]*tare decisis* is of fundamental importance to the rule of law."[17] **Case law** (opinions written by courts) and **statutory law** (laws written by legislatures) make for predictability in the law. Prosecutors, criminal defendants, and their attorneys entering a modern courtroom can generally gauge with a fair degree of accuracy what the law will expect of them. In the words of the Court: "acknowledgments of precedent serve the principal purposes of *stare decisis*, which are to protect reliance interests and to foster stability in the law."[18] In a strongly worded acknowledgment of the importance of *stare decisis,* the U.S. Supreme Court in *Vasquez v. Hillary* (1986)[19] stated that *stare decisis* "permits society to presume that bedrock principles are founded in the law rather than in the proclivities of individuals, and thereby contributes to the integrity of our constitutional system of government, both in appearance and in fact." Even so, a number of justices have, in various cases, recognized that *stare decisis* "is not an imprisonment of reason."[20] In other words, while *stare decisis* is a central guiding principle in American law, it does not dictate blind obedience to precedent.

While lower courts are bound by the decisions of higher courts, any court is free to set aside its previous decisions, assuming that a higher court has not ruled on the subject. While the rationale undergirding the doctrine of *stare decisis* applies to courts when reviewing their own decisions, the willingness of the highest court of any jurisdiction to set aside its own decisions is more important than for other courts because there is no higher court to correct errors. This reality was captured in *Brown v. Allen* (1953)[21] when Justice Jackson stated, "[w]e are not right because we are infallible, but we are infallible only because we are final."

Many cases, of course, are not subject to *stare decisis* because they are unlike previous cases. They may deal with new subject matter or novel situations, raise unusual legal questions, or fall outside of the principles established by earlier decisions. A case is precedential only if the facts are similar to the case that is being heard. If it is possible to distinguish the facts of a new case from the facts of earlier ones, then the law of the precedential case will not be applied, or only applied in part, to the case under review.

For legal professionals, it is important to remember that there is a hierarchy in American law. While federal and state statutes embody the bulk of criminal law, the U.S. Constitution remains the most superior and powerful form of law in the United States. All other law, including state constitutions, must be consistent with it. After the U.S. Constitution, the United States Code is the highest form of federal law, with administrative regulations following. At the state level, state constitutions fall below the federal constitution, with state codes and then administrative regulations following in that order. As stated earlier, the common law, except interpretations of state and federal constitutions, is a lower form of law than statutes. As such, statutes prevail when in conflict with the common law. Legal professionals should keep this hierarchy of law in mind when reviewing criminal laws, so that they can be sure the standards they are considering are consistent with all superior forms of law.

The Model Penal Code

As briefly identified above, the Model Penal Code (MPC) plays a unique and valuable role in American criminal law. The MPC is not authoritative law, in and of itself, but rather offers models for criminal laws that legislatures can use in developing or revising their statutory codes. The MPC was published as a "Proposed Official Draft" by the American Law Institute (ALI) in 1962, and represented the culmination of efforts that had been ongoing since the ALI's inception.

The **American Law Institute** was organized in 1923, following a study conducted by a group of prominent American judges, lawyers, and teachers who were known as "The Committee on the Establishment of a Permanent Organization for the Improvement of the Law."[22] A report of the committee highlighted two chief defects in American law—uncertainty and complexity—which had combined to produce a "general dissatisfaction with the administration of justice" throughout the country. Accordingly, the committee recommended that a lawyers' organization be formed to improve the law and its administration. That recommendation led to the creation of the ALI.

Law Line 2-10
American Law Institute

American Law Institute
a group of prominent American judges, lawyers, and law professors, organized in 1923, who drafted and maintain the Model Penal Code.

The MPC is just one of ALI's many projects, but it remains one of its most significant resources. It is divided into four parts: general provisions, definitions of specific crimes, treatment and correction, and the organization of correction. The MPC's provisions are based on "the principle that the sole purpose of the criminal law [is] the control of harmful conduct," as opposed to imposing punishment. Because the Code's authors believed that "faultless conduct should be shielded from punishment,"[23] the MPC generally limits criminal liability for a number of law violators—especially those who serve merely as accomplices or who act without an accompanying culpable mental state.

At the federal level, the MPC has been instrumental in the drafting of many criminal statutes. In 1966, Congress established the National Commission on Reform of Federal Criminal Laws in order to assess the propriety of federal standards for crime. This commission used the MPC to produce several recommended revisions for Title 18 of the United States Code, which contains the bulk of federal criminal laws. Congress enacted many of these proposals and they now serve as the primary text for several federal criminal statutes.[24]

No state has adopted the MPC in its entirety. But aspects of the MPC have been incorporated into the penal codes of nearly all the states. As a result, the MPC can serve as an important reference for legal professionals, not only because it serves as a model for many state criminal statutes, but also because it contains legal background and thinking on the purpose of criminal law as shared by many cogent thinkers in American jurisprudence. As a result, there are times when you might refer to MPC provisions as a means of understanding, contrasting, or critiquing existing federal or state statutes. For your reference, the MPC is excerpted in Appendix C.

IN THE FIELD

The multiplicity of sources for criminal law offers both challenges and opportunities for legal professionals. In most cases, legal research is not like searching for the holy grail, where a single statute, case, or regulation will offer the perfect and complete resolution to a legal dispute. Instead, legal professionals will often find themselves using several sources, perhaps from different branches and layers of government. There may be statutory language, court precedent, administrative rules, and possibly even Model Penal Code commentary that are all relevant in addressing a particular issue of criminal law.

In these situations, legal analysis can be much like weaving a tapestry, where different sources of fabric are brought together to produce a common cloth. This dynamic can be challenging because it requires legal professionals to conduct intense and exhaustive research, often with one legal source leading to many others. At times, the plethora of source materials can be confusing, requiring legal professionals to carefully organize, diagram, and brief (addressed in Chapter 1 and Appendix A) cases and other documents before they can be used to draft an official memorandum, motion, or other filing. But multiple sources can also present opportunities for many legal professionals, particularly where an initial case or statute does not offer the most favorable legal standard for a client or employer. In these situations, legal professionals should persist in their legal research, knowing that there may be other sources that offer more favorable insights or precedents for the case.

THE LANGUAGE OF LAW

Once you have found the relevant law in a criminal case, perhaps the bigger challenge will be deciding what to do with it. For some, the obvious answer might be that the law needs to be *applied* to the facts of a case. Indeed, in most civics classes, students are taught that judges or juries simply take the facts of the case, apply the law, and then render a decision. This might be symbolized in the form of the linear equation of $F + L = D$. But for many cases, it is not that easy.

First, the facts of a criminal case (or really any case for that matter) are not always clear. There may be different versions of what occurred, and the degree of relevance of certain claimed events may also be in question. In addition, the law itself may not be written with perfect clarity. Even though the law is spelled out in the statute and the words are written in readily understandable terms, it does not mean everyone will agree on the appropriate meaning of the law's legal mandate. The reality is, words only go so far. After you have located the relevant statutory language, it is really up to those reading and applying the law to give it ultimate meaning and effect.

Take for example the word *disorderly*, as in *disorderly conduct*—a criminal offense under most state statutory schemes. Now we can all read this word. Most of us probably pronounce it the same way. And we may even have a fairly common notion of what behavior it is designed to target. But then comes the hard part. What does this term mean when it is applied to different forms of behavior? Does being drunk in public constitute being disorderly? What about swearing in public? How about being loud? If so, how loud do you have to be? This is where human interpretation of language takes over and people begin to give meaning to the words of the statutes. Read the court's opinion in *In Re Fechuch*, a state criminal case involving a disorderly conduct complaint against a defendant who used "salty" language in public. Notice how the application of words within a criminal statute is not as easy as it might seem.

CAPSTONE CASE *In re Fechuch*, 2005 WL 2002268 (Ohio App. 5 Dist., 2005)

The incident giving rise to this appeal occurred on July 25, 2004. On this date, Barbara Moore left her residence, accompanied by her friend, Donnell Parks, and their children. The two women and their children were going to a local funeral home to assist in the making of funeral arrangements for a friend who had just died in an automobile accident. As the women and children approached Ms. Moore's vehicle, appellant screamed at Ms. Moore and Ms. Parks calling them "fucking bitches." Appellant also "flipped them off" by extending her middle finger. . . .

The police charged appellant with a violation of R.C. 2917.11(A)(2). This statute provides as follows:

"(A) No person shall recklessly cause inconvenience, annoyance or alarm to another by doing any of the following:

"(2) Making unreasonable noise or an offensively coarse utterance, gesture, or display or communicating unwarranted and grossly abusive language to any person."

Initially, we recognize that the First Amendment to the United States Constitution protects an individual's freedom to speak as he or she thinks . . . The First Amendment does not protect categories of speech that form " * * * no essential part of any exposition of ideas, and are of such slight social value as a step to

(continued)

(continued)

truth that any benefit that may be derived from them is clearly outweighed by the social interest in order and morality." . . .

For purposes of this appeal, we are concerned with the unprotected category of speech constituting fighting words. "Fighting words" are words which "by their very utterance inflict injury or are likely to provoke the average person to an immediate retaliatory breach of the peace." In determining whether a defendant's speech constitutes fighting words, evidence in the record must demonstrate that the words inflicted injury upon the addressee or that the words would have likely provoked the average person to an immediate retaliatory breach of the peace.

In the case sub judice, we find appellant's conviction is against the sufficiency of the evidence because even if we determined appellant's comment and gesture constituted fighting words, the record lacks evidence that her comment and gesture inflicted injury or provoked Ms. Moore or Ms. Parks to an immediate retaliatory breach of the peace. The testimony presented at the adjudicator hearing supports this conclusion.

On cross-examination, Ms. Moore testified as follows on the issue of whether appellant's conduct inflicted injury or provoked her to an immediate retaliatory breach of the peace:

Q. When she called you this name on the 25th and lifted her middle finger to you, did you feel like running over there and punching her?

A. No.

Q. Didn't enter your head at all?

A. No.

Q. Did you feel like retaliating against her in any way?

A. No. If I would have felt like that, I would have never went and called the cops. I would have walked over there. That's not what I did, I went in and called the police and had them let me fill out a statement so then something was on record about what happened.

Ms. Parks also testified, on cross-examination, that appellant's conduct did not cause her injury or provoke her to an immediate retaliatory breach of the peace. . . .

Thus, based on the above testimony of Ms. Moore and Ms. Parks, we conclude the evidence presented at the adjudicatory hearing was insufficient to establish that appellant committed the offense of disorderly conduct pursuant to R.C. 2917.11(A)(2). In general, something more than mere profanity is required to constitute fighting words. In all of the cases upholding convictions for disorderly conduct involving profanity, the courts found that the profanity was used in a situation that likely could have become violent.

As noted by the above testimony, there is no evidence from which to conclude that either Ms. Moore or Ms. Parks were likely to respond in a violent manner to appellant's profanity. We conclude appellant's language was not "inherently likely to provoke a violent reaction" from the "ordinary citizen." Although we do not condone appellant's use of profanity, we find that the profanity used by appellant does not fall within an unprotected category of speech. . . .

For the foregoing reasons, the judgment of the Court of Common Pleas, Juvenile Division, Tuscarawas County, Ohio, is hereby reversed.

WHAT DO *YOU* THINK?

1. Were the Appellant's actions sufficient to be fighting words? If not, what additional circumstances could have caused them to be fighting words?

2. Why were the plain words of the disorderly conduct statute insufficient to sustain the conviction?

So how should you go about determining what the words in a criminal law actually mean? There is a common expression among policymakers that advises, "where you stand depends on where you sit." This phrase suggests that your ultimate conclusion on policy matters often will depend on the principles with which you start. The same might be said for interpreting legal provisions within criminal statutes. The way you interpret a word or a phrase within a criminal law may depend on the method of interpretation with which you start. There are a number of different starting places when interpreting the language of criminal statutes.

Strict Constructionism

First, you could start with the plain language of the statute. This is generally referred to as the ***plain meaning*** or ***strict constructionist*** approach. This method seeks to extract meaning from the face of the statute's terms using the definitions of words or phrases provided within the statute itself or, if not found there, by using a dictionary or some other source of linguistic interpretation. In using this method, you should remember that most criminal statutes include a section of the law that provides definitions for words and phrases found within the criminal law. These definitions, however, may not always be sufficient.

Read the opinion in *Watson v. United States* (2007) (below) where the Court was asked to interpret the phrase "uses a gun" found within a federal criminal statute. Notice how even such a simple word, such as "uses," can prove difficult when interpreting statutory language and applying it to particular fact patterns. Also appreciate that even some Supreme Court justices find the use of a basic dictionary helpful in resolving disputes over statutory language.

plain meaning
an approach to interpreting law that suggests the facial wording of a statute or constitutional provision should be central to assigning meaning to words; often relies on dictionary-like tools to discover the meaning of words; also known as the strict constructionist approach.

strict constructionist
an approach to interpreting law that suggests the facial wording of a statute or constitutional provision should be central to assigning meaning to words; often relies on dictionary-like tools to discover the meaning of words; also known as the plain meaning approach.

Law Line 2-11
Everybody's Legal Glossary

Law Line 2-12
Black's Law Dictionary

CAPSTONE CASE   *Watson v. United States,* 128 S. Ct. 579 (2007)

Justice SOUTER delivered the opinion of the Court.

The question is whether a person who trades his drugs for a gun "uses" a firearm "during and in relation to . . . [a] drug trafficking crime" within the meaning of 18 U.S.C. § 924(c)(1)(A). We hold that he does not.

Section 924(c)(1)(A) sets a mandatory minimum sentence, depending on the facts, for a defendant who, "during and in relation to any crime of violence or drug trafficking crime[,] . . . uses or carries a firearm." The statute leaves the term "uses" undefined, though we have spoken to it twice before. . . .

[In this case] petitioner, Michael A. Watson, told a Government informant that he wanted to acquire a gun. On the matter of price, the informant quoted no dollar figure but suggested that Watson could pay in narcotics. Next, Watson met with the informant and an undercover law enforcement agent posing as a firearms dealer, to whom he gave 24 doses of oxycodone hydrocholoride (commonly, OxyContin) for a .50 caliber semiautomatic pistol. When law enforcement officers arrested Watson, they found the pistol in his car, and a later search of his house turned up a cache of prescription medicines, guns, and ammunition. Watson said he got the pistol "to protect his other firearms and drugs."

A federal grand jury indicted him for distributing a Schedule II controlled substance and for "using" the pistol during and in relation to that crime, in violation of § 924(c)(1)(A). Watson pleaded guilty across the board, reserving the right to challenge the factual basis for a § 924(c)(1)(A) conviction and the added consecutive sentence of 60 months for using the gun. The Court of Appeals affirmed on Circuit precedent foreclosing any argument that Watson had not "used" a firearm.

(continued)

(continued)

We granted certiorari to resolve a conflict among the Circuits on whether a person "uses" a firearm within the meaning of 18 U.S.C. § 924(c)(1)(A) when he trades narcotics to obtain a gun. We now reverse.

The Government's position that Watson "used" the pistol under § 924(c)(1)(A) by receiving it for narcotics lacks authority in either precedent or regular English. . . . The question here is whether it makes sense to say that Watson employed the gun at all. . . .

With no statutory definition or definitive clue, the meaning of the verb "uses" has to turn on the language as we normally speak it; there is no other source of a reasonable inference about what Congress understood when writing or what its words will bring to the mind of a careful reader. So, in Smith we looked for "everyday meaning," revealed in phraseology that strikes the ear as "both reasonable and normal." This appeal to the ordinary leaves the Government without much of a case. . . .

The agnosticism on the part of § 924(d)(1) about who does the using is entirely consistent with common speech's understanding that the first possessor is the one who "uses" the gun in the trade, and there is thus no cause to admonish us to adhere to the paradigm of a statute "as a symmetrical and coherent regulatory scheme, . . . in which the operative words have a consistent meaning throughout" . . . or to invoke the "standard principle of statutory construction . . . that identical words and phrases within the same statute should normally be given the same meaning." Subsections (d)(1) and (c)(1)(A) as we read them are not at odds over the verb "use"; the point is merely that in the two subsections the common verb speaks to different issues in different voices and at different levels of specificity. The provisions do distinct jobs, but we do not make them guilty of employing the common verb inconsistently. . . .

Given ordinary meaning and the conventions of English, we hold that a person does not "use" a firearm under § 924(c)(1)(A) when he receives it in trade for drugs. The judgment of the Court of Appeals is reversed, and the case is remanded for further proceedings consistent with this opinion.

It is so ordered.

WHAT DO *YOU* THINK?

1. Was the Court's use of dictionary meanings the best way to resolve this case?
2. What other methods could be employed to determine the meaning of the word *used*?
3. What would happen if different dictionaries offered broader or more narrow meanings of terms?

Original Intent

original intent
an approach to legal interpretation that relies on the original intent of the legislators or other persons who wrote the law.

Another way of approaching the meaning of words is by looking at the original intent of the legislators who wrote the law. This is called the theory of *original intent*. This approach gives priority to the purpose or intent of the law, which might be evidenced by legislative floor speeches and other legislative history that led to the passage of the law. To discover statutory meaning under this method, you will likely have to do a bit of historical research to determine what the drafters of the law actually sought to do with the law. In some cases, this may be an easy task, especially if the lawmakers established their purpose within the text of the law. But in other cases, this may prove to be a difficult task, particularly if the purpose is not readily apparent or if different lawmakers had different intentions when they voted to pass the law.

For example, in *District of Columbia v. Heller* (2008),[25] where the Supreme Court addressed the constitutional right to bear arms, the justices wrote about 150 pages of opinion regarding whether the Second Amendment was intended to preserve a "well-regulated militia" or to protect a person's right to have a gun for self-defense. And in *Boumediene v. Bush* (2008),[26] a case regarding the habeas corpus rights of Guantanamo Bay detainees, members of the Court debated whether the framers of the Constitution intended for the right of habeas corpus to apply to foreign prisoners. These cases illustrate that, even where jurists may agree on original intent as an appropriate method for legal interpretation, they may disagree on the sources and meanings of such intent. See Law Line 2-13.

Law Line 2-13
Original Intent Opinions

Original Understanding

Another approach might be to see how the law was originally understood by those who first received or interpreted the law. This theory is called ***original understanding*** or, in some circles, ***original meaning***. This theory is similar to original intent in that it goes back in time to the passage of the law for its source of meaning. But unlike original intent, original understanding theory wants to know how the law was initially received or understood by the recipients of the law—judges, attorneys, parties, and so on. The approach focuses on how the law would have been understood by the common person in the period during which the law was first implemented. This approach, like original intent theory, will likely require you to do some historical research to discover how the "original" generation of people viewed the law. And like original intent, this approach might yield different interpretations—different people could have had different original understandings of the law.

original understanding
an approach to interpreting law that focuses on how particular words or phrases found within a law were initially received or understood by the recipients of the law; also known as original meaning.

Law Line 2-14
Original Understanding Opinion

Precedent

You could also start by looking at how courts have interpreted the language of the statute. This approach typically focuses on the prior judicial rulings or ***precedent*** of courts and is based on the doctrine of *stare decisis*. As discussed above and in Chapter 1, advocates of this approach believe prior rulings that have interpreted a particular provision of a law should be followed in future cases, so that the legal system can be stable and predictable. This theory is perhaps best supported by the admonition "[l]iberty finds no refuge in a jurisprudence of doubt."[27]

precedent
an approach to interpreting law that relies on prior judicial rulings; used in conjunction with the doctrine of *stare decisis*.

In relying on precedent as a method for interpretation, legal professionals' research skills are paramount, as they attempt to unearth as many cases as possible to support their legal position in a given case. But once they have found applicable precedent for a case, they often find that no two cases are exactly alike and that the facts and/or law found in the prior rulings do not match up perfectly with the ones in the current case. In these cases, legal professionals must conduct legal analysis (discussed in Chapter 1), where they use the findings and conclusions of the precedent to urge a particular finding in their current case. And in situations where the precedent they locate does not assist them or their client, they will have to find reasons to distinguish the facts in their current case from those that preceded it. In rare cases, legal professionals may even ask a court to ignore or reverse a precedent. As the Supreme Court has observed, "[s]*tare decisis* is not an inexorable command; rather, it 'is a principle of policy and not a mechanical formula of adherence to the latest decision.'"[28]

Legal Realism

legal realism

an approach to interpreting law that allows the realities (changing circumstances) of current society to influence the meaning of words.

Finally, another approach to interpreting statutory language is to consider the contemporary and practical realities of the law—its impact and effect on society today. This approach is known as *legal realism*. Proponents of this method maintain that laws need to be flexible and capable of growing with contemporary times. As a result, legal realists believe, to varying degrees, that the realities of the day should be able to inform the meaning of the laws. Supreme Court justice Oliver Wendell Holmes famously captured the notion of legal realism when he stated:

> The life of the law has not been logic; it has been experience. The felt necessities of the time, the prevalent moral and political theories, intuitions of public policy, avowed or unconscious, even the prejudices which judges share with their fellow men, have had a good deal more to do than the syllogism in determining the rules by which men should be governed. The law embodies the story of a nation's development through many centuries, and it cannot be dealt with as if it contained only the axioms and corollaries of a book of mathematics.[29]

Read the Court's opinion in *Begay v. United States* (2008), which interpreted the phrase "violent felony" as used in a federal sentencing statute. Notice how the majority opinion addresses the practical realities and problems of applying the phrase to the criminal offense of driving under the influence of alcohol. Also notice that Justice Alito's dissenting opinion places greater emphasis on the plain language or strict construction of the statute's words.

CAPSTONE CASE *Begay v. United States,* 553 U.S. 137 (2008)

Justice BREYER delivered the opinion of the Court.

The Armed Career Criminal Act imposes a special mandatory 15-year prison term upon felons who unlawfully possess a firearm and who also have three or more previous convictions for committing certain drug crimes or "violent felon[ies]." 18 U.S.C. § 924(e)(1) (2000 ed., Supp. V). The question in this case is whether driving under the influence of alcohol is a "violent felony" as the Act defines it. We conclude that it is not. . . .

The Act defines a "violent felony" as "any crime punishable by imprisonment for a term exceeding one year" that

"(i) has as an element the use, attempted use, or threatened use of physical force against the person of another; or

"(ii) is burglary, arson, or extortion, involves use of explosives, or otherwise involves conduct that presents a serious potential risk of physical injury to another."

We here consider whether driving under the influence of alcohol (DUI), as set forth in New Mexico's criminal statutes, falls within the scope of the second clause. . . .

[W]e assume that the lower courts were right in concluding that DUI involves conduct that "presents a serious potential risk of physical injury to another." Drunk driving is an extremely dangerous crime. In the United States in 2006, alcohol-related motor vehicle crashes claimed the lives of more than 17,000 individuals and harmed untold amounts of property. Even so, we find that DUI falls outside the scope of clause (ii). It is simply too unlike the provision's listed examples for us to believe that Congress intended the provision to cover it.

. . .

In our view, DUI differs from the example crimes—burglary, arson, extortion, and crimes involving the use of explosives—in at least one pertinent, and

(continued)

important, respect. The listed crimes all typically involve purposeful, "violent," and "aggressive" conduct. That conduct is such that it makes more likely that an offender, later possessing a gun, will use that gun deliberately to harm a victim. Crimes committed in such a purposeful, violent, and aggressive manner are "potentially more dangerous when firearms are involved."

By way of contrast, statutes that forbid driving under the influence, such as the statute before us, typically do not insist on purposeful, violent, and aggressive conduct; rather, they are, or are most nearly comparable to, crimes that impose strict liability, criminalizing conduct in respect to which the offender need not have had any criminal intent at all. . . .

In this respect—namely, a prior crime's relevance to the possibility of future danger with a gun—crimes involving intentional or purposeful conduct (as in burglary and arson) are different than DUI, a strict liability crime. In both instances, the offender's prior crimes reveal a degree of callousness toward risk, but in the former instance they also show an increased likelihood that the offender is the kind of person who might deliberately point the gun and pull the trigger. We have no reason to believe that Congress intended a 15-year mandatory prison term where that increased likelihood does not exist. . . .

The distinction we make does not minimize the seriousness of the risks attached to driving under the influence. Nor does our argument deny that an individual with a criminal history of DUI might later pull the trigger of a gun. . . . Rather, we hold only that, for purposes of the particular statutory provision before us, a prior record of DUI, a strict liability crime, differs from a prior record of violent and aggressive crimes committed intentionally such as arson, burglary, extortion, or crimes involving the use of explosives. The latter are associated with a likelihood of future violent, aggressive, and purposeful "armed career criminal" behavior in a way that the former are not.

We consequently conclude that New Mexico's crime of "driving under the influence" falls outside the scope of the Armed Career Criminal Act's clause (ii) "violent felony" definition. And we reverse the judgment of the Court of Appeals in relevant part and remand the case for proceedings consistent with this opinion.

It is so ordered.

Justice ALITO, with whom Justice SOUTER and Justice THOMAS join, dissenting.

The statutory provision at issue in this case—the so-called "residual clause" of 18 U.S.C. § 924(e)(2)(B)(ii)–calls out for legislative clarification, and I am sympathetic to the result produced by the Court's attempt to craft a narrowing construction of this provision. Unfortunately, the Court's interpretation simply cannot be reconciled with the statutory text, and I therefore respectfully dissent. . . .

The Court does not hold that the maximum term of imprisonment that petitioner faced on his felony DUI convictions was less than one year. Nor does the Court dispute that petitioner's offenses involved "a serious potential risk of physical injury to another." The only remaining question, therefore, is whether the risk presented by petitioner's qualifying DUI felony convictions was "serious," *i.e.,* "significant" or "important." See, *e.g.*, Webster's Third New International Dictionary 2073. In my view, it was. . . .

WHAT DO *YOU* THINK?

1. What benchmarks or standards would you have used to determine whether a DUI is a prior violent felony? Do any of your methods involve legal realism?
2. What benefits or drawbacks does the majority opinion's use of legal realism have when compared to Justice Alito's reliance on dictionary definitions?

Five Tools in a Toolbox

Overall, you may want to view these methods of interpretation as five tools within a toolbox—each available for use within a given case. See Figure 2-7. In some cases, the use of these five tools might yield the same interpretive result for a criminal statute's language. In other words, each method could result in discovery of the same meaning. But in other cases, the use of these five methods might produce a wide range of differences in the meaning of words used within a criminal statute.

Just think of your own use of language in personal conversations or written communications. You might say to your girlfriend, "your shirt is so retro." Now, you might mean this as a compliment. This was your original intent. But your girlfriend might view it as an insult, taking it to mean her shirt is outdated. This is her original understanding. You could turn to a dictionary to find definitions of the word *retro*. This might be called the plain meaning or strict constructionist approach. You could also turn to your friends to see how they have used the word in other contexts. This might be seen as a form of precedent. Or you could point to other modern-day experiences with the term found in pop culture. Perhaps the cover of the most recent edition of *Vogue* proclaimed, "Retro is in!" This approach, loosely interpreted, could be viewed as a form of legal realism. Obviously, in this situation, the interpretation of the word *retro* depends heavily on where a person's research starts.

IN THE FIELD

As a legal professional, you must realize that, in many cases, the words printed in a criminal statute will go only so far. Legislatures can define words only to a certain extent. After that, it is largely up to those involved in the criminal justice system—judges, juries, attorneys, probation officers, police officers, and so on—to decide how the words within a statute should be interpreted and applied. Remember that the language in many criminal statutes might be subject to multiple interpretations. For better or worse, law remains largely a social science. If it were not, we could simply input the facts of a case into a computer and allow electronic processing to issue a precise and perfect ruling every time.

FIGURE 2-7 **Methods of Interpreting Criminal Law**

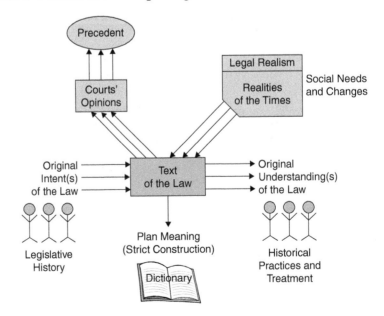

The frequent imprecision of legal language presents both a challenge and an opportunity for legal professionals. On the one hand, it makes it difficult to know exactly how words should be used in every case. Legal professionals looking for perfect certainty when reading criminal statutes may find themselves frequently disappointed. On the other hand, it allows advocates, judges, juries, and other legal professionals the opportunity to use the law for the greater good. Because the law typically is not fixed in stone, those involved in its interpretation and application have a great opportunity to use, shape, and give meaning to the law for the benefit of their particular client. This, in essence, is the heart of legal advocacy.

CHAPTER **SUMMARY**

- American criminal justice takes place in a multilayered and multibranched legal system, where different levels of government (federal, state, and local) and different units of authority (legislative, executive, and judicial) set and apply standards that affect the procedures and outcomes of criminal cases.
- American federalism involves a relationship between a centralized layer of government (the national government) and a group of semiautonomous and decentralized governments (the states).
- The Supremacy Clause ensures that federal standards for criminal justice establish a minimum level of protection that must be afforded in criminal cases. States, however, can provide greater protection or standards than those provided by the federal government.
- Since the middle of the twentieth century, federal authorities have expanded their scope of criminal law, seeking to regulate behavior in areas that were once the exclusive province of the states. Federal authorities often justify this expanded authority as a necessary regulation of activities that substantially affect interstate commerce.
- The federal question doctrine allows federal courts, including the U.S. Supreme Court, to review the actions of state and local authorities, where such actions involve an issue related to a federal source of law.
- The legal systems in the United States are based primarily on adversarial and accusatorial methods, where cases are highly combative in nature and rely on probing investigations and inquiries in order to reach a resolution.
- Criminal laws are most often found in the form of federal and state statutes and local ordinances, but may also be sourced in constitutions, administrative regulations, common law, and the Model Penal Code
- Criminal laws can be interpreted using different methods, including strict construction, original intent, original understanding, precedent, and legal realism.

KEY **TERMS**

accusatorial system
administrative rules
adversarial system
affectation doctrine
American Law Institute
Assistant U.S. Attorneys (AUSA)
Attorney General (AG)
beyond a reasonable doubt standard
burden of proof
case law
Circuit Courts
clear and convincing evidence
Commerce Clause
concurrent jurisdiction
constitution
Department of Justice (DOJ)

District Courts
exclusive jurisdiction
federal question
Federal Register
federalism
intelligible principle
interstate commerce
judicial review
jurisdiction
legal realism
local prosecutor
Model Penal Code (MPC)
ordinances
original intent
original understanding
plain meaning

police powers
precedent
preponderance of the evidence
revised code
separation of powers
state attorney general
statutes
statutory law
strict constructionist
Supremacy Clause
Supreme Court
U.S. Attorney (USA)
United States Code
writ of certiorari
writ of habeas corpus

QUESTIONS FOR **DISCUSSION**

1. How does federalism impact the way criminal justice is administered in the United States?
2. What role does the Supremacy Clause play in American criminal justice?
3. Why is the federal question doctrine important to many criminal cases?
4. Describe instances where the federal government has exceeded its constitutional authority in trying to regulate crime.
5. What effect does the separation of governmental powers have on the creation and implementation of criminal law?
6. Explain how the American judicial system is an adversarial and accusatorial system of resolving disputes.
7. What are the various sources of criminal law?
8. What methods or approaches are used to interpret the meaning of criminal laws and constitutional standards?
9. What function does the Model Penal Code serve in constructing criminal statutes?
10. When interpreting criminal law, what is meant by the admonition "where you stand depends on where you sit?"
11. Are there any areas of criminal law that should be off-limits for federal control and regulated solely by the state governments?
12. Are there any areas of criminal law that should be off-limits to state regulation and controlled exclusively by federal authorities?
13. What role, if any, should state and local law enforcement officers play in regulating illegal immigration, a matter traditionally controlled by the federal government?

REFERENCES

1. Clarence B. Carson, "The Meaning of Federalism," September 20, 2000. Posted at http://www.libertyhaven. com/.
2. James A. Gardner, *Interpreting State Constitutions: A Jurisprudence of Function in a Federal System* (Chicago: University of Chicago Press, 2005).
3. *Gonzales v. Raich*, 545 U.S. 1 (2005).
4. *United States v. Lopez*, 514 U.S. 549 (1995).
5. 529 U.S. 848 (2000).
6. *Id.*
7. *United States v. Morrison*, 529 U.S. 598 (2000).
8. See Daniel E. Hall, *Administrative Law: Bureaucracy in a Democracy*, 4th ed. (Upper Saddle River, NJ: Prentice Hall, 2009).
9. *Marbury v. Madison*, 5 U.S. 137 (1803).
10. *Id.*
11. For a more thorough discussion of judicial review, see Daniel E. Hall and John P. Feldmeier, *Constitutional Values: Governmental Powers and Individual Freedoms*, Ch. 3 (Upper Saddle River, NJ: Prentice Hall 2009).
12. *In re Winship*, 397 U.S. 358 (1970).
13. Although the main thrust of *Winship* was in the area of the rights of juveniles facing adjudication by the juvenile court, the case has been held applicable to adult defendants facing criminal prosecution as well. See, for example, *Victor v. Nebraska*, 511 U.S. 1 (1994).
14. Oklahoma Uniform Jury Instructions—Civil, No. 3.2 (2nd ed., 1993).
15. For more on this subject, see Hall, *Administrative Law*.
16. *California Reduction Company v. Sanitary Reduction Works*, 199 U.S. 306 (1905), citing *Lawton v. Steele*, 152 U.S. 133 (1894).
17. *Welch v. Texas Highways and Public Transp. Dept.*, 483 U.S. 468, 494 (1987).
18. *Itel Containers International Corp. v. Huddleston*, 507 U.S. 60 (1993).
19. *Vasquez v. Hillary*, 474 U.S. 254, 265–66 (1986).
20. *Guardians Assn. v. Civil Service Comm'n of New York City*, 463 U.S. 582, 618 (1983); *United States v. International Boxing Club of New York, Inc.*, 348 U.S. 236, 249 (1955); and *Payne v. Tennessee*, 501 U.S. 808 (1991).
21. 344 U.S. 433 (1953).
22. Some of the material in this section, as well as wording, is taken from "About the American Law Institute," at the American Law Institute's home page on the World Wide Web.
23. Stephen A. Saltzburg, John L. Diamond, Kit Kinports, and Thomas H. Morawetz, *Criminal Law: Cases and Materials* (Charlottesville, VA: Michie, 1994), p. 53.
24. *Id.*
25. 554 U.S. ___ (2008).
26. 553 U.S. ___ (2008).
27. *Planned Parenthood of Southeastern Pa. v. Casey*, 505 U.S. 833, 844 (1992).
28. *Payne v. Tennessee*, 501 U.S. 808, 828 (1991).
29. From the first of twelve Lowell Lectures, delivered by Oliver Wendell Holmes, Jr., on November 23, 1880; the lectures were the basis for *The Common Law*.

APPENDIX
DEVELOPING YOUR LEGAL ANALYSIS

A. THE LAW WHERE YOU LIVE

Assume that you are a legal professional within a county prosecutor's office and that you have been asked to review possible criminal charges in a case. The facts of the case show that I. M. Lowd, a man attending a professional baseball game within your county, engaged in a series of verbal altercations both during and after the game. At the game, Lowd was shouting verbal insults to players from the visiting team. Lowd yelled things like "Your team stinks," "You suck," and "We need a pitcher, not a belly itcher." Many of the fans sitting around Lowd were annoyed by his behavior. Eventually, security officials removed Lowd from the stadium for his verbal assaults. As Lowd was walking back to his car, he continued his insulting antics by telling a police officer, who was across the street, to "Go to hell," and by extending his middle finger to a group of fans driving by in a taxi cab.

Police and prosecutors are reviewing Lowd's behavior and are trying to decide whether to file criminal charges under the state's disorderly conduct statute, which reads:

Disorderly conduct.

A. No person shall recklessly cause inconvenience, annoyance, or alarm to another by doing any of the following:
1. Engaging in fighting, in threatening harm to persons or property, or in violent or turbulent behavior;
2. Making unreasonable noise or an offensively coarse utterance, gesture, or display or communicating unwarranted and grossly abusive language to any person;
3. Insulting, taunting, or challenging another, under circumstances in which that conduct is likely to provoke a violent response;
4. Hindering or preventing the movement of persons on a public street, road, highway, or right-of-way, or to, from, within, or upon public or private property, so as to interfere with the rights of others, and by any act that serves no lawful and reasonable purpose of the offender;
5. Creating a condition that is physically offensive to persons or that presents a risk of physical harm to persons or property, by any act that serves no lawful and reasonable purpose of the offender.

You are asked to prepare a memorandum assessing the potential criminal liability of Lowd in anticipation of criminal charges being filed. You are asked to review and apply the disorderly conduct statute, as well as the leading case on the law—*In re Fechuch* (see above) —and assess whether Lowd should be charged with disorderly conduct. As a part of this assignment, you are asked to review the annotated version of your home state's disorderly conduct statute (or public unruliness law) to see how the courts have interpreted and applied your state's law to different forms of human behavior. In your memo, identify what types of conduct have been found to be criminal, what types of conduct are deemed noncriminal, and whether there are conflicts among the courts within your state regarding certain types of behavior. In addition, identify whether you need additional facts to determine any potential criminal liability under the statute.

B. INSIDE THE FEDERAL COURTS

Assume you work as a legal assistant for the federal public defender's office in your home district. Your office represents a woman who was recently convicted and sentenced under federal law for possessing images of child pornography. According to the charges, the client, Suzie Kidd, had several hundred images of child pornography stored on her home computer. Although there was no evidence that Suzie sent or received these images via the Internet, Suzie was charged under federal anti–child pornography law, which makes it a crime to possess images of child pornography.

Your office is appealing Suzie's conviction to the circuit court of appeals. The public defender on the case wants to make an argument that federal authorities had no jurisdiction to prosecute Suzie because her actions did not involve interstate commerce. Given this argument, the public defender has asked you to prepare a written argument on Suzie's behalf based on the findings of *Jones v. United States* (2000) (see above). Your assignment is to locate and read the Supreme Court opinion, as well as the appellate briefs, filed in *Jones*. Then, using the opinion and the briefs, write a three-page memorandum, asserting that Suzie's conduct cannot be deemed a federal offense.

C. CYBER SOURCES

Assume an attorney in your law office has been asked to handle a criminal case in a neighboring state. Although the attorney is not licensed to practice law in the neighboring state, a long-standing client has been charged with a criminal offense in that state and wants the attorney to handle the matter. The attorney will be filing a *pro hac vice* (admission for this case only) motion with the neighboring court asking for permission to represent the client in that case. The attorney has come to you because he is not familiar with the structure and rules of the judiciary in the neighboring state.

Using electronic resources, prepare a memorandum wherein you identify the names and structure of the courts in the neighboring state (select a state that borders your home state). In the memo, the attorney would like for you to describe the following: What are the various trial courts called? How do attorneys refer to the intermediate courts of appeals in the state? What title is given to the highest court in the state? How many jurists sit on the state's high court? How are they selected—election, appointment, merit-based selection, or other method? How long is their term? In addition, the attorney would like for you to identify the federal district court that has jurisdiction over the relevant location in the neighboring state (select an area within the state). What title is used to refer to this court? Identify the federal circuit court of appeals to which that state has been assigned. Where is it located?

D. ETHICS AND PROFESSIONALISM

Assume that you are working for a small private law firm as a legal assistant. Shelly Collins, a partner in the firm, is handling a state criminal case and will be meeting with the prosecutor tomorrow to discuss a possible plea agreement. Ms. Collins wants to give the prosecutor the strong impression that the defendant is willing to go to trial and that there are a number of attorneys currently working on the matter. She believes this will give her a better bargaining position to negotiate a solid plea agreement for her client. To that end,

Ms. Collins would like for you to "dress up" and attend tomorrow's meeting, where she will introduce you to the prosecutor as her "associate." You will not be required to do or say anything during the meeting.

On a separate matter, Ms. Collins and her law partner, Frank Stanton, would like to add your name to the firm's letterhead when the firm orders new stationary next month. If you agree, your name would be placed two spaces below the names of the two attorneys in the firm.

Draft an e-mail response to Ms. Collins, where you accept, decline, or modify her proposals based on your assessment of the ethics of the situation. Be sure to start by considering any particular ethical standards under the law of your home state. In addition, consider the ethical standards established by the following groups:

American Bar Association

http://www.abanet.org/legalservices/paralegals/downloads/ modelguidelines.pdf

The American Alliance of Paralegals, Inc.

http://www.aapipara.org/Ethicalstandards.htm

National Federation of Paralegal Associations, Inc.

http://www.paralegals.org/displaycommon.cfm?an=1&sub articlenbr=133

National Association of Legal Assistants

http://www.nala.org/code.aspx

chapter **three**

CRIMINAL LIABILITY AND THE ESSENCE OF CRIME

Who thinks the Law has anything to do with Justice? It's what we have because we can't have Justice.

—William McIlvanney (b. 1936)

Law should be like death, which spares no one.

—Montesquieu (1689–1755)

LEARNING OBJECTIVES

After reading this chapter, you should be able to

- Identify the core elements of a criminal statute.

- Define *actus reus* and describe its basic features.

- Explain the concept of *mens rea* and describe the different types of mental states found in the Model Penal Code and contemporary criminal laws.

- Describe strict liability offenses, and explain why some crimes are punished solely on the basis of strict liability.

- Describe how concurrence relates to *mens rea* and *actus reus*.

- Understand and identify the statutory elements of legal causation, resulting harm, and necessary attendant circumstances.

- Identify the basic features of inchoate offenses, including criminal attempt, conspiracy, and solicitation.

- Explain how related actors participating in a crime can be held criminally culpable under the doctrines of accomplice liability, accessory laws, and vicarious liability.

- Explain the nature and realities of criminal liability for corporations.

INTRODUCTION

Near the close of the 1995 California double-murder trial of O. J. Simpson, Judge Lance Ito began providing final jury instructions with these words: "All right, ladies and gentlemen of the jury, you have heard all the evidence, and it is now my duty to instruct you on the law that applies to this case . . . The law requires that I read these instructions to you here in open court. Please listen carefully." Judge Ito's words to the jury that day also included the following instructions:

> The prosecution has the burden of proving beyond a reasonable doubt each element of the crimes charged in the information and that the defendant was the perpetrator of any such charged crimes. The defendant is not required to prove himself innocent or to prove that any other person committed the crimes charged. . . .
>
> The defendant is accused in counts one and two of having committed the crime of murder, a violation of Penal Code, Section 187. Every person who unlawfully kills a human being with malice aforethought is guilty of the crime of murder, in violation of Section 187 of the California Penal Code. In order to prove such crime, each of the following elements must be proved: one, a human being was killed; two, the killing was unlawful; and, three, the killing was done with malice aforethought. . . .

The purpose of these instructions was to inform the jury of the rules of the game. Certainly, we can all appreciate that in criminal cases the trier of fact, whether judge or jury, must sit in judgment of factual and legal allegations. In theory, such judgment could be conducted in a mental vacuum, with judges and juries left to their own independent assessment of whether a crime was committed. Triers of fact could ask themselves: Is the defendant a nice person? Would I want the defendant as my friend? Whose attorney did the better job presenting the case? But in a criminal justice system based on the rule of law, judges and juries are required to base their judgment on the standards set forth in the relevant criminal statutes. These elements found in criminal statutes form the legal benchmark by which all criminal allegations must be measured.

THE CORE ELEMENTS OF CRIMINAL CONDUCT

elements of crime
the statutory components of a criminal offense

In the United States, most criminal statutes share certain basic elements or building blocks. Taken together, these components compose the legal essence of the concept of crime. They are referred to as the ***elements of crime*** and describe the most essential aspects of criminal conduct. All crimes can be said to have these general elements in one form or another. They may be defined by statute in various ways—depending on the jurisdiction.

In most criminal statutes, there are at least three essential elements: (1) the criminal act (also known as the *actus reus*), (2) a culpable mental state (sometimes referred to as the *mens rea*), and (3) a concurrence of these two elements. In some criminal statutes, you may find additional items referenced, including causation, a resulting harm, and necessary attendant circumstances. But the core building blocks for most criminal laws involve a concurrence of a criminal act and a criminal mind. Under some circumstances, a person charged with a criminal offense may present a defense that negates or otherwise refutes the alleged criminal act or mental state. In cases where this occurs, there is no criminal culpability.

FIGURE 3-1 **The Essence of Criminal Culpability**

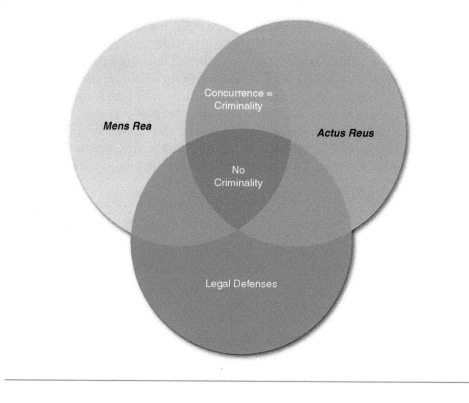

Figure 3-1 illustrates the relationship among the elements of *mens rea*, *actus reus*, and concurrence, identifying criminality where the criminal act and criminal mind concur and where there is no defense to rebut this culpability. Defenses in this figure refer to the zone of individual liberties over which governments have no authority to regulate and to those instances where other factual or legal defenses free an individual from criminal responsibility. As presented in this chapter, the essence of criminal conduct, at a minimum, consists of a concurrence of a criminal act with a culpable mental state. Essentially, this is what distinguishes murder from killing someone accidentally or in self-defense, or sexual assault from consensual sex.

The three core elements of most criminal statutes must be distinguished from the distinct elements defined by statute for *specific crimes*. Because statutes differ between jurisdictions, the specific elements of particular crimes such as murder, assault, robbery, or identity theft may vary. To convict a defendant of a particular crime, prosecutors must prove to a judge or jury that all the required statutory elements are present.[1] If even one element of an offense is not established beyond a reasonable doubt, criminal culpability cannot be found and the defendant must be found not guilty. In Chapters 4–7, we will examine the material elements of *specific* crimes as well as defenses to such crimes. But for now, we will turn our attention to the most fundamental features of criminal statutes.

THE CRIMINAL ACT (*ACTUS REUS*)

Generally, a person must commit some act before being subject to criminal sanctions, and a necessary first feature of most crimes is some act in violation of the law. This act is called the ***actus reus*** of a crime, which is Latin for "guilty act." For

actus reus
Latin for "guilty act"; the act or failure to act that constitutes the conduct of a crime

purposes of the criminal law the word *act* is often said to mean a performance, a deed, or a movement as distinguished from remaining at rest. In keeping with common law tradition, Arizona law, for example, couches the idea of an act squarely in terms of physical conduct. The "definitions" section of the Arizona Revised Statutes says, quite simply, "'Act' means a bodily movement."[2] The same words are found in Part I, Article 1, Section 1.13(2) of the Model Penal Code.

Some bodily movements may appear relatively minor, even though they result in considerable criminal liability. Individuals who hire someone to kill another person, for example, may move only their tongues, but they may still be convicted of murder. As a result, if used to cause unjustifiable harm, words can be deemed criminal acts. In this same regard, given technology, it takes little bodily movement to actually kill someone—merely the pull of a finger on the trigger of a gun.

Being and Doing are Two Different Things

To *be something* is not a crime, but to *do something* might be. Persons who admit (perhaps on a TV talk show) that they are drug users, for example, cannot be arrested purely on that basis. But police detectives who hear the admission might begin gathering evidence to prove some specific law violation in that person's past, or perhaps they may watch that individual for future conduct in violation of the law. An arrest might then occur. If it did, it would be based on a specific action in violation of the law pertaining to controlled substances.

Voluntary Acts

Some forms of human action are inherently noncriminal. The laws of most jurisdictions specify that a person's actions must be voluntary to carry criminal liability. The Indiana Code, for example, reads: "A person commits an offense only if he voluntarily engages in conduct in violation of the statute defining the offense."[3] Similarly, Title 2 of the Texas Penal Code reads: "(a) A person commits an offense only if he voluntarily engages in conduct, including an act, an omission, or possession."[4] These statutes illustrate that involuntary or reflexive actions, or actions undertaken during sleep, under anesthesia, under hypnosis, or otherwise unwittingly, would not be considered criminal, even if they resulted in harm or appeared to constitute violations of the criminal law.

Law Line 3-1
Voluntary Acts

Because the laws of most jurisdictions, like those of Indiana and Texas, require action to be voluntarily undertaken before criminal liability can accrue, a person who kills another during a "bad dream" or while sleepwalking may not be criminally liable for his or her actions. In 1988, in just such a case, a Canadian jury acquitted twenty-four-year-old Kenneth Parks of second-degree murder charges after he admittedly drove fourteen miles to his mother-in-law's home and beat her to death with a tire iron.[5] Parks claimed he was sleepwalking while he committed the killing. During the trial, friends of Parks said he had a history of sleepwalking, and doctors testified that about thirty cases of murder committed by sleepwalkers are known to exist in medical literature.[6]

In 1999, however, forty-three-year-old Scott Falater of Phoenix, Arizona, was convicted in Maricopa County Superior Court of first-degree murder after a jury refused to believe his claim that he stabbed his wife forty-four times, dragged her to a backyard swimming pool, and held her head under water until she died—all while he was sleepwalking.[7] Falater admitted that he must have killed his wife of twenty years, and later removed his bloodstained clothes and hid them and the knife used in the slaying in his car. But, he said, he was asleep at the time of the 1997 killing and had no memory of his actions. Although two sleep experts cited a family history of sleepwalking, job stress, and lack of recent sleep as explanations for Falater's supposedly violent sleepwalking episode, jurors sided with prosecutors, who said that Falater's actions were too deliberate to constitute sleepwalking.

Possession

Possession is generally considered to be another form of action. Possession, like any other act, may not always be voluntary. According to the Texas Penal Code, "possession is a voluntary act if the possessor knowingly obtains or receives the thing possessed or is aware of his control of the thing for a sufficient time to permit him to terminate his control."[8] In like manner, Title 13 of the Arizona Revised Statutes says that "'[p]ossession' means a voluntary act if the defendant knowingly exercised dominion or control over property." Arizona law also says that the word "'[p]ossess' means knowingly to have physical possession or otherwise to exercise dominion or control over property."[9]

As can be inferred from these laws, most jurisdictions draw a distinction between **knowing possession** and **mere possession.** A person who knowingly possesses something is well aware of what he has and probably has taken steps to obtain it. Someone who merely transports something for another, on the other hand, may be unaware of what she possesses. Similarly, a person on whom drugs are "planted," and who remains unaware of their presence, cannot be found guilty of drug possession. Nonetheless, both knowing possession and mere possession constitute **actual possession,** meaning that the person is actually in direct physical control of the object in question.

An individual also may exercise **constructive possession** over property and objects. Constructive possession means that, at a given time, a person may not

knowing possession
the type of possession where a person knowingly possesses something, is well aware of what he or she has, and probably has taken steps to obtain it

mere possession
the actual possession or custody of an object without knowledge of the nature of its contents

actual possession
the direct physical control of the object in question

constructive possession
the type of possession where a person may not have actual physical custody of the material in question but is still able to control or influence it

FIGURE 3-2 **Types of Possession under Law**

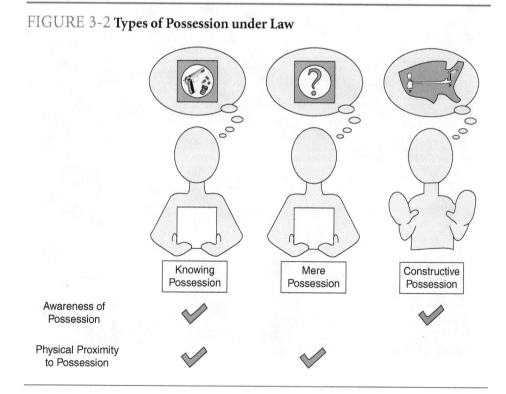

	Knowing Possession	Mere Possession	Constructive Possession
Awareness of Possession	✓		✓
Physical Proximity to Possession	✓	✓	

have actual physical custody of the material in question but is still able to control or influence it. In other words, items that are in a person's desk drawer or safe deposit box are still effectively under his constructive possession, although he may not have them in his immediate presence. So, for example, a person may still be in possession of controlled substances, for purposes of the law, even though the drugs are hidden in a vacation house or other property that the person owns.

Omission or Failure to Act

omission
a failure to act; may constitute a criminal act where the person in question is required by law to do something

An *omission* or **failure to act** may constitute a criminal act where the person in question is required by law to do something. In other words, where a person has a legal duty to act, the failure to do so may constitute criminal conduct. Many duties to act are imposed by law in a number of settings. In general, physicians must report evidence of child abuse to authorities. Adult wage earners must file income tax returns. Men between the ages of eighteen and twenty-six must register for the military draft. Guardians of children must properly respond to the needs of their children. (See the accompanying photo) And in some states, citizens who have knowledge that a felony has been or is being committed must report such information to law enforcement authorities. Under these legal standards, the failure to take appropriate action could be the *actus reus* of a criminal charge.

In some jurisdictions, intentionally withholding needed medication from a critically ill patient may also constitute the basis for a charge of homicide.[10] In a real-life example, Ginger and David Twitchell were convicted in 1990 of involuntary manslaughter after their two-year-old son Robyn died of a bowel obstruction that could have been easily treated surgically.[11] The Twitchells, members of the Christian Science church,[12] believed in the efficacy of "scientific prayer" as the sole

Sharon and David Schoo leave the Kane County Courthouse in Geneva, Illinois, after pleading guilty to contributing to the neglect of a child. The two were accused of leaving their children home alone while vacationing in Mexico. The parents were sentenced to two years each of probation and 200 hours of community service. What other forms of neglect by parents might result in criminal charges?

way to treat illness and refused medical treatment for their son. The Massachusetts Supreme Court later overturned the Twitchells' conviction in 1993, ruling that the couple should have been allowed to argue at trial that they believed they were within their parental rights to choose spiritual treatment. But the underlying dynamic of this case still illustrates the ability of criminal law to punish individuals for their nonaction.

Law Line 3-2
Child Neglect Laws

Threatening to Act

While most forms of speech are protected by the First Amendment of the U.S. Constitution, threatening to act, even without acting, can be a criminal offense. For example, Part II, Article 2, Section 211.3 of the Model Penal Code provides for the offense of "terroristic threat," stating "[a] person is guilty of a felony of the third degree if he threatens to commit any crime of violence with purpose to terrorize another or to cause evacuation of a building, place of assembly, or facility of public transportation, or otherwise to cause serious public inconvenience, or in reckless disregard of the risk of causing such terror or inconvenience." Similarly, in many jurisdictions, telling someone "I'm going to kill you" might result in an arrest for the offense of communicating threats or unlawful intimidation. In addition, threats made for the purpose of illegally acquiring money or other things of value are treated under many penal codes as extortion and blackmail. In general, even in cases where a person does not inflict direct physical harm, a person's threatening behavior, including speech, that unnecessarily causes fear, panic, or intimidation may be sufficient to constitute an *actus reus* under some criminal statutes.

Law Line 3-3
Criminal Harassment Statutes

IN THE FIELD

Many legal professionals working on *actus reus* issues in criminal cases may be tempted to immediately focus on the evidence in the case, seeking to learn what proof exists to support the alleged criminal act. But before turning to these evidentiary matters, legal professionals should carefully review the legal issues associated with the *actus reus* in the case. To start, legal professionals should review the statutory language used to define the criminal act. Read the plain language of the statute. Identify the types of conduct that are prohibited. Determine whether there is any ambiguity in the statute's language. For example, some disorderly conduct statutes prohibit acts that cause "substantial annoyance or alarm." This type of broad language may give rise to both evidentiary issues and constitutional challenges—assertions that the defendant's alleged conduct did not violate the language of the law and/or that the law itself is too vague to constitute a fair and legitimate criminal regulation.

You also should review the case law that has interpreted the language in the statute. How have courts viewed and applied the terms in your statute? Are there issues related to the wording of the criminal act that might apply to your case? Finally, you should review jury instructions used in your jurisdiction for the criminal statute charged in your case. What language is likely to be given to the trier of fact in assessing the alleged criminal act?

By carefully considering the legal issues associated with the *actus reus* of the criminal statute, you can conduct a more informed and thorough review of the evidence available to prove this element of the alleged crime.

MENTAL STATE (*MENS REA*)

mens rea
Latin for "guilty mind";
an element of most criminal
offenses; a person's mental state

A person's mental state or **mens rea** is the second general element found in most criminal statutes. The term *mens rea* means "guilty mind" and refers to the defendant's specific mental state at the time of the alleged harmful conduct. In many cases, the *mens rea* listed in the criminal statute is the most debated element of the crime. The parties to a criminal case often may not dispute the defendant's conduct or *actus reus*. Both sides might openly agree that the defendant did the act alleged in the criminal complaint. But the parties may dispute whether the defendant acted with the requisite state of mind to constitute a crime. And thus, the real issue for the trier of fact in cases like these is the defendant's state of mind at the time the act occurred. This dynamic leads some to observe that "[a]ll crime exists primarily in the mind."[13]

Obviously, a person's state of mind during the commission of an offense can rarely be known directly, unless the person confesses. As a result, judges and juries are often required to assess *mens rea* based on inferences drawn from the defendant's conduct and all the circumstances surrounding those actions. For example, the mental state of a defendant who, while pushing someone, yells, "I hope you die," will likely be deemed more criminally culpable than that of a defendant who commits the same act while saying, "Here, let me help you." Nevertheless, legal professionals should appreciate that proving a person's mental state is often an imperfect and at times subjective process, where the circumstances surrounding a person's conduct frequently lead to conflicting conclusions about the person's state of mind.

Types of Mental States

The Model Penal Code (MPC) establishes a general scheme that outlines four states of mind—purposeful, knowing, reckless, and negligent. These are the most common mental states found in federal and state criminal statutes. Generally speaking, these four mental states are listed in order of criminal culpability, with purposeful conduct regarded as the most culpable and criminally negligent the least culpable. The distinction between these four mental states can be assessed using two primary factors: (1) the defendant's intent to engage in conduct, and (2) the defendant's desire to achieve a particular harmful result.

FIGURE 3-3 **Common Mental States Found in Criminal Statutes**

Mental State	**Intent Regarding Conduct**	**Intent Regarding Result**
Purposeful	Actor consciously engages in harmful conduct	Actor desires harmful result to be caused by such conduct
Knowing	Actor consciously engages in harmful conduct	Actor is aware harmful result will be caused by conduct, but does not necessarily desire such harm
Reckless	Actor is aware that conduct poses a substantial risk of harm but ignores those risks	Actor does not intend harmful results
Negligent	Actor is not aware of risk of harm associated with conduct, but a reasonable person would be aware of such risk	Actor does not intend harmful results

A *purposeful* mental state exists when a person consciously engages in conduct and seeks to achieve a specific harmful result. In short, this mental state involves conscious conduct and a desire to cause a specific harmful result. For example, a person who consciously hits someone with the desire to cause death would have a purposeful mental state with regard to the act of homicide because the person intended to engage in the conduct and desired the particular result.

A *knowing* mental state occurs when a person consciously engages in conduct with the awareness that a harmful result is practically certain to occur. As defined in Ohio law, "[a] person acts knowingly, regardless of his purpose, when he is aware that his conduct will probably cause a certain result or will probably be of a certain nature." This mental state is similar to purposeful, in that it involves consciously harmful conduct. But unlike purposeful acts, persons who act knowingly do not seek to achieve the particular harmful results of their behavior. Yet because they are aware that these results are practically certain to occur, it can be said that they acted knowingly. For example, a person who consciously fires a gun into a crowd of people, with no particular desire to harm or kill anyone, would be acting knowingly with regard to criminal assault (if someone is injured) or homicide (if someone is killed) because reasonable persons would be aware that such harm is

purposeful

a mental state where a person consciously engages in conduct and seeks to achieve a specific harmful result

knowing

a mental state where a person consciously engages in conduct with the awareness that a harmful result is practically certain to occur

FIGURE 3-4 **Comparison of Mental States**

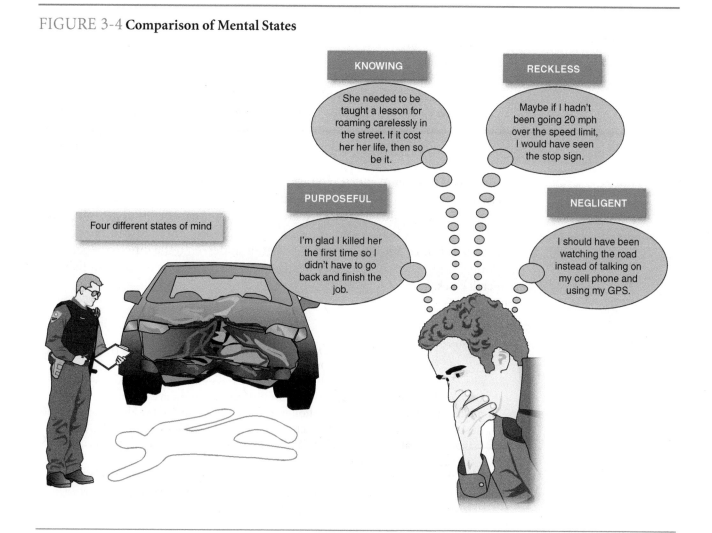

Law Line 3-4
Criminal Mental States

reckless
a mental state where a person is aware that his or her conduct poses a substantial and unjustifiable risk of harm, but ignores that risk and engages in the conduct anyway

criminal negligence
a mental state where a person, while engaging in conduct, fails to be aware of a substantial and unjustifiable risk associated with this conduct

practically certain to occur as a result of their conscious conduct. But if the shooter did not desire to harm or kill anyone, it could not be said that she acted purposely, because this *mens rea* requires the actor to desire the result to happen.

A *reckless* state of mind exists when someone is aware that conduct poses a substantial and unjustifiable risk of harm but ignores that risk and engages in the conduct anyway. In some jurisdictions, this mental state is also known as "willful blindness." Under Arizona law, a person acts recklessly when "with respect to a result or to a circumstance described by a statute defining an offense . . . a person is aware of and consciously disregards a substantial and unjustifiable risk that the result will occur or that the circumstance exists. The risk must be of such nature and degree that disregard of such risk constitutes a gross deviation from the standard of conduct that a reasonable person would observe in the situation." A person who acts recklessly does not necessarily intend to cause any harm. In fact, most reckless drivers are not trying to cause accidents, but their disregard for the substantial and unjustifiable risks associated with their behavior creates conditions for harmful results. For example, people who drive while texting or under the influence of alcohol might be said to be acting with a reckless mental state because, although they do not intend to cause any harm, they intentionally engage in conduct that poses a serious risk of harm and ignore that risk.

Criminal negligence exists when a person, while engaging in conduct, fails to be aware of a substantial and unjustifiable risk associated with this conduct. More specifically, "[a] person acts negligently when, because of a substantial lapse from due care, [a person] fails to perceive or avoid a risk that his conduct may cause a certain result or may be of a certain nature."[14] Negligent persons are not aware that their conduct poses a threat of harm, nor do they seek to cause such harm. But they should have been aware of the substantial and unjustifiable risk of harm associated with their conduct. For example, a home owner who accidentally leaves a car running in a closed garage, thereby causing someone to die of carbon monoxide poisoning, could be prosecuted for negligent homicide.[15]

Even though some negligent acts are criminalized, generally they are not punished as severely as purposeful, knowing, or reckless behavior. As Supreme Court justice Oliver Wendell Holmes once remarked, "Even a dog distinguishes between being stumbled over and being kicked."[16] But keep in mind, negligence in and of itself is not a crime. Negligent conduct can be evidence of crime only when it falls below some acceptable standard of care.[17] Read the court's opinion in *United States v. Hanousek* to better understand the difference between criminal negligence and ordinary negligence, which serves as the basis of liability in civil cases.

CAPSTONE CASE   *United States v. Hanousek,* 176 F.3d 116 (9th Cir. 1999)

> Edward Hanousek, Jr., appeals his conviction and sentence for negligently discharging a harmful quantity of oil into a navigable water of the United States, in violation of the Clean Water Act, 33 U.S.C. §§ 1319(c)(1)(A) & 1321(b)(3). Hanousek . . . argues that section 1319(c)(1)(A) violates due process if it permits a criminal conviction for ordinary negligence.
>
> Hanousek was employed by the Pacific & Arctic Railway and Navigation Company (Pacific & Arctic) as roadmaster of the White Pass & Yukon Railroad, which runs between Skagway, Alaska, and Whitehorse, Yukon Territory, Canada. As

roadmaster, Hanousek was responsible under his contract "for every detail of the safe and efficient maintenance and construction of track, structures and marine facilities of the entire railroad . . . and [was to] assume similar duties with special projects."

One of the special projects under Hanousek's supervision was a rock-quarrying project at a site alongside the railroad referred to as "6-mile," located on an embankment 200 feet above the Skagway River. The project was designed to realign a sharp curve in the railroad and to obtain armor rock for a ship dock in Skagway. The project involved blasting rock outcroppings alongside the railroad, working the fractured rock toward railroad cars, and loading the rock onto railroad cars with a backhoe. Pacific & Arctic hired Hunz & Hunz, a contracting company, to provide the equipment and labor for the project.

At 6-mile, a high-pressure petroleum products pipeline owned by Pacific & Arctic's sister company, Pacific & Arctic Pipeline, Inc., runs parallel to the railroad at or above ground level, within a few feet of the tracks. To protect the pipeline during the project, a work platform of sand and gravel was constructed on which the backhoe operated to load rocks over the pipeline and into railroad cars. The location of the work platform changed as the location of the work progressed along the railroad tracks. In addition, when work initially began, Hunz & Hunz covered an approximately 300-foot section of the pipeline with railroad ties, sand, and ballast material to protect the pipeline, as was customary. After Hanousek took over responsibility for the project no further sections of the pipeline along the 1000-foot work site were protected, with the exception of the movable backhoe work platform.

On the evening of October 1, 1994, Shane Thoe, a Hunz & Hunz backhoe operator, used the backhoe on the work platform to load a train with rocks . . . While using the backhoe bucket to sweep the rocks from the tracks, Thoe struck the pipeline causing a rupture. The pipeline was carrying heating oil, and an estimated 1,000 to 5,000 gallons of oil were discharged over the course of many days into the adjacent Skagway River, a navigable water of the United States.

Following an investigation, Hanousek was charged with one count of negligently discharging a harmful quantity of oil into a navigable water of the United States, in violation of the Clean Water Act. . . .

After a twenty-day trial, the jury convicted Hanousek of negligently discharging a harmful quantity of oil into a navigable water of the United States . . . The district court imposed a sentence of six months of imprisonment, six months in a halfway house and six months of supervised release, as well as a fine of $ 5,000. . . .

Hanousek contends the district court erred by failing to instruct the jury that, to establish a violation under 33 U.S.C. § 1319(c)(1)(A), the government had to prove that Hanousek acted with criminal negligence, as opposed to ordinary negligence, in discharging a harmful quantity of oil into the Skagway River. In his proposed jury instruction, Hanousek defined criminal negligence as "a gross deviation from the standard of care that a reasonable person would observe in the situation." Over Hanousek's objection, the district court instructed the jury that the government was required to prove only that Hanousek acted negligently, which the district court defined as "the failure to use reasonable care." . . .

Sections 1319(c)(1)(A) & 1321(b)(3) of the Clean Water Act work in tandem to criminalize the conduct of which Hanousek was convicted. Section 1319(c)(1)(A) provides that any person who negligently violates 33 U.S.C. § 1321(b)(3) shall be punished by fine or imprisonment, or both.

Neither section defines the term "negligently," nor is that term defined elsewhere in the CWA. In this circumstance, we start with the assumption that the legislative purpose is expressed by the ordinary meaning of the words used.

(continued)

(continued)

The ordinary meaning of "negligently" is a failure to use such care as a reasonably prudent and careful person would use under similar circumstances. . . .

If Congress intended to prescribe a heightened negligence standard, it could have done so explicitly, as it did in 33 U.S.C. § 1321(b)(7)(D). This section of the CWA provides for increased civil penalties "in any case in which a violation of [33 U.S.C. § 1321(b)(3)] was the result of gross negligence or willful misconduct." 33 U.S.C. § 1321(b)(7)(D). This is significant. Where Congress includes particular language in one section of a statute but omits it in another section of the same Act, it is generally presumed that Congress acts intentionally and purposely in the disparate inclusion or exclusion.

We conclude from the plain language of 33 U.S.C. § 1319(c)(1)(A) that Congress intended that a person who acts with ordinary negligence in violating 33 U.S.C. § 1321(b)(3) may be subject to criminal penalties. . . .

The criminal provisions of the CWA constitute public welfare legislation. The criminal provisions of the CWA are clearly designed to protect the public at large from the potentially dire consequences of water pollution, and as such fall within the category of public welfare legislation. . . .

It is well established that a public welfare statute may subject a person to criminal liability for his or her ordinary negligence without violating due process. Where one deals with others and his mere negligence may be dangerous to them, as in selling diseased food or poison, the policy of the law may, in order to stimulate proper care, require the punishment of the negligent person though he be ignorant of the noxious character of what he sells. . . .

Given the fact that a public welfare statute may impose criminal penalties for ordinary negligent conduct without offending due process, we conclude that section 1319(c)(1)(A) does not violate due process by permitting criminal penalties for ordinary negligent conduct. . . .

In light of the plain language of 33 U.S.C. § 1319(c)(1)(A), we conclude Congress intended that a person who acts with ordinary negligence in violating 33 U.S.C. § 1321(b)(3) may be subjected to criminal penalties. These sections, as so construed, do not violate due process. . . . AFFIRMED

WHAT DO *YOU* THINK?

1. Do the dangers of pollution require the approach taken by Congress in the statute involved in this case?
2. Should simple negligence be a basis for criminal liability?

Strict Liability

strict liability
a category of criminal offense that requires no particular mental state

There are some criminal statutes that contain no *mens rea* whatsoever. This narrow category of offenses is **strict liability** or "absolute liability" offenses. These statutes present a significant exception to the principle that all crimes require a conjunction of both *actus reus* and *mens rea*. Strict liability offenses make it a crime simply to *do* something, even if the offender has no intention of violating the law or causing the resulting harm. Strict liability is based on the theory that causing harm is, in and of itself, blameworthy, regardless of the actor's intent. For example, many routine traffic offenses are considered "strict liability" offenses, as they do not require any mental state to accompany the driving-related misconduct. A driver commits minor violations of his state motor vehicle code simply by doing that which is forbidden. As a result, driving

FIGURE 3-5 **Criminal Negligence in *United States v. Hanousek* (1999)**

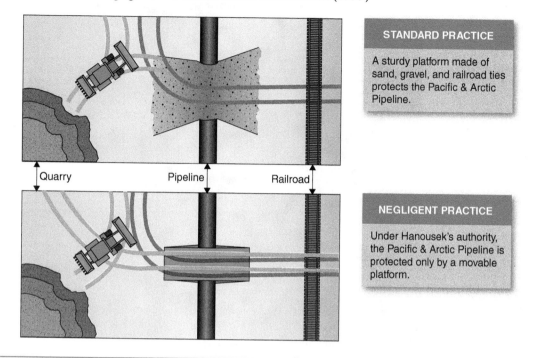

STANDARD PRACTICE

A sturdy platform made of sand, gravel, and railroad ties protects the Pacific & Arctic Pipeline.

NEGLIGENT PRACTICE

Under Hanousek's authority, the Pacific & Arctic Pipeline is protected only by a movable platform.

Quarry　　　Pipeline　　　Railroad

sixty-five miles per hour in a fifty-five-mile-per-hour zone is a violation of the law, even though the driver may be listening to music, thinking, or simply going with the flow of traffic—entirely unaware that his vehicle is exceeding the posted speed limit.

Statutory rape statutes are another example of strict liability offenses.[18] The crime of statutory rape generally occurs between two consenting individuals and requires only that the offender have sexual intercourse with a person under the age of legal consent. Statutes describing the crime routinely avoid any mention of a culpable mental state. California law, for example, identifies the crime of "unlawful sexual intercourse" as "an act of sexual intercourse accomplished with a person who is not the spouse of the perpetrator, if the person is a minor."[19] The law does not require the defendant to act purposely or knowingly; it simply imposes criminal culpability for engaging in the act of sexual intercourse with a minor. Under this law and other statutory rape laws, defendants can be convicted of statutory rape even if the victims lied to them about their age or may have given consent."[20]

Some legal experts maintain that strict liability offenses can never be "true crimes" because they require no element of *mens rea*. And in fact, under the Model Penal Code and some state codes, strict liability offenses are termed "violations," rather than crimes, and are punishable only by fines or forfeiture. As a result, a strict liability standard is often used in regulatory statutes, such as those barring the sale of misbranded items, the possession of a motor vehicle with an altered serial number, or the operation of a car with a burned-out tail light. In addition, many public health and safety regulations are based on strict liability in order to impose strict and strong enforcement of behavior that impacts large numbers of people. As one court noted, "[w]here the offenses prohibited and made punishable are capable of inflicting widespread injury, and where the requirement of proof of

Movie director Roman Polanski walks beside Los Angeles police officers during criminal proceedings. In 1977, Polanski plead guilty to having unlawful sex with a minor, but he fled to Europe prior to his sentencing hearing. In September 2009, Polanski was arrested by Swiss police, whereupon U.S. authorities sought his extradition. In July 2010, Swiss authorities rejected this extradition request and released Polanski from custody, declaring him a "free man."

Law Line 3-5
Strict Liability Law

the offender's guilty knowledge and wrongful intent would render enforcement of the prohibition difficult if not impossible . . . the legislative intent to dispense with *mens rea* as an element of the offense has justifiable basis."[21]

At times, strict liability statutes have been challenged as being unconstitutional. These challenges commonly assert that imposing criminal culpability without *mens rea* violates principles of constitutional due process. With few exceptions, however, strict criminal liability statutes have been deemed constitutional. In *Lambert v. California* (1957),[22] the U.S. Supreme Court stated that it does not agree with "Blackstone in saying that 'a vicious will' is necessary to constitute a crime, for conduct alone, without regard to the intent of the doer, is often sufficient." Yet, in the same case, the Court invalidated a statute that punished a convict's failure to register because it lacked a *mens rea* requirement. The Court's rationale for distinguishing the registration law from other legitimate strict liability crimes was the passive nature of the act, which made it a crime not to register, even if there was no knowledge of the requirement.

When Statutes are Silent on *Mens Rea*

In some cases, courts will review criminal statutes that, on their face, are altogether silent on *mens rea* to determine whether the legislature intended the law to impose strict liability. Because some courts do not favor strict liability crimes, they will sometimes make an effort to determine if a *mens rea* requirement is implicit in the law. Courts can attempt to deduce the statute's meaning by looking at the common law, if it influenced the statute; by examining relevant case law; by looking at similar statutes; by looking to the law of other jurisdictions; and by checking the **legislative history** of the statute. The legislative history is the record of debates, committee reports and meetings, statements of legislators, and other evidence of what the legislature intended when it enacted the law. Read the court's opinion in the accompanying *People v. Jensen* (1998) to see how the Michigan Court of Appeals went into the text of a sex-crime statute, which appeared to impose strict liability, to determine whether the state legislature actually intended to include a *mens rea* requirement for criminal culpability.

legislative history
the record of debates, committee reports and meetings, statements of legislators, and other evidence of what the legislature intended when it enacted a law

CAPSTONE CASE   *People v. Jensen,* 231 Mich. App. 439 (Mich. App. 1998)

Following a jury trial, defendant was convicted of three counts of knowing that she was HIV positive and engaging in sexual penetration without informing her partner of her HIV status, MCL 333.5210; MSA 14.15(5210). Thereafter, the trial court sentenced defendant to concurrent terms of two years and eight months to four years' imprisonment on each of the three counts. . . .

MCL 333.5210; MSA 14.15(5210) states as follows:

A person who knows that he or she has or has been diagnosed as having acquired immunodeficiency syndrome or acquired immunodeficiency syndrome related complex, or who knows that he or she is HIV infected, and who engages in sexual penetration with another person without having first informed the other person that he or she has acquired immunodeficiency syndrome or acquired immunodeficiency syndrome related complex or is HIV infected, is guilty of a felony.

. . .

Defendant . . . argues that the statute is unconstitutional because it does not contain an intent, or *mens rea*, requirement. More specifically, defendant asserts that because the statute does not require a specific intent to harm, one who does not understand or appreciate the consequences of his or her acts can be found criminally responsible. We disagree . . .

With respect to defendant's *mens rea* argument, we note that fewer than half the states have criminal statutes penalizing the exposure of others to the HIV virus, and only a few of those contain an explicit *mens rea* requirement . . . The others, including Michigan's statute, are silent on this topic except to require that the defendant know of his or her HIV or AIDS infection and fail to reveal it before donating blood, engaging in sexual penetration, or engaging a prostitute. . . .

Notably, however, in *People v. Lardie,* 452 Mich 231, 256; 551 NW2d 656 (1996), our Supreme Court recently upheld the constitutionality of the statute that criminalizes causing death by operating a vehicle while intoxicated. The statute was challenged after the trial court held that it unconstitutionally precluded the jury from determining the defendant's mental state or intent, but this Court upheld the statute as creating a "strict liability, public welfare offense" without requiring the prosecutor to prove *mens rea.* In upholding the constitutionality of this statute, our Supreme Court, made the following observations:

In order to determine whether a statute imposes strict liability or requires proof of a mens rea, that is, guilty mind, this Court first examines the statute itself and seeks to determine the Legislature's intent. In interpreting a statute in

(continued)

(continued)

> which the Legislature has not expressly included language indicating that fault is a necessary element of a crime, this Court must focus on whether the Legislature nevertheless intended to require some fault as a predicate to finding guilt. In this statute, the Legislature did not expressly state that a defendant must have a criminal intent to commit this crime.
>
> [But] [w]here a statute is a codification of the common law and that common-law crime includes a mens rea as an element, this Court will interpret that statute to require a mens rea even if the statute is silent regarding knowledge as a necessary element.

Where the offense in question does not codify the common law and omits reference to the element of intent, this Court will examine the Legislature's intent in enacting the legislation to determine whether there is a *mens rea* requirement. . . .

Applying the rationale of *Lardie* to the case at bar, we believe it likely that the Legislature intended to require some type of intent as a predicate to finding guilt under MCL 333.5210; MSA 14.15(5210), but that here the requisite intent is inherent in the HIV-infected person's socially and morally irresponsible actions. . . .

Here . . . [k]nowingly engaging in sexual conduct capable of transmitting the AIDS virus or HIV without telling a partner about one's HIV-positive status, is the culpable state of mind that can cause the partner's resulting infection and eventual death. Accordingly, although the MCL 333.5210; MSA 14.15(5210) contains no express *mens rea* requirement, we presume that the Legislature intended to require that the prosecution prove that the defendant had a general intent to commit the wrongful act, *i.e.*, to engage in sexual penetration with another person while withholding the defendant's positive AIDS or HIV status. Thus, the statute does not require strict liability because if the defendant explains his or her HIV status and the other person consents to the physical contact despite the risks associated with such contact, there is no criminal liability . . . We therefore find that MCL 333.5210; MSA 14.15(5210) is not unconstitutionally infirm on the basis that it lacks an explicit *mens rea* requirement . . .

WHAT DO *YOU* THINK?

1. What kinds of crimes require intent? Which do not?
2. What is the difference between specific intent and general intent? Is either concept relevant in this case? Why?
3. Why does the court find that the statute on which this case is based "does not require strict liability"?
4. Some people argue that the kind of law discussed in this case turns a personal status (being infected with the AIDS virus) into a crime. Do you agree or disagree? Why?

Related Terms and Concepts

willfully
a mental state where a person intentionally seeks to violate the law

Willfulness.   The use of the term ***willfully*** in criminal statutes generally means that, while engaging in conduct, a person intentionally sought to break the law. Under this mental state, prosecutors generally must show that the defendant knew of the criminal law and intentionally sought to break it. For example, under federal law, domestic banks involved in cash transactions exceeding $10,000 must file a report on these transactions with the secretary of the treasury.[23] Federal law makes it illegal for persons to "structure" a bank transaction (divide a single transaction above the reporting limit into two or more separate transactions) in order to avoid the law's reporting requirements. Under 31 U.S.C. § 5322(a), a person who willfully violates this antistructuring law is guilty of a crime.

In *Ratzlaf v. United States* (1994),[24] the Supreme Court ruled that the willfulness requirement of § 5322(a) required the prosecutor to prove that the defendant acted with knowledge of the law's requirements, not simply that the defendant's purpose was to circumvent a bank's reporting obligation. Interestingly, a criminal case involving the *mens rea* of willfulness is one of the few types of cases where the defendant's claim of "ignorance of the law" might be a viable legal defense. See Chapter 7.

Malice.   Some criminal laws use the words ***malice or malicious*** to identify a "life-endangering" or evil-intent state of mind. For example, the Washington Revised Code (RCW) includes the crimes of malicious harassment and malicious mischief. Under each offense, the prosecutor must prove that the defendant acted with malice. RCW 9A.04.110(12) provides that the words *malice* and *maliciously* "shall import an evil intent, wish, or design to vex, annoy, or injure another person [that] . . . may be inferred from an act done in wilful disregard of the rights of another, or an act wrongfully done without just cause or excuse, or an act or omission of duty betraying a wilful disregard of social duty."

In some criminal laws, "malice aforethought" is used to mean that a person wishes to achieve severe consequences by carrying out criminal actions. In some homicide statutes, malice aforethought is used to describe an act committed with ill will or hatred. In some cases, this is viewed as being synonymous with a purposeful *mens rea*.

Scienter.   The term ***scienter*** is a general term that means a defendant's knowledge or "guilty knowledge." Some criminal laws require that in order to obtain a conviction the prosecution must prove that the defendant had knowledge of a given fact. In 1994, for example, the Illinois Supreme Court upheld a state law making it a felony to knowingly expose uninformed others to HIV through sexual contact.[25] Under the law, persons who are aware that they are infected with HIV must avoid sexual contact with persons unaware of their condition or risk felony prosecution. The court held that the law had been properly applied in two cases: that of a woman who knew she was infected with HIV when she had sex with a man without telling him, and that of a man with HIV infection who was charged with raping a woman. In neither case, however, was the purpose of sexual intercourse to intentionally transmit the disease-causing agent.

Motive.   The *mens rea* of a criminal statute is not the same thing as motive. A ***motive*** refers to a person's reason (motivation) for committing a crime. For example, a person may commit a theft or robbery offense in order to further a drug habit or pay off a gambling debt. The underlying drive for committing the offense is the motive, while the mental state held by the defendant during the commission of the criminal act is the *mens rea*. The defendant's motive does not have to be proved as a matter of law. Prosecutors, however, often find it strategically helpful to offer evidence of a motive in order to convince juries of guilt beyond a reasonable doubt. The theory is that jurors will be more likely to find the defendant had sufficient *mens rea* if the defendant had a motive to commit the offense. Conversely, some defendants may attempt to show the lack of motive in order to undermine circumstantial evidence of the prosecution's case.

---

malice
a "life-endangering" or evil intent state of mind; also used as malicious

scienter
a general term meaning a defendant's knowledge or "guilty knowledge"

motive
a person's reason (motivation) for committing a crime

Mental Illness or Insanity.   The ability to form a statute's requisite *mens rea* can be prevented or hindered by mental illness or insanity. Indeed, the insanity defense and other defenses related to mental illness are defenses that seek to rebut the prosecutor's claim of a criminal *mens rea*. These defenses take many forms and there are special rules designed to regulate their use. These will be discussed in Chapter 7. For the moment, be aware that a claim of insanity or other forms of mental illness is an attempt to negate or undermine the *mens rea* listed in the criminal statute and asserted in the criminal charges.

transferred intent

a doctrine holding that a defendant's specific intent to cause harm to one person can be reassigned (transferred) to another person upon whom the harm actually falls

Transferred Intent.   Under the doctrine of ***transferred intent***, a defendant's specific intent to cause harm to one person is transferred to the victim upon whom the harm actually falls. For example, if a defendant purposefully tries to shoot person A, but in so doing, accidentally shoots person B, the purposeful act directed toward person A would be transferred to person B, and the defendant could be convicted of purposeful assault or homicide. For the doctrine of transferred intent to apply, the harm that befalls the unintended victim must be similar to the intended harm, and the transference of intent cannot increase the defendant's criminal liability. So, if a defendant acts in self-defense, but inadvertently harms a third party, the defendant's self-defense applies against the third party, even though that individual posed no threat to the defendant.

Once you have considered all of the legal issues associated with *mens rea*, you can begin to evaluate the evidence surrounding this element. As always, you must consider whether the evidence was obtained through legal means. This is particularly important where the prosecution seeks to use the defendant's statement or confession to prove the mental state. See Chapter 12. In addition, you should review any witness statements, tangible evidence, or other materials that link the defendant to the alleged mental state, always bearing in mind that the evidence is to be judged based on the legal language used to define this *mens rea*.

IN THE FIELD

As identified in this chapter, proving a person's mental state can be a more complex task than proving a person's conduct. We simply do not have brain scan images of defendants while criminal conduct is taking place. In some cases, a person may confess to a particular state of mind, thereby providing some direct insight into the *mens rea* of a criminal act. But in most cases a person's mental state must be proven by circumstantial evidence—using the context or nature of the defendant's conduct to infer a particular state of mind. Despite the increased complexity associated with proving a defendant's mental state, the preparation for this issue parallels that associated with reviewing the defendant's *actus reus*.

Legal professionals should begin with the statutory language and consider how courts have interpreted the mental state set forth in the law. In addition, the jury instructions used to explain the mental state should be reviewed and outlined. In cases where the statute does not contain *mens rea*, you should assess whether the legislature intended this omission and sought to make the crime a strict liability offense, or whether there is an implicit mental state that should be included. Where the statute clearly identifies a strict liability offense, you should consider whether, consistent with the Model Penal Code, such an approach undermines the due process rights of the defendant.

CONCURRENCE

The concurrence of an unlawful act and a culpable mental state provides the third fundamental aspect of crime. **Concurrence** requires that the act and the mental state occur together in order for a crime to take place. If one precedes the other, the requirements of the criminal law are not met. A person may intend to kill a rival, for example. As she carefully drives to the intended victim's house, gun at the ready, fantasizing about how she will commit the murder, the unrecognized victim may be crossing the street on the way home from grocery shopping. If the two accidentally collide, and the intended victim dies, there has been no concurrence of act and intent—even though the driver may later rejoice in her "good fortune" at having killed her enemy without incurring criminal liability.

Some jurisdictions make the issue of concurrence a clear element in their criminal statutes. For example, the California Penal Code requires that "[i]n every crime or public offense there must exist a union, or joint operation of act and intent, or criminal negligence."[26] For other jurisdictions, the need for concurrence of guilty act and guilty mind is more implicit. Under either situation, the criminal act and criminal mind must concur with one another. In the vast majority of cases, this is readily apparent. But in some cases, this criminal element may be less clear, thereby requiring additional evidence and analysis before it can be proven beyond a reasonable doubt.

concurrence
an element of a criminal offense requiring that the criminal act and the mental state occur at the same time

IN THE FIELD

Even though concurrence issues are relatively rare in criminal cases, legal professionals still must account for this element in all criminal cases. In some cases, the evidence alleged to prove a criminal mental state may be divorced in time from the evidence asserted to prove the criminal act. Such a possibility reinforces the need for legal professionals to prepare a detailed chronology for their cases, providing a timeline for all available evidence to ensure that the timing of the alleged criminal act corresponds with the timing of the evidence used to prove the defendant's mental state.

OTHER PRINCIPLES ASSOCIATED WITH CRIMINALITY

In addition to the core elements of *actus reus*, *mens rea*, and concurrence, proving criminality under some statutes may also involve other principles or elements. These items include (1) legal causation, (2) resulting harm, and (3) necessary attendant circumstances. For many, these additional issues are really subissues underlying the core elements of *actus reus* or *mens rea*. But for others, these items are treated as unique and separate elements of crime. Regardless of how they are viewed, these three principles, if presented in a criminal charge, must be proven beyond a reasonable doubt in order to sustain a conviction.

Legal Causation

In general terms, causation refers to an event whereby the concurrence of a guilty mind and a criminal act produce or *cause* harm. Some statutes criminalize only conduct. For instance, laws barring driving while under the influence of alcohol (DUI) target the act of DUI itself without requiring any resulting harm, such as a car accident. But other criminal statutes require a causal connection between the concurrence of crime (*mens rea* and *actus reus*) and a resulting harm or injury. In other words, many statutes require that the offender *cause* a particular result before criminal liability is incurred. For example, the Texas Penal Code defines criminal homicide by stating, "[a] person commits criminal homicide if he intentionally, knowingly, recklessly, or with criminal negligence causes the death of an individual."[27] Under this statute, if there is no death of a human being *caused* by another person, the person cannot be convicted of criminal homicide.

The element of causation can be the source of much debate in some criminal cases. For example, does a person cause the death of another if he fires a weapon at someone intending to kill the person, but misses, and the targeted person drops dead from fright? Does a person cause the death of another if she shoots the person, but he dies six months later in the hospital from pneumonia—never having fully recovered from the gunshot wound? Does a person cause the death of another if he contracts with a witch doctor to curse an individual, and that individual soon dies in an accident or from disease?

When discussing a specific ultimate harm such as "death," which is referred to in homicide statutes, it is necessary to recognize the difference between causation in fact and proximate cause. If there is an actual link between the actor's conduct and the resulting harm, **causation in fact** exists. Even so, a cause in fact cannot be said to be the sole cause, or even the primary cause, of a particular event. If a person fires a gun, for example, and the bullet strikes a building, causing it to ricochet and hit a person standing next to the shooter, it can be said that the person who fired the weapon shot the bystander, or at the very least *caused* him to be shot. In this case, other causes clearly contributed to the event, including the presence and movements of the bystander who was struck, the choices made by the designers of the building as to which materials to use and how to position the structure when it was built, and perhaps even weather conditions (a gust of wind or a particular barometric pressure may have affected the course of the bullet). Each of these features of the event may be said to be causes in fact, for without each being present the harm in question would not have occurred.

To assess causation in fact, some courts use the sine qua non ("without this, that would not be") test. This standard, known as the **but for rule**, considers whether an identifiable injury would have happened *but for* the conduct of the accused. In the example above, the bystander would not have been shot but for the actions of the shooter. Similarly, he would not have been shot but for the fact that someone had chosen to build a wall out of, say, steel-reinforced concrete, which caused the bullet fired by the shooter to ricochet. The following statutory definitions of causation found in Pennsylvania and North Dakota law illustrate the use of the "but for" standard.

Pennsylvania Consolidated Statutes
Title 18, Section 303. Causal relationship between conduct and result.

a. General rule.—Conduct is the cause of a result when:
  1. it is an antecedent but for which the result in question would not have occurred; and
  2. the relationship between the conduct and result satisfies any additional causal requirements imposed by this title or by the law defining the offense. . . .

---

causation in fact
the connection between a person's conduct and a form of harm

but for rule
a standard for determining causation that asks whether a particular form of harm would have occurred but for a person's conduct

FIGURE 3-6 **Cause in Fact Illustrated**

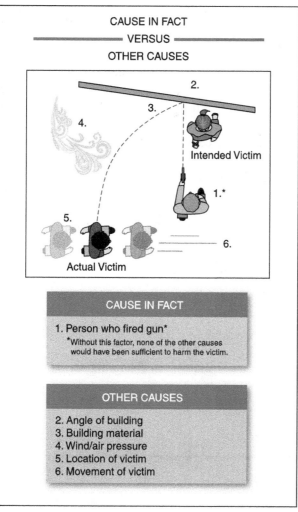

North Dakota Criminal Code
Title 12.1, Section 02-05. Causal relationship between conduct and result.

Causation may be found where the result would not have occurred but for the conduct of the accused operating either alone or concurrently with another cause, unless the concurrent cause was clearly sufficient to produce the result and the conduct of the accused clearly insufficient.

But even where factual cause can be demonstrated, it might not provide the basis for a criminal prosecution, because the government must then prove that it is also a legally recognized cause. As a result, proof of factual cause may be *necessary* for a conviction, but it alone is not *sufficient* for a conviction to result. Instead, the legal standard of proximate cause is used. ***Proximate cause*** holds individuals criminally liable for causing harm when it can logically be shown that the harm caused was ***reasonably foreseeable*** from their conduct. The basic question under this standard is whether a reasonable person engaging in similar harmful conduct would have foreseen or considered the type of harm that ultimately resulted from this harmful conduct.

proximate cause
a legal standard for causation that holds individuals criminally liable for causing harm when it can logically be shown that the harm caused was reasonably foreseeable from their conduct

reasonably foreseeable
a standard used to assess causation in criminal cases; asks whether a reasonable person engaging in similar harmful conduct would have foreseen or considered the type of harm that ultimately resulted from this harmful conduct

If, for example, a woman poisons her husband's dinner, intending to kill him, but he stays late at the office and she puts the meal in the refrigerator, she may still be held liable for the crime of homicide if a boarder staying in the house gets up in the middle of the night, eats the meal, and dies. In this case, the actions of the woman who intended to cause the death of her husband become the proximate cause of the death of the boarder. Proximate cause exists for two reasons. First, the woman set in motion a chain of events with potentially deadly consequences. And second, the boarder's consumption of food in the refrigerator was a reasonably foreseeable event, and his death was therefore a foreseeable consequence of the woman's actions. As a result, even though the wrong person died, a reasonable person engaging in the same conduct likely would have foreseen the possibility of death from this conduct. As a result, legal liability exists.

In most instances, in order to constitute a proximate cause of injury, a person's conduct must also be the primary cause of the harm. The U.S. Supreme Court observed that "'proximate cause' requires some direct relation between the injury asserted and the injurious conduct alleged."[28] If, for example, one person assaults another and chases him out of a building and through a driving rainstorm, the assault cannot be said to be the proximate cause of the victim's death if he is

---

FIGURE 3-7 **Proximate Cause**

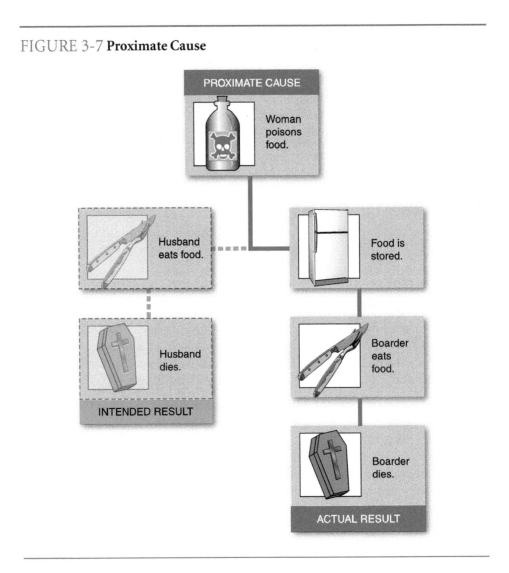

struck by lightning (the primary cause of the death) and killed during the pursuit—even though one might argue that, but for the initial assault, he would not have been exposed to the elements and would therefore have lived. This is so because the lightning strike was not related to the assault, that is, not brought on by it in the same sense that an infection might be produced by a gunshot wound. The bolt of lightning, in this instance, was independent of any harm caused by the assailant and could not have been reasonably foreseen.

It should be noted that the American Law Institute suggests that practitioners use the term *legal cause*, rather than proximate cause, to emphasize the notion of a legally recognizable cause and to preclude any assumption that such a cause must be close in time and space to the result it produces. Legal causes can be distinguished from those causes that produce the result in question (factual cause) but may not be legally viable (legal cause) because they are too complex, too indistinguishable from other causes, not knowable, or not provable in a court of law.

> **legal cause**
> a standard of causation suggested by the American Law Institute, which emphasizes the notion of a legally recognizable cause and precludes any assumption that such a cause must be close in time and space to the result it produces

Resulting Harm

Some criminal statutes also include the need for some identifiable **harm** as a general element of crime. If prohibited conduct had no potential to cause harm, it would make little sense to pass a law prohibiting it. Personal crimes, such as murder and rape, cause specific harm to nameable individuals, while other offenses, such as criminal attempts (attempted murder, attempted assault, and so forth), may seek to inflict harm but fail to achieve it. Still other crimes, such as those against the environment, cause a more general and diffuse kind of harm, the impact of which might be fully felt only in later generations.

> **harm**
> a type of injury caused by a person's actions or inaction

From a legal perspective, it is important to remember that "the question is not whether in some sense, ethical or sociological, the defendant has committed a harm. Rather, the question is whether the defendant's conduct has caused the harm, which the law in question sought to prevent."[29] In some criminal prosecutions, it is not necessary to prove harm as a separate element of a crime, since it is subsumed under the notion of a guilty act. In murder cases, for example, the "killing of a human being" brings about a harm but is, properly speaking, an act that, when done with the requisite *mens rea,* becomes a crime. In other cases, however, a specific and identifiable form of harm is specified by law as an element of an offense.

Under some criminal statutes, the degree of harm can increase the seriousness of an offense. Indiana law, for example, allows greater punishment for the crime of product tampering when harm results. The law reads: "[a] person who: (1) recklessly, knowingly, or intentionally introduces a poison, a harmful substance, or a harmful foreign object into a consumer product; or (2) with intent to mislead a consumer of a consumer product, tampers with the labeling of a consumer product that has been introduced into commerce, commits consumer product tampering, a class D felony. But the offense is increased to a class C felony, if it results in harm to a person, and to a class B felony, if it results in serious bodily injury to another person."[30] North Dakota defines *harm* to means loss, disadvantage, or injury to the person affected, and includes loss, disadvantage, or injury to any other person in whose welfare the affected person is interested.[31]

Where a particular result *is* specified by law as a necessary element of a given crime, however, a successful prosecution requires both a concurrence of *mens rea* and the act, as well as proof of the resulting harm. When the harm that results from criminal activity is different in *degree* from the intended harm, the concurrence requirement is still met. For instance, if a person shoots someone, intending only

---

Law Line 3-6
Harm-Based Criminal Statutes

IN THE FIELD

In cases where a criminal statute requires the defendant to cause a particular form or degree of harm, legal professionals must be sure to document the nature and scope of this harm and treat it as a separate element of the charged offense. This element, like the other elements of an alleged crime, must be proven beyond a reasonable doubt. In many cases, evaluating the nature and degree of harm will involve the use of an expert witness, who will make medical, financial, or scientific judgments regarding the impact of the defendant's alleged acts. For example, in a bank fraud case, a forensic accountant might be used to review complex financial transactions to determine the amount of money lost due to the defendant's alleged conduct. Or in an assault case a medical professional might be used to determine whether the defendant's alleged actions inflicted serious bodily harm (felonious assault) or ordinary bodily harm (simple assault). In these situations, legal professionals will have to consult with forensic experts to prove or rebut factual claims about the degree of harm caused by the defendant's alleged acts.

to wound, but the person dies, the shooter may still be liable for homicide. If, on the other hand, the resulting harm is of a different *kind* than that intended, the needed concurrence may be lacking. If, while breaking into a bank in the middle of the night, a driver leaves a getaway car parked with the engine running in the garage under an apartment, and a person sleeping in the apartment above the car dies from carbon monoxide poisoning, the driver would not be guilty of homicide, even though the driver's actions may have caused a person's death.

Necessary Attendant Circumstances

Finally, some criminal statutes may specify additional elements or circumstances that must be present in order to constitute a crime. These additional items are called **necessary attendant circumstances** and generally refer to the facts surrounding an event, such as the time or place of the conduct or the instrument used to facilitate the harmful act. The term *necessary* suggests that the existence of such statutorily identified circumstances is required in order to sustain a conviction.

Florida law, for example, makes it a crime to "[k]nowingly commit any lewd or lascivious act in the presence of any child under the age of sixteen years . . ."[32] In this case, the behavior in question might not be a crime if committed in the presence of persons older than sixteen. Curfew law offer another example. These laws generally bar juveniles from being in a public place during specified time periods (such as between 11 P.M. or midnight, and 5 or 6 A.M.). The inclusion of necessary attendant circumstances based on time turns perfectly legal conduct performed at 3 P.M. into criminal behavior when performed at 2 A.M.

Sometimes the inclusion of attendant circumstances is used to increase the *degree*, or level of seriousness, of an offense. Under Texas law, for example, the crime of burglary has two degrees, defined by state law as follows: burglary is a "(1) state jail felony if committed in a building other than a habitation; or (2) felony of the second degree if committed in a habitation." As a result, the degree of the offense of burglary changes depending on the nature of the place burglarized. Similarly, Florida law specifies a number of degrees of sexual battery, depending on the amount of force used to commit the crime, the age of the victim, and whether or not more than one perpetrator was involved in the commission of the offense.[33] The relevant statute provides, "[t]he penalty . . . shall be increased as provided in this subsection if it is charged and proven by the prosecution that, during the same criminal transaction or

necessary attendant circumstances circumstances surrounding an event or action; in criminal statutes, these might include the time or place of the conduct or the instrument used to facilitate the harmful act

FIGURE 3-8 **Attendant Circumstances**

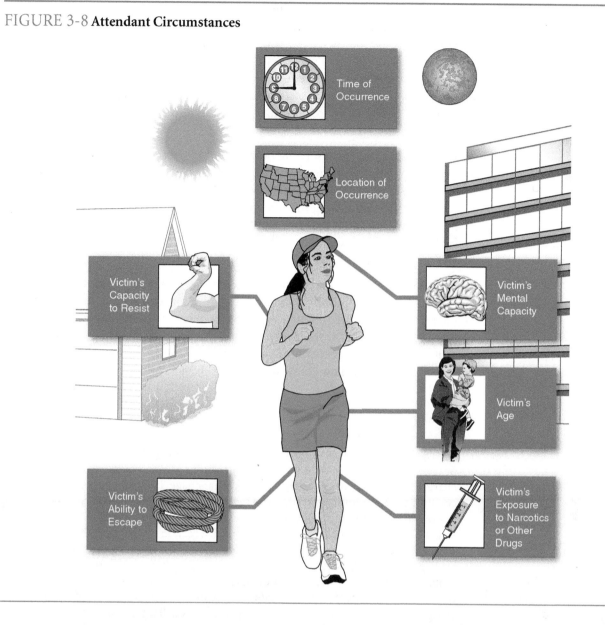

episode, more than one person committed an act of sexual battery on the same victim." Florida law also increases the degree of sexual battery (and associated penalties) "[w]hen the victim is physically helpless to resist . . . ; [w]hen the offender, without the prior knowledge or consent of the victim, administers or has knowledge of someone else administering to the victim any narcotic, anesthetic, or other intoxicating substance, which mentally or physically incapacitates the victim . . . ; [w]hen the victim is mentally defective and the offender has reason to believe this or has actual knowledge of this fact . . . ; [w]hen the victim is physically incapacitated . . . ; when the offender is a law enforcement officer, correctional officer, or correctional probation officer . . . ;" and under other circumstances.

Attendant circumstances surrounding a crime are often discussed in terms of aggravating circumstances (heightening a person's culpability) or mitigating circumstances (reducing a person's culpability). The presence of such factors can be used to increase or lessen the penalty that can be imposed on a convicted offender. In some jurisdictions, necessary attendant circumstances that increase potential criminal punishment are referred to as **specifications**. A specification is a separate

specifications

separate factual allegations made in a charging instrument that serve as a supplement to the base criminal charge

factual allegation made in a charging instrument that serves as a supplement to the base criminal charge. This specification, if proven beyond a reasonable doubt, enhances the possible penalties for the underlying crime. For example, in an indictment for murder (the purposeful killing of another), the grand jury may also include a gun specification (frequently called a "gun spec") that alleges the defendant used a gun to commit the offense. This specification is written in addition to the primary charge of murder contained in the indictment. As an illustration, a gun specification in Ohio reads:

> The Grand Jurors (or insert the person's or the prosecuting attorney's name when appropriate) further find and specify that (set forth that the offender had a firearm on or about the offender's person or under the offender's control while committing the offense and displayed the firearm, brandished the firearm, indicated that the offender possessed the firearm, or used it to facilitate the offense).[34]

Law Line 3-7
Specifications

If proven beyond a reasonable doubt, the gun specification will result in an enhanced criminal sentence, which may include mandatory prison time. See Chapter 14.

Other types of specifications include circumstances arising out of gang activity, sexual motivation, and repeat offenses. The idea behind these specifications and others is to distinguish between crimes committed under aggravating circumstances (use of guns, gangs, or sexual motivation) from those committed under "average" circumstances, and to allow courts to punish such aggravated activity accordingly.

IN THE FIELD

For legal professionals, in most cases involving necessary attendant circumstances or specifications, you should treat these allegations as you would treat traditional charges of criminal wrongdoing. Assess the language and meaning of the words contained in the additional charge and review any judicial interpretations and jury instructions on this supplemental charge. In addition, evaluate all evidence that might be used to support this claim. But realize that, in many cases, the inclusion of attendant circumstances or specifications within the charging instrument may have profound implications for the potential penalties facing the defendant, including, in some cases, mandatory prison time. As a result, one of the first questions often posed to legal professionals in these situations is whether the charges include enhanced or mandatory prison time. All legal professionals should be prepared to answer this question.

CORPUS DELICTI

corpus delicti rule
a common law principle holding that a criminal conviction cannot be based solely on the uncorroborated confession or admission of the accused

One concept used in criminal cases that is often confused with the statutory elements of a crime is the ***corpus delicti rule***. The term *corpus delicti* literally means "body of crime." Generally speaking, the corpus delicti rule is a common law principle holding that a criminal conviction cannot be based solely on the uncorroborated confession or admission of the accused. Under the rule, prosecutors must produce some substantive evidence, independent of the defendant's confession, to show that the crime identified in the confession actually occurred. The purpose of the rule is to ensure that coerced and mentally unstable defendants who make false confessions are not convicted for "crimes" that have not actually occurred.

One way to understand the concept of corpus delicti is to realize that a person cannot be tried for a crime unless it can first be shown that the offense has occurred. In other words, to establish the corpus delicti of a crime, the state has to demonstrate that a criminal law has been violated and that someone violated it. Accordingly, under the corpus delicti rule, a prosecutor must prove (1) that a certain result or injury has occurred, and (2) that a person is criminally responsible for this injury.[35]

For example, the crime of larceny requires proof that the property of another has been stolen—that is, taken unlawfully with the intent to permanently deprive the owner of its possession.[36] As a result, evidence offered to prove the corpus delicti in a larceny trial is insufficient when the evidence fails to prove that property has been stolen from another, or when property found in the accused's possession cannot be identified as having been stolen. Similarly, under an indictment for arson, the corpus delicti would consist of the burning of property and the identification of someone who caused such burning with the requisite criminal intent. If the burning was caused by lightning or other natural or accidental causes, the corpus delicti for arson would not be met.[37]

It is important to note that the federal courts and a few state courts have moved away from applying the corpus delicti rule in criminal cases. Instead, many

---

FIGURE 3-9 **The Corpus Delicti of Crime**

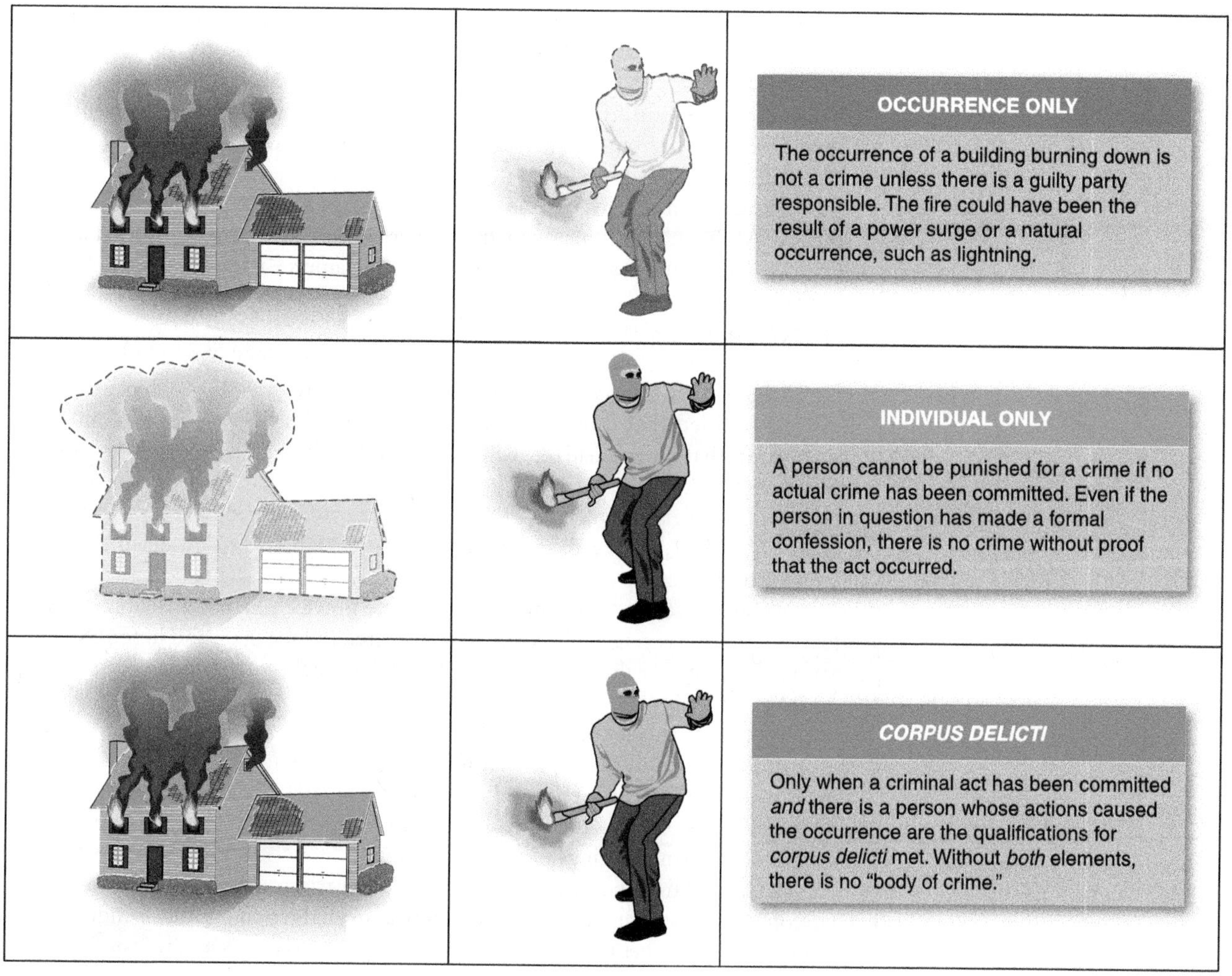

OCCURRENCE ONLY

The occurrence of a building burning down is not a crime unless there is a guilty party responsible. The fire could have been the result of a power surge or a natural occurrence, such as lightning.

INDIVIDUAL ONLY

A person cannot be punished for a crime if no actual crime has been committed. Even if the person in question has made a formal confession, there is no crime without proof that the act occurred.

CORPUS DELICTI

Only when a criminal act has been committed *and* there is a person whose actions caused the occurrence are the qualifications for *corpus delicti* met. Without *both* elements, there is no "body of crime."

corroboration rule

a legal standard requiring prosecutors to simply supplement (corroborate) a defendant's confession with some additional form of independent evidence

of these courts use a more relaxed standard, known as the **corroboration rule,** which requires prosecutors to simply supplement (corroborate) a defendant's confession with some additional form of independent evidence. This additional evidence, however, does not need to show that any crime actually occurred; it just needs to corroborate the defendant's confession.

In *Daniels v. State* (2007),[38] a Texas court of appeals ruled that a confession to sexual assault was inadequate to establish corpus delicti because there was no corroborating evidence. Read the court's opinion in *Daniels* to appreciate the relevance of corpus delicti in criminal law.

CAPSTONE CASE *Daniels v. State,* WL 2460263 (Tex. Ct. App. 2007)

Daniels and his girlfriend, Sherry Washington, moved from Waco to Wichita Falls in late 1993 or early 1994. After getting settled in, Washington began babysitting C.A., a then seven-year-old girl with severe mental retardation. For the next decade, Washington continued, off and on, to babysit C.A.

On Christmas Eve 2004, Washington babysat C.A. at the house that she shared with Daniels. Washington testified that C.A. was asleep on the floor in the spare upstairs bedroom when she and Daniels went to bed just before midnight. Washington further testified that in the early hours of Christmas morning, she was awakened by C.A.'s laughter. Noticing that Daniels was not still in bed with her, Washington got up and went to C.A.'s room. Turning on the light in the hallway, Washington found Daniels in C.A.'s room kneeling over C.A. with his "penis between her butt cheeks." C.A.'s pull-up diaper was pulled down halfway to her knees.

Washington did not call the police. A few days after Christmas, however, she mentioned the incident to some ladies at her church. Washington testified at trial that she told "Sister Jessica" that she had caught Daniels having sex with C.A. After the ladies at the church conferred with the pastor, they phoned police, who thereafter contacted Washington.

Washington told Officer Ronnie Sheehan of the Wichita Falls Police Department that she had seen Daniels having sex with C.A . . . [The arresting officer] testified that during the book-in process, Daniels made the following statement: "that he had had sex with a girl and that he had apologized to his girl-friend about it." . . .

At trial, the State introduced into evidence a video taped interview of Daniels speaking with Detective Tony Fox. On the tape, Daniels [admitted to the 2004 crime, although he claimed his penetration of C.A. was accidental.]

Daniels also made statements on the tape in which he implicated himself in two prior assaults on C.A. alleged to have occurred in June 2002 and June 1995. [He was also charged for these incidents, but no additional evidence of the crimes was presented at trial.]

At the conclusion of the State's case, Daniels moved for an instructed verdict of acquittal as to all three counts of aggravated sexual assault. The trial court overruled the motion. The jury subsequently convicted Daniels of all three counts of aggravated sexual assault and assessed his punishment at twenty-three years' confinement. Daniels brings five points on appeal.

In his first three points, Daniels claims that the trial court erred by overruling his motion for an instructed verdict of not guilty as to all three counts of the indictment. In sum, Daniels argues that the evidence presented in this case is legally insufficient to support the verdict because the State failed to offer any independent evidence of the corpus delicti for the offenses alleged to have been committed in December 2004, June 2002, and June 1995. We disagree as to point one regarding Count 1, and agree as to points two and three regarding Counts 2 and 3, respectively. . . .

As to Counts 2 and 3, the State again needed to produce some evidence, other than the confession itself, that the alleged crimes had occurred. . . .

Here, the State merely attempted to piggyback on the corroboration of Count 1 to establish that Counts 2 and 3 were also sufficiently corroborated. The State failed to offer any independent evidence corroborating Daniels's statements that incidents allegedly occurred in June 2002 and June 1995. Thus, the only evidence offered by the State to support commission of the alleged crimes was the extrajudicial statement itself, in which Daniels implicated himself in two additional incidents of aggravated sexual assault against C.A. Daniels's extrajudicial confession was insufficient to support a conviction for these counts because it was not corroborated. The State argued that Washington's testimony, which was offered to corroborate Daniels's confession regarding Count 1, established Daniels's state of mind, as well as a predatory relationship with the victim. However, we simply cannot agree with the State's argument that Washington's testimony, which appropriately corroborated Daniels's confession as to Count 1, also corroborated his statements regarding the alleged incidents charged in Counts 2 and 3. Washington testified that she had babysat C.A. off and on for over a decade and never had any indication that Daniels did anything inappropriate with C.A. prior to December 2004. Furthermore, the State did not offer any evidence which would make it more probable that Daniels committed the alleged crimes.

The State is asking this Court to infer that Daniels had access to C.A. in 2002 and 1995 because he had a relationship with Washington, who babysat C.A. Furthermore, the State is asking this Court to find that this access serves as corroborating evidence.

The corpus delicti is not satisfied merely because we know that Washington babysat C.A. off and on over a ten-year period, during which defendant may or may not have had the opportunity to be around her.

After reviewing the relevant case law, we have found no authority standing for the proposition that the mere possibility that a person had access to a complainant, without more, is corroborating evidence. As detailed above, the record evidence, other than Daniels's extrajudicial statement, when considered in the light most favorable to the verdict, does not tend to establish that any aggravated sexual assault was committed against C.A. prior to December 2004. Washington's testimony is the only "attempt" the State has made at corroborating Counts 2 and 3, and we fail to see how it was sufficient to corroborate Daniels's confession and satisfy the corpus delicti for alleged criminal conduct committed in 2002 and 1995.

Therefore, although we hold that the eyewitness testimony of Washington was sufficient to corroborate Daniels's confession as to the 2004 assault, we cannot hold that it corroborates Daniels's extrajudicial statement regarding alleged criminal conduct in 2002 and 1995. Aside from Daniels's statement regarding two prior alleged incidents, no evidence at all was offered to establish the corpus delicti of those incidents. Accordingly, we sustain Daniels's second and third points.

WHAT DO *YOU* THINK?

1. Can you give an example of how the prosecutor could have established the corpus delicti for the two earlier assaults?

2. Do you believe that corpus delicti serves an important purpose, or should confessions be allowed to stand alone as evidence to support convictions?

Generally speaking, legal professionals are not likely to use the *corpus delicti* rule or the corroboration rule in very many cases. But professionals are advised to be aware of these doctrines, as well as the jurisdictions in which they apply, particularly in cases where the defendant has offered a confession or other incriminating statement to authorities. Someone may confess to a criminal act, but if there is no independent evidence showing that this act has occurred, the person making the confession cannot be prosecuted. In jurisdictions that apply the *corpus delicti* rule, the important thing is to ensure that there is additional and independent evidence to demonstrate the crime mentioned in the confession or incriminating statement actually occurred. In jurisdictions using the corroboration rule, you must have some evidence that corroborates (supports) the defendant's confession, even though it might not demonstrate evidence that an actual crime occurred.

EXTENDING CRIMINAL LIABILITY: INCHOATE OFFENSES

inchoate crimes
incomplete crimes or anticipatory offenses, such as attempt, conspiracy, or solicitation

Inchoate crimes are incipient or incomplete offenses "which generally lead to other crimes."[39] "Inchoate" means imperfect, partial, or unfinished. Such crimes are also referred to as *anticipatory offenses*. Inchoate crimes include (1) attempt, (2) conspiracy, and (3) solicitation. While language favoring punishment of inchoate misconduct can be found in fourteenth-century judicial opinions, most inchoate crimes were not recognized until the late eighteenth century. Until then, prevailing legal wisdom often held that "a miss is as good as a mile."[40]

Criminal Attempt

criminal attempt
a criminal offense where a person takes a substantial step toward committing a complete crime, but fails to complete all elements of the offense

Under most statutes for *criminal attempt*, there are two basic elements. First, a person must have formed a specific intent to commit a criminal offense. And second, the person must perform a substantial step toward committing the intended offense. Statutory standards for attempt offenses are generally brief.[41] New York, for example, describes the crime of attempt as follows: "[a] person is guilty of an attempt to commit a crime when, with the intent to commit a crime, he engages in conduct which tends to effect the commission of such crime."[42] California's attempt statute provides: "[a] person commits an attempt when, with the intent to commit a specific offense, he does any act which constitutes a substantial step toward the commission of that offense."[43] Illinois offers a similar approach, finding criminal attempt when a person, with the intent to commit an offense, performs any act that constitutes a substantial step toward the commission of that offense.[44]

Law Line 3-8
Criminal Attempt

The Act Requirement.   Attempted criminal activity can include a large amount of conduct. Almost any crime that can be envisioned can be attempted, and under the penal codes of most states, any crime defined by statute has as a companion an attempt to commit that crime. But to charge an attempt as a criminal offense, there must be some type of overt action toward completing an identifiable crime. Generally speaking, courts have held that *mere preparation* to commit an offense is not sufficient to support a charge of attempted criminal activity, and that some specific action must be taken toward the actual completion of the intended offense. Thus, a central task when considering criminal attempt offenses is deciding when the conduct in question moves beyond "mere preparation" for a crime.

Tests Used to Evaluate Acts of Attempt.   Over the years, courts have used various tests to distinguish between mere preparation and the commission of substantial conduct toward a criminal act. At common law, the traditional test was the ***proximity approach***, which maintained that acts remotely leading toward the commission of the offense are not considered attempts to commit the crime, but acts immediately connected with it are. The proximity test was based on the ***last act test***, which required that the accused took the last step or act, performed all that he or she intended and was able to do in an attempt to commit the crime, but for some reason did not complete the crime. Using this test in a murder by shooting, for example, an attempt would not be completed until the accused fired the weapon.

Later, in order to reduce the strict provisions of the last act test, the ***physical proximity test*** was developed. Under the physical proximity test, the substantial step need not be the last act, but it must approach sufficiently near to it in order to stand as a substantial step in the direct movement toward commission of the intended crime. For example, in order to be found guilty of attempted rape, the accused would need to have had the victim under his control and have started taking the necessary steps to force the victim to have sexual relations with him. A modified version of this test, the ***dangerous proximity test***, incorporates the physical proximity standard but is more flexible. According to the dangerous proximity test, a person is guilty of an attempt when her conduct is in "dangerous proximity" to success, which is based on three factors—the nearness of completion, the degree of intended harm, and the degree of apprehension felt by the intended victim.[45]

Some courts have adopted alternatives to the proximity-based tests. These include the ***indispensable element test***, which holds that persons are not guilty of an attempt if they have yet to obtain control of an indispensable feature of the crime; the ***unequivocal test***, which maintains that an act does not become an attempt until it ceases to be equivocal (an act must unequivocally manifest a defendant's criminal intent); and the ***probable desistance approach***, which maintains that a person's conduct constitutes an attempt if it has gone beyond the point where the defendant is likely to voluntarily stop short of completing the offense.

In recent years, most state courts and the federal courts have used the Model Penal Code's ***substantial step test***.[46] Under this approach, a person must commit an overt act that constitutes a substantial step toward committing a crime. Again, the defendant's conduct must go beyond mere preparation, and must strongly confirm that he intended to commit an identified offense. Normally, the prosecutor does not have to prove that the defendant did everything to complete the crime. A substantial step beyond mere preparation is enough. The Model Penal Code lists the following examples of activity that might meet the substantial step criterion, provided that the behavior in question is thought to corroborate the defendant's criminal purpose[47]:

- Lying in wait or searching for or following the contemplated victim;
- Enticing or seeking to entice the contemplated victim of the crime to go to the place contemplated for its commission;
- Reconnoitering the place contemplated for the commission of the crime;
- Unlawful entry of a structure, vehicle, or enclosure in which it is contemplated that the crime will be committed;
- Possession of materials to be employed in the commission of the crime, which are specially designed for such unlawful use or which can serve no lawful purpose of the actor under the circumstances;

proximity approach
a traditional test used to judge whether a person's actions involved a criminal attempt; maintained that acts remotely leading toward the commission of the offense are not considered as attempts to commit the crime, but acts immediately connected with it are

last act test
a part of the proximity test to determine whether an attempt occurred; asks whether the accused took the last step or act toward completing the crime

physical proximity test
a test used to judge criminal attempt cases; maintains that a substantial step need not be the last act toward the completion of a crime, but rather, it must approach sufficiently near to it in order to stand as a substantial step in the direct movement toward commission of the intended crime

dangerous proximity test
a modified version of the physical proximity standard that finds a criminal attempt where a person's conduct is in "dangerous proximity" to success

indispensable element test
a test used to judge attempt cases; holds that persons are not guilty of an attempt if they have yet to obtain control of an indispensable feature of the crime

unequivocal test
attempt standard maintaining that an act does not become an attempt until it ceases to be equivocal; an act must unequivocally manifest a defendant's criminal intent

probable desistance approach
an attempt standard maintaining that a person's conduct constitutes an attempt if it has gone beyond the point where the defendant is likely to voluntarily stop short of completing the offense

substantial step test
the modern approach to judging attempt cases; finds an attempt crime where a person commits an overt act that constitutes a substantial step toward committing a crime

- Possession, collection, or fabrication of material to be employed in the commission of the crime, at or near the place contemplated for its commission, where such possession, collection, or fabrication serves no lawful useful purpose of the actor under the circumstances;
- Soliciting an innocent agent to engage in conduct constituting an element of the crime.

The increased reliance on the MPC's substantial step test reflects a growing trend during the past thirty years to expand liability for attempt offenses. As illustrated by Figure 3-10, this test allows prosecutors to pursue attempt cases in

FIGURE 3-10 **Comparison of Tests to Determine the *Actus Reus* of an Attempt**

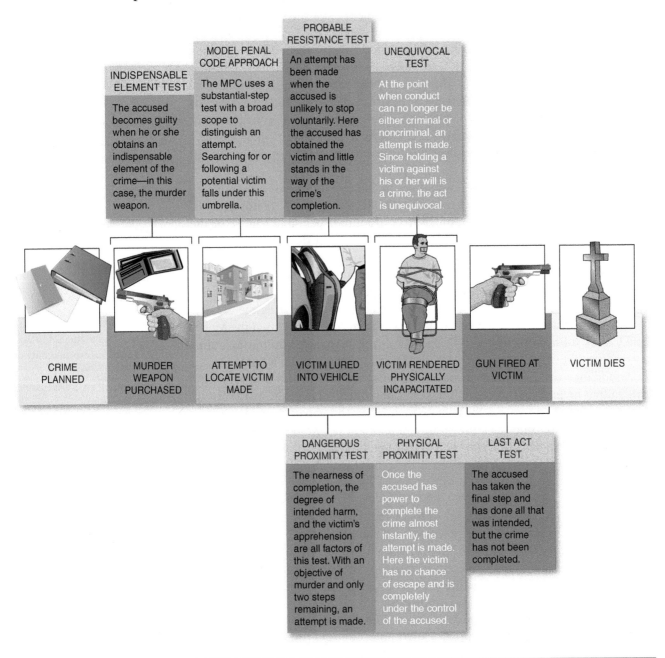

IN THE FIELD

The Model Penal Code's substantial step test presents both challenges and opportunities for legal professionals. The test presents challenges because it lacks concrete benchmarks for determining when persons go beyond mere preparation for a crime. In other words, the test is somewhat subjective, resulting in varied and, at times, inconsistent applications. Nevertheless, the subjectivity of the substantial step test also presents opportunities for both prosecutors and defense attorneys, allowing them to be more creative in their legal advocacy. Legal professionals often must present analogies, hypothetical examples, and other illustrations to courts and juries in an effort to persuade them to find or not to find that a defendant engaged in a substantial step toward the commission of a criminal offense.

situations where most of the other tests would not. As a result, courts have been increasingly more willing to find criminal culpability based on attempt, even where ultimate harm or injury is not imminent.

For example, in some jurisdictions, the crime of attempted sexual contact with a minor requires prosecutors to show that the defendant took a substantial step toward having sexual contact with an underage person. In many cases, defendants make Internet contact with a person they believe to be a minor and arrange to meet them at a particular location. Defendants are then arrested when they drive their car to the location. Is this a substantial step toward sexual contact with a minor? Many courts have said yes, because the defendants made arrangements to meet a person they believed to be a minor and then drove to the location of the meeting. Others disagree, claiming that, because the defendants did not try to engage in any sexual behavior—no removal of clothing and no exposure of private parts—a substantial step toward sexual contact did not occur. In the end, attempt cases often require legal professionals to engage in abstract and creative thinking in an effort to provide meaning and application to the substantial step test.

Criminal Conspiracy

A ***criminal conspiracy*** is an agreement between two or more persons to commit or to effect the commission of an unlawful act, or to use unlawful means to accomplish an act that is not unlawful. More specifically, the elements of conspiracy are (1) an agreement between two or more persons, (2) to carry out an act that is unlawful or one that is lawful but is to be accomplished by unlawful means, and (3) a culpable intent formed by the defendants. The Model Penal Code identifies conspiracy as an offense that serves two primary functions:

> In the first place, conspiracy is an inchoate crime, complementing the provisions dealing with attempt and solicitation in reaching preparatory conduct before it has matured into commission of a substantive offense. Second, it is a means of striking against the special danger incident to group activity, facilitating prosecution of the group, and yielding a basis for imposing added penalties when combination is involved.

Although conspiracy was generally considered to be a misdemeanor under common law, most state and the federal laws today classify it as a felony.

The essence of the crime of conspiracy is an *agreement* for the joint purpose of unlawful ends. Since conspiracy is defined in terms of an agreement, it necessarily

criminal conspiracy
an agreement between two or more persons to commit or to effect the commission of an unlawful act, or to use unlawful means to accomplish an act that is not unlawful

plurality requirement
an element of conspiracy offense that requires at least two persons to participate in an agreement to commit a criminal offense

involves two or more persons. This aspect of the offense is called the ***plurality requirement***. The required agreement does not need to be a "meeting of the minds," such as is required to create an enforceable contract. All that is needed for the crime of conspiracy to occur is that the parties communicate to each other in some way their intentions to pursue a joint and criminal objective, or to pursue a joint objective in a criminal manner.[48]

Some crimes, by their very nature, require two or more criminal participants for their commission. Adultery, for example, requires at least two persons (generally, one of whom must be married to someone else). ***Wharton's Rule*** provides that where the targeted crime by its very nature takes more than one person to commit, then there can be no conspiracy when a single individual participates in the targeted activity. With an adultery crime, for example, there can be no conspiracy to commit adultery unless more than two people are involved in the offense (as when a married couple conspires to lure others into adulterous relationships).[49] Wharton's Rule does not apply to those situations where the crime is defined so as to require two or more persons to commit it, but where only one of the offenders is punishable under the targeted crime statute. The rule is irrelevant, for example, in the case of a statute that punishes the selling of liquor during certain hours of the day but prescribes a punishment only for the seller. In some states and under federal law, Wharton's Rule constitutes only a presumption and does not apply where the legislature clearly indicates that the rule should not preclude conspiracy offenses.[50]

Wharton's Rule
rule providing that where the targeted crime by its very nature takes more than one person to commit, there can be no conspiracy when a single individual participates in the targeted activity

In a conspiracy, the parties do not need to achieve their intended criminal harm to be found criminally culpable. As the U.S. Supreme Court has observed, "the agreement to commit an unlawful act is a distinct evil, which may exist and be punished whether or not the substantive crime ensues."[51] Thus, if two or more people plan to bomb a public building, they can be legally stopped before the bombing. As soon as they take steps to "further" their plan, they have met the requirement for an act. Buying explosives, telephoning one another, or drawing plans of the building may all be actions in "furtherance of the conspiracy."

To prove a conspiracy offense, the government is required to show that the defendant specifically intended to effect the commission of an unlawful act. Courts have held that knowledge of a conspiracy's objective is necessary to show requisite criminal intent.[52] At a minimum, it must be shown that a defendant has knowledge of the conspiracy's illegal purpose when he or she performs acts that further that illicit purpose.[53]

Law Line 3-9
Federal Conspiracy Statute

Parties to a Conspiracy.   When people participate in a conspiracy, the law does not require that each party form an agreement with all of the other parties involved. In complex conspiracies, for example, the parties may not all know one another and may not even be aware of the involvement of all of the other parties. This is particularly true in cases involving organized crime, drug dealing and distribution, illicit gambling, and organized prostitution.

More elaborate conspiracies, where the conspiring parties may not all be aware of one another's identity or even involvement, are sometimes called "wheel" or "chain" conspiracies. In ***wheel conspiracies***, the conspirators deal only with a ringleader and not with each other. The leader of the conspiracy can be thought of as a hub around which each of the others revolve like spokes on a wheel. To establish whether a wheel conspiracy is a single conspiracy or a series of conspiracies for purposes of the law, courts have developed a "community of interests" test. A single conspiracy exists if (1) each spoke knows that other spokes exist, although they need not know the precise identity of the other spokes, and (2) the various spokes have a community of shared interests. In one early case in which such a test was

wheel conspiracy
a type of conspiracy where persons deal only with a ringleader and not with each other

applied, a woman was convicted of conspiracy to perform illegal abortions as part of a wheel conspiracy. The convicted woman had referred pregnant women to a doctor (who was also a defendant) in violation of the law. In declaring that a wheel type of conspiracy existed, the trial court held that the defendant had been aware that others were also referring pregnant women to the same doctor for illegal abortions.[54]

On the other hand, a ***chain conspiracy*** involves a sequence of individuals. Chain conspiracies are often found in illegal drug distribution schemes (in which controlled substances move sequentially from importer, to wholesaler, to retailer, and, ultimately, to the consumer) and in other activities associated with racketeering. The community of interest test may also be used to determine if a chain type of conspiracy consists of a single conspiracy or a group of conspiracies. Under both the wheel and the chain types of conspiracies, the precise identity of the other conspirators is not important, so long as it can be demonstrated that charged conspirators had knowledge of the fact that others were involved in the scheme and that they acted in terms of a shared interest.

chain conspiracy
a type of conspiracy involving a sequence of individuals working in some combination or connectedness

Duration of Conspiracy. In some cases, the duration of a conspiracy may be a critical issue. The longer a conspiracy continues, for example, the greater the chances of successful prosecution, since most statutes of limitation do not begin

FIGURE 3-11 **Types of Conspiracies**

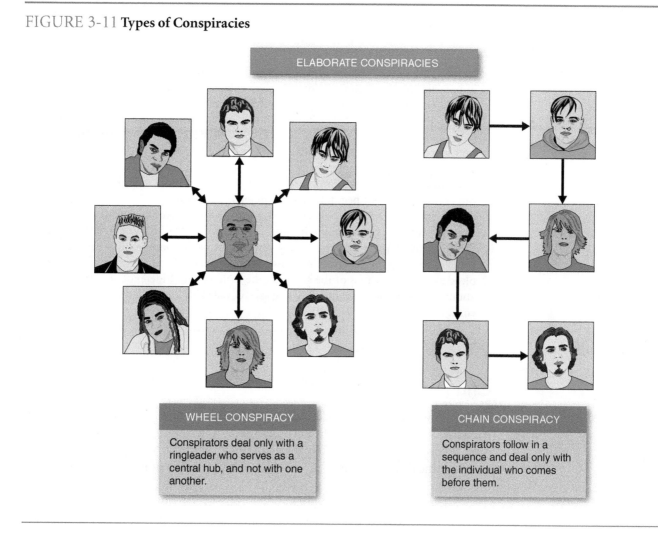

ELABORATE CONSPIRACIES

WHEEL CONSPIRACY

Conspirators deal only with a ringleader who serves as a central hub, and not with one another.

CHAIN CONSPIRACY

Conspirators follow in a sequence and deal only with the individual who comes before them.

measuring time until a crime is complete. Also, in most jurisdictions, declarations of conspirators are admissible against other conspirators if the declarations are made while the conspiracy is still in progress.

Generally speaking, a conspiracy can be said to continue until the crime it seeks to commit is either completed or abandoned by all of the parties involved. If a crime involves multiple conspirators, and a single conspirator withdraws, the conspiracy continues for purposes of the law so long as two or more parties continue to be involved in it. To effectively constitute a withdrawal, a coconspirator generally must give notice of having withdrawn to other conspirators or to law enforcement officials. A person's intent to withdraw is not the same as withdrawal. Under the Model Penal Code guidelines, a person must show that withdrawal was voluntary and that the "success of the conspiracy" was "thwarted."[55] A withdrawal motivated by fear of immediate detection is not considered voluntary.

IN THE FIELD

For legal professionals, conspiracy cases often can be legally complicated and administratively difficult. Many conspiracy cases involve large numbers of defendants, complex evidentiary issues, and intricate factual allegations.[56] In addition, conspiracy statutes often give prosecutors broad authority to charge individuals for what, to some, may appear to be rather nebulous activity. Conspiracy laws can provide extraordinary latitude in prosecuting behavior that would not otherwise be criminal. These cases and the rules by which they are handled offer many procedural advantages to prosecutors, including the use of joint trials, the admission of some hearsay evidence, and the fact that the trial may be held in any jurisdiction where an element of the offense occurred.

Conspiracy indictments also present unique challenges for plea negotiations. In evaluating plea agreement offers in cases with multiple defendants, prosecutors often seek to rank the defendants according to either (1) the level of their participation in the crime, or (2) their potential usefulness (cooperation and testimony) to the prosecution's case. As a result, a substantial amount of advocacy can occur during plea negotiations. For defense attorneys, this means portraying a client as someone who had a relatively minor role in the overall conspiracy and/or someone who has considerable insight into the activities of other coconspirators, thereby providing the prosecutor with a highly valuable cooperating witness, who could either help the government's case at trial or persuade other coconspirators to plead as well. Regardless of the scenario, the reality of multidefendant plea negotiations reinforces the need for good organizational skills and sufficient resources in conspiracy cases.

Criminal Solicitation

criminal solicitation
the request to perform
a criminal act

Under common law, ***criminal solicitation*** is a crime where one person requests or encourages another to perform a criminal act. Unlike conspiracy, criminal solicitation requires no overt act, other than a request. It simply requires a mental state such that the defendant must have intended to induce the other person to perform the crime.

All states have criminal solicitation laws. Florida law, for example, reads: "A person who solicits another to commit an offense prohibited by law and in the course of such solicitation commands, encourages, hires, or requests another person to engage in specific conduct which would constitute such offense or an attempt to commit such offense commits the offense of criminal solicitation . . ."[57] Most states consider it immaterial whether or not the person solicited agrees to perform the act solicited.

Consider a scenario in which Joe asks Jim to kill his wife, Joyce. Since criminal solicitation consists of requesting or encouraging another to commit a crime, Joe's request likely constitutes the crime of solicitation. The crime is completed upon the transmission of the request or the encouragement. If Jim agrees to the request, generally both parties will be guilty of conspiracy when an overt act is taken in furtherance of the conspiracy (such as Jim buying a gun to be used to kill Joe's wife). If Jim does in fact kill Joyce, then both Joe and Jim would be guilty of murder. While solicitation is, in effect, an attempted conspiracy, it is possible to have a conspiracy without a prior solicitation.

In an unusual case, thirty-six-year-old Donald Winniewicz, of Houston, Pennsylvania, was arrested in 2004 and charged with criminal solicitation to commit homicide after he confessed to playing an audiotape to his sleeping ten-year-old stepson.[58] The audiotape, made by Winniewicz, was an apparent attempt to plant suggestions in the sleeping boy's mind that he should smother his four-year-old sibling with a pillow. Those who listened to the tape reported that they heard Winniewicz saying things like, "Why haven't you done this yet? If you love Grandma, you will do this."[59] The tape was discovered by Winniewicz's wife in a drawer in the family's Pittsburgh home and confiscated by police.

Law Line 3-10
Solicitation Statute

IN THE FIELD

For legal professionals, solicitation cases often become "he said/she said" cases, involving competing claims over what, if anything, the defendant said to or requested from another person. In this scenario, solicitation cases essentially result in battles over the credibility of witnesses, with the central question being "did the defendant really say that?" Accordingly, legal professionals can spend considerable time trying to find evidence to bolster the credibility of their witnesses or diminish the credibility of opposing witnesses. This often involves asking some basic questions like: Are there circumstances that make one witness more believable than another? Did the defendant have a motive to solicit? Does the prosecution's witness have a motive to lie? Do any of the witnesses have a history of dishonesty? In the end, unless there is a tangible recording of the defendant's words, solicitation cases are usually won or lost based on whose testimony is more believable.

CRIMINAL LIABILITY FOR RELATED ACTORS

In criminal acts involving multiple actors, some parties can participate in the criminal activity at different stages and in different ways. Common law developed a fairly complex scheme of labeling persons involved in a crime according to their relationship to the criminal act. It distinguished between those who actually committed the crime and others who assisted the perpetrator either before, during, or after the crime had been committed. Categories included (1) the ***principal in the first degree***, who was the individual who actually committed the crime; (2) the ***principal in the second degree***, any person who was present at the crime scene and who aided, abetted, counseled, or encouraged the principal in the commission of

principal in the first degree
a person who actually commits a crime

principal in the second degree
any person who was present at the crime scene and who aided, abetted, counseled, or encouraged the principal in the commission of the crime

FIGURE 3-12 **Parties to Crime**

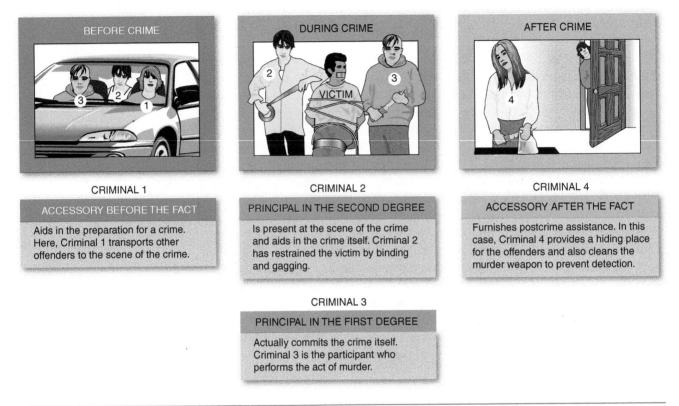

BEFORE CRIME

CRIMINAL 1

ACCESSORY BEFORE THE FACT

Aids in the preparation for a crime. Here, Criminal 1 transports other offenders to the scene of the crime.

DURING CRIME

CRIMINAL 2

PRINCIPAL IN THE SECOND DEGREE

Is present at the scene of the crime and aids in the crime itself. Criminal 2 has restrained the victim by binding and gagging.

AFTER CRIME

CRIMINAL 4

ACCESSORY AFTER THE FACT

Furnishes postcrime assistance. In this case, Criminal 4 provides a hiding place for the offenders and also cleans the murder weapon to prevent detection.

CRIMINAL 3

PRINCIPAL IN THE FIRST DEGREE

Actually commits the crime itself. Criminal 3 is the participant who performs the act of murder.

---

accessory before the fact
a person who aided and abetted in the preparation for the crime but was not present at the crime scene

accessory after the fact
a person who did not participate in the crime, but knew that the crime had been committed and furnished postcrime assistance to keep the criminal from being detected or arrested

the crime; (3) an ***accessory before the fact***, who, like the principal in the second degree, aided and abetted in the preparation for the crime but was not present at the crime scene; and, finally, (4) an ***accessory after the fact***, a person who did not participate in the crime, but knew that the crime had been committed and furnished postcrime assistance to keep the criminal from being detected or arrested.

Today, however, these common law rules largely do not exist in the United States, and any participant in a crime may be tried and convicted even if the individual who actually committed the crime has not yet been apprehended. The degree of criminal liability today rarely depends on a person's presence or absence at the crime scene, and most jurisdictions draw distinctions only between principals and accessories—recognizing a principal as one who directly furthers the criminal act before or while it occurs, and an accessory as one who assists the felon after the crime has been committed.

Federal law, for example, says, "(a) Whoever commits an offense against the United States or aids, abets, counsels, commands, induces or procures its commission, is punishable as a principal. (b) Whoever willfully causes an act to be done which if directly performed by him or another would be an offense against the United States, is punishable as a principal."[60] This section of the United States Code makes clear the legislative intent to punish as a principal not only one who directly commits an offense, as well as one who "aids, abets, counsels, commands, induces or procures" another to commit an offense, but also anyone who *causes* the doing of an act that, if done by him directly, would render him guilty of an offense against the United States. It removes all doubt that one who puts in motion or assists in the illegal enterprise, and thus causes the commission of an indispensable element of the offense by another agent or instrumentality, is guilty as a principal even though he intentionally refrained from the direct act that constituted the completed offense.

Accomplice Liability

Generally, one who assists in the commission of a crime, but does not commit the *actus reus,* is called an **accomplice**. Unlike a mere accessory, an accomplice is often present or directly aids in the commission of the crime. The relationship between the person who commits the crime and his or her accomplice is one of **complicity**. Accomplice liability is based on the notion that any individual who aids, abets, encourages, or assists another person to commit a crime should share in the criminal liability that accrues under law. In most cases, to be liable as an accomplice, a defendant must (1) know what the criminal is trying to do, (2) intentionally aid or encourage another person to commit a crime, and (3) believe that the aid or encouragement would make the criminal's success likely.[61] For his or her actions to be considered intentional, the defendant must have intended to (1) commit the acts that in fact gave aid or encouragement, and (2) bring about the other party's commission of the offense by committing those acts.

accomplice
a person who assists in the commission of a crime, but does not commit the *actus reus*

complicity
the relationship between the person who commits the crime and other individuals who assist in the crime

Law Line 3-11
Reappraising Complicity

Accessory

Under the laws of most jurisdictions today, one who knowingly gives assistance to a person who has committed a felony for the purpose of helping that individual avoid apprehension or detection is guilty as an accessory. For example, the United States Code says: "Whoever, knowing that an offense against the United States has been committed, receives, relieves, comforts or assists the offender in order to hinder or prevent his apprehension, trial or punishment, is an accessory after the fact."[62] In addition, some states have created more specialized "after-the-fact" criminal offenses, including aiding and abetting, aiding a felon, aiding an escape, interference with a police officer, and obstruction of justice.

Proving an accessory's guilt generally requires a showing that (1) a crime has been completed, (2) the defendant knew that the crime had been committed, (3) the defendant knew that the crime was committed by the individual who was being assisted, and (4) the defendant personally gave assistance to the individual who committed the crime. A person who is coerced or forced into giving assistance to a criminal offender, however, will not generally be charged as an accessory after the fact since the assistance was given unwillingly. This would likely be the case where an innocent bystander is forced to drive a getaway car at gunpoint and is later released.

Vicarious Liability

There are times when individuals can be held criminally liable for the harmful act of another, even though they have no knowledge of or intent to commit the criminal act. This is known as **vicarious liability**. For example, a person who loans a vehicle to someone who parks it in a fire zone may be responsible for paying the resulting ticket. Vicarious liability imposes criminal responsibility on one party for

vicarious liability
a legal theory that allows individuals to be held criminally liable for the harmful acts of others

the criminal acts of another party based on the relationship between the two parties. The theory is that a person can commit a criminal act (vicariously) through the acts of another, if a substantial and legally significant relationship exists between the two parties. In many settings, the basis of this relationship is principal/agent or employer/employee.

Vicarious criminal liability is often associated with regulatory crimes, the most common form occurring where an employer is held liable for the criminal acts of employees. In many cases, the criminal liability that is created under the concept of vicarious liability is punishable only by a fine. But there are notable exceptions to this rule, particularly where the law places an affirmative duty on a person to perform a specified act. For example, in *United States v. Parks* (1975),[63] a federal court upheld the conviction and one-year prison sentence of a company president for the shipment of adulterated foods. The FDA statute under which the official had been prosecuted placed an affirmative duty on company officers to ensure that no adulterated food was shipped. Even though, in this case, employees shipped adulterated food without the knowledge of their company's president, his conviction under this vicarious liability statute was upheld by the U.S. Supreme Court.

It is important to distinguish between accomplice liability and vicarious liability. Accomplice liability is based on a person's affirmative participation in a crime, whereas vicarious liability is based solely on the relationship between the defendant (principal) and the perpetrator of the crime (agent). Many states require that, before vicarious liability may be imposed on an individual, the individual must have some form of control over the perpetrator. Accordingly, in these states, vicarious liability is limited to employer–employee relationships and similar situations.[64] Much of the case law limits vicarious liability to situations in which the potential for punishment is not extreme. This "punishment limitation" is based on the fact that although there are social interests in imposing some degree of vicarious liability, anyone who lacks knowledge of an offense should not be too severely punished because of it, even when technically liable for its prevention.[65] While strict liability and vicarious liability are both forms of liability without fault, they dispense with the fault requirement in entirely different ways. Strict liability is imposed in situations in which the *mens rea* requirement has been eliminated. Vicarious liability, on the other hand, may be imposed in situations in which the act requirement has been eliminated.

ETHICAL PRINCIPLES

DELEGATED TASKS IN CRIMINAL CASES

American Bar Association Model for the Utilization of Paralegal Services Guideline 2

Provided the lawyer maintains responsibility for the work product, a lawyer may delegate to a paralegal any task normally performed by the lawyer except those tasks proscribed to a nonlawyer by statute, court rule, administrative rule or regulation, controlling authority, the applicable rule of professional conduct of the jurisdiction in which the lawyer practices, or these guidelines.

Courtesy of the American Bar Association

Criminal Liability of Corporations

Can a corporation be a criminal defendant? Today, the answer is yes. Both a corporation, as a legal entity, and the agents thereof can be held accountable under criminal laws. And in recent years, there has been increasing interest in pursuing criminal charges against corporations and many high-level corporate officials for inflicting financial harm on individuals. Corporate crime can come in many forms, including deficient and harmful work standards, securities fraud, insider trading (using confidential and inside information to benefit through stock trading), and the destruction of business records. But the underlying theory of a corporate criminal case is the same as that used to prosecute individuals for criminal offenses. Prosecutors allege that a corporate entity engaged in behavior that violated criminal laws, thereby resulting in harm to persons or entities.

The 2008 stock market crisis, which caused many individual corporate shareholders and bank customers to lose a substantial amount of money, has led many legislators and prosecutors to place an increasing focus on corporate crime and scandal. The conduct of such financial giants as Lehman Brothers, AIG, Goldman Sachs, Bank of America, and other corporations has blanketed much of the news, leading to many congressional hearings and several criminal and regulatory investigations. But the notion of corporate crime is not new.

Law Line 3-12
Criminal Charges against Corporations

In 2007, for example, Massachusetts prosecutors charged Powers Fasteners, a New York company, with manslaughter in the collapse of concrete ceiling panels in Boston's Big Dig tunnel construction project after one of the panels fell on a car, crushing it and killing a passenger in the vehicle.[66] According to prosecutors, the company was criminally negligent in the tunnel collapse. In 2008, however, prosecutors dropped criminal charges against the company after it agreed to pay $16 million to settle a civil suit stemming from the incident.[67] Powers Fasteners also agreed to take steps to prevent future use of the wrong type of epoxy by its customers.

Other corporate criminal cases include the 2002 federal trial involving accounting firm Arthur Andersen, wherein the corporation was convicted on obstruction of justice charges after its employees shredded documents related to the bankruptcy of Enron Corporation. This conviction was later overturned by the U.S. Supreme Court, based on a finding that the trial judge had improperly instructed the jury on the elements of the offense. See Law Line 3-13. In 1978, the Ford Motor Company was convicted on three counts of reckless homicide in the deaths of three teenage girls in a Ford Pinto whose gas tank exploded in a crash. Exxon Corporation agreed to pay $100 million in criminal fines (and more than $1 billion in civil damages) in charges stemming from the 1989 Exxon Valdez oil spill in Alaska. And in 1990, General Electric was convicted on charges of defrauding the U.S. Army.[68]

Law Line 3-13
Arthur Andersen v. United States (2005)

The Legal Basis for Corporate Criminal Culpability.   The laws regarding corporate criminal liability are still developing. This is especially true in the realm of large multinational corporations that, for the most part, are the product of twentieth-century industry and free enterprise. As some have observed, "[t]here has been a gradual expansion in the . . . law of corporate criminal liability, both of the range of offenses a corporation is capable of committing and in the means by which an offense is imputed to a corporation. There are now very few offenses which a corporation cannot commit. . . ."[69]

Criminal fault is imputed to corporations based upon two legal theories: (1) the principle of vicarious liability (discussed above), and (2) the identification

identification doctrine
a legal theory that allows corporations to be held criminally liable based on unlawful actions of corporate officers and senior officials, whose initiatives are identified with those of the company

doctrine. The principle of vicarious liability grew out of the idea of the liability a master (or employer) holds for the actions of his servant (or employee). The principle of vicarious liability has mostly been used to hold a corporate body accountable for violations of regulatory offenses. Under the **identification doctrine**, however, a corporation can be held responsible for more serious criminal offenses—including those that require mental elements, or *mens rea*, for their commission. The identification doctrine views a corporation as an abstract entity with no mind of its own, but which is actively directed by its officers and senior officials, whose initiatives can be *identified* with those of the company. Identification liability stops at wrongdoing in the boardroom, while vicarious liability extends corporate responsibility to the acts of all employees.[70]

Although some criminal statutes explicitly state that corporations can be treated, for purposes of the law, as persons, others are less clear. As a result, courts often must decide whether a company can be held criminally liable for violation of a particular statute.[71] Under the Model Penal Code,[72] a corporation may be criminally liable if:

1. The offense is a minor offense, and the conduct was performed by an agent acting on the corporation's behalf within the scope of the agent's employment.
2. The offense is defined by another statute and made applicable to corporations.
3. The offense consists of a failure to perform a specific duty imposed upon the corporation by law, for example, failing to file a tax return.
4. The criminal acts were approved, authorized, permitted, or recklessly tolerated by the board of directors or a high management official acting on behalf of the corporation and within the scope of his or her employment.

In addition, some jurisdictions take the approach that a corporation may be held criminally liable for offenses committed by any employee who has been given the power and duty, or responsibility and authority, to act on behalf of the corporation. This approach is based on the belief that it should be incumbent on boards of directors and high management officials to be sufficiently informed so as not to condone criminal misconduct on behalf of the corporation.

Courts have adopted a number of doctrines that enlarge the scope of corporate liability for employee misconduct. One of the most significant, the collective knowledge doctrine, imputes to a corporation the knowledge of all employees, thereby imposing liability on companies even where no single employee has sufficient knowledge to be liable.[73] As some authors have observed,[74] the court in the prosecution of Arthur Andersen (above) seemed to go even one step further, creating a kind of collective corporate liability by instructing the jury that it could convict Andersen without agreeing on which employee committed the crime. Another doctrine adopted by the courts is the "willful blindness" doctrine under which criminal liability can accrue where a corporation deliberately disregards criminal misconduct.[75]

The Future of Corporate Criminal Law. In the not-too-distant past, corporate officers and business managers had only limited legal ability to effectively protect their companies. Until recently, federal law made no provision for leniency in cases in which corporations reported wrongdoing by their employees, and managers could not effectively reduce corporate liability either by attempting to prevent crime or by reporting it to the government once it had been detected within the company. Today, however, official U.S. Department of Justice policy encourages federal prosecutors not to indict a corporation for employee wrongdoing if the corporation had in place an effective program to deter wrongdoing at the time the crimes were committed or if it reported wrongdoing that was detected to the government and cooperated fully in further investigations.[76] Moreover, new federal sentencing guidelines, enacted in 2003, protect businesses that have established effective compliance and ethics programs for their employees.[77]

Congress and some state authorities continue to debate whether additional criminal statutes are needed to specifically regulate crime within the financial industry. Some of these measures include greater regulatory requirements for corporations and their agents. For example, in 2002, Congress enacted the federal *Sarbanes–Oxley Act*, which is officially entitled the Public Company Accounting Reform and Investor Protection Act.[78] This act places limitations on accounting firms in the way they perform audits and other services for corporate clients and publicly traded companies to make disclosures and other filings with the Securities and Exchange Commission (SEC) (a federal regulatory agency) regarding financial dealings and conflicts of interest. The law threatens criminal and civil penalties for violating its provisions and creates additional protections for corporate whistleblowers.

In addition, other federal statutes allow the SEC and other federal agencies to pursue civil claims against corporations for conduct that violates federal criminal laws. In some cases, these civil complaints resemble criminal charges. For example, in April 2010, the SEC filed civil charges against Goldman Sachs, a large investment banking and securities firm, alleging fraud in trading mortgage-backed securities and other financial products. See Law Line 3-14.

Sarbanes–Oxley Act
a federal law enacted in 2002; places limitations on accounting firms in the way they perform audits and other services for corporate clients and publicly traded companies to make disclosures and other filings with the Securities and Exchange Commission (a federal regulatory agency) regarding financial dealings and conflicts of interest

---

Law Line 3-14
SEC complaint filed against Goldman Sachs

IN THE FIELD

Legal professionals are likely to find extended liability cases particularly challenging. Where prosecutors seek to extend criminal liability to parties not directly involved in the criminal act and/or to parties who have no direct intent to commit the act, the critical questions for the case often become what the defendants knew, when they knew it, what the law required them to know, and what their relationship was to the primary criminal actor. Prosecutors generally must show that the defendant had some legal obligation for the primary criminal actor's conduct. Defense attorneys often must try to minimize the defendant's knowledge about the criminal conduct and try to negate the legal relationship between the defendant and the primary criminal actor. In many cases where a legal relationship is established between the defendant and primary criminal actor (e.g., employer/employee), defendants may attempt to argue that the criminal act occurred outside of this relationship (the employee went beyond his legitimate employment duties), and thus, the defendant should not be held vicariously liable for these acts.

CHAPTER **SUMMARY**

- The legal essence of crime consists of three essential elements: *actus reus* (an act in violation of the law), *mens rea* (a guilty mind), and the concurrence of an act in violation of the law and a culpable mental state.
- Some scholars suggest that there are other elements inherent in the concept of crime, which include causation, a resulting harm, and necessary attendant circumstances.
- In contrast to the elements common to all crimes, particular offenses are statutorily defined in terms of specific statutory elements. To convict a defendant of a given crime, prosecutors must prove to a judge or jury that all of the statutory elements of a crime are present. If even one statutory element of an offense cannot be established beyond a reasonable doubt, criminal liability will not have been demonstrated, and the defendant will be found not guilty.
- The *actus reus* or criminal act can involve conduct of either omission or commission. At times a person's failure to act may result in criminal culpability.
- Degrees of culpability, or types of *mens rea*, can be distinguished. Today, the four most common mental states found in statutes are purposeful, knowing, reckless, and negligent.
- Strict liability offenses, which are based on the presumption that causing harm in itself is blameworthy, represent an exception to general understandings of the nature of crime, since they require no accompanying culpable mental state.
- The element of concurrence requires that the culpable act and mental state occur at the same time (concurrently).
- Causation refers to the fact that the concurrence of a guilty mind and a criminal act may produce or *cause* harm.
- There are two primary types of causation—factual and legal. If there is an actual link between the actor's conduct and the resulting harm, causation in fact is said to exist. Legal cause or proximate cause requires a defendant's actions to play a substantial part in causing the injury. It also requires that the injury be reasonably foreseeable under the circumstances.

- Necessary attendant circumstances are "facts surrounding an event" and include such things as time, place, and instruments used to commit an offense.
- The term *corpus delicti* literally means "body of crime." The corpus delicti rule holds that a criminal conviction cannot be based solely on the confession or admission of an accused. The rule requires prosecutors to show some independent evidence that the crime mentioned in a confession actually occurred.
- Inchoate offenses are incipient crimes that generally lead to other crimes. "Inchoate" means imperfect, partial, or unfinished. Inchoate crimes include (1) attempts, (2) solicitation, and (3) conspiracies.
- To constitute an attempt, an act of some sort is necessary. Mere preparation to commit an offense is not sufficient to support a charge of attempted criminal activity.
- The elements of the crime of conspiracy are (1) an agreement between two or more persons, (2) to carry out an act that is unlawful or is lawful but is to be accomplished by unlawful means, and (3) a culpable intent on the part of the defendants.
- Under common law, criminal solicitation occurs when one requests or encourages another to perform a criminal act. Criminal solicitation, unlike conspiracy, requires no overt act. The required mental state is one in which the defendant must have intended to induce the other person to perform the crime. In addition, a successful prosecution must establish that the defendant possessed the mental state required for the completed crime.
- To be held guilty as an accomplice, a defendant must have intentionally aided or encouraged another person to commit a crime.
- One who knowingly gives assistance to a person who has committed a felony for the purposes of helping that individual avoid apprehension or detection is guilty as an accessory after the fact.
- Corporations can also be charged with criminal offenses. Corporate criminal liability is based on either vicarious liability (holding an entity liable for the acts of its agents) or identification liability, where the criminal acts of corporate directors are treated (identified) as the criminal acts of the entity.

KEY **TERMS**

accessory after the fact
accessory before the fact
accomplice
actual possession
actus reus
but for rule

causation in fact
chain conspiracy
complicity
concurrence
constructive possession
corpus delicti rule

corroboration rule
criminal attempt
criminal conspiracy
criminal negligence
criminal solicitation
dangerous proximity test

elements of crime

harm

identification doctrine

inchoate crimes

indispensable element test

knowing

knowing possession

last act test

legal cause

legislative history

malice

mens rea

mere possession

mere preparation

motive

necessary attendant

    circumstances

omission

physical proximity test

plurality requirement

principal in the first degree

principal in the second degree

probable desistance approach

proximate cause

proximity approach

purposeful

reasonably foreseeable

reckless

Sarbanes-Oxley Act

scienter

specifications

strict liability

substantial step test

transferred intent

unequivocal test

vicarious liability

Wharton's Rule

wheel conspiracy

willfully

QUESTIONS FOR **DISCUSSION**

1. What are the three fundamental elements of crime? How is each central to the concept of crime?

2. Describe the different forms in which a criminal act can occur.

3. What are the four primary types of *mens rea* used in criminal statutes? How do they differ?

4. What is strict liability? Why are some crimes punished solely on the basis of strict liability? What is the difference between a criminal mental state and a criminal motive?

5. How does the concept of concurrence relate to *mens rea* and *actus reus*?

6. What is the difference between causation in fact and proximate cause? What is meant by "but for" causation? By "legal cause?"

7. What are victimless crimes? Why are they sometimes called social order offenses? Do you think that such law violations are truly victimless? Why or why not?

8. What is a necessary attendant circumstance? How does this concept relate to the inclusion of specifications in some criminal charges?

9. Explain the concept of *corpus delicti*. How does the corpus delicti of a crime differ from the elements of a crime?

10. Sometimes people mistakenly say that the body of a murder victim provides the *corpus delicti* of the crime of murder. What actually constitutes the corpus delicti of murder?

11. Why is it necessary to require a "substantial step" before mere plans become a criminal attempt?

12. Why are courts hesitant to punish a person for "evil thoughts" alone?

13. What is the difference between conspiracy and criminal solicitation?

14. Why is it easier for prosecutors to build a case when they are not required to establish whether the defendant is a principal in the first degree, or in the second degree, or an accomplice?

15. When is a corporation liable for the acts of its officers?

16. Under the statutes of many states, a bar owner is criminally liable when an employee-bartender sells liquor to juveniles. What if the bar owner instructs the bartender not to sell liquor to juveniles, but the bartender disregards those instructions and sells to juveniles anyway? Should the owner then be held criminally liable? Why or why not?

17. Should vicarious criminal liability exist? What are the implications of holding a corporation liable for the actions of its employees? What about holding parents criminally liable for the acts of their children? Who benefits and who can be harmed by such liability?

REFERENCES

1. Common law crimes, of course, are not based on statutory elements.

2. Arizona Revised Statutes, Title 13, Section 105.

3. Indiana Code, Title 35, Article 41, Chapter 2, Section 1.

4. Texas Penal Code, Title 2, Section 6.01.

5. The woman, Barbara Woods, was also stabbed.

6. "Sleepwalker Acquitted in Mother-in-Law Slaying," *San Francisco Examiner,* May 28, 1988, p. 1.

7. Matt Kelley, "Jury Convicts Husband in Sleepwalking Murder Trial," Associated Press online, June 27, 1999, 42, http://www.trib.com/HOMENEWS/WASH/Sleepwalk Trial.html.

8. Texas Penal Code, Title 2, Section 6.01.

9. Arizona Revised Statutes, Title 13, Section 105, paragraphs 30 and 31.

10. See Jonathan Turley, "When a Child Dies, Faith Is No Defense: Why Do Courts Give Believers a Pass?" *Washington Post,* November 15, 2009.

11. For additional information see Fred Bayles, "Spiritual Healing," Associated Press online, November 27, 1993.

12. The Boston-based church is officially known as "The First Church of Christ, Scientist."

13. *Gordon v. State,* 52 Ala. 3008, 23 Am. Rep. 575 (1875).

14. Ohio Revised Code, Section 2901.22 (D).

15. But not for more serious degrees of homicide, since leaving a young child alone in a tub of water, even if intentional, does not necessarily mean that the person who so acts intends the child to drown.

16. Oliver Wendell Holmes, *The Common Law,* Vol. 3 (Boston: Little Brown, and Co., 1881).

17. All Arizona definitions in this section are taken from Arizona Revised Statutes, Title 13, Section 105.

18. There is disagreement, however, among jurists as to whether or not the crime of statutory rape is a strict liability offense. Some jurisdictions treat it as such, and will not accept a reasonable mistake about the victim's age. Others, however, do accept such a mistake as a defense.

19. California Penal Code, Part 1, Title 9, Chapter 1, Section 261.5.

20. *State v. Stiffler,* 763 P.2d 308 (Idaho App. 1988).

21. *United States v. Greenbaum,* 138 F.2d 437 (3d Cir. 1943).

22. 355 U.S. 225 (1957).

23. See 31 U.S.C. § 5313(a).

24. 510 U.S. 135 (1994).

25. Gregory Tejeda, "Supreme Court Backs State Law Making Knowing HIV Transmission a Crime," United Press online, January 20, 1994.

26. California Penal Code, Preliminary Provisions, Section 20.

27. Texas Penal Code, Title 5, Chapter 19, Section 1.

28. *Holmes v. Securities Investor Protection Corporation,* 503 U.S. 258 (1992).

29. John S. Baker, Jr., et al., *Hall's Criminal Law: Cases and Materials,* 5th ed. (Charlottesville, VA: Michie, 1993), p. 135.

30. Indiana Code, Article 45, Chapter 8, Section 3.

31. N.D.C.C. § 12.1-01-04

32. The statute also says, "A mother's breastfeeding of her baby does not under any circumstance violate this section."

33. Florida Statutes, Section 794.011.

34. Ohio Revised Code Section 2941.145.

35. *Willoughby v. State* (1990), Ind., 552 N.E.2d 462, 466.

36. See *Maughs v. Commonwealth,* 181 Va. 117, 120, 23 S.E.2d 784, 786 (1943).

37. *Williams,* South Carolina Supreme Court, LLR 1996.SC17; and *State v. Blocker,* 205 S.C. 303, 31 S.E.2d 908 (1944).

38. WL 2460263 (Ct. App. Texas 2007).

39. Joseph R. Nolan and Jacqueline M. Nolan-Haley, *Black's Law Dictionary: Definitions of the Terms and Phrases of American and English Jurisprudence, Ancient and Modern,* 6th ed. (St. Paul, MN: West, 1990), p. 761.

40. Jerome Hall, *General Principles of Criminal Law,* 2d ed. (Charlottesville, VA: Michie, 1960).

41. Stanford H. Kadish and Stephen J. Schulhofer, *Criminal Law and Its Processes,* 6th ed. (Boston: Little, Brown, 1995), p. 581.

42. N.Y. Penal Law, Section 110.0.

43. California Penal Code, Section 664.

44. Illinois Ann. Stat. Ch. 38, Section 8–4.

45. *People v. Rizzo,* 246 N.Y. 334, 158 N.E. 888 (1927).

46. Model Penal Code, Section 5.01(2).

47. Model Penal Code, Sections 5.01(2)(a) through (g).

48. *Williams v. United States,* 218 F.2d 276 (4th Cir. 1954).

49. *Gebardi v. United States,* 287 U.S. 112 (1932).

50. *Iannelli v. United States,* 420 U.S. 770 (1975).

51. *United States v. Recio,* U.S. Supreme Court, No. 01–1184 (2003), and *Salings v. United States,* 522 U.S. 52, 65 (1997).

52. *United States v. Klein,* 515 F.2d 751, 753 (3d Cir. 1975).

53. See, e.g., *United States v. Austin,* 786 F.2d 986, 988 (10th Cir. 1986).

54. *Anderson v. Superior Court,* 177 P.2d 315 (Cal. Super. Ct. 1947).

55. Model Penal Code, Section 5.03(6).

56. Paul Marcus, "Criminal Conspiracy Law: Time to Turn Back from an Ever Expanding, Ever More Troubling Area," *Bill of Rights Journal* 1, (1992): 8–11.

57. Florida Penal Code, Chapter 777, Section 4, paragraph 2.

58. "Stepfather Accused of Fratricide Plot," *USA Today*, January 23, 2004, p. 3A.

59. Stu Brown, "Winniewicz Ordered to Stand Trial," WPXI.com, January 28, 2004, http://articles.orlandosentinel.com/keyword/killed-his-brother (accessed November 2, 2004).

60. 18 U.S.C. § 2.

61. *United States v. Ortega,* 44 F.3d 505 (7th Cir. 1995).

62. 18 U.S.C. § 3.

63. *United States v. Parks,* 421 U.S. 658 (1975).

64. *People v. Forbath,* 5 Cal. App. 2d 767 (1935).

65. *Commonwealth v. Koczwara,* 155 A.2d 825 (Pa. 1959).

66. Elizabeth M. Taurasi, "Big Dig Epoxy Provider Pleads Not Guilty to Involuntary Manslaughter," *Design News*, September 5, 2007, http://www.designnews.com/article/1304-Big_Dig_Epoxy_Provider_Pleads_Not_Guilty_to_Involuntary_Manslaughter.php. (accessed December 3, 2008).

67. "Company Pays Millions in Big Dig Settlement," *Palm Beach Post*, December 18, 2008, p. 8A.

68. *Defense and Health Care Industries: Rather Than Clean Up Their Act. They Attack the Act* (Washington, D.C.: Project on Government Oversight, February 1997).

69. Celia Wells, "The Millennium Bug and Corporate Criminal Liability," *Journal of Information, Law and Technology* 2 (1999), http://elj.warwick.ac.uk/jilt/ 99–2/wells.html.

70. *Id.*

71. *Id.*

72. Model Penal Code, Section 2.07.

73. See *United States v. Bank of New England, N.A.,* 821 F.2d 844, 856 (1st Cir. 1987).

74. Seth C. Farber and Melanie R. Moss, "Cooperating with the Government in Corporate Criminal Investigations: Has Andersen Changed the Landscape?" in *The Criminal Litigation Newsletter* (Winter 2002–3): 3–10.

75. See *United States v. Bank of New England, N.A.,* 821 F.2d 844, 856 (1st Cir. 1987).

76. Jennifer Arlen and Reinier Kraakman, "Controlling Corporate Misconduct: An Analysis of Corporate Liability Regimes," *New York University Law Review* 72 (1997): 687, 702.

77. Federal guidelines for the sentencing of organizations and businesses are set out in the *U.S. Sentencing Guidelines Manual,* §§ 8A 1.1–8E1.3. The guidelines are used by federal judges to determine appropriate sentences for businesses and other organizations that have been convicted of crimes.

78. Pub. L. No. 107-204, 116 Stat. 745 (July 30, 2002).

APPENDIX
DEVELOPING YOUR LEGAL ANALYSIS

A. THE LAW WHERE YOU LIVE

Assume that you have been assigned to work on a criminal case within your home-state jurisdiction and your supervising attorney wants to know the details on the elements of the crimes alleged in the case. Locate a criminal indictment (or felony criminal complaint) processed by your local prosecutor's office. Review the indictment or complaint and identify the criminal charges alleged therein, as well as the text of the relevant criminal statute(s). Based on the wording of the statute and the allegations in the indictment, prepare a memorandum (or outline) for an attorney working on the case—either prosecutor or defense attorney—in which you break down the elements of each offense by identifying the *actus reus*, *mens rea*, concurrence, and if applicable, any proximate cause, resulting harm, or necessary attendant circumstances that are included in the statute and criminal charge and that must be proven beyond a reasonable doubt. You can use the accompanying form to help organize your memorandum on these elements. In addition, assume that your supervising attorney wants to know the appropriate evidentiary standard in criminal cases involving confessions. Does your home state use the *corpus delicti* rule or does it use some form of the corroboration rule?

ELEMENTS OF THE OFFENSE
[Sample Review Sheet]

Case Name: [State of Ohio v. Smith]

Judge: [Joanne Johnson]

Court: [Mason Municipal Court]

Count 1: [Negligent Homicide]

Offense Level: [M1]

Statute: ["No person shall negligently cause the death of another by means of a deadly weapon or dangerous ordnance"]

Criminal Complaint: ["On September 25, 2009, Pat Smith negligently caused the death of Will Stevens by means of her automobile."]

Elements of Offense: [break down elements of the criminal law]

	Evidence in Support	Evidence Against
Actus Reus [Cause death of another]		
Mens Rea Negligence [define]		
Concurrence Negligent mental state + causing death of another + means of deadly weapon or dangerous ordnance.		

Causation [Defendant's negligent conduct must be the proximate cause of victim's death]	Evidence in Support	Evidence Against
Resulting Harm [Death of victim]	Evidence in Support	Evidence Against
Attendant Circumstances [Use of deadly weapon or dangerous ordnance] [Is a car considered a deadly weapon or dangerous ordnance under the statute?]	Evidence in Support	Evidence Against

B. INSIDE THE FEDERAL COURTS

Using the same worksheet from Assignment A (above), prepare a memorandum outlining the elements of the following federal criminal offenses:

Bank Fraud (18 U.S.C. § 1344)
Money Laundering (18 U.S.C. § 1956)
Structuring (31 U.S.C. § 5324(a))

Be sure to identify requisite criminal acts, mental states (including federal definitions), concurrences, and where applicable, any proximate cause, harm, and necessary attendant circumstances required by these statutes.

C. CYBER SOURCES

Assume you have been asked to work on a jury trial in a federal criminal case. As a part of your work, you are asked to review and prepare jury instructions for each of the following counts:

Count 1: Conspiracy (18 U.S.C. § 371)
Count 2: Health Care Fraud (18 U.S.C. § 1347)
Count 3: Obstruction of a Criminal Investigation (18 U.S.C. § 1510(a))

After identifying the requisite elements in each count, use electronic or Internet resources to locate the standard jury instructions used in your federal jurisdiction for each of these elements. If you have trouble locating instructions for your particular jurisdiction, you may use one of the following resources used in other federal jurisdictions:

http://www.ca7.uscourts.gov/pjury.pdf
http://www.juryinstructions.ca8.uscourts.gov/
criminal_instructions.htm
http://www.lb5.uscourts.gov/juryinstructions/

D. ETHICS AND PROFESSIONALISM

Assume that you are working as a legal assistant for a well-known and very busy criminal defense attorney, Chester Brown. Mr. Brown is handling the matter of *State v. Steve Kinser*, a driving under the influence of alcohol case. The case is scheduled for a pretrial conference later today in a local courtroom. However, Mr. Brown has just sent a text message to you, asking for your assistance. It seems Mr. Brown has to attend an emergency hearing in another courtroom at the same time as the *Kinser* pretrial. As a result, Mr. Brown will not be able to meet Mr. Kinser or attend his pretrial conference. Mr. Brown is asking you to go to the courtroom in the *Kinser* case and get a continuance (a rescheduling) of the pretrial conference.

You believe that you could complete the task Mr. Brown has delegated to you, but you are concerned about whether it would be ethically appropriate for you to obtain the continuance in the manner Mr. Brown has requested. Review any ethical standards from your home-state jurisdiction regarding the delegation of lawyer work that might apply to this situation, as well as the ethical standards for delegated tasks set forth in the following sources, and then draft a text response to Mr. Brown regarding his request.

American Bar Association

http://www.abanet.org/legalservices/paralegals/downloads/modelguidelines.pdf

The American Alliance of Paralegals, Inc.

http://www.aapipara.org/Ethicalstandards.htm

National Federation of Paralegal Associations, Inc.

http://www.paralegals.org/

chapter **four**

PERSONAL CRIME: HOMICIDE, ASSAULT, SEX CRIMES, AND KIDNAPPING

LEARNING OBJECTIVES

After reading this chapter, you should be able to

- Identify and describe the different types of criminal homicide.

- Discuss the causation problems that are characteristic of criminal homicide prosecutions.

- Explain the concept of corpus deliciti as it relates to criminal homicide.

- Distinguish between murder and voluntary manslaughter.

- Explain the felony murder rule.

- Discuss the nature of criminal liability attached to assisted suicide.

- Explain the differences between the common law crimes of assault and battery.

- Discuss how mayhem differs from other types of battery.

- Identify the features and significance of domestic violence laws.

- Explain the difference between the crime of rape and other forms of sexual assault.

- Provide an example of false imprisonment, and explain how false imprisonment differs from kidnapping.

"Murder" is never more than a shortening of life; if [a] defendant's culpable act has significantly decreased [the] span of human life, the law will not hear him say that [the] victim would thereafter have died in any event.
      —*People v. Phillips,* 64 Cal. 2d 574, 414 P.2d 353 (Cal. 1966)

A battery committed by a person while in a state of voluntary intoxication is no less criminal by reason of his having been in such condition.
      —Justice Traynor, in *People v. Hood,* 1 Cal. 3d 444 (1969)

Rape is nothing more or less than a conscious process of intimidation by which all men keep all women in a state of fear.
      —Susan Brownmiller, *Against Our Will* (1975)

INTRODUCTION

One of the most fundamental purposes of government is to protect people from being harmed. Criminal statutes are often used to fulfill this obligation. By imposing punitive sanctions for conduct that injures persons, governments seek to protect individuals from personal harm. The emphasis in this chapter is on the legal and social dimensions of personal crimes, including homicide, assault and battery, domestic violence, sexual offenses, and kidnapping.

CRIMINAL HOMICIDE

Some deaths are accidental or natural. Others are caused by human intent, recklessness, or negligence. An accidental death or one that is caused by unexpected or unintended means can be distinguished from an accidental killing, which is the result of a purposeful human act lawfully undertaken in the reasonable belief that no harm will result.

Homicide is the killing of one human being by another human being. More precisely, homicide can be defined as "the killing of one human being by the act, procurement, or omission of another human being."[1] There are three basic types of homicide: justifiable, excusable, and criminal. *Justifiable homicides* are those that are permitted under law, as in the case of a state-ordered execution or a military killing of an enemy soldier in the line of duty. A death caused by the legitimate use of self-defense is sometimes classified as a justifiable homicide, although it may also be considered an excusable homicide. See Chapter 7.

Excusable homicides are those homicides that may involve some fault but not enough for the act to be considered criminal. A death caused by a vehicular accident in which the driver was not negligent, for example, would probably be excusable. The term *criminal homicide* refers only to those homicides to which criminal liability may attach. Generally speaking, any homicide that is not classified as justifiable or excusable may be considered criminal.

homicide
the killing of one human being by another human being

justifiable homicides
homicides permitted under law

excusable homicides
homicides that may involve some fault but not enough for the act to be considered criminal

criminal homicide
homicide for which there may be criminal culpability

Corpus Delicti

As discussed in Chapter 3, the *corpus delicti* of a crime is the body of evidence that supports the substance of the criminal charge. In homicide cases, the corpus delicti generally consists of two things: the death of a human being and the fact that the death was caused by the criminal act or agency of another person. These two basic elements include the requirement that the victim's death was the natural and probable consequence of another person's unlawful conduct.[2] Accordingly, in homicide cases, the prosecutor must establish the corpus delicti of the crime by proving that a person died and that the death was caused by the defendant's criminal conduct.

Although discovery of the body of the murder victim may not be necessary to prove criminal homicide in courts today, a conviction requires prosecutors to prove that the death in question was caused "by the act, agency, procurement, or omission of the accused."[3] In *Williams v. State* (1981),[4] for example, the defendant was convicted after he confessed to shooting the victim at close range with a shotgun, although the victim's body was never recovered. In addition, several witnesses testified that the victim was dead and that they helped the defendant dispose of the body. A Texas appellate court, which upheld Williams's conviction, ruled that the State had successfully established that the victim was dead, even though no body had been found, and that the State had established that the victim's death was caused by the criminal act of the accused—thus meeting the requirements for proving criminal homicide under state law.

Defining Death

A central issue in criminal homicide cases is the definition of death, which is needed before criminal prosecution begins in order to establish that death has actually occurred. The Model Penal Code provides no definition of death. The Code's *Commentary* cites two reasons for this failure: (1) contemporary scientific understandings of death were not available when the code was first drafted, making death difficult to define at the time; and (2) the delicate contemporary interplay between criminal law and advances in medical science is still too nebulous to reduce to statutory formulation.[5]

Uniform Determination of Death Act (UDDA)
a set of standards outlined by legal and medical professionals to evaluate when a death occurs; adopted within many state statutes for assessing death in homicide cases

Today, many jurisdictions rely on the *Uniform Determination of Death Act (UDDA)*[6] to evaluate death. The UDDA provides that "[a]n individual who has sustained either: (1) irreversible cessation of circulatory and respiratory functions, or (2) irreversible cessation of all functions of the entire brain, including the brain stem, is dead."[7] The UDDA is supported by the American Medical Association, the American Bar Association, and the National Conference itself.[8] More than thirty states have adopted a "cessation of brain function" approach to defining death. Many states have defined death by statute. For example, the Texas Health and Safety Code Section 671.001 provides:

a. A person is dead when, according to ordinary standards of medical practice, there is irreversible cessation of the person's spontaneous respiratory and circulatory functions.

b. If artificial means of support preclude a determination that a person's spontaneous respiratory and circulatory functions have ceased, the person is dead when, in the announced opinion of a physician, according to ordinary standards of medical practice, there is irreversible cessation of all spontaneous brain function. Death occurs when the relevant functions cease.

c. Death must be pronounced before artificial means of supporting a person's respiratory and circulatory functions are terminated.

Despite the common usage of the brain-death standard, there is still "deep disagreement" among some physicians as to "whether brain death is synonymous with death," since "[d]eath of the brain is not the same as death in a traditional sense."[9] Accordingly, in some cases, the legal determination of death may be disputed, resulting in a battle of evidence offered by medical experts and competing interpretations of the jurisdiction's standards for death. See Figure 4-1.

Time of Death

year and a day rule
a common law rule used to determine the element of causation in homicide cases to assess whether the death of a person was caused by the unlawful actions of another; to hold a defendant accountable for causing the death of another, the victim must die within a year and one day after being injured by the defendant

Sometimes victims of homicidal acts suffer injuries but do not die immediately. Death may occur sometime after the fatal injury. In such cases, homicide prosecutions under common law required that the death of the victim occurred within a year and a day from the time that the ultimately fatal act took place. The requirement was termed the *year and a day rule.* The rule was based on the belief that proof of causation (i.e., the ability to show that actions by the accused were the cause of the victim's death) becomes ever more difficult with the passage of time—resulting in potentially unjustified prosecutions and convictions.[10]

The year and a day rule is still influential in some parts of the country. For example, in 1991, a North Carolina judge cited the rule in dismissing a murder

FIGURE 4-1 **Determining Death**

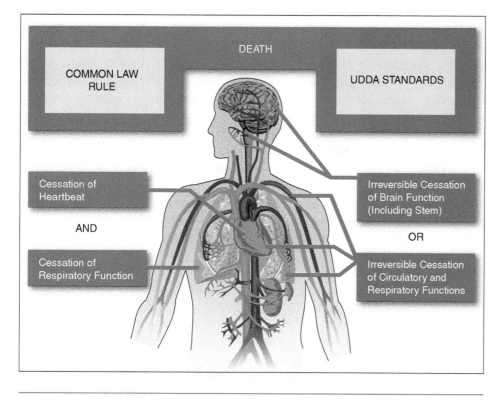

indictment against Terry Dale Robinson.[11] Evidence in the case plainly showed that Robinson had brutally beaten his estranged wife, Gina Robinson, with his hands, feet, and a shotgun that he used as a club. After the beating, he ran her over several times with an automobile. But Gina Robinson did not die immediately after sustaining these assaults. Instead, she remained comatose from the time of the assaults until her death—almost three years later. After her death, prosecutors sought to indict her former husband on murder charges, but the defendant's lawyer moved to dismiss the indictment, citing the fact that the victim's death occurred more than a year and a day after the assault. Although the trial court agreed with the attorney, the State challenged the ruling. Upon appeal, the North Carolina Court of Appeals reinstated the indictment and ordered that Robinson be tried for murder. The appellate court said, "[w]e hold, on the facts before us, that the relevant date of Mrs. Robinson's murder . . . is the date upon which she died."[12]

Today, only a few jurisdictions still follow the year and a day rule. Others, like California, have extended the time limit for homicide prosecutions, requiring the victim's death to occur within three years and a day from the time of the act.[13] In other jurisdictions, the timing and connection between the defendant's alleged conduct and a person's death is assessed based on general legal standards of proximate cause. See Chapter 3 and below.

Proximate Cause and Homicide

Criminal homicide must be the result of an affirmative act, an omission to act, or criminal negligence. For criminal liability to accrue, the cause of death must not be so remote as to fail to constitute natural and probable consequences of the defendant's act. In other words, for charges of homicide to be brought successfully, a person's death must be the proximate result of a human act. As discussed in Chapter 3, the legal standard of proximate cause holds individuals criminally liable for causing harm when it can logically be shown that the harm caused was reasonably foreseeable from their conduct. The basic question under this standard is whether a reasonable person engaging in similar harmful conduct would have foreseen or considered the type of harm that ultimately resulted from this harmful conduct. In homicide cases, a determination of proximate cause requires that death be a natural, probable, and reasonably foreseeable consequence of a person's unlawful conduct.

In most homicide cases, there will be little dispute as to the proximate cause of the victim's death. In most cases involving gunshots, stabbings, or car accidents, the parties readily agree on the cause of the victim's death. But in rare cases, the parties may debate the proximate cause of the victim's death. If, for example, a victim is shot by the accused, sustaining a nonfatal wound, but the victim later dies during an operation to remove the bullet, the shooting will likely be considered to be the proximate cause of death.[14] In *People v. Moan* (1884),[15] the defendant injured a victim who was already deathly ill, and this injury accelerated the victim's death. Despite the victim's near-death state of being, the court found the defendant's conduct to be the proximate cause of death.

It is important to note that to be the proximate cause of death an injurious act need not be the only or sole cause of a person's death.[16] Where concurring causes contribute to a victim's death, an accused may be held criminally liable by reason of conduct that directly contributes to the fatal result. For example, in *People v. Brackett* (1987), an Illinois man raped and severely beat an eighty-five-year-old woman. Following the incident, the victim was moved to a nursing home, where she became depressed and refused to eat. Because of injuries sustained during the beating, the victim could not be fed through a nasal tube, and the woman consequently died of asphyxiation during an attempted feeding. The rapist was convicted of homicide. An appellate court upheld the conviction, finding that the defendant's criminal acts set in motion a series of events that eventually caused the victim's death.[17]

Types of Homicide

Most states today follow the Model Penal Code, recognizing three types of criminal homicide: (1) murder (of which there may be various degrees), (2) manslaughter (of which there may be various kinds), and (3) negligent homicide (which some define as involuntary manslaughter). Generally, the circumstances surrounding a person's death and the mental state of the person who caused the death determine the type (or degree) of criminal homicide that will be charged. The terminology applied to different categories and subcategories of homicide, however, varies considerably between jurisdictions.

MURDER

murder
the intentional killing of another without justification or excuse; generally involves an unlawful killing of a human being, with malice aforethought

Murder is the first of the three types of criminal homicide. Generally, **murder** is the intentional killing of another without justification or excuse. The core elements of a standard murder offense are

- an unlawful killing
- of a human being
- with malice aforethought

In most states, murder is divided into two categories: first degree and second degree. Generally speaking, *first-degree murder* includes any willful, deliberate, and premeditated unlawful killing. The term *premeditation* (which is discussed in greater detail later in this chapter) means the act of deliberating, meditating on, or planning a course of action, such as a crime. For purposes of the criminal law, premeditation requires the opportunity for *reflection* between the time the intent to act is formed and the act itself is committed. See Figure 4-2. Thus, murder would likely be charged in the first degree when it is committed by poisoning or by lying in wait, or when it involves torture. This offense is often punishable by death or by life in prison.

In states in which only two degrees of murder are recognized, all murders other than first degree are said to constitute *second-degree murder.* Some states, like Pennsylvania, recognize three or more degrees of murder. Where three degrees of murder are found, they are usually (1) murders that are committed willfully and deliberately and are premeditated; (2) murders committed during the perpetration or attempted perpetration of an enumerated felony, such as arson, rape, robbery, or burglary; and (3) all other types of murder.

Malice Aforethought

In many jurisdictions, malice is an essential element of a murder offense. Under common law, the "grand criterion" that "distinguished murder from other killing" was malice on the part of the killer, and this malice was not necessarily "malevolent to the deceased particularly" but "any evil design in general; the dictate of a wicked, depraved, and malignant heart."[18] As a contemporary legal term, *malice* refers to the intentional commission of a wrongful act without just cause or legal excuse. Malice encompasses both the intentional carrying out of a hurtful act without

first-degree murder
any willful, deliberate, and premeditated unlawful killing

premeditation
the act of deliberating, meditating on, or planning a course of action

second-degree murder
all forms of murder other than first-degree murder, in states where only two degrees of murder are recognized

malice
in homicide cases, an intention to kill

FIGURE 4-2 **Premeditation**

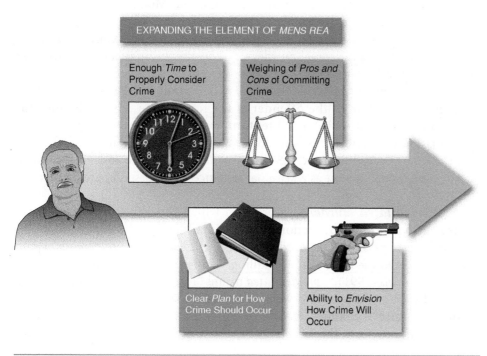

malice aforethought
a historical term that indicates a malicious (evil) design to kill or injure

depraved heart murder
a common law term used to describe homicides committed through a person's extreme cruelty or indifference to human suffering

capital murder
murder offenses for which the death penalty is authorized by statute

premeditated murder
murder in which the intent to kill is formed pursuant to preexisting reflection rather than as the result of a sudden impulse or the heat of passion

cause and the hostility of one individual toward another. In cases of homicide, the term means "an intention to kill."

First-degree murder is often described as requiring **malice aforethought**, a historical term that connotes a malicious design to kill or injure. In contemporary murder statutes, the term *malice aforethought* is generally understood to mean a killing while in any one of the following five mental states: (1) an intent to kill, (2) an intent to inflict great bodily injury, (3) an intent to commit a felony (as in felony murder), (4) an intent to resist a lawful arrest, or (5) an awareness that one is engaged in conduct that carries with it a high risk of someone else's death. The fifth mental state, which describes unjustifiable conduct that is extremely reckless, is sometimes called **depraved heart murder** when it results in the death of a human being.[19]

Although, technically speaking, malice aforethought is planned malice, emphasis today is on the *malice* aspect of the term rather than on any kind of planning that includes the opportunity for reflection. In the modern context, the term can be understood as "the intention to kill, actual or implied, under circumstances which do not constitute excuse or justification or mitigate the offense to manslaughter."[20] It is important to realize that neither malice nor malice aforethought requires an ill will or hatred of the victim.

Malice may exist where the killing is unpremeditated, and malice may be inferred from surrounding circumstances. Pointing a firearm at an individual and firing it, for example, creates the presumption that the defendant actually intended to kill the victim. Malice may also be established by proving that the defendant intended to inflict serious bodily injury, even though not consciously desiring the death of the victim.[21]

Capital Murder

Thirty-five states and the federal government presently authorize the death penalty for some types of murder. In some states, murders for which the death penalty is authorized are treated as a separate class of murder called **capital murder.** In Florida, Georgia, Idaho, Louisiana, Mississippi, Missouri, Nebraska, New Hampshire, New Mexico, North Carolina, Tennessee, and Wyoming, all murders in the first degree fall into the capital crimes category. The most common statutory requirement of first-degree murder is that the killing had to have been *premeditated* and *deliberate.*

The concepts of premeditation and deliberation are attempts to encapsulate the mental state of the offender at the time of the crime. The idea that only those who kill with clear intention, or who envision killing before the commission of their crimes, should be subject to capital punishment is well supported by decisions of the U.S. Supreme Court. The use and constitutionality of capital punishment as a criminal sentence is discussed in greater detail in Chapter 14.

Premeditated murder is murder in which the intent to kill is formed pursuant to preexisting reflection rather than as the result of a sudden impulse or the heat of passion. The word *premeditated* means that the defendant must have considered the act before the killing. As observed by a California court in *People v. Daniels* (1991),[22] *premeditated* means "formed or determined upon as a result of careful thought and weighing of considerations for and against the proposed course of conduct." In *Daniels*, the court concluded that the true test of premeditation was not the duration of time available for thought but the extent of reflection.

Scott Peterson talks to his Defense Attorney, Mark Geragos, during proceedings in his California capital murder case. Peterson was charged with killing his wife, Lacy Peterson, and the couple's unborn child. A jury convicted Peterson of capital murder and he was sentenced to die. Peterson is currently on death row in a California state prison while his case is on appeal.

Following the lead of the Model Penal Code, some states have rejected premeditation and deliberation as the basis for identifying a murder as one that deserves the death penalty. Those states have legislatively defined capital murder as murder plus one or more specific aggravating factors, constituting what is sometimes called *aggravated murder.* The term *aggravated murder* is found in the statutes of some states (such as Utah, Washington, and Ohio), although other states depict capital murder as "first-degree murder with aggravating factors" or with "special circumstances." Illinois law, for example, defines capital murder as first-degree murder with any one of fifteen aggravating circumstances, while capital murder in Ohio consists of "aggravated murder with one of eight aggravating circumstances."[23]

Essentially, the concept of aggravated murder encompasses the notion that certain identifiable factors surrounding the circumstances of a particular murder may so enhance the culpability of the murderer that punishment of the first degree is warranted. While the term *aggravated murder* is used to describe murders that are punishable by death in most jurisdictions, the term can also refer to murders punishable by life imprisonment in jurisdictions where there is no death penalty.

aggravated murder
a term used in some jurisdictions to refer to a murder committed under special circumstances, like premeditation or with malice; used in some statutes to refer to first-degree murder

Felony Murder

Under common law, a defendant was guilty of murder if, while perpetrating a felony, or in the attempt to perpetrate a felony, another person died as a consequence of the crime or as a consequence of the attempt. This is known as the *felony murder rule.* Even in cases where the victim's death is not intentional or foreseen, the offender can be found guilty of murder.

Although often criticized, the felony murder rule is used in most states today, where it can be synonymous with first-degree murder. See Figure 4-3. For example, Ohio Revised Code Section 2903.02 provides that anyone who causes the death of another as a proximate result of the offender's committing or attempting to

felony murder rule
common law rule that allowed a person to be convicted of murder if, while perpetrating a felony, or in the attempt to perpetrate a felony, another person died as a consequence of the crime; used in many statutory schemes today to define a form of murder that involves the death of another during the commission of certain identified felonies

FIGURE 4-3 **Felony Murder**

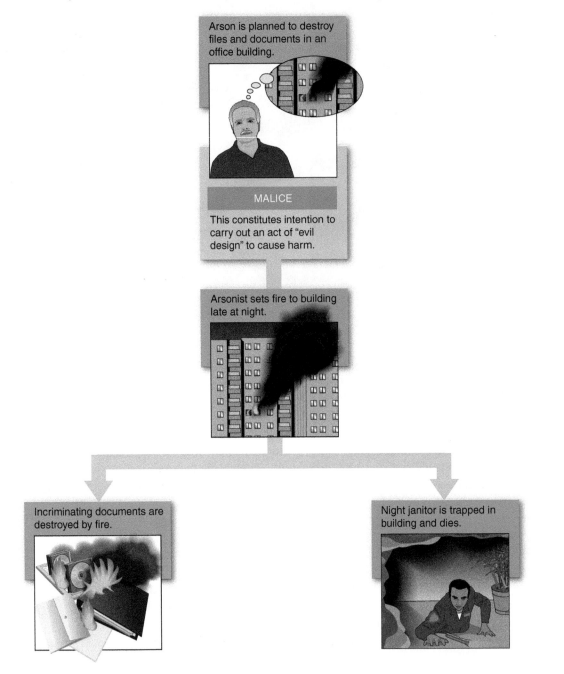

Arson is planned to destroy files and documents in an office building.

MALICE

This constitutes intention to carry out an act of "evil design" to cause harm.

Arsonist sets fire to building late at night.

Incriminating documents are destroyed by fire.

Night janitor is trapped in building and dies.

commit an offense of violence is guilty of murder. In most states, a death that results from the commission of a serious or violent felony, such as arson, rape, robbery, burglary, and the like, is classified as first-degree murder. If the death results from the commission of a less serious offense, perhaps even a misdemeanor, then the homicide may be classified as either second-degree murder or a form of manslaughter.

Because the felony murder rule applies whether the defendant kills the victim intentionally, recklessly, negligently, accidentally, or unforeseeably (rather than purposefully or intentionally), it creates a form of strict criminal liability for any

TABLE 4-1 **The *Mens Rea* of Homicide at Common Law and under the Model Penal Code**

Common Law *Mens Rea*	Crime	Model Penal Code *Mens Rea*
Malice aforethought	Murder	Purposeful, knowing, and reckless with extreme indifference to the value of life
All other unexcused homicides	Manslaughter	Reckless, except the extreme indifference standard for murder
Not recognized at common law	Negligent Homicide	Negligence

death that results from the intentional commission of a felony. As a result, some courts have struggled with the felony murder rule because a murder conviction under the rule does not require malice or intent. But generally speaking, courts have justified felony murder rules in two ways: (1) by holding that the rule dispenses with the requirement for malice, and (2) by holding that malice is implied from the intentional commission of a felony.

MANSLAUGHTER

Manslaughter is the second of the three general types of criminal homicide discussed in this chapter. ***Manslaughter*** is the unlawful killing of a human being without malice. Manslaughter differs from murder in that the homicide is committed without malice or premeditation. Accordingly, the basic elements of manslaughter are

manslaughter
the unlawful killing of a human being without malice

- an unlawful killing
- of a human being
- without malice

Typically, manslaughter occurs without deliberation, planning, or premeditation and may be voluntary or involuntary. As a result, criminal statutes generally recognize two forms of manslaughter—voluntary manslaughter and involuntary manslaughter.

Voluntary Manslaughter

"Voluntary manslaughter is the unlawful killing of a human being, without malice, which is done intentionally upon a sudden quarrel or in the heat of passion."[24] In other words, ***voluntary manslaughter*** is a homicide associated with a sudden fit of rage or passion. Such a killing, although intentional, is neither premeditated nor motivated by a basic evil intent (malice). Voluntary manslaughter would otherwise be murder, except that it is committed in response to adequate provocation, as when a person finds his or her spouse in bed with another person. See Figure 4-4.

voluntary manslaughter
a homicide associated with a sudden fit of rage or passion

Provocation is said to be "adequate" if it would cause a reasonable person to lose self-control.[25] Adequate provocation is also termed *reasonable provocation*. Under common law, only a limited set of circumstances fell into this category, including mutual combat, serious assault or battery, an unlawful arrest, the commission of a crime against a close relative or family member, and the witnessing of one's spouse in an act of adultery. Generally, provocative words alone do not provide adequate provocation to reduce a willful killing to

FIGURE 4-4 **Murder and Voluntary Manslaughter Compared**

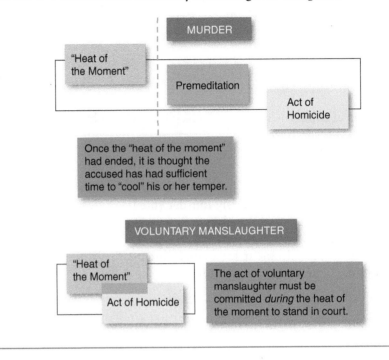

manslaughter. There are, however, exceptions to this rule. See *Commonwealth v. Schnopps* (1981) (below).

Voluntary manslaughter is usually committed with one of the states of mind required for malice aforethought, but the presence of adequate provocation negates the state of mind—resulting in a lesser charge or a lowered sentence. For example, under Texas law, the murder statute provides, "[a]t the punishment stage of a trial, the defendant may raise the issue as to whether he caused the death under the immediate influence of *sudden passion* arising from an *adequate cause.* If the defendant proves the issue in the affirmative by a preponderance of the evidence, the offense is a felony of the second degree [voluntary manslaughter]."[26] Under Texas law, adequate cause means a cause that would commonly produce a degree of anger, rage, or terror in a person of ordinary temper, sufficient to render the mind of the defendant incapable of objective reflection. Sudden passion means passion directly caused by and arising out of provocation by the victim or by another person acting with the victim. In Texas and many other jurisdictions, the burden is on the defendant to establish the facts to reduce the crime from murder to voluntary manslaughter.

The Model Penal Code approach to voluntary manslaughter is similar, except that it does not contain a "sudden passion" requirement. Section 210.3 (b) states, "[c]riminal homicide constitutes manslaughter when . . . a homicide which would otherwise be murder is committed under the influence of extreme mental or emotional disturbance for which there is reasonable explanation or excuse. The reasonableness of such explanation or excuse shall be determined from the viewpoint of a person in the actor's situation under the circumstances as he believes them to be." As a result, the MPC offers a broader possible defense for defendants seeking to reduce the offense level of their murder charges.

CAPSTONE CASE *Commonwealth v. Schnopps*, 417 N.E.2d 1213 (Mass. 1981)

On October 13, 1979, Marilyn R. Schnopps was fatally shot by her estranged husband George A. Schnopps. A jury convicted Schnopps of murder in the first degree, and he was sentenced to the mandatory term of life imprisonment. Schnopps claims that the trial judge erred by refusing to instruct the jury on voluntary manslaughter. We agree. We reverse and order a new trial. . . .

We summarize those facts. Schnopps testified that his wife had left him three weeks prior to the slaying. He claims that he first became aware of the problems in his fourteen-year marriage at a point about six months before the slaying. According to the defendant, on that occasion he took his wife to a club to dance, and she spent the evening dancing with a coworker. On arriving home, the defendant and his wife argued over her conduct. She told him that she no longer loved him and that she wanted a divorce. Schnopps became very upset. He admitted that he took out his shotgun during the course of this argument, but he denied that he intended to use it.

During the next few months, Schnopps argued frequently with his wife. The defendant accused her of seeing another man, but she steadfastly denied the accusations. On more than one occasion Schnopps threatened his wife with physical harm. He testified he never intended to hurt his wife but only wanted to scare her so that she would end the relationship with her coworker.

One day in September, 1979, the defendant became aware that the suspected boyfriend used a "signal" in telephoning Schnopps' wife. Schnopps used the signal, and his wife answered the phone with "Hi, Lover." She hung up immediately when she recognized Schnopps' voice. That afternoon she did not return home. Later that evening, she informed Schnopps by telephone that she had moved to her mother's house and that she had the children with her. She told Schnopps she would not return to their home. Thereafter she "froze [him] out," and would not talk to him. During this period, the defendant spoke with a lawyer about a divorce and was told that he had a good chance of getting custody of the children, due to his wife's "desertion and adultery."

On the day of the killing, Schnopps had asked his wife to come to their home and talk over their marital difficulties. Schnopps told his wife that he wanted his children at home and that he wanted the family to remain intact. Schnopps cried during the conversation and begged his wife to let the children live with him and to keep their family together. His wife replied, "No, I am going to court, you are going to give me all the furniture, you are going to have to get the Hell out of here, you won't have nothing." Then, pointing to her crotch, she said, "You will never touch this again, because I have got something bigger and better for it."

On hearing those words, Schnopps claims that his mind went blank, and that he went "berserk." He went to a cabinet and got out a pistol he had bought and loaded the day before, and he shot his wife and himself. When he "started coming to" as a result of the pain of his self-inflicted wound, he called his neighbor to come over and asked him to summon help. The victim was pronounced dead at the scene, and the defendant was arrested and taken to the hospital for treatment of his wound.

The issue raised by Schnopps' appeal is whether in these circumstances the judge was required to instruct the jury on voluntary manslaughter. Instructions on voluntary manslaughter must be given if there is evidence of provocation deemed adequate in law to cause the accused to lose his self-control in the heat of passion and if the killing followed the provocation before sufficient time had elapsed for the accused's temper to cool.

(continued)

(continued)

Schnopps argues that "[t]he existence of sufficient provocation is not foreclosed absolutely because a defendant learns of a fact from oral statements rather than from personal observation." Schnopps asserts that his wife's statements constituted a "peculiarly immediate and intense offense to a spouse's sensitivities." He concedes that the words at issue are indicative of past as well as present adultery. Schnopps claims, however, that his wife's admission of adultery was made for the first time on the day of the killing, and hence the evidence of provocation was sufficient to trigger jury consideration of voluntary manslaughter as a possible verdict.

The Commonwealth quarrels with the defendant's claim, asserting that the defendant knew of his wife's infidelity for some months, and hence the killing did not follow immediately upon the provocation. Therefore, the Commonwealth concludes, a manslaughter instruction would have been improper. The flaw in the Commonwealth's argument is that conflicting testimony and inferences from the evidence are to be resolved by the trier of fact, not the judge.

Withdrawal of the issue of voluntary manslaughter in this case denied the jury the opportunity to pass on the defendant's credibility in the critical aspects of his testimony. The portion of Schnopps' testimony concerning provocation created a factual dispute between Schnopps and the Commonwealth. It was for the jury, not the judge, to resolve the factual issues raised by Schnopps' claim of provocation.

We do not question the propriety of the verdict returned by the jury. However, based on the defendant's testimony, voluntary manslaughter was a possible verdict. Therefore, it was error to withhold "from the consideration of the jury another verdict which, although they might not have reached it, was nevertheless open to them upon the evidence."

For the reasons stated, the judgment of the Superior Court is reversed, the verdict of murder in the first degree is set aside, and the case remanded for a new trial.

WHAT DO *YOU* THINK?

1. Were the wife's comments so shocking as to be tantamount to the defendant's actually catching her in an adulterous act with her lover?
2. What are the implications of extending the provocation doctrine in infidelity cases from actually witnessing a spouse committing adultery to learning about it verbally?

Involuntary Manslaughter

involuntary manslaughter
an unlawful homicide that is unintentionally caused and that either (1) is the result of an unlawful act other than a dangerous felony (or of a lawful act done in an unlawful way) or (2) occurs as the result of criminal negligence or recklessness

Involuntary manslaughter is an unlawful homicide that is unintentionally caused and that either (1) is the result of an unlawful act other than a dangerous felony (or of a lawful act done in an unlawful way) or (2) occurs as the result of criminal negligence or recklessness. The central distinguishing feature between voluntary and involuntary manslaughter is the absence in involuntary manslaughter of the intention to kill or to commit any unlawful act that might reasonably produce death or great bodily harm. In other words, in cases of voluntary manslaughter, killing is intentional, while it is unintentional in instances of involuntary manslaughter. For example, Pennsylvania law states, "[a] person is guilty of involuntary manslaughter when, as a direct result of the doing of an unlawful act in a reckless or grossly negligent manner, or the doing of a lawful act in a reckless or grossly negligent manner, he causes the death of another person."[27] An "unlawful act other than a dangerous felony" generally refers to a misdemeanor involving danger of injury.

An involuntary manslaughter conviction may be based on an accidental death caused by the defendant during the commission of an unlawful act. The unlawful act may be any misdemeanor or felony that is not included under the felony murder rule. In some states, when death occurs as the result of an unlawful act that is a misdemeanor involving danger of injury, a charge of misdemeanor manslaughter may be brought under what is known as the *misdemeanor manslaughter rule*, which still operates in about a dozen states. Whether the unlawful act is a felony or a misdemeanor, there must be a causal relationship between the act and the death of the victim. In those situations in which the wrongful act is a serious felony, however, the requirement of proximate cause is generally suspended. The Model Penal Code does not define *manslaughter* in relationship to other unlawful behavior except to say generally that "[c]riminal homicide constitutes manslaughter when (a) . . . it is committed recklessly."[28] The MPC does recognize the fact that the act that causes death is unlawful and that this may have an evidentiary bearing on whether it is reckless.

Law Line 4-2
Manslaughter Statutes

IN THE FIELD

It goes without saying that murder and other intentional homicide cases provide some of the most intense and dramatic moments in criminal law. The magnitude of the alleged harm and the severity of the potential punishment of the defendant if convicted make intentional homicide cases extraordinarily challenging. The pressure is felt from all corners of the case.

For prosecutors, homicide cases can involve complex forensic evidence, expert witnesses, and difficult evidentiary matters. But the basic process is the same as in more low-profile cases. Prosecutors must outline the elements of the homicide statute and ensure that they have sufficient evidence to support each element. Prosecutors must have proof beyond a reasonable doubt that a person died and that this death was proximately caused by the defendant's conduct. Prosecutors must also show that the defendant acted with the requisite intent (purposeful, knowingly, with malice, or premeditated) to satisfy the statutory *mens rea*. Unless there is a valid confession to the crime, the defendant's mental state is often proven through circumstantial evidence. What were the circumstances surrounding the defendant's conduct? Did the defendant say or do something that might show his intent? Did he have a motive that might be used as evidence of intent?

For defense attorneys, the stakes obviously are high. But again, the basic process for assessing the law is the same—identify the elements of the charged offense and assess the evidence the prosecutor seeks to use to prove these elements. Each element and item of evidence must be outlined and reviewed with an eye toward undermining (creating reasonable doubt in) the government's case. Are the government's witnesses credible and otherwise trustworthy? Is the prosecutor's tangible evidence reliable? Are there other explanations for the victim's death or the defendant's alleged conduct? Are there any legal or factual defenses to disprove one or more of the elements of the offense?

In many cases, where the evidence connecting the defendant's conduct to the victim's death is strong, the focus will be on the defendant's mental state. Is there mitigating evidence that suggests the defendant should be convicted of a lesser degree of homicide than the one currently charged—second-degree murder instead of first-degree murder or manslaughter instead of murder? This consideration is important for at least two reasons. First, it can be instructive during plea negotiations between the parties. And second, if the case goes to trial, defense attorneys may ask the judge to include in the jury instructions the elements of lower degrees of homicide than the one charged in the indictment, so that a jury might consider finding guilt on a "lesser included" offense, thereby reducing the potential sanctions for the defendant.

RECKLESS AND NEGLIGENT HOMICIDE

reckless homicide
the unlawful death of a person caused by the reckless behavior of another person

negligent homicide
the unlawful of a person death caused by the criminal negligence of another

In some jurisdictions, unintentional homicides can also be classified as reckless homicides or negligent homicides. The offense of **reckless homicide** is the death of a person caused by the reckless behavior of another person. Similarly, the offense of **negligent homicide** is a death caused by the criminal negligence of another. In many statutes, these criminal offenses are written in very simple terms. Ohio's reckless homicide law states in part, "[n]o person shall recklessly cause the death of another." And Alabama's negligent homicide law says, "[a] person commits the crime of negligent homicide if he causes the death of another person by criminal negligence."[29] Under most statutory schemes, reckless homicide is treated as a more serious offense than negligent homicide.

As addressed in Chapter 3, criminal recklessness and criminal negligence are distinct mental states. A person acts recklessly when he or she consciously disregards a substantial and unjustified risk of harm.[30] For example, a person behaves recklessly if he knows it is dangerous to drive a car on a sidewalk, but does it anyway. In reckless homicide cases, the critical factor is that the defendant knowingly ignored the fact that his behavior posed a serious and unjustifiable threat of death to another. Even though death is not intended, the fatal consequences of reckless behavior can result in criminal culpability.

gross negligence
a substantial deviation from the duty to engage in due care

Criminal negligence, on the other hand, is the failure to recognize a substantial and unjustifiable risk of harm. More specifically, criminal negligence or **gross negligence** is defined as "a substantial deviation from the duty to engage in due care." For example, under normal circumstances, a motorist acts negligently if she fails to see an oncoming car before making a left turn. In negligent homicide cases, the critical factor is that the defendant failed to be aware that her conduct posed a threat of death to another person. Keep in mind that criminal negligence is a more culpable mental state than **ordinary negligence,** which is often used in civil cases and is typically regarded as "the lack of ordinary care." To constitute criminal negligence, a defendant's lapse of due care must be substantial.

ordinary negligence
the lack of ordinary care

vehicular homicide
a charge used to prosecute drivers who operate their motor vehicles in a negligent manner, thereby causing the death of another

Some states use the standards of recklessness and negligence to establish specific homicide offenses for deaths caused by motor vehicles. Under some statutory schemes, the offense of **vehicular homicide** is used to prosecute drivers who operate their motor vehicles in a negligent manner, thereby causing the death of another. For example, this offense might be charged for a death caused by a simple traffic accident, where the at-fault driver accidentally fails to yield or misses a stop sign. In more serious cases, the offense of **aggravated vehicular homicide** is used to charge those drivers whose reckless operation of their car results in the death of another. For example, this offense might be more appropriate where death is caused by a driver who is under the influence of alcohol or traveling at an excessive rate of speed.

aggravated vehicular homicide
a charge used to prosecute drivers who recklessly operate their cars, resulting in the death of another

IN THE FIELD

For legal professionals working on reckless or negligent homicide cases, there are atleast two basic tasks. First, you must identify the legal "duty of care" that was allegedly breached by the defendant. What obligation of the defendant was breached, either by willful ignorance (recklessness) or the failure to appreciate (negligence)? Regardless of whether the defendant was driving a car, handling firearms, doing construction work, or engaging in another task, legal professionals must research the statutes, administrative rules, case law, and any other recognized body of standards to identify the legal duty of care held by the defendant.

Second, you must identify the manner by which the defendant allegedly ignored or failed to know this duty. Again, in reckless homicide cases, the prosecutor must show that the defendant consciously disregarded a substantial and unjustifiable risk of harm. And in negligence cases, the evidence must show that the defendant substantially deviated from a duty of care. Legal professionals must closely examine the evidence of the case in light of any statutory, administrative, judicial, or other relevant source of law, to determine whether the defendant breached the assigned duty of care.

SUICIDE

Under early common law, **suicide** (self-inflicted death) was murder, and anyone who assisted another in committing suicide was a party to murder. But generally the modern view is that suicide is not murder because murder involves the killing of another individual. Thirty-five states, however, have created the statutory crime of aiding or assisting suicide. Section 401 of the California Penal Code, for example, provides that any person who deliberately aids, advises, or encourages another to commit suicide is guilty of a felony. In addition, nine states criminalize assisted suicide through common law,[31] although successful prosecutions based on common law may be difficult to obtain. Three states have abolished common law crimes and do not have statutes criminalizing assisted suicide. Only Oregon and Washington permit physician-assisted suicide.

suicide
self-inflicted death

Assisted suicide statutes often target behavior that is comparatively passive in nature. But in many cases, those who take affirmative steps to end the life of another person could be charged with murder, even if the actions were taken at the request of the decedent. For example, Dr. Jack Kevorkian, a well-known and outspoken Michigan physician, was convicted and sent to prison for second-degree murder in the 1998 poisoning death of Thomas Youk. Youk was suffering from Lou Gehrig's disease and had requested Kevorkian's assistance to end his life. His video-taped suicide was shown on national television.[32] Kevorkian also acknowledged assisting in 130 deaths since 1990.[33] The doctor was paroled in 2006 at the age of seventy-eight. In some cases, it may be difficult to determine when a defendant crosses the line between aiding suicide and committing murder. If, for example, a defendant buys potentially deadly drugs for someone else, such conduct might be considered simply "aiding suicide." But if the defendant actually administers the drugs to the other person, such conduct might be found to be proactive, thereby constituting a form of murder.

Legislators, courts, and voters continue to debate the appropriateness of criminalizing assisted suicide. In 1997, Oregon enacted the Death with Dignity Act, allowing for physician-assisted suicide. In 2008, voters in the state of Washington approved a physician-assisted suicide law. And the U.S. Supreme Court has found that states have the authority to allow for physician-assisted suicide or, if they choose, to criminalize the act of assisted suicide.

In the companion cases of *Vacco v. Quill* (1997)[34] and *Washington v. Glucksberg* (1997),[35] the Court upheld laws in New York and the state of Washington that made assisted suicide a criminal offense. The Washington law stated that "[a] person is guilty of [promoting suicide] when he knowingly causes or aids another person to attempt suicide." The plaintiffs challenging these criminal laws had argued that an individual's right to personal liberty, as protected by the Fourteenth Amendment's Due Process Clause, should allow persons to decide whether to engage in physician-assisted suicide. The Supreme Court, however, disagreed, ruling that state prohibitions against causing or aiding a suicide do not violate individual rights to due process because the history and practice within the United States has not recognized such conduct as a fundamental liberty interest protected by the Due Process Clause. Accordingly, the Court ruled that states could continue their ban on physician-assisted suicide.

But in *Gonzales v. Oregon* (2005),[36] the Court upheld an Oregon law that explicitly allowed for physician-assisted suicide in some circumstances. While the underlying validity of the law was not challenged in the case, the U. S. Attorney General had threatened to revoke the license to prescribe controlled substances of any Oregon physician that assisted in a suicide under the state law. The Attorney General argued that using federally controlled narcotics to assist in suicide was not a legitimate medical practice under the federal Controlled Substances Act. In a 6-3 ruling, however, the Supreme Court rejected this argument, holding that the federal government could not prohibit Oregon doctors from prescribing regulated drugs for used in physician-assisted suicide matters permitted under state law.

ASSAULT, BATTERY, AND MAYHEM

assault
common law name for an attempted or threatened battery that places another person in a state of fear; in some settings, used interchangeably with the term *battery*

battery
an action that causes unlawful personal injury to another

There are three basic criminal offenses used to regulate bodily injury to persons—assault, battery, and mayhem. An **assault** is an attempted or threatened battery that places another person in a state of fear. A **battery,** on the other hand, is a consummated assault or an action that causes personal injury to another. And **mayhem** is a battery that causes great bodily harm or disfigurement. See Figure 4-5. In addition, most jurisdictions also have statutes prohibiting a more particularized form of personal injury known as domestic violence. **Domestic violence** is a battery committed against a person within a statutorily defined family or household relationship.

FIGURE 4-5 **Assault, Battery, and Mayhem**

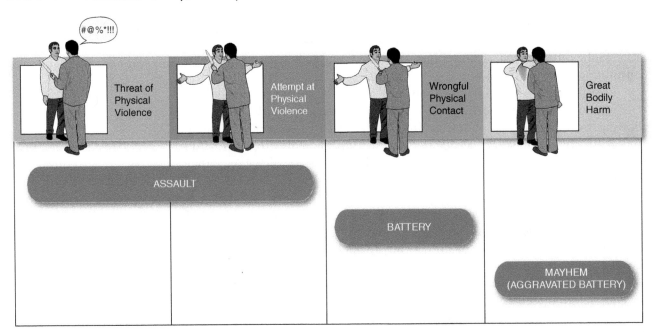

Assault

Under common law, there are two types of assault: an attempted battery and a threatened battery. An attempted battery occurs when the defendant takes a substantial step to commit a battery. A threatened battery occurs when the defendant places another in fear of imminent injury. The difference is that the first form of assault is an actual attempt to commit a battery, while the second form creates a fear in another person's mind that a battery will occur. Accordingly, the common law elements of assault are

- an unlawful attempt or threat
- with present ability
- to commit a battery

Assault as Attempted Battery

A number of states today, including California, do not recognize the second type of common law assault (threatened battery). Instead, California statutes define *assault* as "an unlawful attempt, coupled with a present ability, to commit a violent injury on the person of another." Specifically, California's Penal Code provides:

Section 240. An assault is an unlawful attempt, coupled with a present ability, to commit a violent injury on the person of another. . . .

Section 241.4. An assault is punishable by fine not exceeding one thousand dollars ($1,000), or by imprisonment in the county jail not exceeding six months, or by both. . . .

Section 242. A battery is any wilful and unlawful use of force or violence upon the person of another.

Section 243. (a) A battery is punishable by a fine not exceeding two thousand dollars ($2,000), or by imprisonment in a county jail not exceeding six months, or by both the fine and imprisonment. . . .

(d) When a battery is committed against any person and serious bodily injury is inflicted on the person, the battery is punishable by imprisonment in a county jail for a period of not more than one year or imprisonment in the state prison for two, three, or four years.

Under some circumstances, the victim need not be aware of the attempt to constitute an attempted-battery type of assault. The victim, for example, may be unconscious at the time of the assault. To constitute assault, there must be an overt act from which the inference can be drawn that a violent injury was intended; mere words alone are insufficient.

Similarly, any attempt to commit an injury or an offensive touching must be unlawful. Accordingly, the attempt to inflict injury on a person in a valid self-defense situation is not an unlawful attempt. The use of force by law enforcement officers in effecting a valid arrest is also not unlawful, nor is the reasonable use of force in a boxing match or football game. If, however, the force used or attempted to be used is not authorized or is used in an unauthorized manner, it may be unlawful.

The present ability element of the crime of assault requires that the defendant be physically capable of carrying out the attempted act and that the method he intends or threatens to use will in fact inflict an injury or offensive touching if carried out. Simply put, present ability, as used in assault statutes, means that the offender is physically capable of immediate battery. Present ability relates solely to the ability of the person attempting or threatening the unlawful injury or offensive touching. It does not, in most jurisdictions, refer to the fact that for some reason or condition unknown to and not controlled by the defendant, the intended injury

mayhem

a battery that causes great bodily harm or disfigurement

domestic violence

an assault or battery perpetrated against a statutorily identified family member or person within a domestic relationship could not actually be inflicted. If, for example, the defendant fires a pistol at someone in an automobile, but, unknown to the defendant, the automobile was constructed with bulletproof glass and armor plating, the defendant would still be guilty of assault.

The term *bodily injury*, which appears in many assault and battery statutes, has a special meaning. It does not mean that the injury attempted must be a severe one or must cause great physical pain. It merely refers to an unlawful application of physical force on the person of the victim. As one court noted, for assault crimes the terms *violence* and *force* are synonymous and include any application of force, even if it entails no pain or bodily harm or leaves no mark.[37]

Assault as Placing Another in Fear

The second type of assault under common law, the threatened-battery type, was the placing of another in fear of imminent injury. In some jurisdictions, the crime is described as *intentional-frightening assault.* As noted earlier, not all jurisdictions recognize this form of assault. The threatened-battery type of assault requires that the defendant intend to create fear of imminent injury in the victim. In most cases, words alone do not suffice, and some overt act must occur before the crime can be said to have been committed. Telling a person, for example, "I'm going to kill you!" is generally not an assault unless accompanied by some overt act, such as pointing a gun at the person.

Some threats to commit bodily injuries are based on conditions. For example, the bank robber might say to a bank teller, "One false move and I'll shoot!" The robber has not stated definitively that he will shoot, but has asserted a condition under which such harmful conduct will occur. This is regarded as a **conditional assault** and generally will be treated as a criminal assault if the defendant is not entitled to assert such condition against the victim. For example, the bank robber above had no right to threaten the bank teller, and thus, his conditional threat to the teller likely would be an assault. But if a property owner tells a trespasser, "leave my property or I'll throw you off," such a conditional threat may not constitute an assault because the owner may have a right to protect her property.

conditional assault
a threat to commit bodily harm if a condition is not met; generally will be treated as a criminal assault if the defendant is not entitled to assert such condition against the victim

Aggravated Assault

In most jurisdictions, a simple assault is one unaccompanied by aggravating circumstances. Simple assaults are classified as misdemeanors. In addition, most jurisdictions also identify a variety of felonious assaults, which they call **aggravated assaults.** These are generally assaults with intent to commit some other offense, such as rape or murder. As a result, aggravated assault is sometimes called *assault with intent*, and indictments for specific offenses, such as assault with intent to kill, are not unusual. Aggravated assault was not an offense under common law.

aggravated assault
an assault that is committed with the intention of committing an additional crime or an assault that involves special circumstances

Special categories of assaults—such as assault with a dangerous weapon, assault on a peace officer, assault on a school official or teacher, assault on a prison guard or correctional worker, and so on—have also been classified in various jurisdictions as aggravated assault. As a result, the term *aggravated assault* may mean (1) an assault that is committed with the intention of committing an additional crime or (2) an assault that involves special circumstances. See Figure 4-6. Generally, to prove an aggravated assault, prosecutors must show that an assault took place as part of another, more serious offense or that an assault occurred with an aggravating element specified by law.

FIGURE 4-6 **Aggravated Assault**

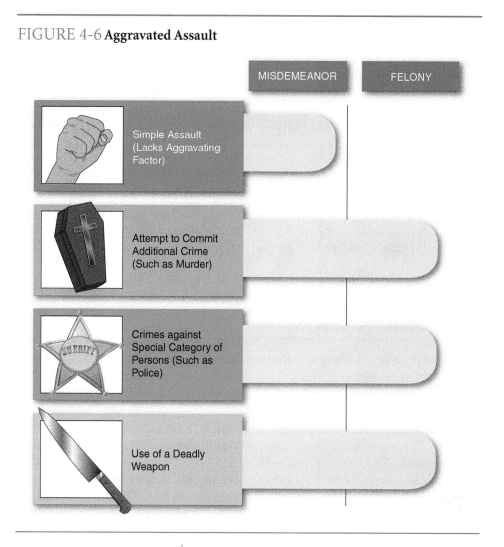

Where assault is considered to be aggravated when committed with a dangerous weapon, the weapons are usually said to be of two types: (1) those that are inherently dangerous or deadly (as a loaded gun would be) and (2) those that are not dangerous per se but that can be used in a dangerous fashion (such as a rope used in a strangling). Some courts have held that a dog used in an attack is a dangerous weapon,[38] others have held that hands and fists can be deadly weapons even if the person has not had martial arts or combat training,[39] and still others have held that human teeth are *not* deadly weapons.[40]

Stalking and Harassment

The strict requirements needed to establish a criminal assault have led many to believe that traditional assault laws are not adequate to punish the conduct of stalkers. Accordingly, many jurisdictions have extended the scope of their assault statutes to include intentional scaring or stalking. The first antistalking statute was enacted in California. California's statute reads as follows: "[a]ny person who wilfully, maliciously, and repeatedly follows or harasses another person, and who makes a credible threat with the intent to place that person in reasonable fear of death or great bodily injury is guilty of the crime of *stalking*."[41] The statute defines *harassment* as "a knowing and wilful course of conduct directed toward a specific

stalking
the act of placing another person in a state of fear of death or bodily injury by way of acts of intimidation or threat

person which seriously harms, annoys, torments, or terrorizes that person, and which serves no legitimate purpose." *Credible threat* means a verbal or written threat implied by a pattern of conduct or a combination of verbal or written statements and conduct made with the intent and apparent ability to carry out the threat so as to cause the person who is the target of the threat to reasonably fear for his safety or for the safety of his immediate family.[42]

Similarly Section 42.072 of the Texas Penal Code defines stalking as follows:

---

§ 42.072. Stalking

(a) A person commits an offense if the person, on more than one occasion and pursuant to the same scheme or course of conduct that is directed specifically at another person, knowingly engages in conduct, including following the other person, that:

1. the actor knows or reasonably believes the other person will regard as threatening:
   (A) bodily injury or death for the other person;
   . . .

2. causes the other person or a member of the other person's family or household to be placed in fear of bodily injury or death . . . ; and

3. would cause a reasonable person to fear:
   (A) bodily injury or death for himself or herself.

Law Line 4-3
Attorney General's Report on Cyberstalking

Stalking and harassing activities regularly extend into cyberspace. As a result, most states have amended their criminal stalking and harassment laws to include conduct committed through electronic communications, including the use of cell phones, computers, video recorders, and other electronic devices.[43] For example, in June 2008, Missouri amended its criminal harassment laws to include cyberbullying. This new law followed the much-publicized suicide of Megan Meier, a thirteen-year-old Missouri girl who killed herself after receiving insulting electronic messages from the mother of one of her friends (see accompanying photo). Among other things, the new law prohibits the use of electronic communications to frighten, intimidate, or cause distress to another person. In cases where the defendant is twenty-one years old or older and the victim is seventeen years old or younger, the crime is classified as a felony.

Law Line 4-4
Missouri Cyberbullying Statute

Battery

As noted earlier, the crime of battery is either the causing of bodily injury or the offensive touching of the person of another. According to Florida law, for example, "[t]he offense of battery occurs when a person: (1) actually and intentionally touches or strikes another person against the will of the other; or (2) intentionally causes bodily harm to another person." Battery has three elements

- the willful and unlawful
- use of force, violence, or offensive contact
- against the person of another

Any unjustified offensive touching constitutes a battery. As one court noted: "[n]o injury to the victim need occur; indeed the touching need not have left any mark at all upon the victim."[44] It is not necessary for the victim to actually fear physical harm as the result of the touching or the injury. The unwelcome touching of a woman's breast, for example, is a battery. To determine if the touching is offensive, the court considers whether a reasonable person would be offended by the touching. And although in most cases battery is an intentional crime, it may also be committed recklessly or with criminal negligence.[45] The Texas Penal Code, for example, makes it a crime to "intentionally, knowingly, or recklessly [cause] bodily injury to another."[46]

Lori Drew leaving the U.S. Federal Courthouse. The Myspace suicide trial ended today with three guilty verdicts against Lori Drew, the forty-nine-year-old Missouri mother who created a fake MySpace account used to torment a thirteen-year-old girl who wound up committing suicide. Lori Drew was not convicted of the more serious charges of using a computer to intentionally inflict emotional distress on thirteen-year-old Megan Meier. Megan's mother Tina Meier spoke at a press conference afterwards and acknowledged she had wished for guilty verdicts on all four felonies, but she called the three misdemeanor convictions "a victory" and hoped the national attention the trial received would focus attention on the dark side of the Internet. "This is not about vengeance," she said. "This is about justice for Megan—and making sure this does not happen to anyone else. I don't want another family to have to endure this." In 2009, the judge in the case acquitted Ms. Drew of the misdemeanor charges as well, finding the federal law used to convict her of the misdemeanors was unduly vague.

In most jurisdictions, the crime of battery is a misdemeanor unless there are special conditions associated with it that aggravate the crime. The most common special conditions include battery on a peace officer, battery with the intent to inflict death or serious bodily injury, battery that results in serious bodily injury, and sexual battery. *Serious bodily injury* includes loss of consciousness, concussion, bone fracture, protracted loss or impairment of any bodily member or organ, a wound that requires extensive suturing, and disfigurement.

Aggravated Battery

As with assault offenses, some jurisdictions have created the statutory crime of **aggravated battery,** which is a battery perpetrated under more severe circumstances or resulting in more serious harm. Aggravated battery may involve the use of a deadly weapon, the intention of committing another crime (rape or murder), or the result of serious injury. In cases of serious injury, the degree of harm inflicted on the victim determines whether a crime is chargeable as simple or aggravated battery. Kansas law, for example, provides that aggravated battery is "[i]ntentionally causing great bodily harm to another person or disfigurement of another person."[47] Florida

aggravated battery
a battery committed under more severe circumstances or resulting in more serious harm

law says that a person commits aggravated battery if he or she (1) intentionally or knowingly causes great bodily harm, permanent disability, or permanent disfigurement; or (2) uses a deadly weapon.[48] Although the definition of a deadly weapon may be open to dispute, some courts have held that hands can be deadly weapons,[49] as can a simple pair of panty hose used in an attempt to strangle someone.

A few states define the crime of aggravated battery to include the battery of special categories of people, such as those who are pregnant or have a physical handicap or who are teachers or emergency personnel operating in a professional capacity. In some jurisdictions, a simple battery offense is classified as a misdemeanor, whereas aggravated battery is a felony.

Mayhem

Common law did not recognize aggravated forms of assault and battery. Instead, the crime of mayhem developed as an alternative and was useful in punishing a perpetrator for a violent attack that did not end in death. Mayhem is a battery that inflicts serious permanent injury upon another. Initially, under common law, the injury had to diminish the victim's ability to defend himself. Later, the resulting injuries were broadened to include bodily disfigurement. In most jurisdictions today, mayhem requires an intent to cause serious injury or death to the victim. Under most statutes, there are three basic elements to the crime of mayhem[50]

- an unlawful battery
- involving maliciously inflicting or attempting to inflict violent injury
- with one or more disabling or disfiguring injuries resulting from the illegal act

California law states that "[e]very person who unlawfully and maliciously deprives a human being of a member of his body, or disables, disfigures, or renders it useless, or cuts or disables the tongue, or puts out an eye, or slits the nose, ear, or lip, is guilty of mayhem."[51] A more serious form of mayhem, that of aggravated mayhem, can be defined as "causing permanent disability or disfigurement of another human being, or depriving another human being of a limb, organ, or member of his or her body under circumstances manifesting extreme indifference to the physical or psychological well-being of that person."[52]

For example, in 2009, two purported gang members in Fresno, California, were charged with aggravated mayhem after they inked a gang-symbol tattoo on a seven-year-old boy. One of the men charged was Enrique Gonzalez, the father of the boy. According to authorities, Gonzalez restrained his son while another man tattooed a dog-paw symbol on the boy's right hip. Prosecutors asserted that these actions intentionally caused permanent disfigurement to the young boy. In June 2010, a jury found the two men not guilty of the alleged crime.

While most jurisdictions have enacted the common law crime of mayhem in their criminal statutes, the Model Penal Code does not recognize mayhem as a separate offense. Under the code, it falls into the category of aggravated assault.[53] A few jurisdictions have enacted torture statutes, which may be closely related to mayhem laws. The California torture statute, for example, reads: "Every person who, with the intent to cause cruel or extreme pain and suffering for the purpose of revenge, extortion, persuasion, or for any sadistic purpose, inflicts great bodily injury . . . upon the person of another, is guilty of torture."[54]

IN THE FIELD

In criminal cases involving personal injuries, there are typically four primary legal questions that must be addressed by legal professionals: (1) Did the defendant cause harm to the victim? (2) If so, what was the defendant's intent at the time of harmful conduct? (3) Is there any justification or excuse for the defendant's conduct? and (4) How serious were the victim's injuries? In cases where the answers to the first three questions point to guilt, the defendant's level of culpability will often depend on the severity of harm caused to the victim. For example, under many assault laws, the difference between an aggravated assault and a simple assault often depends on whether the victim sustained serious injuries or less severe injuries. For legal professionals, this legal question often results in a battle over expert testimony and medical evidence.

ETHICAL PRINCIPLES

ASSISTING ATTORNEYS IN CRIMINAL CASES

National Association of Legal Assistants Code of Ethics and Professional Responsibility

CANON 3

A paralegal must not: (a) engage in, encourage, or contribute to any act which could constitute the unauthorized practice of law; and (b) establish attorney-client relationships, set fees, give legal opinions or advice or represent a client before a court or agency unless so authorized by that court or agency; and (c) engage in conduct or take any action which would assist or involve the attorney in a violation of professional ethics or give the appearance of professional impropriety.

Courtesy of the National Association of Legal Assistants

Domestic Violence

Most jurisdictions have a special category of assault and battery offenses know as domestic violence or "DV" laws. These laws seek to punish physical, and in some cases emotional, harm that occurs between family members or others within intimate relationships. For example, Section 2919.25 of the Ohio Revised Code provides the following:

a. No person shall knowingly cause or attempt to cause physical harm to a family or household member.

b. No person shall recklessly cause serious physical harm to a family or household member.

c. No person, by threat of force, shall knowingly cause a family or household member to believe that the offender will cause imminent physical harm to the family or household member.

Notice that sections (a) and (b) address physical harm, which reflects the common law offense of battery, while section (c) covers activity that is commonly associated with an assault. For the most part, DV laws function the same as assault and battery laws. The prosecutor must show that the defendant caused the requisite harm to the victim. The primary difference is that, with domestic violence laws, the prosecutor must prove that the victim was a member of the offender's family or household. Under many statutes, this includes a spouse, person living as a spouse, former spouse, parent, or child of the offender, who is residing or has resided with the offender.

In addition, many jurisdictions impose a number of administrative requirements in DV cases. One such requirement is a ***mandatory arrest policy*** that requires law enforcement officers to make an arrest when they find evidence of bodily harm and where the perpetrator of such harm can be identified. Under mandatory arrest policies, officers must make an arrest at the scene of a reported act of domestic violence. In addition, many courts impose ***protective orders*** during the early stages of domestic violence cases, requiring the defendant to stay away from the alleged victim and/or the household where the crime allegedly occurred.

Domestic violence is also a crime under federal law, if the offender travels or otherwise uses interstate commerce to commit an act of violence against a family or household member. Under 18 U.S.C. § 2261(A)(1), it is a crime for a person to travel interstate with the intent to injure, harass, or intimidate that person's intimate partner when in the course of or as a result of such travel the defendant intentionally commits a violent crime and thereby causes bodily injury. The term *intimate partner* includes a spouse, a former spouse, a past or present cohabitant (if the parties cohabited as spouses), and parents of a child in common. But under the federal statute, an intimate partner does not include a girlfriend or boyfriend with whom the defendant has not resided unless this relationship is protected by state law.

mandatory arrest policy
law that requires police officers to make an arrest in a domestic violence case when they find evidence of bodily harm and where the perpetrator of such harm can be identified

protective orders
court orders used in domestic violence cases and other matters, requiring a person to stay away from an identified person

Law Line 4-5
Domestic Violence Laws

IN THE FIELD

For many criminal justice professionals, domestic violence cases will become all too familiar. The basic preparation for these cases is quite similar to the typical assault or battery case—the prosecution must show that the defendant caused harm to the identified victim. The primary difference in "DV" cases is that the prosecutor must also show a sufficient family or household relationship between the defendant and victim.

In some cases, prosecutors may find it difficult to get the alleged victim to cooperate as a witness. For a variety of reasons, many DV victims do not wish to pursue charges against the defendant. And in cases where the victim is the only witness to the alleged harm, the prosecutor's case can largely depend on the cooperation of the victim.

For defense attorneys, the early stages of DV cases can bring many tasks. In jurisdictions with mandatory arrest laws, the defendant will need to be bonded out of jail. And in cases where a protective order is issued, defendants must be informed of the legal parameters and consequences of this order, so that they do not violate it, thereby resulting in another criminal charge.

In addition, DV cases can present defense professionals with some difficult ethical issues, particularly when dealing with the alleged victim in a case. One the one hand, DV victims are witnesses in the case, and as with all witnesses, defense professionals should attempt to contact and interview them. But realize that, because there may be a protective order against the defendant, defense professionals must ensure they do not vicariously violate the terms of this order. In addition, there may be times when DV victims begin asking defense professionals for legal advice, posing questions like "Should I testify" or "What should I say to the prosecutor?" Realize that such questions might present a conflict of interest to you, and that, as a representative of the defendant, you cannot offer legal advice to the alleged victim.

SEX OFFENSES

Few areas of criminal law have attracted as much attention in the past twenty-five years as the attempt to place legislative controls on sexual behavior. On the one hand, sexual activity is generally viewed as an intimate activity that should not be supervised by government. On the other hand, sexual conduct—especially when nonconsensual—can inflict considerable harm, thereby warranting government intervention. People generally agree, however, that unwanted and nonconsensual sexual activity should be subject to criminal prosecution and that sex with children under the age of legal consent should be criminalized.

There are many classifications of sex offenses. But generally speaking, criminal statutes are organized around two forms sexual activity—sexual conduct and sexual contact. *Sexual conduct* (also known as sexual intercourse) is intercourse (insertion) involving sex organs. Sexual conduct includes vaginal intercourse, anal intercourse, *fellatio* (oral stimulation of the penis), and *cunnilingus* (oral stimulation of the female vaginal area). Under many statutes, intercourse is defined as the insertion of any body part or artificial instrument into the vaginal or anal opening of another. *Sexual contact* is a less-invasive form of sexual activity involving the sexual touching of another without intercourse. Sexual contact includes the touching of the anus, breast, or any part of the genitals of another person with intent to arouse or gratify the sexual desire of any person.

Using these two forms of sexual activity, criminal statutes classify sex offenses into several categories, including rape, sexual assault, sexual battery, sexual imposition, and unlawful sexual conduct or contact with a minor. In addition, many other criminal acts are classified as sex offenses, including importuning, voyeurism, and prostitution.

Rape

Under common law, any sexual penetration of the female vagina by the male penis was sufficient to complete the crime of rape. It was not necessary that emission occur; as one English court put it, "the least penetration makes it rape . . . although there be no *emissio seminis*."[55] Common law convictions for the crime of rape required that the penetration be of the vagina; penetration of the anus or mouth was referred to as *deviate sexual intercourse.* In contrast, the modern tendency is to define *rape* as any nonconsensual sexually motivated penetration of any orifice of the victim's body.

In most jurisdictions today, the elements of the crime of rape are

- sexual intercourse with a person who is not the spouse of the perpetrator
- through force, through the threat of force, or by guile
- or without the lawful consent of the victim

In the past, many rape statutes emphasized the role of force in the crime of rape, giving rise to the term *forcible rape.* Maryland law, for example, reads: "[a] person is guilty of rape in the second degree if the person engages in vaginal intercourse with another person . . . [b]y force or threat of force against the will and without the consent of the other person."[56] Today, however, some states have supplemented or replaced the element of force with the element of nonconsent. Utah law, for example, says simply, "[a] person commits rape when the actor has sexual intercourse with another person without the victim's consent."[57] The result is that state laws vary considerably in their description

sexual conduct
intercourse (insertion) involving sex organs; also known as sexual intercourse

fellatio
oral stimulation of the penis

cunnilingus
oral stimulation of the female vaginal area

sexual contact
a form of sexual activity involving the sexual touching of another without intercourse; includes the touching of the anus, breast, or any part of the genitals of another person with intent to arouse or gratify the sexual desire of any person

deviate sexual intercourse
term used at common law to refer to forms of unlawful sexual intercourse

rape
unlawful sexual intercourse through force, threat of force, or deception

forcible rape
a rape offense committed by use of physical force or threat

of rape, with some states requiring the element of force or coercion, while others incorporate the element of nonconsent.

Lawful Consent.   Lawful consent can be lacking during sexual intercourse under any number of circumstances, ranging from the use of force or threats to achieve compliance, to intercourse with an unconscious or mentally incompetent individual. In individual cases, however, the question of whether intercourse occurred with or without the consent of the victim may be a difficult question to answer. If the victim is incapable of giving legally effective consent, then intercourse with the victim is rape even if he or she expressed words indicating consent. The fact that the victim consented to sexual foreplay does not mean that the victim consented to intercourse, nor does the fact that the victim had in the past consented to intercourse with the defendant constitute consent on the present occasion.

Under common law, a husband could not rape his wife, since it was believed that when a woman married, she consented to sexual intercourse. This rule, called the *marital exemption*, held that "a wife is irrebuttably presumed to consent to sexual relations with her husband, even if forcible and without consent."[58] But state laws today no longer exempt spouses from rape statutes.[59]

Same-Sex Rape.   The common law definition of *rape* required both (1) penetration and (2) an unwilling *female* victim. Accordingly, it was generally held that there was no crime of homosexual rape under common law. Today, however, a majority of jurisdictions have rape statutes that are gender neutral. In those jurisdictions, intercourse between people of the same gender may be rape, if all of the other elements of the crime are present.

Statutory Rape.   All jurisdictions have laws defining **statutory rape**. Under such laws, anyone who has intercourse with a child below a certain specified age is guilty of statutory rape, whether or not the child consented. Statutory rape, in most jurisdictions, is a strict liability crime. As addressed in Chapter 3, strict liability crimes can be committed when the offender engages in activity that is legally prohibited, even if the offender is unaware of breaking the law or did not intend to do so. As a result, a man who has sexual intercourse with a consenting female under the age specified by statute can still be found guilty of statutory rape even though he thought she was older. Most jurisdictions hold that even a reasonable belief on the part of the defendant that the victim was over the age of consent at the time of the offense is no defense to a charge of statutory rape.[60] In some instances, men have been convicted of statutory rape even though they had been duped by a female below the age of consent into thinking that the girl was older. The Model Penal Code and a minority of jurisdictions, however, allow the defense of reasonable mistake as to age.[61]

Sexual Assault

A recent trend in the United States is to combine all nonconsensual sexual offenses into one crime called **sexual assault**. Where such broad laws exist, sexual assault encompasses far more than the common law crime of rape. Sexual assault may also be used to reference the common law crimes of deviate sexual intercourse, unlawful sexual contact, and **sodomy** (a term that under some statutes includes anal intercourse, fellatio, and cunnilingus). As a result, there are many instances where the phrase "sexual assault" will be used to describe a broad array of sex offenses.

The MPC and a few jurisdictions, however, give a much more specific meaning to the term. Section 213.4 of the MPC defines sexual assault as sexual

statutory rape
unlawful sexual intercourse with a minor below a certain age specified by statute; often treated as a strict liability crime

sexual assault
a classification of crime used in some jurisdictions to refer to nonconsensual sexual offenses

sodomy
a term used in some statutes to refer to anal intercourse, fellatio, and cunnilingus

contact with another person (not one's spouse) knowing that contact to be offensive to the other person. The MPC defines sexual assault to include sexual contact that occurs when the victim is (1) suffering from mental disease or defect that leaves him or her unable to consent; (2) unaware that a sexual act is being committed; (3) less than ten years old; (4) substantially impaired through actions of the offender, such as the administering of drugs; or (5) less than sixteen years old and the actor is at least four years older; and under a few other circumstances.

Law Line 4-6
National Sexual Violence Resource Center

Sexual Battery

Some jurisdictions identify sexual battery as a sexual offense. In some states, *sexual battery* occurs when a person unlawfully touches an intimate part of another person's body against that person's will and for the purpose of sexual arousal, gratification, or abuse. For example, California Penal Code Section 243.4 (a) states, "[a]ny person who touches an intimate part of another person while that person is unlawfully restrained by the accused or an accomplice, and if the touching is against the will of the person touched and is for the purpose of sexual arousal, sexual gratification, or sexual abuse, is guilty of sexual battery."

sexual battery
the unlawful touching of an intimate part of another person's body against that person's will and for the purpose of sexual arousal, gratification, or abuse

In other states, the crime of sexual battery is limited to unlawful sexual conduct (intercourse) between persons who are barred by law from having sexual relations. For example, some sexual battery statutes make it a crime for a teacher to engage in sexual conduct with a student, a medical professional to have sex with a patient, a clergy member to have sex with a congregant, or other specified authority figures to have sex with those subject to their supervision or authority. This form of sexual activity is treated as criminal, even if it occurs between two "consenting" adults, based on the occupational or familial relationship between the individuals. These are often referred to as "status-based" crimes because they are based on the professional, social, or relationship status of the individuals. Read the Ohio Supreme Court's opinion in *State v. Lowe* (2007) (below), which upheld the sexual battery conviction of a man who had consensual sex with his twenty-two-year-old stepdaughter.

CAPSTONE CASE *State v. Lowe,* 112 Ohio St. 3d 507, 861 N.E.2d 512 (2007)

The Stark County Grand Jury indicted defendant-appellant, Paul Lowe, on one count of sexual battery, a felony violation of R.C. 2907.03(A)(5), as a result of his consensual sex with his 22-year-old stepdaughter, the biological daughter of his wife, on March 19, 2003. Lowe pleaded not guilty and filed a motion to dismiss, claiming that the facts alleged in the indictment did not constitute an offense under R.C. 2907.03(A)(5), because the use of the term "stepchild" in the statute signified a "clear legislative intent to have the law apply to children, not adults." In the alternative, Lowe argued that the statute was unconstitutional as applied to his case because the government has no legitimate interest in regulating sex between consenting adults.

After the trial court overruled his motion, Lowe changed his plea to no contest, was convicted, and was sentenced to 120 days of incarceration and three years of community control. The trial court also classified him as a sexually oriented offender. The Fifth District Court of Appeals upheld Lowe's conviction....

(continued)

(continued)

We accepted the case on a discretionary appeal. Lowe argues that in enacting R.C. 2907.03(A)(5), the General Assembly intended to protect children against adults in positions of authority who harmed them. He claims that the statute is unconstitutional when applied to consensual sexual conduct between adults related only by affinity. We will address these arguments in order.

Ohio's Incest Statute

R.C. 2907.03(A) states:

"No person shall engage in sexual conduct with another, not the spouse of the offender, when any of the following apply: . . .

"(5) The offender is the other person's natural or adoptive parent, or a stepparent, or guardian, custodian, or person in loco parentis of the other person."

The statute does not limit its reach to children, as Lowe argues. R.C. 2907.03(A)(5) states that "[n]o person shall engage in sexual conduct with another, not the spouse of the offender when any of the following apply ***." The statute goes on to list guardians and custodians as well as natural and adoptive parents and persons in loco parentis. Thus, the statute is not limited to protecting minors from those in a position of authority over them. . . .

In other words, although the statute does indeed protect minor children from adults with authority over them, it also protects the family unit more broadly. . . .

Lowe would have the statute's prohibition against sexual conduct be limited to conduct with minors. We have held that a court may not add words to an unambiguous statute, but must apply the statute as written. But the plain language of R.C. 2907.03(A)(5) clearly prohibits sexual conduct with one's stepchild while the stepparent-stepchild relationship exists. It makes no exception for consent of the stepchild or the stepchild's age. . . .

Lowe argues that he has a fundamental right to engage in sexual activity with a consenting adult and that his conduct was private conduct protected by the Constitution. He therefore argues that, as applied to him, R.C. 2907.03(A)(5) violates the Fourteenth Amendment to the United States Constitution, which protects him against deprivation of "life, liberty, or property, without due process of law." . . .

Lowe cites *Lawrence v. Texas*, 539 U.S. 558 (2003) to argue that he has a constitutionally protected liberty interest to engage in private, consensual, adult sexual conduct with his stepdaughter when that activity does not involve minors or persons who may be easily injured or coerced. In *Lawrence*, a Texas statute criminalizing homosexual conduct was held to be unconstitutional as applied to adult males who had engaged in private and consensual acts of sodomy. Lowe contends that Lawrence named a new fundamental right to engage in consensual sex in the privacy of one's home.

However, the statute in *Lawrence* was subjected to a rational-basis rather than a strict-scrutiny test, with the court concluding that the Texas statute furthered no legitimate state interest that could justify intrusion into an individual's personal and private life. In using a rational-basis test to strike down the Texas statute, the court declined to announce a new fundamental right arising from the case. . . .

Using the rational-basis test, we conclude that, as applied in this case, Ohio's statute serves the legitimate state interest of protecting the family unit and family relationships. . . .

Accordingly, as applied in this case, R.C. 2907.03(A)(5) bears a rational relationship to the legitimate state interest in protecting the family, because it reasonably advances its goal of protection of the family unit from the destructive influence of sexual relationships between parents or stepparents and their children or stepchildren. If Lowe divorced his wife and no longer was a stepparent to his wife's daughter, the stepparent-stepchild relationship would be dissolved. The statute would no longer apply in that case.

We hold that HN12R.C. 2907.03(A)(5) is constitutional as applied to consensual sexual conduct between a stepparent and adult stepchild, because it bears a rational relationship to the state's legitimate interest in protecting the family. The judgment of the Court of Appeals for Stark County is affirmed.

Judgment affirmed.
PFEIFER, J., dissenting.

. . .

I suspect that the statute was not employed in this case as a means to preserve Ohio's fractured extended families. Rather, the state used R.C. 2907.03(A)(5) as a means to prosecute a strict-liability, slam-dunk sex offense that does not allow the defendant to present any evidence regarding the consent of the victim. R.C. 2907.03(A)(5) provides a shortcut to a conviction. This sort of use of the statute demeans its true purpose. The consent of the alleged victim should remain a valid defense in cases involving adults.

WHAT DO *YOU* THINK?

1. How would you have interpreted Ohio's sexual battery law?
2. Do you agree with the Ohio Supreme Court that the statute does not interfere with a liberty interest to engage in consensual, adult sexual activity?
3. Is there a larger societal purpose served by the court's decision?

The theory behind "status-based" sexual battery crimes is that a person who is subject to the authority of another person may not always feel free to reject the sexual activity. Put another way, the person may feel compelled or pressured to consent to the sexual activity. In ordinary cases, the effective consent of the victim, also referred to as *legal consent*, is a defense to the charge of sexual battery, if the defendant's conduct did not threaten to inflict or actually inflict serious bodily injury. But in status-based sexual battery cases, the law presumes that the person subject to the authority figure's control cannot give effective consent to sexual activity with the authority figure. Thus, the law requires a person to be of proper age, mental capacity, and relationship in order to give a valid form of consent. Effective consent cannot be obtained by fraud or by force, and it cannot be given by a person who does not have the capacity to consent.

Sexual Imposition

Some states use the crime of **sexual imposition** to punish unlawful sexual contact or touching of another. Like the sexual battery and sexual assault laws used in other states, sexual imposition statutes generally target nonconsensual sexual touching of another person's anus, breast, or any part of the genitals. Typically, under these statutes, the touching must be done with the intent to arouse or gratify the sexual desire of at least one of the parties involved. Sexual imposition statutes are often used in cases where the defendant imposes upon another person unwelcome sexual activity that does not rise to the level of sexual intercourse.

sexual imposition
a crime involving the unlawful sexual contact or touching of another

Unlawful Sexual Conduct with a Minor

All states have some form of criminal statute that prohibits persons from engaging in sexual conduct with persons below a specific age. Under some statutes, the term *minor* refers to anyone below the age of eighteen. In other statutes, the age of the victim is more tailored. For example, Ohio Revised Code Section 2907.04 (A) provides: "No person who is eighteen years of age or older shall engage in sexual conduct with another, who is not the spouse of the offender, when the offender knows the other person is thirteen years of age or older but less than sixteen years of age, or the offender is reckless in that regard." This offense is classified as a fourth-degree felony. But Ohio law also accounts for some potential disparities that may occur between the ages of the defendant and victim, reducing the crime to a first-degree misdemeanor if the defendant is less than four years older than the victim, and increasing the crime to a third-degree felony if the defendant is more than ten years older than the victim.

To constitute a crime under most unlawful-sexual-conduct-with-a-minor statutes, it does not matter whether the minor consented to the sexual activity. These statutes generally are based on the presumption that minors are not sufficiently competent to consent to sexual conduct.

Sexual Solicitation of a Minor (Importuning or Enticement)

One of the most notorious and widely observed sexual offenses in recent years is the online sexual solicitation of children. This is often referred to as the offense of importuning or enticement. ***Importuning*** (enticement) is the solicitation of a minor for sexual activity. Importuning and enticement statutes typically are written to address two scenarios: (1) cases where the person being solicited for sex is a real minor (no person shall solicit a minor to engage in sexual activity with the offender); and (2) cases where the minor is fictional (no person shall solicit another by means of a telecommunications device to engage in sexual activity with the offender; the other person is a law enforcement officer posing as a minor and the offender believes that the other person is a minor).

Many have watched popular television programs where the program host uses an Internet sting operation to catch persons soliciting minors for sex. In most cases, these crimes involve no real children. Instead, law enforcement officials or private groups pose as underage persons within Internet chat rooms and wait for someone to solicit them for sex. A meeting is arranged between the solicitor and the fictitious minor, and when the solicitor shows up, he is arrested.

The crime of importuning or enticement occurs when a person solicits a minor (or under some statutes a person believed to be a minor) for sexual activity. The solicitor does not need to attempt sexual activity (e.g., drive to a location to meet the "minor") to constitute the offense. The mere solicitation (request) for sex is enough. In cases where the solicitor engages in a substantial step toward meeting the "minor" for sexual activity, he can also be charged with attempted sexual conduct with a minor (discussed above).

Voyeurism

Voyeurism is another sexual offense found in most state statutes. Generally, voyeurism laws prohibit persons from invading another person's privacy for the purpose of sexual gratification. For example, Ohio's voyeurism statutes reads: "[n]o person, for the purpose of sexually arousing or gratifying the person's self,

importuning
the unlawful solicitation or enticement of another for sexual activity

voyeurism
a crime that involves the invasion of another person's privacy for the purpose of sexual gratification

NEW YORK — April 6, 2003 — NY-UNDERCOVER-COPS — Using a computer, Detective Michael Smith of the New York Police Department tries to identify sexual predators, often by posing as a teenage girl on the internet. Smith, in his office in Manhattan, March 27, 2003. (*Michelle V. Agins/The New York Times*)

shall commit trespass or otherwise surreptitiously invade the privacy of another, to spy or eavesdrop upon another."

Voyeurism offenders are often referred to as "Peeping Toms," fostering the image of a person peering through the window of another's home. But many voyeurism cases today involve the use of electronic equipment, where offenders have installed hidden cameras to tape others during private moments or used portable recording devices to capture private body images of others in public spaces. To combat these technological instruments of crime, many states have amended their voyeurism statutes to prohibit the surreptitious recording of another person (1) in a state of nudity, or (2) for the purpose of viewing the body of, or the undergarments worn by, that other person.[62]

IN THE FIELD

Criminal cases involving sex offenses can present many unique legal challenges. In addition to the normal issues of whether the defendant committed the alleged act with the requisite state of mind, legal professionals often face questions about privacy implications, professional consequences, and sex offender registration requirements that may accompany a sex crime. The reality is that, in most jurisdictions today, cases involving many sex offenses have far more consequences than just a potential criminal sentence.

In many cases, the stigma associated with disclosing matters involving sexual conduct—for both defendant and alleged victim—can present psychological issues of embarrassment, shame, and/or additional trauma. In addition, for defendants working in some professions—teaching, health care, child care, and the like—a sex offense conviction can end a career. And beyond that, a sex crime conviction can bring years or even a lifetime of sexual offender registration requirements, restricting where defendants can live and requiring their neighbors to be notified of their criminal history.

As a result, legal professionals must learn to view cases involving sex offenses in a more global fashion. Whether working for prosecutors or defense attorneys, you must consider all of the potential consequences—legal, professional, administrative, social, and psychological—facing both the defendant and the alleged victim.

KIDNAPPING AND FALSE IMPRISONMENT

kidnapping
the unlawful removal or transportation of a person against that person's will, and through the use of force, fraud, threats, or some other form of intimidation

false imprisonment
the unlawful detention or restraint of another

Kidnapping and false imprisonment are crimes that intimately invade a person's privacy and take away his or her liberty—often in abrupt and forceful fashion. *Kidnapping* is generally defined as the unlawful removal or transportation of a person against that person's will, and through the use of force, fraud, threats, or some other form of intimidation. *False imprisonment* is the unlawful detention or restraint of another. The two crimes are similar, except that false imprisonment does not involve the "carrying away" of the victim.

Kidnapping

asportation
the unlawful carrying away or transportation of a person

Under early common law, kidnapping consisted of the forcible abduction or stealing away of a person from his own country and into another. Later this requirement was modified to require involuntary movement merely from one county to another. Today, most jurisdictions hold that any unlawful movement of the victim that is "substantial" is sufficient to satisfy the movement (asportation) requirement inherent in the crime of kidnapping. For courts today, the primary issue in kidnapping cases is whether a person is forcefully moved against his or her will and not the degree of movement or distance involved.[63] Even so, the movement involved must be "substantial," meaning that merely forcing someone out of one's way or pushing a person a few feet or even across the street would not constitute kidnapping within the meaning of the law. Accordingly, the general elements of kidnapping are

- an unlawful taking and carrying away (***asportation***)
- of a human being
- by force, fraud, threats, or intimidation
- and against the person's will

In some jurisdictions, kidnapping may also be committed by the use of *deadly* force to confine the victim or by confining the victim for purposes of extortion, ransom, or sexual assault. Kidnapping for ransom (or *aggravated kidnapping*, as these crimes are sometimes called) is a more serious form of kidnapping and is usually punished more severely than the crime of simple kidnapping. See Figure 4-7. The same may be true when state statutes specify that the release of a victim in a place that is not safe raises the degree of the crime committed.

The laws of some jurisdictions provide for more than one type of kidnapping. California law, for example, recognizes four different kidnapping offenses: (1) forcible kidnapping, (2) kidnapping with intent to commit certain specified felonies, (3) kidnapping with intent to take the victim out of state, and (4) bringing a kidnapped victim into the state. California law also specifies penalty enhancements for kidnappings that are committed for the purposes of committing a sexual offense, ransom, extortion, or robbery and for kidnapping a child under the age of fourteen.

Florida law, which is essentially an aggravated kidnapping law, defines the crime as follows: "The term 'kidnapping' means forcibly, secretly, or by threat confining, abducting, or imprisoning another person against his will and without lawful authority, with intent to: (1) hold for ransom or reward or as a shield or hostage, (2) commit or facilitate commission of any felony, (3) inflict bodily harm upon or to terrorize the victim or another person, [or] (4) interfere with the performance of any governmental or political function."[64] Were the law to end

FIGURE 4-7 **Aggravated Kidnapping**

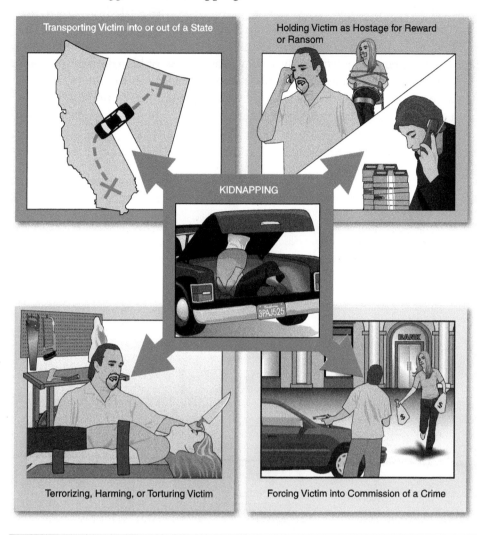

after the words "without lawful authority," this definition would describe a simple kidnapping.

In an effort to combat the abduction of children, which is sometimes called *child stealing*, Florida law also provides that "[c]onfinement of a child under the age of thirteen is against his will within the meaning of this subsection if such confinement is without the consent of his parent or legal guardian."[65] The abduction of children might occur in instances of contested divorce or child custody battles. Under the federal Parental Kidnapping Prevention Act, states are required to enforce the child custody determinations made by other states.[66]

False Imprisonment

Not all states have false imprisonment statutes, and in those that do, the offense is usually classified as a misdemeanor. The elements of false imprisonment are

- an unlawful restraint by one person
- of another person's freedom of movement
- without the victim's consent or without legal justification

The defendant must have compelled the victim to remain against his will or to go where he did not want to go.[67] While the confinement must be accomplished by actual physical restraint, the application of force is not essential. Confinement may be accomplished by threats or by some other action of the defendant that restrains the victim's freedom of movement. For example, a defendant might be found guilty of false imprisonment for intentionally driving a car too fast for his passenger to leave.[68]

In cases in which the confinement is accomplished by threat, the victim must be aware of the threat. Similarly, it is not false imprisonment to prevent a person from going in one direction, as long as the person may go in a different direction

FIGURE 4-8 **Kidnapping versus False Imprisonment**

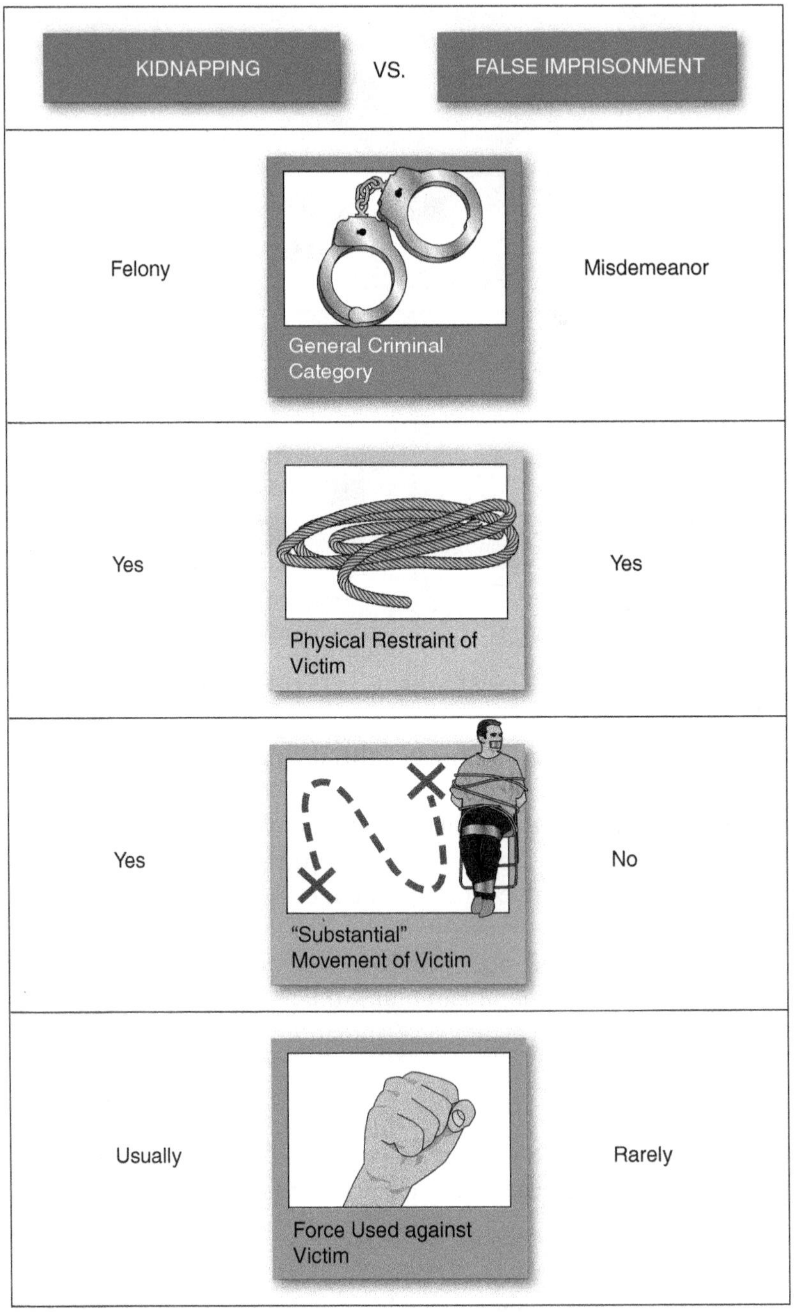

and is aware of this opportunity. Also, the confinement must be unlawful in that there must be no legal authority for the person's involuntary restraint. For example, an arrest that is made without proper legal authority constitutes false arrest—a form of false imprisonment.

False imprisonment is essentially a lesser included offense of the crime of kidnapping. Some authors note that kidnapping is also an aggravated form of false imprisonment. This approach is reflected under Florida law, which defines false imprisonment to mean "forcibly, by threat, or secretly confining, abducting, imprisoning, or restraining another person without lawful authority and against his will."[69] As with kidnapping, the statute also provides that "[c]onfinement of a child under the age of thirteen is against his will within the meaning of this section if such confinement is without the consent of his parent or legal guardian." Some jurisdictions, which define false imprisonment simply as "restraining another unlawfully so as to interfere substantially with his liberty," would consider false imprisonment achieved through the use of force or threats as "aggravated false imprisonment."

Read the Texas Court of Appeals opinion in *Schweinle v. State* (1996) to further understand the similarities and differences between kidnapping and false imprisonment.

CAPSTONE CASE   *Schweinle v. State,* 915 S.W.2d 17 (Texas Ct. App. 1996)

A jury convicted appellant of aggravated kidnapping and assessed his punishment at confinement for fifteen years in the penitentiary. The conviction was affirmed. We granted discretionary review. . . .

Appellant and the complainant became engaged after a brief courtship, and the complainant, who had formerly lived with her parents, moved into appellant's house. However, the couple began arguing, and the complainant moved back to her parents' house, although she would occasionally spend the night with appellant. On October 23, 1991, they had planned that appellant would pick up some food for dinner, and the complainant would meet appellant at his father's liquor store, where appellant worked. The complainant was alone at her parents' house changing clothes when she heard a door slam. Appellant came into the bedroom, enraged because the complainant had not met him at the liquor store as planned. The complainant testified appellant told her she was coming with him, that he had some food in the car and she was going to eat every bite of it. He grabbed her by the arm, dragged her down the hall and slapped her. The complainant told appellant she did not want to go with him, but appellant insisted she was coming with him and walked her to the truck. As appellant was driving, he smeared a steak sandwich in the complainant's face and pointed a gun at her, telling her he would shoot her if she tried to escape. Appellant drove the truck to a subdivision near his house in which roads had been built but no houses constructed. There, he threw another sandwich at her and hit her in the stomach with his fist. He then drove to his house, where he continued to beat her with a belt and a rolled-up newspaper covered with duct tape. The next morning appellant took the complainant to her parents' house.

In ground four, appellant contends the Court of Appeals erred by holding that the lesser included offense of false imprisonment was not raised by the evidence. Whether a charge on a lesser included offense is required is determined by a two-pronged test. First, we must determine whether the offense constitutes a lesser included offense. . . . Second, the lesser included offense must be raised by the evidence at trial. In other words, there must be some evidence which would permit

(continued)

(continued)

a rational jury to find that if guilty, the defendant is guilty only of the lesser offense. . . . Anything more than a scintilla of evidence from any source is sufficient to entitle a defendant to submission of the issue. . . .

Under V.T.C.A. Penal Code, Section 20.03, a person commits the offense of kidnapping if he intentionally or knowingly abducts another. "'Abduct' means to restrain a person with intent to prevent his liberation by: (A) secreting or holding him in a place where he is not likely to be found; or (B) using or threatening to use deadly force." "'Restrain' means to restrict a person's movements without consent, so as to interfere substantially with his liberty, by moving him from one place to another or by confining him. Restraint is 'without consent' if it is accomplished by force, intimidation, or deception. . . ." V.T.C.A. Penal Code, Section 20.01.

A person commits the offense of false imprisonment if he "intentionally or knowingly restrains another person." V.T.C.A. Penal Code, Section 20.02. Kidnapping is accomplished by abduction, which includes restraint, but false imprisonment is committed by restraint only. Thus, false imprisonment is a lesser included offense of kidnapping and aggravated kidnapping. . . .

The Court of Appeals' analysis is flawed in two respects. First, the Court of Appeals determined that the subdivision where appellant stopped his truck to throw more food on the complainant and beat her was a place where she was not likely to be found, without considering whether a rational jury could have reached the opposite conclusion under the evidence. . . .

Appellant testified that the complainant's parents lived on Woodforest, which was a main thoroughfare, and the subdivision where appellant lived was off Woodforest, two to three minutes away from the complainant's parents' house. Appellant described the area where he stopped his truck as a few blocks from his house and in his neighborhood. He testified he turned right off of Woodforest going into his neighborhood, and "as we got around the corner there, I had to make another left to cut down to go to my house." He testified the area where he stopped was very small, "two or three streets there, it's all cleaned out." He further explained, "It's developed, there is just no houses there. . . . It's not really what I would call secluded." The complainant testified that the area was "not very far off Woodforest, but it's just a little—just a little bit secluded. There is like some trees and it's right by the school." Pictures of this area were admitted into evidence. From this evidence, a rational jury could have believed that the street where appellant stopped his truck was not a place where the complainant was not likely to be found.

Secondly, by holding that appellant did not raise the lesser included offense because his testimony refuted both the greater and lesser offenses, the Court of Appeals erred. . . . We [have] pointed out that the defendant's denial of committing any offense does not automatically foreclose submission of a lesser included offense.

Applying those principles to this case, a rational jury could have believed the complainant's testimony that she did not go freely with appellant. Appellant testified that he did not threaten to shoot the complainant, did not touch the gun during the drive from her parents' house to his, and did not point the gun at her at any time. He admitted that the gun was lying on the seat of his truck during the offense, but explained that he habitually carried the gun in his truck either on the seat next to him or on the floor next to the gearshift. . . . From this evidence, a rational jury could have found that despite the presence of a gun on the seat, appellant did not use or threaten to use deadly force to prevent the complainant's liberation.

Similarly, the jury could have believed that appellant held the complainant in his house against her will but believed appellant's house was not a place where the complainant was not likely to be found. Evidence was presented that the complainant had a key to appellant's house, had formerly lived there, and had spent the night there the past three or four nights before the offense. In addition, the complainant's mother testified that when she came home on the night of the offense and found the house in disarray and her daughter missing, she became afraid for her daughter's safety and drove by appellant's house. From this evidence, a jury could have rationally concluded that the complainant was restrained at appellant's house, but his house was not a place where she was not likely to be found. In sum, the jury could have found that appellant had restrained but not abducted the complainant and thus was guilty only of false imprisonment. Therefore, the Court of Appeals erred by holding this lesser included offense was not raised by the evidence.

Accordingly, we reverse the judgment of the Court of Appeals and remand the case to that court....

WHAT DO *YOU* THINK?

1. What are the differences between false imprisonment and kidnapping?
2. Based on the facts contained in the court's opinion, did the accused commit any offense other than kidnapping and false imprisonment? If so, what?

CHAPTER **SUMMARY**

- Homicide is the killing of a human being by another human being. Criminal homicides are those homicides for which criminal liability accrues. Generally, any homicide that is not excusable or justifiable is considered criminal homicide.
- Murder is the unlawful killing of another person with malice aforethought. The statutory elements of the crime of murder are (1) an unlawful killing (2) of a human being (3) with malice.
- Felony murders are deaths that result from the commission of a dangerous felony.
- Manslaughter is the unlawful killing of a human being without malice. The statutory elements of the crime of manslaughter are (1) an unlawful killing (2) of a human being (3) without malice. Manslaughter may be of two types: voluntary or involuntary.
- Voluntary manslaughter is the unlawful killing of a human being, without malice, which is done intentionally during a sudden quarrel or in the heat of passion. Voluntary manslaughter is homicide committed in response to adequate provocation.
- Involuntary manslaughter is an unintended killing caused during the commission of an unlawful act not amounting to a dangerous felony or as the result of criminal negligence or recklessness.
- Reckless homicide occurs when a person consciously disregards a substantial and unjustifiable risk, thereby causing the death of another.
- Negligent homicide occurs when a person substantially deviates from a duty of care, thereby causing the death of another.
- Many states have created the statutory crime of aiding suicide, although someone who actively ends the life of a suicidal individual may be guilty of murder.
- Although the terms *assault* and *battery* are often used together or interchangeably, they should be distinguished

- for purposes of the criminal law. An assault is an attempted or threatened battery. A battery is a consummated assault. Mayhem is a battery that causes great bodily harm.
- Some jurisdictions have combined assault and battery crimes into one offense called *assault*.
- The term *aggravated assault* may mean (1) an assault that is committed with the intention of committing an additional crime or (2) an assault that involves special circumstances.
- Many jurisdictions have enacted antistalking statutes designed to prevent the intentional harassing, annoying, or threatening of another person.
- The crime of battery is an intentional crime, but it may be committed through reckless or criminally negligent conduct. To constitute battery, the offense need cause no injury, and the victim need not fear the force intended to be applied.
- There are several crimes that are classified as sexual offenses. Traditionally, *rape* is defined as unlawful sexual intercourse with a female without her effective consent. The rape statutes of an increasing number of jurisdictions today, however, are not gender specific and also permit charges of spousal rape.
- Some jurisdictions have consolidated sexual offenses into one broad crime of sexual assault.
- Sexual solicitation and importuning are sexual offenses where a person requests sexual activity from another person, typically a person under the age of eighteen.
- Kidnapping is the unlawful removal of a person from the place where he or she is found, against that person's will, and through the use of force, fraud, threats, or some other form of intimidation.
- False imprisonment is the unlawful violation of the personal liberty of another. False arrest, or an arrest that is made without proper legal authority, is a form of false imprisonment.

KEY **TERMS**

aggravated assault
aggravated battery
aggravated murder
aggravated vehicular homicide
asportation
assault
battery
capital murder
conditional assault
criminal homicide
cunnilingus
depraved heart murder
deviate sexual intercourse
Domestic violence
Excusable homicides
False imprisonment
fellatio
felony murder rule
first-degree murder

forcible rape
gross negligence
Homicide
Importuning
Involuntary manslaughter
Justifiable homicides
Kidnapping
malice
malice aforethought
mandatory arrest policy
Manslaughter
mayhem
murder
negligent homicide
ordinary negligence
Premeditated murder
premeditation
protective orders
rape

reckless homicide
second-degree murder
sexual assault
sexual battery
Sexual conduct
Sexual contact
sexual imposition
sodomy
stalking
statutory rape
suicide
Uniform Determination of Death
    Act (UDDA)
vehicular homicide
voluntary manslaughter
Voyeurism
year and a day rule

QUESTIONS FOR **DISCUSSION**

1. What distinguishes noncriminal homicide from criminal homicide?

2. What are the three types of criminal homicide? Describe them.

3. What causation problems are presented in many criminal homicide prosecutions?

4. Explain the concept of corpus delicti as it relates to criminal homicide.

5. What is the difference between murder and voluntary manslaughter?

6. What is the felony murder rule?

7. Can a prosecutor charge a person with a homicide crime without having located a dead body?

8. How does voluntary manslaughter differ from involuntary manslaughter?

9. Explain the difference between reckless homicide and negligent homicide and provide examples of each.

10. What are the differences between the common law crimes of assault and battery?

11. How does mayhem differ from other types of battery?

12. How does a domestic violence offense differ from the crime of battery?

13. Explain the difference between common law rape and modern statutes describing sexual assault.

14. What is importuning and how does it relate to modern developments in criminal justice?

15. Should prosecutors be able to charge a person with soliciting a minor for sex during an Internet chat when the person solicited was really an adult police officer playing the role of an underage minor?

16. How have stalking and voyeurism statutes evolved to keep pace with modern technology?

17. Give an example of false imprisonment. How does false imprisonment differ from kidnapping? How does it differ from false arrest?

REFERENCES

1. *Black's Law Dictionary,* Abridged 5th ed. (1983), p. 375.

2. *Follis v. State,* 101 S.W.2d 242 (1947).

3. *Jones v. State,* 151 Tex. Crim. 114, 205 S.W.2d 603 (1947).

4. *Williams v. State,* 629 S.W.2d 791 (Tex. Ct. App. 5th Cir. 1981).

5. Model Penal Code, Section 210.1, *Commentary,* 11.

6. See National Conference of Commissioners on Uniform State Laws, *Uniform Determination of Death Act and Report,* 12 Uniform Laws Annotated 320 (1990 Supp).

7. *Id.*

8. The National Conference of Commissioners on Uniform State Laws is a nonprofit association comprising state

commissions on uniform laws from each state, the District of Columbia, the Commonwealth of Puerto Rico, and the U.S. Virgin Islands. The National Conference of Commissioners on Uniform State Laws has worked for the uniformity of state laws since 1892. The conference promotes the principle of uniformity by drafting and proposing specific statutes in areas of the law where uniformity between the states is desirable. No uniform law is effective until a state legislature adopts it.

9. P. A. Byrne, S. O'Reilly, and P. M. Quay, "Brain Death: An Opposing Viewpoint," *Journal of the American Medical Association* 242 (1979): 1985–90.

10. See the dissenting opinion in *Commonwealth v. Ladd*, 166 A.2d 501 (Pa. 1960).

11. Guilford County (North Carolina), No. 91CRS20076, October 31, 1991.

12. North Carolina Court of Appeals, No. 9118SC1298, May 18, 1993.

13. California Penal Code, Section 194.

14. *People v. Freudenberg*, 121 Cal. App. 2d 564 (1953).

15. *People v. Moan*, 65 Cal. 532 (1884).

16. *People v. Fowler*, 178 Cal. 657 (1918); *People v. Lewis*, 124 Cal. 551 (1899).

17. *People v. Brackett*, 510 N.E.2d 877 (Ill. 1987).

18. *Commonwealth v. Malone*, 47 A.2d 445 (Pa. 1946).

19. In some jurisdictions, the term *depraved heart murder* means the killing of a human being with extreme atrocity.

20. *People v. Morrin*, 187 N.W.2d 434 (Mich. 1971).

21. *People v. Geiger*, 159 N.W.2d 383 (Mich. 1968).

22. *People v. Daniels*, 52 Cal. 3d 815 (1991).

23. Tracy L. Snell, "Capital Punishment, 1995," Bureau of Justice Statistics bulletin, December 1996.

24. Kansas Statutes Annotated, Section 21-3403.

25. John Kaplan and Robert Weisberg, *Criminal Law: Cases and Materials*, 2nd ed. (Boston: Little, Brown, 1991), p. 248.

26. Texas Penal Code, Section 19.02. Emphasis added.

27. Crimes Code of Pennsylvania, Section 2504(a).

28. Model Penal Code, Section 210.3.

29. Alabama Code, 13A-6-4.

30. Model Penal Code, Section 2.02(2)(c).

31. As reported by Euthanasia.com, http://www.euthanasia.com/bystate.html (accessed April 24, 2001).

32. "Supreme Court Turns Down Kevorkian," CNN.com Law Center, November 2, 2004, http://www.cnn.com/2004/LAW/11/01/scotus.rulings.ap (accessed February 10, 2005).

33. David Shepardson, "Kevorkian Loses Appeal in Top Court," *Detroit News*, November 2, 2004, http://www.detnews.com/2004/metro/0411/02/b01-322446.htm (accessed January 10, 2005).

34. 521 U.S. 793 (1997).

35. 521 U.S. 702 (1997).

36. 526 U.S. 243 (2005).

37. *People v. James*, 9 Cal. App. 2d 162 (1935).

38. *State v. Bowers*, 239 Kan. 417, 721 P.2d 268 (1986).

39. *People v. Ross*, 831 P.2d 1310, 1314 (Colo. 1992).

40. *Commonwealth v. Davis*, 406 N.E.2d 417, 419 (Mass. App. Ct. 1980).

41. California Penal Code, Section 646.9.

42. *Id.*

43. California Penal Code, Section 646.9.

44. *State v. Bowers*, 239 Kan. 417, 721 P.2d 268 (1986).

45. *Fish v. Michigan*, 62 F.2d 659 (6th Cir. 1933).

46. Texas Penal Code, Section 22.01, subparagraphs (1) and (3).

47. Kansas Statutes Annotated, Section 21-3414 (a) (1)(A).

48. Florida Statutes, Section 784.045.

49. *Dixon v. State*, 1992 Fla. App. LEXIS 2401; 17 Fla. L. W. D. 700 (1992). The original decision was rendered by a three-member panel of the appellate court. The full court later ruled that "bare hands . . . are not deadly weapons for purposes of alleging or proving the crime of aggravated battery."

50. Harvey Wallace and Cliff Roberson, *Principles of Criminal Law* (White Plains, NY: Longman, 1996), p. 164.

51. California Penal Code, Section 203.

52. California Penal Code, Section 205.

53. Model Penal Code, Section 211.1.

54. California Penal Code, Section 206.

55. East's Pleas of the Crown 436 (1803).

56. Maryland Code, Article 27, Section 463(a)(1).

57. Utah Code Annotated, Section 76-402.

58. *State v. Bell*, 90 N.M. 134, 560 P.2d 925, 931 (1977).

59. Some legal scholars have noted that it is not the sexual component of spousal rape that is illegal, but the violence with which it is perpetrated.

60. *State v. Randolph*, 528 P.2d 1008 (Wash. 1974).

61. Model Penal Code, Section 213.6 (1).

62. See Ohio Revised Code, Section 2907.08.

63. *State v. Padilla*, 474 P.2d 821 (Ariz. 1970).

64. Florida Penal Code, Section 787.01.

65. *Id.*

66. 28 U.S.C.A. § 1738A.

67. *People v. Agnew*, 16 Cal. 2d 655 (1940).

68. *Dupler v. Seubert*, 69 Wis. 2d 373, 230 N.W.2d 626, 631 (1975).

69. Florida Penal Code, Section 787.02.

APPENDIX
DEVELOPING YOUR LEGAL ANALYSIS

A. THE LAW WHERE YOU LIVE

Assume that you are assigned to work on a criminal case where the defendant is charged with murder and rape. The indictment alleges that on December 6, 2010, Robert Jones, an eighteen-year-old man, used force to coerce Tara Stevens, an eighteen-year-old woman, into having sexual intercourse and then intentionally shot and killed her in an effort to stop her from calling the police. Jones is charged with one count of first-degree murder and one count of forcible rape. Jones, however, strongly disputes the charges, asserting that he had consensual sex with Stevens and that, afterward, Stevens killed herself as a part of a suicide pact she had made with Jones. According to Jones, the couple had agreed to commit suicide after Stevens' parents told her that they would disinherit and disown Tara if she continued dating Jones. Jones claims that the couple agreed to engage in one final act of "love" and then commit suicide, with each partner shooting themselves with separate guns. Jones claims that he brought two guns to his apartment–one for each of them–but after Stevens shot herself, he could not go through with his end of the deal.

Based on these facts, Jones asserts that he is not guilty of murder or rape. His attorney wants the jury to be given instructions on lesser degrees of homicide, as well as the offense of assisted suicide. You have been asked to prepare proposed jury instructions for the case, where you identify and outline the elements for the following offenses under your state's criminal statutes: (1) first-degree murder, (2) other lesser-degree homicide offenses that might be applicable, (3) assisted suicide, and (4) forcible rape. You may assume you are working for either the defense or the prosecutor, but be sure to analyze all of the elements of each offense and document the standard jury instructions for the offenses.

B. INSIDE THE FEDERAL COURTS

Assume you are working with an Assistant U. S. Attorney (AUSA) in reviewing a criminal case for presentation to a grand jury. As understood by the AUSA, the facts of the case involve a thirty-five-year-old man, Stan Motts, who forcibly removed Kim Scott, a six-month-old child, from her mother's home in Michigan and took her to Canada in order to have DNA testing conducted on the child. It seems that Kim's mother, Sheila Scott, had told Motts that he was Kim's biological father and that he would have to start paying child support for the baby. Motts questioned the paternity of the

child, but Scott refused to consent to a paternity test for the child. Stan then made arrangements for a DNA test in Toronto, Canada, which would involve a blood sample being taken from Kim. Over Sheila's objection, Motts took Kim from her mother's Michigan home and drove her to Toronto, where the DNA test was conducted. Later that day, Motts returned Kim safely to her mother. There is no word as to the results of the DNA test.

The AUSA wants to know which, if any, of the following federal offenses should be presented to the grand jury in this case.

Federal Kidnapping Act — 18 U.S.C. § 1201
International Parental Kidnapping Crime Act — 18 U.S.C. 1204
Interstate travel to commit Domestic Violence — 18 U.S.C. § 2261
Interstate stalking — 18 U.S.C. §2261A
Interstate travel to violate a protection order — 18 U.S.C. § 2262

Accordingly, your assignment is to prepare a memorandum for the AUSA where you review the elements of these federal offenses under the facts of the case. The AUSA wants to know which criminal charges if any you would recommend and why. The AUSA also wants to know if there are any additional facts that might be needed to evaluate the criminal charges.

C. CYBER SOURCES

Assume that XYZ, a national television news agency, wants to conduct an online "sting" operation in which they try to catch Internet "predators" seeking sex from minors. Similar to other television programs of its kind, XYZ wants to create an Internet setting, whereby fictional minors are placed in an online chat room or other Internet forum to see if they will be solicited for sex. If so, the news agency will try to arrange meeting with the solicitors, at which time they will be identified, videotaped, and otherwise exposed as "online predators." Producers would then turn over the information to local authorities for possible prosecution.

XYZ, however, is not sure where to conduct this sting operation. Producers are looking at sites in Texas, but are willing to consider locations in other states. As a legal professional, you are asked to prepare a legal memorandum in which you evaluate and outline the importuning or enticement laws of Texas and other states to see if there are any major differences in the criminal laws that punish online sexual solicitation of minors. In particular, XYZ producers want to know: Do all states have laws against the online solicitation of minors? How is this crime classified—as a felony or misdemeanor? Would XYZ's sting operation result in possible convictions under some state laws, but not others? In which states would an adult XYZ employee posing as a minor qualify as a "minor" for purposes of charging someone with soliciting a minor for sex? Use the following sources to facilitate your response.

National Center for Missing and Exploited Children

http://www.missingkids.com/missingkids/servlet/
NewsEventServlet?LanguageCountry=en_US&PageId=2947

Online Solicitation of a Minor (Texas Penal Code § 33.021)

http://www.statutes.legis.state.tx.us/

D. ETHICS AND PROFESSIONALISM

Assume that you are assisting a state prosecutor with a homicide case before a local grand jury. You have put many hours into organizing the exhibits, writing and editing questions for the hearing, and preparing the subpoenas for the witnesses. You know the case very well. During the grand jury hearing, you have worked closely with the prosecutor and things are going quite well. The prosecutor is using the questions you prepared to obtain testimony from the last witness in the case. With just a few more questions to go, the prosecutor receives a message from a family member about an emergency. The prosecutor must leave the grand jury room immediately. There are only three more questions left for the last witness and they are basic and short questions, already printed clearly on a piece of paper. The prosecutor does not want to interrupt the witness's testimony or otherwise disrupt the proceeding and has directed you to ask the last three questions of the witness. You are very comfortable with the facts of the case and the witness who is on the stand. But you are concerned about the ethical propriety of the prosecutor's request. How do you respond to the prosecutor?

chapter **five**

PROPERTY, THEFT, AND COMPUTER CRIMES

LEARNING OBJECTIVES

After reading this chapter, you should be able to

- Explain the common law crime of larceny and how it relates to modern theft statutes.

- Explain the difference between embezzlement and false pretenses.

- Distinguish between robbery and extortion.

- Explain the differences between the crimes of theft, robbery, burglary, and embezzlement.

- Identify the common elements of modern-day arson statutes.

- Identify the different types of computer crime and the unique features of each one.

- Discuss how criminal laws are written to protect individuals from identity theft.

- Appreciate the legal challenges associated with writing criminal laws to regulate harmful conduct occurring within cyberspace.

It is not a crime to make a fool of another by delivering fewer goods than ordered.

—*Rex v. Wheatly*, 97 E.R. 746 (1761)

More money has been stolen at the point of a fountain pen than at the point of a gun.

—Woody Guthrie

As surely as the future will bring new forms of technology, it will bring new forms of crime.

—Cynthia Manson and Charles Ardai[1]

INTRODUCTION

In general, property crimes involve the taking of or interference with the property of another. Property offenses come in many forms, including larceny, fraud, burglary, robbery, criminal trespass, arson, computer crimes involving misappropriation, and identity theft. **Theft** is a general term used to describe many situations where someone unlawfully interferes with the property rights of another. Criminal laws that define theft and other property crimes are designed to "promote security of property by threatening aggressors with punishment."[2]

Crimes of theft are sometimes called **acquisitive offenses**, *wrongful acquisition crimes*, or *crimes of misappropriation* since they involve the unlawful acquisition or appropriation of someone else's property. The Model Penal Code *Commentaries* note that laws defining theft as a crime are the result of "a long history of expansion of the role of the criminal law in protecting property."[3] Although common law originally concerned itself only with crimes of violence, the law expanded, through application of the principle of trespass, "to cover all taking of another's property from his possession without his consent, even though no force was used."[4]

A fundamental principle of common law crimes against property was their concern with the wrongful acquisition of property. Early on, many acquisitive offenses, including larceny, embezzlement, false pretenses, robbery, and the receiving of stolen property, required such precise elements that some courts were slow to expand those crimes to cover novel and emerging situations. Even today, courts and legislatures have difficulty fitting certain offenses, such as computer and high-technology crimes, into the category of theft. The problem stems from the fact that it is sometimes difficult to prove that something was stolen when the "rightful" owner still has possession of the property (as can happen with the theft of software). In addition, modern property crimes also are complicated by the fact that "in a commercial society no clear line can be drawn between greedy antisocial acquisitive behavior on the one hand, and on the other hand, aggressive selling, advertising, and other entrepreneurial activity that is highly regarded or at least commonly tolerated."[5]

The modern trend in some jurisdictions has been to consolidate all acquisitive crimes into the single crime of theft. In such jurisdictions, the consolidated crime of theft includes what had been the common law crimes of larceny, embezzlement, obtaining property by false pretenses, receiving stolen property, robbery, extortion, and burglary. Other jurisdictions treat each of these crimes separately. In this chapter, we discuss each, along with forgery and identity theft.

LARCENY (THEFT)

Larceny was the only property crime punished under early English common law. It was defined as "the wrongful taking and carrying away by any person of the mere personal goods of another, from any place, with a felonious intent to convert them to his own use, and make them his own property, without the consent of the owner."[6]

Today, criminal statutes contain many other forms of property crimes, including robbery, burglary, identity theft, and computer-related offenses. But the crime of larceny or theft, as it is called in some jurisdictions, remains the most basic form of property crime. Similar to its common law roots, **larceny** today is generally understood as the wrongful taking of personal

theft
a general term used to describe many situations where someone unlawfully interferes with the property rights of another

acquisitive offenses
a term for theft offenses; similar to *wrongful acquisition crimes*, or *crimes of misappropriation*

larceny
common law term used to describe theft offenses; the only property crime punished under common law; today understood as the wrongful taking of personal property from the possession of another

Law Line 5-1
Theft Statute

property from the possession of another. The core elements of most larceny or theft offenses are

- trespassory (wrongful) taking
- and carrying away (asportation)
- of the personal property of another
- with the intent to permanently deprive the owner of the use or value of the property

Trespassory Taking

A *taking* generally consists of a physical seizure by which one exercises dominion and control over the property in question.[7] To constitute larceny, however, a taking must also be trespassory. A **trespassory taking** is merely a taking without the consent of the victim. Consent induced by fraud may constitute trespassory taking. It is important to note that a trespassory taking, as the term is used in conjunction with larceny cases, has no relationship to the idea of trespass where real estate or land is concerned. Under common law, a trespassory taking was called *trespass de bonis asportatis* (trespass for goods carried away) to distinguish it from other forms of trespass.

A trespassory taking can also be understood as the taking of possession, even when the thief does not take physical possession of the stolen merchandise. For example, a person out playing tennis who finds an unattended tennis racket and offers to sell it to a passerby is guilty of larceny if the passerby consummates the transaction and walks off with the racket. In such a case, the unwary purchaser assumes that the person offering to sell the racket is the lawful owner, and the thief need never touch the racket in order for it to be stolen. If, on the other hand, the legitimate owner of the tennis racket returns before it can be carried off by the purchaser, the defendant may be guilty of receiving money under false pretenses, although he could not be found guilty of larceny.

Other issues arise when a person finds lost or mislaid property. If a person takes the property and intends to keep it at the time it is carried away, she has committed a trespassory taking and is thus guilty of larceny. For example, in 1997, a Brinks armored truck overturned on Interstate 95 in the desperately poor Overtown section of Miami, Florida. The truck, loaded with an estimated $3.7 million, split open, dropping an unknown amount of money onto the highway and spilling dollar bills, quarters, and fifty-pound bags of money onto a street below the overpass on which the accident happened. Money floated into trees, covered the highway, and showered down onto people, cars, and houses. Those on the scene said it seemed to be raining money. "People walking by, people driving by, anybody that was a witness got money," said Florida Highway Patrol spokesperson Lieutenant Ernesto Duarte.[8] Police estimated that about $550,000 disappeared before police arrived on the scene. In this incident, the rightful owner of the spilled cash was clearly known to the people who picked it up. As a result, those who took the money and kept it likely committed larceny. As Miami Police Lieutenant Bill Schwartz stated, "[t]he money does not belong to them. It is theft, whether you picked up a quarter or $100,000. Collecting the quarters, nickels, and dimes will be hard," said Schwartz. "But the big bills, we'll be counting on people's consciences."[9] The detective also noted that police might be investigating previously poor people found suddenly "strutting the street with wads of cash."

On the other hand, if a finder of lost property does not know who the owner is and has no reason to believe that he or she can find the property's owner, the finder may legally be considered the new owner of the property. If a person finds

trespassory taking
a taking without the consent of the victim

lost property, he or she may take possession of the lost item without incurring criminal liability if he or she intends to return it to the rightful owner. As a result, a person who discovers a lost wallet may lawfully take the wallet home with him if he or she intends to call the local "lost and found" bureau (or other authority) and to return the wallet and all of its contents to its lawful owner.

Similar rules apply when property has been delivered to a person by mistake; that is, a person who receives misdelivered property has a duty to return it and has no right to keep what was not intended for him or her. A person who receives misdelivered property is guilty of larceny if he or she realizes the mistake and intends to keep the property. Under the Model Penal Code, however, and the laws of some states, a defendant's intent at the time she receives the property is irrelevant, and the defendant becomes liable for theft if she, with the purpose of depriving the owner thereof, fails to take reasonable measures to restore the property to the person entitled to it.[10]

Carrying Away

In most jurisdictions, to constitute larceny, the property that is taken must be carried away. The technical term for carrying away is **asportation**. Even the slightest movement of an object, if done in a "carrying-away" manner, is sufficient to constitute asportation.[11]

asportation
the taking away or removal of property

A furtive shoplifter wearing a gray sweater sneaks cold medicine into a black bag with a body outline design at a pharmacy.

Objects may, however, be moved in a manner other than one consistent with carrying away those items. Jewelry on a jewelry counter, for example, might be picked up, turned over for examination, and even tried on without carrying-away movements. As soon as the object is concealed, however, as in the case of shoplifters who "palm" small items by hiding them in their closed hands, a carrying-away movement can be said to have occurred. Similarly, a fallen bicycle may be picked up off the ground, righted, and moved back into a bicycle stand by a good Samaritan. If the person mounts the bicycle and begins to ride off, however, a carrying-away movement occurs.

In many jurisdictions, the asportation requirement is viewed merely as a means of ensuring that the defendant had dominion and control over the property in question. If, for example, a thief puts his hand into the pocket of an intended victim and begins to lift the victim's wallet, asportation sufficient for prosecution has occurred even though the wallet is not completely removed from the victim's pocket.

Some jurisdictions have eliminated the requirement that an object be carried away for a charge of larceny to be brought. The unlawful taking of the property of another with intent to steal constitutes larceny in those jurisdictions. Carrying away may not occur, for example, in cases of misdelivery, as when furniture is delivered to the wrong address. In such a case, accepting delivery of misdelivered property may involve no physical movement of the property beyond the placement of the furniture by delivery people. In such cases, larceny could still be said to have occurred without the need for legal fictions in support of the carrying-away requirement.

Property of Another

Larceny can be committed only against a person who has possession of the property in question. It is sometimes said that a person cannot be convicted of larceny if the property he or she carried away was his or her own. It is important, however, to draw distinctions between the concepts of (1) ownership, (2) possession, and (3) custody. Because the crime of larceny builds on possession rather than ownership, it is possible, in at least some jurisdictions, for the rightful owner of property to unlawfully steal his or her own property when it is in the temporary possession or custody of another. As one court put it: "[t]he phrase 'of another' in the definition of larceny has reference to possession rather than to title or ownership. . . . Even the owner himself may commit larceny by stealing his own goods if they are in the possession of another and he takes them from the possessor wrongfully with intent to deprive him of a property interest therein."[12]

When a demand of return is made, of course, property must be returned to its rightful owner unless some other condition exists that would lawfully preclude such a return. Conditions barring return of property might include a lien on the property, a contract granting possession of the property to another person for a specified period of time, or the fact that the property has been pawned or that it has been repaired and an outstanding repair bill must still be paid. A person who owns a car may, for example, sign a rental contract whereby she agrees to temporarily relinquish possession of the vehicle. If the owner then secretly steals the vehicle back when the renter is asleep, she may be guilty of larceny.

Property that is free and clear of all attachments, however, may still be stolen by its rightful owner if it is in the possession of another. Imagine, for example, that the owner of some property—say, gold jewelry—entrusts it to the care of another for safekeeping. If the owner then enters the place where the jewelry is being stored and secretly removes it (in order, perhaps, to later file a fraudulent insurance claim), the owner would then be guilty of larceny because she had unlawfully taken the property from another's possession.

Custody over an item is not the same thing as ownership or possession. A person who owns something may legally possess it but may also relinquish custody of it temporarily. A woman who hands her purse to a man, asking him to hold it while she goes on a ride at an amusement park, for example, has relinquished custody of her purse but is still the owner and maintains possession from a legal point of view. If she asks the man to hold her purse for safekeeping while she vacations for a few weeks, the man may be said to have both custody of the purse and temporary possession of it. He is still not the purse's owner, however. Assuming that the man complies with the woman's wishes and returns the purse when asked, no legal issues arise. If, however, he sells the purse to another or gives it to his wife as a present, he has taken possession of it and has misappropriated it. Even so, he is still not the lawful owner of the purse, nor is his wife. Under common law, a defendant who was a co-owner of the taken property could not be found guilty of larceny. A few jurisdictions, however, have changed this rule by statute.

Intent to Steal

Larceny is a crime that can only be committed intentionally. It cannot be committed negligently or recklessly. If, for example, a defendant picks up a notebook computer on an airport luggage return rack, thinking that it is hers, and walks off with it, she is not guilty of larceny. An unreasonable, but honest, belief in ownership or right to possession is sufficient to constitute a valid defense to larceny. Such a defense is called the ***claim of right*** and is recognized in most jurisdictions.

The "intent to steal" element of the crime of larceny is sometimes said to mean that the offender intends to permanently dispossess the rightful owner of the property in question. It would, however, be more accurate to say that the offender intends to wrongfully deprive the lawful possessor of an item (not necessarily its owner) of the continued useful possession of that item. So, for example, a man could not be charged with larceny if he "borrows" a tie he finds on a restaurant coat stand upon learning that the restaurant has a dress code and then returns the tie when leaving the restaurant.[13] On the other hand, one who "borrows" a full can of paint and later returns it empty is guilty of larceny because he has deprived the legitimate owner of the value that had been inherent in the paint contained within the can.

The requirement of intent to steal in the crime of larceny often makes it difficult to obtain larceny convictions in cases where someone uses another person's vehicle for a joyriding adventure. These situations may not involve a larceny because the "stolen" vehicle is only "borrowed" and may be returned even before the owner notices that it is missing. Accordingly, most jurisdictions have statutorily created the crime of joyriding, which involves the unauthorized use of a motor vehicle, even when no intent to steal—in the sense of permanently depriving the rightful owner of possession of the vehicle—can be demonstrated. The Model Penal Code, for example, provides that a person commits a misdemeanor if he or she operates another's automobile, airplane, motorcycle, or other motor-propelled vehicle without the consent of the owner.[14]

claim of right
an unreasonable, but honest, belief in ownership or right to possession; can be legally sufficient to constitute a valid defense to larceny

MODERN THEFT STATUTES

Larceny or theft offenses can be organized in progressive categories of seriousness. The most common terms used to divide larceny offenses are petty theft, theft, grand theft, and aggravated theft. In general, the different forms of theft involve the

FIGURE 5-1 **Classification of Theft Offenses under Ohio Law**

Value of Property Taken	Name of Criminal Offense	Level of Criminal Offense
Less than $500	Petty theft	First-degree misdemeanor
$500 to less than $5,000	Theft	Fifth-degree felony
$5,000 to less than $100,000	Grand Theft	Fourth-degree felony
$100,000 to less than $500,000	Aggravated Theft	Third-degree felony
$500,000 to less than $1,000,000	Aggravated Theft	Second-degree felony
$1,000,000 or more	Aggravated Theft	First-degree felony

same basic criminal act—the unlawful deprivation of property of another. But the primary distinction between the forms is the value of the property unlawfully taken. For example, under Ohio law, if a person takes property valued at less than $500, the crime is classified as a petty theft, a misdemeanor of the first degree. If, however, the property stolen is worth between $500 and $5,000 dollars, the offense is theft, a fifth-degree felony. This graduated scheme of classification continues based on the value of the property unlawfully taken. As the value increases, the nature of the offense and the corresponding level of punishment are enhanced. See Figure 5-1.

In other jurisdictions, theft is classified based on the nature of the property stolen, such as firearms, fruit, and cattle. Sections 486–87 of the California Penal Code, for example, read:

> Grand theft is theft committed in any of the following cases: (a) When the money, labor, or real or personal property taken is of a value exceeding four hundred dollars ($400). . . . (b) Notwithstanding subdivision (a), grand theft is committed in any of the following cases: (1) (A) When domestic fowls, avocados, olives, citrus or deciduous fruits, other fruits, vegetables, nuts, artichokes, or other farm crops are taken of a value exceeding one hundred dollars ($100). . . . (2) When fish, shellfish, mollusks, crustaceans, kelp, algae, or other aquacultural products are taken from a commercial or research operation which is producing that product, of a value exceeding one hundred dollars ($100). (3) Where the money, labor, or real or personal property is taken by a servant, agent, or employee from his or her principal or employer and aggregates four hundred dollars ($400) or more in any consecutive twelve-month period. (c) When the property is taken from the person of another. (d) When the property taken is an automobile, firearm, horse, mare, gelding, any bovine animal, any caprine animal, mule, jack, jenny, sheep, lamb, hog, sow, boar, gilt, barrow, or pig.

tangible property
property that has physical form and is capable of being touched

personal property
anything of value that is subject to ownership and that is not land or fixtures

fixtures
items that are permanently affixed to land or a piece of real property

Section 487e of the California Penal Code goes on to read, "[e]very person who feloniously steals, takes, or carries away a dog of another which is of a value exceeding four hundred dollars ($400) is guilty of grand theft."[15]

One of the biggest challenges of modern theft statutes is defining the term *property*. Under common law, only tangible personal property could be subject to the crime of larceny. *Tangible property* is property that has physical form and is capable of being touched. It is "movable" property in the sense that it can be taken and carried away. *Personal property* is anything of value that is subject to ownership and that is not land or *fixtures* (i.e., items that are permanently affixed to the land).[16] Common law, however, excluded intangible property from the realm of larceny. ***Intangible property*** is property that has no value in and of itself but that represents value. A deed to a piece of occupied land, for example, is a kind of intangible property. While a deed might be taken and carried away without the owner's consent, the rightful owner would still retain both legal ownership and possession of the land itself—that is, the thing that had real value.

The distinction between tangible and intangible property was especially valid in early society, where populations were sparse and individuals and families were generally known to one another. In modern complex society, however, proof of ownership may be more difficult to establish. As a result, while most of today's larceny arrests are still made for the stealing of tangible property, larceny law has become much more complex. In many American jurisdictions today, goods and services, minerals, crops, fixtures, trees, utility services, software, intellectual property rights, and other intangibles can all be stolen and are the subject of various laws designed to deter theft. Some jurisdictions have enacted larceny statutes designed to criminalize the misappropriation of property that, although it has value, cannot be touched.

For example, Texas defines "property" as "(A) real property; (B) tangible or intangible personal property, including anything severed from land; or (C) a document, including money, that represents or embodies anything of value."[17] The Model Penal Code, although a bit more complex, defines property as "anything of value, including real estate, tangible and intangible personal property, contract rights, choses-in-action [things to which an owner has a contractual or legal right] and other interests in or claims to wealth, admission or transportation tickets, captured or domestic animals, food and drink, electric and other power."[18] Under the Model Penal Code and the laws of a number of states, the theft of electricity from the company that generates it constitutes larceny, as does the theft of computer software, processing time, or proprietary information. Other jurisdictions have created special laws criminalizing the theft of intellectual property and other intangibles. In the accompanying case of *Dowling v. United States* (1985),[19] the U.S. Supreme Court addressed whether intellectual property satisfies the property requirement for a theft statute.

intangible property
property that has no value in and of itself but that represents value; for example, a deed to a tract of land

CAPSTONE CASE *Dowling v. United States,* 473 U.S. 207 (1985)

JUSTICE BLACKMUN delivered the opinion of the Court.

The National Stolen Property Act provides for the imposition of criminal penalties upon any person who "transports in interstate or foreign commerce any goods, wares, merchandise, securities or money, of the value of $5,000 or more, knowing the same to have been stolen, converted or taken by fraud." 18 U.S.C. § 2314. In this case, we must determine whether the statute reaches the interstate transportation of "bootleg" phonorecords, "stolen, converted or taken by fraud" only in the sense that they were manufactured and distributed without the consent of the copyright owners of the musical compositions performed on the records. . . .

The offenses stemmed from an extensive bootleg record operation involving the manufacture and distribution by mail of recordings of vocal performances by Elvis Presley. The evidence demonstrated that sometime around 1976, Dowling, to that time an avid collector of Presley recordings, began in conjunction with codefendant William Samuel Theaker to manufacture phonorecords of unreleased Presley recordings. They used material from a variety of sources, including studio

(continued)

(continued)

outtakes, acetates, soundtracks from Presley motion pictures, and tapes of Presley concerts and television appearances. . . . The bootleg entrepreneurs never obtained authorization from or paid royalties to the owners of the copyrights in the musical compositions. . . .

The eight § 2314 counts on which Dowling was convicted arose out of six shipments of bootleg phonorecords from Los Angeles to Baltimore and two shipments from Los Angeles to Miami. The evidence established that each shipment included thousands of albums, that each album contained performances of copyrighted musical compositions for the use of which no licenses had been obtained nor royalties paid, and that the value of each shipment attributable to copyrighted material exceeded the statutory minimum. . . .

Federal crimes, of course, "are solely creatures of statute." Accordingly, when assessing the reach of a federal criminal statute, we must pay close heed to language, legislative history, and purpose in order strictly to determine the scope of the conduct the enactment forbids. Due respect for the prerogatives of Congress in defining federal crimes prompts restraint in this area, where we typically find a "narrow interpretation" appropriate . . . [T]he Court has stressed repeatedly that when choice has to be made between two readings of what conduct Congress has made a crime, it is appropriate, before we choose the harsher alternative, to require that Congress should have spoken in language that is clear and definite.

Applying that prudent rule of construction here, we examine at the outset the statutory language. Section 2314 requires, first, that the defendant have transported "goods, wares, [or] merchandise" in interstate or foreign commerce; second, that those goods have a value of "$5,000 or more"; and, third, that the defendant "[know] the same to have been stolen, converted or taken by fraud." Dowling does not contest that he caused the shipment of goods in interstate commerce or that the shipments had sufficient value to meet the monetary requirement. He argues, instead, that the goods shipped were not "stolen, converted or taken by fraud." In response, the Government does not suggest that Dowling wrongfully came by the phonorecords actually shipped or the physical materials from which they were made; nor does it contend that the objects that Dowling caused to be shipped, the bootleg phonorecords, were "the same" as the copyrights in the musical compositions that he infringed by unauthorized distribution of Presley performances of those compositions. The Government argues, however, that the shipments come within the reach of § 2314 because the phonorecords physically embodied performances of musical compositions that Dowling had no legal right to distribute. According to the Government, the unauthorized use of the musical compositions rendered the phonorecords "stolen, converted or taken by fraud" within the meaning of the statute.

We must determine, therefore, whether phonorecords that include the performance of copyrighted musical compositions for the use of which no authorization has been sought nor royalties paid are consequently "stolen, converted or taken by fraud" for purposes of § 2314. We conclude that they are not.

The courts interpreting § 2314 have never required, of course, that the items stolen and transported remain in entirely unaltered form. Nor does it matter that the item owes a major portion of its value to an intangible component. . . .

It follows that interference with copyright does not easily equate with theft, conversion, or fraud. The Copyright Act even employs a separate term of art to define one who misappropriates a copyright: Anyone who violates any of the exclusive rights of the copyright owner, that is, anyone who trespasses into his exclusive domain by using or authorizing the use of the copyrighted work in one of the five ways set forth in the statute, is an infringer of the copyright. There is no dispute in this case that Dowling's unauthorized inclusion on his bootleg albums of performances of copyrighted

(continued)

compositions constituted infringement of those copyrights. It is less clear, however, that the taking that occurs when an infringer arrogates the use of another's protected work comfortably fits the terms associated with physical removal employed by § 2314. The infringer invades a statutorily defined province guaranteed to the copyright holder alone. But he does not assume physical control over the copyright; nor does he wholly deprive its owner of its use. While one may colloquially link infringement with some general notion of wrongful appropriation, infringement plainly implicates a more complex set of property interests than does run-of-the-mill theft, conversion, or fraud. As a result, it fits but awkwardly with the language Congress chose—"stolen, converted or taken by fraud"—to describe the sorts of goods whose interstate shipment § 2314 makes criminal. And, when interpreting a criminal statute that does not explicitly reach the conduct in question, we are reluctant to base an expansive reading on inferences drawn from subjective and variable understandings. . . .

Congress always has had the bestowed authority to legislate directly in this area. Article I, § 8, cl. 8, of the Constitution provides that Congress shall have the power:

> To promote the Progress of Science and useful Arts, by securing for limited Times to Authors and Inventors the exclusive Right to their respective Writings and Discoveries.

By virtue of the explicit constitutional grant, Congress has the unquestioned authority to penalize directly the distribution of goods that infringe copyright, whether or not those goods affect interstate commerce. Given that power, it is implausible to suppose that Congress intended to combat the problem of copyright infringement by the circuitous route hypothesized by the Government. Of course, the enactment of criminal penalties for copyright infringement would not prevent Congress from choosing as well to criminalize the interstate shipment of infringing goods. But in dealing with the distribution of such goods, Congress has never thought it necessary to distinguish between intrastate and interstate activity. Nor does any good reason to do so occur to us. In sum, the premise of § 2314—the need to fill with federal action an enforcement chasm created by limited state jurisdiction—simply does not apply to the conduct the Government seeks to reach here.

WHAT DO *YOU* THINK?

1. When you use the word *stolen*, what do you mean by it?
2. Do you agree with the Court's interpretation of the word? Why or why not?

IN THE FIELD

Most legal professionals in the criminal justice system routinely handle theft or larceny cases. In most of these cases, the value of the property taken is relatively small, ranging from the small-dollar shoplifting case to the few-hundred-dollar cash theft. For legal professionals working on these cases, the primary task is to ensure there is sufficient evidence to show that the defendant took the property in question and that the value of the property is properly identified. Keep in mind, the value of the allegedly stolen property will largely determine the level of the theft offense charged. Under some statutory schemes, if a person steals $499, it is a misdemeanor, but if $500 is taken, it is a felony. And in cases where the stolen property is not currency, its value may not be clear. For example, if someone steals a laptop computer from a store, prosecutors, defense attorneys, and the store owner/victim may debate whether to use the wholesale price, the retail price, or the sale price to determine the proper value of the computer.

(continued)

> In larger theft cases, it may be more difficult to determine the exact value of the property taken. Sometimes, property is stolen over the course of months or even years. And as a result, tracing the amount of loss can be tricky and contested, often requiring the use of a forensic accountant or other investigator.

EMBEZZLEMENT

embezzlement
the unlawful conversion of the personal property of another by a person to whom it has been entrusted by, or for, its rightful owner

As mentioned earlier, larceny requires a trespassory *taking* of another's property. Under some circumstances, however, property may be misappropriated without the need for a trespassory taking. Generally, *embezzlement* is the unlawful conversion of the personal property of another by a person to whom it has been entrusted by, or for, its rightful owner. The standard elements of an embezzlement offense are

- a deceptive or fraudulent conversion
- of property
- belonging to another
- by a person entrusted with custody or control of this property

Embezzlement is essentially a larceny or theft offense committed by someone in violation of a position of trust. For example, Virginia Code Section 18.2-111 is entitled, "Embezzlement deemed larceny; indictment," and addresses embezzlement as follows:

> If any person wrongfully and fraudulently use, dispose of, conceal or embezzle any money, bill, note, check, order, draft, bond, receipt, bill of lading or any other personal property, tangible or intangible, which he shall have received for another or for his employer, principal or bailor, or by virtue of his office, trust, or employment, or which shall have been entrusted or delivered to him by another or by any court, corporation or company, he shall be guilty of embezzlement. Proof of embezzlement shall be sufficient to sustain the charge of larceny. Any person convicted hereunder shall be deemed guilty of larceny and may be indicted as for larceny. . . .

conversion
an element of embezzlement, whereby property is converted to an unauthorized use

Generally, an embezzlement offense is not a crime against possession but one against ownership because the embezzler already has lawful possession of the property in question. The central feature of the crime of embezzlement is unlawful ***conversion***. Although the original taking of possession occurs legally, embezzled property is converted to an unauthorized use. For example, if a woman's employer gives her money to take to the bank for deposit into the company's account, but the employee takes the money and spends it instead, she is guilty of embezzlement. One can be guilty of embezzlement only if the embezzled property belongs to another, since transferring ownership of an item to one who already owns it is not a crime.

Law Line 5-2
Embezzlement

To commit embezzlement, employees must occupy a position of financial trust and must be sufficiently familiar with company procedures to steal and to cover up their wrongdoings. As a consequence, most embezzlers appear to be law-abiding citizens until they are discovered. Embezzlers are sometimes called *white-collar criminals* because of the relatively prestigious positions they often occupy within the business world.

In some jurisdictions, embezzlement is known as *fraudulent conversion* since it involves the misappropriation of property entrusted to one's care (Figure 5-2). In

FIGURE 5-2 **Embezzlement**

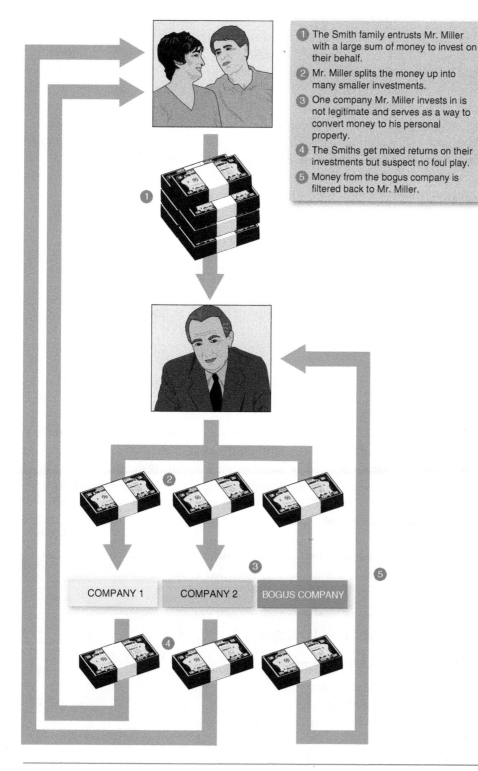

1. The Smith family entrusts Mr. Miller with a large sum of money to invest on their behalf.
2. Mr. Miller splits the money up into many smaller investments.
3. One company Mr. Miller invests in is not legitimate and serves as a way to convert money to his personal property.
4. The Smiths get mixed returns on their investments but suspect no foul play.
5. Money from the bogus company is filtered back to Mr. Miller.

COMPANY 1   COMPANY 2   BOGUS COMPANY

other jurisdictions, embezzlement is not classified as a separate criminal offense. Instead, thefts committed by persons holding a position of trust are prosecuted by way of basic theft or larceny statutes, which can increase the offense level and/or potential sentence in cases where the theft was facilitated by the defendant's breach of trust.

FRAUD (FALSE PRETENSES AND LARCENY BY TRICK)

false pretenses
a form of theft that involves transfer of ownership or title

Theft or larceny also can be committed through the use of falsehoods, deception, or trickery. There are at least three different forms of criminal laws used to address such conduct. Some statutes identify the crime of obtaining property by *false pretenses*, a form of theft that involves transfer of ownership or title. In general, false pretenses can be defined as knowingly and unlawfully obtaining title to, and possession of, the lawful property of another by means of deception and with intent to defraud. To constitute a crime, the false pretenses (false representation) must be material, that is, it must play an important role in a reasonable person's decision whether to enter into the fraudulent transaction. Accordingly, the core elements of a false pretenses offense are

- obtaining title
- to the property belonging to another person
- by intentional or knowing deception or misrepresentation of a material fact
- with the intent to deceive or defraud the possessor or owner of property

larceny by trick
a common law form of larceny that involves a person using trickery to gain possession, not title, to another's property

Other jurisdictions identify the crime of *larceny by trick*, which involves a person using trickery to gain possession, not title, to another's property. If, for example, a defendant obtains a car from an automobile dealership, takes it for a test-drive, and keeps the car, the defendant obtains only possession and not title— leading to a possible charge of larceny or larceny by trick. If, however, the defendant obtains both the car and title to the vehicle by paying for the car with a worthless check, then the defendant has committed, at a minimum, the offense of obtaining property by false pretenses.

fraud
a modern-day crime involving the act of defrauding; generally includes the knowing act of obtaining property by deception

But perhaps the most common legislative method used to address theft by deception comes in the form of criminal fraud statutes. A *fraud*, or the act of defrauding, is generally defined as "to knowingly obtain, by deception, some benefit for oneself or another, or to knowingly cause, by deception, some detriment to another." There are many different statutory forms of fraud offenses, including mail fraud, wire fraud, bank fraud, insurance fraud, and so forth. See Figure 5-3. Fraud statutes are widely used in federal criminal cases to prosecute individuals who use deceptive measures to cause the loss of property, services, or other benefits

FIGURE 5-3 **Federal Fraud Offenses**

Title 18 U.S. Code Chapter 63—Mail Fraud and Other Fraud Offenses

- ☐ § 1341. Frauds and swindles
- ☐ § 1342. Fictitious name or address
- ☐ § 1343. Fraud by wire, radio, or television
- ☐ § 1344. Bank fraud
- ☐ § 1345. Injunctions against fraud
- ☐ § 1346. Definition of "scheme or artifice to defraud"
- ☐ § 1347. Health care fraud
- ☐ § 1348. Securities fraud
- ☐ § 1349. Attempt and conspiracy
- ☐ § 1350. Failure of corporate officers to certify financial reports
- ☐ § 1351. Fraud in foreign labor contracting

to others. If a person's fraudulent conduct involves interstate commerce, including the use of U.S. mail services, interstate roadways, the Internet, phone lines, or other forms of interstate commerce, federal criminal laws generally will apply.

The basic structure of a criminal fraud statute is simple. For example, 18 U.S.C. § 1344, (the federal bank fraud law), reads:

Whoever knowingly executes, or attempts to execute, a scheme or artifice—

1. to defraud a financial institution; or
2. to obtain any of the moneys, funds, credits, assets, securities, or other property owned by, or under the custody or control of, a financial institution, by means of false or fraudulent pretenses, representations, or promises; shall be fined not more than $1,000,000 or imprisoned not more than 30 years, or both.

Similarly, 18 U.S.C. § 1343, the federal wire fraud law provides in part:

Whoever, having devised or intending to devise any scheme or artifice to defraud, or for obtaining money or property by means of false or fraudulent pretenses, representations, or promises, transmits or causes to be transmitted by means of wire, radio, or television communication in interstate or foreign commerce, any writings, signs, signals, pictures, or sounds for the purpose

Law Line 5-3
National Fraud Information Center

IN THE FIELD

For some criminal practitioners, particularly those who handle federal cases, fraud-based offenses can be a regular part of the daily practice of law. Many of these cases will involve highly complex financial transactions and detailed accounting materials, which are often not readily understood by most legal professionals. As a result, both prosecutors and criminal defense lawyers often employ a forensic accountant or other financial expert to review the evidence and determine whether fraudulent activity is present. The challenge for many legal professionals is learning the financial details of a case, so that they may be applied under the legal standards.

For example, in March 2009, Bernard Madoff, a New York stock broker and investment banker, entered a federal plea agreement to eleven counts of fraud-related offenses. As a part of his plea agreement, Madoff admitted to running one of the largest Ponzi schemes in American history, which resulted in investors losing billions of dollars. A ***Ponzi scheme*** is a form of investment fraud, whereby payments are made to current investors from money contributed by new investors. In Madoff's case, this scheme occurred over the course of many years. Federal authorities had investigated Madoff earlier, but due to the elaborate and complex nature of Madoff's financial scheme, many agents could not figure out what he was doing. It took several years and ultimately a confession from Madoff to finally confirm this as a criminal scheme. On June 29, 2009, a federal judge sentenced Madoff to 150 years in prison. See the accompanying photo of Madoff.

Legal professionals often learn that, in a free market economy, there are times when there is a fine line between fraud and effective salesmanship. In other words, in some criminal fraud cases, prosecutors may view defendants' conduct as unduly deceptive, while defendants may argue that their behavior was within acceptable standards of selling a particular product or service. As a result, legal professionals will often find themselves debating the concept and meaning of "fraud" or "defraud" under the relevant criminal code.

Ponzi scheme
a form of investment fraud, whereby payments are made to current investors from money contributed by new investors

Bernard L. Madoff arrives on March 12, 2009, at federal court in Manhattan, where he pleaded guilty to charges in connection with a $65 billion Ponzi scheme. On June 29, 2009, the court sentenced Madoff to 150 years in prison.

Law Line 5-4
Ponzi Scheme

of executing such scheme or artifice, shall be fined under this title or imprisoned not more than 20 years, or both. . . .

Along with other fraud-related statutes, these two criminal laws provide federal prosecutors with substantial tools to target and punish individuals who dupe others out of property or other valuables.

FORGERY

The legal principles underlying the crime of false pretenses extend to many other illegal activities, including the writing of bad checks, credit card fraud, the unlawful altering of wills, counterfeiting, and any other crimes through which ownership of property is obtained by fraud. A number of such crimes, however, have been separately codified by legislative action and are worthy of separate mention. One such offense is forgery.

forgery
the making of a false written instrument or the material alteration of an existing genuine written instrument

uttering
the offering, passing, or attempted passing of a forged document with knowledge that the document is false and with intent to defraud

Forgery is the making of a false written instrument or the material alteration of an existing genuine written instrument. Forgery is complete when the perpetrator either makes or passes a false instrument with intent to defraud. The gist of the crime of forgery is the actual intent to defraud, and the act of defrauding is itself not required. The common law crime of forgery, however, included the act of "uttering" a forged document, and the crime was sometimes referred to as *forgery and uttering. Uttering* is the offering, passing, or attempted passing of a forged document with knowledge that the document is false and with intent to defraud. Today, most jurisdictions have established a separate statutory crime of uttering a forged document.[20] The most common elements of forgery are

- a false signature or material alteration
- signed or altered without authority
- of a writing or other instrument that, if genuine, would have legal significance
- with intent to defraud

The elements of the crime of uttering, passing, publishing, or attempting to pass are

- possession or creation of a forged document that, if genuine, would have legal significance
- uttering, passing, publishing, or attempting to pass the forged document
- with intent to defraud

For an instrument to be subject to forgery, the instrument—if it were genuine—would have to create some legal right or obligation with apparent legal significance. If the instrument has no legal significance, then it is not subject to forgery. Instruments said to have legal significance include checks, wills, college transcripts, college diplomas, insurance proof-of-loss forms, divorce decrees, badges, stamps, credit cards, credit card receipts, and trademarks.

Many jurisdictions have enacted the statutory crime of **criminal simulation**.[21] Criminal simulation is different from forgery in that the item or document falsified need not have any apparent legal significance. Making a piece of furniture to pass off as an antique, for example, constitutes the crime of criminal simulation. Criminal simulation, like forgery, requires an intent to defraud or harm another. It is generally classified as a misdemeanor. For example, Ohio Revised Code Section 2913.32 prohibits criminal simulation by stating:

> (A) No person, with purpose to defraud, or knowing that the person is facilitating a fraud, shall do any of the following:
>
> 1. Make or alter any object so that it appears to have value because of antiquity, rarity, curiosity, source, or authorship, which it does not in fact possess;
> 2. Practice deception in making, retouching, editing, or reproducing any photograph, movie film, video tape, phonograph record, or recording tape;
> 3. Falsely or fraudulently make, simulate, forge, alter, or counterfeit any wrapper, label, stamp, cork, or cap prescribed by the liquor control commission . . . falsely or fraudulently cause to be made, simulated, forged, altered, or counterfeited any wrapper, label, stamp, cork, or cap prescribed by the liquor control commission . . . or use more than once any wrapper, label, stamp, cork, or cap prescribed by the liquor control commission . . .
> 4. Utter, or possess with purpose to utter, any object that the person knows to have been simulated. . . .

Criminal laws against forgery and against criminal simulation have undergone sweeping changes, in an effort to keep pace with advancements in electronic documents. Such documents, which may never be printed on paper, provide for critically needed authentication and identification during financial and other transactions conducted via computer and over telephone and radio communications. As a result, legislators have amended statutory language to account for this expanded concept. For example, the word *writing* has been redefined to include "any computer software, document, letter, memorandum, note, paper, plate, data, film, or other thing having in or upon it any written, typewritten, or printed matter, and any token, stamp, seal, credit card, badge, trademark, label, or other symbol of value, right, privilege, license, or identification."[22] As new methods of creating, storing, and altering information become available, legislators likely will continue to amend criminal simulation and forgery statutes.

criminal simulation
a crime similar to forgery, but involves the falsification or reclassification of an item for material gain; the item or document falsified need not have any apparent legal significance, such as a fake antique

RECEIVING STOLEN PROPERTY

receiving stolen property
knowingly taking possession of, or control over, property that has been unlawfully stolen from another

Another form of theft is ***receiving stolen property***, which is generally defined as knowingly taking possession of, or control over, property that has been unlawfully stolen from another. In most statutes, *receiving* means the taking possession of, acquiring control over, or taking title to any property. Under early common law, receiving stolen property was not a crime. But today, all U.S. jurisdictions have the statutory crime of receiving stolen property, although in some criminal codes, it is written as part of a general theft statute. There are four elements to the crime of receiving stolen property[23]

- receiving
- stolen property
- which the receiver knew was stolen
- where the property was received with the intent to deprive the rightful owner of its possession

If the property in question has not been stolen, then the crime of receiving stolen property cannot take place. Property that has been stolen and recovered can no longer be considered stolen property. If law enforcement officers recover stolen property and then attempt to entrap a person into receiving stolen property by selling it or delivering it to him, the crime of receiving stolen property cannot be charged. This conclusion is based on the principle that once property has been recovered by lawful authorities, it is no longer stolen.

Similarly, in almost all jurisdictions, the crime of receiving stolen property requires that the defendant know or have reason to know that the property was stolen. For example, Ohio Revised Code Section 2913.51 (A) provides, "No person shall receive, retain, or dispose of property of another knowing or having reasonable cause to believe that the property has been obtained through commission of a theft offense." Such knowledge may be established by circumstantial evidence, such as when a defendant pays an unreasonably low price for the merchandise.

In addition, in most jurisdictions, a person's receipt of stolen property does not have to involve the actual possession of the property. Instead, individuals may receive stolen property where they constructively possess the stolen items. This might involve a situation where a person arranges to have the stolen property placed in a designated location or makes arrangements for an immediate sale of the property to a third person. Under these circumstances, the person did not have actual possession of the property, but rather exercised sufficient dominion and control over the items to constitute ***constructive possession***.

constructive possession
the exercise of sufficient dominion and control over property without physically possessing the item

The crime of receiving stolen property is different from the theft of the property itself, and a defendant who steals property cannot be convicted of receiving the same property. In other words, thieves cannot receive stolen property from themselves.[24]

ROBBERY

robbery
the unlawful taking of property that is in the immediate possession of another by force or threat of force

The Federal Bureau of Investigation (FBI) classifies robbery as a violent personal crime. We classify it here as a property crime, rather than as a personal crime, because the *object* of robbery is the unlawful acquisition of property, even though the property may be forcefully taken from the personal possession of another. ***Robbery*** is the unlawful taking of property that is in the immediate possession of another by force or threat of force. Section 160.00 of New York's

Criminal Code identifies robbery as "forcible stealing." This law further provides:

> A person forcibly steals property and commits robbery when, in the course of committing a larceny, he uses or threatens the immediate use of physical force upon another person for the purpose of:
>
> 1. Preventing or overcoming resistance to the taking of the property or to the retention thereof immediately after the taking; or
> 2. Compelling the owner of such property or another person to deliver up the property or to engage in other conduct which aids in the commission of the larceny.

One view of robbery is that it is simply an aggravated form of larceny. But in addition to the elements of a basic larceny offense, a robbery offense typically requires two more elements: (1) that the property be taken from a person or removed from the victim's presence and (2) that the taking occur through the use of force or by putting the victim in fear. As the last element indicates, actual force need not be used, and the threatened use of force suffices to constitute robbery. Accordingly, the elements of the crime of robbery are

- the felonious taking of personal property
- from the person or immediate presence of another
- against the will of the victim
- and accomplished by means of force or by putting the victim in fear of imminent harm

Some crimes, such as pocket picking and purse snatching, also involve the unlawful taking of property from the immediate possession of another person. Accordingly, under some statutory schemes, these offenses might be classified as crimes of larceny or robbery. But in other jurisdictions, these types of actions are not classified as larceny or robbery because the stolen property is taken before the victim is aware of what is happening and no violence or intimidation is used in committing such crimes. If a purse snatcher or pickpocket misses the target on the first "grab," however, and a struggle ensues before the purse or wallet is taken, then the offender is guilty of robbery.

In cases of robbery, it is generally easy to establish that property has been taken *from a person*—as happens in instances of armed robbery, where the robber demands a person's wallet or jewelry that he or she is wearing. Problems arise, however, when property is not taken from a person but is merely removed *from the presence of the victim*. The test to determine if the property is taken from the presence of the victim is whether the victim, at the time of the offense, was in a location where the taking could have been prevented had the defendant not intimidated or forcibly restrained the victim from stopping the taking of property. In cases where property is stolen from a person who is unconscious or dead, the crime might be basic larceny, rather than robbery, because no force is used and the "victim" is not threatened. If, however, the person from whom valuables are stolen is unconscious, and if the cause of unconsciousness was some intentional action on the part of the thief, then most courts would hold that robbery has occurred.

It is important to note that robbery, in most jurisdictions, requires either using or threatening to use imminent force *or* putting the victim in fear of imminent harm. One or the other will suffice. *Fear* means "intimidation." Some states use an objective standard to determine whether intimidation occurred; they ask whether the circumstances would have induced fear in the mind of a reasonable person. Other states use a subjective standard; they ask whether the person robbed actually experienced fear. Accordingly, in such jurisdictions, if the victim is unusually timid, robbery can occur even though the average person would not have felt apprehensive under similar circumstances. For example, Ohio Revised Code Section 2911.02 defines robbery as the following:

(A) No person, in attempting or committing a theft offense or in fleeing immediately after the attempt or offense, shall do any of the following:

1. Have a deadly weapon on or about the offender's person or under the offender's control;
2. Inflict, attempt to inflict, or threaten to inflict physical harm on another;
3. Use or threaten the immediate use of force against another.

Most jurisdictions recognize various degrees of robbery. First-degree robbery, for example, may be armed robbery, which is a robbery committed with the use of a dangerous or deadly weapon or robbery in which the victim is seriously injured. First-degree robbery is sometimes termed *aggravated robbery.* Second-degree robbery, sometimes called *strong-arm robbery,* may be robbery in which no weapon is used or where the victim is not seriously injured. In many jurisdictions, the primary difference between aggravated robbery (first-degree) and robbery (second-degree) is the seriousness of the injuries sustained by the victim. Crimes involving little or no injuries are often classified as robbery, while those involving more serious harm are deemed aggravated robberies. Some states, like New York, make even finer distinctions and have three or more degrees of robbery defined by statute.

In deciding what degree of robbery a defendant can be charged with, it is important to know (1) what constitutes a deadly weapon and (2) what constitutes a serious injury. *Serious bodily injury* has often been interpreted to mean an injury that requires medical treatment. The definition of a *deadly weapon* has proved more complex. Some state statutes specify that armed robbery is any robbery committed with a firearm, making the definition of a deadly weapon relatively straightforward. Most statutes, however, avoid use of the term *firearm* and refer instead to *deadly weapon* or *dangerous weapon.*

The dangerousness (or deadliness) of a weapon is sometimes assessed on the basis of its construction and purpose, as well as the use to which it is put during the offense. As a result, guns, knives, screwdrivers, hammers, axes, clubs, sticks, and even dogs and high-heeled shoes and boots have been found to be deadly weapons within the meaning of robbery statutes. Some courts have gone so far as to conclude that a deadly weapon is anything that appears to be such from the point of view of the victim, meaning that even toy guns (and, in at least one case, a hairbrush hidden in a robber's pocket and held to look like a gun) can meet the criteria for a deadly weapon. Finally, some courts have found that a robber in possession of a deadly weapon at the time of the robbery, such as a gun or a knife, has committed armed robbery even though the weapon remained concealed and was never brought to the attention of the victim.

EXTORTION

extortion

under common law, the corrupt collection of an unlawful fee by a public officer under color of office or the attempt to collect such a fee; today, the threat of future actions to wrongfully obtain property or services

Under early common law, **extortion** was the corrupt collection of an unlawful fee by a public officer under color of office or the attempt to collect such a fee. Today, almost all U.S. jurisdictions have expanded the crime of extortion to cover anyone

ETHICAL PRINCIPLES

ATTORNEY SUPERVISION

National Association of Legal Assistants Code of Ethics and Professional Responsibility Canon 2

A paralegal may perform any task which is properly delegated and supervised by an attorney, as long as the attorney is ultimately responsible to the client, maintains a direct relationship with the client, and assumes professional responsibility for the work product.

Courtesy of The National Association of Legal Assistants

who uses the threat of future actions to wrongfully obtain property or services. Statutory extortion is a felony in most jurisdictions. The basic elements of this offense are

- the intent to take or acquire
- the personal property
- belonging to another person
- by a threat of future harm

Under federal law, extortion and blackmail are punished in various forms. For example, 18 U.S.C. § 872 criminalizes extortion by federal government officials; 18 U.S.C. § 873 makes it a crime to blackmail someone who has violated federal law by offering to remain quiet about the violation in exchange for compensation; 18 U.S.C. §§ 875–877 prohibit the use of U.S. mail or interstate commerce to communicate threats with the intent to extort a thing of value; and 18 U.S.C. § 1951, also known as the Hobbs Act, prohibits racketeering, including the use of robbery or extortion, in interstate commerce.[25]

Law Line 5-5
Federal RICO Statute

Extortion differs from the crime of robbery in that robbery occurs when property is taken by force or threat of immediate violence. In extortion, the defendant obtains property by threat of *future* harm to the person being threatened or to someone this person values. The threat of harm can be physical in nature. But some jurisdictions allow the threatened harm to extend to various other forms of injury, such as the threatened accusation of a crime or civil suit. For example, *blackmail* is a form of extortion in which a threat is made to disclose a crime or other social disgrace. Even a threat to cause economic injury or social embarrassment may be sufficient to constitute extortion in most jurisdictions. A threat to bring a lawsuit or to take other official action, unless the property is given or returned to the defendant, may also constitute extortion. It is a defense under such circumstances, however, if the defendant honestly and lawfully claimed the property as restitution or indemnification for harm done, to which the lawsuit or other official action relates, or as compensation for property or other lawful services.[26]

blackmail
a form of extortion in which a threat is made to disclose a crime or other social disgrace

It should be noted that extortion differs from the offense of ***compounding a crime***, also known as *compounding a felony*, which "consists of the receipt of property or other valuable consideration in exchange for an agreement to conceal or not prosecute one who has committed a crime."[27] Compounding a crime usually involves a mutual agreement between parties, whereas extortion is based on a qualified threat.

compounding a crime
obtaining property or valuable items in exchange for an agreement not to expose a criminal act; also known as compounding a felony

IDENTITY THEFT: A TWENTY-FIRST-CENTURY FORM OF FRAUD

identity theft
the unauthorized use of another individual's personal identity information to fraudulently obtain money, goods, or services

Identity Theft and Assumption Deterrence Act (1998)
a federal law that makes it a crime to knowingly transfer or use, without lawful authority, a means of identification of another person with the intent to commit a crime.

Identity theft is rapidly becoming the most important new theft crime of the twenty-first century. In general, identity theft is viewed as the unauthorized use of another individual's personal identity information to fraudulently obtain money, goods, or services; to avoid the payment of debt; or to avoid criminal prosecution.

At the federal level, one of the primary legislative tools used to fight identity theft is the *Identity Theft and Assumption Deterrence Act (1998)* (also known as the *Identity Theft Act*).[28] This law makes it a federal offense to knowingly transfer or use, without lawful authority, a means of identification of another person with the intent to commit, or to aid or abet, any unlawful activity that constitutes a violation of federal law or that constitutes a felony under any applicable state or local law.[29] The statute defines *means of identification* to include "any name or number that may be used, alone or in conjunction with any other information, to identify a specific individual," including, among other things, name, address, Social Security number, driver's license number, biometric data, access devices (e.g., credit cards), electronic identification number or routing code, and telecommunications identifying information. In addition, some forms of identity theft may also violate more traditional criminal statutes, including identification fraud (18 U.S.C. § 1028), credit card fraud (18 U.S.C. § 1029), computer fraud (18 U.S.C. § 1030), mail fraud (18 U.S.C. § 1341), wire fraud (18 U.S.C. § 1343), or bank fraud (18 U.S.C. § 1344).

At the federal level, the Federal Trade Commission (FTC) runs a clearinghouse for complaints by victims of identity theft. Although the FTC does not have the authority to bring criminal cases, the commission provides victims of identity theft with information to help them resolve the financial and other problems that can result from such illegal activity.

Most states also have statutes criminalizing identity theft. Following are two examples of identity theft statutes from Arizona and Connecticut.

Arizona Criminal Code Section 2708

  A. A person commits taking the identity of another person if the person knowingly takes the name, birth date or Social Security number of another person, without the consent of that other person, with the intent to obtain or use the other person's identity for any unlawful purpose or to cause loss to a person.

  B. Taking the identity of another person is a class 5 felony.

Connecticut Public Act No. 99-99

  A. A person is guilty of identity theft when such person intentionally obtains personal identifying information of another person without the authorization of such other person and uses that information for any unlawful purpose including, but not limited to, obtaining, or attempting to obtain, credit, goods, services or medical information in the name of such other person without the consent of such other person. As used in this section, "personal identifying information" means a motor vehicle operator's license number, Social Security number, employee identification number, mother's maiden name, demand deposit number, savings account number or credit card number.

  B. Identity theft is a class D felony.

State identity theft laws are typically used to punish comparatively minor forms of the crime not governed by the federal Identity Theft Act, which typically only covers thefts of $50,000 or more. The FTC says that identity theft can be perpetrated based on simple low-tech practices, such as stealing someone's mail or "dumpster diving" through a person's trash to find identifying information. But other cases involve far more sophisticated schemes. In a practice known as *skimming*, identity thieves use computers to read and store the information encoded on the magnetic strip of an ATM or credit card when that card is inserted through either a specialized card reader or a legitimate payment mechanism. Once stored, the information can be reencoded onto any other card with a magnetic strip, instantly transforming a blank card into a machine-readable ATM or credit card identical to that of the victim.[30]

Law Line 5-6
Identity Theft

CONSOLIDATION OF THEFT CRIMES

Because of the complexities that can surround any given instance of theft, it has traditionally been difficult for prosecutors to know how to properly charge some defendants. The fine distinctions drawn by statutes, combined with the many statutory varieties of theft in some jurisdictions, have exacerbated the problem. As a result, attorneys and legal scholars suggested some years ago to consolidate the crimes of larceny, embezzlement, and false pretenses. The suggestions were based on the belief that the misappropriation of property by stealth, conversion, and deception represent different aspects of one general type of harm. The 1962 draft of the Model Penal Code incorporated a consolidated theft provision (Section 223.1) that has since been adopted by many states. The MPC provision covers larceny, embezzlement, and false pretenses, as well as extortion, blackmail, and receiving stolen property. In effect, the MPC provision encompasses all nonviolent crimes involving the misappropriation of property, while placing robbery (because it involves violence or the threat of violence) in a separate category.

Today, in recognition of the common principles underlying theft offenses, a fair number of jurisdictions, including New York, Texas, and California, have statutorily consolidated all or most common law theft crimes under one heading. As is the case with the Model Penal Code, such laws generally combine two or more of the crimes of larceny, embezzlement, extortion, receiving stolen property, and false pretenses into one crime called *theft* or, as in New York, *larceny*. The New York law, in contrast to the consolidated theft statutes of some other states, does not include the crime of receiving stolen property, although it does incorporate the offense of acquiring lost property.

BURGLARY

Burglary is another wrongful acquisition crime directed against property. Burglary involves more than theft, however, and under common law it was considered to be a crime against habitation (or one's dwelling). Under common law, burglary consisted of the breaking and entering of the dwelling house of another at night with intent to commit a felony. In most jurisdictions today, however, the crime of **burglary** involves the following elements

- the use of force (breaking) or deception
- to enter
- a building, locked automobile, boat, and so on
- with the intent to commit a felony or theft

burglary
the use of force (breaking) or deception to enter a building or vehicle with the intent to commit a felony or theft

Most jurisdictions divide the crime of burglary into burglary in the first and second degrees. Burglary in the first degree is burglary of an inhabited dwelling. All other burglaries are second-degree burglaries. Some jurisdictions maintain the nighttime distinction, classifying burglaries of inhabited dwellings that occur at night as more serious than other burglaries.

Breaking or Use of Force

Some burglary statutes require the offender to actually break into a property. The "breaking" requirement does not necessitate any damage to the property burglarized, although it is usually interpreted as requiring the use of actual or constructive force to create an opening in the thing burglarized. The opening of any part of a structure with the slightest amount of force will suffice. As a result, while an entry through an already open door is not sufficient to meet the breaking requirement of burglary in most jurisdictions, the simple act of opening a closed door, even one that is unlocked, is sufficient. Many jurisdictions hold that the application of force to enlarge an already existing opening also satisfies the breaking requirement, while other jurisdictions hold that enlargement is not sufficient.[31]

Some years ago, one court explained the amount of force necessary to constitute a breaking this way: "The gist of burglarious breaking is the application of force to remove some obstacle to entry, and the amount of force employed is not material. The exercise of the slightest force is sufficient. The breaking consists of the removal by the intruder, by the exercise of force, of an obstruction which, if left untouched, would prevent entrance. Accordingly, the application of force to push further open an already partly open door or window to enable a person to enter a room or building, is a breaking sufficient to constitute burglary if the other essential elements of the offense are present."[32] In other words, although a breaking needs only the tiniest physical force, the concept of breaking requires more than merely passing over or through an imaginary line or threshold separating one defined space from another (Figure 5-4). Most jurisdictions hold that the use of force merely to exit does not constitute burglary,[33] although a few follow an old common law rule that "breaking out of a building in making an exit is sufficient"[34] for the "breaking" requirement.

In other jurisdictions, a burglary offense can be committed without using force to break into a property. In those settings, burglaries can be committed through deceptive or less destructive means. For example, Ohio Revised Code Section 2911.12 (A)(1) defines burglary by stating:

> (A) No person, by force, stealth, or deception, shall do any of the following:
> (1) Trespass in an occupied structure or in a separately secured or separately occupied portion of an occupied structure, when another person other than an accomplice of the offender is present, with purpose to commit in the structure or in the separately secured or separately occupied portion of the structure any criminal offense;

In some courts, obtaining entry by fraud, by threatening to use force against another person, by entering through a chimney, and by having a coconspirator open a door from within have all been held sufficient to constitute *constructive* breaking. Jurisdictions differ, however, on whether defendants who have entered without a breaking—whether constructive or actual—commit the crime of burglary when they use force to exit the structure, as when they hide in a department store washroom before closing and break out of the store during the night with purloined merchandise.

The Need for Trespass

Generally speaking, breaking must be trespassory. As a result, a defendant who has permission to enter a structure cannot be found guilty of burglary in most

FIGURE 5-4 **Defining "Breaking" in Burglary Cases**

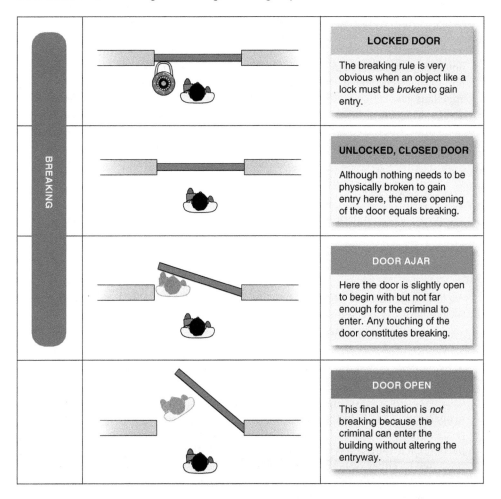

BREAKING

LOCKED DOOR

The breaking rule is very obvious when an object like a lock must be *broken* to gain entry.

UNLOCKED, CLOSED DOOR

Although nothing needs to be physically broken to gain entry here, the mere opening of the door equals breaking.

DOOR AJAR

Here the door is slightly open to begin with but not far enough for the criminal to enter. Any touching of the door constitutes breaking.

DOOR OPEN

This final situation is *not* breaking because the criminal can enter the building without altering the entryway.

jurisdictions.[35] Courts will examine any purported consent to determine whether the defendant in fact had permission to be on the premises at the time in question and to be in the particular part of the structure he entered. To constitute a defense, consent to enter must have been given by the owner of the structure entered or by a person legally authorized to act on behalf of the owner. Consent is not effective if given by a person the defendant knows is not legally authorized to provide it. Read the court's opinion in *Folsom v. State* (1995), where the issue was whether an estranged spouse's forcible entry into the marital home was trespassory.

CAPSTONE CASE *Folsom v. State,* 668 So. 2d 114 (Ala. Crim. App. 1995)

The appellant, Paul Folsom, was convicted of sexual abuse in the first degree and of burglary in the first degree, violations of § 13A-6-66 and 13A-7-5, Code of Alabama 1975, respectively.

The appellant asserts that there was not sufficient evidence to convict him of burglary. He specifically contends that because his wife, from whom he was

(continued)

(continued)

separated at the time of the offense, owned the house, and because he had lived there during the marriage, he could not lawfully be convicted of burglary.

The state's evidence tended to show that the appellant and Patricia Criddle were married in August 1992 and that the appellant then moved into Criddle's house. Shortly after the marriage, the appellant became abusive and Criddle asked him to leave. The appellant had stayed in the house for approximately 35 days. The appellant gave Criddle the house keys in September 1992, and Criddle filed for divorce in October 1992. Criddle testified that on several occasions the appellant came to her house and kicked the door open. On December 13, 1992, the appellant kicked the back door open and lunged at Criddle with a knife.

The issue whether a spouse can burglarize the residence of the other spouse was addressed in depth in this court's opinion in *White v. State*, 587 So. 2d 1218 (Ala. Cr. App. 1990). This court stated:

> In Alabama, burglary, like trespass, is an offense against the possession, and hence the test for the purpose of determining in whom the ownership of the premises should be laid in an indictment is not the title, but the occupancy or possession at the time the offense was committed. A person "enters or remains unlawfully" in or upon premises when he is not licensed, invited or privileged to do so. Ala. Code 1975, § 13A-7-1(4). Under Alabama law, a person who is licensed or privileged to enter premises cannot commit criminal trespass or burglary. Johnson v. State, 473 So. 2d 607, 609 (Ala.Cr.App. 1985).

At the time of the crime, the defendant and his wife were separated. Some authorities broadly state that a man cannot burglarize his wife's home, and it is considered that the burglary statute is not designed to protect against entries by persons occupying a marital or immediate familial relationship with the legal possessor of property. So, it is held that in the absence of a legal separation agreement, or restraining order, or court decree limiting or ending the consortium rights of the parties, each spouse has a legal right to be with the other spouse on premises possessed by either or both spouses so long as the marriage exists, and entry onto such premises by either spouse cannot be a burglary, although a court order will negate any rights to enter the premises.

While the offense [of burglary] is not committed by one who breaks and enters his own dwelling or other building, it has, however, also been held that the mere existence of the marriage relationship does not preclude the one spouse from committing burglary against the other spouse.

We agree with the holding of the Florida Supreme Court in Cladd v. State, 398 So. 2d 442, 443-44 (Fla. 1981):

> The sole issue presented for review is whether a husband, who is physically but not legally separated from his wife, can be guilty of burglary when he enters premises, possessed only by the wife and in which he has no ownership or possessory interest, without the wife's consent and with intent to commit an offense therein. . . . We hold that under the particular facts of this case, the defendant could be guilty of burglary of his estranged wife's apartment. . . .

> The factual situation is narrow. The defendant and his wife had been separated for approximately six months, although there was no formal separation agreement or restraining order. He had no ownership or possessory interest in his wife's apartment and had at no time lived there. One morning, he broke through the locked door of her apartment with a crowbar, struck her, and attempted to throw her over the second floor stair railing. . . .

(continued)

We reject the defendant's contention that the marriage relationship and the right of consortium deriving therefrom preclude the State from ever establishing the nonconsensual entry requisite to the crime of burglary. . . . Since burglary is an invasion of the possessory property rights of another, where premises are in the sole possession of the wife, the husband can be guilty of burglary if he makes a nonconsensual entry into her premises with intent to commit an offense, the same as he can be guilty of larceny of his wife's separate property. In State v. Herndon, 158 Fla. 115, 27 So. 2d 833 (1946), discussing a wife's separate property rights, we held that a husband could be charged with the larceny of his wife's separate property, and we explained:

> In a society like ours, where the wife owns and holds property in her own right, where she can direct the use of her personal property as she pleases, where she can engage in business and pursue a career, it would be contrary to every principle of reason to hold that a husband could ad lib appropriate her property. If the common-law rule was of force, the husband could collect his wife's paycheck, he could direct its use, he could appropriate her separate property and direct the course of her career or business if she has one. We think it has not only been abrogated by law, it has been abrogated by custom, the very thing out of which the common law was derived.

> The defendant's consortium rights did not immunize him from burglary where he had no right to be on the premises possessed solely by his wife independent of an asserted right to consortium. . . .

The facts were sufficient to present the case to the jury on the issue whether the appellant was guilty of burglary.

The appellant further contends that there was not sufficient evidence to find him guilty of sexual abuse. Criddle testified that the appellant kicked open the door to her house, dragged her to the bedroom, forcibly placed an object in her vagina, and then had sexual intercourse with her. The victim's testimony alone was sufficient to present the case to the jury on the issue whether the appellant was guilty of sexual abuse. . . .

For the foregoing reasons, the judgment in this cause is due to be, and it is hereby, affirmed.

WHAT DO YOU THINK?

1. At what point does marriage give a spouse the right to enter the property of his or her marriage partner?
2. What test did the court apply in order to determine that the husband had no right to enter the home?
3. Are there other relationships that should also hold special legal status and established privileges similar to those of legal spouses at issue in this case? What challenges are involved in enforcing such privileges?

In addition to breaking, an actual or constructive entry into the structure is required for a burglary to occur. The slightest intrusion by the burglar or by any part of the burglar's body into the burglarized structure is sufficient to satisfy the requirement of an actual entry. Entry can also be accomplished by the insertion of a tool or other instrument into the structure burglarized. Drilling a hole into the floor of a granary, for example, in order to steal the grain that runs through the hole, would be considered an entry for purposes of the crime of burglary.[36]

constructive entry
causing another person or instrument to enter the property of another

A *constructive entry* occurs when the defendant causes another person (or a robot) to enter the structure to commit the crime or to achieve the felonious purpose. Sending an innocent six-year-old child into a house, for example, to retrieve something for the burglar would be a constructive entry. In one early case, an individual was convicted of burglary when he sent his dog into a house to retrieve the desired object. All American jurisdictions recognize the concept of a constructive entry in burglary cases.

Under common law, the burglarized structure had to be an occupied dwelling. Currently, in most jurisdictions, the burglarized structure must be an occupied dwelling to constitute first-degree burglary. Courts have generally held that as long as the structure that is burglarized is used to sleep in on a regular basis, it is an occupied dwelling for purposes of the law,[37] and it does not matter if the building is also used for business or other functions. During the temporary absence of the residents, an occupied dwelling is still considered "occupied," but it ceases to be an occupied dwelling when the residents permanently move out.[38] All jurisdictions now recognize at least one form of burglary that does not require that the structure in question be a dwelling. Most still require, however, that it be a building, although the definition of a *building* may be liberally interpreted. In one case, for example, a car wash, which was completely open on both ends, was considered to be a building.[39] In many states, including California, even though an automobile is not a building in the everyday sense of the word, a locked vehicle is also subject to being "burglarized."

Common law also required that the breaking and entry had to occur during hours of darkness. It did not matter if the dwelling was brightly illuminated with artificial light. No jurisdictions presently limit breaking and entering offenses to nighttime hours, although in many jurisdictions, burglary during the hours between sunset and sunrise is a higher degree of burglary than one committed under the same circumstances during daylight.

Burglary under common law also required the defendant to have intended to commit a felony, like rape, murder, or a theft offense, at the time of the entry. Presently, most jurisdictions follow this requirement. The theft offense in many jurisdictions, however, may be a misdemeanor (e.g., petty theft). In some jurisdictions, all that is necessary is that the defendant intend to commit any crime, and in a few, it is not necessary that the burglar intend to commit that crime in the burglarized structure. Entering a structure in order to be a lookout or to hide until another crime can be completed elsewhere, for example, may constitute burglary in some jurisdictions. Intent, however, does not require that an identifiable offense actually be committed. As a result, someone who breaks and enters someone else's house with murderous intent still commits burglary even if she is unable to find the intended victim.

The crime of burglary is completed when entry is made. Defendants who, for example, enter a building to steal something but, after entry, change their minds are still guilty of burglary. Generally, the crime of burglary is a felony, although most jurisdictions also recognize the statutory crimes of criminal trespass and looting.

Criminal Trespass, Looting, and Possession of Tools

criminal trespass
a lesser included offense of burglary; entering or remaining on the property or in the building of another when entry is forbidden or failing to depart after receiving notice to do so

criminal mischief
the intentional or knowing damage or destruction of the tangible property of another

Criminal trespass is a lesser included offense of burglary. Criminal trespass is entering or remaining on the property or in the building of another when entry is forbidden or failing to depart after receiving notice to do so.[40] A similar statutory crime against property is *criminal mischief*. Criminal mischief is the intentional or knowing damage or destruction of the tangible property of another. It is committed by those who deface or destroy property. In most jurisdictions, it is a misdemeanor.

Looting is another crime against property and can be defined as burglary committed within an affected geographic area during an officially declared state of emergency or during a local emergency resulting from an earthquake, fire, flood, riot, or other disaster.

Some jurisdictions also criminalize the possession of burglary tools—that is, the possession of tools that serve a special purpose in breaking and entering a secured structure. The **possession of burglary tools** is only a crime when it can be shown that the possessor had the intent to use those tools for the purpose of burglary.

ARSON

Under common law, **arson** was the malicious burning of the dwelling of another. Under this view, the crime was committed against habitation, not against property. But the modern statutes have expanded the scope of arson crimes to include many items other than structures, effectively transforming the crime into one against property. In the state of Washington, for example, arson includes the burning of hay, a bridge, a motor vehicle, and many other things. To constitute arson in the contemporary sense of the offense, there is no requirement that an entire structure be burned or even that a fire, in the normal sense of the word, ensue. Arson occurs with even the slightest malicious burning, although a discoloration or blackening by heat or smoke would not be regarded as sufficient to constitute a burning.

In almost all modern jurisdictions, arson requires the knowing and malicious burning of the fixture or personal property of another, and it includes the burning of one's own property if the purpose is to collect insurance money. Arson cannot be committed by negligent or reckless conduct, and there is no felony arson rule, as there is in the case of felony murder. In determining the pecuniary loss in arson cases, courts generally consider the fair market value of the property at the time it was destroyed or, in the case of damaged property, the cost of restoring it. Most states, like Washington, have divided arson into first and second degrees, with first-degree arson being the more aggravated form of arson.

Most jurisdictions also have statutes to punish those who recklessly start a fire or who unlawfully cause a fire. Such offenses differ from arson in that they may not include the "knowing and malicious" requirement necessary for the crime of arson. Section 452 of the California Penal Code, for example, provides that a person is guilty of unlawfully causing a fire when he or she recklessly sets fire to, burns, or causes to be burned any structure, forest land, or other property. Accordingly, a person may be convicted of unlawfully causing a fire because of recklessness. Under California law, the crime is a misdemeanor.

COMPUTER AND HIGH-TECHNOLOGY CRIMES

Criminal statutes often have trouble keeping pace with on rapidly changing nature of criminal theft activity. This is particularly true when it comes to the growth of technology, and especially computer technology, that has brought with it new types of property crimes. Many of these crimes involve the theft of electronic forms of **intellectual property**, specifically the proprietary information stored in computers and digital devices and on electromagnetic, optical, and other storage media. During the past twenty years, all of the states, the federal government, and

looting
a burglary committed within an affected geographic area during an officially declared state of emergency or during a local emergency resulting from an earthquake, fire, flood, riot, or other disaster; a crime against property

possession of burglary tools
the possession of instruments with the intent to use those tools for the purpose of burglary

arson
at common law, the malicious burning of the dwelling of another; today, a much broader crime involving many forms of malicious burning

intellectual property
protected and proprietary information stored in computers and digital devices and on electromagnetic, optical, and other storage media

computer crime
crimes involving the use or acquisition of computers or other electronic devices or the use of computerized technology

---

Law Line 5-7
Computer Crime Laws by State

---

the District of Columbia have enacted statutes for ***computer crime*** designed to facilitate the prosecution of high-technology and computer-related offenses.

Many traditional forms of crime, including fraud, drug dealing, theft, espionage, pornography, and extortion, can be committed using computers and the Internet. The fact that computers can be used to commit crimes, however, does not necessarily make those crimes computer crimes. Generally, only crimes that cannot be committed without computer technology are classified as *computer crimes.* Crimes that simply target computer machinery (such as the theft of computer equipment, and the arson of computer facilities) or that utilize computer facilities for the commission of more mundane crimes (such as theft, blackmail, and extortion) may be more appropriately prosecuted under other laws.

Computer Crime Laws

By 1990, all fifty states and the federal government had enacted computer crime statutes. The first state to pass a computer crime law was Florida in 1978, while the last state to enact such a law was Massachusetts in 1990. Federal statutes identifying crimes committed with or against computer equipment and software include the following:

- Federal Wiretap Act of 1968[41]
- National Stolen Property Act[42]
- Computer Fraud and Abuse Act of 1984[43] and its amendments, especially Section 290001 of Title 29 of the Violent Crime Control and Law Enforcement Act of 1994[44] (the Computer Abuse Amendments Act of 1994)
- Electronic Communications Privacy Act of 1986[45]
- Communications Decency Act[46]
- No Electronic Theft Act of 1997[47]
- Digital Theft Deterrence and Copyright Damages Improvement Act of 1999[48]
- Cyber Security Enhancement Act of 2002[49]

For the most part, federal laws protect equipment owned by the federal government or a financial institution or computers that are accessed across state lines without prior authorization.[50] The Computer Fraud and Abuse Act defines as criminal the intentional unauthorized access to a computer used exclusively by the federal government or any other computer used by the government when such conduct affects the government's use. The same statute also defines as criminal the intentional and unauthorized access to two or more computers in different states involving conduct that alters or destroys information and causes loss to one or more parties in excess of $1,000.[51]

Central to the law is a provision that makes it a federal crime to access, without authorization, any data-processing system if the data-processing system is involved in or used in relationship to interstate commerce. The act also makes it a crime to use a public telephone system to access, without authority, any data-processing system, and the act prohibits those who have the authority to access a data-processing system from using that authority in an unauthorized manner. Punishment specified under federal law is a maximum sentence of five years and a fine of up to $250,000 upon conviction. The Computer Abuse Amendments Act of 1994, however, adds the provision that "any person who suffers damage or loss by reason of a violation of [this] section . . . may maintain a civil action against the violator to obtain compensatory damages and injunctive relief or other equitable relief."[52]

The Cyber Security Enhancement Act (CSEA) of 2002, which is part of the Homeland Security Act of 2002, directed the U.S. Sentencing Commission to take several factors into account in creating new sentencing guidelines for computer criminals. The law told commission members to consider not only the financial loss caused by computer crime but also the level of planning involved in the offense, whether the crime was committed for commercial or private advantage, and whether malicious intent existed on the part of the perpetrator. Under the law, computer criminals can face up to life in prison if they put human lives in jeopardy. The law also makes it easier for police agencies to obtain investigative information from Internet service providers (ISPs) and shields from lawsuits ISPs who hand over user information to law enforcement officers without a warrant. But the information in question should be that which poses an immediate risk of injury or death.

The Digital Theft Deterrence and Copyright Damages Improvement Act of 1999 amended Section 504(c) of the Copyright Act and increased the amount of damages that could be awarded in cases of copyright infringement, a crime that is intimately associated with software piracy. Enacted in 1997, the No Electronic Theft Act (NETA or NETAct) criminalizes the willful infringement of copyrighted works, including by electronic means, even when the infringing party derives no direct financial benefit from the infringement (such as when pirated software is freely distributed online). The law was created in response to a 1994 case in which David LaMacchia, a Massachusetts Institute of Technology student, distributed more than $1 million worth of copyrighted commercial software on an unauthorized MIT Internet bulletin board. LaMacchia could not be prosecuted under the federal Copyright Act because he did not profit from the distribution.[53] NETA makes it a federal crime to distribute or possess unauthorized electronic copies of copyrighted materials valued at more than $1,000. Possessing ten or more illegal documents worth more than $2,500 carries a three-year prison term and a $250,000 fine. In keeping with NETA requirements, the U.S. Sentencing Commission enacted amendments to its guidelines in 2000 to increase the penalties associated with electronic theft.

The 1996 Communications Decency Act (CDA) is Title 5 of the Telecommunications Act of 1996.[54] It sought to protect minors from harmful material on the Internet. A portion of the CDA criminalized the knowing transmission of obscene or indecent messages to any recipient under eighteen years of age. Another section prohibited knowingly sending or displaying to a person under eighteen any message "that, in context, depicts or describes, in terms patently offensive as measured by contemporary community standards, sexual or excretory activities or organs." The law provided acceptable defenses for those who took "good faith . . . effective . . . actions" to restrict access by minors to prohibited communications and for those who restricted such access by requiring certain designated forms of age proof, such as a verified credit card or an adult identification number.

Shortly after the law was passed, however, the American Civil Liberties Union (ACLU) and a number of other plaintiffs filed suit against the federal government, challenging the constitutionality of the law's two provisions relating to the transmission of obscene materials to minors. In 1996, a three-judge federal district court entered a preliminary injunction against enforcement of both challenged provisions, ruling that they contravened First Amendment guarantees of free speech. The government then appealed to the U.S. Supreme Court. The Court's 1997 decision, *Reno v. ACLU*,[55] upheld the lower court's ruling and found that the CDA's "indecent transmission" and "patently offensive display" provisions abridge "the freedom of speech" protected by the First Amendment. Justice John Paul Stevens in writing for the majority stated, "[i]t is true that we have repeatedly recognized the governmental interest in protecting children from harmful materials.

But that interest does not justify an unnecessarily broad suppression of speech addressed to adults."

Most other federal legislation aimed at keeping online pornography away from the eyes of children has not fared any better when reviewed by the Court. Enforcement of the 1998 Child Online Protection Act (COPA), for example, was partially barred by a 2004 U.S. Supreme Court ruling that held that measures in the law were too restrictive and jeopardized free speech interests.[56] Subsequent lower court litigation on different issues also found the statute unconstitutional. And although the Court approved the Children's Internet Protection Act (CIPA) of 2000,[57] which requires public and school libraries receiving certain kinds of federal funding to install pornography filters on their Internet-linked computers, most observers acknowledge that the Court has placed the Internet in the same category as newspapers and other print media, where government regulations are viewed with substantial skepticism.

Unauthorized Access to a Computer

Most computer crime laws—whether federal or state—criminalize unauthorized access to computer systems. In essence, these laws prohibit individuals from gaining access to computer systems for which they do not have authorization to access. Although penalties for simple access (or access without harm) are usually not harsh,[58] some jurisdictions still classify the offense as a felony. An interesting feature of many unauthorized access statutes is the way in which they enlarge the common definitions of "access" and "property."

For example, Pennsylvania's unauthorized access statute defines **access** as "[t]o intercept, instruct, communicate with, store data in, retrieve data from, or otherwise make use of any resources of a computer, computer system, computer network, or data base," while stating that property "[i]ncludes, but is not limited to, financial instruments, computer software, and programs in either machine or human readable form, and anything of value, tangible or intangible." Using these and other technical terms, Title 18, Section 3933 of the Pennsylvania Consolidated Statutes prohibits unauthorized access to computers in the following terms:

Unlawful use of computer.

a. Offense defined. A person commits an offense if he:
   1. accesses, alters, damages, or destroys any computer, computer system, computer network, computer software, computer program or data base or any part thereof, with the intent to interrupt the normal functioning of an organization or to devise or execute any scheme or artifice to defraud or deceive or control property or services by means of false or fraudulent pretenses, representations, or promises;
   2. intentionally and without authorization accesses, alters, interferes with the operation of, damages, or destroys any computer, computer system, computer network, computer software, computer program, or computer data base or any part thereof; or
   3. intentionally or knowingly and without authorization gives or publishes a password, identifying code, personal identification number, or other confidential information about a computer, computer system, computer network, or data base.
b. Grading. An offense under subsection (a)(1) is a felony of the third degree. An offense under subsection (a)(2) or (3) is a misdemeanor of the first degree. . . .

In an age where many devices—phones, voice mail accounts, security systems, and the like—operate via computer technology, the potential for crime related to unlawful access to computers appears to be rapidly expanding. Read the Colorado court of appeals' opinion in *People v. Rice* (2008) to appreciate how the concept of "computer access" is interpreted by some courts.

CAPSTONE CASE *People v. Rice,* 2008 Colo. App. LEXIS 811 (Colo. App. 3d 2008)

Defendant, Nina B. Rice, appeals from the judgment of conviction entered upon a jury verdict finding her guilty of computer crime. . . .

I. Background Evidence at trial established that, in 2003, defendant filed for unemployment compensation benefits with the Colorado Department of Labor and Employment. To do so, she utilized the Department's CUBLine, an interactive computer system with which unemployment claimants communicate over the telephone.

For over five months, defendant contacted the CUBLine to make biweekly claims for unemployment benefits. Each time she contacted the CUBLine, the computer system asked defendant if she had worked during the week for which she claimed unemployment benefits. Each time, she pressed the number on her telephone corresponding to an answer of "no." In fact, she was employed at the time, and she concedes that she lied in her CUBLine responses.

Defendant was charged by information with the crimes of theft and computer crime. The theft count alleged that defendant intended to permanently deprive the Department of money, and the computer crime count alleged that she accessed a computer for the purpose of obtaining money from the Department or committing theft. At trial, she testified that she believed the money she received from her unemployment claims belonged to her and had been withheld from her paychecks issued by her previous employer.

The jury was unable to reach a verdict on the theft count and found defendant guilty of computer crime. The jury also convicted defendant of false swearing, a lesser nonincluded offense submitted to the jury at defendant's request. Defendant was subsequently sentenced to five years probation. This appeal followed.

II. Sufficiency of the Evidence Defendant contends the evidence was insufficient to support the jury's verdict of guilty on the computer crime count. Specifically, she contends the evidence was insufficient to establish that she "accessed" a computer or computer system within the meaning of the term "access" as used in section 18-5.5-102(1)(c)-(d), C.R.S. 2007. We disagree. . . .

The prosecution charged defendant with computer crime pursuant to subsections (c) and (d) of section 18-5.5-102(1). Under those subsections,

A person commits computer crime if the person knowingly:

. . .

(c) Accesses any computer, computer network, or computer system, or any part thereof to obtain, by means of false or fraudulent pretenses, representations, or promises, money; property; services; passwords or similar information through which a computer, computer network, or computer system or any part thereof may be accessed; or other thing of value; or

(d) Accesses any computer, computer network, or computer system, or any part thereof to commit theft. . . .

§ 18-5.5-102(1)(c)-(d).

Here, the prosecution presented evidence that defendant made biweekly unemployment benefits claims by calling an automated phone system, the CUBLine, maintained by the Department. An employee of the Department testified that the CUBLine is a "computerized system, which uses interactive voice response technology." She further testified that an unemployment benefits claimant identifies himself or herself by entering a Social Security number and a personal identification number using numbers on a telephone when prompted by the system. The system then asks the claimant a number of questions related to "weekly eligibility requirements,

(continued)

(continued)

such as . . . did you work during the weeks you are claiming?" The claimant responds by pressing "1" for "yes" and "9" for "no." This procedure is described in a brochure that was admitted into evidence at trial and, according to the record, was given to defendant to review before she made her first biweekly claim. When the computer system determines a claimant is eligible for unemployment benefits, a computer prints a check that is automatically sent to the claimant. Typically, an eligible claimant completes a claim and receives a check without interacting with a person.

The evidence showed that defendant used the CUBLine to make biweekly claims for unemployment benefits. Each time the computer system asked if she worked during the week for which she was claiming benefits, defendant entered "9" for "no," even though she was, in fact, working.

Defendant contends that she did not "access" a computer within the meaning of section 18-5.5-102(1)(c)-(d) by making a phone call and pressing telephone buttons in response to the CUBLine questions. We disagree. . . .

"Access" is not defined in the Colorado Criminal Code. However, it is a term of common usage, and persons of ordinary intelligence need not guess at its meaning. We, therefore, begin with the dictionary definition in determining the plain and ordinary meaning of "access." *See People v. Janousek*, 871 P.2d 1189, 1196 (Colo. 1994); *Black's Law Dictionary* 14 (8th ed. 2004) defines the word "access" as "[a]n opportunity or ability to enter, approach, pass to and from, or communicate with."

Viewing the evidence in the light most favorable to the prosecution, *Sprouse*, 983 P.2d at 777, we conclude defendant accessed, within the ordinary meaning of the term, a computer system, because she communicated with the CUBLine by inputting data in response to computer-generated questions. Also, the CUBLine was described in testimony at trial sufficient to support a finding that it was a "computer system" as that term is defined in section 18-5.5-101(6), C.R.S. 2007. . . .

In any event, we disagree with defendant's various arguments in support of a narrower definition of "access." . . .

Second, because we conclude the term "access," as used in section 18-5.5-102(1)(c)-(d), is not ambiguous, we reject defendant's contention that the rule of lenity requires us to adopt her interpretation.

Third, we reject defendant's contention that section 18-5.5-102(1)(c)-(d) would be rendered unconstitutionally vague if the term "access" were given its ordinary meaning. . . .

The ordinary meaning of "access" is not confusing or overly technical, and is readily understandable by an ordinary person of reasonable intelligence. *Cf. id.* Contrary to defendant's contention, the term is not susceptible of application to an endless set of facts. Rather, the language in section 18-5.5-102(1) limits its application by providing that "[a] *person* commits computer crime if *the person knowingly* . . ." (emphasis added).

Here, defendant's act of direct communication with a computer system falls within the ordinary meaning of "access." *See Black's Law Dictionary* 14. We thus conclude section 18-5.5-102(1)(c)-(d) will not be rendered unconstitutionally vague, either on its face or as applied here, if the term "access" is given its ordinary and plain meaning.

[The court then reversed and remanded the case based on other grounds.]

Courtesy of LexisNexis

WHAT DO *YOU* THINK?

1. Would an ordinary person agree that making selections in a telephone system qualifies as accessing a computer system or network?

2. Excluding the crimes she was charged with, what other crime(s) did the defendant commit?

The Nature of Computer Crime Laws

Most state computer crime laws are comprehensive statutes, often taking the form of an independent title in a state's criminal code called the Computer Crimes Act or the Computer Crime Prevention Act.[59] In contrast, some states have created a patchwork quilt of modifications to existing laws to cover a variety of crimes, such as computer trespass and theft with a computer. Ohio, for example, has inserted a series of computer crime definitions in its general theft statute, has added one section on denying access to a computer, and has placed computer systems, networks, and software used in committing any offense within its general definition of "contraband."[60]

Many state computer crime statutes occupy a middle ground and can be found under other statutory categories, such as crimes against property, fraud, theft (as is the case in California), or business and commercial offenses. Arizona, for example, has placed its computer crime provisions under the section of its penal code entitled Organized Crime and Fraud, while North Dakota places such legislation under its Racketeer Influenced and Corrupt Organizations (RICO) statute.

Because legislatures often see themselves as creating new laws to deal with emerging and rapid social and technological changes, computer crime laws frequently set forth a number of definitions unique to such legislation. Typically defined by such laws are terms like these: *access, computer, computer network, computer program, computer software, computer system*, and *computer data*. A few states have attempted to define specific terminology like *computer control language* (Maryland), *computer database* (Maryland), *computer hacking* (South Carolina), *system hacker* (Tennessee), *computer supplies* (Wisconsin), *database* (New Jersey and Pennsylvania), *private personal data* (Connecticut and Delaware), and *supporting documentation* (Wisconsin).

The Electronic Frontier Foundation (EFF) points out that "state statutes do not always give computer offenses specific names."[61] The EFF notes that such laws "use a variety of descriptions to state exactly what they are prohibiting." It found that the following descriptive titles are among the most commonly used: access to defraud, access to obtain money, computer fraud, offenses against computer users, offenses against intellectual property, offenses against computer equipment and supplies, unauthorized access, and unauthorized or unlawful computer use.

Generally speaking, computer crime laws attempt to apply the concept of common law trespass to computers. As a result, computer crimes are usually defined as unauthorized entry onto someone else's property. Where no criminal intent beyond curiosity or mischief exists, the crime may be a minor offense, such as computer hacking. Where criminal intent exists, however, criminal laws may allow prosecution for both unauthorized access to a computer and some other crime, usually a fraud, theft, or attempt. Similarly, most computer crime laws contain provisions making it illegal to interfere with another person's legitimate access to computer services or to information stored in a computer. Most states, however, provide for an affirmative defense of authorization when the defendant can demonstrate a reasonable belief that access was authorized.

Types of Computer and Cybercrime

Another term you will often hear used to refer to computer crime is *cybercrime*. Simply put, cybercrime is crime committed with or through the use of computers. Generally speaking, five types of cybercrime are found in today's law, although the names given each type vary considerably between jurisdictions. The five types are (1) computer fraud, (2) computer trespass, (3) theft of computer services, (4) personal trespass by computer, and (5) computer tampering, or the dissemination of computer viruses, worms, and Trojan horses. Even though the names assigned to these criminal offenses can vary, some common elements are found within each category of crime.

computer fraud
a fraud offense committed through the use of a computer or other electronic device

Computer fraud is a fraud offense committed through the use of a computer or other electronic device. The basic elements of a computer fraud offense are

- the use a computer or computer network
- without authority
- and with the intent to (1) obtain property or services by false pretenses, (2) embezzle or commit larceny, or (3) convert the property of another

In computer fraud cases, the computer or other electronic device is the tool used to commit some form of a larceny offense. But unlike standard larceny crimes, where the theft is committed in a direct and personal manner, computer fraud involves the use of "virtual" conduct that results in tangible loss of property or other items of value.

computer trepass
the unlawful transgression upon or access to the computer or other electronic system of another

Computer trespass offenses involve the unlawful transgression upon or access to the computer or other electronic system of another. The elements of computer trespass are

- the use of a computer or computer network
- without authority
- and with the intent to (1) remove computer data, computer programs, or computer software from a computer or computer network; (2) cause a computer to malfunction; (3) alter or erase any computer data, computer programs, or computer software; (4) effect the creation or alteration of a financial instrument or of an electronic transfer of funds; (5) cause physical injury to the property of another; or (6) make or cause to be made an unauthorized copy of data stored on a computer or of computer programs or computer software

In computer trespass cases, the computer or other electronic device is the property upon which someone has trespassed. Unlike traditional trespass cases involving a home, land, or other real estate property, computer trespass offenses treat a person's computer as the forum upon which someone has transgressed.

theft of computer services
a particularized form of a theft offense where the services offered by an electronic systems provider are deemed to be the property unlawfully taken

The *theft of computer services* is a particularized form of theft offense where the services offered by an electronic systems provider are deemed to be the property unlawfully taken. In many jurisdictions, legislators found it necessary to carve out a specialized statute for this crime because when electronic or computer services are stolen, the property taken is virtual, not tangible, and many traditional theft offense statutes did not cover nontangible forms of property. The elements of a basic theft of computer services offense are

- the use of a computer or computer network
- with intent to obtain computer services
- without authority

personal trespass by computer
the use of a computer as an instrument to gain access to someone else's property

A related criminal offense in some jurisdictions is *personal trespass by computer*, which makes it illegal to use a computer as an instrument to gain access to someone else's property. Again, in these situations, the property trespassed upon is usually virtual, not tangible, thereby requiring statutes to address the electronic or virtual nature of property. The core elements of a personal trespass by computer offense are

- use of a computer or computer network
- without authority
- and with the intent to cause physical injury to an individual

Under some statutes, there are different degrees of this offense, depending on the seriousness of the defendant's conduct and the degree of harm that is inflicted.

Finally, many jurisdictions have enacted laws against **computer tampering** in order to address threats involving computer viruses, worms, and "Trojan horses," which are sometimes called *rogue programs.* Generally, computer tampering has four elements:

- the insertion of or attempt to insert a "program" into a computer
- while knowing or believing
- that the "program" contains information or commands
- that will or may damage or destroy that computer (or its data) or any other computer (or its data) accessing or being accessed by that computer, *or* that will or may cause loss to the users of that computer or the users of a computer that accesses or that is accessed by such "program"

computer tampering
the insertion of or attempt to insert a "program" into a computer, while knowing or believing that the "program" contains information or commands that will or may damage or destroy that computer or its data

Individual computer tampering statutes may define the terms *program* and *loss* more precisely, although they do not do so in all cases.[62] A number of such special laws were passed after the arrest of Robert Morris, whose 1988 release of an Internet worm that spread to computers throughout the country (and the world) in a matter of hours, slowing them down and necessitating special administrative measures, became a watershed event in the history of computing. Morris's experiment in malicious programming cost thousands of hours of operator time to repair and an untold amount of monetary damage. Following Morris's arrest and prosecution, California modified its computer crime legislation to specifically refer to both worms and viruses, calling them "computer contaminants."[63] Maine and Texas both changed their laws to include computer viruses, while other states used terminology like *destructive computer programs* and *computer tampering* to describe the same phenomena.

Law Line 5-8
Computer Crime

IN THE FIELD

Computer-related criminal cases are a regular part of any criminal practitioner's landscape. With high degrees of regularity, computers are either the tools or the targets of criminal conduct. As a result, legal professionals must be knowledgeable of the terminology and technology associated with electronic storage and communications or at least have access to a good computer forensics expert who can help navigate the legal professional though these areas.

Although professionals may generally grasp computer-related terms such as *access*, *intercept*, and *storage*, which are found in criminal statutes, the real challenge is applying these terms to real criminal contexts. For example, if someone without authorization listens to voice mail messages stored on another person's phone, does that constitute an interception of an electronic communication? Or if a person without permission uses the garage door opener of another to gain entry to a house, does that involve the unauthorized use of a computer? These and other issues provide both challenges and opportunities for legal professionals to be creative and innovative in their legal work.

Remember, much of the cyberspace world is very different from tangible, everyday human conduct. Things found in cyberspace are not always as they appear. As a result, the legal terminology found in traditional statutes is not always a good fit to address computer-related criminal activity. Be sure to read the terms of the criminal statute carefully, understand the details of the computer-related activity, and where you do not fully understand a computer concept or legal term, research this item more thoroughly.

CHAPTER **SUMMARY**

- Most property crimes are crimes of theft. They are sometimes called *acquisitive offenses*, *wrongful acquisition crimes*, or *crimes of misappropriation* because they involve the unlawful acquiring or appropriation of someone else's property.
- Larceny was the only form of theft originally punished under early common law. In early times, it was a capital offense.
- In most jurisdictions today, the statutory crime of larceny consists of the wrongful taking and carrying away (or *asportation*) of the personal property of another with the intent to permanently deprive the owner of possession of the property.
- Almost all jurisdictions have divided larceny into petit, or petty, larceny and grand larceny. Grand larceny (also known as *grand theft*) usually consists of the theft of property that has a market value of more than a certain amount or of the theft of certain property listed in the statute, such as firearms and cattle.
- Embezzlement is the unlawful conversion of the personal property of another by a person to whom it has been entrusted by (or for) its rightful owner. Embezzlement is fundamentally a violation of trust. As with larceny, one can be guilty of embezzlement only if the embezzled property belongs to another. Embezzlement is also known as *fraudulent conversion*.
- The crime of obtaining property by false pretenses, usually referred to simply as *false pretenses*, occurs when the taking of property with the passing of title is predicated on a false representation of a material fact. The crime occurs when a person uses false pretenses to obtain both possession of, and title to, the property in question.
- Forgery is the making of a false instrument or the material alteration of an existing genuine instrument. Forgery is complete when one either makes or passes a false instrument with the intent to defraud. The gist of the crime of forgery is the intent to defraud.
- Uttering is the offering, passing, or attempted passing of a forged document with the knowledge that the document is false and with the intent to defraud. Today, most jurisdictions have established the separate statutory crime of uttering a forged document.
- Receiving stolen property is another form of theft. Receiving stolen property can be defined as taking possession of, or control over, property that has been unlawfully stolen from another, knowing that it has been stolen.
- Robbery is an aggravated form of larceny. In addition to the elements necessary to constitute larceny, robbery involves two additional aspects: (1) The property must be taken from a person or removed from the presence of the victim, and (2) the taking must be by use of force or by putting the victim in fear.
- Under early common law, extortion was the corrupt collection of an unlawful fee by a public officer under color of office. It was a misdemeanor. Almost all American jurisdictions today have expanded the crime of extortion to cover anyone who uses a future threat to wrongfully obtain property. The contemporary crime of extortion can be defined as the taking of personal property by a threat of future harm. Statutory extortion is a felony in most jurisdictions.
- Blackmail is a form of extortion in which a threat is made to disclose a crime or other social disgrace. Even a threat to cause economic injury or social embarrassment may be sufficient to constitute blackmail in most jurisdictions.
- Identity theft, which is the unauthorized use of another individual's personal identity to fraudulently obtain money, goods, or services, is quickly becoming the most important new theft crime of the twenty-first century. Common forms of identity theft include taking over an existing credit card account and making unauthorized charges to it, taking out loans in another person's name, writing fraudulent checks using another person's name or account number, and using personal information to access and transfer money out of another person's bank or brokerage account.
- Under common law, burglary was the breaking and entering of the dwelling house of another in the nighttime with the intent to commit a felony. In most jurisdictions today, however, the crime of burglary is statutorily defined as the breaking and entering of a building, locked automobile, boat, and so on with the intent to commit a felony or theft. Many jurisdictions divide burglary into burglary in the first or second degree. First-degree burglary is the burglary of an inhabited dwelling, and all other burglaries are second-degree burglaries.
- Looting, another crime against property, can be defined as burglary committed within an affected geographic area during an officially declared state of emergency or during a local emergency resulting from an earthquake, fire, flood, riot, or other disaster.
- Under common law, arson was the malicious burning of a structure of another. The modern trend is to increase the types of items that may be subject to arson. In almost all jurisdictions today, arson is defined in terms of knowingly and maliciously causing a fire. Arson cannot be committed by negligent or reckless conduct.
- Computer crime is a form of crime that could not be committed without computer technology. All fifty states and the federal government have enacted special laws, known as *computer crime statutes*, against cybercrime.
- Generally speaking, there are five types of cybercrime found in today's law: (1) computer fraud, (2) computer trespass, (3) theft of computer services, (4) personal trespass by computer, and (5) computer tampering, or the dissemination of computer viruses and worms.

KEY **TERMS**

acquisitive offenses
arson
asportation
blackmail
burglary
claim of right
compounding a crime
computer crime
computer fraud
computer tampering
computer trespass
constructive entry
constructive possession
conversion

criminal mischief
criminal simulation
criminal trespass
embezzlement
extortion
false pretenses
fixtures
forgery
fraud
identity theft
Identity Theft and Assumption
    Deterrence Act (1998)
intangible property
intellectual property

larceny
larceny by trick
looting
personal property
personal trespass by computer
Ponzi scheme
possession of burglary tools
receiving stolen property
robbery
tangible property
theft
theft of computer services
trespassory taking
uttering

QUESTIONS FOR **DISCUSSION**

1. How do larceny and embezzlement differ, and why are these differences important?

2. What are the rules regarding the keeping of found property?

3. What types of property were subject to the common law crime of larceny?

4. What is the difference between embezzlement and false pretenses?

5. It is often stated that "only people you trust can embezzle from you." Do you agree or disagree with this statement? Explain your answer.

6. What are the advantages to consolidating the wrongful acquisition crimes into a single crime of theft? What are the disadvantages?

7. What test do the courts use in robbery cases to determine whether property was taken from the presence of the victim?

8. How does extortion differ from robbery?

9. Explain the concept of constructive entry as applied to burglary crimes.

10. What are the five types of computer crime discussed in this chapter? What are the unique features of each?

11. Describe the details of a criminal statute banning unlawful access to a computer.

REFERENCES

1. Cynthia Manson and Charles Ardai, *Future Crime: An Anthology of the Shape of Crime to Come* (New York: Donald I. Fine, 1992), p. ix.

2. Louis B. Schwartz, "Theft," in *The Encyclopedia of Crime and Justice,* edited by Sandord Kadish, 4:1537–51 (New York: Macmillian Library Reference, 1983).

3. American Law Institute, *Model Penal Code and Commentaries,* comment to Section 223.1 at p. 127–32 (1980).

4. *Id.*

5. Schwartz, "Theft," 1537.

6. East's *Pleas of the Crown* 553 (1803).

7. *Thompson v. State,* 10 So. 520 (Ala. 1891).

8. Frances Robles, "Truck Crash Turns I-95 into Road to Riches," *Miami Herald,* January 9, 1997.

9. *Id.*

10. Model Penal Code, Section 223.5.

11. *State v. Jones,* 65 N.C. 395 (1871).

12. *Id.,* 297, 298.

13. Although not "larceny," other laws might criminalize such behavior.

14. Model Penal Code, Section 223.9.

15. The statute also effectively eliminates any common law vestiges of the classification of dogs as "base" animals.

16. *State v. Jackson,* 11 S.E.2d 149 (N.C. 1940).

17. Texas Penal Code, Section 28.01(3).

18. Model Penal Code, Section 223.0(6).

19. 473 U.S. 207 (1985).

20. See, for example, California Penal Code, Section 475.

21. See, for example, Texas Penal Code, Section 32.22.

22. Ohio Revised Code, Section 2913.01 (F).

23. *State v. George,* 173 S.W. 1077 (Mo. 1915).

24. *People v. Taylor,* 4 Cal. App. 2d 214 (1935).

25. See Blackmail and Extortion - Modern Federal Statutes http://law.jrank.org/pages/568/Blackmail-Extortion-Modern-federal-statutes.html

26. Model Penal Code, Section 223.4.

27. Stephen A. Saltzburg, et al., *Criminal Law: Cases and Materials* (Charlottesville, VA: Michie, 1994), p. 562.

28. 18 U.S.C. § 1028(a)(7).

29. *Id.*

30. *Id.*

31. *State v. Sorenson,* 138 N.W. 411 (Iowa 1912).

32. *State v. Hill,* 520 P.2d 946 (Wash. App. 1974), citing *State v. Rosencrans,* 167 P.2d 170, 172 (Wash. 1946).

33. *Rolland v. Commonwealth,* 82 Pa. 306 (1876).

34. John S. Baker, Jr., et al., *Hall's Criminal Law: Cases and Materials,* 5th ed. (Charlottesville, VA: Michie, 1993), p. 496, citing *Lawson v. Commonwealth,* 169 S.W. 587 (Ky. 1914), and *People v. Toland,* 111 N.E. 760 (N.Y. 1916). See also *Rolland v. Commonwealth,* 82 Pa. 324 (1876).

35. *Smith v. State,* 362 P.2d 1071 (Alaska 1961).

36. *Mattox v. State,* 101 N.E. 1009 (Ind. 1913).

37. *State v. Hudson,* 430 P.2d 386 (N.M. 1967).

38. *Henderson v. State,* 86 So. 439 (Fla. 1920).

39. *People v. Blair,* 288 N.E.2d 443 (Ill. 1952).

40. Texas Penal Code, Section 30.05.

41. 18 U.S.C. § 2510.

42. And as amended by the National Information Infrastructure Protection Act of 1996; Pub. L. No. 104-294.

43. 18 U.S.C. § 1030 (Pub. L. No. 98-473).

44. Pub. L. No. 103-322.

45. Pub. L. No. 99-508.

46. Title 5 of the Telecommunications Act of 1996, Pub. L. No. 104-104, 110 Stat. 56.

47. Pub. L. No. 105-147.

48. Pub. L. No. 106-160.

49. Section 225 of the Homeland Security Act, Pub. L. No. 107-296.

50. 18 U.S.C. § 1029.

51. As described in M. Gemignani, "Viruses and Computer Law," *Communications of the ACM* 32 (June 1989): 669.

52. This section is taken in part from Frank Schmalleger, *Criminology Today: An Interactive Introduction,* 4th ed. (Upper Saddle River, NJ: Prentice Hall, 2006).

53. See "David LaMacchia Cleared; Case Raises Civil Liberties Issues," *The Tech* (MIT), February 7, 1995, http://tech.mit.edu/V114/N68/lamacchia.00n.html (accessed January 20, 2005).

54. Pub. L. No. 104-104, 110 Stat. 56.

55. *Reno v. ACLU,* 521 U.S. 844 (1997).

56. *Ashcroft v. ACLU,* 542 U.S. 656 (2004).

57. Pub. L. No. 106-554.

58. For a good discussion of the development of computer crime laws, see Richard C. Hollinger and Lonn Lanza-Kaduce, "The Process of Criminalization: The Case of Computer Crime Laws," *Criminology* 26 (1988): 101.

59. See, for example, the Alabama Computer Crime Act, Alabama Code, Sections 13-A-8-100 to 103; the Florida Computer Crimes Act, Florida Statutes, Sections 815.01 to 815.07; and the Illinois Computer Crime Prevention Law, Illinois Revised Statutes, Chapter 38, Section 5/16D-1 to 5/16D-7.

60. See Ohio Revised Code Annotated, Sections 2913.01, 2913.81; and Ohio Revised Code Annotated, Section 2901.01 (m)(10).

61. Visit the Electronic Frontier Foundation on the Web at http://www.eff.org.

62. See, for example, Illinois Revised Statutes, Chapter 38, Section 5/16D-3 (a)(4), from which the elements used in our definition of *computer tampering* are derived.

63. California Penal Code, Section 502 (b)(10).

APPENDIX

DEVELOPING YOUR LEGAL ANALYSIS

A. THE LAW WHERE YOU LIVE

Assume that you are asked to evaluate the possible criminal charges in a multidefendant theft case. According to the facts, four individuals went into a large local department store and removed items of merchandise without paying for them. Sheila allegedly stole three packs of cigarettes, which were priced at $5.00 per pack. Thomas allegedly took ten DVDs, each valued at $30.00, but had a coupon in his pocket for buy-one-get-one-free that would have applied to the entire purchase. Myra purportedly stole a small laptop computer that retailed for $600.00, but that the store obtained for the wholesale price of $300.00. And Stanley allegedly stole a diamond necklace that normally sold for $2,500.00, but was on sale for $999.99.

Using your state and local criminal theft/larceny statutes, prepare a legal memorandum where you address what criminal offenses, if any, should be used to charge each of the above-named defendants. In addition to the name of the alleged offense, be sure to identify the level (felony or misdemeanor) and degree of each offense. For each defendant, identify the value of the property taken and how you determined this amount.

B. INSIDE THE FEDERAL COURTS

Assume you have a client, Ima Sellin, who is a sales representative for the XYZ Corporation, a medical equipment manufacturer and distributor. As a part of her job, Ima is responsible for identifying and contacting new clients for the sale of XYZ's medical equipment. Last month, Ima was having lunch with a friend, Isell Too, who sells similar medical equipment for a competing company. During the lunch, Isell went to the bathroom and left his mobile phone/communications device on the table.

While Isell was gone, his phone rang and Ima answered it. The call was from a prospective client who was inquiring about the purchase of some medical equipment. Ima took the client's name and contact information and promised to get back to him. As Ima hung up the phone, she also noticed a number of text messages appearing on the phone that were sent to Isell from what appeared to be clients seeking medical equipment. Ima jotted down the contact information for these individuals as well. Finally, becoming even more curious, Ima also took a peak at the names and numbers stored in Isell's electronic phone book.

Federal law enforcement officials want to talk to Ima about this activity and she is coming to your law office seeking advice. In advance of this meeting, you have been asked to review a federal law dealing with electronic communications to determine whether Ima faces any potential criminal liability. Accordingly, prepare a legal memorandum where you assess Ima's criminal culpability under 18 U.S.C. §§ 2510 and 2511—Wire and Electronic Communications Interception and Interception of Oral Communications. Be sure to identify what, if any, provisions Ima may have violated and explain why you have drawn these conclusions.

C. CYBER SOURCES

Assume you are working as a summer intern for a local prosecutor's office. The elected prosecutor has been asked to give a talk/presentation to a group of law enforcement officers and private cybersecurity officials regarding the nature and severity of cybercrime. You are asked to put together a PowerPoint presentation (or another form of presentation) that outlines some of the more interesting or outrageous computer crimes committed in recent years.

To that end, your project is to access and review the website maintained by the Computer Crime and Intellectual Property Section of the U. S. Department of Justice, located at http://www.justice.gov/criminal/cybercrime/. Using the materials and cases provided in this source, prepare a presentation where you identify at least six cases of computer crime, provide an adequate explanation of the facts of each case, and identify and explain the nature of the criminal offenses used to prosecute the criminal conduct.

D. ETHICS AND PROFESSIONALISM

Assume that you are working for Stacey Adams, a criminal defense attorney, who is working on a motion to suppress the breathalyzer test results in a Driving Under the Influence of Alcohol (DUI) case. Ms. Adams will be arguing that the blood alcohol results (BAC) should be excluded from evidence during trial because they were improperly obtained by the police officer in the case. To support her motion, Ms. Adams needs an affidavit (a sworn statement of facts) from the client. Ms. Adams is currently out of the office. Accordingly, she has instructed you to call the client, obtain his factual account of what the police officer did during the DUI traffic stop, use this information to prepare an affidavit, and then have the client come to the office to sign the affidavit. Ms. Adams will return to the office in a few days.

When she returns, she will attach the affidavit to her motion and file it with the trial court.

You are comfortable doing this task, but you have some reservations about completing it without Ms. Adams supervising your work. Review any ethical standards from your home state jurisdiction regarding the delegation of lawyer work that might apply to this situation, as well as the ethical standards for delegated tasks set forth in the following sources, and then write an e-mail response to Ms. Adams regarding her request.

American Bar Association

http://www.abanet.org/legalservices/paralegals/downloads/ modelguidelines.pdf

The American Alliance of Paralegals, Inc.

http://www.aapipara.org/Ethicalstandards.htm

National Federation of Paralegal Associations, Inc.

http://www.paralegals.org/

chapter **six**

PUBLIC ORDER AND MORALITY-BASED CRIMES

Whatever differences of opinion may exist as to the extent and boundaries of the police power . . . there seems to be no doubt that it does extend to . . . the preservation of good order and the public morals.
— *Boston Beer Co. v. Massachusetts* (1878)[1]

The criminal law is society's most destructive and intrusive form of intervention.
— Law Reform Commission of Canada (1977)

Vulgar statements directed at police officers . . . [are] not sufficient to constitute disorderly conduct.
— *People v. Stephen* (1992)[2]

LEARNING OBJECTIVES

After reading this chapter, you should be able to

- Identify the different categories of social-order crimes described in this chapter, and explain how they differ from one another.

- Explain the differences between disorderly conduct, riot, rout, fighting, and breach of the peace.

- Explain the legal challenges in regulating immigration.

- Identify the distinguishing features of antiterrorism laws.

- Summarize arguments for and against the regulation of firearms.

- Summarize the differences between perjury, bribery, and contempt, and explain how criminal contempt differs from civil contempt.

- Explain the legal basis for criminalizing public indecency, prostitution, sodomy, and other consensual sexual behavior.

- Identify the differences between profanity, pornography, obscenity, and child pornography.

- Discuss the conditions under which marijuana might be legalized or decriminalized.

- Address some of the legal and practical realities for driving under the influence cases.

- Explain the legal and social challenges in regulating controlled substances.

INTRODUCTION

This chapter discusses crimes against the social order and morality-based criminal offenses. These offenses can be organized in six basic categories: (1) crimes against public order, including disorderly conduct, unlawful fighting, carrying concealed weapons, gambling, alcohol-related offenses, and illegal immigration; (2) crimes challenging the legitimacy of government, including terrorism and treason; (3) crimes against justice and the administration of government, including perjury and obstruction of justice; (4) crimes involving sex acts, including public indecency, prostitution, sodomy, and other consensual sexual behavior; (5) offenses involving materials depicting sexuality, including obscenity and child pornography; and (6) offenses involving controlled substances.

It is important to note that some of these offenses involve entirely consensual behavior. In many cases of prostitution, deviate sex acts, criminal drug use, and illegal gambling, the participants willingly engage in the activity. As such, some of these crimes do not have readily identifiable *individual* victims. This leads some to call these offenses ***victimless crimes***. See Figure 6-1. For others, however, these offenses are not seen as victimless, but rather they are viewed as perpetrating harm upon the whole of society. Accordingly, for some observers, these crimes are social-order offenses or crimes against public order.

victimless crimes
a term used by some to describe criminal offenses that do not have readily identifiable *individual* victims

CRIMES AGAINST PUBLIC ORDER

Public-order offenses are those that disturb or invade society's peace and tranquillity. Public-order offenses include the following: breach of peace (sometimes called disturbing the peace), disorderly conduct, fighting, affray (fighting in public), vagrancy, loitering, illegally carrying weapons, keeping a disorderly (or "bawdy") house, public intoxication (whether by alcohol or other controlled substances), disturbance of public assembly, inciting to riot, rioting, unlawful assembly, rout, and obstructing public passage. Laws criminalizing such activities rest on the assumption that public order is inherently valuable and should be maintained—and that disorder is not to be tolerated and should be reduced, when it occurs, through the application of the criminal law.

Breach of Peace

As some authors point out, all crimes, when viewed from a philosophical perspective, are breaches of peace and disruptions of public order.[3] A murder, for example, not only victimizes the individual killed but also violates the orderliness of social interaction and lessens the overall integrity of the social order. Some crimes, however, do not just *theoretically* disturb public tranquillity but are themselves *actual* disturbances of public tranquillity or cause such disturbances—and these are the crimes that concern us here.

breach of peace
any unlawful activity that unreasonably disturbs the peace and tranquillity of the community

Under common law, ***breach of peace*** was the term used to describe any unlawful activity that unreasonably disturbed the peace and tranquillity of the community. *Breach of peace*, as used today, is "a flexible term, occasionally defined by statute, for a violation of public order; [or] an act calculated to disturb the public peace."[4] Breach of peace can also be described as "a public offense done by violence, or one causing or likely to cause an immediate disturbance of public order."[5] The term itself "embraces a great variety of conduct destroying or menacing public order and tranquility. It includes not only violent acts, but acts and words likely to produce violence in others."[6]

FIGURE 6-1 **Victimless Crimes versus Victim-Based Crimes**

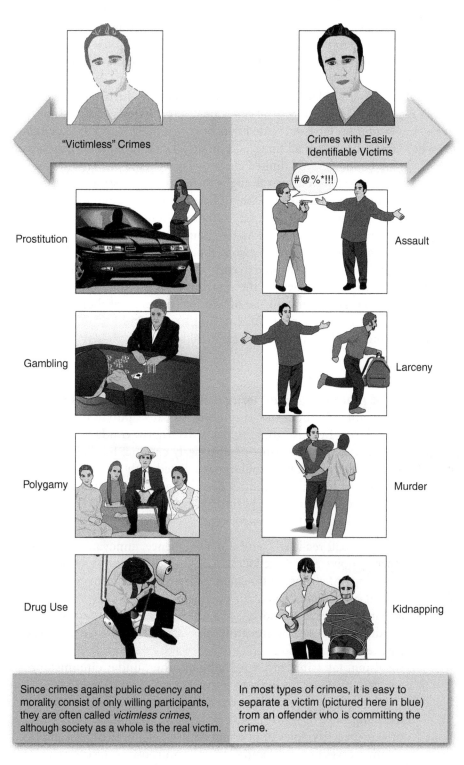

"Victimless" Crimes

Prostitution

Gambling

Polygamy

Drug Use

Since crimes against public decency and morality consist of only willing participants, they are often called *victimless crimes*, although society as a whole is the real victim.

Crimes with Easily Identifiable Victims

#@%*!!!

Assault

Larceny

Murder

Kidnapping

In most types of crimes, it is easy to separate a victim (pictured here in blue) from an offender who is committing the crime.

All jurisdictions have statutes that prohibit conduct likely to cause breaches of the public peace. Contemporary statutes, building on the common law emphasis on public tranquillity, specifically prohibit disorderly conduct, unlawful fighting, challenging a person to fight, the use of "fighting words," and so on.

Certain types of conduct may be considered a breach of peace in one jurisdiction but be called disorderly conduct in another. Accordingly, there is significant overlap between the two offenses, as will be obvious from our discussion in this section.

The California breach of peace statute contains the phrase "offensive words," referring to the use of fighting words. *Fighting words* are utterances that are intended to provoke those at whom they are directed. Impugning another's parentage provides an oft-cited example of fighting words. Fighting words are not protected by the free speech clause of the First Amendment to the U.S. Constitution, a position made clear by the U.S. Supreme Court in *Chaplinsky v. New Hampshire* (1942).[7] In *Chaplinsky*, the Court ruled that "it is well understood that the right of free speech is not absolute at all times and under all circumstances. There are certain well-defined and narrowly limited classes of speech, the prevention and punishment of which have never been thought to raise any Constitutional problem. These include the lewd and obscene, the profane, the libelous, and the insulting or 'fighting' words—those that by their very utterance inflict injury or tend to incite an immediate breach of the peace." As the Court explained, "[i]t has been well observed that such utterances are no essential part of any exposition of ideas, and are of such slight social value as a step to truth that any benefit that may be derived from them is clearly outweighed by the social interest in order and morality." In short, the Court was saying that the use of "epithets or personal abuse is not in any proper sense communication of information or opinion safeguarded by the Constitution" and may be punished as a criminal act.

Disorderly Conduct

While breach of peace is a general term, *disorderly conduct* refers to specific, purposeful, and unlawful behavior that tends to cause public inconvenience, annoyance, or alarm. Because there was no disorderly conduct crime under common law, the modern-day crime of disorderly conduct has been created by statute. One of the constitutional problems associated with attempting to outlaw disorderly conduct, however, is accurately describing just what forms of behavior constitute the offense. For example, a basic disorderly conduct offense is defined in Ohio Revised Code Section 2917.11 as follows:

A. No person shall recklessly cause inconvenience, annoyance, or alarm to another by doing any of the following:
   1. Engaging in fighting, in threatening harm to persons or property, or in violent or turbulent behavior;
   2. Making unreasonable noise or an offensively coarse utterance, gesture, or display or communicating unwarranted and grossly abusive language to any person;
   3. Insulting, taunting, or challenging another, under circumstances in which that conduct is likely to provoke a violent response;
   4. Hindering or preventing the movement of persons on a public street, road, highway, or right-of-way, or to, from, within, or upon public or private property, so as to interfere with the rights of others, and by any act that serves no lawful and reasonable purpose of the offender;
   5. Creating a condition that is physically offensive to persons or that presents a risk of physical harm to persons or property, by any act that serves no lawful and reasonable purpose of the offender.

Notice how many words and phrases within this statute are open to interpretation. Words like *inconvenience, annoyance, alarm,* and *insulting,* and phrases like *turbulent behavior, coarse utterance, grossly abusive language,* and *physically*

---

fighting words
utterances that are intended to provoke those at whom they are directed

---

Law Line 6-1
Chaplinsky v. New Hampshire (1942)

---

disorderly conduct
specific, purposeful, and unlawful behavior that tends to cause public inconvenience, annoyance, or alarm

offensive might cause many to question exactly what type of behavior is prohibited by the law. Such vague language found in many disorderly conduct statutes frequently leads to constitutional challenges and factual debates over the validity and applicability of the law.

In October 2001, for example, not long after the September 11 terrorist attacks, fifty-four-year-old William Harvey, of Long Island City, New York, was arrested near the World Trade Center site and charged with disorderly conduct for staging a speech in which he heralded Osama bin Laden and told onlookers that the attacks had been in retaliation for the U.S treatment of Islamic countries. Although Harvey claimed that he was asserting his First Amendment rights to free speech, Judge Neil E. Ross of the Manhattan Criminal Court found that Harvey created a public disturbance. Judge Ross stated, "[i]t is the reaction which speech engenders, not the content of the speech, that is the heart of disorderly conduct."[8] The judge concluded that it was reasonable to infer that Harvey was aware of the substantial risk of public alarm that his speech would engender and that he consciously chose to disregard that risk.

Fighting and Affray

One form of disorderly conduct that is often described by statute is unlawful public fighting. While some fights may be officially sanctioned, as in the case of regulated sporting events, spontaneous and unregulated physical altercations that occur in a place open to public view constitute disorderly conduct. Many jurisdictions have statutes outlawing **affray**, which can be defined as "the fighting

affray
fighting in a public place that causes others to be afraid

This booking photo released by the Cambridge, Mass., Police Dept., shows Harvard scholar Henry Louis Gates, Jr., who was arrested while trying to force open the locked front door of his home near Harvard University Thursday, July 16, 2009. Gates, a pre-eminent African-American scholar, accused Cambridge police of racism after he was arrested on a disorderly conduct charge based on what police called "exhibited loud and tumultuous behavior." He was released later that day on his own recognizance and the case was later dismissed. The incident led the well publicized "beer summit" at the White House between President Obama, Vice President Biden, Gates, and the police officer.

of persons in a public place to the terror of the people."[9] The term *affray* derives from the word *afraid* and means an altercation that tends to alarm the community.

Fighting is a mutual event and thus differs from assault. If one person attacks another, the attacker may be guilty of assault, since the accosted person may be an innocent victim. But when two people willingly and publicly fight one another, both are guilty of the crime of affray. **Prize fighting**, which is unlawful public fighting undertaken for the purpose of winning a prize, is specifically prohibited by statute in many jurisdictions. Participants in boxing matches that occur under public auspices, however, are exempted from prosecution, as long as they follow the rules of the game.

Riot and Unlawful Assembly

In most jurisdictions, an **unlawful assembly** happens when three or more people assemble for the purpose of committing an unlawful act or of committing a lawful act in a violent, boisterous, or tumultuous manner. Unlawful assembly is a specific-intent crime and therefore requires that those who are assembled must intend to commit an unlawful act or a lawful act in a prohibited manner.

A **rout** can be described as the preparatory stage of a riot.[10] A rout occurs when an unlawful assembly makes an attempt to advance toward the commission of an act that would be a riot. The difference between an unlawful assembly and a rout is that a rout requires both an unlawful assembly and an overt act. A **riot** is the culmination of unlawful assembly and rout, and can be defined as a tumultuous disturbance of the peace by three or more people assembled of their own authority. See Figure 6-2).[11]

As noted earlier, unlawful assembly, rout, and riot all require a common purpose by three or more people. The requirement of *three* or more people stems

prize fighting
unlawful public fighting undertaken for the purpose of winning a prize

unlawful assembly
an assembly of three or more people for the purpose of committing an unlawful act or of committing a lawful act in a violent, boisterous, or tumultuous manner

rout
the preparatory stage of a riot

riot
the culmination of unlawful assembly and rout; can be defined as a tumultuous disturbance of the peace by three or more people assembled of their own authority

FIGURE 6-2 **Riot and Related Offenses**

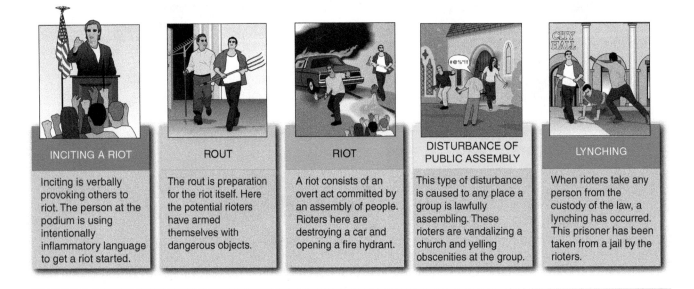

INCITING A RIOT

Inciting is verbally provoking others to riot. The person at the podium is using intentionally inflammatory language to get a riot started.

ROUT

The rout is preparation for the riot itself. Here the potential rioters have armed themselves with dangerous objects.

RIOT

A riot consists of an overt act committed by an assembly of people. Rioters here are destroying a car and opening a fire hydrant.

DISTURBANCE OF PUBLIC ASSEMBLY

This type of disturbance is caused to any place a group is lawfully assembling. These rioters are vandalizing a church and yelling obscenities at the group.

LYNCHING

When rioters take any person from the custody of the law, a lynching has occurred. This prisoner has been taken from a jail by the rioters.

from common law, although some states have statutorily reduced the required number of participating individuals to two. In any case, a single individual acting alone cannot commit these offenses. However, a single individual acting alone can commit the crime of urging or **inciting a riot**. Inciting a riot is the use of words or other means to intentionally provoke a riot. To establish the crime of urging or inciting a riot, the prosecution must prove that the defendant's acts were done with the intent to cause a riot.

inciting a riot
the use of words or other means to intentionally provoke a riot

Another offense against the public order is **disturbance of public assembly**, sometimes termed *disturbing a public or religious meeting*. The crime occurs when one or more people purposely disturb a public gathering collected for a lawful purpose. Disturbing public assembly is a statutory crime in most jurisdictions and generally involves the *willful* disturbance of a public or religious meeting without legal authority. For example, the offense might be appropriate for a person who, in order to prevent official action during a school board meeting, begins shouting at the board members and refuses to leave the meeting.

disturbance of public assembly
a crime that occurs when one or more people purposely disturb a public gathering collected for a lawful purpose

Vagrancy and Loitering

Under common law, **vagrancy** was the act of going about from place to place by a person without visible means of support, who was idle, and who, though able to work for his or her maintenance, refused to do so and lived without labor or on the charity of others.[12] A **vagrant** (also called a *vagabond*) was initially considered "a wanderer; an idle person who, being able to maintain himself by lawful labor, either refuses to work or resorts to unlawful practices, e.g., begging, to gain a living."[13] The term *common vagrant* was often applied at common law to distinguish one whose condition or mode of life was that of a vagrant from one who might be temporarily vagrant.

vagrancy
the act of going about from place to place by a person without visible means of support

vagrant
a person who engages in identifiable forms of behavior that amount to begging, loitering, or other nuisances to the public; also called a *vagabond*

When common law vagrancy was enacted into law in the United States, vagrancy statutes were often successfully attacked as being vague and overbroad and as encouraging "arbitrary enforcement by failing to describe with sufficient particularity what a suspect must do in order to satisfy the statute."[14] As a result, many early vagrancy statutes were invalidated by state courts—and by the U.S. Supreme Court, which in *Papachristou v. City of Jacksonville* (1972)[15] held that many traditionally worded vagrancy statutes were void for vagueness because they failed "to give a person of ordinary intelligence fair notice that his contemplated conduct is forbidden by the statute and because [they] encourage arbitrary and erratic arrests and convictions." A little more than a decade later, in *Kolender v. Lawson* (1983),[16] the Supreme Court found unconstitutional a California statute that prohibited loitering or wandering about without apparent reason or business and refusing to identify oneself when asked to do so by police, because it vested too much discretionary power in the police.

Law Line 6-2
Kolender v. Lawson

States that today retain vagrancy statutes have typically rephrased their description of the crime to require some specific form of behavior. The California vagrancy statute, for example, couches vagrancy in terms of **loitering**, which it defines as "to delay, to linger, or to idle about a school or public place without lawful business for being present." By specifying the circumstances under which loitering could occur, legislatures have sought to deemphasize a person's status as a determinant of criminality.

loitering
lingering in a public place without lawful purpose

Weapons-Related Offenses

In the United States today, criminal laws regulating firearms or other weaponry generally target three primary types of firearm-related activity—the carrying (possession) of weapons, the sale of guns, and the use of firearms.

Possession Offenses.   All states have passed a variety of laws intended to control gun ownership and possession, as well as the possession of weapons of "mass destruction," such as explosives and "heavy weapons." The thrust of most substantive weapons laws in this country are laws banning the carrying of concealed weapons. For example, Ohio Revised Code Section 2923.12 provides:

A. No person shall knowingly carry or have, concealed on the person's person or concealed ready at hand, any of the following:
   1. A deadly weapon other than a handgun;
   2. A handgun other than a dangerous ordnance;
   3. A dangerous ordnance.

concealed weapon
a weapon that is carried on or near one's person and is not discernible by ordinary observation

Under most statutory schemes, a **concealed weapon** is one that is carried on or near one's person and is not discernible by ordinary observation.

Laws regulating the possession of weapons vary greatly from state to state. Moreover, many municipalities have enacted local ordinances even more restrictive than the laws of the states in which they are located. Most state gun control statutes (1) outlaw concealed weapons; (2) limit access to, or ownership of, handguns; (3) severely restrict ownership of modified shotguns and rifles, such as those that have been "sawed off"; and (4) criminalize possession of high explosives and weapons of mass destruction. Most states also have laws controlling the possession of guns by underage youths and laws that make it a crime to carry guns on school property or to discharge a firearm under specified circumstances. Many state codes go to considerable lengths in describing those to whom handgun and weapons laws do not apply, such as law enforcement officers, correctional personnel, and military personnel.

In recent years, however, and in response to growing crime rates and citizens' fears of victimization, a number of states have enacted laws permitting the carrying of concealed weapons by citizens who meet certain licensing requirements. Such requirements typically include handgun training and background checks or a demonstrated need to carry a weapon for protection.

Some individuals and groups, such as the National Rifle Association, argue that American citizens have a fundamental right to own firearms. Arguments in support of the right to own or carry weapons are often based on the Second Amendment to the U.S. Constitution, which reads, "[a] well regulated Militia, being necessary to the security of a free State, the right of the people to keep and bear Arms, shall not be infringed." Others, however, say that the individual ownership of handguns, rifles, shotguns, and other similar weapons has no place in a civilized society like ours. They argue that the Second Amendment is merely a restriction on the actions of the federal Congress—and that states are free to regulate or limit gun ownership as they see fit.

In recent years, the U.S. Supreme Court has addressed these and other debates surrounding the Second Amendment and the right to bear arms. In *McDonald v. Chicago* (2010), the Court held that the right to "keep and bear arms" is an individual right protected by the Second Amendment that applies to both the federal and state governments. In a 5-4 decision, the Court found that the Second Amendment was incorporated through the Fourteenth Amendment and thereby applicable to state and local authorities. The Court, however, did not state exactly what limitations the Second Amendment placed on state and local governments when they seek to regulate firearm possession. The Court even cautioned that some firearm restrictions, such as those "prohibit[ing] . . . the possession of firearms by felons or mentally ill" and "laws forbidding the carrying of firearms in sensitive places such as schools and government buildings, or laws imposing conditions and qualifications on the commercial sale of arms" would still likely be permissible. The Court's ruling in *McDonald* is likely to generate a substantial number of new legal challenges to current state and local firearm possession laws.

Law Line 6-3
McDonald v. Chicago (2010)

In *District of Columbia v. Heller* (2008),[17] the Supreme Court considered whether a District of Columbia law barring the registration of handguns, prohibiting carrying a pistol without a license, and requiring all lawful firearms to be kept unloaded and either disassembled or trigger locked violated the Second Amendment right of civilians seeking to possess firearms for private use. In a 5-4 ruling, the Court struck down the law, holding that the Second Amendment protects an individual's right to possess a firearm in nonmilitia settings and allows persons to use firearms for lawful purposes, like self-defense within the home. The ruling essentially rejected the theory that the Second Amendment protects only a collective right to bear arms for the purposes of maintaining a well-regulated militia.

Law Line 6-4
District of Columbia v. Heller (2008)

And in *United States v. Lopez* (1995), the Court invalidated the Gun-Free School Zones Act of 1990,[18] which made it a federal offense "for any individual knowingly to possess a firearm at a place that the individual knows, or has reasonable cause to believe, is a school zone."[19] In a 5-4 ruling, the Court agreed with the lower court's dismissal of charges against a twelfth-grade student who had carried a concealed .38-caliber handgun and five bullets into the Edison High School in San Antonio, Texas. The Court found that the law was not consistent with Congress's authority to regulate interstate commerce under Article I, section 8 of the U.S. Constitution. The Court found that, to uphold the law, "we would have to pile inference upon inference in a manner that would bid fair to convert congressional authority under the Commerce Clause to a general police power of the sort retained by the States."[20]

Gun Sales. Federal law provides a number of restrictions on the sale of firearms. Most notably, the so-called Brady Act[21]—the Brady Handgun Violence Prevention Act of 1994 —provides for a five-day waiting period before the purchase of a handgun[22] and for the establishment of a national instant criminal background-checking system to be used by firearms dealers before the transfer of any handgun. Originally, the law required licensed gun dealers to notify their chief local law enforcement officer of all handgun applications. But in 1997, the U.S. Supreme Court held that to impose such a requirement on local law enforcement officers was unconstitutional. In *Printz v. United States*[23] and *Mack v. United States*,[24] the Court found that principles of federalism precluded the federal government from exercising direct control over state officers. Writing for the majority, Justice Scalia noted that "the Court's jurisprudence makes clear that the Federal Government may not compel the States to enact or administer a federal regulatory program."

Although the cooperation of local law enforcement officers in conducting background checks can no longer be required, the general thrust of the Brady Law remains in effect. A federal National Instant Criminal Background Check System (Instacheck, or NICS) has since become operational and is used by gun dealers throughout the country. The system, run by the FBI's Criminal Justice Information Services (CJIS) Division, performs fast computerized criminal background checks and effectively zeros out the waiting period required for purchases. It has made gun sales cash-and-carry transactions in areas where they are not further restricted by state or local law.[25] Under Instacheck, a licensed importer, licensed manufacturer, or licensed dealer can verify the identity of an applicant using a valid photo ID (such as a driver's license) and can contact the system to receive a unique identification number authorizing the purchase before transfer of the handgun is made. Three years after the Brady Law went into effect, the Justice Department noted that the law had blocked gun sales to 186,000 criminals and others not allowed to buy firearms under its provisions.[26]

In addition, the Violent Crime Control and Law Enforcement Act of 1994 further regulated the sale of weapons within the United States, banning the manufacture of nineteen military-style assault weapons, including those with specific combat features, such as high-capacity ammunition clips that are capable of holding more than ten rounds. The act also specifically prohibited the sale or transfer of a gun to a juvenile, as well as the possession of a gun by a juvenile, and it prohibited gun sales to, and possession by, people who are subject to family violence restraining orders. Congress did not renew the assault weapons ban, however, and it expired in September 2004.

The Use of Firearms.   As addressed in Chapter 3, the use of a firearm in the commission of a criminal offense can bring enhanced consequences for the defendant. In some cases, the use of a gun will enhance the nature of the criminal charge (felonious assault with a firearm). In other cases, the use of a weapon will be treated as an aggravating circumstance of the underlying crime, resulting in a gun specification being included in the indictment as an attendant circumstance of the base level offense. Either way, if proven, a defendant's use of a firearm during the commission of a criminal offense can lead to increased sentencing measures, including mandatory prison time. See Chapter 3.

Crimes Involving Gambling and Gaming

Gambling is sometimes categorized under the heading "organized crime and vice offenses." We treat it here as an offense against morality because it has all of the characteristics of such an offense—although it may also frequently be associated with organized criminal activity. *Gambling* can be defined as the wagering of money, or of some other thing of value, on the outcome or occurrence of an event. It is illegal where made so by law. Gambling is sometimes called *gaming* in recognition of the fact that it may involve games of chance—that is, contests or events whose outcomes are determined at least in part by luck or chance.

Gambling was not a crime under common law unless conducted in such a manner that it constituted a public nuisance. Today, games of chance, including those based on lotteries as well as those making use of slot machines, are regulated

gambling
the wagering of money, or of some other thing of value, on the outcome or occurrence of an event

in all jurisdictions, and violations of those regulations constitute the statutory crime of gambling. The laws of U.S. jurisdictions vary considerably, however, as to what constitutes illegal gambling. For example, North Carolina law states, "[i]f any person plays at any game of chance at which any money, property, or other thing of value is bet, whether the same be in stake or not, both those who play and those who bet thereon shall be guilty of a misdemeanor."[27] North Carolina is among those states having no officially sanctioned "state lottery." States that have stringent antigaming laws generally also have statutes making it illegal to keep or own slot machines (unless disabled), "punchboards," gaming tables, and other gambling accouterments.

In Nevada, on the other hand, many games of chance—such as blackjack, poker, and "shooting dice"—are authorized but strictly regulated and closely controlled. In a number of other jurisdictions, only state-run lotteries are permitted. Some states allow on-track participants to bet on dog and horse races, while in other states no gambling or lottery of any type is allowed (although exceptions are frequently made for church raffles, bingo games, and fund-raisers sponsored by nonprofit organizations). Under federal law, Native Americans are allowed to conduct games of chance on Indian reservations that are recognized by the U.S. government as independent jurisdictions. As a general rule, however, it is fair to conclude that in most jurisdictions any form of gambling not specifically authorized by statute is considered illegal, although state laws regulating gambling vary considerably.

Several federal statutes also restrict gambling, including 18 U.S.C. § 1955, which prohibits on federally controlled property illegal gambling that is in violation of the local or state law; 18 U.S.C. § 1084, which prohibits the interstate transmission by wire communications of wagering information by persons engaged in illegal betting; 18 U.S.C. § 1952, which prohibits similar activities using the U.S. Postal Service; and 18 U.S.C. § 1953, which regulates the interstate transportation of gambling devices. A federal study of gambling, conducted some years ago, came to the conclusion that (1) illegal gambling is a growing industry in the United States, (2) the legalization of commercial gambling has not reduced illegal gambling, and (3) social gambling generally has been decriminalized by society.[28]

Alcohol-Related Crimes

Alcohol abuse is commonplace in American society today. As a result, most legal professionals working in the criminal justice system will regularly work with alcohol-related offenses. Two of the most common crimes involving alcohol are public drunkenness and driving while intoxicated.

To constitute the crime of *public drunkenness*, one must, while in a public place, be in a state of intoxication to such a degree that one is unable to care for oneself. It is not, however, a crime in most jurisdictions to be intoxicated in a private place, such as one's home. Some jurisdictions have established the statutory crime of being drunk and disorderly. As the name implies, this crime generally requires that the person be both drunk and disorderly for the offense to occur.

The crime of *driving while intoxicated (DWI)* is also referred to as *driving under the influence (DUI)* or *operating a motor vehicle while under the influence of alcohol or drugs (OMVI)*. These statutes generally have been expanded to encompass the operation of a motor vehicle while under the influence of drugs

public drunkenness
being in a public place while intoxicated to such a degree that one is unable to care for oneself

driving while intoxicated (DWI)
operating a motor vehicle while intoxicated

driving under the influence (DUI)
operating a vehicle while physically impaired

operating a motor vehicle while under the influence of alcohol or drugs (OMVI)
a charge akin to DUI or DWI

or other mind-altering substances. Generally, a person's first DUI conviction is counted as a misdemeanor, but subsequent offenses might be classified as felonies.

In most jurisdictions, there are two types of DUI offenses. The first form of DUI occurs whenever a person operates a motor vehicle while under the influence; the person's blood alcohol level is immaterial as long as his or her ability to operate a motor vehicle is impaired. The second type of DUI is the crime of operating a motor vehicle with a blood alcohol content (BAC) specified by statute to be at or above a certain level. This is often referred to as a *per se* DUI because it is based on the result of a person's BAC test. It does not require that the individual's driving skills be impaired, only that his blood alcohol level has reached a certain measurable level.

In recognition of this distinction, some jurisdictions have modified their statutes to include the phrase **driving with an unlawful blood alcohol level (DUBAL)**. The normal blood alcohol level for most DUBAL crimes is generally set by law as either 0.10 percent or 0.08 percent (alcohol content of blood by volume), with a lower level usually specified for operating an aircraft or boat. In addition, most jurisdictions make it a crime for a juvenile to operate a motor vehicle, boat, or airplane with any trace of alcohol in his blood. Others use a level of 0.05 percent for juveniles.

Some jurisdictions have established a third type of DUI, which involves a person operating a motor vehicle with an excessively high BAC. In Ohio, for example, individuals who drive with a BAC of 0.17 percent or higher are subject to enhanced penalties, including a mandatory six-day jail sentence. A few jurisdictions use blood alcohol level tests only to establish a presumption that a person has been operating a vehicle while under the influence of alcohol. In those jurisdictions, evidence may be admitted as to the effect that a certain level of blood alcohol is likely to have had on the defendant. Another variation, used in a few jurisdictions, considers blood alcohol levels below 0.06 percent to establish the presumption that a person was not under the influence of alcohol; levels of 0.07 percent to 0.10 percent to establish a presumption that the driver was under the influence; and levels of over 0.10 percent as irrefutable evidence that the person was under the influence of alcohol.

As with all statutes, some terminology is specific to DUI statutes. The term *under the influence* means, for example, that "alcohol or drugs or a combination thereof [has] so affected the nervous system, the brain, or muscles as to impair to an appreciable degree the ability of the person to operate a motor vehicle in an ordinary and cautious manner."[29]

Operating or driving a vehicle normally involves some intentional movement of the driver's vehicle. But in some jurisdictions, the vehicle does not need to be engaged or operating in order for a driver to be operating the vehicle under the law. Instead, under some statutes, if individuals have potential control over a vehicle, which may include having the car keys in their pockets or within reach, this may be considered to be operating a vehicle for DUI purposes. In some cases, drivers who are sleeping in their vehicle while the engine is turned off have been convicted of DUI.

The definition of motor vehicles generally includes animal-drawn vehicles, go-carts, forklifts, snowmobiles, bulldozers, mopeds, and mobile cranes.[30] Almost all jurisdictions, however, also have statutes that prohibit operating an aircraft, boat, or locomotive while under the influence of alcohol or drugs. The operator or driver is usually defined as the person who "drives," or is in actual physical control of the vehicle. See Figure 6-3).

driving with an unlawful blood alcohol level (DUBAL)
operating a motor vehicle while under the influence of drugs or other mind-altering substances

FIGURE 6-3 **Driving Under the Influence**

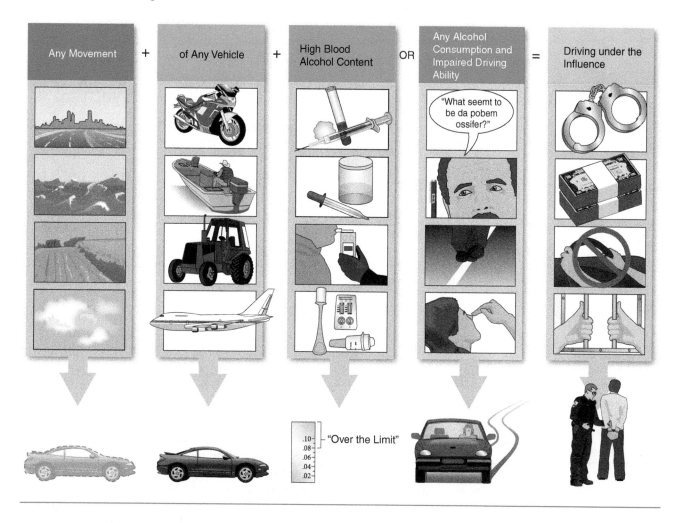

IN THE FIELD

Most legal professionals in the criminal justice system regularly handle DUI and other related cases, especially early in their careers. And although they are common, these cases are often technical in nature because many of them rely on scientific testing—BAC tests—to prove guilt. As a result, to be effective in these cases, legal professionals will often work with very technical terms and evidence regarding the science and technology behind BAC testing and other facets of DUI cases. The National Highway Traffic Safety Administration offers an Impaired Driving Safety Program for Traffic Safety and other materials, which provide background and training on the technical and legal standards for DUI cases.[31]

In addition, because there are so many legal, social, and financial ramifications for DUI defendants, it is important for legal professionals to consider these cases from a global perspective. A DUI conviction can bring incarceration, fines, alcohol treatment, driver's license suspension, job loss, and other consequences to many defendants. For example, most jurisdictions provide for the administrative suspension of a DUI defendant's driver's license for a high BAC test or the refusal to take the test.[32] And DUI cases can be particularly serious for a defendant who has a commercial driver's license (CDL) or otherwise depends on driving a motor vehicle for a living. Accordingly, legal professionals must consider all of the consequences for a DUI defendant before rendering legal assistance.

Immigration-Related Offenses

Congress has substantial constitutional power to regulate immigration, including the use of criminal laws to enforce its immigration policies. Federal criminal laws regulate immigration in two primary ways. First, they provide sanctions against those who enter the United States illegally. And second, for those immigrants legally present in the United States, immigration laws provide legal grounds for removal (deportation) if an alien commits a domestic criminal offense, including a crime at state or local level.

At the outset it must be observed that Article I, section 8 specifically authorizes Congress to "establish a uniform Rule of Naturalization." In addition, the Fourteenth Amendment provides that U.S. citizens include "persons born or naturalized in the United States, and subject to [its] jurisdiction." Based primarily on these two constitutional provisions, federal law classifies persons as either U.S. citizens or aliens. Generally, persons born or naturalized in the United States are *citizens*, while individuals who are not U.S. citizens are regarded as *aliens*. Under federal law, there are four primary categories of aliens: (1) lawful permanent residents (those with green cards), (2) immigrant visa holders, (3) temporary lawful visitors, and (4) undocumented illegal aliens.

Aliens who have entered and remain in the United States illegally face removal from the United States and possible criminal sanctions based on their inadmissibility under federal immigration law. The *Immigration and Nationality Act (INA)*[33] outlines several crimes related to a person's illegal entry into the country. For example, 8 U.S.C. § 1325 bars aliens from entering the United States without legal authorization, and 8 U.S.C. § 1326 prohibits a previously deported alien from reentering the country without obtaining the prior consent of the attorney general to reapply for admission. See Figure 6-4.

In addition, the INA also provides for the removal of aliens who are legally admitted to the United States, when the person commits a serious criminal offense or engages in another prohibited form of conduct. Section 237(a)(2) of the INA outlines the types of criminal offenses that might result in deportation, and they include crimes involving firearms and controlled substances, acts of moral turpitude, and aggravated felonies. Under this provision of federal law, the government must prove that a noncitizen is deportable under the INA by showing through clear and convincing evidence that the alien was convicted of a deportable offense.

citizens

persons born or naturalized in the United States

aliens

individuals who are not U.S. citizens

Immigration and Nationality Act (INA)

federal law that outlines several crimes related to a person's illegal entry into the country, including barring aliens from entering the United States without legal authorization

---

IN THE FIELD

Legal professionals increasingly are presented with immigration-related issues in many of their criminal cases. Such issues range from getting a court-appointed interpreter to help them and the court communicate with the client during the case to assessing whether the defendant will face deportation if convicted of the criminal charges. These and other matters often require legal professionals to seek assistance from other professionals, including Immigration and Naturalization Service (INS) officials, immigration attorneys, and translating services in order to provide effective legal assistance to the client.

FIGURE 6-4 **Illegal Reentry**

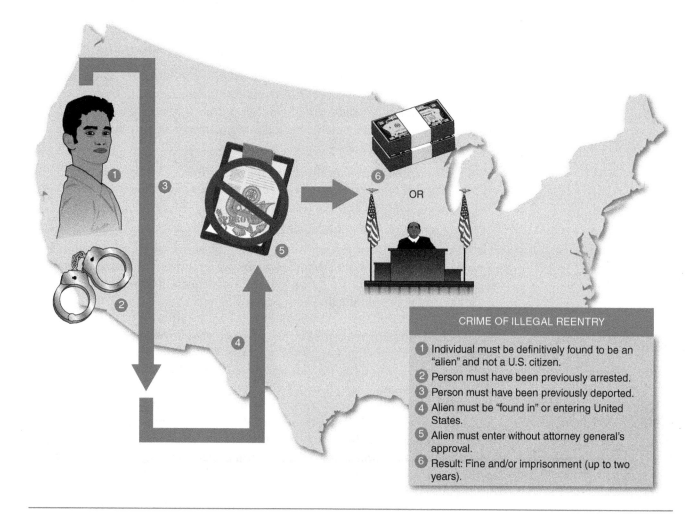

CRIME OF ILLEGAL REENTRY

1. Individual must be definitively found to be an "alien" and not a U.S. citizen.
2. Person must have been previously arrested.
3. Person must have been previously deported.
4. Alien must be "found in" or entering United States.
5. Alien must enter without attorney general's approval.
6. Result: Fine and/or imprisonment (up to two years).

CRIMES CHALLENGING THE LEGITIMACY OF GOVERNMENT

Another class of social-order offenses involves crimes that challenge the legitimacy and sovereignty of the government. This is a broad category of offenses, some of which can involve large-scale amounts of harm. Offenses in this category include terrorism, treason, misprision of treason, criminal syndicalism, rebellion, espionage, and sedition.

Terrorism

The federal government and the governments of all the states have terrorism laws. Acts of terrorism usually involve crimes against people and crimes against property. But terrorism is more than an attack on an individual or an individual's property. It is an attack on a government, using people or property as tools. The primary federal terrorism statute is 18 U.S.C.§ 2331, which defines **domestic terrorism** as activities that

domestic terrorism
criminal activities that are intended to coerce a population or influence a government through intimidation or fear

A. involve acts dangerous to human life that are a violation of the criminal laws of the United States or of any State;

B. appear to be intended—
  i. to intimidate or coerce a civilian population;
  ii. to influence the policy of a government by intimidation or coercion; or
  iii. to affect the conduct of a government by mass destruction, assassination, or kidnapping; and
C. occur primarily within the territorial jurisdiction of the United States.

Federal law also defines international terrorism in much the same manner, except that the harmful acts occur in territorial jurisdictions outside the United States. In addition, most states also define terrorism using similar or the same language. From these and other laws, the following common elements of the crime of terrorism can be extracted:

- the commission of an already established crime
- intended to coerce a population or influence a government
- through intimidation or fear

Beyond standard definitions of terrorism, there are several other terrorism-related crimes, which are found in a variety of subject-specific statutes. For example, bioterrorism, aiding terrorists, financing terrorists, and using weapons of mass destruction in terrorism are separate federal crimes. In some cases, terrorism law is embedded in a statute that addresses a different subject.

In addition, there are many statutes defining the authority and responsibilities of law enforcement officers and agencies that investigate, prevent, and prosecute acts of terrorism. One of the most significant federal laws affecting some terrorism investigations is the *Foreign Intelligence Surveillance Act of 1978 (FISA)*.[34] FISA stands apart from other federal criminal laws because it recognizes the special nature of foreign intelligence work. Under FISA, secret court orders authorizing foreign surveillance by officers of the United States are permitted, even though such orders would not be permitted in standard criminal cases within the United States. The rationale for the distinction is that such orders are not intended to further a prosecution but to advance the gathering of foreign intelligence needed to protect the nation.

Another law involved in the investigation of terrorism and other criminal offenses is the *USA PATRIOT Act*. In response to the attacks on the United States on September 11, 2001, Congress enacted the Uniting and Strengthening America by Providing Appropriate Tools Required to Intercept and Obstruct Terrorism Act of 2001, popularly known as the USA PATRIOT Act. The act, which was reauthorized in 2006, amended many existing laws, including FISA and the Electronic Communications Privacy Act of 1986. The changes included the following:

- The Attorney General was given greater authority to deport suspected alien terrorists.
- Federal law enforcement officials were given expanded authority to secure data about individuals held by third parties, including physicians, Internet providers, and libraries, based only on an assertion that the data will further an ongoing terrorism investigation. Previously, the government had to prove that the individual was an agent of a foreign power.
- The authority of federal law enforcement officials to monitor e-mail, voice mail, and other forms of communication was increased.

In many cases, acts of terrorism are perpetrated by individuals who do not represent another sovereign state or national power. This nonstate nature of

---

Foreign Intelligence Surveillance Act (FISA)
federal law that provides secret court orders authorizing foreign surveillance by officers of the United States

Law Line 6-5
FISA

USA PATRIOT Act
law passed in 2001 following September 11 attacks; allows expanded powers to federal authorities to investigate crime, including terrorism; stands for Uniting and Strengthening America by Providing Appropriate Tools Required to Intercept and Obstruct Terrorism Act;

FIGURE 6-5 **Traditional Crime versus Terrorism**

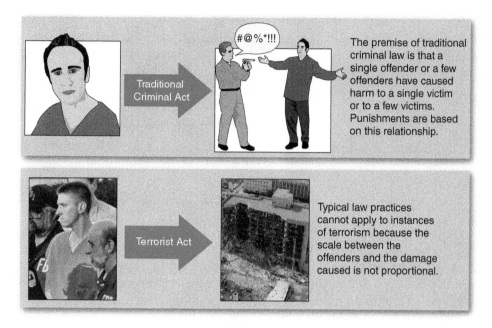

many terrorism offenses confounds the application to terrorism of the laws of war. In addition, it also challenges the traditional criminal justice model used to sanction harmful acts of human behavior. See Figure 6-5. The criminal justice model is premised on the notion of a single actor or a few actors who harm or steal from a single victim or a few victims. As addressed in Chapter 2, the U.S. criminal justice system's due process model is based on constitutional, adversarial, and accusatorial principles and is intended to protect individual liberties, sometimes at the expense of releasing wrongdoers without punishment. For example, a court may suppress critical evidence against the defendant when police engage in an unreasonable search and seizure under the Fourth Amendment. See Chapter 11.

Some believe that terrorism offenses should be treated differently. For some, laws against terrorism should be based as much on the prevention of harmful acts as on the prosecution and punishment of these acts. Some argue that the due process–based protections used in the traditional criminal justice system should not apply to some terrorism cases because the social costs of not detecting and preventing terrorism are more akin to the damages inflicted by war than the costs associated with traditional crimes. Some also claim that domestic courts are less knowledgeable and experienced in national security matters, and that to maintain the separation of powers, they should extend considerable deference to the judgments of the executive branch in matters of national security, foreign affairs, and war.[35] But many civil libertarians have challenged these and other arguments about the rule of law in terrorism cases, asserting that the model of due process should not be compromised, even though the nature of the harm may be different from more conventional criminal cases. See Figure 6-6 for a summary of the differences between individual crimes, war, and terrorism.

Law Line 6-6
USA PATRIOT Act

FIGURE 6-6 **Comparison of Individual Crimes, War, and Terrorism**

Model	Actors	Motive of Actors	Target of Action	Support	Harm
Individual crime	Individual or small group	Personal: money, anger, vengeance, etc.	Individuals or property	Individual actors	One or a few people killed or injured, small amounts of property loss
War	State	Political	State	State	States, large numbers of people killed or injured, significant property loss
Terrorism	Individual or small group	Personal but often furthering a state's or religion's objectives	State indirectly through people and property	Individual, group, state	States, small to large numbers of people killed or injured, small to moderate property loss

Treason

treason
the attempt to overthrow the government of the society of which one is a member

Treason can be defined as the attempt to overthrow the government of the society of which one is a member. Under early common law, it was considered high treason to kill the king or to promote a revolt in the kingdom. Treason under common law was neither a felony nor a misdemeanor but was thought to be in a class by itself. Much the same is true today, and treason is the only crime specifically mentioned in the U.S. Constitution, which says "[t]reason against the United States, shall consist only in levying War against them, or in adhering to their Enemies, giving them Aid and Comfort."[36] Federal statutes use wording similar to the Constitution: "[w]hoever, owing allegiance to the United States, levies war against them or adheres to their enemies, giving them aid and comfort within the United States or elsewhere, is guilty of treason and shall suffer death, or shall be imprisoned not less than five years and fined under this title but not less than ten thousand dollars ($10,000); and shall be incapable of holding any office under the United States."[37] Because treason is a breach of allegiance, persons who have lost or renounced their American citizenship cannot commit treason against the United States.[38]

The crime of treason requires some overt act, such as affirmative encouragement of the enemy. Disloyal thoughts alone are not sufficient to constitute treason. In addition, treason is a specific-intent offense, and conviction for treason requires that the defendant must have intended to betray the government. If the defendant acts with knowledge that her conduct will benefit the enemy, specific intent can be demonstrated. The U.S. Constitution provides: "[n]o Person shall be convicted of Treason unless on the Testimony of two Witnesses to the same overt Act, or on Confession in open Court."[39]

Treason is also a crime under the laws of most states. Some states, like California, have legislatively created the crime of treason, while in others the crime is constitutionally defined. Florida's constitution, for example, which mirrors wording in the U.S. Constitution, says: "[t]reason against the state shall consist only in levying war against it, adhering to its enemies, or giving them aid and comfort, and no person shall be convicted of treason except on the testimony of two witnesses to the same overt act or on confession in open court."[40]

Related Offenses Involving Threats to Government

misprision of treason
the concealment or nondisclosure of the known treason of another

A number of other criminal offenses involve threatening behavior that challenges the legitimacy of government. ***Misprision of treason*** is the concealment or nondisclosure of the known treason of another. It is punishable under federal law and under the laws of most states. ***Rebellion*** is the "deliberate, organized resistance, by force and arms, to the laws or operations of the government, committed by a subject."[41] Under federal law, rebellion is committed when a person incites or engages in any rebellion against the United States.[42] A related crime is that of advocating the overthrow of government. Federal law prohibits knowingly or willfully advocating the overthrow or destruction of the government of the United States or of any state.[43] It is also an offense in many jurisdictions to advocate, teach, or aid and abet ***criminal syndicalism***. Criminal syndicalism consists of advocating the use of unlawful acts as a means of accomplishing a change in industrial ownership or of controlling political change.[44]

Similar to treason is the crime of ***espionage***, or spying for a foreign government. Espionage is defined under the federal Espionage Act[45] as "gathering, transmitting or losing" information or secrets related to the national defense with the intent or the reasonable belief that such information will be used against the United States.

Finally, the crime of ***sedition*** consists of a communication or agreement intended to defame the government or to incite treason. Under federal law, the crime of seditious conspiracy is defined as follows: "[i]f two or more persons in any State or Territory, or in any place subject to the jurisdiction of the United States, conspire to overthrow, put down, or to destroy by force the Government of the United States, or to levy war against them, or to oppose by force the authority thereof, or by force to prevent, hinder, or delay the execution of any law of the United States, or by force to seize, take, or possess any property of the United States contrary to the authority thereof, they shall each be fined under this title or imprisoned not more than twenty years, or both."[46]

rebellion
the purposeful use of force to resist and otherwise rebel against governmental authority

criminal syndicalism
advocating the use of unlawful acts as a means of accomplishing a change in industrial ownership or of controlling political change

espionage
spying for a foreign government

sedition
crime consisting of a communication or agreement intended to defame the government or to incite treason

CRIMES AGAINST THE ADMINISTRATION OF GOVERNMENT

Another class of social-order offenses consists of crimes against the administration of government. Like terrorism offenses, this category of offenses also involves conduct that undermines the role and function of government. But typically the harm inflicted is on a much smaller and more individual scale. Offenses in this category include perjury, subornation of perjury, criminal contempt, obstruction of justice, resisting arrest, escape, misconduct in office, and bribery.

Perjury and Contempt

Under common law, ***perjury*** was the willful giving of false testimony under oath in a judicial proceeding. Most jurisdictions have enlarged the conduct prohibited under the crime of perjury to include any false testimony given under any lawfully administered oath. Accordingly, perjury may be committed if false testimony or a false statement is made under oath before any body that has lawful authority to administer an oath to witnesses who appear before it. For example, Pennsylvania law states, "[a] person is guilty of perjury, a felony of the third degree, if in any official proceeding he makes a false statement under oath or equivalent affirmation, or swears or affirms the truth of a statement previously made, when the statement is material and he does not believe it to be true."[47] Jurisdictions that have broadened the law of perjury sometimes call the offense *false swearing*.

To constitute perjury or false swearing, however, the false statement, as noted by the Pennsylvania law cited above, must be material. In other words, a false statement made under oath that concerns a matter that has no bearing on

perjury
the willful giving of false testimony under oath in a judicial proceeding

the proceedings at hand is not perjury. Again, Pennsylvania law provides, "[f]alsification is material, regardless of the admissibility of the statement under rules of evidence, if it could have affected the course or outcome of the proceeding. It is no defense that the declarant mistakenly believed the falsification to be immaterial. Whether a falsification is material in a given factual situation is a question of law."[48]

subornation of perjury
procuring another person to commit perjury

Subornation of perjury occurs when one person procures another to commit perjury. Federal law provides, "[w]hoever procures another to commit any perjury is guilty of subornation of perjury, and shall be fined under this title or imprisoned not more than five years, or both."[49] To commit this crime, the defendant must have known that the testimony to be given by a witness would be false, and the defendant must have caused the witness to actually give the false testimony.[50] For example, an attorney who calls a witness who the attorney knows will commit perjury is guilty of subornation of perjury in some jurisdictions. In other jurisdictions, the attorney would be considered to be a principal of the offense, and thus guilty of perjury.

criminal contempt
deliberate conduct calculated to obstruct or embarrass a court of law or conduct intended to degrade the role of a judicial officer in administering justice

Criminal contempt consists of deliberate conduct calculated to obstruct or embarrass a court of law or conduct intended to degrade the role of a judicial officer in administering justice. Criminal contempt harms the judicial process itself. It differs from civil contempt in that criminal contempt is a violation of criminal law,[51] which essentially is a violation of common law and of the statutory criminal law of most jurisdictions, whereas civil contempt is a sanction that a court can impose on a person who defies the court's lawful demands made on behalf of another party. Violating a court order to pay alimony, for example, may lead to a civil contempt charge, while being verbally abusive within the courtroom might constitute criminal contempt. In addition, two types of criminal contempt can be distinguished: (1) direct contempt, which consists of acts committed in the presence of the court, and (2) indirect contempt, which consists of acts committed outside of the court's presence. Direct contempt might consist, for example, of a physical assault on a judge while a hearing or trial is in progress. Indirect contempt might involve actions by a juror outside the courtroom that are contrary to the court's instructions, such as discussing the case with family or friends when ordered not to do so.

Although it is generally recognized that both forms of contempt are crimes, instances of direct contempt are usually dealt with summarily; that is, the judge in whose court the contempt occurs informs the "contemner" of the contempt accusation and asks him why he should not be found guilty of contempt. Lacking a satisfactory answer, the court will enter a judgment against the offender and will impose punishment. Individuals charged with indirect contempt must be afforded an opportunity to prepare a defense and may be represented by counsel.

Obstruction of justice

obstruction of justice
interfering with the administration of public justice

Obstruction of justice or the attempt to interfere with the administration of public justice, was a misdemeanor under common law. Today, obstruction of justice is statutorily defined by both the states and the federal government and may be either a felony or a misdemeanor, depending on the seriousness of the offense. As with common law, the statutory crime of obstruction of justice might involve jury tampering; interfering with the activities of an officer of the law or of the court; tampering with or suppressing evidence; threatening witnesses; or bribing judges, jurors, or witnesses.

Martha Stewart walking past the media as she arrives at federal court in 2004 in New York City, after she was charged with obstruction of justice, securities fraud, lying to investigators, and conspiracy. Stewart was later found guilty and sentenced to five months in prison, five months of home confinement, and two years probation.

Under federal law, there are many forms of obstruction of justice. See Figure 6-7. For example, 18 U.S.C. § 1507 provides, "[w]hoever, with the intent of interfering with, obstructing, or impeding the administration of justice, or with the intent of influencing any judge, juror, witness, or court officer, in the discharge of his duty, pickets or parades in or near a building housing a court of

FIGURE 6-7 **Federal Offenses Classified as Obstruction of Justice**

Title 18 U. S. Code Chapter 73—Obstruction of Justice

- § 1501. Assault on process server
- § 1502. Resistance to extradition agent
- § 1503. Influencing or injuring officer or juror generally
- § 1504. Influencing juror by writing
- § 1505. Obstruction of proceedings before departments, agencies, and committees
- § 1506. Theft or alteration of record or process; false bail
- § 1507. Picketing or parading
- § 1508. Recording, listening to, or observing proceedings of grand or petit juries while deliberating or voting
- § 1509. Obstruction of court orders
- § 1510. Obstruction of criminal investigations
- § 1511. Obstruction of State or local law enforcement
- § 1512. Tampering with a witness, victim, or an informant
- § 1513. Retaliating against a witness, victim, or an informant
- § 1514. Civil action to restrain harassment of a victim or witness
- § 1514A. Civil action to protect against retaliation in fraud cases
- § 1515. Definitions for certain provisions; general provision
- § 1516. Obstruction of Federal audit
- § 1517. Obstructing examination of financial institution
- § 1518. Obstruction of criminal investigations of health care offenses
- § 1519. Destruction, alteration, or falsification of records in Federal investigations and bankruptcy
- § 1520. Destruction of corporate audit records
- § 1521. Retaliating against a Federal judge or Federal law enforcement officer by false claim or slander of title

the United States, or in or near a building or residence occupied or used by such judge, juror, witness, or court officer, or with such intent uses any sound-truck or similar device or resorts to any other demonstration in or near any such building or residence, shall be fined under this title or imprisoned not more than one year, or both."[52]

Additionally, some states have made it a crime to refuse to render aid to law enforcement personnel in the official performance of their duties or to give false or misleading evidence to investigators. Other states have also created the crimes of endeavoring to obstruct justice and conspiring to obstruct justice.

One of the most common forms of obstruction of justice is **resisting arrest.** All states make it a crime to resist a lawful arrest. Some even require that a person submit to arrest by police officers who are carrying out their duties, even though the arrest may be unlawful. The defense of resisting unlawful arrest is discussed in Chapter 7. Oregon law, for example, provides, "[a] person commits the crime of resisting arrest if the person intentionally resists a person known by the person to be a peace officer in making an arrest."[53] Some states employ more generic statutes that take the focus off arrest and place it on resisting any public officer in the performance of his or her duties. North Carolina law, for example, states, "[i]f any person shall wilfully and unlawfully resist, delay or obstruct a public officer in discharging or attempting to discharge a duty of his office, he shall be guilty of a Class 2 misdemeanor."[54]

Escape

Under common law, prisoners who left lawful custody without permission committed the crime of **escape.** If force was used in the escape, the offense was termed *prison break* or *breach of prison.* While all jurisdictions have enacted statutes criminalizing escape, some state statutes apply only to those who leave correctional custody without permission, while others apply as well to those who leave the custody of law enforcement personnel. Generally, escape laws require intent on the part of the escapee, but even where they don't, the courts have typically held that intent is a necessary element of the crime of escape. Otherwise it would be possible to imagine, for example, the arrest and conviction of a sleeping work crew prisoner whom authorities inadvertently left behind when they returned to prison.

Some jurisdictions make it lawful for prisoners to escape if they are under extreme duress or facing threats. As a result, a prisoner who believes he is about to be murdered or raped by other inmates might lawfully escape in order to avoid being attacked. If such were to happen, however, the law would likely require that he turn himself in to authorities as soon as possible.

All jurisdictions make it illegal for anyone to help with an escape. Visitors to penal institutions, for example, may be guilty of the crime of aiding escape if they smuggle items into the facility that might be used in an escape attempt. Inmates who provide other prisoners with the tools or other means needed for an escape may also be charged with aiding or facilitating escape, as may correctional personnel who help inmates escape.

Misconduct in Office and Bribery

A public official who, under color of law or in his or her official capacity, acts in such a way as to exceed the bounds of the office may be guilty of **misconduct in office.** This offense includes acts "which the office holder had no right to perform, acts performed improperly, and failure to act in the face of an affirmative duty to

resisting arrest
conduct that is designed to make it more difficult for law enforcement officers to effectuate a lawful arrest

escape
a prisoner's act of leaving lawful custody without permission

misconduct in office
unlawful behavior by a person holding public office

act."[55] ***Malfeasance*** involves doing an act that the officeholder has no right to do. ***Misfeasance***, on the other hand, refers to official acts performed improperly. And ***nonfeasance*** describes failing to do that which should be done.

Misconduct can sometimes be the result of bribery. ***Bribery*** consists of "the offense of giving or receiving a gift or reward intended to influence a person in the exercise of a judicial or public duty."[56] As the definition notes, both the act of giving and the act of taking can constitute bribery—and a person who offers a bribe is just as guilty of the crime of bribery as the one who accepts it. The crime of bribery concerns only *official* acts, and no crime occurs when merely personal actions outside the official sphere are influenced by a bribe. As a result, under the laws of most jurisdictions, only public officeholders, state officials, or state employees acting in some official capacity can be found guilty of accepting bribes. Bribes may be offered, for example, to a jailer in an attempt to win the release of a prisoner, to a judge or juror to ensure the acquittal of a defendant in a criminal trial or a favorable verdict in a civil hearing or civil trial, to an elections official to win or influence an election, to a government decision maker to win a government contract, or to a legislator to gain passage of a favored bill.

CRIMES INVOLVING CONSENSUAL SEX ACTS

In Chapter 4, we discussed several types of sexual offenses, involving cases where sexual conduct is performed without the full consent of the victim. But there are other criminal offenses involving sexual activity or other conduct where the participants fully consent to the activity. The crime of prostitution offers one of the most common examples. Some argue that prostitution (and other such crimes) lowers the moral quality of life for everyone and demeans the status of women in society, thereby resulting in identifiable victims of such offenses. Others claim, however, that the freedom to make choices about one's intimate associations is one of the most basic features of a free society, which should not be regulated by government.

Prostitution and Other Consensual Sex Offenses

Most jurisdictions criminalize the act of ***prostitution***, which is generally defined as "sexual activity for hire." In essence, prostitution is sexual activity, including both sexual conduct and sexual contact, as a part of a commercial transaction. Under most prostitution statutes, the commercial nature of the sexual activity does not depend on a monetary transaction. Other items of value—drugs, alcohol, or merchandise—can constitute sufficient consideration for the sexual activity to be "for hire." Generally speaking, the elements of the crime of prostitution are

- engaging in or offering to perform
- a sexual act
- for hire

Prostitutes can be of either gender, and in most states both the prostitute and his or her customer can be found guilty of prostitution.

North Carolina law defines prostitution as "the offering or receiving of the body for sexual intercourse for hire [as well as] the offering or receiving of the body for indiscriminate sexual intercourse without hire."[57] Georgia law, on the other hand, limits the crime of prostitution to sexual intercourse for hire. Georgia law reads, "[a] person commits the offense of prostitution when he performs or offers or consents to perform an act of sexual intercourse for money."[58] A conviction

malfeasance
an officeholder's performance of an act that the officeholder has no right to do

misfeasance
official acts performed improperly

nonfeasance
failing to do that which should be done

bribery
providing a thing of value in exchange for a benefit from a public officeholder

prostitution
exchanging sexual activity for compensation

for prostitution does not require that the sexual act in question actually take place. An offer to perform the act, or consent to do so, is sufficient to constitute prostitution.

In addition to the primary act of prostitution, most state statutes also prohibit the associated acts of **compelling prostitution** (no person shall compel another to engage in sexual activity for hire), **procuring prostitution** (no person shall entice or solicit another to patronize a prostitute or procure a prostitute for another to patronize), **soliciting prostitution** (no person shall solicit another to engage with such other person in sexual activity for hire),[59] and **promoting prostitution** (profiting or attempting to profit by using others to engage in prostitution).[60]

compelling prostitution
compelling a person to engage in sexual activity for hire

procuring prostitution
enticing or soliciting a person to patronize a prostitute or procure a prostitute for another to patronize

soliciting prostitution
requesting services of prostitution

promoting prostitution
profiting or attempting to profit by using others to engage in prostitution

fornication
sexual relations outside of marriage

adultery
sexual conduct with a person who is married to another

Adultery

Although they may strike anyone with modern sensibilities as strange or outdated, laws against **fornication** and **adultery** (sexual relations outside of marriage or sexual conduct with a person who is married to another) continue to exist in some states. Holdovers from an earlier age, many such laws were passed in the late nineteenth or early twentieth centuries, when a strong family and sexual chastity were being promoted. As a result, many consensual sex offenses are still termed offenses against the family.

Contemporary Georgia law, for example, says, "[a]n unmarried person commits the offense of fornication when he voluntarily has sexual intercourse with another person and, upon conviction thereof, shall be punished as for a misdemeanor."[61] As the law indicates, fornication can only be committed by an unmarried person. Sexual intercourse that occurs between a male and a female, at least one of whom is married to someone else, is adultery. Under Georgia law, "[a] married person commits the offense of adultery when he voluntarily has sexual intercourse with a person other than his spouse and, upon conviction thereof, shall be punished as for a misdemeanor."[62] But despite the presence of adultery and fornication laws in the statute books, many of these laws are not regularly enforced or are considered unconstitutional infringements upon personal privacy, per the Supreme Court's ruling in *Lawrence v. Texas* (2003) (below).

Crimes against Nature

In some jurisdictions, the law books may contain a category of crime called crimes against nature. This is a general and rather outdated legislative grouping that, at times, has included statutes barring anal intercourse (insertion of an object into the anus of another), oral intercourse, including fellatio (involving oral stimulation of the penis) and cunnilingus (involving oral stimulation of the vaginal area), and bestiality (sexual relations with animals). Some laws also prohibit the act of sodomy, which although commonly understood to mean anal intercourse, also includes acts of fellatio and cunnilingus under some legislative definitions. In addition, some statutes have also included acts of homosexuality and heterosexual intercourse conducted in positions other than the "missionary" position.

Because crime against nature was long considered an unspeakable crime, statutes rarely provided precise definitions of the activities they outlawed. For example, a Rhode Island statute is entitled "Abominable and Detestable Crime Against Nature," and states, "[e]very person who shall be convicted of the abominable and detestable crime against nature, either with mankind or with any beast, shall be imprisoned not exceeding twenty (20) years nor less than seven (7) years."[63] Similarly, an Idaho law provides, "[e]very person who is guilty of the infamous crime against nature, committed with mankind or with any animal, is punishable by imprisonment in the state prison not less than five (5) years."[64] The Idaho Penal Code further states, "[a]ny sexual penetration, however slight, is sufficient to complete the crime against nature."[65] The lack of precise statutory definition of crimes against nature has some historical precedent. Blackstone's *Commentaries on the Laws of England*, for example, said that "the very mention of [such offense] is a disgrace to human nature" and referred to crime against nature as "a crime not fit to be named."[66]

In some cases courts have chosen to offer their own definitions of *crime against nature*. One North Carolina court, for example, held, "[t]he crime against nature is sexual intercourse contrary to the order of nature. It includes acts with animals and acts between humans per anum and per os."[67] Another court ruled that "[c]rime against nature embraces sodomy, buggery, and bestiality, as those offenses were known and defined at common law."[68] And in one case, the court even held that "[i]n charging the offense of crime against nature, because of its vile and degrading nature, there has been some laxity of the strict rules of pleading. It has never been the usual practice to describe the particular manner or the details of the commission of the act."[69] In earlier time, some states included homosexual behavior as a crime against nature, calling it "deviate" sexual intercourse. South Carolina, for example, criminalized homosexual acts as the "abominable crime of buggery."

But in modern times, where statutory interpretations are lacking or criminal laws unduly interfere with the rights of personal privacy, courts can strike down such laws as being unconstitutionally vague, unnecessarily overbroad, or an infringement of personal liberty interests. In *Lawrence v. Texas* (2003),[70] the Supreme Court struck down a Texas sodomy law that prohibited individuals of the same sex from engaging in sodomy. The law did not bar heterosexual sodomy. The Court invalidated the law on due process grounds, concluding that it infringed upon "the liberty of the person both in its spatial and more transcendent dimensions." Writing for the majority, Justice Anthony Kennedy noted that, at the

John Lawrence, left, and Tryon Garner, right, arrive at the state courthouse in Houston to face charges of homosexual conduct under Texas sodomy law, in this November 20, 1998 photo. Their case went before the U.S. Supreme Court, where the Court ruled that the sodomy laws in Texas and other states were unconstitutional.

heart of liberty, "is the right to define one's own concept of existence, of meaning, of the universe, and of the mystery of human life." In effect, the Court concluded that private sexual acts between consenting adults are a part of the personal liberties protected by the Due Process Clause of the Constitution. Such liberties include personal decisions about marriage, procreation, family relationships, and education.[71] The *Lawrence* decision effectively struck down all antisodomy laws, except those involving force or victimized individuals who, by reason of age or impairment, are not able to give effective legal consent.

Read the majority opinion in *Lawrence* (below) and try to assess what future impact this decision may have on other criminal laws that attempt to control private and consensual behavior.

CAPSTONE CASE *Lawrence v. Texas*, 539 U.S. 558 (2003)

Justice Kennedy delivered the opinion of the Court.

Liberty protects the person from unwarranted government intrusions into a dwelling or other private places. In our tradition the State is not omnipresent in the home. And there are other spheres of our lives and existence, outside the home, where the State should not be a dominant presence. Freedom extends beyond spatial bounds. Liberty presumes an autonomy of self that includes freedom of thought, belief, expression, and certain intimate conduct. The instant case involves liberty of the person both in its spatial and more transcendent dimensions. . . .

The question before the Court is the validity of a Texas statute making it a crime for two persons of the same sex to engage in certain intimate sexual conduct.

In Houston, Texas, officers of the Harris County Police Department were dispatched to a private residence in response to a reported weapons disturbance. They entered an apartment where one of the petitioners, John Geddes Lawrence, resided. The right of the police to enter does not seem to have been questioned. The officers observed Lawrence and another man, Tyron Garner, engaging in a sexual act. The two petitioners were arrested, held in custody over night, and charged and convicted before a Justice of the Peace.

The complaints described their crime as "deviate sexual intercourse, namely anal sex, with a member of the same sex (man)." The applicable state law is Tex. Penal Code Ann. § 21.06(a) (2003). It provides: "A person commits an offense if he engages in deviate sexual intercourse with another individual of the same sex."

* * *

We conclude the case should be resolved by determining whether the petitioners were free as adults to engage in the private conduct in the exercise of their liberty under the Due Process Clause of the Fourteenth Amendment to the Constitution . For this inquiry we deem it necessary to reconsider the Court's holding in *Bowers* [*Bowers v. Hardwick* (1986)]. . . .

The facts in *Bowers* had some similarities to the instant case. A police officer, whose right to enter seems not to have been in question, observed Hardwick, in his own bedroom, engaging in intimate sexual conduct with another adult male. The conduct was in violation of a Georgia statute making it a criminal offense to engage in sodomy. One difference between the two cases is that the Georgia statute prohibited the conduct whether or not the participants were of the same sex, while the Texas statute, as we have seen, applies only to participants of the same sex. Hardwick was not prosecuted, but he brought an action in federal court to declare the state statute invalid. He alleged he was a practicing homosexual and that the criminal prohibition violated rights guaranteed to him by the Constitution. . . .

It must be acknowledged, of course, that the Court in *Bowers* was making the broader point that for centuries there have been powerful voices to condemn homosexual conduct as immoral. The condemnation has been shaped by religious beliefs, conceptions of right and acceptable behavior, and respect for the traditional family. For many persons these are not trivial concerns but profound and deep convictions accepted as ethical and moral principles to which they aspire and which thus determine the course of their lives. These considerations do not answer the question before us, however. The issue is whether the majority may use the power of the State to enforce these views on the whole society through operation of the criminal law. "Our obligation is to define the liberty of all, not to mandate our own moral code." . . .

In our own constitutional system the deficiencies in *Bowers* became even more apparent in the years following its announcement. The 25 States with laws prohibiting the relevant conduct referenced in the *Bowers* decision are reduced now to 13, of which 4 enforce their laws only against homosexual conduct. In those States where sodomy is still proscribed, whether for same-sex or heterosexual conduct, there is a pattern of nonenforcement with respect to consenting adults acting in private. The State of Texas admitted in 1994 that as of that date it had not prosecuted anyone under those circumstances. . . .

In explaining the respect the Constitution demands for the autonomy of the person in making these choices, we stated as follows:

"These matters, involving the most intimate and personal choices a person may make in a lifetime, choices central to personal dignity and autonomy, are central to the liberty protected by the Fourteenth Amendment. At the heart of liberty is the right to define one's own concept of existence, of meaning, of the universe, and of the mystery of human life. Beliefs about these matters could not define the attributes of personhood were they formed under compulsion of the State."

Persons in a homosexual relationship may seek autonomy for these purposes, just as heterosexual persons do. The decision in *Bowers* would deny them this right. . . .

Equality of treatment and the due process right to demand respect for conduct protected by the substantive guarantee of liberty are linked in important respects, and a decision on the latter point advances both interests. If protected conduct is made criminal and the law which does so remains unexamined for its substantive validity, its stigma might remain even if it were not enforceable as drawn for equal protection reasons. When homosexual conduct is made criminal by the law of the State, that declaration in and of itself is an invitation to subject homosexual persons to discrimination both in the public and in the private spheres. The central holding of *Bowers* has been brought in question by this case, and it should be addressed. Its continuance as precedent demeans the lives of homosexual persons.

The stigma this criminal statute imposes, moreover, is not trivial. The offense, to be sure, is but a class C misdemeanor, a minor offense in the Texas legal system. Still, it remains a criminal offense with all that imports for the dignity of the persons charged. The petitioners will bear on their record the history of their criminal convictions. Just this Term we rejected various challenges to state laws requiring the registration of sex offenders. We are advised that if Texas convicted an adult for private, consensual homosexual conduct under the statute here in question the convicted person would come within the registration laws of at least four States were he or she to be subject to their jurisdiction. This underscores the consequential nature of the punishment and the state-sponsored condemnation attendant to the criminal prohibition. Furthermore, the Texas criminal conviction carries with it the other collateral consequences always following a conviction, such as notations on job application forms, to mention but one example. . . .

(continued)

(continued)

The present case does not involve minors. It does not involve persons who might be injured or coerced or who are situated in relationships where consent might not easily be refused. It does not involve public conduct or prostitution. It does not involve whether the government must give formal recognition to any relationship that homosexual persons seek to enter. The case does involve two adults who, with full and mutual consent from each other, engaged in sexual practices common to a homosexual lifestyle. The petitioners are entitled to respect for their private lives. . . .

Had those who drew and ratified the Due Process Clauses of the Fifth Amendment or the Fourteenth Amendment known the components of liberty in its manifold possibilities, they might have been more specific. They did not presume to have this insight. They knew times can blind us to certain truths and later generations can see that laws once thought necessary and proper in fact serve only to oppress. As the Constitution endures, persons in every generation can invoke its principles in their own search for greater freedom.

The judgment of the Court of Appeals for the Texas Fourteenth District is reversed, and the case is remanded for further proceedings not inconsistent with this opinion.

It is so ordered.

WHAT DO *YOU* THINK?

1. Do you agree with the above rationale provided by the Court for overruling *Bowers v. Hardwick*?
2. Was this a case where the U.S. Supreme Court changed its ruling based on public and international criticism?

Bigamy

Another public morality crime is bigamy—the crime of marrying one person while still legally married to another person. Bigamy is categorized as a crime against the family. While not a crime under early common law, bigamy was an ecclesiastical offense (that is, a crime against the church). In 1603, the British Parliament declared bigamy a capital offense. Today, under the Model Penal Code and the laws of many states, it is a misdemeanor.

Generally, the crime of bigamy is not committed if a person marries without divorcing from a prior spouse if the defendant's wife or husband has been absent for an extended period (generally about seven years) and the defendant honestly believes that the husband or wife is dead—or if there was a judgment of divorce or dissolution that was later declared void. Bigamy does not necessarily fall into the category of victimless crimes, since the second spouse of one who is already legally married may be unaware of the previous marriage. Even so, as one court recently held: "At common law and under this section bigamy is an offense against society rather than against the lawful spouse of the offender."[72]

Some jurisdictions have also created the companion crime of marrying the spouse of another. As the name implies, this offense occurs when a person knowingly and willfully marries the husband or wife of another. A similar offense, polygamy, is the marrying of, or cohabiting with, more than one spouse at a time in the purported exercise of the right of plural marriage. In most jurisdictions, polygamy is a felony. And in many cases, especially those involving minors, the criminal charge of bigamy or polygamy is accompanied by additional charges of rape, statutory rape, or other forms of sexual assault.

Incest

Incest is another offense frequently viewed as a crime against nature. This crime generally consists of unlawful sexual intercourse with a relative through blood or marriage, such as one's brother, sister, mother, or father. One court defined incest as "sexual intercourse within or outside the bonds of marriage between persons related within certain prohibited degrees."[73] Incest is sometimes termed *prohibited sexual contact*. While many incest cases involve consensual behavior, others do not and can involve child sexual abuse or other serious crimes. Georgia's incest law provides, "[a] person commits the offense of incest when he engages in sexual intercourse with a person to whom he knows he is related either by blood or by marriage as follows: (1) Father and daughter or stepdaughter; (2) Mother and son or stepson; (3) Brother and sister of the whole blood or of the half blood; (4) Grandparent and grandchild; (5) Aunt and nephew; or (6) Uncle and niece."[74] The law also stipulates that "[a] person convicted of the offense of incest shall be punished by imprisonment for not less than one nor more than 20 years."

IN THE FIELD

In cases involving taboo—yet consensual—sex acts, legal professionals must be mindful of the constitutional limitations on the regulation of privacy and expression. A number of legal scholars have criticized the notion of crimes against public decency and morality—calling them "legal moralism"—and saying that they represent little more than attempts "to achieve conformity with private moral standards through use of the criminal law."[75] While one could argue that all laws—even those condemning murder, rape, and other violent crimes—are based on socially shared conceptualizations of morality, the essential question for legal professionals considering morality-based criminal statutes is how far into the private lives of citizens may government-sanctioned views of morality properly intrude?

The Supreme Court's ruling in *Lawrence v. Texas* (2003) (opinion excerpt above) provides some insight into answering this question and offers defendants some of the most effective constitutional defenses to laws regulating private and consensual behavior. This decision provides grounds for defendants charged with offenses of prostitution, consensual incest, or other purported crimes against nature to challenge the criminal statutes as being an unconstitutional interference with personal privacy and individual expression. As a result, legal professionals must be thoroughly familiar with *Lawrence* and understand the relevance of the ruling to their individual cases.

CRIMES INVOLVING SEXUAL MATERIALS

In addition to laws banning particular forms of sexual activity between two or more persons, some criminal statutes also regulate materials that depict sexual activity. Generally, these laws are designed to protect individuals from viewing materials that may offend their sensibilities or those of society and to otherwise guard against so-called harmful *secondary effects* that may be associated with depictions of human sexuality. These laws attempt to regulate five forms of human sexuality—pornography, obscenity, child pornography, lewdness, and sexually oriented entertainment.

Pornography and Obscenity

Two of the most common terms used in criminal statutes that regulate the depictions of human sexuality are *pornography* and *obscenity*. These terms, while related to one another, have separate and distinct legal meanings. Pornography can be defined as "the depiction of sexual behavior in such a way as to excite the viewer sexually."[76] In other words, pornography is the depiction of sexuality for the purpose of sexual arousal. Pornographic materials are also referred to as *sexually oriented materials* or *adult materials* in some statutes. Generally speaking, the Supreme Court has ruled that nonobscene pornography depicting consenting adults is a protected form of expression under the First Amendment. As a result, government cannot completely ban adult pornography and must provide sufficient justification before it can regulate the time, place, or manner of its distribution or use.

Obscene materials, however, are a different matter. Unlike pornography, the Supreme Court has held that obscenity is an unprotected form of expression under the First Amendment, thereby allowing government to prohibit such materials as criminal contraband.[77] All jurisdictions have laws that punish the sale and distribution of obscene material. Obscenity involves a more precise legal definition than pornography. In *Miller v. California* (1973),[78] the Court held that to be obscene, material must meet all of the following requirements:

1. The average person, applying contemporary community standards, would find that the work, taken as a whole, appeals to the prurient interest.
2. The work depicts or describes, in a patently offensive way, sexual conduct specifically defined by the applicable statute.
3. The work, taken as a whole, lacks serious literary, artistic, political, or scientific value. [79]

Consistent with the Court's ruling in *Miller*, modern California law defines *obscene matter* as "matter, taken as a whole, that to the average person, applying contemporary statewide standards, appeals to the prurient interest, that, taken as a whole, depicts or describes sexual conduct in a patently offensive way, and that, taken as a whole, lacks serious literary, artistic, political, or scientific value."[80] As used in the definition, prurient interest means "[o]bsession with lascivious and immoral matters."[81]

Law Line 6-7
Miller v. California

While the production, mailing, and sale of obscene material may be subject to criminal sanctions, the U.S. Supreme Court has made it clear that overarching issues of privacy protect a person's right to read or view such materials within the confines of his or her own home. In *Stanley v. Georgia* (1969),[82] the Court held, "[w]hatever may be the justification for other statutes regulating obscenity, we do not think they reach into the privacy of one's own home. If the First Amendment means anything, it means a State has no business telling a man, sitting alone in his own home, what books he may read or what films he may watch." The "right of privacy," however, does not protect the public exhibition of obscene matter nor the involvement of minors.[83]

Child Pornography Laws

One special area of recent concern in pornography legislation is the sexual exploitation of children, or child pornography. The Supreme Court has identified child pornography as unprotected expression. In *New York v. Ferber* (1982)[84] the U.S. Supreme Court held that a New York law against the distribution of child pornography was valid even though the material in question did not necessarily meet the legal standards for obscenity—it did not appeal to the prurient interest of the average person and was not displayed in what could be regarded as a patently offensive manner. The Court reasoned that, because real children can be harmed during the production of child pornography, governments can ban such materials without running afoul of the First or Fourteenth Amendments. Accordingly, the possession, production, or distribution of child pornography is prohibited by all state and federal authorities, including the federal Child Protection Act of 1984, which makes it a crime to knowingly receive through the mail a "visual depiction [involving] a minor engaging in sexually explicit conduct."

The Supreme Court, however, has placed some limitations on child pornography laws. In *Ashcroft v. Free Speech Coalition* (2002).[85] the Court invalidated portions of the federal Child Pornography Prevention Act (CPPA) that prohibited pornographic *virtual* images of children. The CPPA criminalized depictions that *appeared to be* of children engaging in sex or that *conveyed the impression* that children were engaging in sexual activity. The Court found these two phrases were unconstitutionally overbroad because their facial language applied to many mainstream movies, including *Traffic*, *American Beauty*, and *Titanic*, which depicted scenes of teenage sexuality but were not produced using actual children.

Subsequently, in 2008, the Supreme Court reviewed the Prosecutorial Remedies and Other Tools to End the Exploitation of Children Today Act of 2003 (PROTECT Act), which among other things prohibited a person from promoting or presenting real or purported material as being child pornography. The Supreme Court upheld the validity of some portions of this law in *United States v. Williams* (2008) (below).

Law Line 6-8
Ashcroft v. Free Speech Coalition

CAPSTONE CASE *United States v. Williams*, 553 U.S. 285 (2008)

Justice Scalia delivered the opinion of the Court.

Section 2252A(a)(3)(B) of Title 18, United States Code, criminalizes, in certain specified circumstances, the pandering or solicitation of child pornography. This case presents the question whether that statute is overbroad under the First Amendment or impermissibly vague under the Due Process Clause of the Fifth Amendment....

We have long held that obscene speech—sexually explicit material that violates fundamental notions of decency—is not protected by the First Amendment. But to protect explicit material that has social value, we have limited the scope of the obscenity exception and have overturned convictions for the distribution of sexually graphic but nonobscene material.

Over the last 25 years, we have confronted a related and overlapping category of proscribable speech: child pornography. See *Ashcroft v. Free Speech Coalition*, 535 U.S. 234 (2002). This consists of sexually explicit visual portrayals that feature children. We have held that a statute which proscribes the distribution of all child pornography, even material that does not qualify as obscenity, does not on its face violate the First Amendment. Moreover, we have held that the government may criminalize the possession of child pornography, even though it may not criminalize the mere possession of obscene material involving adults.

The broad authority to proscribe child pornography is not, however, unlimited. Four Terms ago, we held facially overbroad two provisions of the federal Child Pornography Protection Act of 1996 (CPPA). *Free Speech Coalition*. The first of these banned the possession and distribution of "any visual depiction" that "is, or appears to be, of a minor engaging in sexually explicit conduct," even if it contained

(continued)

(continued)

only youthful-looking adult actors or virtual images of children generated by a computer. This was invalid, we explained, because the child-protection rationale for speech restriction does not apply to materials produced without children. . . .

After our decision in *Free Speech Coalition*, Congress went back to the drawing board and produced [the statute being reviewed today,] . . . relevant portions of which now read as follows:

"(a) Any person who—
"(3) knowingly—

. . .

"(B) advertises, promotes, presents, distributes, or solicits through the mails, or in interstate or foreign commerce by any means, including by computer, any material or purported material in a manner that reflects the belief, or that is intended to cause another to believe, that the material or purported material is, or contains—

"(i) an obscene visual depiction of a minor engaging in sexually explicit conduct; or
"(ii) a visual depiction of an actual minor engaging in sexually explicit conduct,

. . .

"shall be punished as provided in subsection (b)."

The Act's express findings indicate that Congress was concerned that limiting the child-pornography prohibition to material that could be *proved* to feature actual children, as our decision in *Free Speech Coalition* required, would enable many child pornographers to evade conviction. The emergence of new technology and the repeated retransmission of picture files over the Internet could make it nearly impossible to prove that a particular image was produced using real children. . . .

On April 26, 2004, respondent Michael Williams, using a sexually explicit screen name, signed in to a public Internet chat room. A Secret Service agent had also signed in to the chat room under the moniker "Lisa n Miami." The agent noticed that Williams had posted a message that read: "Dad of toddler has 'good' pics of her an [sic] me for swap of your toddler pics, or live cam." The agent struck up a conversation with Williams, leading to an electronic exchange of nonpornographic pictures of children. (The agent's picture was in fact a doctored photograph of an adult.) Soon thereafter, Williams messaged that he had photographs of men molesting his 4-year-old daughter. Suspicious that "Lisa n Miami" was a law-enforcement agent, before proceeding further Williams demanded that the agent produce additional pictures. When he did not, Williams posted the following public message in the chat room: "HERE ROOM; I CAN PUT UPLINK CUZ IM FOR REAL—SHE CANT." Appended to this declaration was a hyperlink that, when clicked, led to seven pictures of actual children, aged approximately 5 to 15, engaging in sexually explicit conduct and displaying their genitals. The Secret Service then obtained a search warrant for Williams's home, where agents seized two hard drives containing at least 22 images of real children engaged in sexually explicit conduct, some of it sadomasochistic.

Williams was charged with one count of pandering child pornography under §2252A(a)(3)(B) and one count of possessing child pornography under §2252A(a)(5)(B). He pleaded guilty to both counts but reserved the right to challenge the constitutionality of the pandering conviction. The District Court rejected his challenge and sentenced him to concurrent 60-month sentences on the two counts. The United States Court of Appeals for the Eleventh Circuit reversed the pandering conviction, holding that the statute was both overbroad and impermissibly vague. . . .

(continued)

According to our First Amendment overbreadth doctrine, a statute is facially invalid if it prohibits a substantial amount of protected speech. The doctrine seeks to strike a balance between competing social costs. On the one hand, the threat of enforcement of an overbroad law deters people from engaging in constitutionally protected speech, inhibiting the free exchange of ideas. On the other hand, invalidating a law that in some of its applications is perfectly constitutional—particularly a law directed at conduct so antisocial that it has been made criminal—has obvious harmful effects. In order to maintain an appropriate balance, we have vigorously enforced the requirement that a statute's overbreadth be *substantial*, not only in an absolute sense, but also relative to the statute's plainly legitimate sweep. . . .

A number of features of the statute are important to our analysis:

First, the statute includes a scienter requirement. The first word of §2252A(a)(3) —"knowingly"—[applies to the provisions under which Williams was prosecuted]. . . .

Second, the statute's string of operative verbs—"advertises, promotes, presents, distributes, or solicits"—is reasonably read to have a transactional connotation. That is to say, the statute penalizes speech that accompanies or seeks to induce a transfer of child pornography—via reproduction or physical delivery— from one person to another. . . .

Third, the phrase "in a manner that reflects the belief" includes both subjective and objective components. "[A] manner that reflects the belief" is quite different from "a manner that would give one cause to believe." The first formulation suggests that the defendant must actually have held the subjective "belief" that the material or purported material was child pornography. . . .

Fourth, the other key phrase, "in a manner . . . that is intended to cause another to believe," contains only a subjective element: The defendant must "intend" that the listener believe the material to be child pornography and must select a manner of "advertising, promoting, presenting, distributing, or soliciting" the material that *he* thinks will engender that belief—whether or not a reasonable person would think the same. . . .

Fifth, the definition of "sexually explicit conduct" (the visual depiction of which, engaged in by an actual minor, is covered by the Act's pandering and soliciting prohibition even when it is not obscene) is very similar to the definition of "sexual conduct" in the New York statute we upheld against an overbreadth challenge in *Ferber*. . . .

We now turn to whether the statute, as we have construed it, criminalizes a substantial amount of protected expressive activity. . . .

Offers to engage in illegal transactions are categorically excluded from First Amendment protection. . . .

To be sure, there remains an important distinction between a proposal to engage in illegal activity and the abstract advocacy of illegality. The Act before us does not prohibit advocacy of child pornography but only offers to provide or requests to obtain it. There is no doubt that this prohibition falls well within constitutional bounds. The constitutional defect we found in the pandering provision at issue in *Free Speech Coalition* was that it went *beyond* pandering to prohibit possession of material that could not otherwise be proscribed. . . .

In sum, we hold that offers to provide or requests to obtain child pornography are categorically excluded from the First Amendment. . . .

WHAT DO *YOU* THINK?

1. Should speech in the form of an offer to engage in a criminal act be sufficient to establish criminal liability?

2. Does your opinion change if there is no apparent ability to commit the act?

3. Should there be a hard-line rule that applies to all crimes, or should the First Amendment be interpreted flexibly, allowing legislatures to distinguish between crimes, depending on perceived risks and harm?

Lewdness Statutes

In addition to laws against obscenity and child pornography, some jurisdictions have strictures against lewdness. Lewd behavior consists of intimate activity by a single individual where such activity is intended to be sexually arousing. New Jersey law defines *lewd acts* to "include the exposing of the genitals for the purpose of arousing or gratifying the sexual desire of the actor or of any other person."[86] Under common law, it was a misdemeanor for persons to intentionally expose their private parts in a public place. Most of today's laws follow in this tradition.

Lewd behavior is sometimes written alongside the term *lascivious*. Lascivious refers to something that is obscene or lewd or tends to cause lust. Lewd and lascivious conduct is sometimes also termed *public indecency* or indecent exposure. Georgia law, for example, states, "[a] person commits the offense of public indecency when he or she performs any of the following acts in a public place: (1) An act of sexual intercourse; (2) A lewd exposure of the sexual organs; (3) A lewd appearance in a state of partial or complete nudity; or (4) A lewd caress or indecent fondling of the body of another person."[87] New Jersey confronts lewdness in the following terms:

New Jersey Code, Section 14-4

    a. A person commits a disorderly person's offense if he does any flagrantly lewd and offensive act which he knows or reasonably expects is likely to be observed by other non-consenting persons who would be affronted or alarmed.

    b. A person commits a crime of the fourth degree if:

        1. He exposes his intimate parts for the purpose of arousing or gratifying the sexual desire of the actor or of any other person under circumstances where the actor knows or reasonably expects he is likely to be observed by a child who is less than thirteen years of age where the actor is at least four years older than the child.

        2. He exposes his intimate parts for the purpose of arousing or gratifying the sexual desire of the actor or of any other person under circumstances where the actor knows or reasonably expects he is likely to be observed by a person who because of mental disease or defect is unable to understand the sexual nature of the actor's conduct.

    c. As used in this section: "lewd acts" shall include the exposing of the genitals for the purpose of arousing or gratifying the sexual desire of the actor or of any other person.

Sexually Oriented Business Laws

Many jurisdictions also have enacted laws regulating nude dancing and other forms of adult entertainment. These laws are identified as sexually oriented business or "SOB" laws because they regulate the time, place, and manner in which sexually oriented entertainment can be offered to patrons. Such laws are often challenged on First Amendment grounds, presenting a conflict between the police power of government and the expressive freedoms of individuals. The Supreme Court addressed the proper balance between these two interests in *City of Erie v. Pap's A.M* (2000).

As you read the Court's opinion in *Pap's*, notice that, while still affording sexual expression some constitutional protection, the Supreme Court has regarded such expression to be on the outer limits of First Amendment safeguards. As a result, the Court generally has allowed legislatures to enact reasonable time, place, and manner regulations on adult entertainment, as long as they afford sufficient due process protections, including prompt judicial review and sufficient governmental justification, when implementing the regulations.

CAPSTONE CASE *City of Erie v. Pap's A.M.*, 529 U.S. 277 (2000)

Justice O'Connor announced the judgment of the Court....

On September 28, 1994, the city council for the city of Erie, Pennsylvania, enacted Ordinance 75-1994, a public indecency ordinance that makes it a summary offense to knowingly or intentionally appear in public in a "state of nudity." Respondent Pap's, a Pennsylvania corporation, operated an establishment in Erie known as "Kandyland" that featured totally nude erotic dancing performed by women. To comply with the ordinance, these dancers must wear, at a minimum, "pasties" and a "G-string." On October 14, 1994, two days after the ordinance went into effect, Pap's filed a complaint against the city of Erie, the mayor of the city, and members of the city council, seeking declaratory relief and a permanent injunction against the enforcement of the ordinance....

Being "in a state of nudity" is not an inherently expressive condition. As we explained in *Barnes*, however, nude dancing of the type at issue here is expressive conduct, although we think that it falls only within the outer ambit of the First Amendment's protection....

To determine what level of scrutiny applies to the ordinance at issue here, we must decide "whether the State's regulation is related to the suppression of expression." If the governmental purpose in enacting the regulation is unrelated to the suppression of expression, then the regulation need only satisfy the "less stringent" standard from *O'Brien* for evaluating restrictions on symbolic speech. If the government interest is related to the content of the expression, however, then the regulation falls outside the scope of the *O'Brien* test and must be justified under a more demanding standard....

In *Barnes*, we analyzed an almost identical statute, holding that Indiana's public nudity ban did not violate the First Amendment, although no five Members of the Court agreed on a single rationale for that conclusion. We now clarify that government restrictions on public nudity such as the ordinance at issue here should be evaluated under the framework set forth in *O'Brien* for content-neutral restrictions on symbolic speech.

The city of Erie argues that the ordinance is a content-neutral restriction that is reviewable under *O'Brien* because the ordinance bans conduct, not speech; specifically, public nudity. Respondent counters that the ordinance targets nude dancing and, as such, is aimed specifically at suppressing expression, making the ordinance a content-based restriction that must be subjected to strict scrutiny....

The ordinance here, like the statute in *Barnes*, is on its face a general prohibition on public nudity. By its terms, the ordinance regulates conduct alone. It does not target nudity that contains an erotic message; rather, it bans all public nudity, regardless of whether that nudity is accompanied by expressive activity. And like the statute in *Barnes*, the Erie ordinance replaces and updates provisions of an "Indecency and Immorality" ordinance that has been on the books since 1866, predating the prevalence of nude dancing establishments such as Kandyland....

The State's interest in preventing harmful secondary effects is not related to the suppression of expression. In trying to control the secondary effects of nude dancing, the ordinance seeks to deter crime and the other deleterious effects caused by the presence of such an establishment in the neighborhood....

Similarly, even if Erie's public nudity ban has some minimal effect on the erotic message by muting that portion of the expression that occurs when the last stitch is dropped, the dancers at Kandyland and other such establishments are free to perform wearing pasties and G-strings. Any effect on the overall

(continued)

(continued)

expression is *de minimis*. And as *Justice Stevens* eloquently stated for the plurality in *Young v. American Mini Theatres, Inc.*, 427 U. S. 50, 70 (1976), "even though we recognize that the First Amendment will not tolerate the total suppression of erotic materials that have some arguably artistic value, it is manifest that society's interest in protecting this type of expression is of a wholly different, and lesser, magnitude than the interest in untrammeled political debate," and "few of us would march our sons or daughters off to war to preserve the citizen's right to see" specified anatomical areas exhibited at establishments like Kandyland. If States are to be able to regulate secondary effects, then *de minimis* intrusions on expression such as those at issue here cannot be sufficient to render the ordinance content based.

We conclude that Erie's asserted interest in combating the negative secondary effects associated with adult entertainment establishments like Kandyland is unrelated to the suppression of the erotic message conveyed by nude dancing. The ordinance prohibiting public nudity is therefore valid if it satisfies the four-factor test from *O'Brien* for evaluating restrictions on symbolic speech. . . .

Applying that standard here, we conclude that Erie's ordinance is justified under *O'Brien*. The first factor of the *O'Brien* test is whether the government regulation is within the constitutional power of the government to enact. Here, Erie's efforts to protect public health and safety are clearly within the city's police powers. The second factor is whether the regulation furthers an important or substantial government interest. The asserted interests of regulating conduct through a public nudity ban and of combating the harmful secondary effects associated with nude dancing are undeniably important. . . .

WHAT DO *YOU* THINK?

1. While the complete logic of the Pennsylvania Supreme Court is not provided in this summary opinion, why do you think that court found nude dancing to be a protected form of expression? On what basis might such an argument be made?

2. Did the U.S. Supreme Court contradict the Pennsylvania Supreme Court's finding relative to the nature of nude dancing as expressive conduct? If not, then how did the U.S. Supreme Court reach a conclusion that was different from that of Pennsylvania's high court?

IN THE FIELD

Invariably, criminal cases involving obscenity, child pornography, lewdness statutes, or adult entertainment law require legal professionals to be thoroughly familiar with constitutional law, particularly the doctrines, standards, and cases relating to the freedom of expression, privacy, and due process. In addition, many of these cases also require legal professionals to understand the complexities of computer technology, as many obscenity and child pornography cases involve materials downloaded to or distributed via computers. There can be many forensic issues that relate to the legal elements of the criminal statute. Most obscenity and child pornography statutes require the defendant to "knowingly possess or distribute" the banned materials. But in cases where the materials are stored on a computer, there can be evidentiary questions regarding who had access to the computer and whether the materials were intentionally downloaded by the user or stored on the hard drive by some unauthorized source.

CRIMES INVOLVING CONTROLLED SUBSTANCES

The word drug is a generic term applicable to a wide variety of substances that have any physical or psychotropic effect on the human body. Over the years, drugs have been defined by social convention. While today, for example, most everyone would agree that heroin and cocaine are drugs, they were not always seen as such. Similarly, although alcohol, nicotine, and even caffeine probably fall into the "drug" category in the minds of most people today, their categorization as drugs is relatively recent, having occurred during the past two or three decades.[88] Both the law and social convention make strong distinctions between drugs that are socially acceptable and those that are not. See Figure 6-8.

Another important distinction can be made between two major classes of drugs: (1) those that are biologically active and (2) those that are psychologically active. Psychotropic substances, or drugs that affect the mind, are said to have psychoactive properties. Bioactive substances, on the other hand, are drugs that affect the body. While bioactive drugs are subject to considerable regulation and control, most drug laws concern themselves with the manufacture, sale, and possession of psychoactive substances. The term *controlled substance* refers to specifically defined bioactive or psychoactive chemical substances that come under the purview of the criminal law.

FIGURE 6-8 **Drug Terminology**

Drug: Any chemical substance defined by social convention as bioactive or psychoactive. Not all drugs are socially recognized as such, although those that are may not be well understood. Among recognized drugs, some are legal and readily available, whereas others are closely controlled.

Controlled substance: A specifically defined bioactive or psychoactive chemical substance that is proscribed by law.

Drug abuse: The frequent, overindulgent, or long-term use of a controlled substance in a way that creates problems in the user's life or in the lives of those with whom the user associates.

Psychological addiction: A craving for a specific drug that results from long-term substance abuse. People who are psychologically addicted use the drug in question as a "crutch" to deal with the events in their lives. Also called *psychological dependence.*

Physical addiction: A biologically based craving for a specific drug that results from frequent use of the substance. Also called *physical dependence.*

Addict: Generally, someone who abuses drugs and is psychologically dependent, physically dependent, or both.

Soft drugs: Psychoactive drugs with relatively mild effects whose potential for abuse and addiction is substantially less than for hard drugs. By social convention, soft drugs include marijuana, hashish, and some tranquilizers and mood elevators.

Hard drugs: Psychoactive substances with serious potential for abuse and addiction. By social convention, hard drugs include heroin, methaqualone (Quaaludes), LSD, mescaline, peyote, psilocybin, and MDA. Cocaine and its derivative, crack, and methamphetamine (speed) are often placed in the hard-drug category.

Recreational drug user: A person who uses drugs relatively infrequently and whose use occurs primarily among friends and in social contexts that define drug use as pleasurable. Most addicts began as recreational users.

Source: Frank Schmalleger, *Criminal Justice Today: An Introductory Text for the Twenty-first Century,* 8th ed. Copyright 2005, p. 680. Reprinted by permission of Pearson Education, Inc., Upper Saddle River, NJ.

Anti-Drug Abuse Legislation

Controlled Substances Act (CSA)
federal law that identifies and
organizes controlled substances
into five schedules

In 1970, Congress enacted the Comprehensive Drug Abuse Prevention and Control Act,[89] which still forms the basis of federal drug enforcement efforts today. Title II of the act is the **Controlled Substances Act (CSA)**. The CSA sets up five schedules (see Figure 6-9) that classify psychoactive drugs according to their degree of psychoactivity and abuse potential.[90]

- *Schedule I controlled substances* have no established medical usage, cannot be used safely, and have great potential for abuse. Included in this category

FIGURE 6-9 **Schedules of the Federal Controlled Substances Act**

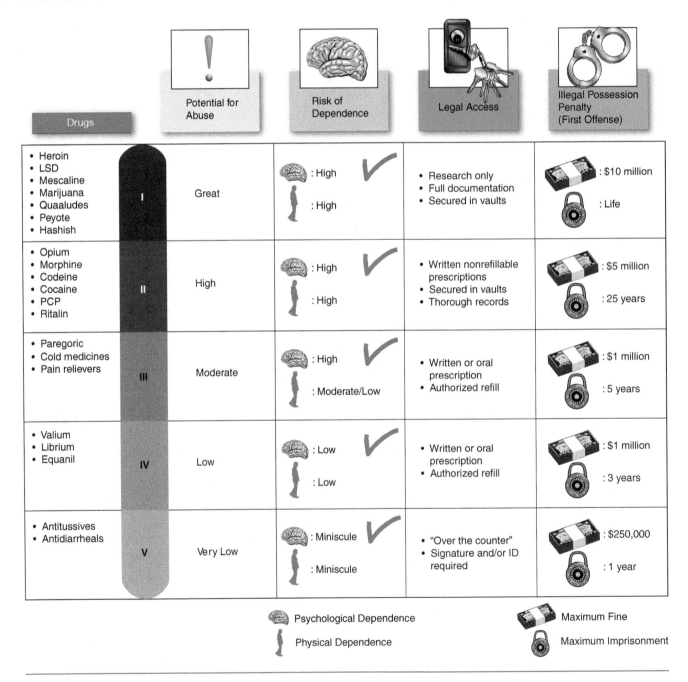

are heroin, LSD, mescaline, peyote, methaqualone (Quaaludes), psilocy-bin, marijuana, and hashish. Penalties for a first-offense possession and sale of Schedule I controlled substances under the federal Narcotic Penalties and Enforcement Act of 1986 range up to life imprisonment and a $10 million fine. Penalties increase for subsequent offenses.

- *Schedule II controlled substances* are defined as drugs with high abuse potential for which there is a currently accepted pharmacological or medical use. Most Schedule II substances are also considered to be addictive. Drugs that fall into this category include opium, morphine, codeine, cocaine, phencyclidine (PCP), and their derivatives. Certain other stimulants, such as methylphenidate (Ritalin) and phenmetrazine (Preludin), and a few barbiturates with high abuse potential also come under Schedule II. Penalties for first-offense possession and sale of Schedule II controlled substances range up to twenty years' imprisonment and a $5 million fine under the federal Narcotic Penalties and Enforcement Act. Penalties increase for subsequent offenses.

- *Schedule III controlled substances* involve lower abuse potential than do those in previous schedules. Common low-dosage antidiarrheals, such as opium-containing paregoric, and cold medicines or pain relievers with low concentrations of codeine fall into this category. Anabolic steroids, whose abuse by professional athletes has come under increased scrutiny, were added to the list of Schedule III controlled substances by congressional action in 1991. Maximum penalties associated with first-offense possession and sale of Schedule III controlled substances under federal law include five years' imprisonment and fines of up to $1 million.

- *Schedule IV controlled substances* have a relatively low potential for abuse (when compared to higher schedules), are useful in established medical treatments, and involve only a limited risk of psychological or physical dependency. Depressants and mild tranquilizers, such as Valium, Librium, and Equanil, fall into this category. Maximum penalties associated with first-offense possession and sale of Schedule IV substances under federal law include three years in prison and fines of up to $1 million.

- *Schedule V controlled substances* are prescription drugs with a low potential for abuse and with only a very limited possibility of psychological or physical dependence. Cough medicines (antitussives) and antidiarrheals containing small amounts of opium, morphine, or codeine are found in Schedule V. Maximum federal penalties for first-offense possession and sale of Schedule V substances include one year in prison and a $250,000 fine.

Pharmacologists, chemists, and botanists are constantly discovering and creating new drugs. Likewise, street corner "chemists" in clandestine laboratories churn out inexpensive designer drugs—psychoactive substances with widely varying effects and abuse potential.

The Anti–Drug Abuse Act of 1988

In 1988, the federal Anti–Drug Abuse Act was passed. Under the law, penalties for "recreational" drug users were substantially increased,[91] and it became more difficult for suspected drug dealers to purchase weapons. The law also denied federal benefits to convicted drug offenders, ranging from loans (including student loans) to contracts and licenses.[92] Earned benefits like Social Security, retirement, and health and disability benefits were not affected by the legislation, nor were welfare payments or existing public housing arrangements. But separate legislation does provide for termination of public housing tenancy for drug offenses. Under the law, civil penalties of up to $10,000 may be assessed against convicted "recreational" users for possession of even small amounts of drugs.

The 1988 legislation also included the possibility of capital punishment for drug-related murders. The killing of a police officer by offenders seeking to avoid apprehension or prosecution is specifically cited in the law as carrying a possible sentence of death, although other murders by major drug dealers also fall under the capital punishment provision.[93] Other significant federal antidrug legislation exists in the form of the Crime Control Act of 1990 and the Violent Crime Control and Law Enforcement Act of 1994.

Law Line 6-9
Drug Enforcement Administration

State-Level Antidrug Laws

Antidrug laws at the state level show a surprising degree of uniformity. Such standardization is due to the fact that almost all states have adopted some version of the Uniform Controlled Substances Act, which was proposed in 1972 by the National Conference of Commissioners on Uniform State Laws. The Uniform Controlled Substances Act is similar to the federal Drug Abuse and Prevention Control Act in that it also groups controlled substances into five schedules. The schedules are quite similar to those under federal law.

Most jurisdictions have also categorized controlled substances into penalty groups, with penalties ranging from first-degree felonies to misdemeanors. The possession of drugs or substances listed in Schedules I and II are generally felonies, and the possession of drugs or substances listed in Schedules III to V may be either felonies or misdemeanors. Under the laws of most jurisdictions, the crime of possessing a controlled substance involves a person's possession or right to exercise control over a controlled substance; his or her knowledge of the presence of the controlled substance and of its nature as a controlled substance; and possession of a usable quantity of the controlled substance. Generally speaking, the elements of the offense of unlawful possession of a controlled substance are as follows:

- possession (except as otherwise provided by law)
- of any controlled substance (as classified by law)
- unless upon the written prescription of a physician, dentist, podiatrist, or veterinarian licensed to prescribe such a drug

Other than possession, jurisdictions generally criminalize the manufacture, sale, and purchase of a controlled substance. Florida law, for example, says that "it is unlawful for any person to sell, manufacture, or deliver, or possess with intent to sell, manufacture, or deliver, a controlled substance."[94] Similar to the laws of other states, Florida law also criminalizes the sale, manufacture, and possession with intent to sell or deliver a controlled substance "within one thousand feet of the real property comprising a public or private elementary, middle, or secondary school between the hours of 6 A.M. and 12 A.M." As in other states, Florida law also makes it "unlawful for any person to purchase, or possess with intent to sell, a controlled substance," except as allowed by law (that is, with a license, through prescription, and so on). Finally, Florida law states, "[i]t is unlawful for any person to be in actual or constructive possession of a controlled substance unless such controlled substance was lawfully obtained from a practitioner or pursuant to a valid prescription or order of a practitioner while acting in the course of his professional practice or to be in actual or constructive possession of a controlled substance except as otherwise authorized by this chapter."

Most jurisdictions have also created special penalties for adults who sell drugs to juveniles and for adults who employ juveniles in the illegal drug trade. Florida law, for example, states, "[e]xcept as authorized by this chapter, it is unlawful for any person eighteen years of age or older to deliver any controlled substance to a person under the age of eighteen years, or to use or hire a person under the age of eighteen years as an agent or employee in the sale or delivery of such a substance, or to use such person to assist in avoiding detection or apprehension for a violation of this chapter."

Most states and the federal government also control the sale and possession of *precursor chemicals*, or those chemicals that may be used in the manufacture of a controlled substance. Similarly, most states have enacted antiparaphernalia laws similar to the Model Drug Paraphernalia Act, which prohibits possession, manufacture, delivery, or advertising of drug paraphernalia. Drug paraphernalia may include "bongs," hypodermic needles, "roach clips," crack pipes, and other specially described items normally used in the distribution and consumption of controlled substances.

precursor chemicals
chemicals that may be used in the manufacture of a controlled substance

IN THE FIELD

Most legal professionals working in the criminal justice system will regularly be assigned drug cases, as these matters occupy a large percentage of both state and federal court dockets. For many of these cases, there are two primary legal questions: (1) Were the drugs and the defendant seized in a constitutional manner under the Fourth Amendment? and (2) What is the quality and quantity of drugs that can be attributed to the defendant's conduct?

As to the first question, legal professionals must be prepared to file and defend against motions to suppress evidence and other legal claims in which the defendant asserts that the drugs were obtained in violation of the Fourth Amendment. As a result, legal professionals should understand the process for such motions and become knowledgeable in the details of Fourth Amendment law. See Chapter 10.

As to the second question, most criminal drug laws categorize the severity of the crime and the potential punishment based on the amount and nature of the drugs involved in the offense. Larger quantities of drugs typically lead to more serious charges. As a result, legal professionals must pay attention to the manner in which confiscated narcotics are weighed and otherwise evaluated. In cases where the volume or weight of the drugs is in question, additional expert analysis should be requested.

CHAPTER **SUMMARY**

- Public-order offenses are those that disturb or invade society's peace and tranquillity. They include breach of peace, disorderly conduct, fighting, affray, vagrancy, loitering, illegally carrying weapons, keeping a disorderly house, public intoxication, disturbance of public assembly, inciting to riot, rioting, unlawful assembly, rout, and obstructing public passage.

- Laws criminalizing public-order offenses rest on the assumption that public order is inherently valuable and should be maintained—and that disorder is not to

be tolerated and should be reduced, when it occurs, through the application of the criminal law.

- Some court decisions have focused specifically on fighting words, or those utterances that are an affront to the public peace and that are intended to provoke those at whom they are directed. According to the U.S. Supreme Court, fighting words are not protected under free speech constitutional guarantees.

- Public intoxication is a common offense, and many people are arrested annually for driving while intoxicated (DWI) or driving under the influence (DUI).

- Vagrancy, a crime under common law, has been largely recast today in terms of loitering. Traditional vagrancy laws often ran afoul of the constitutional prohibition against vagueness because they criminalized a person's status rather than his or her conduct.
- A special category of public-order offense is that of illegally carrying weapons. Considerable debate exists within the United States today over the issue of gun control, with persuasive arguments being advanced on both sides of the controversy.
- Another class of social-order offense discussed in this chapter is that of crimes against the administration of government. Offenses in this category include treason, misprision of treason, rebellion, criminal syndicalism, espionage, sedition, perjury, subornation of perjury, criminal contempt, obstruction of justice, resisting arrest, escape, misconduct in office, and bribery.
- Increasingly, legislatures have fashioned criminal laws to address acts of terrorism. In general, terrorist acts are criminal acts designed to influence government policy.
- Crimes against public decency and morality constitute a third type of social-order offense. They typically include not only prostitution, gambling, and drug use, but also pornography, obscenity, and various other consensual sex offenses—such as bestiality, deviate sexual relations, lewdness, indecency, seduction, fornication, adultery, and bigamy.
- Crimes against public decency and morality are sometimes termed *victimless crimes* by virtue of the fact that they generally involve willing participants.
- Pornography is the depiction of sexual behavior in such a way as to excite the viewer sexually. Obscenity, a related crime, can be defined as material that appeals to a prurient interest in sex, is patently offensive, and lacks serious literary, artistic, political, or scientific value. Sex and obscenity are not synonymous, and obscenity is not constitutionally protected under First Amendment free speech guarantees.
- An emerging concern in the area of crimes against public decency and morality is the availability of pornography via the Internet. Lawmakers (especially at the federal level) have attempted to restrict access to pornographic materials.
- Drug use and abuse and lawfully controlled substances represent an area of special interest to many Americans today. Controlled substances are specifically defined as bioactive or psychoactive chemical substances that come under the purview of the criminal law.
- Under federal law and the laws of many states, controlled substances are classified according to five schedules. Schedules are an attempt to categorize controlled substances according to their abuse potential.

KEY **TERMS**

adultery
affray
aliens
breach of peace
bribery
citizens
compelling prostitution
concealed weapon
Controlled Substances Act (CSA)
criminal contempt
criminal syndicalism
disorderly conduct
disturbance of public assembly
domestic terrorism
driving under the influence (DUI)
driving while intoxicated (DWI)
driving with an unlawful blood alcohol
   level (DUBAL)
escape
espionage

fighting words
Foreign Intelligence Surveillance
   Act (FISA)
fornication
gambling
Immigration and Nationality
   Act (INA)
inciting a riot
loitering
malfeasance
misconduct in office
misfeasance
misprision of treason
nonfeasance
obstruction of justice
operating a motor vehicle while under
   the influence of alcohol or drugs
   (OMVI)
perjury
precursor chemicals

prize fighting
procuring prostitution
promoting prostitution
prostitution
public drunkenness
rebellion
resisting arrest
riot
rout
sedition
soliciting prostitution
subornation of perjury
treason
unlawful assembly
USA PATRIOT Act
vagrancy
vagrant
victimless crimes

QUESTIONS FOR **DISCUSSION**

1. What are victimless crimes? Do you agree that some crimes are truly victimless? Why or why not?

2. What are the categories of social-order crimes? How do they differ? With which two categories is this chapter most concerned?

3. What are fighting words? How can they be distinguished from protected forms of speech?

4. Explain the differences between rout, riot, and unlawful assembly.

5. What is vagrancy? Why have traditional laws against vagrancy been held to be unconstitutional?

6. Should the possession of handguns be regulated? Summarize the arguments on both sides of the issue.

7. What is the difference between treason and espionage?

8. Explain the differences between perjury, bribery, and contempt. How does criminal contempt differ from civil contempt?

9. What are the constitutional standards for obscenity cases?

10. Should prostitution remain illegal in most jurisdictions? Explain.

11. Should marijuana use be legalized under certain conditions? If so, what conditions?

REFERENCES

1. 97 U.S. 25, 33, 24 L. Ed. 989 (1878).

2. 153 Misc. 2d 382, 581 N.Y.S.2d 981 (N.Y. Crim. Ct. 1992).

3. Rollins M. Perkins and Ronald N. Boyce, *Criminal Law*, 3rd ed. (Mineola, NY: Foundation Press, 1982), p. 477.

4. *Id.*

5. *Id.*

6. *Cantwell v. Connecticut*, 310 U.S. 296, 308, 60 S. Ct. 900 (1940).

7. *Chaplinsky v. New Hampshire*, 315 U.S. 568 (1942).

8. *People v. Harvey*, 2001 NY 078439.

9. Wesley Gilmer, *The Law Dictionary*, 6th ed. (Cincinnati, OH: Anderson, 1986), p. 54.

10. Derald D. Hunt, *California Criminal Law Manual*, 8th ed. (Edina, MN: Burgess, 1996).

11. *Id.*

12. *Id.*

13. Gilmer, *The Law Dictionary*, p. 334.

14. *Papachristou v. City of Jacksonville*, 405 U.S. 156 (1972).

15. *Id.*

16. *Kolender v. Lawson*, 461 U.S. 353 (1983).

17. 554 U.S. ___, 128 S. Ct. 2783 (2008).

18. 18 U.S.C. § 922.

19. 18 U.S.C. § 922(q)(1)(A) (1988 ed., Supp. V).

20. *United States v. Lopez*, 514 U.S. 549 (1995).

21. 18 U.S.C. § 922.

22. The five-day waiting period will be phased out after a planned national instant background-checking system becomes fully operational.

23. *Printz v. United States*, 521 U.S. 98 (1997).

24. *Mack v. United States*, 521 U.S. 98 (1997). Combined with *Printz v. United States*, 521 U.S. 98 (1997).

25. To learn more about the system, see Michael F. Cahn, James M. Tien, and David M. Einstein, *Assessment and Resolution of Replicated Firearm Eligibility Checks* (Washington, DC: Structured Decisions Corporation, 2004).

26. "Brady Bill Backers Hail 3rd Anniversary Friday," Reuters, February 28, 1997.

27. North Carolina General Statutes, Section 14-292.

28. G. R. Blakey and H. A. Kurland, "Development of Federal Law on Gambling," *Cornell Law Review* 63 (1978): 923.

29. *People v. Byrd*, 125 Cal. 3d 1054 (1985).

30. *People v. Jordan*, 75 Cal. 3d Supp. 1 (1979).

31. See National Highway Traffic Safety Administration website at www.nhtsa.gov

32. California Penal Code, Section 23157.

33. 8 U.S.C. § 1326.

34. 50 U.S.C. § 36.

35. *Zadvydas v. Davis*, 533 U.S. 678, 696 (2001).

36. U.S. Constitution, Article III, section 3, clause 1.

37. 18 U.S.C. § 2381.

38. *Kawakita v. United States*, 343 U.S. 717 (1952).

39. U.S. Constitution, Article III, section 3.

40. Florida Constitution, Section 20.

41. *Id.*

42. 18 U.S.C. § 2383.

43. 18 U.S.C. § 2385.

44. *Id.*

45. 18 U.S.C. § 793.

46. 18 U.S.C. § 2384.

47. Pennsylvania Code, Title 18, Section 4902(a).

48. Pennsylvania Code, Title 18, Section 4902(b).

49. 18 U.S.C. § 1622.

50. *Niehoff v. Sahagin*, 103 A.2d 211 (Me. 1954).

51. See *Bloom v. Illinois*, 391 U.S. 194, 88 S. Ct. 1477 (1968).

52. 18 U.S.C. § 1507.

53. Oregon Revised Statutes, Section 162.315(1).

54. North Carolina General Statutes, Chapter 14, Section 223.

55. Joseph R. Nolan and Jacqueline M. Nolan-Haley, *Black's Law Dictionary: Definitions of the Terms and Phrases of American and English Jurisprudence, Ancient and Modern*, 6th ed. (St. Paul, MN: West, 1990), p. 999.

56. *Id.*

57. General Statutes of North Carolina, Section 14-203.

58. Official Code of Georgia Annotated, Section 16-6-9.

59. Note, however, that North Carolina law (and the law of some other states) makes "indiscriminate sexual intercourse" a crime—even when no money changes hands.

60. Model Penal Code, Section 251.2(2).

61. Official Code of Georgia Annotated, Section 16-6-18.

62. *Id.*, Section 16-6-19.

63. Rhode Island General Laws, Section 11-10-1.

64. Idaho Penal Code, Section 18-6605.

65. *Id.*, Section 18-6606.

66. William Blackstone, *Commentaries on the Laws of England*, Vol. 4 (Oxford: Clarendon Press, 1769), p. 215.

67. *State v. Chance*, 3 N.C. App. 459, 165 S.E.2d 31 (1969).

68. *State v. Stokes*, 1 N.C. App. 245, 161 S.E.2d 53 (1968).

69. *Id.*

70. *Lawrence v. Texas*, 539 U.S. 558 (2003).

71. Tony Mauro, "U.S. Supreme Court Strikes Down Law Banning Gay Sex," *Legal Times*, June 27, 2003.

72. *State v. Williams*, 220 N.C. 445, 17 S.E.2d 769 (1941).

73. *Haller v. State*, 232 S.W.2d 829 (Ark. 1950).

74. Official Code of Georgia Annotated, Section 16-6-22.

75. Sanford H. Kadish, "The Crisis of Overcriminalization," *Annals of the American Academy of Political and Social Science* 374 (1967): 157.

76. William Kornblum and Joseph Julian, *Social Problems*, 8th ed. (Upper Saddle River, NJ: Prentice Hall, 1995), p. 115.

77. *Roth v. United States*, 354 U.S. 476 (1957).

78. *Miller v. California*, 413 U.S. 15 (1973).

79. David R. Simon, *The American Standard Law Dictionary*, 1995, via Cybernation online, http://www.e-legal.com (accessed March 4, 2003).

80. California Penal Code, Section 311(a).

81. *Id.*

82. *Stanley v. Georgia*, 394 U.S. 557 (1969).

83. *Paris Adult Theatre v. Slaton*, 413 U.S. 49 (1973).

84. *New York v. Ferber*, 458 U.S. 747 (1982).

85. *Ashcroft v. Free Speech Coalition*, 535 U.S. 234 (2002).

86. New Jersey Code of Criminal Justice, Section 14-4.

87. Official Code of Georgia Annotated, Section 16-6-8.

88. Some of the material in this section has been adapted from Frank Schmalleger, *Criminal Justice Today: An Introductory Text for the Twenty-first Century*, 10th ed. (Upper Saddle River, NJ: Prentice Hall, 2008).

89. 21 U.S.C. § 801 et seq.

90. For a good summary of the law, see Drug Enforcement Administration, *Drugs of Abuse*, http://www.justice.gov/dea/pubs/abuse/index.htm (accessed April 5, 2009).

91. This provision became effective on September 1, 1989.

92. "Congress Gives Final OK to Major Antidrug Bill," *Criminal Justice Newsletter* 19, no. 21 (November 1, 1988): 1–4.

93. *Id.* at 2.

94. Florida Statutes, Section 893.13.

APPENDIX

DEVELOPING YOUR LEGAL ANALYSIS

A. THE LAW WHERE YOU LIVE

In recent years, there have been many news stories about so-called sexting—the process of sending nude pictures or other sexually suggestive materials of oneself via electronic message. In many cases, this activity has involved persons under the age of eighteen sharing images of themselves with their friends or romantic partners. These underage images, even though produced and sent voluntarily by the imaged persons themselves, may nonetheless constitute criminal contraband under most state and federal child pornography laws.

Assume that you are asked to work on a criminal case involving Ima Yung, a sixteen-year-old girl who allegedly sent nude pictures of herself to her seventeen-year-old boyfriend. Based on a review of your home state's child pornography statute and the Supreme Court's rulings in *New York v. Ferber* (1986) and *Lawrence v. Texas* (2003), prepare a two-page memorandum addressing why the child pornography charges filed under your state's statute should be dismissed against Ms. Yung. Within the memorandum, address how Ms. Yung's alleged conduct should be protected from prosecution based on the Court's rulings in *Ferber* and *Lawrence*. Alternatively, using the same materials, play the role of prosecutor and prepare a legal memorandum opposing the dismissal of the charges.

B. INSIDE THE FEDERAL COURTS

As discussed above, for many years, the Supreme Court has deemed obscene materials to be unprotected expression under the First Amendment. This unprotected status has allowed federal and state authorities to criminalize many activities associated with obscenity. Specifically, federal statutes ban the sale, transmission, or distribution of obscene materials within interstate commerce. See 18 U.S.C. §§ 1461, 1462, and 1465.

But after the Court's ruling in *Lawrence v. Texas* (2003), many defendants charged with obscenity-related offenses have challenged obscenity laws, asserting that they are unconstitutional because they interfere with rights of personal privacy and unduly restrict individual decisions about what they wish to view in their home. And in at least one case, a court has agreed with this argument. In *United States v. Extreme Associates* (2005), federal District Court Judge Gary Lancaster found the federal obscenity statute unconstitutional under the Supreme Court's ruling in *Lawrence*. This ruling was later reversed on procedural grounds by the Third Circuit Court of Appeals, but the basic constitutional question about whether the federal government can continue to ban obscene materials in light of *Lawrence* still remains.

Assume you are assigned to work on a federal obscenity case. You are asked to prepare a legal memorandum where you address whether the federal obscenity statutes are still constitutional based on the Court's ruling in *Lawrence*. As a part of this memorandum, review and outline the federal obscenity statutes (cited above) and the *Lawrence* ruling, and then discuss whether you find the federal laws are still constitutionally valid. Be sure to explain why you have drawn these conclusions.

C. CYBER SOURCES

Assume you are clerking for a national public interest group that is interested in assessing the state of American laws and morality. You are asked to prepare an electronic slide presentation (or another form of presentation) that outlines some of the more interesting or disturbing laws that attempt to regulate adult, consensual behavior, all in the name of maintaining or promoting morality. As a part of this project, you are asked to review the materials found in the following websites:

Weird Sex Laws—http://weirdsexlaws.com
Strange U.S. Sex Laws—http://www.lectlaw.com/files/fun23.htm
Sexlaws—http://www.sexlaws.org

Based on your review, prepare a presentation where you discuss the nature of current morality-based crime in America and whether these criminal laws, in reality, could still be enforced through criminal prosecution.

D. ETHICS AND PROFESSIONALISM

Assume you have been working with Joe Taylor, criminal defense attorney, for the last five years. You have worked on many types of cases, met hundred of clients, and feel like you thoroughly understand the attorney's approach to the practice of law. Assume further that Joe is scheduled to meet with Stacey Johnson, a possible new client. Ms. Johnson was arrested and charged with disorderly conduct after getting into a fight with a friend outside a bar. Also assume that Ms. Johnson has arrived at the law firm for her appointment, but Joe is still in a court hearing and will not return to the office for another hour. In Joe's absence, he wants you to (1) meet with Ms. Johnson, (2) obtain the information about her case, including making a copy of her citation, (3) share background information with her about the law firm and Joe's practice, (4) explain the standardized and preprinted legal fees and retainer agreement for Joe's services, and (5) have Ms. Johnson sign the retainer agreement.

You are quite comfortable with doing the initial client interview with Ms. Johnson. But the office manager of your firm is questioning whether this assignment is ethically appropriate. Review any ethical standards from your home state jurisdiction regarding the initial contacts and interviews with clients that might apply to this situation, as well as the ethical standards for delegated tasks set forth in the following sources. Based on your review, prepare a response to your office manager regarding her concerns.

American Bar Association

http://www.abanet.org/legalservices/paralegals/downloads/modelguidelines.pdf

The American Alliance of Paralegals, Inc.

http://www.aapipara.org/Ethicalstandards.htm

National Association of Legal Assistants

http://www.nala.org/code.aspx

chapter **seven**

LEGAL DEFENSES: JUSTIFICATIONS AND EXCUSES

Men use thought only to justify their wrongdoings.

—Voltaire (1694–1778)

Ignorance of the law excuses no man; not that all men know the law, but because 'tis an excuse every man will plead, and no man can tell how to refute him.

—John Selden (1584–1654)

Two wrongs don't make a right, but they make a good excuse.

—Thomas Szasz (b. 1920)

LEARNING OBJECTIVES

After reading this chapter, you should be able to

- Explain the purpose of a defense to a criminal charge and the nature of affirmative defenses.

- Describe the difference between justifications and excuses, and give examples of justifications that might serve as defenses.

- Summarize the differences between the defenses of necessity and duress.

- Illustrate when force and deadly force may be used in self-defense.

- List the main distinguishing features of an excuse.

- Explain why voluntary intoxication is usually not accepted as a defense to a criminal charge.

- Explain the defense of mistake, and explain when it is most useful.

- Discuss the minimum age at which people should be held criminally liable for their actions.

- Elaborate upon the difference between the subjective and objective approaches to assessing entrapment.

- Describe syndrome-based defenses, and provide some examples of this type of defense.

- Distinguish incompetency to stand trial from insanity at the time a crime is committed.

- Distinguish between the various legal "tests" for assessing insanity.

FIGURE 7-1 **Legal and Factual Defenses**

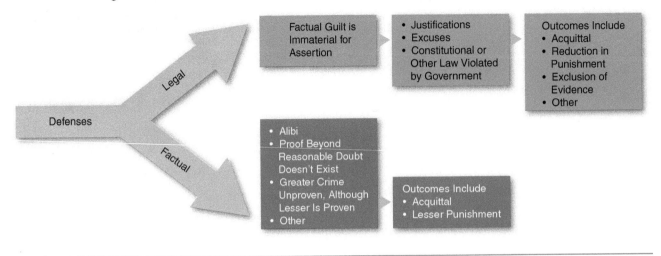

INTRODUCTION

defense
a criminal defendant's response
stating why defendant should not
be held liable for a criminal charge

factual defense
a defendant's assertion that
defendant did not commit a
criminal act as a matter of fact

alibi
a defense based on asserted fact
that defendant was "elsewhere" at
the time of the crime

legal defense
a defense based on a legal theory,
as opposed to a factual claim

justification
a defendant's admission to
performing the harmful act in
question but assertion that the act
was necessary to avoid some
greater evil

excuses
defendants' assertions that a
physical or psychological condition
at the time of the allegedly criminal
act negates the voluntariness of the
conduct or prevented the charged
mental state from being formed

A *defense* to charges of criminal culpability consists of evidence and arguments offered by defendants and their attorneys to show why that person should not be held liable for a criminal charge. Generally, there are two types of defenses—factual and legal. See Figure 7-1. A *factual defense* is one in which defendants simply assert that they didn't do it. For example, an *alibi* can be used as a factual defense. Defendants can assert an alibi by providing evidence that they were not present during or otherwise involved in the alleged criminal offense. Defendants often introduce witnesses or other evidence to show that they were somewhere else at the time of the crime. But in some cases, even when a defendant *has* committed the illegal act in question, a *legal defense* may be available to avoid a conviction of the charged offense. It is therefore possible for a defendant to have committed an allegedly criminal act but face no legal liability.

Types of Legal Defenses

There are two types of legal defenses—justifications and excuses. A *justification* involves the defendant admitting to performing the harmful act in question but claiming it was necessary to avoid some greater evil. *Excuses* involve defendants asserting that a physical or psychological condition at the time of the allegedly criminal act negates the voluntariness of the conduct or prevented the charged mental state from being formed. In other words, "[a] justified actor engages in conduct that is not culpable because its benefits outweigh the harm or evil of the offense; an excused actor admits the harm or evil but nonetheless claims an absence of personal culpability."[1]

Generally speaking, a justification involves harmful conduct that a person believes is necessary to avoid a greater harm or evil. As a result, justifications often involve situations where people find themselves facing a choice between a lesser of two evils. If the defendant makes the "right choice" between these two harms, as determined by judges and/or juries after the fact, this may reduce or eliminate criminal liability for the alleged offense. For example, even though intentionally set fires that cause damage to others are often charged as arson, if firefighters set a controlled fire in order to create a firebreak to avoid greater damage to the larger community, this may be justifiable behavior in the eyes of the community *and* in the eyes of the law.

Law Line 7-1
Defenses

An excuse, in contrast, does not claim that a person's harmful conduct was justified. Rather, an excuse maintains that at the time of the harmful conduct, the actor was not physically or psychologically capable of forming the criminal mental state necessary to constitute the criminal offense, and therefore is not criminally culpable for the harmful conduct. For example, a person who assaults a police officer thinking that the officer is really a space alien who has come to abduct him may use an insanity or diminished capacity excuse to defend against criminal assault charges.

The Nature of Defenses

When considering justifications and excuses, it is important to realize that not all states have codified these defenses, and even those jurisdictions that have do not necessarily apply them in a uniform and predictable manner. As the Model Penal Code (MPC) explains, "[t]he main aim of a criminal code is to differentiate conduct that warrants criminal sanctions from conduct that does not. If it is clear that conduct will not be subject to criminal sanctions, the effort to establish precisely in each case whether that conduct is actually justified or only excused does not seem worthwhile."[2]

Justifications and excuses are ***affirmative defenses***, that is, they must be raised or asserted by the defendant independently of any claims made by the prosecutor. This is different from the general rule that places the burden of production and persuasion on the prosecutor in a criminal case. In most cases, defendants have the burden of production in raising a legal defense, that is, they must timely assert the defense and provide some evidence that it is applicable to the criminal charges. A defendant's failure to raise an affirmative defense in a timely manner acts as a waiver of the defense. States vary about the burden of persuasion placed on the defendant. Some require the defendant to prove the defense; others shift the burden to the prosecution to disprove the defense.

affirmative defenses
defenses that must be raised or asserted by the defendant independently of any claims made by the prosecutor

A successfully raised defense may have the effect of completely exonerating the defendant of any criminal liability. At times, however, the defense raised is less than perfect—that is, the defendant is unable to meet all of the requirements necessary to demonstrate that a particular justification or excuse should be entirely accepted in his case. When claims offered by the defendant are not sufficient for a verdict of not guilty, they may still mitigate the defendant's liability and result in a lesser punishment.

Since many criminal cases are complex, it is difficult to be certain whether a specific defense will be accepted by a judge or jury in a given instance. Moreover, those charged with crimes may be particularly inventive in their efforts to expand traditional defenses in order to apply them to their cases. Other defendants may offer creative excuses that have not previously been heard in American courts. In one case, a defendant offered a "twinkie defense," whereby he claimed that his harmful conduct was the product of a sugar high he suffered as the result of eating too many sweets. This attempted defense received substantial publicitiy, but in the end was unsuccessful. Still others may attempt to apply traditionally accepted defenses under novel circumstances. All this makes it difficult to generalize about the applicability of any particular defense to a given set of circumstances.

Legal professionals should become familiar with the technical requirements for asserting an affirmative defense. This includes understanding the timing, format, scope, and substance of a defendant's disclosure to the prosecutor and court regarding a planned defense.

For example, in most jurisdictions, defendants wishing to raise an alibi defense must timely file a notice of alibi with the court, notifying the court and the prosecutor of the nature and details of the claimed alibi. Thus, Rule 12.1(a) of the Federal Rules of Criminal Procedure states:

(a) **Notice by defendant.** Upon written demand of the attorney for the government stating the time, date, and place at which the alleged offense was committed, the defendant shall serve within ten days, or at such different time as the court may direct, upon the attorney for the government a written notice of the defendant's intention to offer a defense of alibi. Such notice by the defendant shall state the specific place or places at which the defendant claims to have been at the time of the alleged offense and the names and addresses of the witnesses upon whom the defendant intends to rely to establish such alibi.

Legal professionals working on behalf of defendants must fully appreciate the importance of filing timely notices of alibi where the circumstances warrant such a filing. If the defendant fails to properly file a notice of alibi, the trial court may prohibit alibi evidence from being introduced. Legal professionals working with prosecutors will typically use the defendant's notice of alibi to conduct an additional investigation to determine the credibility of the defendant's claims. In cases where the investigators find merit to the defendant's alibi, the prosecutor may seek to dismiss the criminal charges. But in cases where the defendant's alibi cannot be substantiated, the prosecutor must be prepared to rebut the defendant's claims in court.

JUSTIFICATION AS A DEFENSE

Conduct that violates the law may be justifiable. A person who kills another in self-defense, for example, may be completely innocent of criminal homicide. Justifications include (1) necessity, (2) self-defense, (3) defense of others, (4) defense of home and property, (5) resisting unlawful arrest, and (6) consent. The applicability of any particular defense may vary between jurisdictions. Some jurisdictions have codified a wide number of defenses, while others continue to follow common law tradition in the acceptability of some defenses.

Necessity

Strictly speaking, the concept of *necessity* forms the basis of all justifications. See Figure 7-2. A defendant offering the defense of necessity makes the claim that it was necessary to commit some unlawful act in order to prevent or avoid a greater harm. Sometimes the harm avoided is one that otherwise would have affected the defendant; sometimes it is a harm that would have affected others. In a third type of situation, both the person taking the necessary action and others whom he or she was acting to protect might have been harmed.

Some jurisdictions do not recognize the necessity defense as a justification for certain types of crimes, particularly those bringing about substantial bodily injury to others. But the Model Penal Code (MPC) says that the principle of necessity "is essential to the rationality and justice of the criminal law." And official commentaries on the code recognize specific instances in which necessity may

Law Line 7-2
Notice of Alibi Form

necessity
a defense based on the claim that it was necessary to commit some unlawful act in order to prevent or avoid a greater harm

FIGURE 7-2 **Defense of Necessity**

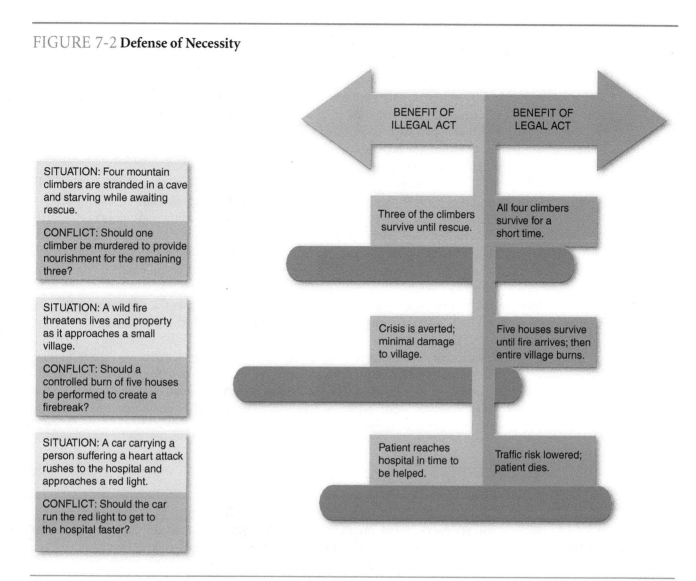

provide an effective defense to a criminal charge, including the running of a red light by an emergency vehicle, the jettisoning of cargo to save a sinking ship, the breaking and entering of someone seeking shelter in a blizzard, and the emergency dispensing of medication by a pharmacist without a prescription.

A number of state laws refer specifically to the defense of necessity, while the Model Penal Code contains a "choice of evils" provision under which necessity is subsumed.[3] MPC Section 3.02, entitled "Justifications Generally: Choice of Evils," reads:

> Conduct that the actor believes to be necessary to avoid a harm or evil to himself or to another is justifiable, provided that: (a) the harm or evil sought to be avoided by such conduct is greater than that sought to be prevented by the law defining the offense charged, and the actor was not negligent or reckless in bringing about the situation requiring a choice of harms or evils in appraising the necessity for his conduct.[4]

As the Model Penal Code points out, necessity can only be claimed where the "evil" to be avoided is greater than the harm caused. The actions of a person who throws luggage out of a falling aircraft to save the aircraft and its passengers will be far more justified in the eyes of the law than, for example, a person who kills another to avoid a financial loss. Texas law includes this concept. Section 9.22 of the state's penal code provides: Conduct is justified if (1) the actor reasonably believes the conduct is immediately necessary to avoid imminent harm; (2) the desirability and urgency of avoiding the harm clearly outweigh, according to ordinary standards of reasonableness, the harm sought to be prevented by the law proscribing the conduct; and (3) a legislative purpose to exclude the justification claimed for the conduct does not otherwise plainly appear.

For example, in March 2008, a defendant in Amarillo, Texas, successfully asserted a necessity defense to earn an acquittal in a possession of marijuana case. Tim Stevens suffered from an HIV infection and was using marijuana to relieve the severe vomiting effects that came with this condition. Stevens's vomiting was so bad that he had to be hospitalized and receive blood transfusions. Stevens was charged with possessing marijuana after a witness complained to police that Stevens was smoking a joint on the porch of a friend's home. At trial, Stevens relied on testimony from a medical expert to demonstrate that the harm associated with his HIV infection outweighed that associated with his marijuana usage.[5]

Overall, necessity defenses in criminal cases have been far more effective in protecting defendants facing grave and imminent physical threats than it has been in protecting defendants who are facing economic or psychological challenges. For example, a person who destroys a house to stop a fire advancing on a town is far less likely to incur criminal liability than one who steals because of hunger or another who breaks into a pharmacy to acquire the drugs needed to feed a powerful addiction.

Self-Defense

self-defense
a necessity-based defense asserting that individuals have an inherent right to protect themselves

Defense of self has long been accepted as justification for activities that might otherwise confer criminal liability. *Self-defense* is based on the recognition that individuals have an inherent right to protect themselves and that to reasonably defend oneself from unlawful attack is a natural response to threatening situations. Similarly, it can be argued that a person who acts in self-defense lacks the requisite *mens rea* for the commission of a crime; that is, a person who kills an attacker does not have as his primary purpose the taking of another's life, but rather the preservation of his own.

Texas law provides "[a] person is justified in using force against another when and to the degree he reasonably believes the force is immediately necessary to protect himself against the other's use or attempted use of unlawful force."[6] The Model Penal Code's provision is similar. It states that "[t]he use of force upon or toward another person is justifiable when the actor believes that such force is immediately necessary for the purpose of protecting himself against the use of unlawful force by such other persons on the present occasion."[7] But there is a significant difference between the two statutes when it comes to defining the reasonableness of the actor's belief about the need for protection. Under the Texas law, judges and juries must assess the actor's decision *objectively*—that is, from the point of view of a reasonable person. The Model Penal Code, on the other hand, requires the trier of fact to decide whether the defendant *subjectively* believed that the use of force was necessary. The difference between these two standards can have important consequences for many criminal cases.

As addressed below, the requirement that the use of force in self-defense be reasonable mandates that the accused behave as a reasonable person would under

Law Line 7-3
Self-Defense

the same circumstances. The concept of a ***reasonable person*** envisions a person who acts with common sense and who has the mental capacity of an average, normal, sensible human being (whatever that means). In many ways, the concept of a reasonable person is a legal fiction—that is, there is no actual person who is introduced into evidence as a reasonable person. Instead, when judging any activity, the reasonable person criterion requires the trier of fact to make assumptions about whether the defendant acted in an objectively reasonable manner. As a result, generally speaking, defendants motivated by special needs or driven by unique psychological conditions often struggle to assert self-defense as a viable justification in jurisdictions imposing an objective standard of reasonableness.

Apparent danger is another concept associated with self-defense. See Figure 7-3. Apparent danger exists when the conduct or activity of an attacker makes the threat of danger obvious. Danger, for example, becomes apparent when a threatening individual draws a gun or a knife and approaches another person in a menacing fashion. The emphasis on "immediacy" and "present occasion" found in many state codes classifies forceful activities undertaken in self-defense as justifiable only when they occur within the context of a face-to-face encounter. As a result, while a person who uses force to fight off an unlawful attack is justified in doing so, someone who stalks and kills a potential attacker in a preemptive strike would be hard-pressed to claim self-defense. Likewise, a person who "takes the law into her own hands" and exacts vengeance on a person who has previously victimized her cannot be said to be acting in self-defense. In short, "the victim had it coming" typically is not a valid self-defense justification.

The concept of **force**, as used in most self-defense standards, means physical force; it generally does not extend to emotional, psychological, economic, psychic,

reasonable person
a concept used to judge acts of self-defense; envisions a person who acts with common sense and who has the mental capacity of an average, normal, sensible human being

apparent danger
a concept associated with self-defense; considers the danger perceived by the defendant, as opposed to the actual danger present

FIGURE 7-3 **Apparent Danger**

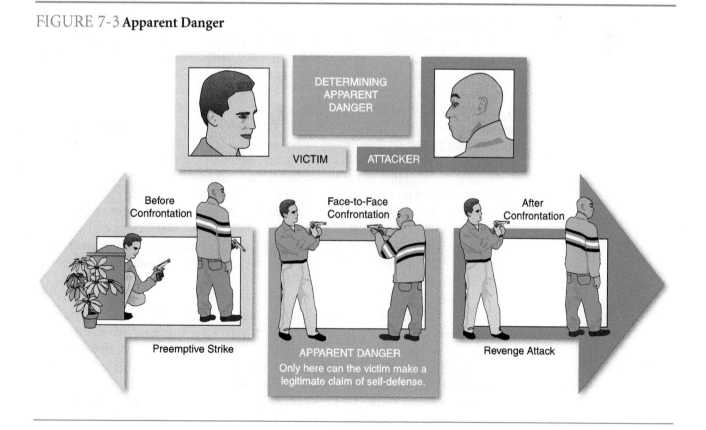

or other forms of coercion. A person who turns the tables on a robber and assaults him during the robbery attempt, for example, may be able to claim self-defense, but a businessperson who assaults a financial rival to prevent a hostile takeover of her company likely will have no such recourse.

Individuals may also protect themselves in the face of threats when the threat implies that danger is present in a given situation even though the precise nature of that danger may not be immediately apparent. Situations involving present danger include circumstances in which threatened individuals can anticipate the danger that they are about to face. For example, if a threatening individual says, "I'm going to kill you!" and advances on another while reaching into his pocket, the threatened individual can reasonably assume that the attacker is reaching for a weapon and can act on that basis. Difficulties may arise, however, when defensive force is used on an attacker who may be incapable of carrying out the threat. Someone who says, "I'm going to kill you," while searching for the key to a locked gun cabinet would appear to represent a less immediate danger than one who has the key in hand. Most jurisdictions recognize, however, that a reasonable amount of force can be used to protect oneself in the face of threats that seem to clearly imply that the use of unlawful force is imminent.

The amount of force used by those who seek to defend themselves from unlawful attack must be proportionate to the amount of force or the perceived degree of threat that they are defending themselves against. As a result, ***reasonable force*** is the degree of force that is appropriate and not excessive in a given situation. Reasonable force can also be thought of as the minimum degree of force necessary to protect oneself, one's property, a third party, or the property of another in the face of a substantial threat.

Deadly Force. ***Deadly force*** is the highest degree of force and is considered reasonable only when used to counter an immediate threat of death or great bodily harm (as may be the case in situations involving attempted murder, rape, kidnapping, and attempted assault). Deadly force cannot be used against nondeadly force. If a lesser degree of injury can be anticipated or if a lesser degree of force affords an effective defense, it must be used. Similarly, once danger has been averted, the use of force must cease. A person who overcomes an attacker, leaving him incapable of further attack, is unjustified in then taking the attacker's life. Once a threat has been deterred, it is improper for a person who has successfully defended himself to continue using force. Doing so effectively reverses the role of attacker and victim. For example, a person walking home alone at night might be accosted by a robber who beats him. If the would-be victim turns the tables on the robber by using a can of pepper spray, disabling and temporarily blinding the robber, he would be unjustified if he then picked up a rock and smashed the skull of the incapacitated robber.

Similarly, a person who is facing assault cannot exceed the bounds of necessary force in repelling the attack. If a large and robust person is struck by an unarmed small, weak—but angry—individual, for example, it would be unreasonable for the much stronger person to break the smaller person's neck if instead he could merely restrain the attacker.

The claim of self-defense is usually unavailable to those who precipitate or incite an attack on themselves. In other words, one who initiates a confrontation cannot later be reasonably afforded the protection of a self-defense claim. A verbally and physically abusive person, for example, generally cannot claim self-defense if the victim responds with force and the situation escalates into a brawl or leads to a homicide. Under such circumstances, the law recognizes the inherent validity of the claim often heard from children: "He started it!" This principle is illustrated in *United States v. Thomas* (1994),[8] extracts of which appear in this chapter.

reasonable force
the degree of force that is appropriate and not excessive in a given situation

deadly force
the highest degree of force; considered reasonable only when used to counter an immediate threat of death or great bodily harm

CAPSTONE CASE   *United States v. Thomas*, 34 F.3d 44 (2nd Cir. 1994)

On October 30th, 1990, Wallie Howard, a Syracuse police officer working undercover for the Federal Drug Enforcement Administration (DEA), was shot and killed during a cocaine "buy-bust" taking place in the parking lot of "Mario's Big M Market" in Syracuse....

Morales met with Agent Howard and Gregory at Gregory's apartment, and they agreed to do the deal in the parking lot of Mario's Big M. When the buyers arrived at the parking lot, Morales told Gregory to come with him to Morales' apartment to check the quality of the cocaine. When they arrived at Morales' apartment, Lawrence and Stewart emerged with guns drawn. They bound and gagged Gregory, breaking his wrist in the process. Morales, Lawrence, and Stewart then returned to Mario's Big M. While Morales waited in his car, Lawrence and Stewart, both armed, approached Gregory's vehicle, where Agent Howard was seated in the passenger seat. Stewart proceeded to the driver's side and got in the driver's seat, while Lawrence went around the back of the vehicle to the passenger side....

At that point, conversation ceased and background noises are heard on the recording. According to trial testimony, Stewart had the loaded .22 in his hand and tried to shoot but was unsuccessful because no round had been placed in the chamber. Agent Howard got three shots off, one of which struck Stewart in the shoulder. From behind Howard, Lawrence, who was standing at the rear passenger side of the vehicle, fired the .357 at Agent Howard, striking him in the rear of the head and killing him. Stewart was arrested seconds later, slumped against a wall with the .22 nearby. Morales and Lawrence attempted to flee but were both apprehended within moments; the murder weapon was recovered from the floor of Morales' vehicle. Both Morales and Stewart waived their *Miranda* rights, made admissions, and signed confessional affidavits....

In his confession, Morales recounted the events of the day largely as outlined above. He stated that seated in his car in the parking lot, he saw Stewart draw a gun and get shot by Howard. He further testified that Lawrence then shot Howard in the head, threw his gun into Morales' car, and started to run....

At trial, the defendants-appellants were found guilty as charged. All of the defendants were sentenced to life....

The defendants contend that the district court erred in not specifically charging the jury that it was the government's obligation to prove the absence of self-defense beyond a reasonable doubt. The government generally has the burden of disproving self-defense beyond a reasonable doubt once it is raised by a defendant. For reasons not clear, Judge McCurn agreed to give only a portion of the requested self-defense charge (which was taken virtually verbatim from Leonard B. Sand et al., *Modern Federal Jury Instructions*, 1993). He declined to give the last two paragraphs of the requested charge, which expressly placed the burden on the government to prove beyond a reasonable doubt that the defendants did not act in self-defense. The defendants claim that this omission was error....

The defense of self-defense is not available to one who acts as the aggressor, and commits his aggression threatening deadly force, even though the intended victim responds with deadly force so that the original aggressor will be killed if he does not first kill.

It has long been accepted that one cannot support a claim of self-defense by a self-generated necessity to kill. The right of homicidal self-defense is granted only to those free from fault in the difficulty; it is denied to slayers who incite the fatal attack, encourage the fatal quarrel or otherwise promote the necessitous occasion for taking life.... In sum, one who is the aggressor in a conflict culminating in death cannot invoke the necessities of self-preservation.

(continued)

(continued)

Under this principle, the defendants had no entitlement to any self-defense charge. The unrebutted evidence showed that with guns drawn, Lawrence, Stewart, and Morales bound and gagged Gregory, breaking his wrist in the process; they then returned to the parking lot where Stewart and Lawrence, armed with a .22 and a .357 respectively, approached Howard's car from two opposite sides; Lawrence banged on the window, and they demanded the money Howard was carrying. At least Lawrence, and possibly both Lawrence and Stewart, had their guns drawn as they confronted Howard and demanded the $40,000. Moreover, in finding the defendants guilty of felony murder under Count VI, the jury necessarily found that the killing was done in the attempted perpetration of a robbery. Upon this evidence, it is clear that Lawrence and Stewart were the aggressors, and that their felonious aggression was accompanied at the outset by the threat of deadly force. There was no evidence to the effect that Howard menaced Stewart and Lawrence prior to their assault on him. Even if one believes Stewart's contention that he did not draw his gun until Howard drew on him, that claim would not alter the uncontested evidence that Lawrence menaced Howard with his gun while Lawrence and Stewart approached him. Thus, even on Stewart's asserted facts, the defendants were the first to threaten deadly force. They therefore did not raise an issue of fact calling for an instruction on self-defense.

The charge was therefore unnecessarily favorable to the defendants in that it offered the jury the option to acquit by reason of self-defense. The judge's failure to make clear that the burden on the issue of self-defense rests on the government cannot have prejudiced the defendants when they had no right to have the jury consider the issue at all.

The judgments of conviction are affirmed.

WHAT DO *YOU* THINK?

1. Lawrence fired at Agent Howard and killed him after Howard had already drawn his weapon and fired. Why was Lawrence unable to claim self-defense in the shooting? Do you think he should have been allowed to raise this claim? Why or why not?

2. In this case, the U.S. Court of Appeals for the Second Circuit said: "It has long been accepted that one cannot support a claim of self-defense by a self-generated necessity to kill." What is the logic behind this principle? Do you agree with it? Explain.

3. Under what circumstances, if any, might the defendants have been justified in using force against Agent Howard? Under what circumstances might they have been justified in using deadly force?

Law Line 7-4
United States v. Thomas

---

retreat rule

a legal standard used in some jurisdictions that requires a person being attacked to retreat, where possible, to avoid the necessity of using force

Duty to Retreat.   A minority of jurisdictions impose a **retreat rule** upon those who would claim self-defense. Those jurisdictions require that the person being attacked retreat to avoid the necessity of using force if retreat can be accomplished with "complete safety." Jurisdictions that follow a retreat rule, however, often specify that actors are not obliged to retreat from specific locations, such as their home or place of work, before responding forcefully when threatened or assailed. Actors who do not retreat may be judged according to other criteria, such as whether the amount of force with which they responded was reasonable and proportionate to the threat at hand. Some jurists argue that a person who is under attack should have no obligation to retreat since he or she has a natural right to resist an unprovoked attack under any circumstances.

A number of jurisdictions, like North Carolina, have developed the notion of **perfect self-defense**. When deadly force is used, perfect self-defense is established "when the evidence, viewed in the light most favorable to the defendant, tends to show that at the time of the killing it appeared to the defendant and she believed it to be necessary to kill the decedent to save herself from imminent death or great bodily harm. That belief must be reasonable, however, in that the circumstances as they appeared to the defendant would create such a belief in the mind of a person of ordinary firmness. Further, the defendant must not have been the initial aggressor provoking the fatal confrontation. A killing in the proper exercise of the right of perfect self-defense is always completely justified in law and constitutes no legal wrong."[9] **Imperfect self-defense** may exist when any of the conditions required for perfect self-defense are lacking. In jurisdictions where the concepts of perfect and imperfect self-defense are employed, imperfect self-defense may lower criminal liability but not eliminate it.

> **perfect self-defense**
> a situation where the bulk of evidence demonstrates that defendant's use of force was performed out of a reasonable perception of necessity

> **imperfect self-defense**
> a situation where some evidence suggests that defendant's use of force was necessary to avoid a greater harm

Defense of Others

The use of force to defend oneself has generally been extended to permit the use of reasonable force to defend others who are, or who appear to be, in imminent danger. This doctrine is called **defense of others** or defense of a third person. Generally speaking, this defense allows a person to stand in the shoes of the victim and to use whatever force the victim could use in that person's defense.

The defense of others, however, is often circumscribed in some jurisdictions by the **alter ego rule**. See Figure 7-4. The alter ego rule holds that a person can defend a third party only under circumstances and only to the degree that the third party could act. As a result, a person who aids a third party whom he sees being accosted may be criminally liable if the third party initiated the attack or if the assault on the third party is a lawful one—that is, being made by a law enforcement officer conducting a lawful arrest of a person who is resisting.

> **defense of others**
> use of reasonable force to defend others who are, or who appear to be, in imminent danger

> **alter ego rule**
> a legal standard maintaining that a person can defend a third party only under circumstances and only to the degree that the third party could act

Some jurisdictions, like Texas (see below), follow Model Penal Code standards and do not recognize the alter ego rule. Instead, they allow a person to act in defense of another if "the actor reasonably believes that his intervention is immediately necessary to protect the third person." Even though a person may misperceive a situation and act in defense of a third party, thinking that party is in immediate danger, the requisite *mens rea* that might otherwise make the action a crime would be lacking.

Texas Penal Code § 9.33 Defense of Third Person

A person is justified in using force or deadly force against another to protect a third person if:

1. Under the circumstances as the actor reasonably believes them to be, the actor would be justified under Section 9.31 or 9.32 in using force or deadly force to protect himself against the unlawful force or unlawful deadly force he reasonably believes to be threatening the third person he seeks to protect; and
2. The actor reasonably believes that his intervention is immediately necessary to protect the third person.

§ 9.34. Protection of Life or Health.

(a) A person is justified in using force, but not deadly force, against another when and to the degree he reasonably believes the force is immediately necessary to prevent the other from committing suicide or inflicting serious bodily injury to himself.

(b) A person is justified in using both force and deadly force against another when and to the degree he reasonably believes the force or deadly force is immediately necessary to preserve the other's life in an emergency.

Generally, the defense of others cannot be claimed by an individual who joins an illegal fight merely to assist a friend or family member. Likewise, one who intentionally aids an offender in an assault, even though the tables have turned and the offender is losing the battle, cannot claim defense of others. In other words, defense of others always requires that defenders be free from fault and that they act to aid an innocent person who is in the process of being victimized. The restrictions that apply to self-defense also apply to defense of a third party. A defender must act in response to an immediate threat to another person, cannot use deadly force against less-than-deadly force, and must act only to the extent and use only the degree of force needed to repel the attack.

FIGURE 7-4 **The Alter Ego Rule**

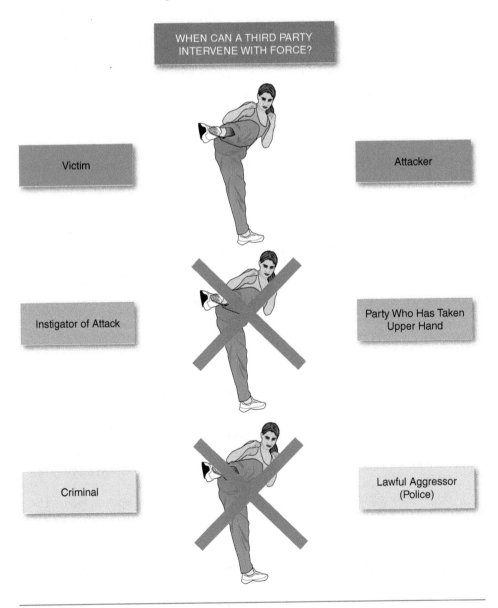

Defense of Home and Property

Defense of property, also called ***protection of property***, can apply in the following situations: (1) protection of personal property, (2) defense of home or habitation, (3) defense of another's property, and (4) use of a mechanical device to protect property.

    In most jurisdictions, the owner of property can justifiably use reasonable *nondeadly* force to prevent others from unlawfully taking or damaging that property. As a general rule, however, the preservation of human life outweighs protection of property, and the use of deadly force to protect property is not justified unless the perpetrator of the illegal act may intend to commit, or is in the act of committing, a violent act against another human being. A person who shoots a trespasser, for example, cannot use the defense of property to avoid criminal liability, but one who shoots and kills an armed robber while being robbed can. The difference is that a person facing an armed robber has a right to protect his property but is also in danger of death or serious bodily harm. An unarmed trespasser represents no such serious threat.[10]

    The use of mechanical devices to protect property is a special area of law. Since, generally speaking, deadly force is not permitted in defense of property, the setting of booby traps—such as spring-loaded shotguns, electrified grates, explosive devices, and the like—is generally not permitted to protect property that is unattended and unoccupied. Of course, another problem may arise in the use of such devices: the death or injury of an innocent person. Booby-trapped property may be entered by children trying to recover a baseball, by fire fighters called to extinguish a fire, or by law enforcement officers with a lawful search warrant. If an individual is injured as a result of a mechanical device intended to cause death or injury in the protection of property, criminal charges may be brought against the person who set the device.

    These principles were well summarized by the California Supreme Court in *People v. Ceballos* (1974),[11] where the court found, "[i]n the United States, courts have concluded that a person may be held criminally liable under statutes proscribing homicides and shooting with intent to injure, or civilly liable, if he sets upon his premises a deadly mechanical device and that device kills or injures another.... However, an exception to the rule that there may be criminal and civil liability for death or injuries caused by such a device has been recognized where the intrusion is, in fact, such that the person, were he present, would be justified in taking the life or inflicting the bodily harm with his own hands."[12]

    In other circumstances, however, harmful acts that would otherwise be criminal may carry no criminal liability if undertaken to protect one's home. For purposes of the law, one's "home" is one's dwelling, whether owned, rented, or merely "borrowed." Hotel rooms, rooms onboard vessels, and rented rooms in houses belonging to others are all considered, for purposes of the law, one's "dwelling." The retreat rule, referred to earlier, which requires a person under attack to retreat when possible before resorting to deadly force, is subject to what some call the castle exception. The ***castle exception*** maintains that "[a] man's house is his castle—for where shall a man be safe if it be not in his house?"[13] The castle exception generally recognizes that a person has a fundamental right to be in his or her home and also recognizes the home as a final and inviolable place of retreat (i.e., the home offers a place of retreat from which a person can be expected to retreat no farther). As a result, it is not necessary for one to retreat from one's home in the face of an immediate threat, even where such retreat is possible, before resorting to deadly force in protection of the home. A number of

protection of property
use of force to defend property

Law Line 7-5
People v. Ceballos

castle exception
a legal standard recognizing that a person has a fundamental right to be in his or her home; often used to negate the duty to retreat

court decisions have extended the castle exception to include one's place of business, such as a store or office. See the discussion of self-defense and duty to retreat (above).

The law describing defense of home is far from clear, however. Part of the problem comes from the fact that people defending their home against intrusion are often acting out of self-defense or defense of family. Another problem arises because not all states have codified the conditions under which the use of force in defense of the home is justifiable. Some states follow the old common law rule that permits the use of deadly force to prevent an unlawful entry of any kind into the home. Other states, however, especially those that have enacted statutes designed to give the weight of legal authority to defense of one's home, qualify the use of deadly force by authorizing it only for purposes of preventing a felony. Under such statutes, a person would be authorized in using force against a burglar who has illegally entered his or her home with the intent to steal, but the person would not be authorized in using force against someone who mistakenly or lawfully enters the residence.

Finally, property in the possession of a third person, or the home of a third person, may be protected by one who assists that person to the same degree and in the same manner that the owner of the property or the home would have been privileged to act. Tennessee's protection of property law (below) is similar to Model Penal Code Section 3.06 and many other state laws.

Tennessee Criminal Code

Title 39, Section 11-614. Protection of property.

(a) A person in lawful possession of real or personal property is justified in threatening or using force against another when and to the degree it is reasonably believed the force is immediately necessary to prevent or terminate the other's trespass on the land or unlawful interference with the property.

(b) A person who has been unlawfully dispossessed of real or personal property is justified in threatening or using force against the other when and to the degree it is reasonably believed the force is immediately necessary to reenter the land or recover the property if the person threatens or uses the force immediately or in fresh pursuit after the dispossession; and:

   1. The person reasonably believes the other had no claim of right when the other dispossessed the person; and

   2. The other accomplished the dispossession by threatening or using force against the person.

(c) A person is not justified in using deadly force to prevent or terminate the other's trespass on real estate or unlawful interference with personal property.

Title 39, Section 11-615.

Protection of third person's property.

A person is justified in threatening or using force against another to protect real or personal property of a third person if, under the circumstances as the person reasonably believes them to be, the person would be justified under 39-11-614 in threatening or using force to protect the person's own real or personal property.

Title 39, Section 11-616.

Use of device to protect property.

(a) The justification afforded by §§ 39-11-614 and 39-11-615 extends to the use of a device for the purpose of protecting property only if:

   1. The device is not designed to cause or known to create a substantial risk of causing death or serious bodily harm;

2. The use of the particular device to protect the property from entry or trespass is reasonable under the circumstances as the person believes them to be; and

3. The device is one customarily used for such a purpose or reasonable care is taken to make known to probable intruders the fact that it is used.

(b) Nothing in this section shall affect the law regarding the use of animals to protect property or persons.

Resisting Unlawful Arrest

All jurisdictions today have laws making it illegal for a person to resist a lawful arrest. Under common law, however, it was lawful to use force to resist an *unlawful* arrest. Following common law tradition, some jurisdictions today continue to consider resistance in the face of an unlawful arrest justifiable, and many have codified statutory provisions detailing the limits imposed on such resistance and the conditions under which it may be used. The Texas statute cited in the preceding section, for example, makes it clear that a person may use a reasonable amount of force, other than deadly force, to resist an unlawful arrest or an unlawful search by a law enforcement officer if the officer "uses or attempts to use greater force than necessary to make the arrest or search" and "when and to the degree the actor reasonably believes the force is immediately necessary to protect himself against the peace officer's use or attempted use of greater force than necessary." A provision of the law makes it inapplicable to cases in which the defendant is the first to resort to force, and deadly force to resist arrest is not justified unless the law enforcement officer resorts to deadly force when it is not called for.

On the other hand, some states require a person to submit to any arrest by an authorized law enforcement officer acting on official business. The rationale for this rule is that resisting arrest can be a dangerous undertaking for all the parties involved and in the heat of the moment it can sometimes be difficult to determine whether an arrest is lawful or not. Moreover, in contrast with common law days, the ready availability of defense counsel makes it unlikely that anyone unlawfully arrested will spend much time in jail. In some jurisdictions, it is an affirmative defense to prosecution if the peace officer involved was out of uniform and did not identify himself or herself as a peace officer by showing credentials to the person whose arrest was attempted.

Most jurisdictions provide statutory protections to law enforcement officers who find it necessary to use force to effectuate an arrest or to prevent individuals in their custody from escaping. Such statutes provide an **execution of public duty defense** and preclude the possibility of arresting officers being prosecuted on charges of assault or battery (if force is needed to effect the arrest or to maintain custody) as long as the officers acted in a lawful manner. Requirements of a lawful arrest typically include (1) making the purpose of the arrest known to the person arrested and (2) using a valid arrest warrant (if the arrest is to be made on the authority of a warrant—something that is not necessary if the crime was committed in the officer's presence). Execution of public duty statutes also protect anyone carrying out the order of a lawful court or tribunal, anyone performing the duties or functions of a public officer, and anyone lawfully involved in the execution of legal processes defined by law. Blanket statutes of this sort legitimize the lawful behavior of public servants, government employees, and elected officials.

The use of deadly force by law enforcement officers is of special concern. If police officers attempting to make a lawful arrest meet resistance, they may use reasonable force to effectuate the arrest and to protect themselves. General rules of

execution of public duty defense a statutory protection for law enforcement officers to use force to effectuate an arrest or to prevent individuals in their custody from escaping

self-defense apply in such situations. But even in those states requiring citizens to retreat before using deadly force, an officer is not required to retreat rather than make an arrest.

Prior to the U.S. Supreme Court's ruling in *Tennessee v. Garner* (1985),[14] which specified the conditions under which deadly force could be used in the apprehension of suspected felons, most law enforcement departments throughout the United States operated under the **fleeing felon rule**. The fleeing felon rule permitted officers to shoot a suspected felon who attempted to flee from a lawful arrest. But in *Garner*, the Court ruled that "the use of deadly force to prevent the escape of all felony suspects, whatever the circumstances, is constitutionally unreasonable."[15] According to *Garner*, deadly force may be applied only to prevent death or the threat of serious injury to the public or to protect the law enforcement officer from a defendant who resorts to the use of deadly force. Because *Garner* was a civil case, however, the actions of police officers, while they might violate criteria established by *Garner*, may still not be criminal.

fleeing felon rule
a legal standard permitting officers to shoot a suspected felon who attempts to flee from a lawful arrest

Law Line 7-6
Tennessee v. Garner

Consent

consent
a legal defense to some crimes where the victim agreed to sustain the injury or accepted the possibility of injury

The defense of **consent** makes the claim that the person suffering an injury either (1) agreed to sustain the injury or (2) accepted the possibility of injury before the activity was undertaken. In either case, consent must be voluntarily and legally given if the defense is to be useful. It is also important to note that consent is available as a defense only if lack of consent is an element of the crime. For example, in the crime of rape, the lack of consent to sexual conduct is often included as an essential element of the offense.

Consent can be inherent in some situations. As one observer puts it, "[t]he act of one who grabs another by the ankles and causes him to fall violently to the ground may result in a substantial jail sentence under some circumstances, but receive thunderous applause if it stops a ball carrier on the gridiron."[16] A person injured in an athletic contest cannot, under most circumstances, bring a charge of battery against another player, since both consented to participate in the game. Of course, some sporting events are much more likely to produce injuries than others, and some involve far more personal contact than others. Football players, for example, are routinely expected to tackle one another, while tennis players are not. If an assault continues beyond the point permitted by the rules of the sport, it may become illegal. Fistfights between basketball players, even though they occur on court, provide an example of such illegal activity.

In 2004, for example, five Indiana Pacers players and five Detroit Pistons fans were charged with assault and battery in connection with one of the worst brawls in American sports history. See accompanying photo. The fight broke out near the end of a game in Michigan after an on-court dispute over a foul. Some fans at the game exacerbated the situation by throwing cups and other objects at some of the players. Local authorities charged five players with assault, and all five were convicted and sentenced to a year on probation with community service. Similarly, violent sports that are not recognized as legitimate by government authorities may leave the participants liable to a criminal charge. Contestants in bare-knuckle or street fighting, for example, can be charged with assault, even though the contest may have been informally arranged by the "local community" and sanctioned by numerous observers.

Sexual activity is another area in which the defense of consent is frequently employed. A man might claim in defense to a charge of rape, for example, that a woman consented to his sexual advances and therefore agreed to sexual intercourse. Consent to one thing (sexual advances), however, does not constitute

Indiana Pacers forward Ron Artest is grabbed by fans after he went into the seats during a brawl with the Detroit Pistons with just 45.9 seconds left in the game Friday, November 19, 2004, in Auburn Hills, Mich. Artest was later charged and convicted of misdemeanor assault based on the incident and was sentenced to one-year of probation, sixty hours of community service, and a $250 fine.

consent to another (sexual intercourse). Problems may arise when one of the parties to a sexual act wrongly believes that the other has consented and proceeds to engage in sexual activity on the basis of that belief. For example, Joel Valdez , a defendant is a 1993 Austin, Texas, rape case, claimed that his alleged victim consented to sexual intercourse. Valdez, who was drunk and armed with a knife at the time of the attack, argued that his victim's request to use a condom during the attack amounted to consent. Valdez's victim pledged not to resist, and in fact did not resist, in exchange for Valdez agreeing to use a condom. The jury in the case, however, rejected Valdez's claim and found him guilty of rape.[17]

Although cases like the "condom rapist" may be easy to decide, questions of consent in other sexual assault cases may prove more difficult. For many, some sexual activity proceeds on the basis of nonverbal cues, which require a fair degree of subjective interpretation, and both the cues and the manner of their interpretation can be the products of strong cultural influences. To address this dynamic, some sought to establish an express consent requirement. Express consent is a verbally expressed willingness to engage in a specified activity, and in the heterosexual arena it generally places the burden of ensuring that consent has been obtained on the man. In 1990, for example, Antioch College instituted a requirement of "willing and verbal consent for each individual sexual act." The Antioch policy requires express consent from both partners at each stage as the level of sexual activity increases. Although the college's policy does not carry the force of law, it is indicative of the complexities involved in determining consent.

Because the public has an interest in the protection of citizens, consent is generally not available as a defense in cases of homicide or where the injury inflicted causes serious bodily harm. Reflecting such concerns, consent, or lack thereof, is not an element specified by laws contravening homicide and many other crimes. A killer who shoots another person, for example, after being told, "There's the gun. Go ahead and shoot me!" cannot effectively offer a consent defense, even though the victim's comments may be substantiated by witnesses.[18] Similarly, most jurisdictions do not permit one to consent to one's own death, and consent is not a valid defense in cases of euthanasia, especially where the defendant played an *active* role in the decedent's death or directly caused the death.

IN THE FIELD

Legal professionals can spend a lot of time considering and preparing justification-based defenses. Many of these defenses—self defense, defense of others, consent, and so forth—often boil down to the substance and credibility of what the defendant perceived while committing the harmful act. Did the defendant reasonably believe she would be harmed? Did the defendant reasonably believe that the victim was consenting to his conduct? For both defense and prosecutorial professionals, these issues involve difficult assessments of whether the trier of fact will buy the defendant's claims. To this end, some legal professionals might test a defendant's justification prior to trial by using mock trial simulations. Others with more limited resources might informally test the defendant's justification by asking friends, family, and laypersons to comment on the perceived reasonableness of the defendant's claims.

ETHICAL PRINCIPLES

RESPONDING TO CLIENTS' QUESTIONS

National Association of Legal Assistants Code of Ethics and Professional Responsibility Canon 5

A paralegal must disclose his or her status as a paralegal at the outset of any professional relationship with a client, attorney, a court or administrative agency or personnel thereof, or a member of the general public. A paralegal must act prudently in determining the extent to which a client may be assisted without the presence of an attorney.

Courtesy of the National Association of Legal Assistants

EXCUSE AS A DEFENSE

Unlike justifications, which assert that the allegedly criminal act was in fact legally permitted, an excuse acknowledges the act's criminality but asserts that the defendant should not be blamed for it.[19] In other words, excuses admit that the action committed by the defendant was wrong and that it violated the criminal law but claim that the defendant should be excused from criminal liability by virtue of special conditions or circumstances that suggest that the actor was not responsible for his or her deeds. The majority of excuses are personal in nature, that is, they claim that the defendant acted on the basis of some disability or some abnormal condition, such as intoxication, insanity, or immaturity. Even when defendants suffer from a disability, however, that disability alone is not sufficient to excuse them from criminal responsibility. Only when the disability in some way contributes to the criminal activity will defendants be excused. Like justifications, excuses are affirmative defenses and must be raised by the defendant.

Over the years, and to various degrees, some jurisdictions have recognized a variety of legal excuses, including (1) duress, (2) involuntary intoxication, (3) mistake, (4) age, (5) entrapment, (6) insanity, and (7) diminished responsibility. In addition, some defendants have also presented other unique syndrome-based conditions as legal excuses.

Duress

The Model Penal Code (MPC) states that "[i]t is an affirmative defense that the actor engaged in the conduct charged to constitute an offense because he was coerced to do so by the use of, or a threat to use, unlawful force against his person or the person of another, which a person of reasonable firmness in his situation would have been unable to resist."[20] The defense of **duress**, sometimes also called *compulsion*, is based on the belief that people do not willfully engage in acts they are compelled or coerced to perform. As a result, the mother forced to rob a bank by someone holding her children hostage, the captured military officer compelled to provide secrets to an enemy under threat of torture, and the pilot of an airplane who flies off course after her plane has been commandeered by terrorists are all forced to commit acts they would not otherwise perform.

duress
a defense that asserts the defendant was compelled or coerced to perform an illegal act

Some legal scholars say that duress may qualify as either a justification or an excuse. The main difference, they point out, is that necessity (a justification) is brought about by acts of nature or natural events, whereas duress is imposed by one human being on another. But in most jurisdictions, the effective use of the duress defense must be based on a showing that the defendant feared for his or her life or was in danger of great bodily harm—or that the defendant was acting to prevent the death or bodily harm of another.[21] Likewise, the threat under which the defendant acted must have been immediate, clear, and inescapable and must not have arisen from some illegal or immoral activity of the defendant.

Generally speaking, duress is a defense only when the crime committed is less serious than the harm avoided. Some jurisdictions limit the applicability of the duress defense to less serious crimes; others state that it cannot be used as a defense to a charge of homicide; and still others broaden the ban to all crimes of personal violence. For example, the California Penal Code limits the duress defense to non-capital crimes in which the actor's life was threatened.

Intoxication

A defendant's claim of intoxication is generally not regarded as an effective defense, even when the intoxication results from alcoholism. Laws that codify intoxication-related defenses usually limit the use of these defenses to cases where intoxication is involuntary. These laws generally hold that those who voluntarily put themselves in an intoxicated state are accountable for any resulting consequences. In some jurisdictions and for certain crimes, however, voluntary intoxication may reduce the level of a defendant's criminal liability when it prevents the person from forming the necessary *mens rea* for the offense. For example, a defendant might try to defend against a first-degree premeditated murder charge by arguing that his intoxicated state made it impossible to form the specific intent to kill or any degree of premeditation. If successful, this defense might result in a second-degree murder or manslaughter conviction. Such a dynamic is illustrated by the jury instruction given in *People v. Walker*,[22] where the jury was told:

> In the crime of attempted murder of which the defendant is accused in count 1 of the information, a necessary element is the existence in the mind of the defendant of the specific intent to kill. If the evidence shows that the defendant

was intoxicated at the time of the alleged crime, you should consider that fact in determining whether defendant had such specific intent. If from all the evidence you have reasonable doubt whether the defendant formed such specific intent, you must find that he did not have such specific intent.

The essence of any defense based on intoxication can be found in the effect that an intoxicating substance has on the mental state of the defendant. Of course, intoxication may make it impossible to commit a crime. A man charged with rape, for example, could conceivably use expert testimony to support his contention that it was impossible for him to achieve an erection because of his highly intoxicated condition at the time of the alleged offense. Such a claim, however, does not reference the mental state of the defendant, but instead relies on the assertion that the crime in question did not actually occur because the defendant was too intoxicated to commit it. This kind of defense is far different from the claim that the requisite mental state needed to commit an offense was lacking.

There is a critical difference between voluntary and involuntary intoxication. The California Penal Code says that "***voluntary intoxication*** includes the voluntary ingestion, injection, or taking by any other means of any intoxicating liquor, drug, or other substance."[23] ***Involuntary intoxication***, in contrast, generally results from the unknowing ingestion of an intoxicating substance. Involuntary intoxication may result from secretly "spiked" punch or LSD-laced desserts, from following medical advice, and from situations in which an individual is tricked or forced into consuming an intoxicating substance.

Involuntary intoxication also may result from the use of prescription or over-the-counter drugs containing substances with which the user is unfamiliar. In one case,[24] a trial court acquitted a hunter charged with assaulting members of his hunting party, based on the defendant's claim that he suffered from toxic psychosis brought on by his excessive use (twelve boxes in twenty-four hours) of cough drops containing the chemical dextromethorphan hydrobromide. In other cases, criminal defendants have asserted defenses based on the side effects of Ambien, a popular sleeping medication. For example, in 2006, Ki Yong O was driving his car in Middlesex County, Massachusetts, when he struck and killed another motorist. Authorities charged Yong O with operating a motor vehicle under the influence and motor vehicle homicide. In his defense, Yong O claimed that his fatal driving was brought on by the unexpected side effects associated with his use of Ambien. And in fact, blood tests revealed toxic levels of the sleeping agent in the defendant's system. At trial, the judge acquitted Yong O, finding that "the court is unable to conclude beyond a reasonable doubt that the defendant was voluntarily intoxicated when he operated his motor vehicle."

Accordingly, in some jurisdictions, involuntary intoxication may serve as a defense, if it either creates in defendants an incapacity to appreciate the criminality of their conduct or creates an incapacity to conform their behavior to the requirements of the law.

Mistake

An honest ***mistake of fact*** can preclude criminal liability in cases where the defendant's harmful conduct would have been lawful had the situation been as the defendant reasonably believed it to be. In some circumstances, a person's mistake of fact eliminates or reduces the ability to form the necessary *mens rea* to commit an offense. An *honest mistake* is one that is genuine and sincere and not a pretext offered merely to hide criminal intent. For example, fashion model Jerry Hall was

voluntary intoxication
the voluntary ingestion, injection, or taking by any other means of any intoxicating liquor, drug, or other substance; not recognized as a viable defense in most jurisdictions and for most crimes

involuntary intoxication
the unknowing ingestion of an intoxicating substance; can serve as the basis for a viable defense by negating the requisite *mens rea* for a crime

mistake of fact
a legal defense based on claimed misunderstanding of factual reality

arrested after she picked up a marijuana-filled suitcase in the baggage claim area of a Barbados airport. Hall, who was the girlfriend of the rock musician Mick Jagger, claimed that she mistakenly grabbed the bag because it looked just like one she owned. Hall convinced authorities that her mistake was genuine, and she was released after spending a night in jail.

A *reasonable mistake* is one that might be made by a typically competent person acting under the same set of circumstances. A man who forces a woman whom he does not know to accompany him on a journey she does not want to take may, for example, be guilty of kidnapping even though he believed she acquiesced to his requests to accompany him. In just such a case, the Indiana Supreme Court found a defendant guilty of kidnapping a woman who offered no physical resistance out of fear of the defendant—although she expressed verbal reservations. Any reasonable man, under the same circumstances, said the court, would have realized that she did not want to go with him. In the words of the court:

> Appellant's assertion that he did not "force" the victim out of the laundromat provides some evidence that he honestly so believed. It is, however, no evidence of the reasonableness of that belief. . . . Apart from this statement, we find nothing in the record to suggest that a reasonable man in appellant's position would have interpreted the victim's actions as indicative of her free consent to accompany appellant. By appellant's own version of the encounter the facts are such that no reasonable person could have believed as appellant alleges he did.[25]

Mistake of fact is different from an ***ignorance of fact***. Ignorance of fact refers to a lack of knowledge of some fact relating to the matter at hand, while mistake of fact refers to a misinterpretation or misunderstanding of the facts at hand. Both can be defenses to a criminal charge. As a defense, both ignorance of fact and mistake of fact may negate the *mens rea* required for a specific offense. As one court stated, "[t]he criminal intention being of the essence of crime, if the intent is dependent on a knowledge of particular facts, a want of such knowledge, not the result of carelessness or negligence, relieves the act of criminality."[26]

Some mistakes do not relieve a defendant of criminal liability. A drug dealer who mistakenly purchases heroin, thinking it is cocaine, will still be found guilty of trafficking in a controlled substance.[27] Likewise, when a person intends to commit one crime but actually commits another, his mistake will be no defense. For example, a burglar who breaks into the wrong house seeking money he has heard is hidden under a mattress is still guilty of burglary even though he is unable to locate the cash.

Another form of mistake is ***mistake of law***. Generally speaking, however, courts have held that neither ***ignorance of the law*** (where one does not know a law exists) nor a misunderstanding of the law provides for an acceptable defense, and criminal proceedings assume that "every one capable of acting for himself knows the law."[28] This assumption does not mean, of course, that everyone is actually familiar with each and every law, but it effectively compels people to learn the standards set by the law in their sphere of activity. In effect, ignorance of the law is a kind of culpable ignorance in which an individual's failure to exercise ordinary care to acquire knowledge of the law may result in criminal liability.

Although quite rare in practice, ignorance or mistake of law may be a defense in cases where the charged offense requires a specific intent or where a mistake of law negates the *mens rea* required by the statute. Ignorance of the law also may be an excuse where the law is not adequately published or is incapable of being known. An individual who violates a federal law against "knowingly making false statements" by placing her signature on a complicated government form may, for example, raise

ignorance of fact
lack of knowledge of some fact relating to the matter at hand; different from mistake of fact, which refers to a misinterpretation or misunderstanding of the facts at hand

mistake of law
a misunderstanding of the legal standards for a given situation; typically not a viable defense

ignorance of the law
a situation where one does not know a law exists; not usually a viable defense

just such a defense. In one such case, a defendant signed a federal form required to obtain a firearm, but the form contained references to federal statutes by numbered sections and subsections, without explaining the content or purpose of the law it cited. Although the defendant was technically in violation of the law (he was a convicted felon, and the laws referred to on the form prohibited a convicted felon from purchasing a gun), he claimed that he did not knowingly make a false statement because he was ignorant of what the legal nomenclature on the form meant. Although he was convicted, a federal appeals court reversed his conviction, saying that "many lawyers would not have understood" the language of the form and that it was therefore unreasonable to expect a layman to understand it.[29]

Finally, mistake of law may be a valid defense to a criminal charge if made in good faith under circumstances involving a bona fide attempt to ascertain the meaning of the law through reliance on a public official who is in a position to interpret the statute or through the use of appropriate legal counsel. In some jurisdictions, a defendant may effectively raise such a defense where "before engaging in the conduct, the defendant made a bona fide, diligent effort, adopting a course and resorting to sources and means at least as appropriate as any afforded under our legal system, to ascertain and abide by the law, and where he acted in good faith reliance upon the results of such effort."[30]

Mistake of fact can be asserted by a defendant to show that, based on the defendant's belief at the time of the illegal activity, no crime occurred because the requisite *mens rea* was lacking. Read the accompanying opinion in *People v. Tolbert* (1996),[31] where a California appellate court held that a reasonable but mistaken belief in a victim's death prior to movement of that person by the defendant precludes conviction for kidnapping.

CAPSTONE CASE *People v. Tolbert,* 56 Cal. Rptr. 2d 604 (Cal. Ct. App. 1996)

[California] Penal Code, Section 26, recites, generally, that one is incapable of committing a crime who commits an act under a mistake of fact disproving any criminal intent. Penal Code Section 20 provides, "In every crime . . . there must exist a union, or joint operation of act and intent, or criminal negligence." The word "intent" in Section 20 means "wrongful intent." "So basic is this requirement [of a union of act and wrongful intent] that it is an invariable element of every crime unless excluded expressly or by necessary implication."

The kidnapping statute "neither expressly nor by necessary implication negate[s] the continuing requirement that there be a union of act and wrongful intent. The severe penalties imposed for th[is] offense . . . and the serious loss of reputation following conviction make it extremely unlikely that the Legislature intended to exclude as to th[is] offense the element of wrongful intent."

Mistake of fact is an affirmative defense. The defendant therefore has the burden of producing evidence that "he had a *bona fide* and reasonable belief that the [victim] consented to the movement. . . ." The Supreme Court has since held that this burden may be met with evidence supplied by the prosecution. However, because wrongful intent is an element of the crime, the ultimate burden of persuasion is on the people; the defendant is "only required to raise a reasonable doubt as to whether he had such a belief."

We find ourselves unable to distinguish a mistake of fact about whether the kidnapping victim consents from a mistake of fact about whether the kidnapping victim is alive. If the victim is dead, he or she is no longer a "person" who can be kidnapped, precisely because he or she can no longer give or withhold consent to the asportation. It does appear that . . . knowledge that the victim was alive is not an element of the crime of kidnapping, which the prosecution must prove in all cases; but if there is any evidence that the defendant honestly and reasonably believed the victim was dead, the people must prove beyond a reasonable doubt that the defendant lacked such a belief. . . .

Here, there was ample evidence that defendant reasonably believed Killingbeck was dead before the asportation began. Indeed, it seems amazing that Killingbeck stayed alive for any time at all. He had been shot in the right eye by a shotgun held six to twelve inches away; there was an exit wound behind his right ear. Some of the pellets left through the exit wound, but "lots of them" remained inside. The force was sufficient to leave his head "slightly deformed." He was rendered unconscious instantly; the wound was inevitably fatal. The pathologist testified that Killingbeck was able to live for a little while because the left side of his brain was uninjured, but this would hardly have been obvious to a layman. The fact that defendant believed Killingbeck was dead is further evidenced by his comment to Tim that there was "a dead body" in the car, even though Killingbeck actually was still alive at the time.

Thus, it is inferable that defendant reasonably believed Killingbeck died immediately after he was shot. On the other hand, there is no evidence that defendant did not reasonably believe Killingbeck died immediately. Certainly one could imagine all sorts of scenarios in which defendant could have realized Killingbeck was still alive; he might have noticed that Killingbeck was still breathing before he closed the trunk; or he might have stopped the car at some point and opened the trunk to check on Killingbeck. "But speculation is not evidence, less still substantial evidence." . . .

The only sufficient asportation here consisted of the movement of the car around Rubidoux with Killingbeck in the trunk. There was substantial evidence that at this point defendant honestly and reasonably believed Killingbeck was dead; there was no substantial evidence to the contrary. Accordingly, the kidnapping for robbery conviction must be reversed. Retrial is barred by double jeopardy. . . .

The kidnapping for robbery conviction is reversed, and the case is remanded for resentencing. In all other respects, the judgment is affirmed.

WHAT DO *YOU* THINK?

1. Should mistake of fact exonerate a defendant who, through criminal activity, brings about a situation (as in this case) that causes him to mistake the facts?

2. The court imagined could "all sorts of scenarios in which defendant could have realized Killingbeck was still alive." What possible scenarios might these include?

Age

Legal defenses based on age generally make the claim that the defendant should not be held criminally responsible for their activities by virtue of their youth. In some jurisdictions, this is also called an ***infancy defense*** or immaturity defense. Under common law, children below the age of seven were presumed to be without criminal capacity—that is, to be incapable of forming the *mens rea* needed for criminal activity. Today that rule still holds, and in most states children below the age of seven cannot be charged even with juvenile offenses, no matter how serious their actions.

infancy defense
an age-based or maturity-based defense

Law Line 7-7
People v. Tolbert

But in a startling 1994 case, prosecutors in Cincinnati, Ohio, charged a twelve-year-old girl with murder after she confessed to drowning her toddler cousin ten years earlier—when the girl was only two years old. The cousin, thirteen-month-old Lamar Howell, drowned in 1984 in a bucket of bleach mixed with water. Howell's drowning had been ruled an accidental death until his cousin confessed. In discussing the charges with the media, the prosecutor acknowledged that the girl could not be successfully prosecuted. "Frankly," he said, "anything under seven cannot be an age where you form criminal intent."[32] According to the prosecutor, his goal was simply to "make sure she gets the counseling she needs."

Most jurisdictions today do not impose full criminal culpability on children under the age of eighteen, while a number of states set the age of responsibility at sixteen and some at seventeen. Children who violate the criminal law are officially referred to as **juvenile offenders**, rather than as "criminals" to avoid the sort of stigmatization that might follow them throughout their lives. Juvenile offenders may be adjudicated "delinquent" or "responsible," but generally they are not found "guilty." See Figure 7-5.

Children under the age of criminal responsibility are often subject to juvenile court jurisdiction, rather than adult criminal courts, although almost all states allow older children to be transferred to adult criminal court if their conduct is especially serious or if the children are habitually in trouble with the law. In most cases, transfer to adult court requires a showing by the prosecution that the child was able to "appreciate the wrongfulness of [his or her] conduct," that the child had "a guilty knowledge of wrongdoing," or that the child was "competent to know the nature and consequences of his [or her] conduct and to know that it was wrong." Some states specify that juvenile courts have no jurisdiction

juvenile offenders
a name given to children who violate the criminal law

FIGURE 7-5 **Age as a Defense**

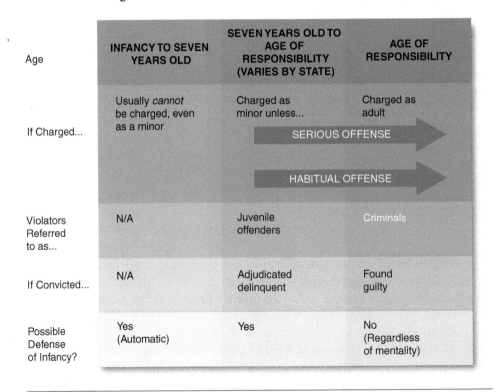

Age	INFANCY TO SEVEN YEARS OLD	SEVEN YEARS OLD TO AGE OF RESPONSIBILITY (VARIES BY STATE)	AGE OF RESPONSIBILITY
If Charged...	Usually *cannot* be charged, even as a minor	Charged as minor unless... SERIOUS OFFENSE / HABITUAL OFFENSE	Charged as adult
Violators Referred to as...	N/A	Juvenile offenders	Criminals
If Convicted...	N/A	Adjudicated delinquent	Found guilty
Possible Defense of Infancy?	Yes (Automatic)	Yes	No (Regardless of mentality)

over certain excluded offenses. Delaware, Louisiana, and Nevada, for example, do not allow juvenile court jurisdiction over children charged with first-degree murder.

Entrapment

The defense of ***entrapment*** is based on a claim that, had it not been for government instigation, no crime would have occurred. Entrapment defenses may be raised where public law enforcement officials or people acting on their behalf induce or encourage an otherwise law-abiding person to engage in illegal activity. In effect, the defense of entrapment claims that law enforcement officers are guilty of manufacturing a crime where none would otherwise exist.

Entrapment activities can involve a number of inducements to crime, but the two most common are (1) false representation by enforcement agents that are calculated to induce the belief that the illegal behavior is not prohibited and (2) the use of inducements to crime that are so strong that a person of average will and good intent could not resist. See Figure 7-6.

Entrapment cannot be effectively raised as a defense, however, where government employees "merely afford opportunities or facilities for the commission of the offense" or where law enforcement officers or their representatives engage in the "mere fact of deceit."[33] In other words, an undercover "sting" operation set up by the government to lure burglars and thieves who want to sell stolen goods would be legal, while government enticements to steal might not be.

U.S. Supreme Court cases have distinguished the subjective approach to reviewing entrapment cases from the objective approach, which developed later. See Figure 7-7. The ***subjective test*** excludes from criminal liability people who are

entrapment
a legal defense claiming that, but for government instigation, no crime would have occurred

subjective test
a type of entrapment defense based on the subjective beliefs of the defendant

---

FIGURE 7-6 **Entrapment**

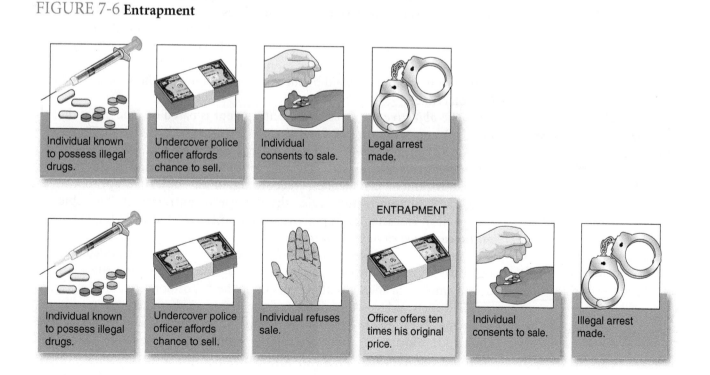

| Individual known to possess illegal drugs. | Undercover police officer affords chance to sell. | Individual consents to sale. | Legal arrest made. |

| Individual known to possess illegal drugs. | Undercover police officer affords chance to sell. | Individual refuses sale. | ENTRAPMENT — Officer offers ten times his original price. | Individual consents to sale. | Illegal arrest made. |

FIGURE 7-7 **Entrapment: Summary of Tests**

Entrapment Test	Standard	Evidence	Effect	Where Used
Subjective test	Is defendant predisposed to commit the crime?	Defendant's record, statements, etc.	If defendant is predisposed, then he or she will be convicted regardless of government conduct	Federal government and majority of states
Objective test	Does government behavior create substantial risk that someone not predisposed will commit the offense?	Government's conduct	If government's conduct is excessive, then defendant will be acquitted regardless of predisposition	MPC and minority of states

"otherwise innocent, who have been lured to the commission of the prohibited act through the Government's instigation."[34] The subjective test attempts to distinguish between those who are blameworthy and those who are not, by asking whether a person "caught" by the government was predisposed to commit the crime in question. In doing so, it distinguishes "unwary criminals," who are ready and willing to commit the offense when presented with a favorable opportunity, from those who are not.

Some courts have held that predisposition can be established by demonstrating a defendant's (1) prior convictions for similar crimes, (2) reputation for committing similar crimes, or (3) readiness to engage in a crime suggested by the police.[35] The subjective test for entrapment uses the criterion of "origin of intent." It asks whether "the criminal intent start[ed] in the mind of the officers, or [whether] the defendant [was] 'predisposed' to commit the offense when the officer first appeared on the scene?"[36] As a result, under the subjective approach, traps may be legitimately laid by the government only for those who are already bent on crime.

The **objective test** to assessing entrapment is based on "the belief that the methods employed on behalf of the Government to bring about conviction cannot be countenanced."[37] If government agents have acted in a way that is likely to instigate or create a criminal offense, regardless of the defendant's predisposition to crime, then—according to the objective approach—the defendant can successfully raise the defense of entrapment. The objective approach to assessing entrapment is sometimes referred to as the defense of **outrageous government conduct:**

In *Jacobson v. United States* (1992),[38] the U.S. Supreme Court ruled that "[i]n their zeal to enforce the law ... government agents may not originate a criminal design, implant in an innocent person's mind the disposition to commit a criminal act, and then induce commission of the crime so that the government may prosecute."[39] All states recognize the defense of entrapment, and some have even codified it. Most states follow a subjective approach in assessing a defendant's claims of entrapment. At least a dozen states follow an objective approach. But no

objective test
a type of entrapment defense based on what an objectively reasonable person would have believed

outrageous government conduct
a type of entrapment defense that considers the reasonableness of the government's conduct

Law Line 7-8
Jacobson v. United States

jurisdiction permits the excuse of entrapment to serve as a defense to serious crimes, such as murder and rape. Read a Florida court's ruling in *Madera v. State* (2006) to see how some courts analyze entrapment defenses.

CAPSTONE CASE *Madera v. State*, 943 So. 2d 960 (Fla. App. 4th Dist. 2006)

The appellant pled no contest to charges of trafficking in MDMA [a controlled substance with the street name Ecstasy], conspiracy to traffic in MDMA, and delivery of MDMA, reserving his right to appeal the trial court's denial of his motion to dismiss. The motion asserted that, on the undisputed facts, he was entrapped as a matter of law. We agree and reverse....

The State argues that because it denied that the defendant lacked a predisposition to commit the crime, a material issue of fact was in dispute, and thus the motion was properly denied. This argument, however ignores the distinction between a subjective and objective theory of entrapment. In the former, a predisposition to commit the crime will defeat the affirmative defense of entrapment. In the latter, predisposition is not an issue. Rather, the question is whether the conduct of law enforcement was so egregious as to violate the due process rights of the defendant.

The facts alleged in the motion that were not specifically denied by the state include the following: The defendant was 37 years old with absolutely no criminal history, unknown to law enforcement officers, and gainfully employed in lawful activity at the time the confidential informant first approached him. The defendant became romantically interested in the CI and she led him to believe that she was similarly interested in him. She first brought up the topic of illegal drug use and continually asked the defendant if he knew where to buy drugs or if he could obtain drugs for her. The defendant repeatedly told her that he did not use or sell illegal drugs, and that, being new to the area, he did not know anyone who used or sold drugs.

The CI made promises of an intimate relationship, to include sexual relations, if the defendant would assist her in obtaining drugs. She discussed her personal medical problems with the defendant and played on his sympathy, indicating that she needed the drugs to cope with the pain and the stress of cancer. The CI was herself a convicted drug trafficker who had recently received a below guidelines suspended sentence and probation. Unbeknownst to the defendant at the time, the CI was involved in similar transactions with several other individuals, whom she also pretended to befriend....

[I]n this case, there would have been no crime without the CI's prodding and improper conduct. At the time, the defendant was gainfully employed at a lawful occupation, had no prior criminal history, and was not even suspected of criminal activity. The CI was used here, not to detect crime, but to manufacture it. Thus, as in *Curry*, we find that the defendant's due process rights were violated by this egregious conduct and that he was objectively entrapped as a matter of law.

Accordingly, the judgment and sentence are hereby reversed with directions to set them aside and grant the motion to dismiss.

WHAT DO *YOU* THINK?

1. Was the conduct of law enforcement in this case so egregious that it was entrapment under both the objective and subjective tests?

2. Is the promise of a romantic relationship, including sex, so alluring or immoral that it is always wrong for the government to use this approach?

3. Would the outcome of this case have been different if the offer had been made by a male confidential informant to a female target?

Syndrome-Based Defense Enhancements

In the past several years, some defendants have offered new and innovative defense strategies based on claimed "syndromes." In the medical literature, a **syndrome** is defined as "a complex of signs and symptoms presenting a clinical picture of a disease or disorder."[40] If it can be demonstrated that a person charged with a crime was "suffering" from a known syndrome at the time that the crime was committed, such a showing may lower or eliminate criminal liability in at least three ways: (1) it may help support the applicability of a traditional defense (including a justification); (2) it may expand the applicability of traditional defenses (including justifications) to novel or unusual situations or to situations in which such defenses might not otherwise apply; or (3) it may negate the *mens rea* needed to prove the offense, leading the jury or trial judge to conclude that a crucial element necessary to prove the crime is missing. Some suggest a fourth possibility, which is "the creation of new affirmative defenses."[41] This would allow for more novel and unique defenses beyond those currently recognized. Defenses predicated on, or substantially enhanced by, the acceptability of syndrome-related claims are termed syndrome-based defenses. See Figure 7-8.

As a matter of constitutional law, a defendant generally is entitled to introduce evidence that might disprove any element of the charged crime. Consequently, many defendants have attempted to use syndromes as proof that they lacked the *mens rea* required for conviction. Some defendants, for example, have asserted battered woman's syndrome (BWS) as a part of a *self-defense* defense of their actions. But syndrome-based defenses are not always *convincing* because relatively few syndromes are medically well documented, and fewer still have found an established place within American legal tradition.

Although courts have been reluctant to recognize the claim that syndromes negate *mens rea*, the use of syndromes in expanding the applicability of traditional defenses has met with greater success. In such a role, syndromes provide neither a justification nor an excuse for otherwise criminal behavior. Rather, they are used to explain why a given individual in a particular situation should be held to different standards than those to which a typical "reasonable person" is held. For example, one might assert that the reasonableness of action by a battered woman should be judged according to the criterion of a "reasonable battered woman," rather than that of a "reasonable (nonbattered) person."

Battered Woman's Syndrome.   **Battered woman's syndrome (BWS)** is the best known of the syndromes on which today's innovative defenses are based. BWS is also referred to as *battered spouse syndrome* or *battered person's syndrome*. Battered woman's syndrome has been defined by the New Jersey Supreme Court as "a series of common characteristics that appear in women who are abused physically and psychologically over an extended period of time by the dominant male figure in their lives; a pattern of psychological symptoms that develop after somebody has lived in a battering relationship; or a pattern of responses and perceptions presumed to be characteristic of women who have been subjected to continuous physical abuse by their mate[s]."[42]

As is the case with syndromes generally, BWS is not in itself a defense. It is a *condition* said to characterize women who live in abusive relationships. BWS, however, may provide additional justification for a woman who kills a battering spouse during an episode of battering—when the threat of serious bodily harm or death is imminent. As an excuse for killings that do not occur within the context of an

syndrome
a disease or disorder of the mind that causes or contributes to purported criminal behavior

battered woman's syndrome
(BWS) a mental condition brought about by physical or psychological abuse inflicted by a spouse or domestic partner

FIGURE 7-8 **The Structure of a Syndrome-Based Defense**

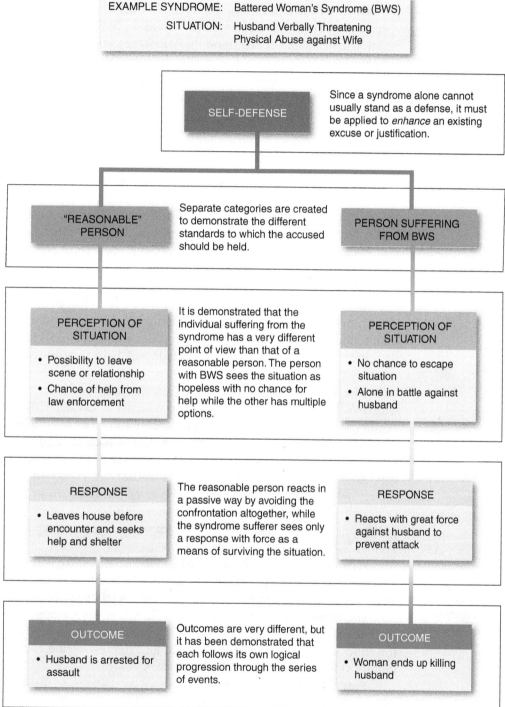

immediate threat, however, BWS has proven less effective in eliminating criminal liability, although it may lessen it, as provocation generally does (resulting, for example, in a manslaughter conviction rather than a conviction for first-degree or second-degree murder).

BWS is an area of the law that is still in flux. Some states, such as California, specifically permit expert testimony regarding BWS concerning "the physical, emotional, or mental effects upon the beliefs, perceptions, or behavior of victims of domestic violence,"[43] while others make no specific provision for the admissibility of BWS testimony. Such testimony, however, where available, may help juries better understand claims of self-defense made by battered women. As a Kansas court explained, "[e]xpert testimony on the battered woman syndrome would help dispel the ordinary lay person's perception that a woman in a battering relationship is free to leave at any time. The expert evidence would counter any 'common sense' conclusions by the jury that if the beatings were really that bad the woman would have left her husband much earlier. Popular misconceptions about battered women would be put to rest, including the beliefs the women are masochistic and enjoy the beatings and that they intentionally provoke their husbands into fits of rage."[44] At the same time, defense initiatives based on BWS *as a syndrome* one day may effectively extend the role of BWS beyond that of merely expanding self-defense claims and into the role of an excuse, such as duress or diminished capacity.

Other Syndrome-Based Defenses.   While BWS was one of the first syndromes to be raised as a defense enhancement in American courtrooms, many others have since followed, including adopted child syndrome (mental conditions resulting from the knowledge of being an adopted child), false memory syndrome (a condition where a person's behavior is based on a memory of a false traumatic experience),[45] premenstrual syndrome (PMS) (where a woman's behavior is affected by her menstrual cycle), Holocaust survival syndrome (involving behavior influenced by the trauma of being a Holocaust survivor),[46] attention deficit disorder (ADD) (a mental condition affecting the ability to concentrate), fetal alcohol syndrome (behavior caused by being exposed to alcohol or drugs while in the womb), Gulf War syndrome (behavior influenced by exposure to trauma during war), Munchausen by proxy syndrome (wherein a caregiver injures his or her children to gain attention), and posttraumatic stress disorder (conduct influenced by being exposed to traumatic events).[47]

Internet addiction disorder (IAD) a claimed syndrome maintaining that a person's dependence on Internet and other electronic resources can result in serious antisocial behavior

One recent syndrome addressed in medical literature is ***Internet addiction disorder (IAD)***, which maintains that a person's dependence on Internet and other electronic resources can result in serious antisocial behavior, including criminal acts. The claim is that people with IAD tend to lose control over their daily activities and crave the use of the Internet. They even have withdrawal symptoms when forced to forgo access to the Internet for an extended period of time. Some have found IAD to be as real as alcoholism.

Since syndromes are clinically viewed as diseases or disorders, we might anticipate the development of defenses based on other disorders as well, including hypoglycemia, senility, Alzheimer's disease, sleep disorders, postpartum disorders, preexisting genetic conditions, alcoholism, and drug addiction. Remember, there are two major elements of all crimes: *mens rea* and *actus reus*. And if an involuntary physical condition causes one to commit a crime (for example, if an epileptic batters someone during a seizure), this may negate the *mens rea* for the offense.

The use of syndrome-based defenses and other excuses often requires legal professionals to be familiar with in psychiatric and other sciences. Legal professionals are encouraged to evaluate the totality of circumstances surrounding a defendant's alleged harmful acts and to assess what factors—physiological, psychological, or environmental—may have caused or contributed to the defendant's conduct. There are just so many unknowns about mental science—things like the side effects of medicine and food, the effects of personal trauma, and the exposure to environmental harms, like lead or radiation. Given these and other possible factors, legal professionals must consider all possible contributors to criminal acts before proceeding with a particular strategy. And in cases where the science is complicated, legal professionals must consult medical and psychiatric experts for additional diagnosis

MENTAL INCOMPETENCY

Mental competency is an important concept in criminal law. A defendant's mental state can be assessed using different legal standards at various points in the criminal justice system. See Figure 7-9. There are two primary questions that legal professionals face in criminal cases: (1) Is the defendant competent to stand trial? and (2) Was the defendant mentally competent at the time of the alleged crime?

Competency to Stand Trial

Due process requirements prohibit the government from prosecuting a defendant who is legally incompetent to stand trial. Competency to stand trial may become an issue when a defendant appears to be incapable of understanding the proceedings against him or is unable to assist in his own defense due to mental disease or defect. Conversely, a person is **competent to stand trial** if he, at the time of trial, has sufficient

competency to stand trial
a defendant's ability to consult with his or her lawyer with a reasonable degree of understanding and a rational as well as factual understanding of the trial events

FIGURE 7-9 **Insanity and Competency**

AT TIME OF ACT	AT TRIAL	AT SENTENCING	POSTSENTENCE
An individual's act may be excused if, at the time of the crime, he or she is legally insane under the applicable standard (M'Naughten, MPC, etc.).	An accused may not be tried if not rational or if incapable of assisting in his or her own defense.	Insane and mentally retarded convicts may not be executed but may otherwise be punished.	Some states provide for mandatory psychological assessment of specific offenders (e.g., sexual predators) for dangerousness. If dangerous, civil commitment is used to continue detention.
If not guilty by reason of insanity, accused is assessed and committed if dangerous. If not, he or she is released.	Trial may proceed when defendant regains ability to assist in defense. Temporary detention is permitted while awaiting competency restoration. Longer detentions must occur through civil commitment procedures.		
If guilty but mentally ill, convict is provided treatment during incarceration/ punishment.			

FIGURE 7-10 **Competency to Stand Trial**

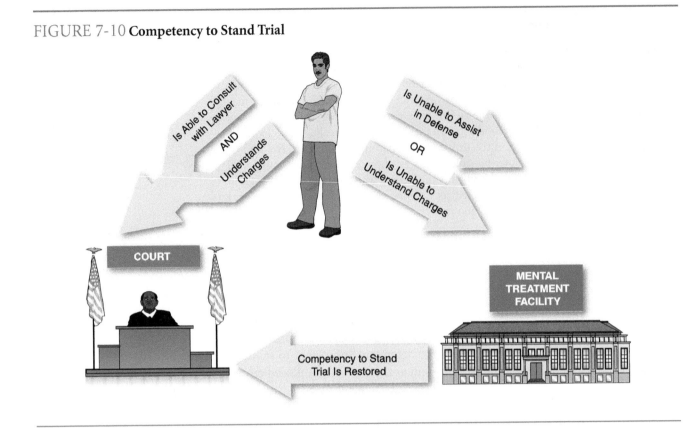

present ability to consult with his lawyer with a reasonable degree of understanding and a rational as well as factual understanding of the proceedings.[48] See Figure 7-10.

Competency to stand trial focuses on the defendant's condition at the time of trial, rather than at the time of the crime. As a result, it is not considered to be a formal defense to a crime as much as it is a rule of criminal procedure. But the end result, which is the avoidance of criminal culpability, may be the same.

The U.S. Supreme Court has held that "[f]undamental principles of due process require that a criminal defendant who is legally incompetent shall not be subjected to trial."[49] In *Pate v. Robinson* (1966), the Court held that a failure to observe procedures adequate to protect a defendant's right not to be tried or convicted while incompetent to stand trial deprives the defendant of the right to a fair trial.[50] The federal test to determine whether a defendant is competent to stand trial was set forth in *Dusky v. United States* (1960), in which the Supreme Court held that the "test must be whether he has sufficient present ability to consult with his lawyer with a reasonable degree of rational understanding—and whether he has a rational as well as factual understanding of the proceedings against him."[51]

Section 4241 of Title 18 of the U.S. Code, "Determination of Mental Competency to Stand Trial," reads:

> If . . . the court finds by a preponderance of the evidence that the defendant is presently suffering from a mental disease or defect rendering him mentally incompetent to the extent that he is unable to understand the nature and consequences of the proceedings against him or to assist properly in his defense, the court shall commit the defendant to the custody of the Attorney General. The Attorney General shall hospitalize the defendant for treatment in a suitable facility.[52]

Once sanity has been recovered, the defendant may be brought to trial.

In *Cooper v. Oklahoma* (1996), the U.S. Supreme Court ruled that states must let criminal defendants avoid trials if it is more likely than not that they are incompetent.[53] Until *Cooper*, Oklahoma defendants (and defendants in Pennsylvania, Connecticut, and Rhode Island) were required to provide clear and convincing evidence that they were mentally incompetent and therefore unable to participate in their own trials in a meaningful way. As discussed in Chapter 2, clear and convincing evidence is that which establishes the reasonable certainty of a claim, although the standard requires less than proof beyond a reasonable doubt. In *Cooper*, the Court held that the clear and convincing evidence standard was too strict and ruled that criminal defendants must be allowed to avoid trials if they show by a preponderance of the evidence that they are mentally unfit.

Law Line 7-10
Cooper v. Oklahoma

Once the issue of incompetency is raised, some states and the federal government require the defendant to prove the lack of competency in order to avoid trial, while other states require that the prosecution prove the defendant competent before trial can proceed. Arizona offers a typical approach, which follows the Supreme Court's ruling in *Dusky*. Arizona law states that the term incompetent to stand trial means that, "as a result of a mental illness, defect, or disability, a defendant is unable to understand the nature and object of the proceeding or to assist in the defendant's defense." Arizona law, however, cautions that "[t]he presence of a mental illness, defect, or disability alone is not grounds for finding a defendant incompetent to stand trial."

Typically, many procedural requirements are associated with a defendant's competency to stand trial. In Arizona, for example, after the prosecutor has initiated criminal charges, a defendant can request an examination to determine competency "to stand trial, to enter a plea, or to assist the defendant's attorney." And within three working days after this request is made, the parties are required to "provide all available medical and criminal history records to the court," and the "court may request that a mental health expert assist the court in determining if reasonable grounds exist for examining a defendant." Arizona law also provides that "[w]ithin thirty days after the report is filed, the court shall hold a hearing to determine a defendant's competency to stand trial." If the court finds that the defendant is competent to stand trial, the proceedings can proceed. But "[i]f the court initially finds that the defendant is incompetent to stand trial, the court shall order treatment for the restoration of competency unless there is clear and convincing evidence that the defendant will not be restored to competency within fifteen months. The court may extend the restoration treatment by six months if the court determines that the defendant is making progress toward the goal of restoration."

When competency cannot be restored, Arizona law stipulates that "[i]f the court finds that a defendant is incompetent to stand trial and that there is no substantial probability that the defendant will regain competency within twenty-one months after the date of the original finding of incompetency, any party may request that the court: (1) Remand the defendant to the custody of the department of health services for the institution of civil commitment proceedings. . . . (2) Appoint a guardian. . . . (3) Release the defendant from custody and dismiss the charges against the defendant."[54]

Insanity at the Time of the Crime

For some defendants, questions of mental competency relate to the time of the alleged offense. In these cases, legal professionals must assess whether the defendant was insane or otherwise mentally impaired at the time of the alleged crime.

not guilty by reason of insanity (NGRI) a legal defense based on medical conclusions that the defendant was not mentally sane at the time of the criminal act

Law Line 7-11
Insanity Defense in Criminal Law

insanity
a social term referring to a person's mental competency

DSM-IV
the *Diagnostic and Statistical Manual of Mental Disorders*; the definitive work on mental disorders, published by the American Psychiatric Association

Law Line 7-12
Categories of Mental Disorders

Insanity and other forms of mental impairment can influence criminal liability in two ways: (1) It may result in a finding that the *mens rea* required for a specific crime was lacking, leading the court to conclude that no crime occurred, or (2) it may lead to a showing that although the requisite *mens rea* was present at the time of the crime, the defendant should be excused from legal responsibility because of mental disease or defect. The first perspective allows that a given mental condition may negate an element of an offense, while the latter recognizes that a crime took place but excuses the perpetrator due to a lack of moral blameworthiness. If *mens rea* cannot be proven by the prosecution, a finding of not guilty should result. If the defendant possessed the necessary *mens rea* but was insane at the time of the act, a **not guilty by reason of insanity (NGRI)** verdict should be returned. In short, *as a defense*, insanity recognizes that some people, by virtue of mental disease or mental defect, cannot morally and justly be held accountable for their actions.

At the outset, it must be noted that defendants rarely employ an insanity defense. According to the American Bar Association, "[t]he best evidence suggests that the mental nonresponsibility defense is raised in less than 1 percent of all felony cases in the United States and is successful in about a fourth of these."[55] As a result, most legal professionals are unlikely to deal with many, if any, insanity defenses.

Black's Law Dictionary warns that the term **insanity** is "a social and legal term rather than a medical one." *Black's* defines insanity as "a condition which renders the affected person unfit to enjoy liberty of action because of the unreliability of his behavior with concomitant danger to himself and others."[56] *Black's* continues, saying that the term "is used to denote that degree of mental illness which negates the individual's legal responsibility or capacity." In other words, the law has its own definition of insanity, which is sometimes at odds with the psychiatric definition of mental illness. A person may be mentally ill or mentally abnormal and yet be legally sane, and vice versa.

As *Black's* observes, the term *insanity* has no place in the medical literature—which speaks instead of *mental disorders*, a term also used in some statutes. The definitive work on mental disorders is the *Diagnostic and Statistical Manual of Mental Disorders*, published by the American Psychiatric Association.[57] The *Manual* is referred to as **DSM-IV** and lists twelve major categories of mental disorders. See Law Line 7-12. Over the years, researchers have identified many different mental illnesses of varying severities and complexities. From a psychiatric perspective, it is far too simplistic to describe a severely mentally ill person merely as "insane." In fact, the vast majority of people with a mental illness would be judged "sane" if current legal tests for insanity were applied to them.[58] As a result, while mental illness may explain a person's behavior, it seldom excuses it.

Even though the term *insanity* is a legal term and not a psychiatric one, legal insanity, as a concept, is still predicated on a disease or disability of the mind. As one judge observed, "[i]t is not enough, to relieve from criminal liability, that the prisoner is morally depraved. It is not enough that he has views of right and wrong at variance with those that find expression in the law. The variance must have its origin in some disease of the mind."[59]

The M'Naughten Rule: The Original Standard

The insanity defense is rooted in the 1843 case of Daniel M'Naughten, a woodcutter from Scotland, who killed another man while suffering from a purported case of paranoia. The judge in M'Naughten's case, Lord Chief Justice Tindal, allowed M'Naughten to assert an insanity defense and instructed the jury as follows:

The question to be determined is whether at the time the act in question was committed, the prisoner had or had not the use of his understanding, so as to know that he was doing a wrong or wicked act. If the jurors should be of opinion that the prisoner was not sensible, at the time he committed it, that he was violating the laws both of God and man, then he would be entitled to a verdict in his favour; but if, on the contrary, they were of the opinion that when he committed the act he was in a sound state of mind, then their verdict must be against him.

Applying these instructions to the facts of the case, the jury acquitted M'Naughten, finding him to be insane.

The ***M'Naughten rule*** includes two possibilities: (1) a lack of *mens rea* (the person didn't know what he or she was doing) and (2) an acceptable legal excuse (the person didn't know that it was wrong). *Either* alternative provides an acceptable defense under M'Naughten. Central to the second alternative is the possibility that defendants may be able to demonstrate insanity by showing that, while they knew what they were doing, they did not know that their behavior was "wrong."

But sources disagree as to whether the word *wrong* refers to defendants' ability to appreciate the *legal* or the *moral* wrongfulness of their acts. To appreciate legal wrongfulness, defendants must be aware that their conduct is against the law. But under statutes with a moral wrongfulness standard, defendants who understand the illegal nature of their conduct may still be found insane if they believe their conduct to be morally acceptable or even righteous. The Model Penal Code, federal law, and most state statutes all contain some form of the wrongfulness test, and all make use of the word *wrong* or *wrongfulness* in attempting to assess a defendant's mental condition at the time of the crime.

For example, defense attorneys successfully asserted the insanity defense in the 2006 capital murder trial of Andrea Yates, a Texas mother who was accused of drowning her five young children in a bathtub. The State of Texas employed a modified version of the M'Naughten rule that required defendants who claim insanity to prove that they did not know that the unlawful act they committed was wrong. The law read, "[i]t is an affirmative defense to prosecution that, at the time of the conduct charged, the actor, as a result of severe mental disease or defect, did not know that his conduct was wrong."[60]

Yates was initially tried and convicted of murder. But an appellate court reversed this conviction based on procedural errors relating to the insanity defense. See Law Line 7-13. During Yates's second trial, her attorneys offered evidence intended to show that Yates, who was strongly influenced by religious fundamentalism, believed she was saving her children from eternal damnation by killing them.[61] Testimony from various defense experts purported to show that this distorted belief was the product of delusions and hallucinations from which Yates suffered, which were made worse by postpartum depression following the birth of her last child. From her deranged perspective, the experts suggested, she believed that she was doing right and not wrong.[62] Defense attorneys also pointed to Yates's long history of psychological problems, including confinement in mental institutions, suicide attempts, and a history of prescribed antidepressive drug treatments. Prosecutors countered by pointing to the fact that Yates had rationally and calmly phoned 911 almost immediately after the killings to inform police of what she had done—evidence, they said, that she understood that the killings were criminal. Based on this evidence, the jury found Yates not guilty by reason of insanity. See accompanying photo. The judge then committed Yates to a state hospital.

M'Naughten rule
a form of insanity defense based on a claim that the defendant did not know what he or she was doing or did not know that his or her acts were wrong

Law Line 7-13
Opinion Reversing Andrea Yates's Conviction

HOUSTON, TX—JULY 26: Andrea Yates (R) sits with her attorney, George Parnham, after the not guilty by reason of insanity verdict was read in her retrial July 26, 2006, in Houston. Yates admitted to drowning her five children in a bath tub in 2001 and pleaded guilty by reason of insanity.

By the early 1900s, it was generally accepted that a strict application of the M'Naughten rule often deprived the trier of fact of many of the insights yielded by modern psychiatry. As a result, other proposals for assessing legal insanity were made—primary among them the irresistible impulse test, the Durham rule, and the American Law Institute test.

The Irresistible Impulse Test: Control Rules

The wrongfulness component of the M'Naughten rule has been criticized because it focuses only on the cognitive component of the personality. In other words, to *know* that one's actions are wrong requires the ability to think and to judge. Moreover, the M'Naughten rule does not allow for degrees of insanity. Under the rule, either a person knows what he is doing, and knows that it is wrong, or he does not. There is no middle ground. Recognizing this, some authors have concluded that "[t]he essence of *M'Naughten* is that for mental disease or defect to incapacitate, it must be of such a degree as to leave the person irrational—that is, no rational person lacks criminal capacity by reason of insanity."[63] It is possible to imagine a situation, however, in which a person knows what she is doing, knows that it is wrong, and is still unable to stop doing it. A famous potato chip commercial of a few years ago, for example, challenged viewers with the phrase, "You can't eat just one!" The advertisement claimed that once a person tasted one of the chips, she would be unable to resist having more.

Although there is nothing legally or morally "wrong" with eating potato chips, it may be that some people find it equally impossible to control other forms of behavior that are against the law. During the 1920s, in the belief that some forms of behavior could not be controlled, many states modified the M'Naughten rule to permit "irresistible impulse" defenses. Defenses based on the ***irresistible impulse test*** claim that at the time the crime was committed, a mental disease or disorder prevented the defendant from controlling his or her

irresistible impulse test

a form of insanity defense asserting that at the time the crime was committed, a mental disease or disorder prevented the defendant from controlling his or her behavior

FIGURE 7-11 **Insanity Tests: Expanding Concepts**

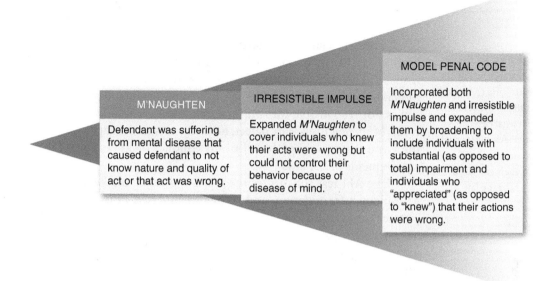

MODEL PENAL CODE

Incorporated both *M'Naughten* and irresistible impulse and expanded them by broadening to include individuals with substantial (as opposed to total) impairment and individuals who "appreciated" (as opposed to "knew") that their actions were wrong.

IRRESISTIBLE IMPULSE

Expanded *M'Naughten* to cover individuals who knew their acts were wrong but could not control their behavior because of disease of mind.

M'NAUGHTEN

Defendant was suffering from mental disease that caused defendant to not know nature and quality of act or that act was wrong.

behavior. See Figure 7-11. Some jurisdictions that use the irresistible impulse provision employ a "policeman at the elbow" jury instruction. Jurors are told that "if the accused would not have committed that act had there been a policeman present, he cannot be said to have acted under irresistible impulse."

Critiques of the irresistible impulse test point out that it may be impossible to really know who can and who cannot control their behavior in specific situations and that such an excuse might apply to all who commit crimes. In the case of the second claim, the inability to control one's impulses might be a general characteristic of criminal personalities, making it possible to argue that all criminal offenders engage in illegal behavior because of lessened behavioral controls. Were it not for such a lack of control, some people suggest, criminals would be law-abiding citizens.

The Durham Rule: Crime as a Product of Mental Disease

In *Durham v. United States* (1954),[64] the U.S. Court of Appeals for the District of Columbia concluded that all existing tests to determine legal sanity were flawed. The court then went on to develop its own standard, stating that the rule "is simply that an accused is not criminally responsible if his unlawful act was the *product* of mental disease or mental defect." The **Durham rule**, also known as the *product rule*, built on the court's belief that an inability to distinguish right from wrong is merely a symptom of mental disease and that behavior resulting from the disease is a more apt determinant of legal insanity.

Unfortunately, however, few mental health professionals could be found who expressed the relationship between mental illness and behavior as the court did. As a result, the Durham rule was quickly criticized as being out of touch with medical realities. Others claimed that it was far too vague and provided little guidance to the jury, potentially resulting in far too many acquittals. As one

Durham rule
an insanity defense, also known as the *product rule*; claims that a criminal act was the product of a mental disease

federal appellate court held, "[t]he most significant criticism of *Durham* . . . is that it fails to give the factfinder any standard by which to measure the competency of the accused."[65]

The American Law Institute Test: Substantial Capacity

substantial capacity test

the insanity test established by the American Law Institute (ALI) and incorporated into the Model Penal Code; provides a legal defense where defendants lack substantial capacity either to appreciate the wrongfulness of their acts or to conform their acts to the law

In an effort to clarify standards for assessing legal insanity, the American Law Institute (ALI) incorporated a **substantial capacity test** into the Model Penal Code.[66] The ALI substantial capacity test is a modernized version of the M'Naughten rule, blended with control rules. This standard provides that "[a] person is not responsible for criminal conduct if at the time of such conduct, as a result of mental disease or defect, he lacks substantial capacity either to appreciate the criminality [wrongfulness] of his conduct or to conform his conduct to the requirements of the law."[67]

The ALI test substitutes the word *appreciate* for *know*, used in the original M'Naughten formulation, and recognizes the role of impulse through use of the phrase "conform his conduct to the requirements of the law." The test also recognizes modern psychiatric knowledge through use of the word *substantial*, which acknowledges that, while some portions of a defendant's mental state might be identified as insane, other portions might still be medically sound. In some settings, people refer to this condition as temporary insanity. But this is not a legal term. In the end, whether partial or complete, a defendant's claim of insanity must be judged by the jurisdiction's applicable legal standards.

CONSEQUENCES OF AN INSANITY FINDING

Few defendants found not guilty by reason of insanity or guilty but mentally ill are immediately released, as would be a person who is acquitted of a crime, although nondangerous defendants may not by law be kept longer than necessary to assess their condition. Generally, those found not guilty by reason of insanity or guilty but mentally ill are subject to a hearing to determine whether they are still mentally ill and dangerous to themselves or others and whether confinement in a treatment facility is justified.[68] Most are so confined, and studies show that people found NGRI are, on average, held at least as long as people found guilty and sent to prison.[69]

After a period of time, a person so confined may request a hearing to determine whether he or she is still a danger to self or others or is eligible to be released. At such a hearing, in order for confinement to continue, the State must demonstrate by clear and convincing evidence that the person poses a danger to self or others and requires continued confinement. Such proceedings are civil, not criminal. Accordingly, the constitutional protections afforded criminal defendants do not automatically extend to the subjects of civil commitment proceedings. Of course, however, basic notions of due process apply, and because individuals determined to be dangerous will experience a significant loss of liberty, something more than typical civil law constitutional protections exist. Furthermore, many legislatures have provided by statute for protections similar to those available in criminal proceedings.[70]

Guilty but Mentally Ill

A definitive moment in the history of the insanity defense in this country came in 1982 with an NGRI verdict in the trial of John Hinckley, who admitted to trying to assassinate President Ronald Reagan for the delusional purpose of proving his love for actress Jodie Foster. After weeks of conflicting testimony, the judge instructed jurors to weigh the issue of insanity in terms of the Model Penal Code's approach and to return a verdict of "not guilty" unless they could agree "beyond a reasonable doubt" that Hinckley was sane. Since the expert witnesses could not agree among themselves as to Hinckley's sanity, the jury instruction virtually ensured the NGRI verdict—and one was promptly returned.

Public outcry at the *Hinckley* verdict led about half of the states to rewrite their insanity statutes, with many returning to M'Naughten-like standards. Before *Hinckley*, the Model Penal Code definition of insanity had been adopted by ten of the eleven federal courts of appeals and by more than half of the states. After *Hinckley*, a few states (Idaho, Montana, and Utah among them) abolished the insanity defense except insofar as insanity could be shown to affect the specific *mens rea* required by statute for a particular crime. Also in response, Congress passed the 1984 Crime Control and Prevention Act, which included the **Insanity Defense Reform Act of 1984** (IDRA).[71] This law mandated a comprehensive overhaul of the insanity defense as it operated in the federal courts. The act made insanity an affirmative defense to be proven by the defendant by clear and convincing evidence and created a special verdict of not guilty by reason of insanity.[72] Through the IDRA, Congress sought to prohibit the presentation of evidence of mental disease or defect, short of insanity, to excuse conduct.[73] The wrongfulness test has been at the center of controversy since its inception.

The IDRA does not, however, prohibit psychiatric evidence that may be relevant to proving whether a crime occurred. If a subjective state of mind is an element of a crime, for example, evidence regarding the existence or absence of that state of mind is relevant to whether a crime was in fact committed. As federal courts have ruled, "[p]sychiatric evidence which negates *mens rea* . . . negates an element of the offense rather than constituting a justification or excuse"[74] and may be admitted at trial for that purpose. As in federal courts, the use of psychiatric evidence is admissible in all state jurisdictions today to negate *mens rea* where the evidence presented focuses on the defendant's specific state of mind at the time the offense was committed.

The IDRA also created a comprehensive civil commitment procedure under which a defendant found NGRI is held in custody pending a court hearing. The hearing must occur within forty days of the verdict. At the conclusion of the hearing, the court determines whether the defendant should be hospitalized or released.

In a second type of response to the *Hinckley* verdict, ten states adopted statutes that permitted findings of **guilty but mentally ill (GBMI)**. The states patterned their laws after a 1975 Michigan statute that created the possibility of GBMI verdicts in Michigan criminal trials. GBMI statutes require that when the insanity defense is raised at trial, judges must instruct juries that four verdicts are possible: (1) guilty, (2) not guilty, (3) not guilty by reason of insanity, and (4) guilty but mentally ill. A jury must return a finding of guilty but mentally ill if (1) every element necessary for a conviction has been proven beyond a reasonable doubt, (2) the defendant is found to have been *mentally ill* at the time the crime was committed, and (3) the defendant was *not* found to have been *legally insane* at the time the crime was committed. The difference between mental illness and legal insanity is a crucial one.

A finding of GBMI is equivalent to a finding of guilty, and the court will sentence the defendant just as a person found guilty of the crime in question would be sentenced. A GBMI verdict establishes that "the defendant, although mentally ill,

Insanity Defense Reform Act of 1984
(IDRA) federal law changing the way insanity defense is asserted in federal courts; makes insanity an affirmative defense to be proven by the defendant by clear and convincing evidence; also creates a special verdict of not guilty by reason of insanity

guilty but mentally ill
(GBMI) a possible verdict available in some jurisdictions; allows juries to impose guilt, instead of insanity acquittal, upon defendants with mental illness

was sufficiently in possession of his faculties to be morally blameworthy for his acts."[75] According to one source, "[t]he most obvious and important function of the GBMI verdict is to permit juries to make an unambiguous statement about the factual guilt, mental condition, and moral responsibility of a defendant."[76]

Once sentenced, GBMI offenders are evaluated to determine whether hospitalization or psychiatric treatment is needed. Offenders who are hospitalized will join the "regular" prison population on release from the treatment facility. Time spent in the hospital and in prison both count toward sentence completion, and the offenders will be released from custody after the sentence has been served, even if they still suffer from mental disease.

The Doctrine of Settled Insanity

For legal purposes, insanity is insanity, regardless of its underlying cause. As a result, "insanity at the time of an alleged criminal act generally constitutes a defense, regardless of how the condition may have come about."[77] Consequently, insanity may be a useful defense even if it is brought on by the defendant's own actions.

As addressed above, intoxication is generally not regarded as a defense to a criminal charge because it is a condition brought about by the intoxicated person's willful consumption of alcohol or other intoxicants. Under the **doctrine of settled insanity**, however, the habitual and long-term use of intoxicants or other drugs that results in permanent mental disorders "that are symptomatically and organically similar to mental disorders caused by brain disease"[78] can create the basis for a claim of insanity, provided that the defendant can meet the required definition of insanity in the relevant jurisdiction.

According to some sources, "the nearly unanimous rule is that a mental or brain disease or defect caused by the long-term effects of intoxicants constitutes a mental state that warrants an insanity defense."[79] The same is not true, however, of "mere addiction" to narcotics, alcohol, or other mind-altering substances. Courts in twenty-nine states and the District of Columbia have recognized the defense of settled insanity, while only one state has rejected it.[80] Twenty states have yet to consider the issue.

Diminished Capacity

The defense of **diminished capacity**, also called *diminished responsibility*, is available in some jurisdictions. Although the terms *diminished responsibility* and *diminished capacity* do not have universally accepted meanings,[81] this defense generally is based on a mental condition that would not qualify as an "official" mental disease, such as insanity, but it still might reduce the level of criminal culpability.[82]

Diminished capacity is similar to the insanity defense in that it depends on showing that the defendant's mental state was impaired at the time of the crime. As a defense, diminished capacity is most useful when it can be shown that, because of some defect of reason or mental shortcoming, the defendant's capacity to form the *mens rea* required by a specific crime was impaired. Unlike an insanity defense, however, which can result in a finding of not guilty, a diminished capacity defense is built on the recognition that "[m]ental condition, though insufficient to exonerate, may be relevant to specific mental elements of certain crimes or degrees of crime."[83] For example, defendants might present evidence of mental abnormality in an effort to reduce first-degree murder to second-degree murder, or second-degree murder to manslaughter, when a killing occurs under extreme emotional

doctrine of settled insanity
an insanity-based defense claiming that the habitual and long-term use of intoxicants or other drugs can result in mental disorders akin to insanity   .

diminished capacity
a defense available in some jurisdictions; based on the defendant's mental deficiency as opposed to outright insanity, in an effort to reduce or avoid certain levels of *mens rea*

disturbance. Similarly, in some jurisdictions very low intelligence will, if proved, serve to reduce first-degree murder to manslaughter.[84]

The Model Penal Code limits the diminished capacity defense to cases in which capital punishment might be imposed. The code provides, "[w]henever the jury or the Court is authorized to determine or to recommend whether or not the defendant shall be sentenced to death or imprisonment upon conviction, evidence that the capacity of the defendant to appreciate the criminality [wrongfulness] of his conduct or to conform his conduct to the requirements of law was impaired as a result of mental disease or defect is admissible in favor of sentence of imprisonment."[85]

Like the insanity defense, the diminished capacity defense has been entirely eliminated in some jurisdictions. The California Penal Code, for example, provides that "[t]he defense of diminished capacity is hereby abolished."[86] The code adds that "[a]s a matter of public policy there shall be no defense of diminished capacity, diminished responsibility, or irresistible impulse in a criminal action or juvenile adjudication hearing."[87] Although California law limits the use of certain excuses that might be raised to negate *mens rea*, a showing that the required *mens rea* was in fact lacking can still lead to acquittal. California does allow that "evidence of diminished capacity or of a mental disorder may be considered by the court at the time of sentencing or other disposition or commitment."[88]

Law Line 7-14
Diminished Capacity

IN THE FIELD

Legal professionals in the criminal justice system frequently work with defendants and victims who suffer from mental illness. Recent reports suggest that large percentages of inmates at U.S. penal facilities have some degree of mental illness. But defendants are often reluctant to assert insanity or other mental capacity defenses due to the social stigma, uncertain consequences, or lack of resources associated with asserting these defenses. Where mental illness is suspected, legal professionals are encouraged to take the time to find the resources to thoroughly evaluate defendants and victims before proceeding with pleas or trials in their criminal cases. And of course, legal professionals must be able to convey to their clients the possible consequences of proceeding with defenses based on mental illness.

CHAPTER **SUMMARY**

- A defense consists of evidence and arguments offered by a defendant and his attorney(s) to show why he should not be held liable for a criminal charge.
- Defenses may be built upon these bases: (1) alibi, (2) justifications, and (3) excuses.
- Justifications and excuses are affirmative defenses. They must be raised or asserted by the defendant independently of any claims made by the prosecutor.
- Justifications include (1) necessity, (2) self-defense, (3) defense of others, (4) defense of home and property, (5) resisting unlawful arrest, and (6) consent.
- The defense of necessity claims that it was necessary to commit some unlawful act in order to prevent or to avoid a greater harm.
- Self-defense is based on the recognition that individuals have an inherent right to protect themselves and

that to defend oneself from unlawful attack is a natural response to threatening situations.
- The use of force to defend oneself has generally been extended to permit the use of reasonable force to defend others who are, or who appear to be, in imminent danger. Property in the possession of a third person, or the home of a third person, may be protected by one who assists that person to the same degree and in the same manner that the owner of the property or the home would have been privileged to act.
- The defense of consent claims that the person suffering an injury either agreed beforehand to sustain the injury or accepted the possibility of injury before the activity was undertaken.
- Excuses are another category of defenses. Excuses admit that the law-breaking actions committed by a

defendant were wrong and that they violated the criminal law but that the defendant should nonetheless be excused from criminal liability because of special circumstances.

- Excuses recognized by law include (1) duress, (2) intoxication, (3) mistake, (4) age, (5) entrapment, (6) insanity, (7) diminished capacity, and, to a limited degree, (8) various "syndromes."
- The defense of duress, sometimes also called *compulsion*, is based on the notion that people do not willfully engage in acts that they are compelled or coerced to perform.
- Voluntary intoxication is generally not a defense because individuals are responsible for their impaired state, and the law generally holds that those who voluntarily put themselves in a condition of having little or no control over their actions must be held to have intended whatever consequences ensue.
- Involuntary intoxication may serve as a defense if it creates in the defendant either an incapacity to appreciate the criminality of her conduct or an incapacity to conform her behavior to the requirements of the law.
- Mistake of fact will preclude criminal liability when the actions undertaken would have been lawful had the situation been as the acting person reasonably believed them to be. However, mistake of law, or ignorance of the law, rarely provides an effective defense.
- Infancy, or immaturity, defenses claim that certain individuals should not be held criminally responsible for their activities by virtue of their youth.
- The entrapment defense is built on the assertion that had it not been for government instigation, no crime would have occurred. Two approaches to assessing entrapment can be found in the law: the subjective and the objective.
- Although courts have been reluctant to recognize the claim that syndromes negate *mens rea*, the use of syndromes in expanding the applicability of traditional defenses has met with greater success.
- Competency to stand trial focuses on the defendant's condition at the time of trial rather than at the time of the crime. Competency to stand trial exists when a defendant has sufficient present ability to consult with his lawyer with a reasonable degree of rational understanding and has a rational as well as factual understanding of the proceedings against him.
- The insanity defense recognizes that some people, by virtue of mental disease or mental defect, cannot morally and justly be held accountable for their actions.
- There are many forms of the insanity defense, including the M'Naughten rule, the irresistible impulse rule, the Durham rule, and the substantial capacity test.
- A guilty but mentally ill (GBMI) verdict establishes that a defendant, although mentally ill, was sufficiently in possession of her faculties to be morally blameworthy for the criminal act.
- The defense of diminished capacity, also called *diminished responsibility*, is available in some jurisdictions. It is based on claims that a defendant's mental condition at the time of the crime, although not sufficient to support the affirmative defense of insanity, might still lower criminal culpability.

KEY **TERMS**

affirmative defenses
alibi
alter ego rule
apparent danger
battered woman's syndrome (BWS)
castle exception
competency to stand trial
consent
deadly force
defense
defense of others
diminished capacity
doctrine of settled insanity
DSM-IV
duress
Durham rule
entrapment
excuses

execution of public duty
 defense
factual defense
fleeing felon rule
guilty but mentally ill (GBMI)
ignorance of fact
ignorance of the law
imperfect self-defense
infancy defense
insanity
Insanity Defense Reform Act
 of 1984 (IDRA)
Internet addiction disorder (IAD)
involuntary intoxication
irresistible impulse test
justification
juvenile offenders
legal defense

M'Naughten rule
mistake of fact
mistake of law
necessity
not guilty by reason of
 insanity (NGRI)
objective test
outrageous government conduct
perfect self-defense
protection of property
reasonable force
reasonable person
retreat rule
self-defense
subjective test
substantial capacity test
syndrome
voluntary intoxication

QUESTIONS FOR **DISCUSSION**

1. What is the purpose of a defense to a criminal charge? What is an affirmative defense?

2. What is the difference between justifications and excuses? Give examples of justifications that might serve as defenses.

3. What fundamental claim is raised by the defense of necessity? When are claims of necessity most successful?

4. When may force be used in self-defense? When may deadly force be used?

5. Explain the execution of public duty defense. When and by whom might such a defense be used?

6. What are the main distinguishing features of an excuse?

7. What are the conditions needed for the successful use of the defense of duress? Why is the defense inapplicable in cases of serious law violations like murder and rape?

8. Why is voluntary intoxication usually not accepted as a defense to a criminal charge? Should it be? Why or why not?

9. What is the nature of a mistake that is acceptable as a defense to a criminal charge? What kinds of mistakes are not likely to reduce criminal liability?

10. At what age do you think people should be held criminally liable for their actions? Should there be a minimum age and a maximum age for determining culpability?

11. What is the difference between the subjective and the objective approaches to assessing entrapment? Which do you think is most useful? Why?

12. Is a syndrome an excuse, a justification, or an explanation? Are syndromes best viewed as potentially negating *mens rea*, as widening traditional defenses, or as justifying behavior for a particular class of people? Why?

13. How does the legal notion of insanity differ from psychiatric conceptions of mental disorders? What is the significance of such differences from a legal perspective?

14. How is competency to stand trial assessed? How might defendants who are truly incompetent best be distinguished from those who are "faking it"?

15. What is the difference between a finding that, as a result of mental disease or defect, the defendant lacks the specific *mens rea* required for a given crime and a finding that the defendant is insane?

16. What is the difference between a finding of NGRI and one of GBMI?

17. Compare and contrast the various legal "tests" for assessing insanity that are discussed in this chapter. Which do you think is more useful? Why?

18. Some jurisdictions have eliminated the insanity defense. Why do you think they did so? Do you agree with such reasoning? Explain.

REFERENCES

1. Paul H. Robinson, "Criminal Law Defenses: A Systematic Analysis," *Columbia Law Review* 82 (1982): 190, 203–4.

2. Model Penal Code, Article 3, Commentary.

3. The "Codification of a Principle of Necessity" is discussed in Part I of the code's commentaries.

4. Model Penal Code, Section 3.02.

5. See http://reason.com/blog/2008/03/27/successful-medical-necessity-d

6. Texas Penal Code, Section 9.31.

7. Model Penal Code, Section 3.04 (1).

8. *United States v. Thomas*, 34 F.3d 44 (2nd Cir. 1994).

9. *State v. Norman*, 324 N.C. 253, 378 S.E.2d 8 (1989).

10. The exception, of course, is that of a trespasser who trespasses in order to commit a more serious crime.

11. *People v. Ceballos*, 12 Cal. 3d 470, 526 P.2d 241 (1974).

12. Under common law, exceptions were made in instances of attempted arson and attempted burglary of a dwelling house.

13. Sir Edward Coke, *Third Institute*, p. 162.

14. *Tennessee v. Garner*, 471 U.S. 1, 9–10 (1985).

15. *Id.*

16. Rollin M. Perkins and Ronald N. Boyce, *Criminal Law*, 3rd ed. (Mineola, NY: Foundation Press, 1982), p. 1075.

17. "Rapist Who Agreed to Use Condom Gets 40 Years," *New York Times*, May 15, 1993, http://query.nytimes.com/gst/fullpage.html?sec=health&res=9F0CE2DF173FF936A25756C0A965958260 (accessed March 15, 2009).

18. See, for example, *State v. Fransua*, 85 N.M. 173, 510 P.2d 106, 58 A.L.R. 3d 656 (Ct. App. 1973).

19. Sanford H. Kadish and Stephen J. Schulhofer, *Criminal Law and Its Processes: Cases and Materials*, 6th ed. (New York: Little, Brown, 1995), p. 821.

20. Model Penal Code, Section 2.09.

21. Some jurisdictions specify that the "other" must be an immediate family member.

22. *People v. Walker*, 18 Cal. Rptr. 2d 431 (1993).

23. California Penal Code, Section 22.

24. See *People v. Low*, 732 P.2d 622 (Colo. 1987).

25. *Davis v. State*, 265 Ind. 476, 355 N.E.2d 836 (1976).

26. *Gordon v. State*, 52 Ala. 308, 23 Am. Rep. 575 (1875).

27. Although one who purchases baking powder thinking it is heroin may suffer only from his own mistake, actual possession of a controlled substance is an element of most trafficking offenses.

28. *Gordon v. State*, 52 Ala. 308, 23 Am. Rep. 575 (1875).

29. *United States v. Squires*, 440 F.2d 859 (2d Cir. 1971).

30. *Long v. State*, 44 Del. 262, 65 A.2d 489 (1949).

31. *People v. Tolbert*, 56 Cal. Rptr. 2d 604 (1996).

32. "Girl Charged," Associated Press, February 28, 1994.

33. *United States v. Russell*, 411 U.S. 423 (1973).

34. *Id.*

35. *Cruz v. State*, 465 So. 2d 516, 518 (Fla. 1985).

36. Perkins and Boyce, *Criminal Law*, 1167.

37. *Id.*

38. *Jacobson v. United States*, 503 U.S. 540 (1992).

39. *Id.*

40. *Id.*

41. *Id.* at 3.

42. *State v. Kelly*, 97 N.J. 178 (N.J. 1984).

43. California Evidence Code, Section 1107.

44. *State v. Hodges*, 716 P.2d 563, 567 (Kan. 1986), *supra*, 716 P.2d at p. 567, citing Lenore Walker, *The Battered Woman* (New York: Harper and Row, 1979), pp. 19–31.

45. This list is drawn from Alan M. Dershowitz, *The Abuse Excuse: And Other Cop-Outs, Sob Stories, and Evasions of Responsibility* (Boston: Little, Brown, 1994), pp. 321–41; Richard G. Singer and Martin R. Gardner, *Crimes and Punishment: Cases, Materials, and Readings in Criminal Law*, 2nd ed. (New York: Matthew Bender, 1996), pp. 903–20.

46. *Werner v. State*, 711 S.W.2d 639 (Tex. Crim. App. 1986), in which the son of a Nazi concentration camp survivor claimed that Holocaust syndrome caused him to be overly assertive in confrontational situations. The court hearing the case disallowed the claim.

47. *State v. Kenneth J. Sharp, Jr.*, 418 So. 2d 1344 (La. Sup. Ct., 1982).

48. *United States v. Taylor*, 437 F.2d 371 (4th Cir. 1971).

49. *Pate v. Robinson*, 383 U.S. 375, 86 S. Ct. 836, 15 L. Ed. 2d 815 (1966).

50. *Id.*

51. *Dusky v. United States*, 362 U.S. 402, 80 S. Ct. 788, 789, 4 L. Ed. 2d 824, 825 (1960).

52. 18 U.S.C. § 4241(d).

53. *Cooper v. Oklahoma*, 116 S. Ct. 1373, 134 L. Ed. 2d 498 (1996).

54. Arizona Penal Code, Sections 13-4501, 13-4503, 13-4507, and 13-4510.

55. American Bar Association Standing Committee on Association Standards for Criminal Justice, *Proposed Criminal Justice Mental Health Standards* (Chicago, IL: American Bar Association, 1984).

56. *Id.*

57. American Psychiatric Association, *Diagnostic and Statistical Manual of Mental Disorders*, 4th ed. (Washington, DC: American Psychiatric Association, 1994).

58. American Psychiatric Association website, http://www.psych.org/ (accessed September 20, 1996).

59. *People v. Schmidt*, 110 N.E. 945, 949 (N.Y. 1915).

60. Texas Penal Code, Section 8.01.

61. Andrea Yates, http://en.wikipedia.org/wiki/Andrea_Yates

62. *Id.*

63. Perkins and Boyce, *Criminal Law*.

64. *Durham v. United States*, 94 U.S. App. D.C. 228, 214 F.2d 862, 874–75 (1954).

65. *United States v. Freeman*, 357 F.2d 606, 618–22 (2d Cir. 1966).

66. Model Penal Code, Commentary, Comment on Section 4.01 at 156–60 (Tentative Draft No. 4, 1955).

67. Model Penal Code, Section 4.01(1).

68. Even those who have committed no crime can be confined under civil procedures if found dangerous to themselves or others. See, for example, *Kansas v. Hendricks*, 521 U.S. 346 (1997).

69. American Psychiatric Association website, http://www.psych.org/ (accessed September 20, 1996).

70. *Commonwealth v. Burgess*, 450 Mass. 366 (Mass. 2008).

71. 18 U.S.C. § 17.

72. 18 U.S.C. §§ 17 and 4242(b).

73. See, for example, *United States v. Pohlot*, 827 F.2d 889, 897 (3d Cir. 1987), cert. denied, 484 U.S. 1011, 108 S. Ct. 710, 98 L. Ed. 2d 660 (1988).

74. *United States v. Cameron*, 907 F.2d 1051, 1065 (11th Cir. 1990).

75. Mickenberg, "A Pleasant Surprise: The Guilty But Mentally Ill Verdict Has Both Succeeded in Its Own Right and Successfully Preserved the Traditional Role of the Insanity Defense," 55 U. Cin. L. Rev. 943 (1987).

76. *Id.*

77. *State v. Porter*, 213 Mo. 43, 111 S.W. 529 (1908).

78. A. Levine, "Denying the Settled Insanity Defense: Another Necessary Step in Dealing with Drug and Alcohol Abuse," *Boston University Law Review* 76 (1998): 75–76.

79. L. Johnson, "Settled Insanity Is Not a Defense: Has the Colorado Supreme Court Gone Crazy? *Bieber v. People,*" *Kansas Law Review* 43 (1994): 259–60.

80. Charlotte Carter-Yamauchi, *Drugs, Alcohol and the Insanity Defense: The Debate over "Settled Insanity"* (Honolulu, HI: Legislative Reference Bureau, 1998), p. 22.

81. *United States v. Pohlot,* 827 F.2d 889 (3d Cir. 1987), cert. denied.

82. Peter Arenella, "The Diminished Capacity and Diminished Responsibility Defenses: Two Children of a Doomed Marriage," *Columbia Law Review* 77 (1977): 830.

83. *United States v. Brawner,* 471 F.2d 969 (1972).

84. Bryan A. Garner, ed., *Black's Law Dictionary,* 6th ed. (New York: Thompson West, 2004), p. 458.

85. Model Penal Code, Section 4.03.

86. California Penal Code, Section 25 (a).

87. California Penal Code, Section 28 (b).

88. California Penal Code, Section 25 (c).

APPENDIX
DEVELOPING YOUR LEGAL ANALYSIS

A. THE LAW WHERE YOU LIVE

In the highly acclaimed musical and movie *Chicago*, a fictional group of female prison inmates, who are all charged with murdering their husbands, sing the comedic song "Cell Block Tango." In this number, the women profess that they did not kill their husbands, but even if they did, their husbands deserved it. Assume a similar scenario, where a defendant might reasonably assert a number of possible defenses, including (1) alibi, (2) battered spouse syndrome, and (3) mental incompetence to stand trial.

Specifically, assume that Julie Dunit, a criminal defendant and client, is claiming that she could not have committed the charged criminal offense because she was shopping with a friend, Ima Witness, at a mall several miles away from the crime scene. Review your state's criminal procedure rules for filing a Notice of Alibi, and then, based on Ms. Dunit's assertion, prepare a Notice of Alibi to be filed in the case.

Next, assume that Joe Brawn, a defendant and client, who is charged with killing or seriously assaulting a spouse, wishes to present a battered spouse defense. Research whether this defense is available in your state, and if so, identify what procedures must be followed in order to assert it. Then prepare a memorandum where you outline the availability and details of presenting a battered spouse defense in your state.

Finally, assume further that Mr. Brawn wishes to assert that he is not competent to stand trial. Research your state's procedural standards for pursuing this claim and prepare a motion requesting the trial court to examine the defendant for his competency to stand trial.

B. INSIDE THE FEDERAL COURTS

In recent years, there have been numerous stories about Internet predators—men who use chat rooms to solicit sexual activity from individuals they believe to be minors. This activity was featured on NBC's television program *To Catch a Predator*.

Assume that federal authorities conducted an Internet sting operation where adult federal agents posed as fifteen-year-old girls within an Internet chat room—*Adult Connections*—that is designed to facilitate romantic opportunities between adults. The sign-in page of the chat room clearly states that it is for "adults only" and that users must be atleast eighteen years of age to use it. Assume further that David Lenu, a twenty five-year-old man, was using his computer to talk with other adults in the *Adult Connections* chat room. While online, David has the following conversation with an undercover federal agent posing as a fifteen-year old girl in David's hometown:

- David: Hey, whatcha doin?
- Yng1: Nuthin. Just sitting at home while my parents are away on vacation.
- David: Wanna get together?
- Yng1: For what?
- David: Whatever you want.
- Yng1: I'm 15, so I haven't done much.
- David: That's OK, I'll show you how.
- Yng 1: OK
- David: Let's meet at your house in an hour
- Yng 1: OK, I'm at 704 Houser St.

Based on this online chat, federal agents have charged David with Coercion and Enticement, a criminal offense under 18 U.S.C. § 2422(b), which prohibits a person from using an instrument of interstate commerce to induce or entice a minor to engage in sexual activity.

David wants to claim entrapment and mistake of fact as legal defenses. Using the standards for these defenses (outlined above) and any other research you find under federal law, write a memorandum wherein you either support or refute the validity of David's defenses. In short, explain whether David was entrapped by federal authorities and/or can assert a mistake of fact defense. Also, identify whether, under federal law, any other justifications or excuses were asserted in David's defense.

C. CYBER SOURCES

At times, legal professionals must rely on creative and innovative strategies in order to best serve their clients. There are many criminal cases where the standard practices, defenses, and trial tactics will not suit your client's legitimate interests, whether government or defendant. Using www.findlaw.com or www.law.cornell.edu, both of which offer cases, legal practice materials, and legal news, or another Internet search tool, find at least five unique criminal defenses—justifications or excuses—that defendants have asserted, successfully or not, in criminal cases within the past few years. Then, based on the standards outlined in this chapter, evaluate the legal basis for asserting these defenses and how well they were received by judges and juries.

D. ETHICS AND PROFESSIONALISM

Assume you are working as a legal assistant in a law firm that handles criminal cases. Jay Adams, one of the firm's clients and a criminal defendant charged with a fourth-degree felony of cocaine possession, is on the phone wanting to speak with the attorney assigned to his case. The attorney is unavailable, so the client is asking to speak with you, the legal assistant assigned to the case. The client has a number of questions, including (1) When is the date for my next pretrial conference? (2) Can you explain the second argument raised in the motion to suppress that was filed on my behalf last week? (3) How much prison time am I facing under the current indictment? (4) If we lose the suppression hearing, what defenses can I present at trial? and (5) What are my odds of winning at trial?

You are quite comfortable answering each of these questions. But you are not sure whether you should be the one responding to them. Review any ethical standards from your home state jurisdiction regarding client contacts and inquiries, as well as the ethical standards for delegated tasks set forth in the following sources. Based on your review, identify how you would respond to each of the client's questions.

American Bar Association

http://www.abanet.org/legalservices/paralegals/downloads/ modelguidelines.pdf

The American Alliance of Paralegals, Inc.

http://www.aapipara.org/Ethicalstandards.htm

National Association of Legal Assistants

http://www.nala.org/code.aspx

chapter **eight**

SOURCES OF CRIMINAL PROCEDURES

Criminals do not die by the hands of the law; they die by the hands of other men.

—George Bernard Shaw, *Man and Superman*[1] Irish Dramatist

If the government becomes a law breaker, it breeds contempt for law; it invites every man to become a law unto himself; it invites anarchy. To declare that in the administration of the criminal law the end justifies the means—to declare that the Government may commit crimes in order to secure conviction of a private criminal—would bring terrible retribution.

—Justice Louis D. Brandeis, *Olmstead v. United States*[2] (1928)

The criminal is to go free because the constable has blundered.

—Judge (later Justice) Benjamin Cardozo, *People v. Defore* (1926)[3]

LEARNING OBJECTIVES

After reading this chapter, you should be able to

- Appreciate the differences between criminal law and rules of criminal procedure.

- Identify the many layers of government involved in setting procedural standards for criminal cases.

- Discuss the sources and standards for criminal procedure found in the U.S. Constitution.

- Explain the role of the incorporation doctrine in state and local criminal cases.

- Locate and use the Federal Rules of Criminal Procedure.

- Research and understand your state rules of criminal procedure.

- Identify and use federal, state, and local administrative regulations that impact the procedures of criminal cases.

- Local the local rules for criminal practice within your local federal and state courts.

- Understand the different methods used to interpret and apply the legal language of criminal procedure.

INTRODUCTION

As evidenced in Chapters 1–7, criminal law focuses on the substance of government-enforced prohibitions of certain behavior, or the "guts" of criminal statutes. This might be referred to as the "what" of the criminal justice system—*what* types of behavior are prohibited by the government and *what* elements must be proven in order to demonstrate the alleged crime. ***Criminal procedure***, on the other hand, addresses the processing of criminal cases or the "how" portion of the criminal justice system. Essentially, the primary focus is *how* a suspect or defendant is treated while in the system. Both criminal law and criminal procedure are critical to ensuring a fair and effective criminal justice system. Not only must the laws themselves be written in a way that is just, but the law must also be implemented in a way that is fair.

The manner in which a person is treated during criminal proceedings can have just as much, if not more, of an impact on the final result as the content found within the criminal laws themselves. In some cases, the evidence obtained by law enforcement may form a very strong case for proving all elements of a criminal offense.

For example, in a typical theft case, prosecutors may have evidence that the defendant took property belonging to another person with the intent to permanently deprive the other person of its use. See Chapter 5 on theft offenses. The prosecutors may even have a confession from the defendant or videotaped footage of the heist. Given the basic elements of a theft offense, you might say that the prosecutors have a rather strong case against the defendant. But if law enforcement obtained the evidence in an illegal manner or breached other procedural standards during their investigation, it is possible that these procedural shortcomings could adversely impact the government's case. If, for example, the police used unreasonable tactics to interrogate the defendant and obtain the confession, or used an unreasonable search and seizure to obtain the video evidence, these procedural defects could result in the prosecutor being barred from using the evidence against the defendant to prove the underlying criminal charge. See Chapters 10–12. The exclusion of this evidence, in turn, may make it difficult or impossible for the prosecution to prove its case beyond a reasonable doubt.

In many cases, the substance of a criminal law may be fine. But if the government treats persons unfairly while processing them for violating the law, this mistreatment may be a violation of constitutional or other legal standards of due process. As a legal professional, you must be mindful of both dimensions of legal protection within the criminal justice system. Certainly, you need to account for the substance of the alleged crime. This involves asking questions like, Is the criminal statute in a given case constitutional and otherwise legally sound? What are the elements of the charged offense? And is there enough evidence to prove these elements? But at the same time, you must also be aware of the procedure used to bring a defendant into the criminal justice system. This involves asking questions like, What methods were used to identify and charge the defendant? How did the police obtain the evidence for the case? And how has the defendant been treated while in the criminal justice system? By evaluating criminal cases in a holistic manner, looking at both the legal substance and procedure involved in a case, you will be able to conduct a more complete accounting of the strength of a case and be in a better position to advance your client's interests or needs. See Figure 8-1.

criminal procedure
body of law that regulates the manner in which authorities process criminal cases and treat individual suspects or defendants

Law Line 8-1
National Criminal Justice Reference Service

FIGURE 8-1 **Two Sides of the Same Coin: Criminal Law and Procedure**

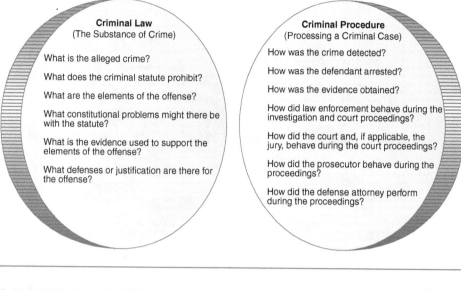

Criminal Law
(The Substance of Crime)

What is the alleged crime?

What does the criminal statute prohibit?

What are the elements of the offense?

What constitutional problems might there be with the statute?

What is the evidence used to support the elements of the offense?

What defenses or justification are there for the offense?

Criminal Procedure
(Processing a Criminal Case)

How was the crime detected?

How was the defendant arrested?

How was the evidence obtained?

How did law enforcement behave during the investigation and court proceedings?

How did the court and, if applicable, the jury, behave during the court proceedings?

How did the prosecutor behave during the proceedings?

How did the defense attorney perform during the proceedings?

MULTIPLE LAYERS OF CRIMINAL PROCEDURE

In Chapter 2, you learned that American criminal justice takes place in a federal system, which contains three primary levels of government—federal, state, and local. You also learned that within each of these levels of governmental authority, there are typically three branches of power—legislative, executive, and judicial. Given these multiple levels and branches of government authority, it is perhaps not surprising that, within this system of federalism and separation of powers, standards of criminal procedure come from many sources.

They come from federal, state, and local constitutions, which provide the basic blueprint for governing within a jurisdiction. They come from federal, state, and local legislative sources in the form of statutes, codes, and ordinances. They come from federal, state, and local administrative agencies, which implement rules pursuant to their statutory authorities. And they come from federal, state, and local courts, which have their own rules of practice and procedure. All told, these multiple sources for criminal procedures create an intricate and sometimes complicated web of rules and standards for legal professionals in their pursuit of criminal justice.

Moreover, among the array of criminal procedures, there is a hierarchy of law, which often allows federal standards to reign supreme over state and local standards and state standards to be superior to those of local government. See Chapter 2 for discussion on the Supremacy Clause.

Overall, legal professionals must be aware that criminal procedure is not a one-dimensional area of the law, where you can regularly go to one source to find all of the rules and standards for a given case. Often you must conduct a "global" review of the legal standards to determine whether all of the standards, at all of the layers of applicable government, and among all branches of government, have been satisfied.

Constitutional Sources

Many standards for criminal procedure come from constitutional authority. At the federal level, the U.S. Constitution contains several provisions related to criminal cases. Similarly, each state has its own constitution, which provides standards for

constitution

agreement between a governing body (an institution of government) and those parties it seeks to govern (the people); typically, a constitution outlines the duties and powers of a government, as well as any rights or protections held by individuals

Political cartoon about Search and Seizure: "We've looked everywhere for the constitutional protection against illegal search and seizure . . . but we haven't found any yet!"

Search and Seizure

"We've looked everywhere for your constitutional protection against illegal search and seizure... but we haven't found any yet!"

By Beattie for The Daytona Beach Morning Journal

criminal procedure. At the local level, counties, townships, cities, villages, and other municipalities may also provide more standards for processing criminal cases.

The U.S. Constitution

The U.S. Constitution has several procedural standards for criminal cases. The entire Constitution may seem fairly long and dense. If so, it may be helpful to view the document as containing four basic sections—the Preamble, seven Articles, a Bill of Rights, and seventeen additional amendments. While the Preamble does not impose any explicit requirements on government and essentially sets forth the basic reasons for writing the Constitution, several provisions affecting criminal procedure are found in the Articles, the Bill of Rights, and the amendments.

The Articles.   The Articles of the Constitution provide the basic blueprint for the federal government and contain numerous provisions regarding the powers and limitations of the three branches of government and, to some extent, the states. Two of the more basic principles found within the Articles are the separation of powers and the system of checks and balances. As addressed in Chapter 2, the **separation of powers** divides governmental authority among different units or branches of power. In the case of the United States, the three primary branches are legislative, executive, and judicial. Under the **system of checks and balances**, each institution or branch of government is given an amount of coequal authority and further allowed to supervise (check) the other institutions. The authority of the legislative, executive, and judicial branches of the U.S. government to check and balance one another is found within Articles I, II, and III of the Constitution.

The elements of separation of powers and of checks and balances can serve as important functions in criminal procedure. They can ensure that legislative authorities do not enact criminal statutes that transgress upon basic rights of individual freedom. They can work to ensure that executive authorities, including police officers and federal agents, do not encroach upon the personal liberties of individuals while pursuing criminal investigations. And they can establish basic requirements for courts that process persons charged with criminal offenses.

Take, for example, the case of former congressman William Jefferson (D–La), who was indicted by federal authorities in 2006 for bribery and government corruption charges. As a part of a corruption investigation, federal authorities raided the congressional office of Representative Jefferson pursuant to a search warrant and took large amounts of materials. The congressman challenged the constitutionality of the government's search of his congressional office and moved for return of the seized property. Specifically, Jefferson argued that the search of his congressional office violated the Speech and Debate Clause found in Article I, section 6 of the Constitution. This section provides, "The Senators and Representatives . . . shall in all Cases, except Treason, Felony and Breach of the Peace, be privileged from Arrest during their Attendance at the Session of their respective Houses, and in going to and returning from the same; and for any Speech or Debate in either House, they shall not be questioned in any other Place."

Law Line 8-2
D.C. Circuit Court of Appeals
Opinion in William Jefferson's case

A federal trial court rejected Jefferson's argument, but the Circuit Court of Appeals for the District of Columbia reversed in part the lower court opinion. The appellate court held that the federal agents' search of Jefferson's paper files in his congressional office violated the Speech or Debate Clause, but that the agents' copying of the congressman's computer hard drives and other electronic media was constitutionally permissible. Accordingly, the court ruled that Jefferson was entitled to the return of his privileged legislative materials but was not entitled to return of nonprivileged materials.[4] Jefferson was later convicted of charges related to soliciting bribes. And in January 2010, a federal district court sentenced Jefferson to thirteen years of imprisonment for these offenses.

The Articles of the Constitution also contain certain explicit rights for criminal suspects and defendants. For example, in Article I, section 9, Congress is prohibited from suspending petitions for a writ of habeas corpus, except when public safety is threatened by rebellion or invasion. A **writ of habeas corpus** is a court order issued to an official (typically, a prison warden) holding or detaining a person (usually, an inmate) that mandates the release of the person being held. Convicted defendants often petition courts for a writ of habeas corpus after they have exhausted their appellate rights. See Chapter 14.

In recent years, however, Congress's authority to suspend the right of habeas corpus has been at the center of the constitutional debate over the federal detention of terrorism suspects. In *Boumediene et al. v. Bush* (2008), the U.S. Supreme Court ruled 5-4 that prisoners held as "enemy combatants" at Guantánamo Bay, Cuba, can immediately file habeas corpus petitions in federal district courts challenging the legality of their confinement. The majority ruled that the provision of the 2006 Military Commissions Act (MCA) stripping Guantánamo Bay prisoners of their habeas corpus rights was unconstitutional.

Law Line 8-3
Boumediene v. Bush

In addition, Article I, section 9 prohibits Congress, and Article I, section 10 prohibits the states, from passing ex post facto laws and bills of attainder. An **ex post facto law** is a law that punishes a person for an act that occurred before the law was enacted. This essentially ensures that authorities give individuals notice of prohibited behavior before they seek to punish them for such behavior. A **bill of attainder** is a law that imposes punishment on individuals without the benefit of trial proceedings. This basically prohibits legislatures from serving as judges and juries in criminal cases by simply convicting persons as criminals by passing legislation.

self-incrimination provision

Fifth Amendment right that provides within a criminal case that persons cannot be forced to provide testimony against themselves

Due Process Clause (Fifth Amendment)

provision stating that the federal government may not deprive a person of life, liberty, or property without due process of law

speedy trial provision

Sixth Amendment right that provides individuals with a right to a speedy trial

public trial provision

Sixth Amendment right that entitles criminal defendants in most serious criminal cases to a public trial

jury trial clause

Sixth Amendment right that allows individuals have their criminal cases decided by an impartial jury (as opposed to a judge) within the jurisdiction where the crime was allegedly committed

information clause

Sixth Amendment provision that requires the government to notify defendants of the nature and cause of the criminal charges

confrontation clause

Sixth Amendment protection that gives accused persons the ability to confront (cross-examine) any witnesses providing testimony against them

compulsory process clause

Sixth Amendment right that allows defendants to compel witnesses to appear on their behalf

assistance of counsel provision

Sixth Amendment right for an accused person to have counsel (an attorney) assist in defending against the criminal charges

excessive bail

prohibition in the Eighth Amendment stating that the amount of bail (the collateral required by a court as a condition for pretrial release of the defendant) cannot be excessive

In the end, in many criminal cases, the constitutional limitations and requirements found in the Articles of the Constitution may not play a critical role. But it is important to keep these principles in mind when assessing the proper procedures for handling a case.

The Bill of Rights.   Most of the specific standards for criminal procedure are found in the **Bill of Rights** (the first ten amendments to the U.S. Constitution). The Bill of Rights was ratified in 1791 and serves as the primary list of civil liberties that cannot be infringed upon by government. See Figure 8-2. These liberties include the right to the free exercise religion, the right to free speech, and the right to bear arms. Standards related to criminal procedure are found primarily in the Fourth, Fifth, Sixth, and Eighth amendments.

In the Fourth Amendment, there are two primary provisions. The **search and seizure clause** bars government from engaging in unreasonable searches and seizures of persons, houses, papers, and effects. And the **warrant provision** requires that the government must demonstrate probable cause before a warrant will be issued by a judge. These two provisions, which are often interrelated, form the basic constitutional context for addressing government searches of persons and places, seizures of evidence, and arrests of individuals.[5]

The Fifth Amendment contains four clauses relevant to criminal procedure. The **grand jury provision** requires government to obtain a **grand jury indictment** (a formal charge by a group of citizens sitting as a jury who have reviewed the evidence and decided that there is sufficient cause to charge a person with a criminal offense) in order to charge a person with a **capital offense** (an offense punishable by death) or an "otherwise infamous crime," which is usually read to mean a **felony** (generally defined to mean a crime for which the punishment may include a year or more of incarceration).[6] The **Double Jeopardy Clause** provides that government may not punish a person twice for the same offense.[7] The *self-incrimination provision* states that, within a criminal case, persons cannot be forced to provide testimony against themselves.[8] And last, the *Due Process Clause* provides that the federal government may not deprive a person of life, liberty, or property without due process of law. This clause, which is repeated in the Fourteenth Amendment and thereby made applicable to the states, requires among other things that government treat individuals fairly during the criminal process. This may include such protections as the right to a fair trial, the right to be free from outrageous conduct by prosecutors or judges, the right to a full and fair appeal of a conviction, and the right to humane conditions of confinement.[9] See the Due Process section (below).

The Sixth Amendment includes several standards for the criminal process. The *speedy trial provision* gives individuals a right to a speedy trial.[10] Similarly, the *public trial provision* states that individuals are also entitled to a public trial.[11] The *jury trial clause* provides that individuals have a right to have their criminal cases decided by an impartial jury (as opposed to a judge) within the jurisdiction where the crime was allegedly committed.[12] The *information clause* requires government to notify defendants of the nature and cause of the criminal charges. The *confrontation clause* provides the accused with the right to confront (generally interpreted as to view and cross-examine) any witnesses testifying against them.[13] The *compulsory process clause* allows defendants to compel witnesses to appear on their behalf.[14] And the *assistance of counsel provision* provides that the accused has the right to have counsel (an attorney) assist in defending against the criminal charges.[15]

Finally, the Eighth Amendment contains three primary provisions. The *excessive bail* provision states that the amount of bail (the collateral required by a

FIGURE 8-2 **Textual Contents of the Bill of Rights**

First Amendment

Bars government from passing laws respecting an establishment of religion

Bars government from prohibiting the free exercise of religion

Bars government from abridging the freedom of speech

Bars government from abridging the freedom of the press

Bars government from abridging the right to peacefully assemble

Bars government from abridging the right to petition government for redress of grievances

Second Amendment

Bars government from infringing on the right to bear arms

Third Amendment

In peacetime, bars government from quartering soldiers in homes without an owner's consent

During war, allows troops to be quartered in a manner prescribed by law

Fourth Amendment

Bars government from violating the right against unreasonable searches and seizures

Requires probable cause, oath or affirmation, and particularity for the issuance of warrants

Fifth Amendment

Requires grand jury indictment for charges of capital or infamous charges

Bars government from trying a person twice for the same offense (double jeopardy)

Bars government from compelling persons to testify against themselves in criminal cases

Bars government from depriving persons life, liberty, or property without due process of law

Bars government from taking private property for public use without just compensation

Sixth Amendment

Provides accused persons with the right to a speedy, public, and jury trial in criminal cases

Provides accused persons with the right to be notified of the criminal charges against them

Provides accused persons with the right to confront witnesses against them

Provides accused persons with the right to compel witnesses to appear on their behalf

Provides accused persons with right to the assistance of legal counsel in criminal cases

Seventh Amendment

Provides the right to a jury trial in civil cases involving disputes valued over twenty dollars

Provides common law rules to be used when federal courts review common law suits

Eighth Amendment

Bars government from imposing excessive bail or fines

Bars government from inflicting cruel and unusual punishment

Ninth Amendment

Provides that the Constitution's enumeration of specific rights should not be interpreted to deny other rights retained by the people

Tenth Amendment

Provides that all powers not given to the United States or taken from the states by the Constitution are reserved to the States or to the people

---

court as a condition for pretrial release of the defendant) cannot be excessive. Under the ***excessive fines*** provision a fine (a postconviction punishment in the form of monetary payment) cannot be excessive. And the ***cruel and unusual punishment clause*** provides that government may not inflict cruel and unusual punishment upon individuals.[16]

Many of the protections within the Bill of Rights are specific to criminal cases. This is particularly true with the Fourth, Fifth, Sixth, and Eighth Amendments. But many of the other general protections within the Bill of Rights

excessive fines
prohibition in the Eighth Amendment providing that a fine (a postconviction punishment in the form of monetary payment) cannot be excessive

cruel and unusual punishment clause

Eighth Amendment right providing that government may not inflict cruel and unusual punishment upon individuals

can also impact the procedure and substance of criminal cases. Criminal laws, investigations, or prosecutions that interfere with the freedom of speech, religion, assembly, press, or other constitutional rights may be restricted by the constitutional protections found in the Bill of Rights. For example, if an officer arrests a person for using profane language or engaging in offense behavior, the person may argue that the arrest infringed upon the First Amendment right to free speech. Or if police used state laws against underage alcohol consumption to arrest a teenager who consumed wine during a Catholic mass, the teenager would assert that this action violated the First Amendment right to the free exercise of religion.

Over the years, many criminal laws and procedures have been invalidated because they violated basic principles of free speech, religion, privacy, or other more general forms of civil liberties. In *Ashcroft v. Free Speech Coalition* (2002),[17] the Supreme Court rejected a federal child pornography law because it intruded on free speech rights. In *The Church of Lukumi Babalu Aye v. City of Hialeah* (1993),[18] the Court invalidated a local ordinance banning animal sacrifice because it infringed upon the free exercise rights of members of the Santerian faith. These are just two of the many cases where the enumerated liberties protected by the Bill of Rights were invoked to restrict government's actions in criminal settings.

Law Line 8-4
Ashcroft v. Free Speech Coalition (2002)

Explicit versus Implicit Rights.   In addition to the specific and enumerated rights found in the Bill of Rights, the Supreme Court has also identified other implicit rights protected by the Constitution. For example, the Court has recognized the rights to privacy, marriage, travel, certain levels of reproductive freedoms, and the freedom of association as fundamental constitutional rights, even though none of these rights is explicitly mentioned in the Bill of Rights. See Figure 8-3. For some, the recognition of implicit constitutional liberties is grounded in the Ninth Amendment, which provides, "[t]he enumeration in the Constitution, of certain rights, shall not be construed to deny or disparage others retained by the people." Some have interpreted this language to mean that the Bill of Rights should not be read as an exhaustive accounting of all rights protected by the Constitution, but rather, a partial list of just some of the personal freedoms enjoyed by individuals against government action.

For others, implicit liberties are found through the Due Process Clause (see below), which ensures that government does not deny individuals liberty without due process of law. Under this approach, the generic term *liberty*, as used in the Due Process Clause, is interpreted as a category of protections, within which the Court can identify rights that are not explicitly referenced in the Constitution.

The recognition of implicit constitutional rights can impact the substance and procedure of criminal cases. For example, in *Griswold v. Connecticut* (1965),[19] doctors in Connecticut were threatened with criminal prosecution if they provided information to patients about certain types of birth control. The Supreme Court, however, struck down this law because it violated a patient's fundamental right to personal

---

FIGURE 8-3 **Implicit Fundamental Rights**

Right to Privacy—*Griswold v. Connecticut* (1965)

Right to Travel—*Shapiro v. Thompson* (1969)

Right to Reproductive Freedoms, including some types of abortion—*Roe v. Wade* (1973)

Freedom of Association—*NAACP v. Alabama* (1958)

Right to Marriage—*Zablocki v. Redhail* (1978)

privacy. Although the right to privacy is not explicitly referenced in the Constitution, a majority of the Court found that it was nonetheless protected as a fundamental right.

Overall, the Bill of Rights contains several provisions that may explicitly or implicitly impact the procedure in a criminal case. In many cases, these provisions will serve as the primary touchstone for determining whether suspects and defendants have received fair treatment in their cases.

Incorporation Doctrine.   It is important to understand that most of the protections afforded in the Bill of Rights apply to all levels of government—federal, state, and local. Despite the fact that the Bill of Rights begins by stating that "*Congress* shall make no law," state and local governments also must comply with most provisions of the Bill of Rights because these provisions have been made applicable to them through the Fourteenth Amendment's Due Process Clause. The theory or doctrine used to require state and local authorities to follow most provisions within the Bill of Rights is known as the ***incorporation doctrine***. This doctrine holds, to varying degrees, that the provisions of the Bill of Rights ought to be applied to state and local governments by "incorporating" them through the Fourteenth Amendment's Due Process Clause. See Figure 8-4.

In essence, the incorporation doctrine maintains that courts do not need to "reinvent the wheel" when it comes to interpreting the liberties and process protected by the Fourteenth Amendment Due Process Clause. Under this doctrine, if a constitutional standard under the Fifth Amendment is good enough to resolve self-incrimination issues involving federal authorities, it is good enough for addressing those disputes in state and local courts as well.

In the aftermath of the Civil War, Congress passed and the states ratified the Fourteenth Amendment, which includes a ***Due Process Clause*** that specifically applies to the states.[20] Section 1 of the Fourteenth Amendment provides, in relevant part, "nor shall any State deprive any person of life, liberty, or property, without due

incorporation doctrine
a constitutional doctrine holding that the provisions of the Bill of Rights ought to be applied to state and local governments by "incorporating" them through the Fourteenth Amendment's Due Process Clause

Due Process Clause (Fourteenth Amendment)
provision stating in relevant part, "nor shall any State deprive any person of life, liberty, or property, without due process of law

FIGURE 8-4 **Incorporation Doctrine: Apply the Bill of Rights to the States**

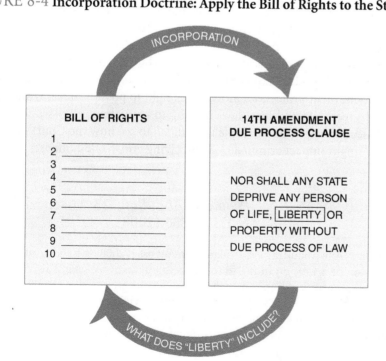

process of law. . . ." The 1868 ratification of this Due Process Clause provided an explicit mandate to the states about protecting life, liberty, and property—a mandate for states that was not in the original Bill of Rights. But even with the Due Process Clause in place, it was not clear that the provisions of the Bill of Rights applied to state and local governments. The Due Process Clause stated only that states must not deny life, liberty, or property without due process of law; it did not explicitly provide any requirement that the states abide by the first ten amendments to the Constitution. And in the wake of the Fourteenth Amendment's ratification, courts began to grapple with two fundamental questions: What types of behavior does the term "liberty" include? And what "process" must be provided by states before liberty can be denied? Since these terms were not defined or further addressed by the Fourteenth Amendment, the scope and meaning of these provisions were uncertain.

Over time, the Supreme Court developed different theories for incorporating provisions within the Bill of Rights and making them apply to state and local authorities through the Fourteenth Amendment Due Process Clause. For example, in *Benyton v. Maryland* (1969),[21] the Court held that the Fifth Amendment right against double jeopardy was incorporated and applied to the states. And in *Malloy v. Hogan*, 378 U.S. 1 (1964),[22] the Court ruled that the states must abide by the Fifth Amendment's protection against self-incrimination.

Between 1896 and 1972, the Court relied on the Fourteenth Amendment's Due Process Clause to incorporate nearly all of the provisions of the Bill of Rights. And today, only four provisions remain unincorporated. Officially, the Court has not incorporated the Third Amendment right against quartering troops in a person's house, the Fifth Amendment right to indictment by grand jury, the Seventh Amendment right to jury trial in civil cases, and the Eighth Amendment right against excessive fines and bail. Many states, however, have their own constitutional protections for these and other liberties.[23]

In recent years, the Court's failure to incorporate the Second Amendment right to bear arms has been a central issue in many state criminal cases involving the possession or use of firearms. The Second Amendment provides: "A well regulated militia, being necessary to the security of a free state, the right of the people to keep and bear arms, shall not be infringed." Many defendants have sought to assert a Second Amendment defense to state-initiated gun crimes. But as addressed in Chapter 6, the Supreme Court ruled in *McDonald v. Chicago* (2010) that the Second Amendment protects an individual's right to possess firearms and restricts, to some degree, state and local laws seeking to regulate gun possession. See Law Line 8-5. Read the opinion of *People v. Abdullah* to see how the Court's decision in *McDonald* might impact criminal cases involving gun-related offenses.

Law Line 8-5
McDonald v. City of Chicago

CAPSTONE CASE *People v. Abdullah*, 23 Misc. 3d 232, 870 N.Y.S.2d 886 (2008)

Defendant, Albi Abdullah, was arraigned on August 1, 2008 on a charge of criminal possession of a weapon in the fourth degree pursuant to Penal Law 265.01(1). Defendant moves for dismissal of the charge on the ground that the PL 265.01 is unconstitutional and that such charge constitutes a violation of defendant's Second Amendment right to keep and bear arms in his home for self protection, pursuant to the US Constitution., Amendments II and XIV; and pursuant to the holding of

(continued)

the U.S. Supreme Court in *District of Columbia v. Heller*, 128 S.Ct. 2783, 171 L.Ed.2d 637 (2008). Defendant further supports his claim of unconstitutionality on the alleged arbitrary and capricious nature of the City's gun licensing process as managed by the New York City Police Department.

The People base their response on the ground that the Supreme Court has repeatedly held that the language of the Second Amendment places limits upon the power of Congress, not upon the powers of the States. The People argue that Heller, by its own terms, is neither applicable to nor binding upon the States, and that it cannot be interpreted to mean that the Second Amendment bars a state's reasonable regulation of gun possession. The court has reviewed the defendant's moving papers, the People's response, relevant statutes and case law, and for the reasons discussed hereafter, denies the defendant's motion.

Pursuant to the complaint, defendant's motion, and the response filed by the People, Police Officer Chiwen Cen was brought to the marital abode in response to a call that defendant was present in the home in violation of a temporary order of protection that had been issued ex parte on the previous day. When defendant was asked if he had any weapons he stated, in substance, that there was a weapon in the top cabinet in the kitchen. The Officer recovered an unloaded .25 caliber semi-automatic pistol from inside a kitchen cabinet. Defendant was arrested for violation of Penal Law § 265.01(1).

The Supreme Court did specifically hold in . . . that the District of Columbia's ban on the possession of handguns in the home violates the Second Amendment but the Court also stated that the right to keep and bear arms as secured by the Second Amendment is not unlimited . . . and that the Second Amendment is neither applicable to nor binding upon the States. The Court then chose not to address the validity of the District of Columbia's licensing requirement and hypothesized that "Assuming that *Heller* is not disqualified from the exercise of Second Amendment rights, the District must permit him to register his handgun and must issue him a license to carry it in the home."

Because New York does not have a complete ban on the possession of handguns in the home and because the District of Columbia is a federal enclave and not a State, *Heller* is distinguishable and its holding does not invalidate New York's gun possession laws or regulations. The Second Amendment has been recently held not to apply to the States and is not incorporated into the Fourteenth Amendment. Therefore, in New York, possession of a firearm remains a criminal act, pursuant to Penal Law Article 265, unless one holds a license to so possess, pursuant to Penal Law § 265.20(a)(3) and Article 400.

Defendant's motion to dismiss on the ground that Penal Law 265.01 violates the Second Amendment of the United States Constitution is denied.

It is worth noting that based on the file presently before the court the complaint is unconverted, as the operability of the firearm recovered is not documented therein.

This opinion constitutes the decision and order of the court.

WHAT DO *YOU* THINK?

1. Given the Supreme Court's incorporation of the Second Amendment, thereby making it applicable to the states, how will this impact the state's ability to regulate the possession and use of firearms?

2. Would it be possible for state and local governments to enact regulations on ammunition (bullets), as opposed to guns, and still comply with the Second Amendment?

The reality today is that most of the provisions found in the Bill of Rights apply to state and local governments through the Due Process Clause of the Fourteenth Amendment. As a result, many of the criminal procedures applicable to state and local cases will be derived from provisions within the federal Bill of Rights. These will be discussed in more detail in the chapters that follow. But in general, legal professionals within the criminal justice system should be aware of the important role the federal constitution plays in many cases, even at the state and local levels.

Due Process Clauses. As mentioned above, there are two due process clauses in the Constitution that serve as important sources for criminal procedure. The Due Process Clause in the Fifth Amendment applies to the federal government. The clause in the Fourteenth Amendment applies to state and local governments. Each ensures that government cannot deprive persons of life, liberty, or property, without due process of law. In other words, when government seeks to interfere with a person's life, liberty, or property, it must go about this process in a fair and just manner.

Given the nature of criminal cases, where the government is essentially trying to deprive defendants of some form of liberty (by probation, detention, arrest, jail, imprisonment), deprive them of property (by fines and restitution), or, in extreme cases, take away their life (by capital punishment), it is not surprising that the Due Process Clause plays an important role in establishing standards for governmental conduct.

Due process has two dimensions—substantive and procedural. **Substantive due process** essentially requires that the substance of the law itself must not unduly interfere with basic notions of liberty and fairness. For example, in *Lawrence v. Texas* (2003),[24] the U.S. Supreme Court struck down a Texas law that criminalized sodomy between persons of the same sex. The law banned same-sex sodomy, but did not prohibit such sexual activity between persons of the opposite sex. A majority of the Court found that the substance of the law interfered with the liberty of individuals to choose the nature of their private and consensual sexual activity. Although the Constitution does not explicitly identify a right to sexual freedom, the Court nonetheless interpreted the word *liberty* as found in the Due Process Clause of the Fourteenth Amendment to include such a right. And based on this conclusion, the Court found the Texas law to violate substantive due process.

As the *Lawrence* case illustrates, a substantive right of due process does not have to be specifically listed in the Bill of Rights in order to be protected. There are explicit substantive due process rights, including the First Amendment rights to free speech and religious exercise, and the Second Amendment right to bear arms. But there are also many substantive due process rights implicitly included in the terms life, liberty, and property. These include the fundamental rights to privacy, travel, and marriage. The Supreme Court has found these and other substantive due process rights to be implicit in the concept of ordered liberty, and thus protected as substantive rights of due process.

Procedural due process protects individuals from being treated unfairly during government proceedings. This dimension of due process essentially requires that persons have a full and fair opportunity to defend themselves and that government authorities not have an unfair advantage during the proceedings. Procedural due process may include such things as the right to sufficient notice of proceedings, the right to speak before sentencing, and the right to appeal.

As with substantive due process, there does not necessarily have to be an explicit provision contained in the Bill of Rights for a procedural right to be protected. Certainly, there are enumerated rights that impact procedural due process, such as the Sixth Amendment rights of a defendant to be informed of the

---

substantive due process
a dimension of due process requiring that the substance of the law itself must not unduly interfere with basic notions of liberty and fairness

---

Law Line 8-6
Lawrence v. Texas

---

procedural due process
a dimension of due process that protects individuals from being treated unfairly during government proceedings

nature and cause of the criminal charges, the right during trial to confront adverse witnesses, and the right to counsel during certain stages of criminal proceedings. But there also are implicit procedural protections, such as the defendant's right to be free from prejudicial forms of judicial, prosecutorial, or jury misconduct, as well as the right of a defendant to receive exculpatory evidence in the possession of the prosecutor. Each of these nonenumerated protections also ensures basic notions of procedural due process.

Both substantive and procedural rights of due process can be intertwined in criminal cases, treated almost like two sides of the same coin. A defendant can claim both that the substance of a criminal law is unfair and also that the manner in which he was processed was unfair. Read the Supreme Court's opinion in *Connecticut Dept. of Public Safety v. Doe* (2003) to see how both substantive and procedural due process can impact the implementation of sexual-offender registration laws.

CAPSTONE CASE *Connecticut Dept. of Public Safety v. Doe,*
538 U.S. 1, 123 S. Ct. 1160 (2003)

Chief Justice REHNQUIST delivered the opinion of the Court.

We granted certiorari to determine whether the United States Court of Appeals for the Second Circuit properly enjoined the public disclosure of Connecticut's sex offender registry. The Court of Appeals concluded that such disclosure both deprived registered sex offenders of a "liberty interest," and violated the Due Process Clause because officials did not afford registrants a predeprivation hearing to determine whether they are likely to be "currently dangerous." . . .

"Sex offenders are a serious threat in this Nation." "[T]he victims of sex assault are most often juveniles," and "[w]hen convicted sex offenders reenter society, they are much more likely than any other type of offender to be re-arrested for a new rape or sexual assault." Connecticut, like every other State, has responded to these facts by enacting a statute designed to protect its communities from sex offenders and to help apprehend repeat sex offenders. Connecticut's "Megan's Law" applies to all persons convicted of criminal offenses against a minor, violent and nonviolent sexual offenses, and felonies committed for a sexual purpose. Covered offenders must register with the Connecticut Department of Public Safety (DPS) upon their release into the community. . . .

The statute requires DPS to compile the information gathered from registrants and publicize it. In particular, the law requires DPS to post a sex offender registry on an Internet Website and to make the registry available to the public in certain state offices. Whether made available in an office or via the Internet, the registry must be accompanied by the following warning: " 'Any person who uses information in this registry to injure, harass or commit a criminal act against any person included in the registry or any other person is subject to criminal prosecution.' " . . .

Petitioners include the state agencies and officials charged with compiling the sex offender registry and posting it on the Internet. Respondent Doe (hereinafter respondent) is a convicted sex offender who is subject to Connecticut's Megan's Law. He filed this action . . . claiming that the law violates, *inter alia,* the Due Process Clause of the Fourteenth Amendment. Specifically, respondent alleged that he is not a " 'dangerous sexual offender,' " and that the Connecticut law "deprives him of a liberty interest—his reputation combined with the alteration of his status under state law—without notice or a meaningful opportunity to be heard." . . .

In *Paul v. Davis* (1976), we held that mere injury to reputation, even if defamatory, does not constitute the deprivation of a liberty interest. Petitioners urge us to reverse the Court of Appeals on the ground that, under *Paul v. Davis,* respondent has failed to establish that petitioners have deprived him of a liberty interest. We find it

(continued)

(continued)

unnecessary to reach this question, however, because even assuming, *arguendo*, that respondent has been deprived of a liberty interest, due process does not entitle him to a hearing to establish a fact that is not material under the Connecticut statute.

In cases such as *Wisconsin v. Constantineau* and *Goss v. Lopez*, we held that due process required the government to accord the plaintiff a hearing to prove or disprove a particular fact or set of facts. But in each of these cases, the fact in question was concededly relevant to the inquiry at hand. Here, however, the fact that respondent seeks to prove—that he is not currently dangerous—is of no consequence under Connecticut's Megan's Law. As the DPS Website explains, the law's requirements turn on an offender's conviction alone—a fact that a convicted offender has already had a procedurally safeguarded opportunity to contest. No other fact is relevant to the disclosure of registrants' information. Indeed, the disclaimer on the Website explicitly states that respondent's alleged nondangerousness simply does not matter.

In short, even if respondent could prove that he is not likely to be currently dangerous, Connecticut has decided that the registry information of *all* sex offenders—currently dangerous or not—must be publicly disclosed. Unless respondent can show that that *substantive* rule of law is defective (by conflicting with a provision of the Constitution), any hearing on current dangerousness is a bootless exercise. It may be that respondent's claim is actually a substantive challenge to Connecticut's statute "recast in 'procedural due process' terms." Nonetheless, respondent expressly disavows any reliance on the substantive component of the Fourteenth Amendment's protections, and maintains, as he did below, that his challenge is strictly a procedural one. But States are not barred by principles of "*procedural* due process" from drawing such classifications. Such claims "must ultimately be analyzed" in terms of substantive, not procedural, due process. Because the question is not properly before us, we express no opinion as to whether Connecticut's Megan's Law violates principles of substantive due process.

Plaintiffs who assert a right to a hearing under the Due Process Clause must show that the facts they seek to establish in that hearing are relevant under the statutory scheme. Respondent cannot make that showing here. The judgment of the Court of Appeals is therefore *Reversed*.

WHAT DO *YOU* THINK?

1. Does the state's publicized disclosure of nonviolent sexual offenders unduly infringe upon their privacy and reputational rights?
2. How important was Connecticut's statutory language barring the use of the registration information to harass a person? If this language were not included in the law, would the law violate Doe's due process rights?

IN THE FIELD

For legal professionals reviewing criminal cases, there may be an occasion to question whether the government is providing sufficient substantive and/or procedural due process. You may have those times when a particular criminal law, police practice, or courtroom policy just does not seem fair or effective enough to protect a person's life, liberty, or property interests. In these situations, such laws, practices, and policies can be challenged as violations of substantive and/or procedural due process. And keep in mind, the government's questionable treatment of the defendant does not have to be explicitly referenced by a specific provision in the Bill of Rights in order for it to be deemed unconstitutional. If the government's treatment of the defendant seems unfair or prejudicial, it can be challenged under the Due Process Clause of the Fifth Amendment (in federal cases) or the Fourteenth Amendment (in state states).

MAINTAINING THE ATTORNEY-CLIENT PRIVILEGE

National Federation of Paralegal Associations, Inc. Model Code of Ethics and Professional Responsibility and Guidelines for Enforcement Rule 1.5

A paralegal shall preserve all confidential information provided by the client or acquired from other sources before, during, and after the course of the professional relationship.

ETHICAL CONSIDERATION 1.5(A)

A paralegal shall be aware of and abide by all legal authority governing confidential information in the jurisdiction in which the paralegal practices.

ATTORNEY-CLIENT PRIVILEGE

Though each jurisdiction has its own rules governing confidential client communications, the attorney-client privilege generally prohibits the unauthorized disclosure of:

1. communications from a client;

2. to the client's attorney (or to the attorney's assistants, including paralegals);

3. relating to the attorney's offering of legal advice;

4. made with the client's expectation of confidentiality;

5. and not in furtherance of a future crime or illegal act;

6. provided the client has not waived the privilege by disclosing the communications to third parties or by consenting to disclosure by attorneys or legal assistants.

Courtesy of The National Federation of Paralegal Associations http://www.paralegals.org

State and Local Constitutions

As most legal professionals know, state and local governments have their own constitutions. In many areas of criminal procedure, the protections afforded by state and local constitutions will basically mirror those protections afforded by the U.S. Constitution. Essentially, in many areas of criminal procedure, state and local governments have chosen to simply model their constitutional requirements after those found in the U.S. Constitution.

Interestingly, although state and local governments must provide at least as much protection to criminal suspects and defendants as that required by the U.S. Constitution, they can, if they choose, provide *more* protection for individuals, as long as such enhanced protection does not conflict or otherwise undermine the federal law. As a matter of state constitutional law or local charter, state and local governments can require their own law enforcement officers to give individuals enhanced protections when it comes to executing search warrants, interrogating suspects, or stopping vehicles.

For example, in *Oregon v. Kennedy* (1982),[25] the U.S. Supreme Court ruled that the Fifth Amendment ban on double jeopardy did not preclude the state from prosecuting a defendant a second time for the same offense after the defendant

Law Line 8-7
State Constitutions

successfully moved for a mistrial in the first case. The Court found that, because the defendant's request for a mistrial was not caused by prosecutorial or judicial conduct *intended* to provoke the defendant into moving for a mistrial, the state could proceed with a second trial. But after the case was remanded to the Oregon Supreme Court, the state court interpreted the state's double jeopardy clause, found in Article I, section 12 of the Oregon Constitution, to preclude a second trial.[26] The state court ruled that, under the state's double jeopardy clause, a second trial is prohibited if (1) the prosecutor's misconduct was so prejudicial that it could not be cured without declaring a mistrial, (2) the prosecutor knew the conduct was improper, and (3) the prosecutor either intended a mistrial or was indifferent to the possibility. In short, the Oregon Supreme Court found that the state constitution gave defendants more protection against double jeopardy than the Fifth Amendment.

State constitutions are particularly important when it comes to a defendant's right to be charged by a grand jury. The Fifth Amendment to the U.S. Constitution states in part: "No person shall be held to answer for a capital, or otherwise infamous crime, unless on a presentment or indictment of a grand jury." But in *Hurtado v. California* (1884)[27] the U.S. Supreme Court refused to apply this requirement to the states by incorporating it through the Fourteenth Amendment Due Process Clause. The Court reasoned that the Due Process Clause was not intended to include the Fifth Amendment's indictment provision, and therefore states were not required under the federal constitution to use grand jury indictments to bring felony charges. Instead, states could use an instrument called an **information**, which allows prosecutors to directly charge a person with a felony without grand jury approval. See Chapter 9.

As explained above, shortly after *Hurtado*, the Court slowly began to incorporate or apply many of the provisions of the Bill of Rights to the states. In fact, between 1896 and 1972, the Court used the Fourteenth Amendment's Due Process clause to incrementally incorporate nearly all of the provisions of the Bill of Rights. But the Court has not reversed its ruling in *Hurtado*, and thus, today the grand jury provision remains inapplicable to the states. Nevertheless, approximately half of all states employ some form of a grand jury indictment system as a requirement under their own state constitutions or statutes. The other half still permit felonies to be charged by way of an information. As a result, in state criminal cases, particularly those involving felony charges, state constitutions play an important role in determining the defendant's grand jury rights.

IN THE FIELD

The important thing for legal professionals to keep in mind in state criminal cases is that, in addition to federal constitutional standards, the home-state constitution can be a critical source for criminal procedure. There may be advantages to your client/employer in providing the criminal court with both areas of constitutional law in the event that the court finds the state or local constitution provides greater standards than those required under the federal constitution. This also can have important implications for appealing or otherwise processing state criminal actions in federal courts. As a result, when preparing legal motions, briefs, or other documents in state cases, it may be important to cite both the federal constitutional standard and the state/local standard for the relevant criminal procedure.

Federal Procedures

Within the United States Code, many laws related to criminal procedure are found in Title 18. Although enacted by Congress in the form of statutes, these laws are often referred to as the *Federal Rules of Criminal Procedure.* These rules provide basic statutory requirements for processing criminal cases. As reflected in Figure 8-5, they include rules requiring that defendants receive preliminary hearings (Rule 5.1), rules explaining how to subpoena a witness (Rule 17), and rules for conducting closing arguments during trial (Rule 29.1).

Law Line 8-8
Federal Rules of Criminal Procedure

Federal Rules of Criminal Procedure
rules of criminal procedure enacted by Congress in the form of statutes

FIGURE 8-5 **Index to Federal Rules of Criminal Procedure**

Federal Rules of Criminal Procedure (2009)

I. **Applicability**
   - 1. Scope; Definitions
   - 2. Interpretation

II. **Preliminary Proceedings**
   - 3. The Complaint
   - 4. Arrest Warrant or Summons on a Complaint
   - 5. Initial Appearance
       5.1. Preliminary Hearing

III. **The Grand Jury, The Indictment, and the Information**
   - 6. The Grand Jury
   - 7. The Indictment and the Information
   - 8. Joinder of Offenses or Defendants
   - 9. Arrest Warrant or Summons on an Indictment or Information

IV. **Arraignment And Preparation For Trial**
   - 10. Arraignment
   - 11. Pleas
   - 12. Defenses and Objections—When and How Presented—By Pleading or Motion—Motion for Judgment on the Pleadings
       12.1. Notice of an Alibi Defense
       12.2. Notice of an Insanity Defense; Mental Examination
       12.3. Notice of a Public-Authority Defense
       12.4. Disclosure Statement
   - 13. Joint Trial of Separate Cases
   - 14. Relief from Prejudicial Joinder
   - 15. Depositions
   - 16. Discovery and Inspection
   - 17. Subpoena
       17.1. Pretrial Conference

V. **VENUE**
   - 18. Place of Prosecution and Trial
   - 19. [Reserved]
   - 20. Transfer for Plea and Sentence
   - 21. Transfer for Trial
   - 22. [Transferred]

VI. **Trial**
   - 23. Jury or Nonjury Trial
   - 24. Trial Jurors

(continued)

FIGURE 8-5 **Continued**

- 25. Judge's Disability
- 26. Taking Testimony
  - 26.1. Foreign Law Determination
  - 26.2. Producing a Witness's Statement
  - 26.3. Mistrial
- 27. Proving an Official Record
- 28. Interpreters
- 29. Motion for a Judgment of Acquittal
  - 29.1. Closing Argument
- 30. Jury Instructions
- 31. Jury Verdict

VII. Post-Conviction Procedures
- 32. Sentencing and Judgment
  - 32.1. Revoking or Modifying Probation or Supervised Release
  - 32.2. Criminal Forfeiture
- 33. New Trial
- 34. Arresting Judgment
- 35. Correcting or Reducing a Sentence
- 36. Clerical Error
- 37. [Reserved]
- 38. Staying a Sentence or a Disability
- 39. [Reserved]

VIII. Supplementary And Special Proceedings
- 40. Arrest for Failing to Appear in Another District
- 41. Search and Seizure
- 42. Criminal Contempt

IX. General Provisions
- 43. Defendant's Presence
- 44. Right to and Appointment of Counsel
- 45. Computing and Extending Time
- 46. Release from Custody; Supervising Detention
- 47. Motions and Supporting Affidavits
- 48. Dismissal
- 49. Serving and Filing Papers
  - 49.1. Privacy Protection For Filings Made with the Court
- 50. Prompt Disposition
- 51. Preserving Claimed Error
- 52. Harmless and Plain Error
- 53. Courtroom Photographing and Broadcasting Prohibited
- 54. [Transferred]
- 55. Records
- 56. When Court Is Open
- 57. District Court Rules
- 58. Petty Offenses and Other Misdemeanors
- 59. Matters Before a Magistrate Judge
- 60. Victim's Rights
- 61. Title

For example, in cases where a defendant is seeking to assert an insanity defense (see Chapter 7) in response to federal criminal charges, the Federal Rules of Criminal Procedure require a defendant to provide notice of such a defense to the prosecutor in advance of trial. Specifically, Rule 12.2(a) provides:

> A defendant who intends to assert a defense of insanity at the time of the alleged offense must so notify an attorney for the government in writing within the time provided for filing a pretrial motion, or at any later time the court sets, and file a copy of the notice with the clerk. A defendant who fails to do so cannot rely on an insanity defense. The court may, for good cause, allow the defendant to file the notice late, grant additional trial-preparation time, or make other appropriate orders.

Keep in mind that this rule, like all other rules of criminal procedure, is established by legislative statute. As a result, its textual requirements and procedural implementation must comply with any and all constitutional standards for criminal procedure. And so, for example, a criminal defense attorney's failure to timely file a notice of an insanity plea pursuant to Federal Rule of Criminal Procedure 12.2(a), thereby resulting in the district court barring the defendant from asserting this defense at trial, may raise constitutional issues in the case. Most notably, the defense attorney's deficient performance may result in constitutional claims of ineffective assistance of counsel under the Sixth Amendment to the U.S. Constitution. See Chapter 13. Accordingly, in reviewing and implementing rules of criminal procedure, legal professionals must always be mindful of other constitutional and statutory standards that might be involved in the case.

IN THE FIELD

Legal professionals would be hard-pressed memorize all of the federal rules related to criminal procedure. And even if you could, it probably would not be a good idea, as these laws and rules can be altered by Congress. The bottom line is that, no matter how much you might think you know the rules or laws that apply to a given case, it is always best to review these standards from scratch for each new case. Even if the standards have not changed, you might read the law in a different light or notice a section you have never used, which in turn might assist your client/employer.

State and Local Procedures

Like their federal counterpart, state legislatures have adopted criminal procedures, which are found within the statutes. Delaware, for example, has placed most of its rules for criminal procedure in Title 11 of its code. As illustrated by Figure 8-6, Title 11 contains several chapters. The topics of these chapters range from arrests to sentencing and from search warrants to extradition. And within these chapters, there are more detailed sections. So, for example, in Title 11 of the Delaware Code you will find Chapter 35, which contains section 3511. This might be cited in a shorthand version as 35 Del.C. 3511. There you will find legislative standards for videotaping the testimony of witnesses under the age of twelve in criminal cases.

In most situations, state statutory procedures for criminal cases must provide at least as much protection for defendants and suspects as that required by the U.S. Constitution. In addition, state statutes must also conform to the home state's constitution. And in some cases, a state's constitutional standards for protecting

FIGURE 8-6 **Index of Delaware Code**

Delaware Title 11—Crimes and Criminal Procedure

- CHAPTER 1 — INTRODUCTORY PROVISIONS
- CHAPTER 2 — GENERAL PROVISIONS CONCERNING OFFENSES
- CHAPTER 3 — PROVING AND DISPROVING CRIMINAL GUILT
- CHAPTER 4 — DEFENSES TO CRIMINAL LIABILITY
- CHAPTER 5 — SPECIFIC OFFENSES
- CHAPTER 15 — ORGANIZED CRIME AND RACKETEERING
- CHAPTER 17 — GENERAL PROVISIONS
- CHAPTER 19 — ARREST AND COMMITMENT; FRESH PURSUIT
- CHAPTER 21 — RELEASE OF PERSONS ACCUSED OF CRIMES
- CHAPTER 23 — SEARCH AND SEIZURE
- CHAPTER 24 — WIRETAPPING, ELECTRONIC SURVEILLANCE AND INTERCEPTION OF COMMUNICATIONS
- CHAPTER 25 — EXTRADITION AND DETAINERS
- CHAPTER 27 — JURISDICTION AND VENUE
- CHAPTER 31 — INDICTMENT AND INFORMATION
- CHAPTER 33 — TRIAL JURORS
- CHAPTER 35 — WITNESSES AND EVIDENCE
- CHAPTER 39 — SENTENCE, JUDGMENT, EXECUTION AND MANDATORY TESTING
- CHAPTER 41 — FINES, COSTS, PENALTIES AND FORFEITURES
- CHAPTER 42 — CLASSIFICATION OF OFFENSES; SENTENCES
- CHAPTER 43 — SENTENCING, PROBATION, PAROLE AND PARDONS
- CHAPTER 45 — APPEAL; STAY OF EXECUTION; POSTCONVICTION REMEDY
- CHAPTER 51 — SUPERIOR COURT
- CHAPTER 53 — COURT OF COMMON PLEAS
- CHAPTER 59 — JUSTICES OF THE PEACE
- CHAPTER 65 — DEPARTMENT OF CORRECTION
- CHAPTER 67 — BOOT CAMP INTENSIVE INCARCERATION
- CHAPTER 82 — CAPITOL POLICE
- CHAPTER 83 — STATE POLICE
- CHAPTER 84 — DELAWARE POLICE TRAINING PROGRAM
- CHAPTER 85 — STATE BUREAU OF IDENTIFICATION
- CHAPTER 86 — DELAWARE CRIMINAL JUSTICE INFORMATION SYSTEM
- CHAPTER 87 — CRIMINAL JUSTICE COUNCIL
- CHAPTER 88 — DELAWARE COUNTY AND MUNICIPAL POLICE/ OFIREFIGHTER PENSION PLAN
- CHAPTER 89 — STATISTICAL ANALYSIS CENTER
- CHAPTER 89A — DELAWARE COUNTY AND MUNICIPAL POLICE/ OFIREFIGHTERS' RETIREE PENSION PLAN
- CHAPTER 90 — COMPENSATION FOR INNOCENT VICTIMS OF CRIME
- CHAPTER 91 — DISTRIBUTION OF MONEYS RECEIVED AS RESULT OF COMMISSION OF CRIME
- CHAPTER 92 — LAW-ENFORCEMENT OFFICERS' BILL OF RIGHTS
- CHAPTER 93 — POLICE CHIEF DUE PROCESS
- CHAPTER 94 — VICTIMS' BILL OF RIGHTS
- CHAPTER 95 — VICTIM-OFFENDER MEDIATION
- CHAPTER 96 — PROTECTION OF WITNESSES

the rights of the accused are more substantial than those required by the federal constitution. As a result, questions can arise as to whether a state's statutory standard measures up to federal or state constitutional requirements. In these cases, the legislative standards should be challenged as being unconstitutional.

Law Line 8-9
State Codes

By way of illustration, consider *Furman v. Georgia* (1972), a case in which the Supreme Court invalidated Georgia's death penalty law because it failed to provide sufficient procedural safeguards to ensure that juries in death penalty cases would not apply capital punishment in an arbitrary and capricious manner. At the time, Georgia (and several other states) had a law that allowed juries to recommend death sentences for convicted defendants under certain circumstances. This law, however, did not provide juries with enough guidelines when considering death sentences. As a result, the Court found the law unconstitutional under the Eighth Amendment provision against cruel and unusual punishment. Later, Georgia revised its statute to include a list of mitigating and aggravating factors that juries had to consider when deliberating on the death penalty. And in *Gregg v. Georgia* (1976), the Court found these revised legislative standards to be constitutionally acceptable.

Local governments may have legislative standards for criminal procedure found within codified ordinances. For example, the City of Grandview, Texas, adopted an ordinance that set standards for the issuance of citations by law enforcement.[28] This ordinance establishes who is authorized to issue citations for criminal violations of the city's code and the manner and form such citations must follow. Specifically, Sections 3.2 and 3.3 of the ordinance provide:

Authority to Issue Citations Pursuant to this Chapter, and the scope of their assigned duties, a citation may be issued by any of the following individuals as may be designated by the City Council:

    a. Police Officer
    b. Animal Control Officer
    c. Building Inspector

Form & Content of Citation A citation issued under this section must be in a form approved by the Municipal Court Clerk that includes the following information:

    a. the name and address (or other identifying information such as date of birth, or driver's license number and physical description, and telephone number) of the person cited;
    b. the offense for which the person is charged;
    c. the date and location of the offense;
    d. an appearance date;
    e. a statement requiring the person receiving the citation to appear at municipal court on or before the appearance date indicated on the citation;
    f. a statement of the person's promise to respond to the citation, pursuant to Article 27.14 of the Code of Criminal Procedure, by the appearance date indicated on the citation, including a place for the person cited to provide the person's signature; and
    g. the signature of the person issuing the citation.

In most criminal cases, local ordinances and resolutions will not provide considerable requirements for criminal procedures. But there are times when local governments do prescribe particular protocols for officers when conducting investigations, administering citations, or making arrests. If so, these standards could be relevant in reviewing a criminal case that is either brought under local law or initiated by local law enforcement.

ordinances or resolutions legislative enactments by local governments

Overall, it is important for legal professionals to carefully read and consider legislative standards that impact their criminal cases. Do not assume that, because you have worked on similar cases in the past, you know how the statutes apply. Laws can change. Legislators can amend, replace, or revoke their statutes. Moreover, in re-reading laws that you may know generally, you may find provisions or words that have new meaning because of the unique facts of your case. Again, do not assume that you know the statutes or rules in a given case. Start from scratch in each case by obtaining the relevant legal standards for your case and reading them thoroughly in light of the facts you have in your present case, and be sure to have them available for all proceedings.

Administrative Rules

administrative rules
legal standards set by executive or independent agencies

Administrative rules, adopted by executive agencies at the federal, state, and local levels, can also play a very important role in processing criminal cases, especially those cases involving highly technical forensic investigations or scientific tests.

As an illustration, most states have administrative regulations regarding the proper method for conducting breathalyzer and other tests on persons suspected of driving under the influence of alcohol or drugs (DUI). Testing a person for blood alcohol content is a scientific procedure, and to be considered credible evidence in a criminal case it must meet certain technical requirements. In Ohio, the state department of health, an administrative agency, establishes the technical requirements or "administrative rules" for performing blood alcohol tests during DUI investigations. See Figure 8-7. These requirements are outlined in the Ohio Administrative Code in the form of administrative rules. One rule is Ohio Administrative Rule 3701-53-04(A), which states:

(A) A senior operator shall perform an instrument check on approved evidential breath testing instruments . . . no less frequently than once every seven days in accordance with the appropriate instrument checklist for the instrument being used. The instrument check may be performed anytime up to one hundred and ninety-two hours after the last instrument check.

Law Line 8-10
Administrative Code

FIGURE 8-7 **Ohio Administrative Code**

Chapter 3701-53 Alcohol and Drug Testing; Permits for Personnel

Rule No.	Title
3701-53-01	Techniques or methods
3701-53-02	Breath Tests
3701-53-03	Blood, urine and bodily substance tests
3701-53-04	Instrument check
3701-53-05	Collection and handling of blood and urine specimens
3701-53-06	Laboratory requirements
3701-53-07	Qualifications of personnel
3701-53-08	Surveys and proficiency examinations
3701-53-09	Permits
3701-53-10	Revocation and denial of permits

A police officer holds a breathalyzer alcohol meter while a dejected young man blows into the machine to register his blood alcohol level after being pulled over for drunk driving.

Under this rule, a breathalyzer machine or other breath-testing equipment must be calibrated properly before its results can be considered valid in a court of law. If officers fail to properly test the equipment or do not conduct the test according to required scientific standards, the test result indicating a person's blood alcohol content may be deemed invalid and thus inadmissible as evidence in a criminal trial. Read the opinion in *State v. Schmitt* to see the role administrative rules can sometimes play in criminal cases, particularly the administrative standards used to perform breathalyzer tests during DUI stops.

CAPSTONE CASE *State v. Schmitt,* 101 Ohio St. 3d 79, 801 N.E.2d 446 (2004)

In case No. 2002-1807, in June 2001, a state trooper stopped a vehicle driven by defendant-appellee, Kevin K. Schmitt, on State Route 219 in Mercer County after observing Schmitt weaving and driving left of center. The trooper smelled a strong odor of alcohol on Schmitt and observed that Schmitt was glassy-eyed and that his speech was slow. The trooper conducted three field sobriety tests: the horizontal gaze nystagmus test ("HGN"), the one-leg-stand test, and the walk-and-turn test. During these exercises, the trooper observed Schmitt's poor balance and inability to follow certain instructions. Schmitt also took a portable breath test, which yielded a result of .143 percent. Based upon the results of these tests and his observations, the trooper placed Schmitt under arrest for driving under the influence ("DUI"). Schmitt refused to take a breathalyzer test.

Having been convicted of three DUI offenses within the last six years, Schmitt was indicted on a charge of a felony DUI pursuant to R.C. 4511.19(A)(1). Schmitt filed a motion to suppress all testimony related to the field sobriety tests. For purposes of the motion, the parties stipulated that the field sobriety tests were not administered in strict compliance with National Highway Traffic Safety Administration ("NHTSA") standards. The trial court granted the motion to suppress. In a two-to-one decision, the court of appeals for Mercer County affirmed the decision of the trial court, citing *State v. Homan* (2000). . . .

(continued)

(continued)

In Homan, 89 Ohio St.3d 421, 732 N.E.2d 952, paragraph one of the syllabus, we held, "In order for the results of a field sobriety test to serve as evidence of probable cause to arrest, the police must have administered the test in strict compliance with standardized testing procedures." In reaching this holding, we noted that even minor deviations from the standardized procedures can bias the test results. Quoting from an NHTSA manual, we stressed that " '[i]f any one of the standardized field sobriety test elements is changed, the validity is compromised.' " Therefore, we affirmed the judgment of the court of appeals, holding that the improper administration of the tests made their results inherently unreliable.

We are initially asked to decide whether our holding in *Homan* precludes noncomplying field sobriety test results from admissibility at trial. The state argues that *Homan* is limited in its scope and that it excludes only the test results for probable-cause purposes. While we recognize that the holding of *Homan* addresses the probable-cause stage of litigation, we now extend our holding to the admissibility of such test results at trial. Whether there is probable cause to arrest depends upon whether an officer has sufficient information to cause a prudent person to believe that the suspect was driving under the influence. In the cases at bar, the issue is whether the elements of driving under the influence can be proven beyond a reasonable doubt. Since we required strict compliance with the field sobriety testing procedures to determine the lesser standard of probable cause, the same standard must apply to a determination of test-result admissibility at trial, where the standard of proof is higher and where the ultimate determination involves the defendant's guilt or innocence. Therefore, we hold that the lower courts properly suppressed the test results where the tests were not administered in accordance with standardized testing procedures.

Since our decision in *Homan*, the General Assembly has amended R.C. 4511.19. Under the amended statute, the arresting officer no longer needs to have administered field sobriety tests in strict compliance with testing standards for the test results to be admissible at trial. Instead, an officer may now testify concerning the results of a field sobriety test administered in substantial compliance with the testing standards. Consequently, we recognize that this portion of our decision will have limited applicability . . . .

With regard to the second issue before us, the following question has been certified to our court: "Does *State v. Homan* [2000] preclude a law enforcement officer from testifying at trial regarding observations made during a defendant's performance of nonscientific standardized field sobriety tests when those tests are not administered in strict compliance with the National Highway Traffic Safety Administration Guidelines?" The defendants contend that where the underlying tests were administered improperly, the reliability of the entire test process is called into question and *all* facts and circumstances related to the testing, including officer observation, are unreliable and should be suppressed. Conversely, the state argues that even if the test results are excluded, the observations made by the arresting officer during even flawed test administration are proper lay testimony admissible under Evid.R. 701.

In *Homan*, although we excluded the noncomplying field test results from our consideration, we nevertheless concluded that the totality of the circumstances surrounding the defendant's arrest supported a finding of probable cause. In particular, we found relevant the officer's observations of the defendant, including the fact that he observed erratic driving, that the defendant's eyes were red and glassy, and that she smelled of alcohol. These observations clearly fall within the realm of Evid.R. 701, since they are rationally based on the perceptions of the witness and are helpful to a clear understanding of a fact in issue.

(continued)

The certified conflict concerns whether an officer's observations regarding a defendant's performance on nonscientific field sobriety tests should likewise be admissible as lay evidence of intoxication. It is generally accepted that virtually any lay witness, including a police officer, may testify as to whether an individual appears intoxicated. Such lay testimony is often crucial in prosecuting drunk driving cases. Moreover, such evidence is relevant and admissible pursuant to Evid.R. 401 and Evid.R. 402. Thus, courts have recognized that "[t]o prove impaired driving ability, the state can rely on physiological factors (*e.g.,* slurred speech, bloodshot eyes, odor of alcohol) and coordination tests (*e.g.,* field sobriety tests) to demonstrate that a person's physical and mental ability to drive is impaired." . . . .

The nonscientific field sobriety tests involve simple exercises, such as walking heel-to-toe in a straight line (walk-and-turn test). The manner in which defendant performs these tests may easily reveal to the average layperson whether the individual is intoxicated. We see no reason to treat an officer's testimony regarding the defendant's performance on a nonscientific field sobriety test any differently from his testimony addressing other indicia of intoxication, such as slurred speech, bloodshot eyes, and odor of alcohol. In all of these cases, the officer is testifying about his perceptions of the witness, and such testimony helps resolve the issue of whether the defendant was driving while intoxicated.

Unlike the actual test results, which may be tainted, the officer's testimony is based upon his or her firsthand observation of the defendant's conduct and appearance. Such testimony is being offered to assist the jury in determining a fact in issue, i.e., whether a defendant was driving while intoxicated. Moreover, defense counsel will have the opportunity to cross-examine the officer to point out any inaccuracies and weaknesses. We conclude that an officer's observations in these circumstances are permissible lay testimony under Evid.R. 701. Therefore, we answer the certified question in the negative and hold that a law enforcement officer may testify at trial regarding observations made during a defendant's performance of nonscientific standardized field sobriety tests.

[W]e find that the trial court properly excluded the results of the noncomplying field sobriety tests. However, the lower courts erred in suppressing the arresting officer's trial testimony concerning his observations of the defendant's performance of the nonscientific standardized field sobriety tests. . . .

WHAT DO *YOU* THINK?

1. Should a police officer's failure to follow strict and technical requirements for administering blood alcohol tests be grounds for excluding evidence of the defendant's intoxication?

2. In what ways do scientific methods and techniques make it more challenging for defendants and prosecutors to litigate DUI cases?

IN THE FIELD

In general, legal professionals must be aware that administrative rules can play an important role in many criminal cases, especially in cases where forensic or other scientific evidence is involved. There also may be times when a medical, engineering, or other technical expert might be needed to review the relevant evidence in the case and to assess it under the administrative rules. But this process all begins with the recognition that there might be a relevant issue of criminal procedure found within administrative rules.

Law Line 8-11
Bureau of Alcohol, Tobacco, and Firearms
www.atf.treas.gov

Local Rules and Practices

Still other standards for criminal procedure might be developed by federal, state, and local courts, through interpretation of constitutional or statutory sources or simply as an expression of their own preferences. These are known as **local rules and practices**. Often these provincial standards come in the form of local rules set forth by the local courts. In the federal judiciary, individual courts are authorized to prescribe rules for the conduct of their business.[29] And although the local court rules must be consistent with federal law and the federal rules of practice and procedure, they can still vary from jurisdiction to jurisdiction.

Many of these rules involve attorney admissions, the appointment of counsel, or technical requirements for filing motions and briefs. Other rules may establish standards for decorum within the courtroom, how to file subpoenas, or whether attorneys are allowed to talk to jurors after a verdict. As illustrated by Figure 8-8, the federal District Court for the Middle District of Alabama has a number of local rules that apply to criminal cases within its courts. Particular standards are set for the appointment of counsel, the facsimile filing of pleadings, and the emergency filing of motions. These rules are unique to the Middle District of Alabama and supplement the constitutional and statutory requirements for criminal procedure that apply in all federal cases.

Even within the same jurisdiction, there are times when different judges or courtroom officials will have different practices for conducting proceedings. Some individual judges may have preferences regarding how motions are to be written, how exhibits must be organized, whether you can talk to a client or associate during the proceedings, or where attorneys must stand during court proceedings. Some judges can be very strict, requiring adherence to formal courtroom policies and expectations. Other judges may have more relaxed standards, imposing few personal preferences outside of the statutory requirements and local rules. For example, under Rule 24(a) of the Federal Rules of Criminal Procedure, in federal jury trials, during voir dire (the jury selection stage of the trial), judges have the discretion to examine prospective jurors themselves or they may permit the attorneys for the parties to do so. Under this rule, the method of jury selection in federal cases is ultimately up to the judge's discretion. Thus, in the federal cases, jury selection is a matter of local practice and preference.

FIGURE 8-8 **Local Rules for the United States District Court
for the Middle District of Alabama**

PART 2. CRIMINAL RULES
[Cite as M.D. Ala. LCrR]

X. General Provisions
44.1 Appointed Counsel.
44.2 Notice of Appearance Required for Retained Counsel.
49.1 Removal of Court Files and Return or Destruction of Exhibits.
49.2 Emergency Filing of Pleadings, Motions and Other Papers.
49.3 Facsimile Filing Restrictions.
49.4 Identification of Counsel on Pleadings, Motions and Other Papers.
55.1 Removal of Court Files and Return or Destruction of Exhibits.
56.1 Emergency Filing of Pleadings, Motions and Other Papers.
57.1 Attorneys: Admission to Practice and Disciplinary Proceedings.
58.1 Forfeiture of Collateral in Lieu of Appearance.
58.2 Assignment of Duties to Magistrate Judges.

IN THE FIELD

As a legal professional, it is important that you not only learn the formal standards, rules, and procedures for each case, but that you get to know the preferences and customs for the particular courtroom and judge assigned to each matter. In learning the local legal culture, you should be aware that particular practices or customs must be constitutional and otherwise legal in order to be valid. There are times when you might see a regular practice in a courtroom, jail, law office, or police station and ask, "why is it done that way?" And in response, you might be told, "that's just the way we do it" or "we've always done it that way." Such explanations, by themselves, do not necessarily satisfy the legal standards for criminal procedure. In these situations, you should analyze the practice or policy in accordance with all of the relevant legal standards you have come to learn regarding criminal procedure.

INTERPRETING SOURCES OF CRIMINAL PROCEDURE

Inevitably, at some point in your career as a legal professional, you will hear a supervisor or lead attorney on a case say, "I need a case that says [fill in the blank]." In this situation, a lawyer has found a rule or standard that might apply to a given case, but realizes that the words found within the legal standard are in need of interpretation and is looking to find a judicial opinion that interprets the standard in the client's favor. This situation illustrates that, no matter how efficient you might be as a legal researcher and no matter how many relevant sources of criminal procedure you locate for a case, these standards amount to just words on a page and ultimately it will depend on human beings to read them, interpret them, and apply them in a particular factual context. In short, words do not define themselves; people define and give meaning to words.

Take for example the cruel and unusual punishment clause of the Eighth Amendment. Generally speaking, this provision is supposed to prohibit government from inflicting cruel and unusual punishment upon individuals. See Chapter 14. The problem, however, is that the words *cruel* and *unusual* are nowhere defined in the Constitution and the words themselves are not self-explanatory. Indeed, one might argue that these terms are highly subjective in nature. What is considered cruel to one person may be perfectly appropriate to another. And what is highly unusual to some may be absolutely ordinary to others. Many of the U.S. Supreme Court's cases on the subject illustrate this point.

For example, in *Atkins v. Virginia* (2002)[30] the Supreme Court held in a 5-4 ruling that the death penalty could not be imposed on individuals with mental retardation. This ruling reversed a 1989 decision that had allowed such executions to occur. And in *Roper v. Simmons* (2005)[31], the Court ruled 5-4 that the Eighth Amendment bars the execution of juveniles (persons who were under eighteen years of age at the time of their offense). This ruling reversed another 1989 opinion, which had allowed persons sixteen-years-of-age and older to be executed. Both of these rulings were sharply divided, revealing that the nine justices, all with extraordinary legal educations and some of the most highly regarded training in the legal profession, could not agree on the meaning of the terms *cruel* and *unusual*. The debate over the meaning of cruel and unusual is further reflected by many other Court rulings regarding the Eighth Amendment. See Figure 8-9.

The point is, printed words only go so far. And within the world of criminal procedure—just like all other areas of law—it is the responsibility of those given

Law Line 8-13

Atkins v. Virginia (2002)

FIGURE 8-9 **What Forms of Punishment are "Cruel and Unusual" Under the Eighth Amendment?**

A. *Graham v. Florida* (2010)
Life without parole for minors in non-homicide cases
B. *Hudson v. McMillian* (1992)
Beating by prison guards of a handcuffed inmate in prison
C. *Ingraham v. Wright* (1977)
Use of corporal punishment in Florida public schools
D. *Roper v. Simmons* (2005)
Death penalty for crime committed when defendant was a minor
E. *Harmelin v. Michigan* (1991)
Life imprisonment for the first-time offense of possession of cocaine
F. *Kennedy v. Louisiana* (2008)
Death penalty for the rape of a child where the victim did not die
G. *Gregg v. Georgia* (1976)
Capital punishment in general
H. *Edmund v. Florida* (1982)
Death penalty for an accomplice to a murder who does not directly kill the victim
I. *Glass v. Louisiana* (1985)
Use of electrocution to execute defendants
J. *Atkins v. Virginia* (2002)
Executing mentally retarded individuals

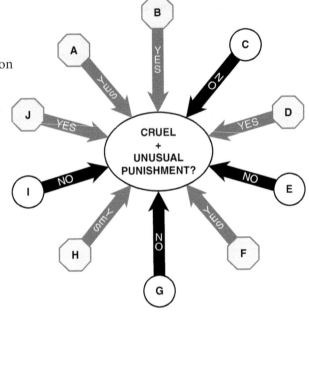

the authority to interpret and apply legal language to give conclusive meaning to the printed words. Many of the legal phrases applied in criminal procedure, such as "unreasonable search and seizure," "speedy trial," "assistance of counsel," "excessive bail," and "probable cause" are not well defined or perfectly prescribed. Law is a social science, not a hard science. As a result, it is ultimately up to jurists to determine the meaning and scope of these terms based on some source of constitutional values. What must a law enforcement officer do to make a search unreasonable? How long must a criminal defendant wait for trial before such trial is no longer speedy? How much evidence constitutes probable cause? These questions, frequently left unanswered by the explicit texts of constitutions, statutes, or rules, ultimately require the application of values from beyond the text. Within the legal jurisprudence of criminal justice, this has resulted in the creation of a variety of doctrines, tests, rules, and exceptions that make criminal procedure one of the most dynamic and fluctuating forms of constitutional law.

In the end, given the linguistic challenges posed by language—regardless of whether it comes from a constitution, statute, administrative rule, or local court policy—the task for many legal professionals will come down to assessing and trying to shape what words should mean in a given case. Ultimately, it will be the legal responsibility of judges and/or juries to given final and authoritative meaning to the words, but legal professionals can play a big role in this process by identifying the relevant procedural standards and providing authorities with materials that assist them in understanding and applying these standards.

IN THE FIELD

To be an effective legal professional in the American criminal justice system, you must be aware that the constitutional standards, statutory requirements, and other rules and practices for criminal procedure do not occur in an isolated forum. They occur in a larger system of legal authorities, with multiple layers of law, and among different branches of government. Because of this, you should consider all layers and branches of authority that might apply to a given case. And once you identify these authorities, do not take it for granted that they automatically conform to the constitutional or legal requirements established for the system as a whole. Effective legal professionals learn to examine a case and its legal underpinnings from different perspectives, and where appropriate, are willing to question and otherwise challenge the standard way of doing things.

CHAPTER **SUMMARY**

- Criminal procedure is a body of law that addresses the process used by authorities to administer a criminal case. Whereas criminal law concerns the substance of the criminal act for which a person is charged, criminal procedure addresses the process used by authorities to investigate or prosecute individuals for violations of criminal statutes.
- Within the American system of justice, criminal procedure occurs within a governmental system of federalism and checks and balances. This involves multiple layers of government—federal, state, and local, and multiple divisions or branches of government—legislative, executive, and judicial. Each layer and branch of governmental authority can impose standards for criminal procedure.
- The Supremacy Clause of Article VI of the U.S. Constitution generally ensures that the standards set forth in the federal constitution are the supreme law of the land, superior in effect to all standards established by state and local authorities.

- Under the incorporation doctrine, state and local authorities must comply with nearly all of the provisions within the Bill of Rights.
- States have their own constitutions, which can afford suspects and defendants even greater legal protections than those found in the federal constitution.
- In addition, statutes passed by legislative branches at all levels of government also contain certain requirements for processing criminal cases.
- Executive agencies may also have standards that impact criminal procedure. These standards are known as administrative rules.
- Local courts also have rules and practices that govern their courtrooms.
- Whatever the source, the written standards for criminal procedure do not define themselves. They are just a starting point. Ultimately, it is up to authorities within the criminal justice system to interpret and apply these standards to a given case.

KEY **TERMS**

administrative rules
assistance of counsel provision
compulsory process clause
confrontation clause
constitution
criminal procedure
cruel and unusual punishment clause
Due Process Clause (Fifth Amendment)

Due Process Clause (Fourteenth Amendment)
excessive bail
excessive fines
federal question
Federal Rules of Criminal Procedure
incorporation doctrine
information clause
jury trial clause

local rules and practices
ordinances or resolutions
procedural due process
public trial provision
revised codes
self-incrimination provision
speedy trial provision
statutes or codes
substantive due process

QUESTIONS FOR **DISCUSSION**

1. What are the differences between criminal law and criminal procedure? What implications do these differences have on legal professionals in the criminal justice system?

2. How does the American system of federalism affect criminal procedure?

3. What are some of the basic procedural safeguards established by the U.S. Constitution for criminal cases?

4. Can state constitutions provide standards for criminal procedure that differ from those set forth in the U.S. Constitution?

5. What is the incorporation doctrine and how does it affect states in administering criminal justice?

6. How might administrative rules impact the procedure for criminal cases?

7. What are local rules and practices? Where are they found and how might they affect the processing of criminal cases?

8. What does it mean to say "words do not define themselves?" How does this observation impact the role of the legal professional in interpreting and applying legal standards for criminal procedure?

REFERENCES

1. Bernard Shaw (1856–1950), *Man and Superman,* "Maxims for Revolutionists," (1903).

2. *Olmstead v. United States,* 277 U.S. 438 (1928), Justice Brandeis dissenting.

3. *People v. Defore,* 242 N.Y. 13, 21, 150 N.E. 585, 587 (1926).

4. *United States v. Rayburn House Office Building, Room 2113, Washington, D.C.,* 497 F.3d 654 (D.C. Cir. 2007).

5. See *Wolf v. Colorado,* 338 U.S. 25 (1949) and *Carroll v. United States,* 267 U.S. 132 (1925).

6. See *Hurtado v. California,* 110 U.S. 516 (1884) (discussing the grand jury provision but refusing to apply it to state prosecutions).

7. See *Benton v. Maryland,* 395 U.S. 784 (1969).

8. See *Malloy v. Hogan,* 378 U.S. 1 (1964).

9. See *Ward v. City of Monroeville,* 409 U.S. 57 (1972) (barring mayor from presiding over trial because of city's financial interest in imposing fines); *Batson v. Kentucky,* 476 U.S. 79 (1989) (precluding prosecutor's use of race to exclude jurors during voir dire).

10. See *Klopfer v. North Carolina,* 386 U.S. 213 (1967).

11. See *In re Oliver,* 333 U.S. 257 (1948).

12. See *Duncan v. Louisiana,* 391 U.S. 145 (1968).

13. See *Pointer v. Texas,* 380 U.S. 400 (1965).

14. See *Washington v. Texas,* 388 U.S. 14 (1967).

15. See *Gideon v. Wainwright,* 372 U.S. 335 (1963) (applicable to felony cases); *Argersinger v. Hamlin,* 407 U.S. 25 (1972) (applicable to misdemeanor cases if sentence includes imprisonment).

16. See *Robinson v. California,* 370 U.S. 660 (1962).

17. *Ashcroft v. Free Speech Coalition,* 535 U.S. 234 (2002).

18. *The Church of Lukumi Babalu Aye v. City of Hialeah,* 508 U.S. 520, 113 S. Ct. 2217 (1991).

19. *Griswold v. Connecticut,* 381 U.S. 479 (1965).

20. Note that the Fifth Amendment contains a due process clause as well; it has been interpreted to apply to the federal government. See *Bolling v. Sharpe,* 347 U.S. 497 (1954).

21. 395 U.S. 784 (1969).

22. 378 U.S. 1 (1964).

23. See Robert Dowlut, "Federal and State Constitutional Guarantees to Arms," University of Dayton Law Review 15 (1989): 1–89.

24. 539 U.S. 558 (2003).

25. 456 U.S. 667 (1982).

26. *State v. Kennedy,* 295 Or. 260, 666 P.2d 1316 (1983); see also, *Bauder v. State,* 921 S.W.2d 696 (Tex. Crim. App. 1996) (Texas Constitution precludes retrial if the prosecutor should have known that his or her conduct might provoke a mistrial.)

27. 110 U.S. 516 (1884).

28. See http://www.cityofgrandview.org/index.php?tag=0fb2f61318f01ebdordinances%5Cgrandview_ordinances_2005_1122.pdf

29. 28 U.S.C. § 2071(a).

30. 536 U.S. 304 (2002).

31. 543 U.S. 551 (2005).

APPENDIX
DEVELOPING YOUR LEGAL ANALYSIS

A. THE LAW WHERE YOU LIVE

As addressed above, in *Hurtado v. California* (1884) the U.S. Supreme Court refused to apply the Fifth Amendment's guarantee of a grand jury indictment in capital or infamous cases (felonies) to the states. As a result, only about half of all states rely on the grand jury system to charge felonies in criminal cases. In the absence of federal constitutional mandate, how does your home state address the need for a grand jury indictment for felony offenses? Does your home state's constitution say anything about the need for grand juries in felony cases? If not, what method is required under your state's constitution or laws? And while you are reviewing your state's constitution, compare other areas of criminal procedure such as rights protecting against unreasonable searches and seizure, self-incrimination, and cruel and unusual punishment. How does the wording match up with the language of the Bill of Rights? Do any differences in the wording of your home state's constitution result in greater protection for criminal defendants?

B. INSIDE THE FEDERAL COURTS

Assume you are working with Sandy Benis, an attorney in a federal criminal case. The matter is *United States v. Thomas* and involves a criminal indictment for multiple counts of drug offenses. Ms. Benis is planning on filing a motion to suppress the drug evidence in the case but needs to know the deadline and other court requirements for filing this motion. Ms. Benis also would like to bring another attorney in on the case to assist in the matter, but the other attorney is not licensed to practice in the federal district where the case is pending. As a result, Ms. Benis will have to file a motion *pro hac vice* (a motion asking the trial court to admit a lawyer to the bar "for this matter only").

Accordingly, research the Federal Rules of Criminal Procedure, as well as any local rules for your federal district court, and identify the requirements for filing both a motion to suppress evidence and a motion *pro hac vice*. Outline these requirements in a two-page memorandum to Ms. Benis.

C. CYBER SOURCES

Assume you are working with Frank Daniels, a local state prosecutor. Authorities have just arrested a man on charges relating to selling child pornography. The alleged crime could be prosecuted both in state and federal courts because the alleged acts constitute a crime under each jurisdiction. Mr. Daniels will be meeting with the representatives from the U.S. Attorney's office to discuss who should file criminal charges against the arrested man. Before the meeting, Mr. Daniels would like to know what sexual offender registration requirements the man would face under your home-state law and what the requirements he would face under federal law.

Using the resources below, as well as any other electronic research method you find credible and helpful, identify the registration requirements for each jurisdiction, assuming that the arrested man will be convicted of selling child pornography.

FBI Crimes Against Children

http://www.fbi.gov/hq/cid/cac/registry.htm

National Center on Sexual Behavior of Youth

http://www.ncsby.org/pages/registry.htm

D. ETHICS AND PROFESSIONALISM

Assume you are working with Jane Sandford, a defense attorney who is representing Abbey Jones, a criminal defendant charged with a complicated scheme of bank fraud. The government's case against Abbey is based on a series of loan documents she provided to XYZ Bank over the course of three months. Authorities alleged that the timing and details of these documents show an intent to defraud the bank. Ms. Sandford and you have met with Abbey, during which time she disclosed many details about her interactions with the bank. This information is considered confidential attorney-client communication. Given the amount of detail, including many dates, times, and specific bank documents, Ms. Sandford has asked Abbey to prepare a written timeline of everything she did and said to XYZ Bank.

Abbey is now calling you to say that she is almost finished with the requested timeline, but would like to have her sister, Tonya, look it over before she sends it to you. It seems that Tonya was with Abbey during many of the bank interactions and may be able to confirm or otherwise assist in putting together the details for the timeline. Abbey is calling you just to make sure that this is OK. Initially, you do not see any problem with this situation, but you are a little concerned about whether Abbey's consultation with her sister might waive the attorney-client privilege that covers the timeline communication with Ms. Sandford. Review the ethical standards for confidential client communications found in the following materials, and then prepare a two-page memorandum explaining how you would respond to Abbey.

American Bar Association

http://www.abanet.org/legalservices/paralegals/downloads/ modelguidelines.pdf

National Federation Of Paralegal Associations, Inc.

http://www.paralegals.org/displaycommon.cfm?an=1& subarticlenbr=133

United States v. Stewart, 287 F. Supp. 2d 461 (S.D.N.Y. 2003).

chapter **nine**

THE BEGINNINGS OF A CRIMINAL CASE

Crime is a socio-political artifact, not a natural phenomenon. . . . We can have as much or as little crime as we please, depending on what we choose to count as criminal.
—Herbert Packer, *The Limits of Criminal Sanction* (1968)

Every society gets the kind of criminal it deserves. What is equally true is that every community gets the kind of law enforcement it insists on.
—Robert Kennedy (1925–1968)

[A]ny prosecutor who wanted to could indict a ham sandwich.
—Sol Wachtler, *After the Madness*[1]
Former New York State Chief Judge

LEARNING OBJECTIVES

After reading this chapter, you should be able to

- Appreciate the many different tasks of legal professionals in initiating and processing cases in the criminal justice system.

- Identify and understand the different ways a criminal case can be initiated by law enforcement officials.

- Understand the importance of bond hearings and the legal standards used to set a defendant's bond.

- Explain the theory and realities of a preliminary hearing.

- Discuss the process of an arraignment and/or initial appearance hearing.

- Identify and explain the difference between the pleas of guilty, not guilty, and no contest.

- Explain the complexities and procedures of grand jury hearings.

EARLY ON: THE MANY TASKS OF LEGAL PROFESSIONALS

The work of legal professionals during the early stages of a criminal case can be some of the most dynamic and challenging in the criminal justice system. In fact, the most active and uncertain time for many criminal cases comes during this initial period. The legal tasks and ethical obligations of legal professionals vary from setting to setting and from case to case. But generally speaking, the primary role of legal professionals during the initial stage of a criminal matter is to gather and transmit information. Defense attorneys, prosecutors, law enforcement officers, judges, and court staff all need information in order to do their jobs during this very dynamic and fast-paced time. Moreover, outside of the court system, victims, family members, and in some cases, news reporters also are seeking basic information about the case.

Criminal Defense

For those working on behalf of criminal defendants, there is often a lot of activity early in a criminal case. Initially, you might receive a phone call from a prospective client or his family or friends. Someone may say to you, "I've just been arrested" or "my son was just picked up by the police." In these situations, one of the first things that must be done is that the attorney with whom you are working must be assured that he or she is being retained by the client. In other words, before you or anyone else with your office can take any official action on behalf of a criminal suspect or defendant, you must be sure that the suspect or defendant wants you to represent him or her. This may involve an office meeting with prospective clients, going to the jail to meet with the prospective client, or working with his family or other representatives. It will also involve preparations for seeking bond for the client. See below.

In other situations, your involvement as a legal professional may begin well before an arrest or formal criminal charge. You or your client may receive a phone call from a detective or other law enforcement official who wants to talk with your client about a situation. In a more formal setting, your client might receive a subpoena to appear as a witness before a grand jury, or perhaps even a petit jury (trial jury). In these situations, the client has not been formally charged with an offense yet. But what he or she says during their testimony can impact their criminal fate.

In other cases, clients may know about the criminal investigation or may even be in custody pending official charges. As a legal professional, your role in this scenario might be to monitor the grand jury's docket each day to see whether your client has been indicted or otherwise charged. In rare cases, you may even be involved in preparing your client for grand jury testimony.

In still other settings, a client may come to you with nothing more than a story about something that occurred. There may be no pending charges or investigation. Some clients just may be concerned that their behavior or the behavior of those around them may have risen to criminal conduct. These situations can be a little tricky. In some cases, clients might be advised to discontinue or avoid certain behavior. In other cases, where the conduct has already occurred, the client may need to decide whether to notify law enforcement about the situation. In many ways, these types of scenarios put criminal defense lawyers in a different role. Usually, in most criminal cases, defense lawyers respond or react to criminal charges that have already been filed. But in precharge settings, the criminal defense lawyer must anticipate what will likely occur depending on the client's decisions.

Law Line 9-1
National Association of Criminal
Defense Attorneys

Prosecution

In prosecutorial settings, the role of legal professionals can vary as well, but the primary obligation is to assist law enforcement officials with the preparation of their case. This may involve working with police to determine what criminal offenses should be charged in a given factual scenario and completing a criminal complaint. In this setting, officers may have questions about what legal elements are involved in a particular offense and what type of evidentiary proof will be necessary to prove the case. Prosecutors themselves ask their legal assistants to research the elements of a case to see how courts have interpreted and applied the language of a given criminal statute.

Legal professionals can also assist during the intake stage. This typically involves meeting with alleged crime victims or other persons who wish to file criminal complaints. During this phase, legal professionals listen to people tell stories about an event that has occurred. But intake also involves the legal professional asking questions. While the crime victim or complainant's primary concern might be the facts of the case, the legal assistant must be mindful of the legal standards that apply to the alleged facts. Facts that are seemingly irrelevant to a victim might be highly relevant to whether a criminal charge should be filed. As a result, legal professionals performing intake duties must learn to ask questions that are helpful in assessing criminality.

In jurisdictions with grand juries, legal professionals can assist prosecutors with reviewing and presenting cases to the grand jury. This may involve obtaining and organizing exhibits, preparing subpoenas to serve on witnesses, working with victims and law enforcement in preparation of their testimony, preparing indictments, or simply keeping interested parties informed as to the status of the case. In jurisdictions where grand juries are not used, legal professionals can perform many of the same tasks. Prosecutors considering the filing of an information also need to be informed of the relevant facts, the credibility of potential witnesses, and strength of the evidence.

In some prosecutors' offices, legal assistants may work with alleged crime victims. Some prosecutors even have an official victim's advocate unit that serves as a liaison between the prosecutor and alleged victims. Legal professionals working with victims must be able to explain the stages and charges to alleged victims and to solicit information from these individuals that might be helpful to the government's case.

Law Line 9-2
Association of Prosecuting Attorneys

Court Assistants

Legal professionals working in court-related offices also play many roles. Some work in pretrial services, which is often an office within the court's probation department. These individuals often obtain the basic information on a defendant in preparation for the court's bond hearing and other early proceedings. In many jurisdictions, those working in pretrial services prepare a formal report or "scoring sheet" for judges to assist them in making decisions regarding the setting of bond and pretrial release. This may involve obtaining the criminal history of the defendant, documenting the nature and severity of injury allegedly caused by the defendant in the current case, and identifying the extent of contact the defendant has with the community. For many judges, these factors are central to determining whether a person will be released pending trial and, if so, under what conditions.

In many jurisdictions, legal professionals performing pretrial services work must be prepared for a fast-paced and substantial case load. When individuals are arrested and brought into the criminal justice system, legal professionals must gather as much of the necessary information as possible before the bond hearing, which in some cases might be as early as the day of the arrest or the next day thereafter.

INITIATING A CRIMINAL CASE

There are many ways a criminal case can officially begin. Perhaps the most familiar way is an *arrest*. An arrest occurs when a law enforcement officer takes a person into governmental custody or substantially restricts the person's freedom of movement under the officer's authority. Before conducting an arrest, an officer must have *probable cause* to suspect that the person being arrested committed a criminal offense. Probable cause is a legal standard that measures the amount of evidence an officer has at the time a person is taken into custody. Jurisdictions can vary as to how they view the probable cause standard, but generally, probable cause "exist[s] where the known facts and circumstances are sufficient to warrant a [person] of reasonable prudence in the belief that contraband or evidence of a crime will be found."[2]

In Chapter 11, you will learn the Fourth Amendment standards for probable cause and how to apply them in a given case for both arrests and searches and seizures. But for now, appreciate that an arrest, by itself, does not charge a person with a crime. Instead, a government-sanctioned document must be produced that officially states the specific offense(s), their elements, and the nature of a criminal accusation. Such an accusation or charge can come in the form of a criminal complaint, an indictment, an information, or a citation.

Criminal Complaint

Most criminal cases begin with the filing of a *criminal complaint*, which is a written accusation of a criminal act that asserts an individual committed an offense against a particular jurisdiction. Rule 3 of the Federal Rules of Criminal Procedure defines a criminal complaint as "a written statement of the essential facts constituting the offense charged. It must be made under oath before a magistrate judge or, if none is reasonably available, before a state or local judicial officer." In short, a criminal complaint is a charging instrument used by law enforcement to notify defendants (as well as the general public) that the government is charging them with criminal activity. See Figure 9-1.

Depending on the jurisdiction, a criminal complaint is officially filed by a prosecutor's office or law enforcement official. After reviewing evidence offered by law enforcement or submitted by private citizens, a prosecutor's office can initiate criminal proceedings by completing a criminal complaint and filing it with the court. Within this document, the prosecutor identifies the name of the jurisdiction bringing the charge(s) (e.g., "United States of America" or "State of Ohio"); the person against whom the charge(s) are brought (identified with the title of "defendant"); the criminal code or statute the person allegedly violated; the basic elements of the asserted offense(s); the date or time period when the offense allegedly occurred; in many cases, the basic facts supporting the legal allegation; and the signature of a person who has authority to officially file a complaint. See Figure 9-2.

Most often a prosecutor-initiated criminal complaint occurs after an intake process has occurred. *Intake* proceedings generally involve a meeting between the prosecutor's office or in some cases a clerk of courts representative and either

arrest
a law enforcement officer's act of taking a person into governmental custody or substantially restricting the person's freedom of movement under the officer's authority

probable cause
the legal standard for making an arrest; requires the arresting officer to have articulable facts that would make a reasonable person believe that the suspect committed a crime

criminal complaint
a written accusation of a criminal act that asserts an individual committed an offense against a particular jurisdiction

intake
the administrative process used to gather information about a suspect when he or she is taken into custody

FIGURE 9-1 **Federal Criminal Complaint Form**

AO 91 (Rev. 08/09) Criminal Complaint

UNITED STATES DISTRICT COURT
for the

United States of America)
v.)
) Case No.
)
)
_____)
Defendant(s)

CRIMINAL COMPLAINT

I, the complainant in this case, state that the following is true to the best of my knowledge and belief.

On or about the date(s) of _____ in the county of _____ in the

_____ District of _____ , the defendant(s) violated:

Code Section   *Offense Description*

This criminal complaint is based on these facts:

❏ Continued on the attached sheet.

_____
Complainant's signature

_____
Printed name and title

Sworn to before me and signed in my presence.

Date: _____

_____
Judge's signature

City and state: _____

_____
Printed name and title

private citizens or police. During this meeting, officers or individuals typically tell a story to authorities about what they believe to be criminal activity. These sessions can be purely narrative in form, or the reporting individual may have other evidence as well—signs of injury, documents, recordings, photos, and so on. The intake official will listen to the story being told and likely ask questions about what is being reported. In most situations, the details of the meeting are then put in a standardized intake form, along with any other submitted evidence or documented statements offered by the officer or individual. The intake form and any other evidence submitted are then used by prosecutors (or in some jurisdictions, a court official) to determine whether an official complaint should be filed against the individual accused of perpetrating the alleged harm. See Law Lines 9-3 and 9-4.

Law Line 9-3
Defense Attorney Intake Form

Law Line 9-4
Prosecutor Intake Form

FIGURE 9-2 **Domestic Violence Complaint Filed by Local Kentucky Authorities**

FAYETTE COUNTY ATTORNEY
CRIMINAL COMPLAINT

DOMESTIC VIOLENCE

Case No. _____

Court _____

Fayette County

COMMONWEALTH OF KENTUCKY   **PLAINTIFF**

V.

Name: STEPHEN NUNN   *MCA - gw met 2/20/09*   **DEFENDANT**
Address (if known) 113 S. WINTER STREET, MIDWAY, KENTUCKY 40347

The Affiant, AMANDA ROSS, whose address is: 541 W. SHORT STREET #35, LEXINGTON, KENTUCKY 40507

Says that on 2/17/2009 in Fayette County, Kentucky, the above-named defendant unlawfully: COMMITTED THE OFFENSE OF ASSAULT 4TH DEGREE: DOMESTIC VIOLENCE

KRS: 508.030   RESPONDENT ID: THE COUNTY ATTORNEY HAS REVIEWED AND RECOMMENDS:
SSN: ███████   ☒ WARRANT
DOB: ███████   ☐ SUMMONS
HGT/WGT: 6'3"/230   ☐ OTHER _____ DATE 2/18/09
HAIR/EYES: BLK/HAZEL   *neul Amanda Ross*
SEX/RACE: M/W

Affiant's grounds of belief as to the commission of this offense are: RESPONDENT INTENTIONALLY OR WANTONLY CAUSED PHYSICAL INJURY TO ANOTHER PERSON TO WIT: AFFIANT ADVISES THAT THE RESPONDENT FORMERLY LIVED WITH THE AFFIANT BUT MOVED OUT IN NOVEMBER 2008. AFFIANT STATES THAT SHE AND THE RESPONDENT WERE ARGUING WHEN THE RESPONDENT BECAME ANGRY AND STRUCK THE AFFIANT ON THE LEFT SIDE OF THE FACE WITH A CLOSED FIST CAUSING RED MARKS AND BRUISING. AFFIANT STATES THE RESPONDENT THEN GRABBED THE AFFIANT BY THE ARMS AND PUSHED THE AFFIANT AGAINST A WALL CAUSING BRUISING TO AFFIANT'S ARMS AND BACK.

Date: 2/18/2009   Signature of Affiant _____

Subscribed and sworn to before me by _Amanda Ross_ this 18th day of _Feb. 2009_
my commission expires 01-07-2012 _Terese Dutton_

       Circuit Clerk/Notary

By: _____ D.C.

In other settings, law enforcement officials themselves can initiate a criminal complaint, usually by completing a complaint form and filing it with the clerk of court's office. In these situations, the officer's sworn statement regarding an incident serves as the factual basis for making a criminal charge. In some jurisdictions, the officer's complaint will be reviewed by the prosecutor's office to ensure it meets all technical and legal requirements. In other cases, the officer's complaint will initiate a court proceeding where a judicial official will decide if the complaint contains sufficient information to maintain the matter as a criminal case.

Upon filing the complaint with the local court, a prosecutor or officer may ask that a warrant be issued for the person's arrest. In these cases, an ***arrest warrant*** may be filed contemporaneously with the criminal complaint, thereby authorizing an officer to physically seize the defendant named in the complaint. See Figure 9-3. In other cases, where the prosecutor or officer is not seeking to arrest the defendant, a summons will be issued to the defendant. A ***summons*** is a court order for a person to appear in court or another official proceeding. See Figure 9-4. It is essentially a government-issued invitation that a person cannot normally refuse. A summons will typically notify a person when and where he or she must be in court for an initial proceeding on the criminal complaint.

arrest warrant
a court order authorizing a law enforcement officer to make an arrest of an identified individual

summons
a court order for a person to appear in court or other official proceeding

FIGURE 9-3 **Federal Arrest Warrant Form**

AO 442 (Rev. 01/09) Arrest Warrant

UNITED STATES DISTRICT COURT
for the

United States of America
v.
)
)
)   Case No.
)
)
)

Defendant

ARREST WARRANT

To: Any authorized law enforcement officer

YOU ARE COMMANDED to arrest and bring before a United States magistrate judge without unnecessary delay
(name of person to be arrested) _____ ,
who is accused of an offense or violation based on the following document filed with the court:

❑ Indictment ❑ Superseding Indictment ❑ Information ❑ Superseding Information ❑ Complaint
❑ Probation Violation Petition ❑ Supervised Release Violation Petition ❑ Violation Notice ❑ Order of the Court

This offense is briefly described as follows:

Date: _____

_____
Issuing officer's signature

City and state: _____

_____
Printed name and title

Return
This warrant was received on *(date)* _____ , and the person was arrested on *(date)* _____ at *(city and state)* _____ .
Date: _____   _____ *Arresting officer's signature*
_____ *Printed name and title*

(continued)

Citation

Perhaps the most familiar form of criminal charge comes in the form of a ***citation*** issued by a law enforcement officer. These are typically presented on a single piece of paper or cardlike form that contains blank lines used by the issuing officer to insert the relevant facts of an offense. See Figure 9-5. In many cases, people refer to citations as "tickets." But in reality, if you look at the fine print of most of these tickets, they are in fact forms of a criminal complaint. Citations will contain all of the information generally found in a formal criminal complaint. They identify the plaintiff and defendant, assert a violation of a criminal code, give basic factual information about the alleged offense, and are signed by the complaining officer. Generally, police officers issue citations in cases where a physical arrest is not

citation
a document used to cite someone with a criminal or traffic offense; also known as a ticket; usually used to charge a person with a minor criminal offense

FIGURE 9-3 **Continued**

This second page contains personal identifiers provided for law-enforcement use only
and therefore should not be filed in court with the executed warrant unless under seal.

(Not for Public Disclosure)

Name of defendant/offender: _____

Known aliases: _____

Last known residence: _____

Prior addresses to which defendant/offender may still have ties: _____

_____

Last known employment: _____

Last known telephone numbers: _____

Place of birth: _____

Date of birth: _____

Social Security number: _____

Height: _____   Weight: _____

Sex: _____   Race: _____

Hair: _____   Eyes: _____

Scars, tattoos, other distinguishing marks: _____

_____

History of violence, weapons, drug use: _____

_____

Known family, friends, and other associates *(name, relation, address, phone number)*: _____

_____

FBI number: _____

Complete description of auto: _____

_____

Investigative agency and address: _____

Name and telephone numbers (office and cell) of pretrial services or probation officer *(if applicable)*:

_____

Date of last contact with pretrial services or probation officer *(if applicable)*: _____

_____

---

mandatory appearance
requirement that a person who
receives a citation must appear in
court, as opposed to just paying
out the ticket

payout ticket
a citation that allows a person to
pay a fine instead of appearing
in court

being made. For example, if police charge a person with disorderly conduct, jay-walking, or traffic violations, they will likely use a citation to initiate criminal proceedings.

A citation will also indicate how a named defendant must or can proceed with the complaint. At the bottom portion of most citations, there is usually a summons form that, once completed by an officer, will indicate whether a defendant must appear in court to address the complaint. This is often referred to as a ***mandatory appearance*** or a summons (see above). In some cases, however, the officer will issue a type of "optional" summons, informing defendants that they have the choice of appearing in court pursuant to the summons, usually contained within the citation, or resolving the citation before the scheduled court appearance, usually by signing a statement of guilt and paying a predetermined fine with the clerk's office. In some circles, this is referred to as a ***payout ticket***, because it allows defendants to avoid court proceedings by admitting responsibility or guilt to the allegations in the citation, by signing a written statement of guilt (often printed on the ticket), and then paying a standardized fine or penalty. "Paying out" a citation or ticket will still result in a criminal offense being recorded against the defendant; it just avoids the need for a court proceeding on the matter.

FIGURE 9-4 **Federal Criminal Summons Form (Page 1 of 2)**

AO 83 (Rev. 06/09) Summons in a Criminal Case

UNITED STATES DISTRICT COURT
for the

United States of America	)	
v.	)	
	)	
	)	Case No.
	)	
	)	
Defendant	)	

SUMMONS IN A CRIMINAL CASE

YOU ARE SUMMONED to appear before the United States district court at the time, date, and place set forth below to answer to one or more offenses or violations based on the following document filed with the court:

❏ Indictment   ❏ Superseding Indictment   ❏ Information   ❏ Superseding Information   ❏ Complaint
❏ Probation Violation Petition   ❏ Supervised Release Violation Petition   ❏ Violation Notice   ❏ Order of Court

| Place: | Courtroom No.: |
| | Date and Time: |

This offense is briefly described as follows:

Date: _____

_____
Issuing officer's signature

_____
Printed name and title

I declare under penalty of perjury that I have:

❏ Executed and returned this summons   ❏ Returned this summons unexecuted

Date: _____

_____
Server's signature

_____
Printed name and title

Indictment

In most jurisdictions, criminal complaints are sufficient charging instruments to begin a criminal case for a **_misdemeanor_** offense. A misdemeanor is generally classified as a criminal offense for which a person faces a year or less of incarceration. But in many jurisdictions, including the federal criminal justice system, a criminal complaint is not sufficient to officially charge a **_felony_**, which is generally regarded as a crime for which a defendant faces a possible penalty of more than one year of incarceration. In these jurisdictions, felony charges must be brought via an **_indictment_**, a charging instrument similar to a criminal complaint in that it officially charges a person with a criminal offense and provides legal and factual details of the accusation; the difference is that it is issued by a grand jury. See Figure 9-6. Rule 7(c)(1) of the Federal Rules of

misdemeanor
a criminal offense for which a person faces a year or less of incarceration

felony
a crime for which a defendant faces a possible penalty of more than one year of incarceration

indictment
an instrument used in some jurisdictions to charge felony offenses; issued by a grand jury as a finding of probable cause that a defendant committed a crime

FIGURE 9-5 **Sample Citation from Georgia**

GEORGIA
UNIFORM TRAFFIC CITATION, SUMMONS AND ACCUSATION

Court Case Number ______ SS NR-GA0950800 NCIC Number ______ Citation Number ______

PORT HAMMOND POLICE DEPT.

SECTION I - VIOLATOR

Upon Month ______ (Day) ______ (Year) ______ at ______ ☐ A.M. ☐ P.M.

Operator License No. ______

License Class or Type ______ State ______ Endorsements ______ Expires ______

Name ______ (Last) (First) (Middle)

Address ______

City ______ State ______ Zip Code ______

DOB ______ Hair ______ Hgt ______ Wgt. ______ Sex ______ Eyes ______

Veh. Yr. ______ Make ______ Style ______ Color ______

Registration No. ______ Yr. ______ State ______

COMMERCIAL DRIVER LICENSE ☐ YES ☐ NO COMMERCIAL VEHICLE ☐ YES ☐ NO ACCIDENT ☐ YES ☐ NO

SECTION II VIOLATION

(ONE VIOLATION PER CITATION) ☐ DRIVER REQUESTED ACCURACY CHECK ☐ VASCAR ☐ LASER ☐ RADAR
Within the State of Georgia, did commit the following offense: SPEEDING - Clocked by ☐ PATROL VEHICLE ☐ OTHER
(Serial # ______ Calibration/Check ______) at ______ MPH in a ______ zone

☐ DUI (Test Administered: ☐ BLOOD ☐ BREATH ☐ URINE ☐ OTHER) DUI Test Results ______
TEST ADMINISTERED BY (If Applicable): ______

OFFENSE (Other than above) ______
In Violation of Code Section ______ of ☐ State Law ☐ Local Ordinance

REMARKS ______

SAMPLE

WEATHER	(A) ROAD	(B)	TRAFFIC	LIGHTING	COMMERCIAL VEHICLE INFORMATION
☐ Clear	☐ Dry	☐ Concrete	☐ Light	☐ Daylight	☐ Commercial Vehicle Violation
☐ Cloudy	☐ Wet	☐ Blacktop	☐ Medium	☐ Darkness	☐ Hazardous Material Violation (PLACARD)
☐ Raining	☐ Ice	☐ Dirt	☐ Heavy	☐ Other	
☐ Other	☐ Other	☐ Other			

SECTION III LOCATION

County of FELIX and ______ miles ______ of (city) ______
on ______ at or near mile post ______, or within (city) PORT HAMMOND
at/on (secondary location) ______
OFFICER (Print) ______ Badge # ______ Div. ______

SECTION IV SUMMONS

You are hereby ordered to appear in Court to answer this charge on the ______ day of ______
______ at ______ ☐ AM ☐ PM in the MUNICIPAL Court
at 1140 S. COOPER HIGHWAY (922) 362-4510
City PORT HAMMOND, Georgia 31620

NOTICE: This citation shall constitute official notice to you that failure to appear in Court at the date and time stated on this citation to dispose of the cited charges against you shall cause the designated Court to forward your driver's license number to the Department of Motor Vehicle Safety, and your driver's license shall be suspended. (Georgia Code 17-6-11 and 40-5-56) The suspension shall remain in effect until such time as there is a satisfactory disposition in this matter or the Court notifies the Department of Motor Vehicle Safety.

SECTION V OFFICER CERTIFICATION

LICENSE DISPLAYED IN LIEU OF BAIL ☐ YES ☐ NO RELEASED TO ______
SIGNATURE ACKNOWLEDGES SERVICE OF THIS SUMMONS AND RECEIPT OF COPY OF SAME

SIGNATURE X ______

ARRESTING OFFICERS CERTIFICATION

The undersigned has just and reasonable grounds to believe, and does believe, that the person named herein has committed the offense set forth, contrary to law.

SIGNATURE ______ Signature of Arresting Officer Badge # ______

AUTHORIZED AND APPROVED PURSUANT TO:
CODE 40-13-1 - D.P.S. REG. 570.19

OFFICER'S COPY

NCIC NO. SS NR-GA0950800

GA-17-5

G.A. THOMPSON, P.O. BOX 720254, DALLAS, TEXAS 75372

FIGURE 9-6 **Indictment in Ohio Murder Case**

DANIEL M. HORRIGAN

·2008 APR -9 PM 1: 28

SUMMIT COUNTY
CLERK OF COURTS   8

IN THE COURT OF COMMON PLEAS
COUNTY OF SUMMIT, OHIO

INDICTMENT TYPE: BINDOVER

CASE NO. 2008-03-0968

INDICTMENT FOR: MURDER (1) 2903.02(B) SF; FELONIOUS ASSAULT (1)
2903.11(A)(1) F-2; ENDANGERING CHILDREN (1) 2919.22(B)(1) F-2; ENDANGERING
CHILDREN (1) 2919.22(A) F-3

In the Common Pleas Court of Summit County, Ohio, of the term of MARCH in the year of
our Lord, Two Thousand and Eight.

The Jurors of the Grand Jury of the State of Ohio, within and for the body of the County
aforesaid, being duly impaneled and sworn and charged to inquire of and present all
offenses whatever committed within the limits of said County, on their oaths, IN THE
NAME AND BY THE AUTHORITY OF THE STATE OF OHIO,

COUNT ONE

DO FIND AND PRESENT That **CRAIG R. WILSON** on or about the 12th day of March,
2008, in the County of Summit and State of Ohio, aforesaid, did commit the crime of
MURDER in that he did cause the death of C.W. (DOB: ████████) as a proximate result of
CRAIG R. WILSON committing or attempting to commit Endangering Children and/or
Felonious Assault, an offense of violence that is a felony of the first or second degree, in
violation of Section 2903.02(B) of the Ohio Revised Code, A SPECIAL FELONY, contrary
to the form of the statute in such case made and provided and against the peace and
dignity of the State of Ohio.

COUNT TWO

And the Grand Jurors of the State of Ohio, within and for the body of the County of Summit
aforesaid, on their oaths in the name and by the authority of the State of Ohio, DO
FURTHER·FIND AND PRESENT, that **CRAIG R. WILSON** on or about the 12th day of
March, 2008, in the County of Summit aforesaid, did commit the crime of **FELONIOUS
ASSAULT** in that he did knowingly cause serious physical harm to C.W. (DOB: ████████ ,
in violation of Section 2903.11(A)(1) of the Ohio Revised Code, A FELONY OF THE
SECOND DEGREE, contrary to the form of the statute in such case made and provided
and against the peace and dignity of the State of Ohio.

COUNT THREE

And the Grand Jurors of the State of Ohio, within and for the body of the County of Summit
aforesaid, on their oaths in the name and by the authority of the State of Ohio, DO
FURTHER FIND AND PRESENT, that **CRAIG R. WILSON** on or about the 12th day of
March, 2008, in the County of Summit aforesaid, did commit the crime of **ENDANGERING
CHILDREN** in that he did recklessly abuse C.W., 2 months, a child under eighteen years
of age (DOB: ██████ , resulting in serious physical harm to said child, in violation of
Section 2919.22(B)(1) of the Ohio Revised Code, A FELONY OF THE SECOND
DEGREE, contrary to the form of the statute in such case made and provided and against
the peace and dignity of the State of Ohio.

COUNT FOUR

And the Grand Jurors of the State of Ohio, within and for the body of the County of Summit
aforesaid, on their oaths in the name and by the authority of the State of Ohio, DO
FURTHER FIND AND PRESENT, that **CRAIG R. WILSON** on or about the 1st day of
January, 2008 to the 12th day of March, 2008, in the County of Summit aforesaid, did

(continued)

FIGURE 9-6 **Continued**

commit the crime of **ENDANGERING CHILDREN** in that he did being a parent, guardian, custody, person having custody or control, or person in loco parentis of C.W., 2 months, a child under eighteen years of age (DOB: ███████), did recklessly create a substantial risk to the health or safety of the child by violating a duty of care, protection or support resulting in serious physical harm to said child, in violation of Section 2919.22(A) of the Ohio Revised Code, A FELONY OF THE THIRD DEGREE, contrary to the form of the statute in such case made and provided and against the peace and dignity of the State of Ohio.

Sherri Bevan Walsh/mk
SHERRI BEVAN WALSH, Prosecutor/pw

Prosecutor, County of Summit, by

Margaret Kanelli
Date: **4-8-08**

A TRUE BILL

Grand Jury foreperson/Deputy Foreperson

Criminal Procedure provides that "[t]he indictment or information must be a plain, concise, and definite written statement of the essential facts constituting the offense charged and must be signed by an attorney for the government. It need not contain a formal introduction or conclusion."

An indictment is organized based on counts. A **count** is a numerically indicated, specific criminal charge contained in an indictment. For example, a defendant charged with three criminal offenses would have three separate counts listed in the indictment, each containing a specific claim of fact and criminal code section. Rule 7(c)(1) of the Federal Rules of Criminal Procedure states that "[a] count may incorporate by reference an allegation made in another count. A count may allege that the means by which the defendant committed the offense are unknown or that the defendant committed it by one or more specified means. For each count, the indictment or information must give the official or customary citation of the statute, rule, regulation, or other provision of law that the defendant is alleged to have violated. . . . " See Figure 9-7.

Indictments are produced by a **grand jury**, which is a group of citizens who meet in secret to determine whether there is enough evidence to charge a person with a criminal offense. See "Grand Jury Hearings" below. Practically speaking, grand juries can issue indictments at any time during the criminal process. Some indictments are issued before a person is arrested. In such cases, individuals may have no idea that they are being charged with criminal activity until they learn of the grand jury's indictment. In other cases, individuals may have some belief that the grand jury is conducting an investigation, and perhaps, as suspects, they may even be summoned to testify before the grand jury. In some of these cases, an indictment may come after a criminal complaint has been filed against a defendant. But in some jurisdictions, because the complaint's allegations involve felony charges, a grand jury must review the case before felony charges can become official. In some of these postcomplaint cases, a grand jury will issue an indictment after a person has been arrested and without hearing from the person. In these cases, individuals who are either detained in some form of custody or released on bail know that a grand jury will be reviewing their case to determine whether charges are appropriate.

count
a numerically indicated, separate criminal charge contained in an indictment

grand jury
a group of citizens who convene secretly to review criminal complaints and investigate facts to determine whether there is probable cause to believe criminal activity has occurred

FIGURE 9-7 **Sample Grand Jury Report**

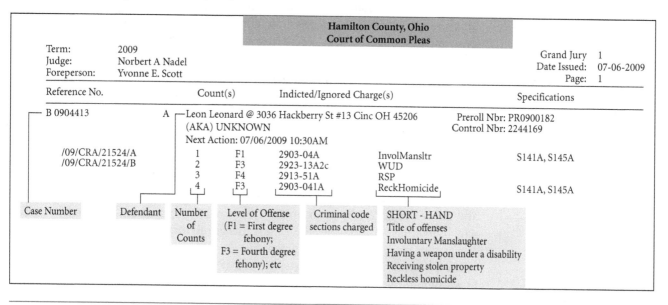

In cases where the grand jury finds sufficient evidence or probable cause that criminal activity has occurred, it will issue an indictment or a ***true bill***. In other cases, where the evidence is insufficient or lacking in probable cause, the grand jury can either formally issue a ***no bill*** or no true bill, indicating that the matter is closed, or can take no action and label the case as ***ignored***. An ignored case means that the grand jury did not find probable cause to issue an indictment but that it may revisit the case if additional evidence becomes available. In most cases, an ignored report by the grand jury means that the case is over. But legally speaking, such a report does leave the door open to a future review and indictment by the grand jury.

In situations where the grand jury takes no action, the case is not truly concluded as a matter of law until the ***statute of limitations*** expires for the suspected offense. A statute of limitations is a law that sets a maximum time period following the alleged criminal act within which prosecutors may bring criminal charges for the offense. The statute of limitations for some minor offenses can be fairly short—perhaps six months. For more serious misdemeanors, the statute of limitations might be two years. For many felonies, the statute of limitations is often five or six years, and for certain federal fraud felonies up to ten years. And for some very serious felonies, such as murder, there may be no statute of limitations at all, meaning charges can be brought at any time.

true bill
another name for an indictment

no bill
an indication that the grand jury is not issuing an indictment in a case; also known as no true bill

ignore
a term used in some jurisdictions to indicate that the grand jury is not indicting, but has not conclusively closed the case

statute of limitations
a law that sets a maximum time period following the alleged criminal act within which prosecutors may bring criminal charges for the offense

IN THE FIELD

For many legal professionals working in the criminal justice field, one of their primary tasks may be to review the grand jury reports from the local courts to see what, if any, action the grand jury has taken against clients or other identified individuals. In many jurisdictions, these reports are available online via the clerk of court's website. In other jurisdictions, the reports are available in hardcopy via the clerk of court's office. Either way, legal professionals are regularly asked to review these reports and any corresponding indictments and explain them to clients, attorneys, and other interested parties. As a result, legal professionals should familiarize themselves with the electronic and manual sources for monitoring grand jury reports.

Information

Slightly more than half of the states in America do not depend, at least exclusively, on grand juries as the legal means to charge individuals with felony offenses. In most of these jurisdictions, prosecutors are allowed to charge individuals with felonies through an *information*. An information is similar to an indictment because it serves as a document that officially charges an individual with a crime, which is usually a felony. But instead of being issued by a grand jury, it is typically written and signed by the prosecuting authority within a given jurisdiction. For example, in California, the state constitution allows a felony case to proceed by information if the district attorney recommends prosecution and a judge agrees that facts exist to warrant prosecution.

Even in jurisdictions where a grand jury indictment is constitutionally required to charge a felony, a defendant or suspect may choose to waive this right and allow the government to proceed by way of information. One may wonder why individuals would waive their right to a grand jury indictment. In some cases, the person has already been indicted and the case is pending before a court. The parties, however, reach a plea agreement that allows the defendant to plead guilty to a different offense than the one alleged in the indictment. Rather than requiring the prosecutor to present the case again to a grand jury, a defendant will waive the right to grand jury indictment, allow the prosecutor to amend the charge without grand jury review, and proceed with an admission of culpability or guilt.

Law Line 9-5
Criminal Information Filed against Frank DiPascali

In other cases, a suspect may agree to an information before the grand jury issues an indictment. In these cases, typically the prosecutor and defendant (likely through a defense lawyer) will negotiate a plea agreement before the grand jury has initiated formal charges. The defendant will then be asked to waive the grand jury presentment requirement and allow the prosecutor to proceed via information. Within each scenario, the waiver of the grand jury requirement is viewed as being in the best interests of the defendant/suspect because a favorable plea agreement has been reached.

BOND HEARINGS

One of the most critical stages of a criminal case is the setting of *bond*. The term *bond* is often used interchangeably with the term *bail*, a more generic term that refers to any form or condition of pretrial release. Bail usually comes in the form of money or other property that a person held in custody provides to a court as a guarantee that the person will appear in court as scheduled. If the person appears in court as ordered, the court will refund the bail at the end of the case. But if the person fails to meet his court appearances, the court may order that the bail be forfeited and that a warrant be issued for the person's arrest.

Today, both bond and bail are used to refer to a court order that allows a defendant to be released from custody pending trial in exchange for certain conditions to be met by the defendant. Whether imposed after a formal hearing, or established directly through a standardized bond schedule (which many courts use— see below), this phase can be one of the most important proceedings for both criminal defendants and prosecutors.

The Constitutional Right to Reasonable Bail

There is some confusion about the constitutional right to bail. On the one hand, the Eighth Amendment to the U.S. Constitution provides that "[e]xcessive bail shall not be required." This might suggest to some that a defendant is entitled to a reasonable bail in all cases. But on the other hand, if you observe bond hearings, you likely will see federal courts and some state court denying any bond to defendants in certain cases, and state courts in some cases setting bonds in amounts nearing or exceeding a million dollars.[3] For most defendants in these cases, there is no reasonable chance that they will be released while awaiting trial.

The original purpose of bail was to afford liberty to arrested persons while criminal charges are pending. Thus, in principle, the amount of bail should be no more than is reasonably necessary to keep defendants from fleeing before their cases are concluded. But in recent years, a second purpose for bond has been offered by courts and legislatures—to protect the community from harm inflicted by defendants while their cases are pending. This second justification is known as *preventive detention* because it is designed to prevent defendants from engaging in additional criminal acts against the public while awaiting trial on initial allegations.

In 1984, Congress passed the *Bail Reform Act of 1984*, which authorized judges to detain defendants charged with serious offenses if the judge found that there were no bail or release conditions that would assure "'the safety of any other person and the community." In *United States v. Salerno* (1988),[4] the Court held that the preventive detention provisions of the Bail Reform Act did not violate the Eighth Amendment. The Court found that the purpose of bail is not limited to preventing defendants from fleeing before trial, stating, "we reject the proposition that the Eighth Amendment categorically prohibits the government from pursuing other admittedly compelling interests through regulation of pre-trial release." The Court further concluded that "the only arguable substantive limitation of the Bail Clause is that the government's proposed conditions of release or detention not be 'excessive' in light of the perceived evil." The Court then held that the pretrial detention of "arrestees charged with serious felonies who are found after an adversary hearing to pose a threat to the safety of individuals or to the community which no condition of release can dispel" met this constitutional standard.

It should be noted that the Court has never officially incorporated the excessive bail provision of the Eighth Amendment and made it applicable to the states. See Chapter 8. But the Court has reviewed state bail standards under the Fourteenth Amendment Due Process Clause. Read the Court's opinion in *Schall v. Martin* (1984), where the Court reviewed a facial challenge to New York's pretrial detention standards for juveniles. Consider whether detaining juveniles without bond before trial satisfies the standards of due process outlined by the Court. Consider too whether the case would be evaluated any differently if the Eighth Amendment provision against excessive bail were applied. Finally, consider whether the excessive bail provision of the Eighth Amendment should be incorporated through the Fourteenth Amendment and made applicable to the states.

In the end, the legal reality is that courts have not interpreted the Eighth Amendment or the Fourteenth Amendment to require courts to provide bail to defendants in all cases. Bail, however, can still be deemed excessive under the Eighth Amendment or perhaps under related protections under state constitutions if the amount or nature of the bond is more than necessary to ensure the return of the defendant for future court proceedings and to protect the community. When defendants believe their bail is excessive, they can file a *motion to modify bond*, which establishes reasons why the defendant is likely to return for future proceedings and does not pose a threat to the community. Keep in mind that in most cases, the judge or magistrate who sets the initial bond in a case will not be the assigned

preventive detention
keeping persons in custody while their criminal case is pending in order to ensure the safety of the community

Bail Reform Act of 1984
a federal statute that allows judges to detain defendants charged with serious offenses if the judge finds that there are no bail or release conditions that would assure the safety of the community; passed by Congress in 1984

motion to modify bond
a petition filed with the court asking for a change in the current conditions of the defendant's bond

trial judge for the trial. Once the case is assigned to a permanent trial judge, defendants can seek review by the trial court. In most jurisdictions, if the motion is denied, defendants can appeal to the court of appeals, and if still unsuccessful, to the supreme court.

CAPSTONE CASE *Schall v. Martin*, 467 U.S. 253 (1984)

Justice REHNQUIST delivered the opinion of the Court.

Section 320.5(3)(b) of the New York Family Court Act authorizes pretrial detention of an accused juvenile delinquent based on a finding that there is a "serious risk" that the child "may before the return date commit an act which if committed by an adult would constitute a crime." Appellees brought suit on behalf of a class of all juveniles detained pursuant to that provision. . . .

We conclude that preventive detention under the FCA serves a legitimate state objective, and that the procedural protections afforded pretrial detainees by the New York statute satisfy the requirements of the Due Process Clause of the Fourteenth Amendment to the United States Constitution. . . .

The statutory provision at issue in these cases, § 320.5(3)(b), permits a brief pretrial detention based on a finding of a "serious risk" that an arrested juvenile may commit a crime before his return date. The question before us is whether preventive detention of juveniles pursuant to § 320.5(3)(b) is compatible with the "fundamental fairness" required by due process. Two separate inquiries are necessary to answer this question. First, does preventive detention under the New York statute serve a legitimate state objective? And, second, are the procedural safeguards contained in the FCA adequate to authorize the pretrial detention of at least some juveniles charged with crimes?

Preventive detention under the FCA is purportedly designed to protect the child and society from the potential consequences of his criminal acts. When making any detention decision, the Family Court judge is specifically directed to consider the needs and best interests of the juvenile as well as the need for the protection of the community. . . . As an initial matter, therefore, we must decide whether, in the context of the juvenile system, the combined interest in protecting both the community and the juvenile himself from the consequences of future criminal conduct is sufficient to justify such detention.

The "legitimate and compelling state interest" in protecting the community from crime cannot be doubted. We have stressed before that crime prevention is "a weighty social objective," and this interest persists undiluted in the juvenile context. The harm suffered by the victim of a crime is not dependent upon the age of the perpetrator. And the harm to society generally may even be greater in this context given the high rate of recidivism among juveniles.

The juvenile's countervailing interest in freedom from institutional restraints, even for the brief time involved here, is undoubtedly substantial as well. But that interest must be qualified by the recognition that juveniles, unlike adults, are always in some form of custody. Children, by definition, are not assumed to have the capacity to take care of themselves. They are assumed to be subject to the control of their parents, and if parental control falters, the State must play its part as *parens patriae*. In this respect, the juvenile's liberty interest may, in appropriate circumstances, be subordinated to the State's "parens patriae interest in preserving and promoting the welfare of the child." . . .

Of course, the mere invocation of a legitimate purpose will not justify particular restrictions and conditions of confinement amounting to punishment. It is axiomatic that "[d]ue process requires that a pretrial detainee not be punished." . . . .

There is no indication in the statute itself that preventive detention is used or intended as a punishment. First of all, the detention is strictly limited in time. If a juvenile is detained at his initial appearance and has denied the charges against him, he is entitled to a probable-cause hearing to be held not more than three days after the conclusion of the initial appearance or four days after the filing of the petition, whichever is sooner. . . .

Detained juveniles are also entitled to an expedited factfinding hearing. If the juvenile is charged with one of a limited number of designated felonies, the factfinding hearing must be scheduled to commence not more than fourteen days after the conclusion of the initial appearance. . . .

Secure detention is more restrictive, but it is still consistent with the regulatory and parens patriae objectives relied upon by the State. Children are assigned to separate dorms based on age, size, and behavior. They wear street clothes provided by the institution and partake in educational and recreational programs and counseling sessions run by trained social workers. Misbehavior is punished by confinement to one's room. We cannot conclude from this record that the controlled environment briefly imposed by the State on juveniles in secure pretrial detention "is imposed for the purpose of punishment" rather than as "an incident of some other legitimate governmental purpose." . . . .

Given the legitimacy of the State's interest in preventive detention, and the nonpunitive nature of that detention, the remaining question is whether the procedures afforded juveniles detained prior to fact-finding provide sufficient protection against erroneous and unnecessary deprivations of liberty. . . .

[In addition] the facts and reasons for the detention must be stated on the record.

In sum, notice, a hearing, and a statement of facts and reasons are given prior to any detention under § 320.5(3)(b). A formal probable-cause hearing is then held within a short while thereafter, if the factfinding hearing is not itself scheduled within three days. These flexible procedures have been found constitutionally adequate under the Fourth Amendment. Appellees have failed to note any additional procedures that would significantly improve the accuracy of the determination without unduly impinging on the achievement of legitimate state purposes. . . .

Given the regulatory purpose for the detention and the procedural protections that precede its imposition, we conclude that § 320.5(3)(b) of the New York FCA is not invalid under the Due Process Clause of the Fourteenth Amendment.

The judgment of the Court of Appeals is Reversed.

WHAT DO *YOU* THINK?

1. Given the fact that the text of the Eighth Amendment says that excessive bail cannot be required, should it be constitutional for courts to detain juveniles without setting a pretrial bond?
2. In cases where bond is set for charged juvenile offenders, what types of conditions might be set to ensure the safety of the community?

The Process of Setting Bond

Obtaining a reasonable and quick bond for clients can be one of the most valuable services criminal defense lawyers can provide during a criminal case. In many criminal cases, particularly misdemeanors or low-level felonies, convicted defendants are not likely to serve any jail or prison time as a part of their criminal sentences. In these cases, their pretrial custody may be their only exposure to incarceration. As a result, it is important for clients to quickly obtain a pretrial bond that is reasonable, given their circumstances. Criminal defense lawyers and their assistants can make a good first impression on clients by arranging a manageable bond in an expedited and smooth manner. Conversely, struggling to obtain what should be a reasonable bond or appearing disorganized in seeking bond may cause their clients to question their legal representation.

A defendant's bond conditions also can be important for prosecutors. In some cases, law enforcement officials are concerned that defendants pose a threat to public safety, and thus seek to have them detained pending trial. In other cases, law enforcement officials might be concerned that the defendant will not return for trial or pretrial hearings if released. Perhaps the defendant has a history of fleeing or the possible punishment in the current case is so substantial as to make it more attractive for the defendant to "jump bail." Prosecutors may come under public criticism if a defendant is released pending trial. Some also believe that a defendant's pretrial detention can aid prosecutors during plea negotiations. The theory is that defendants who have a particularly bad experience while being held in pretrial detention may be more inclined to accept a plea agreement in order to get out of local custody. Regardless of whether this last item is truly a factor in many cases, prosecutors have plenty of incentives to be engaged in the bond-setting process.

For many misdemeanor and low-level felony cases, bond is set based on a standardized and published schedule. This document typically lists criminal offenses and the corresponding amount of money it will take to satisfy the bond conditions. See Figure 9-8. In these scenarios, there is little suspense or surprise regarding the defendant's bond. And in fact, many jails have the bail schedule and allow arrested persons to be released as soon as they post the corresponding amount of money for their alleged criminal offense.

But in other cases, the bond-setting process can take much longer. If the charges are particularly serious or there are extenuating factual circumstances, the court may hold a formal bond hearing where the nature and amount of bond will

---

FIGURE 9-8 Iowa Uniform Bond Schedule

Iowa law provides that under certain circumstances, an arrested person may be released pending an initial appearance if the release is pursuant to pretrial release procedures or a bond schedule approved by the judicial council. The bond schedule shall be used only if the person was arrested for a crime other than a forcible felony and the courts are not in session.

Uniform Bond Schedule (Order: 8/2/07):

- Violation of §124.401(1)(a) & (b) (class "B" felony charge for manufacture or delivery of certain controlled substances, counterfeit substances, or substitute substances, including heroin, cocaine, and meth)—$100,000.
- Violation of §124.401(1)(c) (class "C" felony charge for the above type crimes)—$50,000
- Other class "B" felony—$25,000
- Other class "C" felony—$10,000
- Class "D" felony—$5,000
- Aggravated misdemeanor—$2,000
- Serious misdemeanor—$1,000
- Simple misdemeanor (non-scheduled violation)—$300
- Scheduled violations—amount established in State of Iowa Compendium of Scheduled Violations and Scheduled Fines

Source: http://www.iowacourtsonline.org/District_Courts/Trial_Court_Tools/Uniform_Bond_Schedule/

be debated by the parties. In these more serious cases, judges typically consider two primary factors to determine the type and amount of bond: (1) whether the defendant poses a threat to the community, and (2) whether, if given bond, the defendant will return for all court appearances. In assessing a defendant's threat to the community, judges will likely consider the following factors:

- The nature and seriousness of the criminal charges filed in the current case.
- Any documented injuries allegedly caused by the defendant as a part of the case.
- The defendant's criminal history.
- Any threats made by the defendant to alleged victims or law enforcement.
- Statements from any alleged victims.
- Whether the defendant was out on bond when the current charges were filed.

In determining whether the defendant is likely to return for future court proceedings, a judge will probably consider the following factors:

- Whether the defendant has family members in the community (spouse, parents, children).
- Whether the defendant has lived in the jurisdiction for a substantial time.
- Whether the defendant is employed.
- The extent and nature of the defendant's criminal history.
- Whether the defendant had any problems appearing before the court in other cases.

Once bond is set by the judge during the bond hearing, if either the prosecution or defendant is not satisfied with the bond order, they can seek modifications to the bond conditions. As explained above, defendant can file a motion to reduce bond. But prosecutors can also seek to modify bond conditions by presenting new evidence to the court demonstrating that the defendant poses a flight risk or is a threat to the community.

Types of Bond

Within most jurisdictions, there are several types of bond that judges can issue. The least restrictive form of bond is a ***personal recognizance bond***, also known as an ***own recognizance*** or ***OR bond***. This bond allows defendants to be released based simply on their written promise to return for future court proceedings. The defendant is not required to put down any money or provide the court with any other collateral. This bond is often issued in cases where there are fairly minor criminal charges pending or where the judge believes the defendant to be highly trustworthy, likely to return, and not a danger to the community.

Another form of bond is an ***unsecured bond***, which allows the defendant to be released without providing the court with any money or other form of security. Under this bond, defendants sign a promise to return to court and agree to pay a stated amount of money if they fail to return. Essentially, under this bond, defendants promise to pay the amount listed in the bond if they fail to appear in court as ordered. For example, if the judge issues a $1,000 unsecured bond, the defendant would not have to put any money down to be released, but would be legally obligated to pay $1,000 to the court if he failed to appear in court during the case proceedings.

A judge can also issue a ***secured bond***, which allows defendants to be released from custody if they can provide the court with a stated amount of money or other

personal recognizance or own recognizance (OR) bond
a form of pretrial release that allows defendants to be released based simply on their written promise to return for future court proceedings

unsecured bond
a form of pretrial release that allows defendants to be released without providing the court with any money or other form of security; defendants sign a promise to return to court and agree to pay a stated amount of money if they fail to return

secured bond
a form of pretrial release in which the defendant can provide the court with a stated amount of money or other form of security or collateral

cash bond or straight bond
a form of pretrial release that requires a defendant to pay the full cash amount stated in the bond

10 percent bond
a form of pretrial release that requires the defendant to pay a certain percentage of a stated bond amount

property bond
a form of pretrial release that requires a defendant to provide the court with an interest in property owned by the defendant, typically in the form of real estate

surety bond
a form of pretrial release where the defendant pays the surety (often a bail bondsman) a fee for putting up an amount of bail

form of security or collateral (often, an interest in real property). If defendants return for all court proceedings, the court will return the security (money) to them when the case is concluded. But if a defendant fails to appear as promised, the amount of security can be forfeited. There are a few variations on secured bonds. A judge can order a defendant to pay the full cash amount stated in the bond. This is often referred to as a *cash bond or a straight bond*. For example, if a defendant receives a $1,000 secured bond, she must provide the court with the full amount in order to be released. In some jurisdictions, the judge can also order a percentage bond, using what is called a *10 percent bond*. Under this bond, a judge would issue a bond in a stated amount, but allow the defendant to be released if he or she can provide the court with 10 percent of the stated amount. For example, a $1,000 secured bond at 10 percent requires the defendant to provide $100 to satisfy the bond. But if the defendant fails to make required court appearances as promised, the court may order the defendant to forfeit the $100 and pay the remaining $900 of the stated bond amount.

Finally, in some jurisdictions, the court will issue a *property bond* in addition to a secured cash bond. This requires a defendant to provide the court with an interest in property owned by the defendant, typically in the form of real estate. Under this bond, defendants sign over a legal interest in their home or other real estate to satisfy the bond amount. So, if the judge orders a $1,000 bond, cash or property, the defendant can provide the court with either $1,000 in cash or a $1,000 interest in property.

Oftentimes, defendants do not have the resources to satisfy the court's bond amount and may turn to a bail bondsman or other surety for help. A *surety bond* allows another person or entity to provide the court with the bond amount. In exchange, the defendant pays the surety (often a bail bondsman) a fee for this service. For example, if the court orders a $1,000 cash bond, a defendant could retain a bail bondsman to provide the court with the full amount. In return, the defendant will pay the surety a percentage (often 20 percent) of the amount posted with the court. If the defendant fails to appear in court as promised, the surety's money could be forfeited.

Julie Ann S. Barnes and Thomas S. Levesque appear in Worcester, Mass., District Court January 6, 2000, for a bail hearing. The homeless pair were accused of accidentally starting a December 3, 1999, warehouse blaze that led to the deaths of six firefighters. Levesque's bail was reduced to $250,000 cash or $2.5 million with surety; Barnes' bail was $75,000 cash or $750,000 with surety. Manslaughter charges against the pair were later dropped in exchange for a five-year term of probation.

Finally, with all forms of bond, the judge can order additional conditions that the defendant must satisfy in order to be released. These may include reporting conditions that require the defendant to be supervised by court officials (often, pretrial services) and to report, either in person or via phone, on a scheduled basis to court officials. Other conditions might include (1) travel restrictions, including surrendering of passports; (2) electronic monitoring (often, an electronic ankle bracelet), which allows court officials to track the defendant's whereabouts; (3) regular testing for prohibited substances; (4) restrictions on driving; (5) an order to avoid contact with alleged victims or other individuals; (6) house arrest, which requires defendants to be confined in their home; (7) an order not to possess guns or other dangerous instruments; and (8) an order not to engage in criminal activity. If defendants breach any of these conditions, a judge could revoke their bond and order that they be returned to custody pending the resolution of their case.

IN THE FIELD

Legal professionals can do a number of things in preparation for initial bond hearings or subsequent hearings on motions to modify bond. All of these tasks are directed at the two main factors considered by judges in bond hearings—the dangerousness of the defendant and the likelihood that he or she will return for court proceedings if released. Professionals in the prosecutor's office may want to prepare (1) the defendant's complete and accurate criminal history; (2) statements, exhibits, or testimony from victims or law enforcement to demonstrate the amount of harm allegedly caused by defendant; (3) any statements made by defendant in the form of threats or indications of future harm; (4) information on defendant's lack of ties to the local community (if appropriate); and (5) any evidence suggesting defendant cannot be trusted to return to court for future proceedings.

Criminal defense professionals have several tasks, including (1) obtaining and reviewing the client's criminal history, (2) reviewing evidence regarding the amount of harm allegedly caused by the client, (3) obtaining evidence suggesting that the client has strong ties to the local community and therefore is likely to return for all court proceedings, (4) making arrangements with the client's family or friends so that they can bring necessary resources or documentation to the court to satisfy surety bonds or other conditions, and (5) verifying that the client has a place to stay or, where appropriate, a place of employment if released.

To some observers, the bond-setting process in criminal cases may appear to be a fairly simple and insignificant stage of the court proceedings. But this time can be highly significant and valuable to both prosecutors and criminal defendants, and in some cases can ultimately impact the resolution of the case. It may be the first time clients will see their criminal defense lawyers in action. And first impressions can affect the way the attorney–client relationship develops or whether it continues at all. Moreover, it can be far more difficult and time consuming for attorneys to communicate with defendants in pretrial custody. Attorney–client communications can be more challenging and inhibited in a jail setting. This, in turn, may make it more difficult to prepare for trial. And for prosecutors, the defendant's pretrial custody can also impact the way a case is handled. A detained defendant can calm some of the fears of alleged victims. It may even impact the willingness of defendants to accept plea agreements. As a result, legal professionals will do well to provide particular attention and detail to the bond-setting stage of their criminal cases.

PRELIMINARY HEARINGS

preliminary hearing or probable cause hearing
a court hearing to determine whether the government has probable cause to maintain the current criminal charges

In federal cases and many state jurisdictions, courts hold a ***preliminary hearing*** or ***probable cause hearing*** for defendants shortly after they are taken into custody and often after they have been arraigned. A preliminary hearing is a court hearing to determine whether the government has enough evidence to support the criminal charges and continue the case. The purpose of a preliminary hearing is to provide a safeguard against overzealous or unwarranted prosecutions by allowing a judge to conduct a brief review of the government's evidence before forcing a defendant to endure the full length of a criminal case. The hearing is especially helpful to defendants who are unable to make bond. But even defendants who have been released on bond are entitled to a preliminary hearing in jurisdictions where these proceedings are offered.

The Nature of the Proceedings

Preliminary hearings are conducted by judges, not juries. In cases where the judge finds sufficient evidence to support the criminal charges, the judge will make a finding of probable cause and the case will continue. This occurs in the vast majority of cases. In jurisdictions that use grand juries, this means the case will proceed to a grand jury. But in rare cases, the judge may find that the evidence against the defendant is insufficient and that the case must be dismissed.

Unlike a full criminal trial, judges in preliminary hearings do not decide the guilt or innocence of the defendant. Instead, judges must review the evidence presented by the prosecution and determine whether it satisfies the probable cause standard for criminal activity. In other words, judges must decide whether the government's evidence is sufficient to show a reasonable jury that the defendant committed the offenses charged in the complaint. Keep in mind that the probable cause standard is a lower evidentiary burden than the criminal trial standard of beyond a reasonable doubt. The prosecution, of course, has the burden of proof in preliminary hearings. Normally, prosecutors can call witnesses and introduce tangible evidence in order to meet the probable cause standard. Often a single law enforcement officer is the only witness called. In addition, the rules of evidence are also relaxed during preliminary hearings and the judge may allow more evidence, including hearsay, to be introduced than that permitted during a criminal trial.

Defendants or their attorneys have the opportunity to cross-examine the prosecution's witnesses, review the evidence introduced, and, if they wish, introduce witnesses and evidence on their own. But in most cases, because the burden of proof is so minimal and the likelihood of a probable cause finding is so high, defendants and their attorneys rarely introduce their own witnesses or evidence.

direct indictment or rapid indictment program
a procedure used in some jurisdictions to avoid the use of a preliminary hearing; requires grand juries to review cases soon after the filing of a criminal complaint

It is important to remember that preliminary hearings are not held in every case. In some states, they are only available in felony cases. In other jurisdictions, they are not available at all. Instead, some courts rely on a ***direct indictment*** or ***rapid indictment program*** that requires grand juries to review cases soon after the filing of a criminal complaint. This program allows prosecutors to avoid the preliminary hearing by submitting the case directly to the grand jury, and it ensures that the defendants held in custody have a reasonably quick assessment of probable cause in their case. And even in cases where preliminary hearings are scheduled, the hearing will not be held if the grand jury issues an indictment on the criminal charges before the time of the hearing.

Strategies

Despite the fairly predictable outcome of preliminary hearings (in almost all cases, the court issues a probable cause finding), these proceedings can be valuable to the parties in a criminal case. For defendants, it provides an initial insight into the government's case. Defendants and their attorneys get the opportunity to see some of the evidence and cross-examine the witnesses called by the prosecution. The testimony offered during preliminary hearings, like all other official court proceedings, is given under oath and recorded. And this testimony can become useful to defendants during later proceedings or even at trial. If later during the criminal proceedings a prosecution witness offers different testimony than that given during the preliminary hearing, this can be used to impeach the witness's credibility and create reasonable doubt. As a result, defendants and their attorneys regularly use preliminary hearings as a way to gather information that will help them build their defense.

Preliminary hearings also can be valuable to prosecutors. It offers them a chance to test the strength of their case by seeing some of their evidence in action. It allows them to see how some of their witnesses appear on the witness stand. It gives them the opportunity to hear questions from the judge and defense attorney. And depending on the questions posed by defense counsel during cross-examination, it may give prosecutors some insight into the weaknesses of their case.

IN THE FIELD

Legal professionals can have a number of tasks associated with preliminary hearings. For those working with prosecutors, preparing for these hearings can be a more abbreviated form of trial preparation. You must review the criminal complaint and any corresponding evidence, identify the elements of the criminal charges, and prepare the witnesses and evidence to satisfy these elements. For those working for criminal defendants, preparing for a preliminary hearing can be much like getting ready for a deposition. You are aware that your client's chances of prevailing during the hearing are slim. But your supervising attorney typically will want to extract as much evidence from the prosecution's witnesses as possible, even if the evidence is not immediately helpful or favorable to your client. As a result, you should review the charges with your client, prepare many open-ended questions for the prosecution's witnesses, and generally remember that you are actually in discovery mode (the search for information) during most preliminary hearings. Another practical tool that can be helpful is to provide clients with some paper and a pen during the hearing, so that they can write down any questions or observations.

ARRAIGNMENT/INITIAL APPEARANCE

For many criminal cases, the defendant's first court appearance is the **_arraignment_**. There are two main functions of an arraignment. The first is to inform defendants of the criminal charges filed against them. Typically, the judge will verbally state the charges in open court or ask defendants if they have received a copy of the complaint or indictment. The second function is to afford the defendant an opportunity to respond to the charges by entering a plea to the charges.

In some cases, an arraignment hearing may be combined with a bond hearing. In still other cases, the arraignment may not be a hearing at all, but rather the defendant may enter a written plea of not guilty and ask the court to set the matter

arraignment
a court hearing where the defendant is informed of criminal charges and has an opportunity to respond to the charges by entering a plea

MAINTAINING PROFESSIONAL CONDUCT

National Federation of Paralegal Associations, Inc. Model Code of Ethics and Professional Responsibility Rule 1.3

A Paralegal Shall Maintain a High Standard of Professional Conduct.

ETHICAL CONSIDERATIONS

EC 1.3(a) A paralegal shall refrain from engaging in any conduct that offends the dignity and decorum of proceedings before a court or other adjudicatory body and shall be respectful of all rules and procedures.

EC 1.3(b) A paralegal shall avoid impropriety and the appearance of impropriety and shall not engage in any conduct that would adversely affect his/her fitness to practice. Such conduct may include, but is not limited to: violence, dishonesty, interference with the administration of justice, and/or abuse of a professional position or public office.

Courtesy of The National Federation of Paralegal Associations http://www.paralegals.org

---

for a pretrial conference with the assigned trial judge. Many courts have found the arraignment process to be a mere formality, with most defendants entering not guilty pleas and the case being scheduled for future proceedings. This is particularly true in felony cases. To expedite matters, some courts allow defendants and their attorneys to sign a written plea or written waiver, acknowledging that they have received a copy of the complaint or indictment, they are waiving a formal arraignment hearing, and they wish to enter a plea of not guilty. The filing of a written plea accomplishes the same essential functions as a formal hearing.

Law Line 9-6
Initial Appearance Form for Judges

Types of Pleas

In most jurisdictions, three types of pleas can be entered during an arraignment—guilty, not guilty, or no contest. A ***guilty plea*** means that the defendant admits that the facts alleged in the complaint/indictment are true and that those facts constitute, as a matter of law, the criminal offense(s) charged. Defendants rarely enter guilty pleas during an arraignment when there are serious criminal charges pending. But in cases where minor charges are alleged, including many traffic-related and misdemeanor cases, defendants may enter a guilty plea, in order to complete the case quickly. Many defendants feel that they are not likely to receive any jail time for these minor offenses, and therefore they might as well admit guilt and resolve the case quickly. From a legal standpoint, this can be a risky strategy because it does not afford defendants and their attorneys a reasonable opportunity to review the prosecution's evidence and consider all possible defenses. But many defendants in minor criminal cases just want to be done with the matter as soon as possible.

The safest bet during an arraignment is for defendants to enter a ***not guilty plea***, where they deny both the facts and the legal allegations in the complaint/indictment. This plea is most often entered during arraignments in serious felony cases in state courts and in most federal criminal cases. This plea preserves all of the defendant's trial-related rights, including the right to receive discovery materials (evidence) from the prosecutor and the right to a trial by jury. Defendants often prefer a not guilty plea during an arraignment because, at this stage of the proceedings, they and their

guilty plea
a plea in which the defendant admits that the facts alleged in the complaint/indictment are true and that those facts constitute, as a matter of law, the offense chanrged

not guilty plea
a plea in which the defendant denies both the facts and the legal allegations in the complaint/indictment

attorneys have not had an adequate chance to review the evidence held by the prosecution. They likely do not know whether there are constitutional, legal, or factual challenges that could me made to refute or otherwise challenge the criminal charges. So in order to allow sufficient opportunity to review the matter and consider all possible legal strategies, the safest bet for most defendants, particularly when serious criminal charges are alleged, is to enter a not guilty plea at the arraignment.

In many jurisdictions, defendants may also enter a ***no contest* or *nolo contendere plea*.** Under this plea, defendants admit to the factual allegations contained in the complaint or indictment, but deny that these facts constitute a criminal offense. In most cases where a no contest plea is entered, the judge will listen to the facts as presented by the prosecutor and then enter a finding as to guilt. In the vast majority of cases, judges will find the defendant guilty following a no contest plea. There is usually no significant difference between a no contest plea and a guilty plea; each likely will result in a conviction. But some defendants, particularly those who may have some civil liability associated with the facts of their criminal case (e.g., a car accident), may be advised to enter a no contest plea instead of a guilty plea. The reason is that a guilty plea is an admission of guilt, and as such, it can be used against defendants in later civil proceedings as an admission. In many jurisdictions, however, defendants who enter a no contest plea are not admitting guilt, and thus, their plea cannot be used against them as an admission in later civil proceedings. Thus, to play it safe, in cases where defendants wish to resolve their case with a guilty plea, they may be advised to enter a plea of no contest.

In still other jurisdictions and in rare cases, the defendant may be permitted to enter what is known as an ***Alford plea***. By entering an Alford plea, defendants maintain their innocence but acknowledge that the prosecution likely has enough evidence to obtain a conviction from a reasonable jury.[5] Many jurisdictions may not accept an Alford plea. But such a plea can be important to some defendants who, for a variety of reasons, do not wish to admit to the facts or legal allegations of criminal charge, but also do not want to prolong the case by proceeding to trial. In cases where defendants enter an Alford plea, the judge likely will find them guilty and proceed to sentencing, either immediately thereafter or at a later hearing.

When defendants enter a guilty plea, the judge must assure that they are making the plea knowingly, voluntarily, and intelligently and that they are aware of the rights they are waiving, including the right to a jury trial. Once a judge accepts a defendant's guilty plea, a conviction is entered into the record and the case may proceed to sentencing. In less serious cases, like state misdemeanor matters, the judge will sentence the defendant immediately after a guilty plea is accepted. In other cases, including federal cases and state felony cases, the judge will ask that a sentencing report be prepared by the probation department and then schedule a separate sentencing hearing for a later date. More details about the nature of pleas are discussed in Chapter 10 with respect to plea bargaining. Also see Figure 9-9.

no contest or *nolo contendere* plea
a plea in which the defendant admits to the factual allegations contained in the complaint or indictment, but denies that these facts constitute a criminal offense under the law

Alford plea
a plea allowed in rare cases by which defendants maintain their innocence but acknowledge that they will likely be found guilty of the charged offense; results in a guilty finding by the trial court

---

FIGURE 9-9 **Types of Pleas**

Type of Plea	Factual Allegations	Legal Allegations
Not Guilty	Deny	Deny
Guilty	Admit	Admit
No Contest	Admit	Deny
Alford Plea	Deny, but acknowledge jury likely to find sufficient	Deny, but recognize jury likely to convict

---

For legal professionals working in arraignment settings, the process may seem very bureaucratic. There can be a lot of forms and paperwork being signed and exchanged during this hearing, including the exchange of police reports, the sharing of complaints, and the filing of written pleas. In cases where there is an actual arraignment hearing, the process can be quite short and formulaic, with the judge, defendants, and attorneys saying and doing relatively the same thing in case after case. But there are some essential tasks that legal professionals must perform during arraignments.

If you work for prosecutors you must ensure that defendants receive a copy of their indictment or complaint. And because defendants may actually enter a plea of guilty or no contest during an arraignment for minor offenses, you must also ensure that the prosecutor is prepared to read a statement of facts that contains all elements of the offense. Prosecutors must also be prepared to respond to legal arguments about whether elements are met. And you must be prepared to state the government's position for sentencing. This includes having a complete and accurate accounting of the defendant's criminal history and a sense of the position held by law enforcement officers and any victims involved with the case.

Legal professionals assisting defendants might view arraignments as a quick formality. As discussed above, oftentimes, the defense attorney has not had adequate time to meet the client, review the government's evidence, and evaluate the facts in light of the applicable law. Thus, to safeguard the defendant's rights, lawyers will simply advise the client to enter a not guilty plea or enter such a plea on behalf of the client. This occurs in most felony cases or other matters where defendants may possibly receive incarceration or other serious consequences after their conviction. In cases where the defendant wishes to resolve the matter at the arraignment, such as in traffic-related cases or some misdemeanor cases, defense attorneys must advise clients on the legal and practical consequences of admitting factual or legal culpability. And where clients still do not wish to enter a not guilty plea, they must also be advised on whether they should enter a guilty plea or no contest plea.

GRAND JURY HEARINGS

As explained above, a grand jury is a group of citizens who convene secretly to review criminal complaints and investigate facts to determine whether there is probable cause to believe criminal activity has occurred. In cases where a grand jury makes a probable cause finding, it will issue an indictment formally charging someone with a criminal offense.

For legal professionals working with grand jury hearings, this phase can be one of the more challenging aspects of a criminal case. For one, grand juries meet in secret, with little if any exposure to the public. As a result, most people are not as familiar with grand jury proceedings as they are with other more public stages of a criminal case. Second, grand jury hearings are one-sided affairs, with prosecutors being the only attorneys who normally present evidence to grand jurors. Criminal suspects and their attorneys have no right to participate in the grand jury hearing. Given this level of secrecy and one-sidedness, the grand jury process can be a complicated and uncertain time for many legal professionals.

The Basis for Grand Juries

As discussed in Chapter 8, the legal touchstone for grand juries is found in the Fifth Amendment to the U.S. Constitution, which provides, in relevant part, that criminal charges for all capital and "infamous" crimes be brought by a grand jury indictment.

In 2005, Travis County, Texas District Attorney Ronnie Earle announces the indictment of U.S. House of Representatives Majority Leader Tom DeLay on conspiracy charges. DeLay stepped aside as House majority leader following his indictment by a Texas grand jury on conspiracy and money laundering charges. He is no longer in Congress. In November 2010, a jury convicted Delay of conspiracy and money laundering charges. In January 2011, the trial court sentenced Delay to a minimum of three years in prison.

The Supreme Court has interpreted this provision to mean that felony charges must be issued via a grand jury indictment, unless a defendant waives this right. The Court, however, has not made this provision applicable to the states. As explained in Chapter 8, even though the Court has applied or "incorporated" almost all of the requirements set forth in the Bill of Rights to the states through the Fourteenth Amendment Due Process Clause, it has yet to make states comply with the Fifth Amendment grand jury requirement.[6] Nevertheless, about half of the states have their own constitutional standards requiring grand jury indictments in felony cases. For those states not using grand juries to produce felony cases, prosecutors or courts typically issue felony charges through the filing of an information (see above).

Originally, grand juries were designed to limit the unfettered prosecutorial power of executive authorities, such as monarchs or other autocratic rulers. The belief was that a panel of citizens would provide a more objective and complete review of cases than a centralized and political ruler. In more modern times, grand juries have been justified as an effective and fair administrative mechanism for assessing probable cause in potential criminal matters. The use of grand juries can also lead the general public to believe that a group of citizens (public peers) is making decisions about criminal charges, not an elected or appointed executive official, thereby promoting a notion of democracy in action.

Many critics, however, find these justifications rather hollow. They claim that, for all practical purposes, grand juries serve as a tool for prosecutors seeking criminal indictments and that there are very few limitations placed on prosecutorial authorities by this process. Critics assert that grand juries are controlled by prosecutors, who have no adversarial counterpart present in the grand jury room, and who unilaterally determine what types of evidence and arguments are presented to grand jurors. Critics suggest that grand jurors typically go along with whatever recommendation the prosecutor makes in a case. This has led to the often-used claim that, if they wanted to, prosecutors could indict a ham sandwich. Some also assert that prosecutors use grand juries as a tool to gather evidence in a case, using the grand jury's subpoena power to compel witnesses to produce evidence and testimony that prosecutors and investigators cannot obtain through other methods.

Thus, depending on your perspective, grand juries can be viewed as an important check on executive authority, an institution that promotes democratic government, or simply a practical tool for enhancing prosecutorial power in the pursuit of criminal indictments.

The Form and Function of Grand Juries

In federal courts, there are two types of grand juries—original (regular) and special. A regular grand jury reviews criminal complaints filed in the normal course of criminal investigations and arrests. Cases are likely to include drug trafficking, fraud, and other crimes involving the use of interstate commerce. *Original* or *regular grand juries* are usually convened for a term of eighteen months, but a judge can extend the term for up to six additional months. *Special grand juries* are convened to investigate a particular factual scenario, usually a large case involving complicated facts and a substantial amount of evidence. Like regular grand juries, special grand juries typically sit for eighteen months, but a judge can extend their term in six-month increments for up to eighteen additional months. In state systems using grand juries, the terms vary considerably. But on average, they are convened for approximately one year.

Though methods can vary, a court typically selects members of the community to serve on grand juries, using voter registration lists, driver's license databases, or tax records. A court initiates this process by sending individuals a summons for grand jury duty. A *summons* is a court order commanding a person to appear before a court. As illustrated by Figure 9-10, a **grand jury summons** commands a person to appear for grand jury duty. The size of state grand juries can vary. But usually, they are within the range of federal grand juries, which typically consist of sixteen to twenty-three people. In both the federal and state systems, a grand jury is usually larger than a trial or **petit jury**, which is used during criminal trials. Once summoned to court, grand jurors will appear before a judge who will administer an oath for grand jury members and discuss their legal obligations. And after being assembled, the grand jury elects a member to serve as a foreperson who will generally serve as the coordinator for the group and the signor of any indictments issued by the full grand jury.

Grand juries meet in a designated room that is usually removed from the general courtrooms. In some jurisdictions, the grand jury room is located inside the prosecutor's office. There is no judge present inside the room. Instead, there typically will be a judge assigned to the grand jury who is contacted only when something unusual occurs or there are legal disputes that need to be addressed. Besides the grand jurors themselves, there will be a court reporter to document the proceedings, a prosecutor and perhaps an assistant who will present evidence to the grand jurors, and, when appropriate, a witness may be present as well. Beyond that, the grand jury room is a limited forum, with just a few individuals beyond the grand jurors themselves. In the federal system and in most states, defendants, suspects, and their attorneys do not have a right to present evidence to the grand jury, although in rare cases, prosecutors may invite suspects to testify.

original or regular grand juries
the typical form of grand jury used to investigate crimes as they arise during a given term, usually a term of eighteen months

special grand juries
grand juries convened to investigate a particular factual scenario

Law Line 9-7
Federal Grand Jury Handbook

grand jury summons
a court order commanding a person to appear for grand jury duty

petit jury
a jury used during criminal trials

FIGURE 9-10 **Sample Grand Jury Summons from Massachusetts**

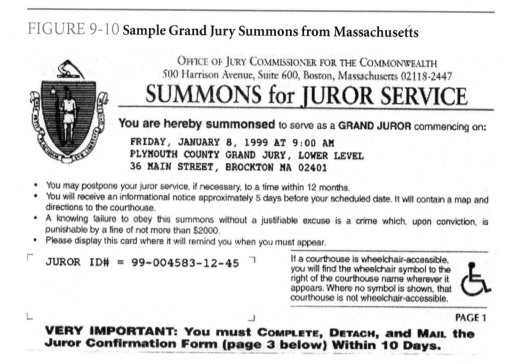

OFFICE OF JURY COMMISSIONER FOR THE COMMONWEALTH
500 Harrison Avenue, Suite 600, Boston, Massachusetts 02118-2447

SUMMONS for JUROR SERVICE

You are hereby summonsed to serve as a **GRAND JUROR** commencing on:

FRIDAY, JANUARY 8, 1999 AT 9:00 AM
PLYMOUTH COUNTY GRAND JURY, LOWER LEVEL
36 MAIN STREET, BROCKTON MA 02401

- You may postpone your juror service, if necessary, to a time within 12 months.
- You will receive an informational notice approximately 5 days before your scheduled date. It will contain a map and directions to the courthouse.
- A knowing failure to obey this summons without a justifiable excuse is a crime which, upon conviction, is punishable by a fine of not more than $2000.
- Please display this card where it will remind you when you must appear.

JUROR ID# = 99-004583-12-45

If a courthouse is wheelchair-accessible, you will find the wheelchair symbol to the right of the courthouse name wherever it appears. Where no symbol is shown, that courthouse is not wheelchair-accessible.

PAGE 1

VERY IMPORTANT: You must COMPLETE, DETACH, and MAIL the Juror Confirmation Form (page 3 below) Within 10 Days.

Once in session, the prosecutor introduces the grand jurors to the facts of a case and presents evidence regarding potential criminal activity. The evidence may include testimony from witnesses, law enforcement officers, or alleged victims, as well as exhibits or other tangible evidence. Prosecutors will then discuss potential criminal charges and will likely have an indictment prepared for the grand jury to consider. The grand jury itself can issue subpoenas to witnesses in order to secure evidence. A ***grand jury subpoena*** is a court order commanding a person to appear before the grand jury. Unlike a summons, a grand jury subpoena seeks evidence, not grand jury service, from individuals. In general, there are two basic forms of subpoenas—a witness subpoena and a subpoena *duces tecum*. As applied to the grand jury setting, a ***witness subpoena*** compels a person to appear before the grand jury and provide oral testimony. A ***subpoena duces tecum*** commands a person to bring certain documents or other evidence for the grand jury's review. In some cases, persons may receive both types of subpoena, thereby compelling both oral testimony and physical evidence within their possession to be presented to the grand jury. See Figure 9-11.

After the evidence is presented in a case, the prosecutor will leave the room and allow the grand jurors to deliberate. Grand jurors must decide whether there is probable cause to believe an identified suspect committed the criminal offense(s) listed in the indictment. If a majority of the grand jury finds probable cause, the foreperson will sign the indictment, thereby resulting in a formal criminal charge against the named defendant. This likely will trigger an arrest warrant or summons (see above) from the criminal court, thereby authorizing law enforcement to apprehend the defendant. In those cases, the defendant will be arrested or summoned to court, where a bond hearing and arraignment will be held. In many cases, when an indictment is issued, the defendant already will be in custody based on an arrest and criminal complaint. In those cases, the court will schedule the case for an arraignment. If a majority of grand jurors do not support an indictment, either the case can be labeled "ignored," which allows the grand jury to revisit the matter at a later time, or the grand jury can issue a "no bill," which reflects that the charges were not supported by probable cause and the case is dismissed.

grand jury subpoena
a court order commanding a person to appear before the grand jury

witness subpoena
a court order compelling a person to appear before the grand jury and provide oral testimony

subpoena *duces tecum*
a court order commanding a person to bring certain documents or other evidence for the grand jury's review

FIGURE 9-11 **Federal Grand Jury Subpoena Form**

AO 110 (Rev. 06/09) Subpoena to Testify Before a Grand Jury

UNITED STATES DISTRICT COURT
for the

SUBPOENA TO TESTIFY BEFORE A GRAND JURY

To:

YOU ARE COMMANDED to appear in this United States district court at the time, date, and place shown below to testify before the court's grand jury. When you arrive, you must remain at the court until the judge or a court officer allows you to leave.

Place:	Date and Time:

You must also bring with you the following documents, electronically stored information, or objects *(blank if not applicable)*:

Date: _____

CLERK OF COURT

_____
Signature of Clerk or Deputy Clerk

The name, address, e-mail, and telephone number of the United States attorney, or assistant United States attorney, who requests this subpoena, are:

Practical Challenges

Because grand jury hearings are not adversarial in nature (only the prosecutor presents evidence), many of these hearings proceed without much legal conflict or dispute. There are, however, some areas that can give rise to conflicts of criminal procedure.

One area of dispute involves the issuance of grand jury subpoenas. When a person receives a grand jury subpoena he or she may object to providing testimony, physical evidence, or both to the grand jury. As ground for this objection, a person may believe the subpoenaed evidence is protected under some legal privilege, such as the attorney/client privilege, physician/patient privilege, or some journalistic privilege. For example, in 2005, *New York Times* reporter Judith Miller tried to avoid a federal grand jury subpoena in what is now known as the "Scooter Libby" case based on her assertion of a reporter's privilege not to disclose the identity of confidential news sources. See Law Line 9-8 and photo. A federal judge, however, rejected this asserted privilege, concluding that, under federal law, reporters cannot withhold the identities of confidential news sources when such information is relevant to grand jury investigations into criminal behavior.[7] Many states, however, provide privileges or shield laws that protect news reporters from disclosing their confidential news sources to state grand juries and other state court proceedings.[8]

Law Line 9-8
Court Opinion Upholding Contempt Order against Judith Miller

In other cases, witnesses who receive a subpoena *duces tecum* may object to the volume or nature of materials they are being asked to submit, they may find the subpoena to be too vague or general, or they may assert that their appearance is too burdensome or their testimony too irrelevant to be compelled.

In these situations, witnesses may respond to the subpoena by filing a motion to quash with the court. As applied to the grand jury setting, a **motion to quash** a subpoena asks the court to quash (invalidate) the grand jury subpoena altogether or, in some cases, to modify the subpoena to constitute a more reasonable request for evidence. If the judge grants the motion to quash, the witness will not have to testify or the parameters of the permitted testimony may be limited through court order. If the judge denies the motion, a witness faces a difficult choice—either comply with the subpoena and testify or refuse testimony and risk being held in contempt by the court. When a court holds someone in **contempt**, it means that it has found the person to have violated or refused a court order. In the case of grand jury testimony, the order violated would be the order to provide testimony to the grand jury. When grand jury witnesses are held in contempt, they can be incarcerated until such time as either (1) they decide to testify, or (2) the grand jury before which they were to appear is dismissed, whichever comes first. In the case of *New York Times* reporter Judith Miller, the court held her in contempt and incarcerated her for twelve weeks for her refusal to disclose her confidential news sources to a federal grand jury in 2005. Miller was released after she negotiated an arrangement with her confidential news source and agreed to testify before the grand jury.[9]

motion to quash
a pleading asking a court to quash (invalidate) the grand jury subpoena

contempt
the situation where a person disobeys a court order

Law Line 9-9
Preparing a Motion to Quash a Grand Jury Subpoeana

New York Times reporter Judith Miller speaks to reporters on September 30, 2005 outside the U.S. District Court House in Washington, DC, after testifying before a grand jury investigating a leak of Central Intelligence Agency information. Miller was released earlier in the day after spending twelve weeks in prison for refusing to testify in a federal probe on the outing of an undercover CIA agent.

Another, area of conflict can occur when witnesses subpoenaed by the grand jury fear that their testimony might lead to criminal charges being filed against them. In these cases, they might have a Fifth Amendment privilege against self-incrimination. See Chapter 12. Witnesses with self-incrimination concerns often are not able to get their grand jury subpoenas quashed, but rather must appear before the grand jury and assert their Fifth Amendment privilege to each question where it might apply. For the witness, this can be challenging because, as explained above, in most jurisdictions, defense attorneys and attorneys for witnesses are not permitted in the grand jury room. So witnesses fearing self-incrimination must work with their attorneys in advance of the grand jury hearing and be prepared to properly assert their Fifth Amendment rights on their own. Typically, courts allow attorneys for witnesses to be present outside the grand jury room and permit the witness to leave the room after each question posed by the prosecutor to consult with the attorney. But unlike most open-court hearings, the attorney is not available to assert objections on the witness's behalf.

A final area of contention occurs when the prosecutor seeks to compel witnesses to testify by offering them a grant of immunity for their testimony. This is one way a prosecutor can respond to a witness's assertion of a Fifth Amendment privilege. There are two primary types of immunity that can be granted to witnesses. The first is *use immunity*, by which the prosecutor agrees not to use any of a witness's testimony (or evidence derived therefrom) against that witness in a criminal case. The second type of immunity is *transactional immunity*, which is a broader form of immunity because it assures the witness that he or she will not be prosecuted for any transaction or event that he or she discusses during his testimony. In most situations where a prosecutor offers immunity to witnesses in exchange for their testimony, it comes in the form of use immunity. Most prosecutors are reluctant to offer transactional immunity to witnesses because it allows a witness to be immunized from prosecution for any event or transaction mentioned during the witness's testimony.

use immunity
a type of legal protection provided by prosecutors, whereby they agree not to use any of a witness's testimony (or evidence derived therefrom) against that witness in a criminal case

transactional immunity
a type of legal protection provided by prosecutors, whereby they assure witnesses that they will not be prosecuted for any transaction or event that they discuss during their testimony

IN THE FIELD

Legal professionals involved in grand jury proceedings can have many tasks. If you are a prosecution assistant, you may be involved with a variety of people and functions. These might include:

- Reviewing criminal complaints to assess whether they should be presented to a grand jury for felony charges.
- Meeting with law enforcement and victims to prepare them for grand jury testimony.
- Preparing exhibits for the grand jury.
- Preparing the indictments for grand jurors to consider.
- Preparing grand jury subpoenas for witnesses.
- Keeping victims and other interested parties informed of the grand jury's actions.

Legal professionals working for defense attorneys will often have a more passive role with most grand juries. For many cases, your role will be to monitor, either online or at the courthouse, the grand jury reports that are issued during the day to see if clients have been indicted. In cases where a client is indicted, you may also be asked to do the following:

- Inform the client and any family members or friends of the grand jury's actions.
- Explain the nature of the charges and the possible penalties.
- Notify the client of the next court appearance.

- If the client has not yet been apprehended and processed, work with prosecutors to allow for clients to turn themselves via a summons rather than be arrested pursuant to an arrest warrant.

In more complicated cases, legal professionals working for criminal defense attorneys may actually be involved in preparing for the grand jury hearing. This may involve performing such tasks as these:

- Explaining the grand jury process to clients and other relevant persons.
- Preparing clients for their testimony before the grand jury.
- Reviewing subpoenas to determine whether there are any grounds for filing a motion to quash the subpoena.
- Preparing and filing a motion to quash the subpoena.
- Helping clients comply with grand jury subpoenas, particularly subpoenas *duces tecum*, to ensure that that have fully and accurately complied with the grand jury's request.
- Rehearsing and role-playing with clients in preparation for the grand jury, including the proper way to assert the Fifth Amendment right against self-incrimination.
- Working with defense attorneys sitting outside the grand jury room as their clients testify.

Overall, in jurisdictions where grand juries are used, the proceedings are usually quite administrative and formulaic in nature, with the prosecutor controlling most of the hearing and cases being presented in a fairly methodical manner. But in more complex or unique cases, grand jury proceedings can be more dynamic events, with more detailed evidence being presented and perhaps even legal challenges being made within the proceedings.

CHAPTER **SUMMARY**

- A criminal case can official begin in many ways, including an arrest and filing of criminal complaint, the receipt of a citation, a grand jury indictment, or the prosecutor's filing of an information.
- The terms *bail* and *bond* are generally used interchangeably and refer to the conditions upon which defendants will be released from government custody pending the resolution of their criminal case.
- In setting bond, judges typically focus on two primary factors: (1) whether the defendant is likely to return for future court proceedings (risk of flight), and (2) whether the defendant poses a risk of harm to the community.
- There are several different types of bond, including personal recognizance bond, unsecured bond, secured bond, cash bond, property bond, and surety bond.
- A preliminary hearing or probable cause hearing is a court hearing to determine whether the government has enough evidence to support the criminal charges and continue the case.
- In most preliminary hearings, the court makes a probable cause finding and the case will continue, either based on the existing criminal complaint or via submission to a grand jury. Preliminary hearings,

however, can serve as important tools for prosecutors and defense attorneys in evaluating the evidence in a case.
- An arraignment is a hearing where defendants are informed of the criminal charges filed against them and given the opportunity to respond by entering a plea to the charges.
- In most jurisdictions, there are three types of pleas—guilty, not guilty, and no contest. In some jurisdictions, defendants may also enter an Alford plea.
- A grand jury is a group of citizens who convene to review criminal complaints and otherwise investigate matters to determine whether there is probable cause to believe criminal activity has occurred. In cases where a grand jury makes a probable cause finding, it will issue an indictment formally charging someone with a criminal offense. In cases where no probable cause is found, the grand jury can issue a no bill or simply state that it is ignoring the case.
- In federal cases, the Fifth Amendment requires that felony charges be filed by a grand jury, unless a defendant waives this right. This constitutional requirement does not apply to the states. But approximately one-half of all states still employ a grand jury in some capacity.

KEY **TERMS**

10 percent bond
Alford plea
arraignment
arrest
arrest warrant
bail
Bail Reform Act of 1984
bond
cash bond or straight bond
citation
contempt
count
criminal complaint
direct indictment or rapid
  indictment program
felony
grand jury
grand jury subpoena

grand jury summons
guilty plea
ignore
indictment
information
intake
mandatory appearance
misdemeanor
motion to modify bond
motion to quash
no bill
no contest or *nolo contendere* plea
not guilty plea
original or regular grand juries
payout ticket
personal recognizance or own
  recognizance (OR) bond
petit jury

preliminary hearing or probable
  cause hearing
preventive detention
probable cause
property bond
secured bond
special grand juries
statute of limitations
subpoena *duces tecum*
summons
summons
surety bond
transactional immunity
true bill
unsecured bond
use immunity
witness subpoena

QUESTIONS FOR **DISCUSSION**

1. What are the different ways a criminal case can officially begin?

2. What is the difference between an indictment and an information?

3. What is the purpose of a preliminary hearing? What standard of proof is required during this hearing?

4. What factors do judges consider in setting bail or bond for defendants? Given the Eighth Amendment's language barring excessive bail, it is constitutionally appropriate for some judges to deny bail altogether for some defendants?

5. What are the different types of bond that can be issued in a case and how do they work?

6. What is an arraignment and when does it occur during the criminal justice process?

7. What are the different types of pleas that a defendant can enter and what are the legal distinctions among them?

8. What is the purpose of a grand jury and how does it conduct its business?

9. Given the openness and transparency of a democratic government, do you find it appropriate for the government to shroud grand jury proceedings in so much secrecy?

10. What is the difference between a summons and a subpoena?

11. What are some of the procedural challenges that can arise during grand jury proceedings?

12. Under what circumstances might you file a motion to quash a grand jury subpoena?

REFERENCES

1. Sol Wachtler, *After the Madness*, e-reads.com, p. 254 (2003).

2. See *Ornelas v. United States*, 517 U.S. 690, 696 (1996); *Illinois v. Gates*, 462 U.S. 213, 238 (1983).

3. See Roxana Hegeman, "Possible Threats Spur $20M Bond for Tiller Suspect," Associated Press, June 16, 2009.

4. 481 U.S. 739 (1988).

5. See *North Carolina v. Alford*, 400 U.S. 25 (1970).

6. See *Hurtado v. California*, 110 U.S. 516 (1884).

7. *In re: Grand Jury Subpoena, Judith Miller*, 405 F.3d 17 (D.C. Cir. 2005).

8. See Ohio Revised Code, Section 2739.04 (applying to broadcast journalists) and Section 2739.12 (applying to print journalists).

9. See Judith Miller, "My Four Hours Testifying in the Federal Grand Jury Room," October 16, 2005, http://www.judithmiller.com/496/my-four-hours-testifying-in-the-federal-grand

APPENDIX
DEVELOPING YOUR LEGAL ANALYSIS

A. THE LAW WHERE YOU LIVE

Assume that you are working with Abe Nizney, a local prosecutor who is assigned to the courtroom that conducts bond hearings for newly arrested state defendants. Mr. Nizney would like to present arguments to the court for denying bond to a defendant in a felonious assault case, or a least urge the court to establish a high bond for the defendant, so that he will not likely be released before trial. The case is based on the defendant's conduct during a fight inside a bar, where another patron received several cuts and a concussion as the result of the defendant's alleged conduct.

Using one of your classmates, friends, or family members to play the role of the defendant, obtain some background information to be used during the bond hearing. Consider the relevant factors for setting bond, as offered in the website below (or other reliable resources). Then based on the information provided by your classmate/friend/family member, as well as the nature of the criminal charge and alleged harm to the victim, assess the best arguments for issuing or not issuing bond for the defendant.

Just Cause Law Collective

http://www.lawcollective.org/article.php?id=49
Offers detailed information and advice on preparing
for bail hearings.

B. INSIDE THE FEDERAL COURTS

Assume that you are working in a law firm that represents criminal defendants in federal court. Janet Smith, one of the newer attorneys in the office, is representing a client who has just been arrested by federal authorities. Ms. Smith is not that familiar with the intake process, that is, the interview/review that will be performed by the Pretrial Services Division of your federal district court's Probation Department. As a result, Ms. Smith is asking you to research the process and obtain the necessary information, so that she can be prepared when she meets with the new client and represents him during the pre-bond interview.

Accordingly, contact the Pretrial Services Division of your federal district court's Probation Department. Identify how the office handles interviews with new federal defendants and otherwise conducts its assessment for the bond hearing. If available, obtain a copy of the intake form used by the office to conduct pretrial interviews and assessments for bond hearings. Ask a probation officer to explain how they tally information for federal judges to consider in bond hearings. Then prepare a memorandum to Ms. Smith outlining your findings.

C. CYBER SOURCES

Assume you are working with Zach Stebbins, a criminal defense attorney who is representing three clients in different criminal cases. Each of the clients is awaiting word from the local state grand jury as to whether he or she will be charged with felony offenses and, if so, on what types of charges. You are asked to monitor the grand jury's report and notify the clients and Mr. Stebbins when the grand jury has issued its findings.

Using your local felony court as the jurisdiction, locate the electronic source for its grand jury reports. Then identify three cases listed in the report and review the report and actual indictment (if available). Assume that the three individuals identified in the cases are clients that Mr. Stebbins represents and that you must explain to each of them the actions of the grand jury. Did the grand jury indict the client? Did it ignore the case or issue a no bill? If an indictment was issued, what criminal offenses were charged? Using the criminal code for your local jurisdiction, what elements must be proven in order for the prosecution to gain a conviction for these charges? Is there any other information that the client should know—the assigned judge, any codefendants, or the date of the next court appearance (often, the arraignment date)?

If your local courts do not have online grand jury reports or you are otherwise having trouble locating this document, you can also use the following websites to perform this exercise:

Hamilton County, Ohio

http://www.courtclerk.org/grand_jury.asp

Miami Dade County, Florida

*http://www.miamisao.com/publications/
grandjuryreports.htm*

D. ETHICS AND PROFESSIONALISM

Assume you are working as a paralegal for a criminal defense attorney who is representing Bill Johnson in a case of felony theft. Mr. Johnson has just learned that his case has been assigned to Judge Lance Tibbins, a ten-year trial judge on the local Superior Court. Mr. Johnson is calling you to ask you about Judge Tibbins. He wants to know if (1) he is a "good" judge; (2) what kind of reputation he has with regard to sentencing; (3) what this assignment means for the strategies in the case; (4) whether you would recommend a bench trial instead of a jury trial; and (5) any other "insider" information on Judge Tibbins.

Assume further that you know Judge Tibbins quite well. Your firm has had many cases with him during the last ten years. And in most cases, the experience for your clients has not been very good. In your assessment, Judge Tibbins is an abrasive judge who does not treat criminal defendants fairly and has a reputation for giving severe sentences in criminal cases. You would like to respond to Mr. Johnson's questions by telling him everything you know about Judge Tibbins, but you are a little concerned about maintaining your ethical duties of professionalism to the court and the local bar. In a two-page memorandum, identify how you would respond to Mr. Johnson's questions based on the information you have and your ethical obligations. Be sure to consider Rule 1.3 and the ethical considerations offered by the National Federation of Paralegal Associations (below), as well as any state or local ethical standards that may apply.

National Federation of Paralegal Associations, Inc.

http://www.paralegals.org/displaycommon.cfm?an=1&subarticlenbr=133

chapter **ten**

PRETRIAL PROCEDURES: DISCOVERY, MOTIONS, THE EXCLUSIONARY RULE, AND PLEA BARGAINING

A wise man proportions his belief to the evidence.

—David Hume

The criminal is to go free because the constable has blundered.
—Judge (later Justice) Benjamin Cardozo, *People v. Defore*[1]

Our cases have consistently recognized that unbending application of the exclusionary sanction to enforce ideals of governmental rectitude would impede unacceptably the truth-finding functions of judge and jury.
—Justice Byron White, *United States v. Leon*[2]

LEARNING OBJECTIVES

After reading this chapter, you should be able to

- Recognize the many events that can occur during the pretrial stage of a criminal case.

- Appreciate the importance of the discovery process of a criminal proceeding and the challenges associated with sharing evidence between the parties.

- Prepare a basic request for discovery or prepare a response to a party's request for discovery.

- Discuss the types of evidence that a criminal defendant is constitutionally entitled to receive from the prosecutor.

- Prepare a basic subpoena, subpoena *duces tecum*, and a motion to quash a subpoena.

- Understand the complexities of plea bargaining and the multiple interests and parties that might be involved in negotiating a plea agreement.

- Recognize the importance and different types of pretrial motions used in a criminal case.

- Prepare a basic motion to suppress evidence and/or memorandum in opposition to a motion to suppress evidence.

- Understand and explain the use of the exclusionary rule and the fruit of the poisonous tree doctrine in criminal cases.

INTRODUCTION

pretrial
a term used to describe the time between the formal criminal charge and trial in a criminal case. In some setting, this term is also used to describe a scheduled conference for the parties and the court to meet and discuss matters related to a case.

One of the most critical time periods of a criminal case occurs after a defendant is formally charged and arraigned, but before the scheduled trial date. This is known as the ***pretrial*** stage of a criminal case. There are many procedures that can occur during this stage of a criminal case. In most cases, the prosecutor and defense attorney are exchanging evidence with one another. The parties also may be filing motions with the court seeking rulings on the admissibility of the evidence or the legal viability of the charges. In addition, the parties might be engaged in plea negotiations during this time. And finally, the parties can be preparing their cases for trial. These and other pretrial proceedings require legal professionals to understand four primary areas of criminal procedure: (1) the discovery process, (2) motion practice, (3) the exclusionary rule, and (4) plea bargaining.

DISCOVERY

discovery
the pretrial process by which the prosecutor and the defendant exchange information and evidence about their respective cases

Discovery is the pretrial process by which the prosecutor and the defendant exchange information and evidence about their respective cases. In some circles, the term *discovery* is used by legal professionals to describe an object or group of objects, such as in "I received discovery" or "I gave discovery." Either way, the discovery phase of a criminal case allows a party to discover eligible materials held or controlled by the opposing party.

request for discovery
written request seeking discovery materials from an opposing party

In most criminal cases, the defendant initiates the discovery process by submitting a ***request for discovery*** to the prosecutor. In some jurisdictions, this document is also filed with the clerk of courts. A request for discovery is similar to a motion (see Figure 10-1) wherein the requesting party asks for copies of or the opportunity to review certain materials held by the opposing party. Depending on the jurisdiction, this might include the names of witnesses, the prosecutor's trial exhibits, exculpatory evidence, and any forensic test results.

In some cases, requests for discovery can be very lengthy and detailed. For example, in cases based on scientific or computer-related evidence, defendants may wish to view, copy, or test forensic materials, such as DNA evidence or computer hard drives. In these situations, legal professionals must be careful when drafting requests for discovery to ensure that all possible materials held or controlled by the prosecutor are formally included in the written request.

In other cases, requests for discovery can be quite generic in nature. For example, in some petty theft or simple assault cases, the government's case might be based purely on eyewitness testimony. As such, legal professionals might use more standardized discovery requests to secure all of the relevant and eligible materials from the prosecutor. Most law offices maintain standardized requests for discovery, which follow the detailed language of the court's rules on discovery. These standardized requests, however, can and should be made more specific where legal professionals have reason to seek more specific forms of evidence.

Before making a request for discovery, legal professionals should read the court rules for this process. Each jurisdiction has its own rules for discovery. These rules identify the types of materials eligible for review and the process by which materials are exchanged. At the federal level, Federal Rule of Criminal Procedure 16 provides the standards for discovery in criminal cases. Many states also list their discovery standards under the "Rule 16" found within their rules of criminal procedure.

At a minimum, requests for discovery should mirror the language found within the applicable discovery rule. All discoverable items listed within Rule 16 (or similar rule) should be included a defendant's or prosecutor's discovery

Law Line 10-1
Discovery Motions

request. But in cases where a party knows of particular items of evidence possibly held by the opposing side or where a party has a particular interest in evidence that might be held by the opposing party, a more detailed request should be included in the request for discovery. For example, if police seek hundreds of documents from a defendant's office, there may be particular items, such as calendars, note pads, or bills, within this large volume of materials that may be useful to the defendant's case. The prosecutor, however, may not recognize these items as being exculpatory or otherwise discoverable under a generic request for discovery. In these and similar situations, legal professionals should include specific items within their discovery request.

The same is true in many cases involving scientific evidence, such as DUI or OMVI cases based on breathalyzer or other blood alcohol (BAC) tests. In addition to requesting basic items of discovery, legal professionals representing defendants

---

FIGURE 10-1 **Basic Discovery Request (Abbreviated)**

MONTGOMERTY COUNTY
MUNICIPAL COURT

STATE OF IDAHO	) Case No.: CMC – 2010-45889
	)
Plaintiff,	) INFORMAL REQUEST FOR DISCOVERY
vs.	)
	)
SAM STEVENS	)
	)
Defendant	)

TO THE PROSECUTING ATTORNEY IN THE ABOVE-ENTITLED ACTION:

Pursuant to Criminal Rule 16, Notice is hereby given that I presently represent Defendant who is charged with a violation of _____. In accordance with the provisions of Penal Code _____ the Defendant requests disclosure and production of the materials and information listed below, within fifteen days of the date of delivery of this request.

1.   Any and all police reports, supplemental reports or the like relating to this case.

2.   Any and all citations or tickets issued in this matter.

3.   Any and all statements, oral, written or otherwise recorded or preserved in any manner, attested to, signed by or not, alleged to have been made by the Defendant to any person at any time regarding the facts or circumstances of this case.

4.   Any and all names, addresses and phone numbers of any persons who may be called to testify against Defendant at trial or any other hearing on issues related to this case.

5.   Any and all statements made by any of the aforementioned witnesses, oral or written, recorded in any manner, attested to or signed or not by them.

6.   Any and all names, addresses and phone numbers of any percipient witnesses to any aspect of the offense, investigation or analysis conducted in this case, whether favorable or unfavorable to the defense, regardless of the prosecution's intent to call these persons as witnesses in any hearing(s).

7.   Any and all statements made by any of the aforementioned witnesses, oral or written, recorded in any manner, attested to or signed, or not, by them.

(continued)

FIGURE 10-1 **Continued**

8.   Any and all audio or visual recordings of the Defendant, the scene, or any other facts or circumstances related to the above offense however recorded and maintained.

9.   Any and all criminal records allegedly relating to this Defendant.

10. NOTICE IS HEREBY GIVEN THAT THE DEFENSE REQUESTS ANY AND ALL ORIGINAL TAPES OF COMMUNICATION REGARDING THIS EVENT BE PRESERVED FOR INSPECTION.

11. The specific name of the State's expert who will testify as a technical supervisor and will interpret the breath test device results.

Defendant asks that this document be treated as a continuing request through the completion of trial.

Thank you in advance for your cooperation.

Sincerely,

J.Q. Attorney
Attorney Registration No. 000000
704 Houser St.
Boise, ID 45555
761-555-5555

---

in these cases may also want detailed discovery items about the instrument used to test the defendant's BAC. This might include the operation manual for the testing instrument, the dates and methods used to calibrate the machine, the qualifications of the officer administering the BAC test, and other scientific/technical information regarding the test. All of these items should be spelled out with specificity in a defendant's request for discovery.

Materials Discoverable from the Prosecutor

Under Federal Criminal Rule 16, upon request, a defendant is entitled to review and/or receive copies of types of materials, if they are within the custody or control of the government. These include (1) the defendant's oral statements, if made "before or after arrest, in response to interrogation by a person the defendant knew was a government agent if the government intends to use the statement at trial"; (2) the defendant's written or recorded statement; (3) if the defendant is an organization, the statements made by the organization's agents; (4) the defendant's prior criminal record; (5) documents and objects within the government's possession, custody, or control, which are material to preparing the defense, are to be used by the government in its case-in-chief at trial, or are obtained from or belong to the defendant; (6) reports of examinations and tests, which are material to preparing a defense or will be used by the government in its case-in-chief; and (7) written summaries of any expert testimony that the government intends to use during its case-in-chief, including the bases and reasons for expert opinions and the witness's qualifications.

But in most cases, Federal Criminal Rule 16 does not allow defendants to obtain or inspect reports, memoranda, or other internal government documents made by an attorney for the government or other government agent in connection with investigating or prosecuting the case. These are known as ***attorney work***

attorney work product under the work product doctrine
documents or other materials made in connection with investigating or prosecuting a case; many are not discoverable by an opposing party

product under the work product doctrine. This doctrine applies to many types of attorney work, not just prosecutorial work product. And in general, this doctrine holds that materials created in preparation for trial, including the mental impressions, opinions, and theories of attorneys and their agents, are not discoverable by an opposing party.

Rule 16 also does not allow the pretrial discovery or inspection of statements made by prospective government witnesses. And unless the defendant can show likely irregularities with the grand jury, Rule 16 does not allow defendants to obtain pretrial discovery or inspection of the grand jury's recorded proceedings.

Materials Discoverable from the Defendant

Under Federal Criminal Rule 16, and under most other court rules, if a defendant does not request and receive discovery from the prosecutor, the prosecutor is not eligible to receive materials from the defendant. But if the defendant requests discovery and the prosecutor properly complies with this request, the prosecutor may request reciprocal discovery from the defendant. For example, under Federal Criminal Rule 16(a)(1)(E), if a defendant requests documents and objects from the government, and the government properly complies with this request, upon request from the prosecutor the defendant must permit the government to inspect and to copy the same type of eligible documents and objects.

Law Line 10-2
Federal Criminal Rule 16

Generally speaking, Rule 16 allows the prosecutor to obtain many of the same materials from the defendant that were eligible for inspection and receipt by the defendant from the prosecutor. These materials include (1) documents and objects within the defendant's custody or control that the defendant intends to use in the defendant's case-in-chief at trial; (2) reports of examinations and tests, which the defendant has and intends to use at trial, and (3) summaries of expert witness opinions and the experts' qualifications.

Under Rule 16, defendants are not required to disclose their work product or the work product of their attorneys and agents made in preparation for trial. Defendants are also not required to provide prosecutors with statements made by the defendant or witnesses.

Motions to Compel

Initially, discovery procedures are handled between the parties themselves, with little if any involvement by the trial court. Normally, the parties submit their requests directly to each other and exchange materials without any judicial direction or control. But in some cases, a defendant or prosecutor may have reason to believe that the opposing party has not fully complied with a discovery request. Legal professionals should carefully review the materials provided as discovery and compare them to the items requested. In cases where legal professionals believe that the opposing party may have forgotten or overlooked discoverable materials within its possession, they might make a follow-up request or phone call to determine the status and availability of the missing items.

In some cases, opposing parties might indicate that they do not have the materials within their possession or control. In other cases, the parties may see their mistake and provide the remaining materials. In still other cases, opposing parties may assert that the materials are not discoverable under the court rules for discovery. If discovery disputes cannot be worked out between the parties themselves, the requesting party may need to seek judicial intervention.

This is often accomplished through a ***motion to compel discovery***, which is a formal motion filed with the trial court asking for an order compelling the opposing

motion to compel discovery
a motion seeking court intervention in obtaining discovery materials from an opposing party

party to comply with the moving party's discovery request. Generally, this motion identifies the extrajudicial measures the moving party used to seek discovery, outlines the moving party's basis for believing the opposing party has not fully complied, and then requests an order from the court compelling the disclosure of the requested discovery materials. In addition, the moving party may also request a hearing on the motion. See Figure 10-2.

FIGURE 10-2 **Motion to Compel Discovery –** *State of Florida v. Anthony* (Abbreviated)

IN THE CIRCUIT COURT OF THE NINTH JUDICIAL CIRCUIT, IN AND FOR ORANGE COUNTY, FLORIDA

STATE OF FLORIDA

CASE NO: 48-2008-CF-15606-O

    Plaintiff,

DIVISION: 16

vs.

CASEY MARIE ANTHONY,

    Defendant.

_____/

STATE OF FLORIDA'S SECOND MOTION TO COMPEL RECIPROCAL DISCOVERY and MOTION FOR DISCOVERY SCHEDULE

COMES NOW, the State of Florida, by and through the undersigned Assistant State Attorney, pursuant to Florida Rule of Criminal Procedure 3.220(d), and moves this Honorable Court for an order compelling CASEY MARIE ANTHONY to provide the names and current addresses of any witnesses she intends to call at hearing or trial in the above-entitled action. The State of Florida also requests this Honorable Court enter a pretrial order outlining a discovery schedule in anticipation of a trial date in the summer of 2010. In support of this request, the State says as follows:

1. At a scheduling conference with the court on July 7, 2009, counsel for defendant Anthony advised that trial preparation in the case would take approximately one year with anticipated filing dates for defense motions shortly after Labor Day, 2009. Counsel suggested that once the motions were filed, she would submit a proposed motions schedule to the court.

2. Understanding the volume of information that counsel needed to review, the Court agreed to a suggested trial status date of January 21, 2010 striking the case from the October 12, 2009 trial docket. As pretrial discovery continued, it was anticipated that by January, 2010, counsel for both parties would be in a better position to address a realistic trial date during the summer of 2010.

3. As previously noted in *State of Florida's Motion to Compel Reciprocal Discovery* filed September 10, 2009, the only response that the defendant has made toward fulfilling her reciprocal obligation was a *Defense Witness List* filed November 20, 2008 and an *Amended Defense Witness List* filed January 22, 2009 due to improper form of the original.

4. In a written response to the original *Motion to Compel Reciprocal Discovery*, as well as during a hearing on the motion on October 16, 2009, counsel for the defendant informed this Court that the defendant understood her reciprocal discovery obligations and was prepared to meet same. Despite these assurances to the Court, Miss Anthony has filed motions with attached statements from witnesses purporting to have information regarding specific aspects of the case. See *Defendant's Motion in Limine to Introduce*

(continued)

FIGURE 10-2 **Continued**

Prior Bad Acts and other Circumstantial Evidence Pertaining to Roy Kronk signed November 18, 2009, but served on the Office of the State Attorney on November 19, 2009 and *Motion to Modify the Court's Order on Defendant's Application for Subpoena Duces Tecum for Documents in the Possession of Texas Equusearch* signed and served on November 23, 2009.

5. Neither motion was filed with a list of the names and addresses of witnesses as required by Florida Rule of Criminal Procedure 3.220(d)(1)(A). Instead, upon inquiry, the undersigned was informed initially via email from Andrea Lyon on Friday, November 20, 2009 that the "potential witnesses should be obvious from the filing", and then ultimately an email was received from Jose Baez on Tuesday, November 24, 2009 with "witness contact information" listing lawyers for Crystal & Brandon Sparks (in Washington DC), Jill Kerley (in Knoxville, TN), and Laura Buchanan (in Woodbridge, NJ). At that point, the undersigned made a specific request for a formal witness list with current addresses as required by the Rule and was advised that the defense feels they have no "further obligation to file anything" and "…the witnesses do not want the media harassing them in the meantime."

6. This unilateral decision on the part of a party to hold the witness addresses confidential runs afoul of the basic tenets of the Rules of Criminal Procedure and well-established case law. The FRCP do not permit any party to hold confidential the names and addresses of witnesses except in certain proscribed circumstances. FRCP 3.220(g)(2) While those circumstances are not applicable here, the case law dealing with the disclosure of the name and address of a confidential informant is instructive. Litigation on this issue in both the Federal and State courts quite naturally deals with the potential constitutional violation when a defendant's ability to confront the witness(es) against him/her is hampered. While the State can not assert a constitutional violation, the issue before this Court is one of fundamental fairness. In Hassberger v. State, 350 So.2d 1 (Fla. 1977), the Supreme Court of Florida cited language in Smith v. Illinois, 390 U.S. 129 (1968) for the proposition that "when the credibility of a witness is in issue, the very starting point in 'exposing falsehood and bringing out the truth' through cross-examination must necessarily be to ask the witness who he is and where he lives. The witness' name and address open countless avenues of in-court examination and out-of-court investigation. To forbid this most rudimentary inquiry at the threshold is effectively to emasculate the right of cross-examination itself."

[Items 7-11 omitted]

WHEREFORE, the State of Florida respectfully requests that this Honorable Court conduct a hearing on this matter, or alternatively, order the defendant to immediately turn over any and all evidence to include the names and addresses of witnesses, any statements or reports generated by those witnesses, and any tangible papers or objects to be used at hearing or trial. The State additionally requests that this Court enter a pretrial order setting discovery, motion, and hearing deadlines, applicable to both parties, so this matter can proceed to trial as expeditiously as possible.

Respectfully Submitted this 9th day of December, 2009,

LINDA DRANE BURDICK
Assistant State Attorney
FL Bar #0826928
415 North Orange Avenue
Orlando, FL 32801
407.836.2402

Before filing a motion to compel discovery, legal professionals should make every effort to obtain discovery without judicial intervention. In addition to filing a clearly worded request for discovery, this may also include submitting a follow-up letter or request to the opposing party, or simply making a phone call to opposing counsel to determine the status of the party's discovery response. But a defendant or prosecutor who has exhausted all reasonable and extrajudicial means to obtain eligible discovery should file a motion to compel discovery when the other efforts have failed.

Under Federal Criminal Rule 16, trial judges reviewing motions to compel discovery have several options if they find that a party has not complied with discovery rules : "(A) order that party to permit the discovery or inspection; specify its time, place, and manner; and prescribe other just terms and conditions; (B) grant a continuance; (C) prohibit that party from introducing the undisclosed evidence; or (D) enter any other order that is just under the circumstances." In most cases, a trial judge will simply order a noncomplying party to provide the outstanding discovery materials. But in more egregious cases involving discovery violations, particularly those discovered after a defendant is convicted, a judge may impose more severe sanctions, including dismissal of the indictment (see below).

The bottom line is that legal professionals working for both prosecutors and defense attorneys must pay careful attention to discovery requests. And where there appears to be a discrepancy between the materials requested and the items supplied, legal professionals must make further inquiry and requests, or even seek court intervention.

Discovery and the Constitution

In some cases, the prosecutor's failure to provide complete and timely discovery to the defendant may violate the defendant's constitutional rights to due process and a fair trial. For example, in 2008, federal prosecutors secured a conviction against then United States Senator Ted Stevens (R-AK) for fraud and corruption charges. But approximately six months after a federal jury convicted Stevens, the judge in the case dismissed the charges because federal prosecutors had improperly withheld evidence from Stevens's lawyers while the case was being processed. In essence, the court found that the prosecutor's failure to provide all eligible discovery materials violated Stevens's right to procedural due process, thereby warranting the dismissal of the indictment.[3] In many other criminal cases, defendants cite the withholding of discovery as constituting prosecutorial misconduct and due process violations.[4]

The U.S. Supreme Court has held that the constitutional right to due process guarantees a criminal defendant's right to receive certain materials from the government for trial purposes. In *Brady v. Maryland* (1963),[5] the Court ruled that, upon request, defendants are entitled to any ***exculpatory evidence*** (items that might lead to the defendant's exoneration) within the prosecutor's control or possession. The Court held that "the suppression by the prosecution of evidence favorable to an accused upon request violates due process where the evidence is material either to guilt or punishment, irrespective of the good faith or bad faith of the prosecution." Under the ***Brady rule***, as it is known, "[t]he question is not whether the defendant would more likely than not have received a different verdict with the evidence, but whether in its absence he received a fair trial, understood as a trial resulting in a verdict worthy of confidence."[6] Generally, the *Brady* rule requires prosecutors to disclose evidence that is favorable to a defendant, which is either exculpatory or impeaching and is material to either guilt or punishment.

In addition, in *Giglio v. United States* (1972),[7] the Court ruled that, upon request, a defendant is also entitled to materials within the prosecutor's possession

exculpatory evidence
items or information that might lead to the defendant's exoneration

***Brady* rule**
legal rule that requires prosecutors to disclose exculpatory evidence to the defendant

Law Line 10-3
Brady v. Maryland (1963)

that may be used to impeach government witnesses. As used by many legal professionals, the phrase **Giglio material** refers to information that might impeach the character or testimony of the prosecutor's witness during a criminal trial. **Impeach** means to challenge the credibility of a witness or piece of evidence. An attorney can use impeachment evidence to undermine the credibility or accuracy of witnesses' testimony by showing that their statements are unreliable or untrustworthy. Impeachment materials might include a witness's prior inconsistent statements, criminal record, or plea agreement with the prosecution. For example, a prosecutor may have agreed not to prosecute a witness in exchange for the witness's testimony. If so, this agreement must be disclosed to the defendant.

In *Jencks v. United States* (1957), the Supreme Court ruled "that the defendant on trial in a federal criminal prosecution is entitled, for impeachment purposes, to relevant and competent statements of a government witness in possession of the [g]overnment touching the events or activities as to which the witness has testified at trial." The Court, however, did not indicate when the prosecution must provide the statements to the defendant. In response to *Jencks*, Congress enacted 18 U.S.C. § 3500, commonly known as the **Jencks Act**, which largely codifies the Court's ruling in *Jencks* requiring the prosecutor to provide defendants with verbatim statements or reports made by government witnesses. But the Jencks Act does not require the prosecutor to provide these statements until *after* the witness has testified during the government's case. Under the act, once the government's witness testifies, and upon the defendant's motion, the trial court must order the prosecutor to produce any statement of the witness in his possession relating to the subject matter as to which the witness testified. The defense attorney can then review these statements and, if desired, use them to cross-examine the government's witness.

Finally, in *Kyles v. Whitley* (1995),[8] the Supreme Court made it clear that prosecutors are also responsible for disclosing exculpatory material held by law enforcement officials. Under *Kyles*, prosecutors have an affirmative obligation to inquire about and disclose any favorable evidence that is in the hands of other government agents working on the case. According to the Court:

> [T]he individual prosecutor has a duty to learn of any favorable evidence known to the others acting on the government's behalf in the case, including the police. But whether the prosecutor succeeds or fails in meeting this obligation (whether, that is, a failure to disclose is in good faith or bad faith), the prosecution's responsibility for failing to disclose known, favorable evidence rising to a material level of importance is inescapable.[9]

Read the Supreme Court's opinion in *Strickler v. Greene* (1999) to see how the Court analyzes alleged *Brady* violations.

Giglio material
information that might impeach the character or testimony of the prosecutor's witness during a criminal trial

impeach
to challenge the credibility of a witness or piece of evidence

---

Law Line 10-4
Giglio v. United States (1972)

Law Line 10-5
Jencks Act

Law Line 10-6
Kyles v. Whitley (1995)

CAPSTONE CASE   *Strickler v. Greene,* 527 U.S. 263 (1999)

Justice Stevens delivered the opinion of the Court.

In the early evening of January 5, 1990, Leanne Whitlock, an African-American sophomore at James Madison University, was abducted from a local shopping center and robbed and murdered. In separate trials, both petitioner and Ronald Henderson were convicted of all three offenses. Henderson was convicted of first-degree murder, a noncapital offense, whereas petitioner was convicted of capital murder and sentenced to death.

(continued)

(continued)

At both trials, a woman named Anne Stoltzfus testified in vivid detail about Whitlock's abduction. The exculpatory material that petitioner claims should have been disclosed before trial includes documents prepared by Stoltzfus, and notes of interviews with her, that impeach significant portions of her testimony. . . .

The first question that our order granting certiorari directed the parties to address is whether the State violated the *Brady* rule. We begin our analysis by identifying the essential components of a *Brady* violation.

In *Brady* this Court held "that the suppression by the prosecution of evidence favorable to an accused upon request violates due process where the evidence is material either to guilt or to punishment, irrespective of the good faith or bad faith of the prosecution." *Brady v. Maryland*, 373 U.S., at 87. We have since held that the duty to disclose such evidence is applicable even though there has been no request by the accused, *United States v. Agurs*, 427 U.S. 97, 107 (1976), and that the duty encompasses impeachment evidence as well as exculpatory evidence, *United States v. Bagley*, 473 U.S. 667, 676 (1985). Such evidence is material "if there is a reasonable probability that, had the evidence been disclosed to the defense, the result of the proceeding would have been different." Moreover, the rule encompasses evidence "known only to police investigators and not to the prosecutor." In order to comply with *Brady*, therefore, "the individual prosecutor has a duty to learn of any favorable evidence known to the others acting on the government's behalf in this case, including the police."

. . .

[T]he term "*Brady* violation" is sometimes used to refer to any breach of the broad obligation to disclose exculpatory evidence—that is, to any suppression of so-called "*Brady* material"—although, strictly speaking, there is never a real "*Brady* violation" unless the nondisclosure was so serious that there is a reasonable probability that the suppressed evidence would have produced a different verdict. There are three components of a true *Brady* violation: The evidence at issue must be favorable to the accused, either because it is exculpatory, or because it is impeaching; that evidence must have been suppressed by the State, either willfully or inadvertently; and prejudice must have ensued.

Two of those components are unquestionably established by the record in this case. The contrast between (a) the terrifying incident that Stoltzfus confidently described in her testimony and (b) her initial perception of that event "as a trivial episode of college kids carrying on" that her daughter did not even notice, suffices to establish the impeaching character of the undisclosed documents. Moreover, with respect to at least five of those documents, there is no dispute about the fact that they were known to the State but not disclosed to trial counsel. It is the third component—whether petitioner has established the prejudice necessary to satisfy the "materiality" inquiry—that is the most difficult element of the claimed *Brady* violation in this case. . . .

Without a doubt, Stoltzfus' testimony was prejudicial in the sense that it made petitioner's conviction more likely than if she had not testified, and discrediting her testimony might have changed the outcome of the trial.

That, however, is not the standard that petitioner must satisfy in order to obtain relief. He must convince us that "there is a reasonable probability" that the result of the trial would have been different if the suppressed documents had been disclosed to the defense. As we stressed in *Kyles* [*v. Whitley*]: "[T]he adjective is important. The question is not whether the defendant would more likely than not have received a different verdict with the evidence, but whether in its absence he received a fair trial, understood as a trial resulting in a verdict worthy of confidence." . . .

The record provides strong support for the conclusion that petitioner would have been convicted of capital murder and sentenced to death, even if Stoltzfus had been severely impeached. . . . Petitioner has satisfied two of the three components of a constitutional violation under *Brady:* exculpatory evidence and nondisclosure of this evidence by the prosecution. . . . However, petitioner has not shown that there is a reasonable probability that his conviction or sentence would have been different had these materials been disclosed. He therefore cannot show materiality under *Brady* or prejudice from his failure to raise the claim earlier. Accordingly, the judgment of the Court of Appeals is Affirmed.

WHAT DO *YOU* THINK?

1. Do you find the three-part *Brady* test established by the Court to be a fair test for both prosecutors and defendants?
2. Do you see any problems with the Court making assessments or predictions about whether the outcome of a criminal trial would have been different had the relevant impeachment materials been provided?

Obtaining Materials from Third-Party Sources

Realize, however, that for some criminal cases, legal professionals may be seeking evidence from a source other than an opposing party. In these situations, a party may not possess or control the evidence sought by the opposing party. For example, in a bank fraud case, the defendant may wish to secure more bank records for his defense than the prosecutor possesses. In this situation, the defendant would need to seek the records from the third-party bank, not the prosecutor.

Typically, the acquisition of evidence from third parties is accomplished through a *subpoena*, which is a court order to produce testimony or evidence. A subpoena is served upon the person or entity that holds the requested evidence. As explained in Chapter 9, there are two basic types of subpoenas. A *witness subpoena* compels a person to attend a court proceeding and provide oral testimony regarding a particular matter. And a *subpoena duces tecum* is a subpoena that commands a person to bring certain documents or other evidence for the party's or court's review. In most jurisdictions, the form for each type of subpoena is the same. See Figure 10-3. And in some cases, persons may receive one subpoena, compelling both oral testimony and physical evidence within their possession to be presented to the requesting party.

For legal professionals, there can be a number of different dimensions to serving a subpoena on a witness. At the outset, most courts maintain their own subpoena forms. Legal professionals typically keep a supply of these forms on hand, either physically or electronically. Upon identifying a witness or source of evidence, legal professionals must closely follow the applicable court rules for completing and serving the document. For example, in federal criminal cases, Federal Criminal Rule 17(a) states that "[a] subpoena must state the court's name and the title of the proceeding, include the seal of the court, and command the witness to attend and testify at the time and place the subpoena specifies."

subpoena
a court order to produce testimony or evidence

witness subpoena
court order compelling a person to attend a court proceeding and provide oral testimony regarding a particular matter

subpoena *duces tecum*
subpoena that commands a person to bring certain documents or other evidence for the party's or court's review

FIGURE 10-3 Subpoena in a Criminal Case (Without proof of service page)

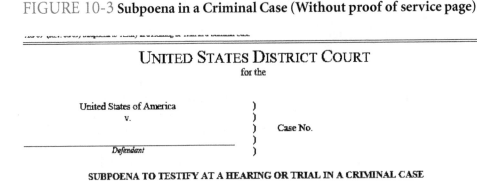

UNITED STATES DISTRICT COURT
for the

United States of America)
v.)
) Case No.
)
_____)
Defendant)

SUBPOENA TO TESTIFY AT A HEARING OR TRIAL IN A CRIMINAL CASE

To:

YOU ARE COMMANDED to appear in the United States district court at the time, date, and place shown below to testify in this criminal case. When you arrive, you must remain at the court until the judge or a court officer allows you to leave.

| Place of Appearance: | Courtroom No.: |
| | Date and Time: |

You must also bring with you the following documents, electronically stored information, or objects *(blank if not applicable)*:

(SEAL)

Date: _____

CLERK OF COURT

_____
Signature of Clerk or Deputy Clerk

The name, address, e-mail, and telephone number of the attorney representing *(name of party)* _____
_____, who requests this subpoena, are:

Most courts also have particular rules about the manner in which subpoenas are served upon witnesses, or the *service of process* as it is called in some courts. In some jurisdictions, subpoenas must be served personally on a witness or a witness's agent. In other courts, service of process may be done by mail or by leaving the subpoena at a person's home or place of business. In other courts, witnesses must be provided with an attendance fee and mileage allowance in order for the subpoena to be properly served. For example, Federal Criminal Rule 17(d) provides:

A marshal, a deputy marshal, or any nonparty who is at least 18 years old may serve a subpoena. The server must deliver a copy of the subpoena to the witness and must tender to the witness one day's witness-attendance fee and the legal mileage allowance. The server need not tender the attendance fee or mileage allowance when the United States, a federal officer, or a federal agency has requested the subpoena.

In cases where an indigent defendant is unable to pay the witness fees and other costs associated with serving a subpoena, the court can order that the subpoena be issued without direct costs to the defendant.

In some offices, the service of process is handled by external agents. In most U.S. Attorneys' offices, the U.S. Marshal's office serves the subpoenas. Some private law firms use process servers to deliver subpoenas. A ***process server*** can be a private company that specializes in handling court-related work, including serving subpoenas. Typically, a law firm will pay a fee to the process server for this service. This eliminates the need for using employees and legal assistants of the law firm to deliver subpoenas. It can also reduce liability concerns that may arise when trying to locate and serve documents on persons who may not wish to be served.

process server
a person who specializes in handling court-related work, including serving subpoenas

Depositions

The discovery rules in some jurisdictions allow the prosecutor and defendant to depose witnesses prior to the criminal trial. A ***deposition*** is typically an out-of-court proceeding wherein witnesses are asked questions and give answers relevant to a pending case. Depositions are quite common in civil cases. But some jurisdictions also allow them in criminal matters as well. Usually, depositions are held at a law office or another out-of-court setting, where the attorneys involved in the case have the opportunity to question (depose) a witness under oath. The proceedings are usually transcribed by a court reporter and/or videotaped. The witness's testimony is transcribed and becomes a part of the trial record. The parties can then use the transcript to prepare their case for trial.

deposition
an out-of-court proceeding wherein witnesses are asked questions and give answers relevant to a pending case

In those jurisdictions that allow for pretrial depositions, defendants have an important tool for discovery. For example, Missouri Revised Statute 545.400 provides:

> **Conditional examination of witnesses**
> The defendant in any criminal cause may also have witnesses examined on his behalf, conditionally, upon a commission issued by the clerk of the court in which the cause is pending, in the same cases and upon the like notice to the prosecuting attorney, with the like effect and in all respects as is provided by law in civil suits; provided, that the notice in such case to the prosecuting attorney shall state the name or names of the witness or witnesses whose depositions are desired or will be taken.

The use of depositions in criminal cases can be particularly useful when expert witnesses are involved. Authorizing parties to question expert witnesses prior to trial allows the technical and detailed opinions to be better understood and analyzed before they are presented to a judge or jury. In Missouri, "[t]he defense may discover by deposition the facts and opinions to which an expert is expected to testify. Unless manifest injustice would result, the court shall require that the party seeking discovery from an expert pay the expert a reasonable hourly fee for the time such expert is deposed."

Where depositions in criminal cases are permitted, the rules for these hearings typically do not allow the defendant to attend the deposition. Some authorities fear that the defendant's presence might cause some witnesses to be intimidated. As a result, absent compelling reason for their participation, defendants generally are excluded from depositions. For example, Missouri Rule of Criminal Procedure 25.12 provides, "[t]he defendant shall not be physically present at a discovery deposition except by agreement of the parties or upon court order for good cause shown. . . . In addition, upon motion of the defense, the court may order the physical presence of the defendant upon a showing of good cause." Keep in mind, however, that even where prosecutors are allowed to conduct depositions as a form of discovery, defendants cannot be compelled to provide testimony. As discussed in Chapter 12, defendants have a Fifth Amendment right not to testify in criminal matters, and this includes depositions taken by prosecutors.

Realize too that most jurisdictions do not allow for general depositions in criminal cases. For defendants, that means that they must wait until trial before they can question government witnesses, which comes in the form of cross-examination. This can put defendants at a distinct disadvantage in preparing a criminal case. In most jurisdictions, prosecutors have the power of a grand jury subpoena that they can use to question witnesses about a possible crime. As a result, they know what their witnesses are going to say before they put them on the stand. But generally, in most jurisdictions, defendants have no corresponding ability to subpoena witnesses for basic pretrial testimony. In fact, as discussed in Chapter 9, defendants have no right to participate in grand jury proceedings and generally are not entitled to the transcripts of grand jury hearings.

Bill of Particulars

bill of particulars a document provided by a prosecutor that offers more specific information about the government's criminal charge

For criminal defendants, another source for discovery or insight into the prosecution's case may come through a bill of particulars. A ***bill of particulars*** is a document provided by a prosecutor that offers more specific information about the government's criminal charge. For example, an indictment may charge a defendant with one count of theft, alleging the defendant stole $2,000 worth of property from the XYZ Company on October 12, 2011. But the indictment may not reveal the type of property stolen or the method allegedly used by the defendant to take the property. In this instance, the defendant may file a ***motion for a bill of particulars***, asking the court to order the prosecutor to provide more details about the alleged criminal offense, including the date and time of the offense, the specific property taken, and the means allegedly used to commit the offense. See Figure 10-4.

motion for a bill of particulars
motion asking the court to order the prosecutor to provide more details about the alleged criminal offense

In terms of procedure, Federal Rule of Criminal Procedure 7(f) provides that "[t]he court may direct the government to file a bill of particulars. The defendant may move for a bill of particulars before or within 14 days after arraignment or at a later time if the court permits. The government may amend a bill of particulars subject to such conditions as justice requires." Generally, when seeking a bill of particulars, defendants must show that the charging instrument —indictment, complaint, or information—is lacking in sufficient specificity to afford the defendant a fair opportunity to understand the nature of the criminal charges. Thus, in addition to asking for specific "particulars," defendants must also be prepared to demonstrate how the charging document is deficient.

If the trial court grants the defendant's motion, the prosecutor will then file a bill of particulars with the court, thereby notifying the defendant and the court of the additional details surrounding the alleged criminal offense. The defendant can then use these details to prepare a defense, assert an alibi, or request and review discovery in the case.

FIGURE 10-4 **Motion for a Bill of Particulars**

UNITED STATES DISTRICT COURT
FOR THE SOUTHERN DISTRICT OF OHIO

UNITED STATES OF AMERICA   :

              VS.   :   **CASE NUMBER xx-0065-04 (CRR)**

JOHN SMITH   :

DEFENDANT'S MOTION FOR A BILL OF PARTICULARS

      Defendant, by and through undersigned counsel, and pursuant to Fed. R. Crim. P. 7(f), and the Fifth and Sixth Amendments to the United States Constitution, hereby move this Court for an order compelling the government to file a bill of particulars, setting forth the following:

COUNT 1 (Conspiracy)

1. Identify the specific locations "elsewhere" where the conspiracy functioned.

2. Identify the "unindicted" co-conspirators with whom the defendant conspired who are "known" to the grand jury.

3. Identify all overt acts not listed in the indictment but upon which the government may rely at trial.

4. Identify the transactions which provide the basis for the allegation that the alleged conspiracy involved greater than 50 grams of cocaine base.

5. Identify the manner and means of the conspiracy.

WHEREFORE, it is respectfully requested that this Motion for Bill of Particulars be granted.

Respectfully submitted,

_____
A.K. Attorney
Assistant Federal Public Defender
250 Main St.
Cincinnati, OH 45202
(513) 555-5555

IN THE FIELD

For legal professionals, the discovery phase of a criminal case is a critical time. Many cases are won, lost, or reshaped based on the information and evidence shared or not shared in advance of trial. Much of this work is done outside of the courtroom, with legal professionals reviewing documents, locating and interviewing witnesses, and testing forensic evidence. At times, discovery-related tasks can be tedious, bureaucratic, and time consuming. And in many cases, the materials acquired and prepared might never actually be used in the criminal proceedings. But a well-prepared case is not just used for trial. It can also signal to your opposing party—whether prosecutor or defendant—that you are confident in your case and are ready for trial. This, in turn, can generate more favorable plea negotiations for your client.

(continued)

(continued)

In jurisdictions with electronic discovery, legal professionals must become proficient in using the software to access and store data. Not only will you need to thoroughly review the materials, you also want to appear competent and capable in the courtroom as you access these electronic materials for the judge or jury. Professionals who struggle to locate and present electronic evidence during proceedings may not only miss critical pieces of information, they may also appear unprepared, thereby diminishing their credibility before the trier of fact.

In those jurisdictions where electronic discovery is not used, legal professionals must be skilled in more traditional forms of document organization, including binder preparation, indexing, and exhibit identification. Above all else, legal professionals must become thoroughly familiar with the rules of the court when organizing exhibits and other trial court materials. Many courts, particularly at the federal level, have specific rules regarding the organization and presentation of exhibits for all court proceedings, not just jury trials. These rules range from whether parties should use numeric or alphabetic symbols for their exhibits, to whether the exhibits must be presented in a bound notebook.

ETHICAL PRINCIPLES

EXERCISING JUDGMENT IN CRIMINAL CASES

National Association of Legal Assistants Code of Ethics and Professional Responsibility Canon 4

A paralegal must use discretion and professional judgment commensurate with knowledge and experience but must not render independent legal judgment in place of an attorney. The services of an attorney are essential in the public interest whenever such legal judgment is required.

Courtesy of the National Association of Legal Assistants

PRETRIAL MOTIONS

Much of the work during the pretrial stage of a criminal case is done with an eye toward going to trial. Criminal charges are filed, defendants are processed, and discovery is shared. All of this is done with the understanding that the matter could end up being decided by a judge or jury. But charging instruments, processing procedures, and discovery materials can also be used as a basis for filing pretrial motions, including motions seeking to have the court exclude or limit evidence during trial or perhaps even dismiss the charges altogether.

In general, a ***motion*** is a request from a litigant requesting a ruling or directive by the trial court on a matter relating to a case. In many situations, motions are quite formal in nature, presented to the court in typewritten form. In other scenarios, including trial settings, motions are made orally by an attorney to the court, such as "I move to strike that testimony" or "motion to voir dire the witness, your honor?" Most pretrial motions are filed in typewritten form, with the moving party identifying the requested court action and the grounds (basis) for seeking it.

At the federal level, Federal Rules of Criminal Procedure 12(b)–(d) outline the general conditions for filing pretrial motions in criminal cases. These rules provide:

Law Line 10-7
Public Defender Motions

motion
a request from a litigant requesting a ruling or directive by the trial court on a matter relating to a case

(b) **Pretrial Motions.**

1. *In General.*

   Rule 47 applies to a pretrial motion.

2. *Motions That May Be Made Before Trial.*

   A party may raise by pretrial motion any defense, objection, or request that the court can determine without a trial of the general issue.

3. *Motions That Must Be Made Before Trial.*

   The following must be raised before trial:

   A. a motion alleging a defect in instituting the prosecution;

   B. a motion alleging a defect in the indictment or information—but at any time while the case is pending, the court may hear a claim that the indictment or information fails to invoke the court's jurisdiction or to state an offense;

   C. a motion to suppress evidence;

   D. a Rule 14 motion to sever charges or defendants; and

   E. a Rule 16 motion for discovery.

4. *Notice of the Government's Intent to Use Evidence.*

   A. *At the Government's Discretion.*

      At the arraignment or as soon afterward as practicable, the government may notify the defendant of its intent to use specified evidence at trial in order to afford the defendant an opportunity to object before trial under Rule 12(b)(3)(C).

   B. *At the Defendant's Request.*

      At the arraignment or as soon afterward as practicable, the defendant may, in order to have an opportunity to move to suppress evidence under Rule 12(b)(3)(C), request notice of the government's intent to use (in its evidence-in-chief at trial) any evidence that the defendant may be entitled to discover under Rule 16.

(c) **Motion Deadline.**

   The court may, at the arraignment or as soon afterward as practicable, set a deadline for the parties to make pretrial motions and may also schedule a motion hearing.

(d) **Ruling on a Motion.**

   The court must decide every pretrial motion before trial unless it finds good cause to defer a ruling. The court must not defer ruling on a pretrial motion if the deferral will adversely affect a party's right to appeal. When factual issues are involved in deciding a motion, the court must state its essential findings on the record.

Notice that under Rule 12, the district courts typically establish a scheduling order setting the due dates for pretrial motions. As a result, motion deadlines in federal courts can vary depending on the needs of the parties and the courts. In some state courts, however, motion deadlines are established by court rule. For example, under Ohio Rule of Criminal Procedure 12(D), most pretrial motions must be filed within thirty-five days after the defendant is arraigned or seven days before trial, whichever is earlier. Ohio courts have the discretion to extend this deadline "in the interest of justice," but generally, parties are advised to follow the standard deadline set forth in Rule 12(D).

At the outset of a criminal case, legal professionals must identify the court rules and deadlines for pretrial motions and make every effort to comply with them. In cases where time constraints, limited resources, or other factors make compliance with these rules difficult or undermine the rights or interests of the client, legal professionals must seek formal relief from the rules by asking the trial court for an extension of time to prepare and file the requisite motions.

Anatomy of a Motion

The format for pretrial motions can vary, depending on the formal court rules for filing motions and the individual preferences of the judge. In some settings, courts ask that motions include a separate legal memorandum outlining the legal basis for the motion. Some courts prefer that each paragraph in the motion be numbered. Some jurisdictions require motions to include as attachments unreported cases and any court orders, transcripts, or materials relied upon in the motion. Some other courts may also want motions to include an attached proposed court order or court entry that allows the judge to simply sign the document and file it with the clerk of courts. Other courts, however, may allow motions to be fairly short and informal, requiring no particular method or format. But generally, a motion should clearly state what the party wants the court to do and provide a basic outline of the legal and factual basis for the requested court action. See Figure 10-5.

FIGURE 10-5 **Outline of Pretrial Motion**

A. Caption (In some jurisdictions, you must also clearly state your request for a hearing, if sought.)

UNITED STATES DISTRICT COURT
FOR THE DISTRICT OF COLUMBIA

UNITED STATES OF AMERICA :

              v. : CASE NUMBER CR-0055-01 (JPF)
                              (Evidentiary Hearing Requested)

JULIE SMIITH :

B. Title of Motion (Be as specific as possible in stating your requested court order.)

MOTION TO SUPPRESS DEFENDANT'S STATEMENTS

C. Motion/Request (In some courts this section might include a legal argument in support.)

Defendant, by and through counsel, respectfully moves for the suppression of certain statements and evidence constituting fruits of such statements taken from Julie Smith in violation of her rights under the Fifth Amendment to the United States Constitution, and requests an evidentiary hearing on this Motion.

D. Memorandum in Support (In some courts, this is a separate document or section that is attached to the motion. In other jurisdictions, each paragraph within the memorandum must be numbered in sequential order).

1. **Background Facts** (Clearly and succinctly state the background facts the court needs to rule on the motion—who did what to whom when and how)

2. **Legal Issue** (Clearly identify the legal question(s) to be decided by the court –"Did the government violate defendant's Fifth Amendment rights against self incrimination?"). This can also be stated in a more authoritative form – "These facts demonstrate that the government violated Defendant's Fifth Amendment rights, and therefore, the statements must be excluded from evidence.").

3. **Rule of Law** (Outline the applicable rule(s) of law, including an insightful yet succinct discussion of all constitutional provisions, relevant statutes, and judicial precedent on the issue.)

(continued)

FIGURE 10-5 **Continued**

4. **Application of law to facts** (Do the legal analysis, whereby you apply the relevant legal standards to the facts of the case in a way that favors your client).

5. **Conclusion** (Establish the legal conclusion you wish the court to make in your client's favor).

E. Attachments
    1. Unreported cases cited in motion.
    2. Copies of critical documents, including transcript pages, needed to rule upon the motion.

F. Attached Order (Required in some jurisdictions or provided as a courtesy in others.)

UNITED STATES DISTRICT COURT
FOR THE DISTRICT OF COLUMBIA

UNITED STATES OF AMERICA   :

            v.   :   CASE NUMBER CR-0055-01 (JPF)

JULIE SMIITH   :

**ORDER GRANTING DEFENDANT'S MOTION TO SUPPRESS
DEFENDANT'S STATEMENTS TO LAW ENFORCEMENT**

Upon Defendant's motion and for good cause shown, the Court orders that all oral statements made by Defendant to law enforcement officials on February 12, 2010, are to be excluded from being introduced as evidence against Defendant during the trial in this matter.

_____
Date

_____
The Honorable Judge Franks

Motion Hearings

In some circumstances, the moving party will also ask the court to conduct a hearing on the motion. There are two basic types of pretrial motion hearings. An *evidentiary hearing* allows the parties to call witnesses and introduce evidence for the purpose of supporting or refuting a motion. For example, some defendants asserting an unlawful search and seizure may request an evidentiary hearing in order to develop sufficient evidence to support the motion, including possible testimony from law enforcement officials who conducted the search.

An *oral hearing* or oral argument, on the other hand, does not involve witnesses or evidence, but rather allows the parties to present their claims orally to the court and affords the trial judge a chance to ask questions of the attorneys. For example, many motions to dismiss the indictment (or other charging instrument) are based on legal claims and case-driven arguments. As a result, there may be little, if any, need for evidence to be introduced. Instead, the parties may present an oral argument to the court, similar to that presented to a court of appeals. See Chapter 14 (appeals).

Under some motions and in some motion hearings, the defendant has the burden of proof. For example, defendants who move to dismiss an indictment based on a claim that the underlying criminal statute is unconstitutional usually have the burden of proving the alleged constitutional defect. In most jurisdictions, criminal laws are presumed to be constitutional, and thus, defendants are required to rebut

evidentiary hearing
proceeding before a trial court that allows the parties to call witnesses and introduce evidence for the purpose of supporting or refuting a motion

oral hearing
proceeding before a trial court that allows the parties to present their claims orally to the court and affords the trial judge a chance to ask questions of the attorneys

this presumption. But in other motions, the burden of proof rests with the prosecutor. For example, where defendants allege an illegal warrantless search and seizure, prosecutors typically have the burden of showing the lawfulness of the evidentiary seizure because it was conducted without prior judicial authorization (a warrant).

In general, before filing pretrial motions, legal professionals must assess whether there is a need for a hearing on the motion, and if so, what type of hearing should be requested. Where a hearing is sought, legal professionals should state a request for a hearing clearly and early in the motion.

Types of Motions

Many types of motions can be made before trial; see Figure 10-6. Some motions focus on the charging instrument, alleging defects in the substance or procurement

---

FIGURE 10-6 **Possible Pretrial Motions and Their Purposes**

BY DEFENDANTS

Motion in Limine
> To exclude or limit the prosecutor or witnesses from referencing unfairly prejudicial material about the defendant (prior convictions or irrelevant personal characteristics) during trial -- often filed under Federal Rules of Evidence 403, 404, 609.

Motion for the Appointment of Counsel or for Funds to Obtain an Expert
> To obtain a court-appointed attorney to represent an indigent defendant or to retain an expert (accountant, forensics examiner, etc.) to assist an indigent defendant in preparing a defense.

Motion to Modify Bail & Pretrial Detention
> To reduce or otherwise modify the terms and conditions of bail for the defendant set during the bond hearing.

Motion for a Bill of Particulars
> To obtain more details about the nature of the criminal charges.

Motion to Determine Competency
> To have defendants evaluated to see whether they are competent to stand trial.

Motion for a Continuance
> To obtain additional time to prepare for trial, motions, or other proceedings.

Requests and Motions for Discovery
> To obtain evidence and information about the criminal charges, including Brady, Jencks, Giglio information.

Motion to Dismiss Charges or Indictment
> To eliminate criminal charges based on unconstitutionality of criminal statute, grand jury irregularities, speedy trial violations, double jeopardy, duplicity of counts, or the failure to state a claim.

Motion to Travel
> To allow the defendant to travel for particular purpose while awaiting trial.

Motion for the Return of Property
> To obtain court order for law enforcement to release seized property (car, computer, documents), which defendant needs for trial preparation or which government has no basis to maintain.

(continued)

FIGURE 10-6 **Continued**

Motion for Judicial Recusal

To have the currently assigned judge step down from the case based due to a conflict of interest or other ethical concerns.

Motion for Severance of Defendants and/or Counts

To seek separate trials for co-defendants or multiple criminal counts where the joinder of these defendants or counts would unfairly prejudice the defendant.

Motion to Suppress

To prevent evidence from being introduced during trial against the defendant based on the assertion that it was illegally obtained by law enforcement.

Motion for Change of Venue

To change the location of the trial, including the geographic territory from which jurors might be selected.

BY PROSECUTORS

Motion in Limine

To exclude or limit the defense from referencing unfairly prejudicial material about the victim or prosecution witnesses (prior convictions or irrelevant personal characteristics) during trial -- often filed under Federal Rules of Evidence 403, 404, 609.

Motion for Protective Order

To protect the victims or witnesses by ordering the defendant not to make contact with these individuals.

Motion to Revoke or Modify Defendant's Bail

To enhance the terms and conditions of bail set during the bond hearing.

Motion for Voice, Handwriting, or Other Exemplars from Defendant

To require defendant to submit voice, handwriting, hair, or other samples for the prosecutor's review.

Motion for a Continuance

To change date or time for proceedings to accommodate prosecutorial needs.

Motion to Compel Discovery

To obtain evidence and information from defendant.

Motion to Amend the Indictment or Complaint

To make adjustments to the charging instrument in order to correct a defect or omission, provided no change is made to the name of the crime charged.

Motion for Judicial Recusal

To have the currently assigned judge step down from the case based due to a conflict of interest or other ethical concerns.

---

of the indictment or complaint. For example, a ***motion to dismiss*** seeks to have the court eliminate some or all of the criminal charges against the defendant. In some cases, motions to dismiss are based on asserted constitutional defects of the underlying criminal statute (see Chapter 2). In other cases, defendants might base their motions on alleged double jeopardy or speedy trial violations (see Chapter 12). And in rare cases, prosecutors may move the court to dismiss a case if they find procedural or evidentiary defects in the matter.

motion to dismiss

request to a trial court to have some or all of the criminal charges against the defendant eliminated

---

Law Line 10-8

Motion to Dismiss

motion to suppress or motion to exclude evidence
request to a trial court to bar the prosecutor from introducing evidence that was allegedly obtained unlawfully by law enforcement officials

motion in limine
request for a trial court to limit the opposing party from introducing evidence that, even though factually accurate and lawfully obtained, is irrelevant or unfairly prejudicial to a party or witness

motion to travel
request to a trial court to allow a defendant to travel beyond the terms and conditions established by the pretrial bond

motion for continuance
request that the court change the date for a hearing or trial

motion to modify bond
request to a court to reduce the conditions for the defendant's pretrial release from jail

motion to revoke bond
prosecutorial request to have the defendant placed in pretrial custody based on alleged violation of pretrial bond conditions

motion for a protective order
prosecutorial request asking for a court order limiting actions of defendant toward an alleged victim

Other pretrial motions seek to exclude or limit the introduction of evidence during trial. For example, a ***motion to suppress*** asks the trial court to bar the prosecutor from introducing evidence that was allegedly obtained unlawfully by law enforcement officials (see below). In a somewhat similar fashion, a ***motion in limine*** asks the court to limit the opposing party from introducing evidence that, even though factually accurate and lawfully obtained, is irrelevant or unfairly prejudicial to a party or witness. For example, some defendants in DUI or OMVI cases may have prior convictions for driving under the influence. But a prior DUI conviction is not factually or legally relevant to whether a defendant committed the alleged crime in a current case. As a result, defendants in these circumstances may file a motion in limine asking the trial court to bar all witnesses from mentioning the defendant's prior convictions during trial.

Still other motions are designed to address more administrative matters. For defendants, this might include a ***motion to travel***, which would allow the defendant to travel beyond the terms and conditions established by the pretrial bond; a ***motion for continuance***, which asks the court to change the date for a hearing or trial; or a ***motion to modify bond***, which seeks to reduce the conditions for the defendant's pretrial release from jail. For prosecutors, such motions might include a ***motion to revoke bond***, which attempts to have the defendant placed in pretrial custody based on alleged violation of pretrial bond conditions; or a ***motion for a protective order***, which asks the trial court to bar the defendant from making contact with the alleged victim or other government witnesses.

Figure 10-6 outlines many of the more common pretrial motions filed by defendants and prosecutors. But realize that pretrial motions can also request less conventional court action that is tailored to the needs of specific clients and cases. For example, prosecutors in a 2008 capital murder trial in Butler County, Ohio, filed a motion asking the trial court to prohibit the defense attorneys in the case from crying in front of the jury. In their motion, prosecutors stated, "defense attorneys have strategically been known to cry on cue and beg for their clients' lives," [thus] "appealing to the emotions of the jury instead of to reason."[10] In the end, legal professionals are likely to find that most of the pretrial motions they prepare and file conform to those listed in Figure 10-6. But legal professionals should also be willing to be creative and innovative and consider other types of pretrial motions that are helpful to the client and within reasonable parameters of the law.

IN THE FIELD

For legal professionals, preparing and filing pretrial motions can be one of the most critical aspects of a criminal case. These motions and the court rulings thereon can essentially determine the ground rules for an ensuing criminal trial. And although most cases never go to trial, the strength of a party's pretrial motion can also substantially affect plea-bargaining negotiations. A prosecutor who believes evidence might be excluded from trial based on the defendant's filing of a motion to suppress may be willing to offer a more favorable plea agreement. Conversely, a defendant who reads the prosecutor's response to a motion to suppress may find little hope that the court will exclude the evidence, and thus may be more eager to resolve the case through a plea agreement.

In the end, parties must have a legitimate basis for filing a pretrial motion. You cannot file motions without a reasonable legal or factual basis. But there can be many different purposes and objectives for seeking pretrial court orders. As a result, legal professionals must learn to evaluate cases, charging instruments, and discovery/evidence thoroughly and thoughtfully. And after such review, professionals must work with their supervising attorneys to adopt strategic and thoughtful motions that further the client's interests.

THE EXCLUSION OF EVIDENCE

In a large percentage of criminal cases, the evidence obtained by law enforcement officials is sufficient (or at least appears sufficient) to support the elements of the charged offense(s). As a result, many defendants see little hope of defending their cases based on the factual evidence. For example, a defendant caught with illegal narcotics in his pants pocket will not likely have a strong factual basis to defend against the criminal charge of drug possession. But in order for the confiscated drug evidence to be used against the defendant, it must also be lawfully obtained by law enforcement officials. If it is not, a defendant can seek to have it excluded from evidence, thereby eliminating the primary factual basis of the government's case. This process involves two basic tools—a motion to suppress and the exclusionary rule.

Motions to Suppress

In cases where defendants believe that law enforcement officers used illegal means to obtain incriminating evidence, they can file a **motion to suppress** or a **motion to exclude evidence**. In this context, the terms *suppress* and *exclude* are used interchangeably. Regardless of the title, a motion to suppress asks the trial court to issue an order barring the prosecutor from introducing certain evidence against the defendant during trial. Where the evidence involves tangible materials, such as computer records, firearms, drugs, money, fingerprints, and so forth, defendants often assert that the Fourth Amendment provision against unreasonable searches and seizures bars the admission of this evidence (see Chapter 11). Where the evidence includes the defendant's statements made while in government custody, the Fifth Amendment provision protecting the right against self-incrimination is often asserted (see Chapter 12). With other evidence, like pretrial identification lineups and privileged communications, defendants may rely upon specific statutory rules of evidence or general principles of due process and/or equal protection to argue that law enforcement officials obtained the evidence illegally.

Motions to suppress can have a huge impact on a criminal case. If granted, these motions can effectively eliminate the evidence the prosecutor needs to proceed to trial. For example, in a case where a defendant is charged with carrying a concealed weapon, if the court finds that the seized gun must be excluded from evidence because law enforcement obtained the weapon through an unlawful search, the prosecutor typically will not be able to proceed to trial without being able to introduce the weapon into evidence. Conversely, if the trial judge denies the motion to suppress, the prosecutor likely will have a rather straightforward case to prove. In still other cases, a court's ruling or anticipated ruling on a motion to suppress can shape the nature and substance of plea negotiations, discussed below. In short, many cases are won, lost, or substantially influenced by motions to suppress.

A motion to suppress normally contains the same basic components as those found in other pretrial motions. Defendants must clearly state what materials or information they are seeking to exclude from evidence during trial and provide a factual and legal basis for this exclusion. In most circumstances, defendants will request an evidentiary hearing to construct a factual record for their motion. See Figure 10-7. At a suppression hearing, the trial court typically hears testimony from law enforcement officers and other witnesses about how the challenged evidence was gathered and preserved. In hearings where there are factual disagreements about what occurred during the evidentiary seizure, trial courts will also make judgments about the credibility of the witnesses' testimony.

FIGURE 10-7 **Sample Motion to Suppress (Abbreviated)**

**IN THE UNITED STATES DISTRICT COURT
FOR THE DISTRICT OF UTAH**

UNITED STATES OF AMERICA,
   Plaintiff,   Criminal Action No. 2010-cr-00111

vs.

JACOB VICKERS,
   Defendant.

DEFENDANT'S MOTION TO SUPPRESS STATEMENTS AND EVIDENCE

  Defendant, by and through counsel, respectfully moves for the suppression of certain statements and evidence constituting fruits of such statements taken from Jacob Vickers in violation of his rights under the Fifth Amendment to the United States Constitution, and requests an evidentiary hearing on this Motion. In support of this Motion, Mr. Vickers states as follows:

I. Facts
1. On or about October 13, 2010, the Utah Bureau of Investigation (UBI) initiated an investigation into alleged misuse of computers at the Utah Crime Information Center (UCIC) and/or the National Crime Information Center (NCIC).

2. On or about October 16, 2010, the Executive Director of the UBI, Cindy Cornwell, telephoned John Stevens, Special Agent in Charge (SAC), to request that he investigate the use of NCIC/UCIC computers by Mr. Vickers. Stevens is the highest ranking UBI official in its office in Salt Lake City. Pursuant to Cornwell's request, Vickers was called into the office of, Robert Moore, Assistant Special Agent in Charge (ASAC).

3. Without providing any admonition or advisement of rights of any kind, Moore asked Vickers whether he had accessed the computer files of an individual in NCIC/UCIC. Vickers answered the question, after which time Moore directed Vickers to accompany him to Stevens' office. Vickers was instructed to answer the same question in Stevens' presence.

[include all other relevant facts known or believed to be true, which are necessary for court to rule in defendant's favor on the motion]

II. Legal Standard
4. The Fifth Amendment to the United States Constitution provides that, "[n]o person . . . shall be compelled in any criminal case to be a witness against himself." U.S. Const. amend. V. It is coercion by the government in compelling testimonial statements that is the concern of the Fifth Amendment. *Colorado v. Connelly*, 479 U.S. 157, 170 (1986).

5. Under the Fifth Amendment and federal statutes, no person may be compelled to answer any question put to him "unless and until he is protected at least against the use of his compelled answers and evidence derived therefrom in any subsequent criminal case in which he is a defendant." *Lefkowitz v. Turley*, 414 U.S. 70, 78 (1973).

(continued)

FIGURE 10-7 **Continued**

6. In the event that Vickers' statements were unconstitutionally obtained, they must be suppressed and all evidence derivative of them must similarly be suppressed. *See Wong Sun v. United States*, 371 U.S. 471, 485 (1963).

[provide all other relevant legal standards for the motion]

III. Argument

7. The environment and circumstances present here were inherently coercive. First, the questioning was done by or at the direction of the most senior official in the region and Vickers's ultimate supervisor. Second, the questioning was done in the respective supervisors' offices. Third, the questioning was done without the presence of any representative for Vickers. Fourth, Vickers was specifically aware of official policy statements and practices threatening him with "removal" or "dismissal" from employment in the event that he refused to answer questions posed to him. Finally, no admonitions or advisements were given to Vickers.

8. Vickers subjectively believed, under all the attendant circumstances, that he could not assert his Fifth Amendment right to remain silent and refuse to answer these questions without facing termination from employment.

[insert all other arguments supporting legal conclusions for the motion]

WHEREFORE, Vickers respectfully requests that the Court suppress the statements at issue here. Further, Vickers requests that all evidence derived from the statements also be suppressed as fruits of the poisonous tree. Vickers requests that an evidentiary hearing be held on this motion.

Dated January 17, 2011
Respectfully submitted,
s/ J.Q. Attorney _____
Attorney & Attorney LLP
704 Houser Street
Salt Lake City, Utah 55555
Phone: (301) 555-5555
Fax: (301) 555-5555

The Exclusionary Rule

At the heart of most motions to suppress is the ***exclusionary rule***, which holds that illegally seized evidence must be excluded from governmental use during trial. Upon finding that the government has engaged in an unreasonable search and seizure under the Fourth Amendment, infringed the right against self-incrimination under the Fifth Amendment, or otherwise unconstitutionally obtained evidence for a criminal case, the central question is what can a court do about it? The Supreme Court's response to this question has gradually, although not consistently or thoroughly, been to exclude from the evidence those items unconstitutionally obtained by the government.

The Court first adopted the exclusionary rule in *Weeks v. United States* (1914),[11] when it recognized the rule as an appropriate judicial method for enforcing constitutional violations of the Fourth Amendment search and seizure provision. The Court justified this rule by observing:

> The tendency of those who execute the criminal laws of the country to obtain conviction by means of unlawful seizures and enforced confessions, the latter often obtained after subjecting accused persons to unwarranted practices

exclusionary rule
a legal doctrine that requires illegally seized evidence to be excluded from governmental use during trial

destructive of rights secured by the Federal Constitution, should find no sanction in the judgments of the courts, which are charged at all times with the support of the Constitution, and to which people of all conditions have a right to appeal for the maintenance of such fundamental rights.

The Court declared the exclusionary rule to apply to evidence unconstitutionally seized by federal authorities.

The Court, however, did not apply the exclusionary rule to state authorities until 1962. In *Mapp v. Ohio* (1962),[12] Cleveland police officers went to Dollree Mapp's house to ask her questions about a recent bombing. After Mapp refused the officers' requests to enter her home, the officers handcuffed Mapp and searched her home, where they seized purportedly obscene materials. The Supreme Court, however, ruled that the exclusionary rule should apply to bar the seized evidence from state criminal proceedings. The Court concluded that the rule applied to the states through the Due Process Clause of the Fourteenth Amendment.

Law Line 10-9
Mapp v. Ohio (1962)

As applied today, the exclusionary rule is designed to deter police misconduct by essentially imposing a type of "death penalty" to evidence that is obtained outside of constitutional parameters. If imposed, the rule bars unconstitutionally obtained evidence from being used by the government against the accused. In many cases, defendants rely upon the exclusionary rule as the primary tool for defending against criminal charges. Many criminal defendants are not in a good position to refute or otherwise undermine the substance of the factual allegations made in the indictment or criminal complaint. As such, they do not view going to trial as a viable option. And in fact, in some circles, going to trial in the face of overwhelming factual evidence of guilt is referred to as a "slow guilty plea." So under these circumstances, many defendants may find the best way to defend against the criminal charges is to challenge the legal pedigree of the government's evidence. In other words, while the substance of the government's evidence may be quite damning for many defendants, the law enforcement methods used to obtain the evidence may preclude the prosecutor from using it in court. If so, the exclusionary rule may apply to bar this evidence from being introduced by the prosecutor against the defendant.

Legal professionals working on state criminal cases also should be aware of additional standards for the exclusionary rule that might exist within state law. For example, Texas Code of Criminal Procedure Article 38.23(a) provides:

No evidence obtained by an officer or other person in violation of any provisions of the constitution or laws of the State of Texas, or of the Constitution or laws of the United States of America, shall be admitted in evidence against the accused on the trial of any criminal case.

In some state courts, the exclusionary rule is broader than that used pursuant to the U.S. Constitution.

And as noted in Chapters 2 and 8, while the Supreme Court's rulings on the exclusionary rule establish the *minimum* standards for this doctrine, individual states can establish more stringent standards for their law enforcement officers. As a result, while the focus of this section is on the national standards for the exclusionary rule under U.S. Supreme Court precedent, in state cases legal professionals should also determine whether their state constitutions, statutes, or judicial precedents offer even greater exclusionary authority for their particular situation and evidence. See the State of Washington's approach to the "good faith" exception (below). These additional standards for law enforcement officers and trial proceedings may work to exclude evidence in ways that the standard exclusionary rule adopted under the U.S. Constitution does not.

Fruit of the Poisonous Tree Doctrine.   In some cases, the Court has applied the exclusionary rule to more than just the initial item of evidence obtained by police in violation of the Constitution, using it to exclude any other evidence derived from the initial piece of evidence. This is known as the "***fruit of the poisonous tree doctrine***." This metaphoric doctrine likens "the poisonous tree" to the evidence initially obtained by police in violation of the Constitution and "the fruit" to all other evidence that "grew" out of the ill-gotten evidence or "poisonous tree."[13] So, for example, if police engage in an unreasonable search and seize of a defendant's house, thereby obtaining the defendant's diary, the entries of which allow authorities to find a corpse, murder weapon, blood stains, and the names of witnesses, a basic application of the fruit of the poisonous tree doctrine would exclude all evidence derived from the illegal search because it is fruit from an original and poisonous search. See Figure 10-8.

In some situations, determining whether law enforcement officers failed to obtain evidence in a constitutional manner is only the first step. If this is shown, the trial court and the parties must then determine what additional evidence sought to be used by the prosecutor may have been obtained as a result of the initial unconstitutional search or interrogation. In some cases, courts or parties may ask for a ***Kastigar hearing***. Technically speaking, a Kastigar hearing is a proceeding to determine whether law enforcement officers improperly obtained evidence from a witness's immunized testimony. This term comes from *Kastigar v. United States* (1972),[14] where the Supreme Court ruled that, where the government

fruit of the poisonous tree doctrine
a legal doctrine that requires any evidence derived from illegally obtained evidence to be excludable at trial

Kastigar **hearing**
a proceeding to determine whether law enforcement officers improperly obtained evidence from a witness's immunized testimony

FIGURE 10-8 **Fruit of the Poisonous Tree Doctrine**

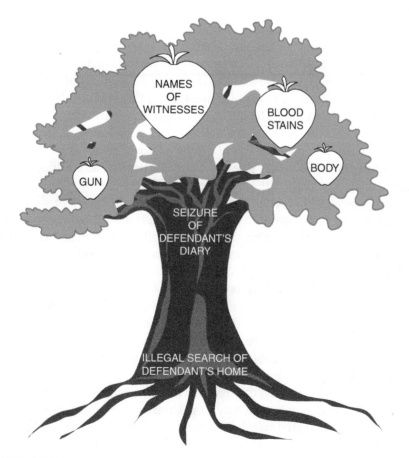

grants a witness immunity in exchange for testimony and then later seeks to prosecute the witness based on other evidence, the government bears the burden of showing that this evidence was "derived from a source wholly independent of the compelled testimony." But in many settings, the term *Kastigar* hearing is used in a more generic manner to refer to any proceeding where the court is asked to trace the pedigree of the prosecutor's evidence to determine whether it was derived from an unconstitutional search or interrogation.

Exceptions to the Exclusionary Rule.   While in theory, the fruit of the poisonous tree doctrine could lead to a substantial expansion of the exclusionary rule in some criminal cases, the Supreme Court also has imposed a number of restrictions on its application. Specifically, the Court has carved out a number of exceptions to the general rule requiring exclusion for illegally obtained evidence.

First, the Court has ruled that, if police can show that the evidence was obtained from a source that is separate or independent from the originally tainted method, they can still use the evidence. This is called the ***independent source rule***. As an example, if police unconstitutionally coerce a suspect into confessing to a crime, they cannot use this confession.[15] But if the police use a valid warrant based on information unrelated to the coerced confession to obtain the same confession from a journal located in the suspect's home, the confession will be admissible as evidence against the defendant.

Second, the Court has adopted the ***intervening circumstances*** exception, whereby evidence is admissible if new circumstances or events break the causal link between the illegal actions of the police and the ill-gotten evidence.[16] For example, if a suspect voluntarily provides to police the same evidence that the officers had originally seized illegally, then the evidence may be admissible due to the intervening event of the confession.

Third, the Court has adopted the ***inevitable discovery*** exception, which allows illegally obtained evidence to be admitted if the government can show that the evidence eventually would have been discovered through proper means.[17] In *Nix v. Williams* (1984), state police were searching for the body of a murdered ten-year-old girl. During the search, police questioned the defendant without providing him *Miranda* warnings. The defendant then told police where the girl's body was located, which turned out to be a public and open location. The Court concluded that, even though police found the girl's body through an unconstitutional interrogation, the exclusionary rule did not apply because authorities would have found the body eventually without the defendant's confession.

The Court also has established a ***good faith exception***, which allows illegally obtained evidence to be introduced if the police can show that they relied in good faith on a judicial order or search warrant. Typically, the good faith exception also includes situations where police act in good faith on laws or rules that they reasonably believe are valid even though they ultimately are found to be invalid.[18] This exception arises out of *United States v. Leon* (1984), where the Court ruled that the exclusionary rule did not apply to evidence obtained by officers acting in reasonable reliance on a search warrant that was issued by neutral and detached magistrate, but ultimately found to be invalid. The Court found that the exclusionary rule serves as a remedy to "substantial and deliberate" Fourth Amendment violations, does not apply to searches and seizures conducted in good faith by law enforcement. (The *Leon* case is discussed further in Chapter 11.)

In *Herring v. United States* (2009), the Court extended the good faith exception to searches conducted based on incorrect information received from police computers. In *Herring*, police searched the defendant and found drugs and a gun

independent source rule
an exception to the exclusionary rule that allows evidence to be admitted if police can show that the evidence was obtained by a source that is separate or independent from the originally tainted method

intervening circumstances
an exception to the exclusionary rule, whereby evidence is admissible if new circumstances or events break the causal link between the illegal actions of the police and the ill-gotten evidence

inevitable discovery
an exception to the exclusionary rule that allows illegally obtained evidence to be admitted if the government can show that the evidence eventually would have been discovered through proper means

Law Line 10-10
Nix v. Williams (1984)

good faith exception
an exception to the exclusionary rule that allows illegally obtained evidence to be introduced if the police can show that they relied in good faith on a judicial order or search warrant

Law Line 10-11
United States v. Leon (1984)

after a police computer wrongly indicated that there was an outstanding arrest warrant for Herring. In a 5-4 ruling, the Court concluded that the exclusionary rule did not apply because the police had acted in good faith when relying on the computer records to arrest and search Herring.

And finally, the Supreme Court has ruled that the exclusionary rule does not apply to grand jury hearings, civil proceedings, and, in some cases, where the prosecution seeks to use illegally obtained evidence to impeach a criminal defendant's testimony during trial.[19] As a result, where applied, the exclusionary rule is often limited to barring tainted evidence from being introduced during the government's case-in-chief. All told, the Court's exceptions and limitations have served to substantially limit the scope of the exclusionary rule and fruit of the poisonous tree doctrine.

CAPSTONE CASE *Herring v. United States,* 129 S. Ct. 695 (2009)

Chief Justice Roberts delivered the opinion of the Court.

On July 7, 2004, Investigator Mark Anderson learned that Bennie Dean Herring had driven to the Coffee County Sheriff's Department to retrieve something from his impounded truck. Herring was no stranger to law enforcement, and Anderson asked the county's warrant clerk, Sandy Pope, to check for any outstanding warrants for Herring's arrest. When she found none, Anderson asked Pope to check with Sharon Morgan, her counterpart in neighboring Dale County. After checking Dale County's computer database, Morgan replied that there was an active arrest warrant for Herring's failure to appear on a felony charge. Pope relayed the information to Anderson and asked Morgan to fax over a copy of the warrant as confirmation. Anderson and a deputy followed Herring as he left the impound lot, pulled him over, and arrested him. A search incident to the arrest revealed methamphetamine in Herring's pocket, and a pistol (which as a felon he could not possess) in his vehicle.

There had, however, been a mistake about the warrant. The Dale County sheriff's computer records are supposed to correspond to actual arrest warrants, which the office also maintains. But when Morgan went to the files to retrieve the actual warrant to fax to Pope, Morgan was unable to find it. She called a court clerk and learned that the warrant had been recalled five months earlier. Normally when a warrant is recalled the court clerk's office or a judge's chambers calls Morgan, who enters the information in the sheriff's computer database and disposes of the physical copy. For whatever reason, the information about the recall of the warrant for Herring did not appear in the database. Morgan immediately called Pope to alert her to the mixup, and Pope contacted Anderson over a secure radio. This all unfolded in 10 to 15 minutes, but Herring had already been arrested and found with the gun and drugs, just a few hundred yards from the sheriff's office.

Herring was indicted in the District Court for the Middle District of Alabama for illegally possessing the gun and drugs. . . . He moved to suppress the evidence on the ground that his initial arrest had been illegal because the warrant had been rescinded. . . .

Because the error was merely negligent and attenuated from the arrest, the Eleventh Circuit concluded that the benefit of suppressing the evidence "would be marginal or nonexistent," and the evidence was therefore admissible under the good-faith rule of *United States v. Leon,* 468 U.S. 897 (1984).

. . .

The Fourth Amendment protects "[t]he right of the people to be secure in their persons, houses, papers, and effects, against unreasonable searches and

(continued)

(continued)

seizures," but "contains no provision expressly precluding the use of evidence obtained in violation of its commands." Nonetheless, our decisions establish an exclusionary rule that, when applicable, forbids the use of improperly obtained evidence at trial. We have stated that this judicially created rule is "designed to safeguard Fourth Amendment rights generally through its deterrent effect."

. . .

The fact that a Fourth Amendment violation occurred—*i.e.*, that a search or arrest was unreasonable—does not necessarily mean that the exclusionary rule applies. Indeed, exclusion "has always been our last resort, not our first impulse," and our precedents establish important principles that constrain application of the exclusionary rule. . . .

To trigger the exclusionary rule, police conduct must be sufficiently deliberate that exclusion can meaningfully deter it, and sufficiently culpable that such deterrence is worth the price paid by the justice system. As laid out in our cases, the exclusionary rule serves to deter deliberate, reckless, or grossly negligent conduct, or in some circumstances recurring or systemic negligence. The error in this case does not rise to that level.

. . .

We do not suggest that all recordkeeping errors by the police are immune from the exclusionary rule. In this case, however, the conduct at issue was not so objectively culpable as to require exclusion. . . .

If the police have been shown to be reckless in maintaining a warrant system, or to have knowingly made false entries to lay the groundwork for future false arrests, exclusion would certainly be justified under our cases should such misconduct cause a Fourth Amendment violation. . . .

Petitioner's claim that police negligence automatically triggers suppression cannot be squared with the principles underlying the exclusionary rule, as they have been explained in our cases. In light of our repeated holdings that the deterrent effect of suppression must be substantial and outweigh any harm to the justice system, we conclude that when police mistakes are the result of negligence such as that described here, rather than systemic error or reckless disregard of constitutional requirements, any marginal deterrence does not "pay its way." In such a case, the criminal should not "go free because the constable has blundered."

The judgment of the Court of Appeals for the Eleventh Circuit is affirmed.

It is so ordered.

WHAT DO *YOU* THINK?

1. Should the exclusionary rule have been applied to encourage police agencies to maintain more accurate and up-to-date records in their computer systems?
2. Do you find that negligent police misconduct should be distinguished from deliberate misconduct when applying the exclusionary rule?

It should be noted, however, that a number of states have not applied some of the exceptions to the exclusionary rule under their own constitutions and statutes. For example, in the state of Washington, the state supreme court has refused to recognize a good faith exception to the Fourth Amendment.[20] Instead, Washington state courts evaluate the exclusion of evidence based on whether the search and seizure was unreasonable. Other states have similarly rejected or limited the U.S. Supreme Court's exceptions to the exclusionary rule.

In addition, the exclusionary rule may not be the only remedy available to those whose rights are violated under the Fourth, Fifth, and Sixth amendments. See Chapters 11 and 12. Individuals may also pursue civil actions, under federal or state law, for money damages against officials who breach their rights of privacy during arrests and searches and seizures.[21]

IN THE FIELD

For many legal professionals, motions to suppress and the exclusionary rule are the heart and soul of criminal practice. In many cases, both sides realize that, if the case goes to trial with the existing body of evidence held by the prosecutor, the defendant likely will be convicted. As a result, there is often a "trial within a trial" that occurs in the form of a suppression hearing. The motions that initiate these court proceedings, as well as the hearings themselves, are important for two reasons.

First, they may have an immediate impact on the trial proceedings, by limiting or allowing certain trial evidence. But in addition, the proceedings and court rulings in suppression hearings may also form the basis for a criminal appeal once the trial court matter has concluded. As noted throughout this text, many criminal cases are resolved though plea agreement. In these cases, the defendant admits some level of criminal culpability to the charged offense. But despite this admission, some defendants may still be able to appeal any adverse trial court rulings on pretrial motions that may have influenced their decision to enter a plea. As a result, pretrial motions, particularly motions to suppress, can impact criminal cases well beyond the trial court.

PLEA NEGOTIATIONS

Although criminal trials receive a lot of attention in the news media and television dramas, the real-life reality is that the overwhelming majority of criminal cases never go to trial. In fact, according to recent findings, less than 5 percent of all criminal cases are actually tried before a judge or jury.[22] The vast majority of the other 95 percent of cases are resolved through some form of plea agreement. As a result, legal professionals are likely to work with far more plea agreements and hearings than actual criminal trials.

That does not mean, however, that trial preparation and pretrial motions are unimportant. In fact, just the opposite is true. In many cases, the level and depth of a party's trial preparation will dictate or at least strongly influence the type of plea agreement that is reached. For example, a prosecutor who puts together a strong and organized case in advance of trial can signal to the defendant that a trial will likely result in a conviction of all current charges. Conversely, a defendant who demonstrates preparedness for trial or solid arguments in pretrial motions, including motions to suppress evidence, can convince a prosecutor that a trial conviction is not guaranteed. In short, prosecutors and defendants generally obtain favorable plea agreements by being prepared for trial.

Plea Agreements

In general, a ***plea agreement*** is a formal resolution of a criminal case made by the prosecutor and defendant and approved by the trial court. In many cases, a plea agreement is written in the form of a contract, wherein the parties actually spell out the terms of their resolution. This written agreement is then filed with the trial

plea agreement
a formal resolution of a criminal case made by the prosecutor and defendant and approved by the trial court

court. In some cases, written plea agreements can be quite lengthy and detailed, identifying very precise facts to which the defendant will admit and explaining exactly what benefits the government will provide the defendant in exchange for the guilty or no contest plea.

In other cases, particularly misdemeanor cases in state or local courts, plea agreements are made informally and orally between the parties. These oral agreements are then placed on the trial court record when the parties explain their understandings to the judge and the court reporter records the terms in the trial transcript. For example, in a basic DUI or OMVI case, the prosecutor might simply say to the judge, "Your honor, the defendant has agreed to plead no contest to the A charge, and in exchange, the state has agreed to dismiss the B and C charges." In this example, the A charge is the DUI or OMVI count, while the B and C charges are likely supplemental DUI charges or driving-related infractions, such as reckless operation of a vehicle or speeding.

plea bargaining
the process by which plea agreements are made

The process by which plea agreements are made is called ***plea bargaining.*** Black's Law Dictionary defines plea bargaining as follows:

> The process whereby the accused and the prosecutor in a criminal case work out a mutually satisfactory disposition of the case subject to court approval. It usually involves the defendant's pleading guilty to a lesser offense or to only one or some of the counts of a multi-count indictment in return for a lighter sentence than that possible for the graver charge.

Generally, plea bargaining can occur at any time during a criminal case, including the middle of a trial. Some trial judges have particular court rules that require the plea agreements to be reached within a certain number of days before trial. But typically, courts will consider plea agreements between the parties made at any time.

The Terms Negotiated

The term *plea bargaining* is something of a misnomer in many cases because the parties really are not negotiating about what plea the defendant will enter. Instead, the parties are trying to resolve other terms related to the termination of the case.

Gary Leon Ridgway initials the plea agreement in court on November 5, 2003 in the King County Courthouse in Seattle, in which he pled guilty to forty-eight murders. Ridgway added in a confession read out by a prosecutor in open court, "I killed so many women I have a hard time keeping them straight." Ridgeway pleaded guilty as part of a plea bargain with prosecutors in which his life would be spared.

There are several items that might be negotiated in a plea agreement besides the plea itself. These include the nature of the charges, the number of counts, the sentence, the facts to which the defendant will plead, the amount of restitution or harm, and, in some cases, other more particular terms.

Bargaining over the plea typically involves the parties agreeing to what the defendant will admit in the form of a legal plea. As outlined in Chapter 9, three primary pleas are used in criminal cases—guilty, not guilty, and no contest (*nolo contendere*). In rare cases, the defendant may be permitted to enter an Alford plea. Where the type of plea is being negotiated, the most common dispute involves whether the defendant will plead guilty or no contest to the charges. As addressed in Chapter 9, a guilty plea involves the defendant admitting to both the facts and legal conclusions outlined by the prosecutor, either in the original charging instrument or a negotiated plea agreement. With a guilty plea, defendants admit to facts as alleged by the prosecutor and admit that those facts constitute the criminal offense asserted in the charging instrument or plea agreement. Both prosecutors and trial courts typically have very little trouble accepting a defendant's guilty plea as a part of a plea agreement.

But in many cases, defendants may wish to plead no contest as a part of a plea agreement. There can be many reasons for this request. First, as mentioned in Chapter 9, a no contest plea may afford defendants some legal protection in related civil cases. In some jurisdictions and to varying degrees, a guilty plea in a criminal case may be used against the defendant in a corresponding civil suit, so some defendants may wish to plead no contest instead. Second, in some jurisdictions, if defendants enter a guilty plea, they waive their right to appeal any adverse pretrial rulings by the trial court, whereas a no contest plea allows them to maintain their rights to appeal these matters. And third, some defendants simply have trouble admitting guilt in some criminal cases, so for them a no contest plea is just a more palatable plea to enter.

Charge bargaining involves discussions over what criminal offense(s) the defendant will accept responsibility for in the plea agreement. Of course, defendants can plead "as charged," meaning they admit to the criminal offense(s) contained in the charging instrument. Or the parties can agree to another criminal offense, which is typically an offense containing a lower degree of criminal culpability. For example, a defendant charged with felonious assault, a fourth-degree felony, might negotiate to plead to a simple assault charge, which is a first-degree misdemeanor. By negotiating for a lower degree of criminal offense, defendants can reduce the severity of their criminal sentence because the reduced charge carries less jail time or lower fines.

Charge bargaining can have other consequences as well. For example, a defendant charged with soliciting a minor for sexual activity (or a similar offense) will likely have to register as a sex offender after being convicted. Under most statutory schemes, this offense carries a mandatory sexual offender registration requirement. But in some jurisdictions, if defendant can negotiate for a plea to attempted importuning, this offense is not listed as a crime requiring mandatory sexual offender registration.

Count bargaining involves negotiation over the number of criminal counts to which the defendant will be pleading. This occurs mostly with indictments containing multiple counts—in some cases a dozen or more criminal charges—and often includes charge bargaining as well. Like charge bargaining, count bargaining is designed to influence the sentence the defendant is likely to receive.

Sentence bargaining involves a negotiated understanding between the prosecutor and the defendant about what sentence is most appropriate.

bargaining over the plea
a type of plea bargaining that involves the parties agreeing to what the defendant will admit in the form of a legal plea (guilty, no contest, etc.)

charge bargaining
a type of plea bargaining that involves discussions over what criminal offense(s) the defendant will accept responsibility for

count bargaining
negotiation over the number of criminal counts to which the defendant will be pleading

sentence bargaining
a negotiated understanding between the prosecutor and the defendant about what sentence is most appropriate

This is a more difficult type of negotiation because, technically, trial judges impose sentences and are not bound by any agreement reached by the parties. In many cases, the parties actually consult with the trial judge about the plea agreement, including any understanding about the recommended sentence. In many courts, judges will let the parties know whether they can abide by the negotiated recommended sentence. In other cases, there is no formal agreement about the sentence, but rather the prosecutor may agree not to push for any particular punishment or promise to remain silent at the sentencing hearing. Sentence bargaining is more common in state and local courts, where the parties have greater and more informal access to the trial judges, which enables discussions about negotiated sentences. In federal courts, however, sentence bargaining is rarely conducted because of the legal requirements for federal sentencing, which are discussed in Chapter 14. Instead, the parties in federal criminal cases can attempt to influence the sentence by engaging in charge or count bargaining or by stipulating to particular facts within the plea agreement.

fact bargaining
negotiation over which facts the defendant will acknowledge in making a plea

Fact bargaining involves negotiations over which facts the defendants will acknowledge in making their pleas. Obviously, there are some facts asserted within a charging instrument that may form the basis of the plea. But in some cases the defendant is not willing to admit all of these items, or there may be other facts not contained in the charging instrument that will be relevant to the trial court's determination of a sentence. In these types of cases, the prosecutor and defendant may agree to a precise factual statement that will support the underlying plea agreement. The factual stipulations agreed upon by the parties can serve as a parameter for judicial consideration during the sentencing hearing. Factual stipulations can involve many different items, including the amount of loss or harm incurred by the victim, the amount of restitution that must be paid by the defendant, whether the defendant has provided substantial assistance to law enforcement authorities, and whether there were any aggravating or mitigating circumstances surrounding the offense.

Other terms can also be negotiated as a part of a plea agreement, as long as they are within the authority of the parties and the trial court to enforce. In some cases, the parties might also negotiate other factors or circumstances. For example, defendants may wish to remain free pending their appeal; they may want a certain amount of time to pay restitution to the victim; or they may wish to receive a particular drug or alcohol treatment program as a part of their sentence. Prosecutors may also want certain terms, such as the defendant's forfeiture of certain property or the defendant's agreement to assist law enforcement officers with their ongoing investigations.

Plea Hearings

Although plea agreements are negotiated by the parties, they must be approved and implemented by the trial court. Generally, trial courts must conduct plea hearings in open court and on the record, and the defendant must be present. During the hearing, trial courts generally have three primary concerns to address before accepting a plea agreement between the parties.

First, the trial court must ensure that defendants are entering plea agreements voluntarily and that they are under no undue form of coercion in changing their plea from not guilty to guilty or no contest. Federal Rule of Criminal Procedure 11(b)(2) states:

---

(2) *Ensuring That a Plea Is Voluntary.*

Before accepting a plea of guilty or *nolo contendere,* the court must address the defendant personally in open court and determine that the plea is voluntary and did not result from force, threats, or promises (other than promises in a plea agreement).

Second, the trial court must certify that defendants are waiving their rights to a trial with a requisite degree of knowledge about the consequences. In other words, the court must make sure defendants are knowingly entering into the plea agreement. Under Federal Criminal Rule 11(b)(1), trial courts must do the following:

(b) Considering and Accepting a Guilty or *Nolo Contendere* Plea.

1. ***Advising and Questioning the Defendant.***

   Before the court accepts a plea of guilty or *nolo contendere*, the defendant may be placed under oath, and the court must address the defendant personally in open court. During this address, the court must inform the defendant of, and determine that the defendant understands, the following:

   A. the government's right, in a prosecution for perjury or false statement, to use against the defendant any statement that the defendant gives under oath;

   B. the right to plead not guilty, or having already so pleaded, to persist in that plea;

   C. the right to a jury trial;

   D. the right to be represented by counsel—and if necessary have the court appoint counsel—at trial and at every other stage of the proceeding;

   E. the right at trial to confront and cross-examine adverse witnesses, to be protected from compelled self-incrimination, to testify and present evidence, and to compel the attendance of witnesses;

   F. the defendant's waiver of these trial rights if the court accepts a plea of guilty or *nolo contendere;*

   G. the nature of each charge to which the defendant is pleading;

   H. any maximum possible penalty, including imprisonment, fine, and term of supervised release;

   I. any mandatory minimum penalty;

   J. any applicable forfeiture;

   K. the court's authority to order restitution;

   L. the court's obligation to impose a special assessment;

   M. in determining a sentence, the court's obligation to apply and calculate the applicable sentencing-guideline range and to consider that range, possible departures under the Sentencing Guidelines, and other sentencing factors under 18 U.S.C. § 3553(a); and

   N. the terms of any plea-agreement provision waiving the right to appeal or to collaterally attack the sentence.

And finally, the court must assess whether there is a proper factual basis to support the charges in the plea agreement and that the terms of the agreement are otherwise appropriate under the circumstances. In most cases, after hearing the terms of the agreement and ensuring that the defendant is knowingly and voluntarily entering the plea, the trial court will accept the defendant's new plea and the terms of the plea agreement. Depending on the jurisdiction, the trial court will then either proceed immediately to sentencing the defendant or schedule the case for a sentencing hearing at a later date.

FIGURE 10-9 **Recommended Plea Hearing Checklist for Alaska Judges**

Alaska

PLEA HEARING CHECKLIST
Criminal Rule 11

Ask the parties or counsel to state any plea agreement.

Ask the defendant if he understands the nature of the charge.

State the maximum and minimum penalties. See Penalty Checklist.

Ask for the defendant's plea.

Tell the defendant that he is giving up the right to appeal a sentence within the limits of the plea agreement.

Ask the attorneys if the defendant is relying on any discussions that are not part of the plea agreement.

[For sex offenses, give the defendant written notice of the sex offender registration requirements using Form Cr-440.]

Tell the defendant that by a plea of guilty or no contest the defendant gives up the right to trail by judge or jury (summarize) and the right to confront adverse witnesses.

Remind the defendant that he has the right to plead not guilty or continue with that plea.

Ask the defendant if the plea is voluntary.

Ask the defendant if the plea results from force or threats or from any promises apart from the plea agreement.

Ask the defendant is sick or under the influence of any drugs, alcohol or medication.

For pleas of guilty, decide whether there is a factual basis for the plea by reviewing the complaint affidavit or taking a statement form the prosecutor.

Make findings on whether the plea is knowing and voluntary, and state whether you accept the plea.

Proceed with the sentencing hearing (most misdemeanors) or schedule the sentencing hearing (most felonies).

In some cases, the trial judge may find that the agreed-upon terms, such as the negotiated charge(s) or sentence, are not proper given the facts of the case. If so, the trial court must inform the parties that it cannot accept the plea agreement as currently stated, and if the defendant has already changed his plea to guilty or no contest, he must be given an opportunity to withdraw it. This is usually a rare event. But in cases where it occurs, the parties must either revise the terms of their plea agreement or begin preparing the case for trial.

Additional Considerations for Plea Bargaining

In addition to the general terms and conditions for plea bargaining, more particularized concerns can exist in some cases, especially those at the federal level. Although plea bargaining regularly occurs in federal cases, the negotiations can be far more complicated than those that occur in state and local cases. Due to sentencing factors found in the United States Sentencing Guidelines (USSG) (see Chapter 14), as well as the more formal nature of federal criminal proceedings, it is often far more difficult for the parties to reach a plea agreement that will provide sufficient certainty or predictability with respect to the eventual sentence.

This dynamic is further complicated by the fact that the U.S. Attorney's Manual (USAM) contains several provisions regarding plea agreements, including

Chapter 9-16.300 (Plea Agreements), which states that plea agreements should "honestly reflect the totality and seriousness of the defendant's conduct," and any departure must be consistent with Sentencing Guideline provisions. In addition, federal district courts rely heavily on the formal presentence investigation reports provided by the U.S. Probation Department when imposing criminal sentences. These reports, however, are compiled after the defendant has entered a plea during the plea hearing. As a result, it is more difficult for the parties in federal cases to control the precise outcome of their plea agreements.

It should also be noted that, in many jurisdictions, prosecutors must consult with the identifiable victim(s) in a criminal case before reaching a final plea agreement with the defendant. The nature and extent of this consultation varies from state to state. But generally, victims must be afforded an opportunity to register their reaction and views on the proposed plea agreement. This is not to say that victims have final veto authority over the terms of plea agreements in these jurisdictions, but their input and reaction to proposed terms can influence the eventual agreement between the parties.

IN THE FIELD

Perhaps more than in any other area of criminal practice, plea bargaining requires a substantial amount of experience and preparation. For inexperienced legal professionals, it may be very difficult to assess whether a plea offer—from either a prosecutor or a defendant—is a good deal, unless you know enough about your case and the personal circumstances of the defendant. As a result, the cardinal rule of plea bargaining is "know thy case."

In addition to understanding the standard items, such as the degree of the offense, the possible sentence, and the risks of going to trial (outlined above), legal professionals also must consider the particular effect a plea agreement will have on an individual defendant. In some cases, even if a plea agreement may be considered a "good deal" for most criminal defendants, it may nonetheless have more adverse and long-term consequences for other defendants. For some defendants, a plea to a felony offense may result in losing their jobs or being barred from applying for some future job opportunities. For other defendants, a plea to a sexual offense will likely result in sexual offender registration requirements that may impact where they can live or work. For defendants who are not U.S. citizens, a plea to some criminal offenses may result in deportation or other immigration problems. For defendants who work in medicine, law, teaching, or commercial driving occupations, a plea to certain offenses may cause them to lose their professional licenses. And for defendants in drug cases, plea agreements that place them on probation in exchange for their completion of a drug treatment program might ultimately not benefit defendants who believe they cannot successfully complete the treatment program.

The bottom line is that legal professionals must fully explore all of the potential consequences of a plea agreement. For criminal defense attorneys , the details for these agreements must be fully explained to clients. And for prosecutors, plea agreements often must also be presented and explained to victims in some cases. In addition, legal professionals working with attorneys may also receive calls and other inquiries from clients, family members of the client, and others with questions about proposed or pending plea agreements. In these situations, legal professionals must be careful to remain within their ethical role as legal assistants and not provide legal advice or perform other attorney-only functions when responding to these questions.

CHAPTER **SUMMARY**

- The pretrial stage of a criminal case, which occurs after a defendant is formally charged and arraigned, but before the scheduled trial date, involves four primary areas of criminal procedure: (1) the discovery process, (2) motion practice, (3) the exclusionary rule, and (4) plea bargaining.
- Discovery is the pretrial process by which the prosecutor and the defendant exchange information and evidence about their respective cases.
- In most criminal cases, the defendant initiates the discovery process by submitting a request for discovery, where the requesting party asks for copies of or the opportunity to review certain materials held by the opposing party.
- At the federal level, Federal Rule of Criminal Procedure 16 provides the standards for discovery in criminal cases. Many states also list their discovery standards under the Rule 16 found within their rules of criminal procedure. Under Rule 16, defendants and prosecutors are not required to disclose their work product or the work product of their attorneys and agents made in preparation for trial.
- In cases where legal professionals believe that the opposing party may have forgotten or overlooked discoverable materials within its possession, they may have to file a motion to compel discovery, a formal motion filed with the trial court asking for an order compelling the opposing party to comply with the moving party's discovery request.
- Typically, the acquisition of evidence from third parties is accomplished through a subpoena, which is a court order to produce testimony or evidence. There are two basic types of subpoenas—a witness subpoena and a subpoena *duces tecum*.
- For criminal defendants, another source for discovery or insight into the prosecution's case may come through a bill of particulars, a document provided by a prosecutor that offers more specific information about the government's criminal charge.
- A pretrial motion is a request from a litigant for a ruling or directive by the trial court on a matter relating to a case. In general, a motion should clearly state what the party wants the court to do and provide a basic outline of the legal and factual basis for the requested court action.
- Many types of motions can be made before trial, including a motion to dismiss, motion to suppress, motion in limine, motion to travel, motion for continuance, motion to modify bond, motion to revoke bond, and motion for a protective order.
- In cases where defendants believe that law enforcement officers used illegal means to obtain incriminating evidence, they can file a motion to suppress or a motion to exclude evidence.
- At the heart of most motions to suppress is the exclusionary rule, which holds that illegally seized evidence must be excluded from governmental use during trial.
- In some cases, the Supreme Court has applied the exclusionary rule to more than just the initial item of evidence obtained by police in violation of the Constitution and has used it to exclude any other evidence derived from the initial piece of evidence. This is known as the "fruit of the poisonous tree doctrine."
- The Supreme Court has adopted a number of exceptions to the general rule requiring exclusion for illegally obtained evidence. These include the independent source rule, the intervening circumstances exception, the inevitable discovery exception, and the good faith exception.
- The vast majority of criminal cases are resolved through some form of plea agreement. A plea agreement is a formal resolution of a criminal case made by the prosecutor and defendant and approved by the trial court.
- There are several items that might be negotiated in a plea agreement besides the plea itself. These include the nature of the charges, the number of counts, the sentence, the facts to which the defendant will plead, the amount of restitution or harm, and, in some cases, other more particular terms.

KEY **TERMS**

attorney work product under the work
   product doctrine
bargaining over the plea
bill of particulars
Brady rule
charge bargaining
count bargaining
deposition

discovery
evidentiary hearing
exclusionary rule
exculpatory evidence
fact bargaining
fruit of the poisonous tree doctrine
Giglio material
good faith exception

impeach
independent source rule
inevitable discovery
intervening circumstances
Jencks Act
Kastigar hearing
motion
motion for a bill of particulars

motion for a protective order
motion for continuance
motion in limine
motion to compel discovery
motion to dismiss
motion to modify bond
motion to revoke bond

motion to suppress or motion to
   exclude evidence
motion to travel
oral hearing
plea agreement
plea bargaining
pretrial

process server
request for discovery
sentence bargaining
service of process
subpoena
subpoena *duces tecum*
witness subpoena

QUESTIONS FOR **DISCUSSION**

1. How do parties in a criminal case obtain discovery materials from one another?
2. What materials must a prosecutor provide to a defendant, if requested? What materials is the prosecutor not required to provide?
3. What can a party do if she believes the opposing party has not provided complete discovery?
4. How can a defendant or prosecutor obtain materials from a third party?
5. What is the purpose of pretrial motions?
6. Identify at least eight pretrial motions a defendant might file in a criminal case. Identify at least four pretrial motions that might be filed by prosecutors.
7. What are the basic elements or features found in a pretrial motion?
8. What is the purpose of a motion to suppress?
9. Explain how the exclusionary rule works.
10. What are the primary exceptions to the exclusionary rule?
11. What terms or conditions might be negotiated as a part of a plea agreement?
12. What procedures must trial courts follow before accepting a plea agreement?

REFERENCES

1. *People v. Defore*, 242 N.Y. 13, 21, 150 N.E. 585, 587 (1926).
2. *United States v. Leon*, 468 U.S. 902 (1984).
3. http://www.cnn.com/2009/POLITICS/04/07/ted.stevens/index.html.
4. See http://wrongful-convictions.blogspot.com/2009/07/murder-case-against-ralph-armstrong.html.
5. 373 U.S. 83 (1963).
6. *Kyles v. Whitley*, 514 U.S. 419, 434 (1995).
7. 405 U.S. 150 (1972).
8. 514 U.S. 419 (1995).
9. *Kyles*, 514 U.S. at 437–38 (citations omitted).
10. See http://www.digitaljournal.com/article/256701; http://www.time.com/time/nation/article/0,8599,1817551,00.html.
11. 232 U.S. 383 (1914).
12. 367 U.S. 643 (1961).
13. See *Wong Sun v. United States*, 371 U.S. 471 (1963).
14. 406 U.S. 441, 453 (1972).
15. See *Segura v. United States*, 468 U.S. 796 (1984).
16. See *Brown v. Illinois*, 422 U.S. 590 (1975).
17. See *Nix v. Williams*, 467 U.S. 431 (1984).
18. See *United States v. Leon*, 468 U.S. 897 (1984) (invalid search warrant); *Michigan v. DeFillippo*, 443 U.S. 41 (1979) (facially valid statute).
19. See *United States v. Calandra*, 414 U.S. 338 (1974) (grand jury); *United States v. Janis*, 428 U.S. 433 (1976) (civil proceedings); *Harris v. New York*, 401 U.S. 222 (1971) (impeachment).
20. *State v. White*, 97 Wash. 2d 92, 109–10, 640 P.2d 1061 (1982).
21. See Federal Civil Rights Law, 42 U.S.C. § 1983; *Bivens v. Six Unknown Named Agents of the Federal Bureau of Narcotics*, 403 U.S. 388 (1971) (providing monetary relief for a Fourth Amendment violation).
22. See Robert Burns, *The Death of the American Trial* (Chicago: University of Chicago Press, 2009).

APPENDIX
DEVELOPING YOUR LEGAL ANALYSIS

A. THE LAW WHERE YOU LIVE

Assume that you are working in a state public defender's office and have been asked to work on a drug case entitled *State v. Beth Jones*, Case No. 2011-0655. It seems that the State indicted Ms. Jones on one count of cocaine possession—a fourth-degree felony—and the case has been assigned to Judge Mary Gavel.

According to the facts provided by the client, Ms. Jones was driving her car down Main Street when a local police officer activated his lights and siren and caused her to pull her car to the side of the road. The officer told Ms. Jones that she was speeding and asked her to step out of the car. After Ms. Jones complied with the officer's request, the officer reached inside the car and opened the glove box, where he found a plastic bag containing a white substance, which the State asserts is cocaine. Based upon this finding, the police officer arrested Ms. Jones for cocaine possession.

Your assignment is to locate and review your state's rules on obtaining discovery in criminal cases. Based on these rules, and the facts of the case as you know them, prepare a request for discovery to be filed in the case. Be sure to identify all items of information potentially in the State's possession or control that might be helpful to Ms. Jones, either in preparing for trial or filing additional pretrial motions, such as a motion to suppress.

B. INSIDE THE FEDERAL COURTS

Assume you are working in a U.S. Attorney's office in the criminal division. You have been asked to prepare a motion to revoke the defendant's bond in the case of *United States v. Frederick Williams*, Case No. CR-2011-045. The case is assigned to Judge Joseph Parker. The government indicted defendant Williams on two counts of bank fraud under 18 U.S.C. § 1344. According to the indictment, Mr. Williams provided a bank teller at the Union Savings Bank with two fictitious checks in order to obtain cash from the bank. During Mr. Williams's bond hearing, the magistrate judge issued a $10,000 bond, but ordered as a condition of this bond that Mr. Williams have no contact with the bank or bank employees involved in the criminal case. Mr. Williams made this bond and is currently free pending the trial date.

The U.S. Attorney's office has information that Mr. Williams has made contact with the Union Savings Bank and the teller involved in his criminal case. According to reliable information, on July 22 Mr. Williams stopped the bank teller in the parking lot of the bank and said that he wanted to apologize for his actions and for getting her involved as a witness in a criminal case. Mr. Williams did not threaten or harm the teller. But his presence on bank property nonetheless frightened the teller. Witnesses say that Mr. Williams returned to the bank on July 24 to use the ATM machine located on the outside of the building. Mr. Williams obtained cash from the machine, using his account, and then left the premises.

Based on these facts, you are asked to prepare a motion to revoke bond, which will be filed by Jay Peterson, the Assistant U.S. Attorney assigned to the case.

C. CYBER SOURCES

Assume that you have just been hired by a new attorney, Ima Yung, who has just opened a law office and started her private practice of law. As many new attorneys in private practice do, Ms. Yung has gone to the local courthouses and put her name on the list of court-appointed attorneys, so that she can be appointed by the trial courts as a defense attorney in cases involving indigent clients/defendants.

To prepare for this experience, Ms. Yung has asked you to compile a database of motions that she may have to file in criminal cases. Ms. Yung realizes that each of her cases will be different and that each motion will have to be tailored to the particular facts. But she would like to create some basic templates for motions and have them available in the firm's computer. Ms. Yung also wants to review these motions to learn some of the pretrial actions that are available and used in criminal cases.

Using the following websites (or others that you discover), compile at least ten different pretrial motions that might be filed on behalf of defendants in criminal cases. In addition, identify the primary purpose of each motion and its potential benefit to defendants/clients.

http://www.dcfpd.org/motions.html

http://www.dcfpd.org/motions/alaska.htm

D. ETHICS AND PROFESSIONALISM

Assume you are working as a legal assistant in a law firm that is representing Molly Dodd in her state criminal case. Ms. Dodd is charged with possessing methamphetamines under state law, a third-degree felony. Ms. Dodd, who has no prior criminal history, is out on bail and her case is scheduled for trial. If convicted, Ms. Dodd faces up to five years in state prison. The prosecutor has offered Ms. Dodd a plea agreement that would require her to plead guilty as charged and serve thirty days in the local jail.

Ms. Dodd is not sure what to do and is asking you for your advice. She wants to know (1) What are the odds of winning at trial? (2) If convicted at trial, how much time would the judge likely give her? (3) What has occurred in other cases like this that you have worked on? (4) What would it be like serving time in the local jail? and (5) What is your best recommendation as to whether she should accept the plea agreement or go to trial?

Assume you have worked on at least thirty state felony cases involving methamphetamines. You are very familiar with the judge assigned to Ms. Dodd's case and believe you know his approach to sentencing. But you are concerned about the ethical propriety of answering some of Ms. Dodd's questions. Consider the following resources, particularly Canon 4 of the ethics code offered by the National Association of Legal Assistants (below), as well as any state or local ethical standards that may apply. Then draft a two-page response where you reply to each of Ms. Dodd's questions.

American Bar Association

www.abanet.org/legalservices/paralegals/downloads/ modelguidelines.pdf

The American Alliance of Paralegals, Inc.

http://www.aapipara.org/Ethicalstandards.htm

National Association of Legal Assistants

http://www.nala.org/code.aspx

chapter **eleven**

FOURTH AMENDMENT: SEARCHES AND SEIZURES

LEARNING OBJECTIVES

After reading this chapter, you should be able to

- Understand the basic constitutional protections afforded criminal defendants under the Fourth Amendment.

- Appreciate the difference between a seizure of a person, an arrest, and an investigatory detention.

- Explain the process for evaluating the constitutionality of search and seizure issues within criminal cases.

- Read and recognize the different components of a search warrant.

- Understand the legal standard of probable cause as it applies to search and arrest warrants.

- Explain the rationale and realities of a *Terry* stop or a stop and frisk.

- Explain the difference between the legal standards of probable cause and reasonable suspicion, as well as the circumstances where each standard might apply.

- Prepare basic motions to suppress a warrant-based search and a warrantless search.

- Identify the exceptions to the warrant requirement under the Fourth Amendment.

- Prepare a basic memorandum in response to a motion to suppress.

[I]t is not the breaking of a man's doors and the rummaging of his drawers that constitutes the essence of the offense; but it is the invasion of his indefeasible right of personal security, personal liberty and private property, where that right has never been forfeited by his conviction of some public offense.
—Justice Joseph P. Bradley, *Boyd v. United States* (1886)

It is better, so the Fourth Amendment teaches us, that the guilty sometimes go free than the citizens be subject to easy arrest.
—Justice William O. Douglas, *Henry v. United States* (1959)

Justice may be blind, but she has very sophisticated listening devices.
—Edgar Argo

INTRODUCTION

In Chapter 10, we observed that the evidence obtained by law enforcement officials in most criminal cases is sufficient to support the elements of the charged offense(s). But before this evidence can be used at trial to prosecute defendants, it must be shown to be properly obtained by law enforcement. In cases where the government has acquired evidence through unlawful methods of search and seizure, a trial court may bar the prosecution from using the evidence at trial.

As outlined in Chapter 10, the primary tool used by legal professionals in this area is a motion to suppress, which is generally based on the exclusionary rule. Defendants typically file motions to suppress as the means for requesting the exclusion of evidence. And courts generally use the exclusionary rule as the basis for limiting evidence from trial. Where the challenged evidence involves tangible materials, such as computer records, firearms, drugs, money, fingerprints, and so forth, defendants often assert that this evidence was obtained through an unlawful search and seizure.

THE FOURTH AMENDMENT

The Fourth Amendment to the U.S. Constitution provides the textual bedrock for governmental searches and seizures. This amendment bars the government from conducting unreasonable searches and seizures of persons, houses, papers and effects. It also requires that warrants be based on probable cause. Specifically, the Fourth Amendment provides:

> The right of the people to be secure in their persons, houses, papers, and effects, against unreasonable searches and seizures, shall not be violated, and no Warrants shall issue, but upon probable cause, supported by Oath or affirmation, and particularly describing the place to be searched, and the persons or things to be seized.

Within this amendment, there are two primary provisions. The ***search and seizure clause*** bars government from engaging in unreasonable searches and seizures of persons, houses, papers, and effects. And the ***warrant provision*** requires that government must demonstrate probable cause before a warrant will be issued by a judge. These two provisions, which are sometimes interrelated, form the basic constitutional context for addressing government searches of persons and places, seizures of evidence, and arrests of individuals.[1] But in general, "[t]he essential purpose of the proscriptions of the Fourth Amendment is to impose a standard of 'reasonableness' upon the exercise of discretion by government officials, including law enforcement agents, in order 'to safeguard the privacy and security of individuals against arbitrary invasions. . . .' "[2]

The Meaning of Searches and Seizures

As you can tell, the terms and standards of the Fourth Amendment are not self-defining. The phrases "unreasonable search and seizure" and "probable cause" are not defined or further addressed by the amendment or any other provision of the Constitution. In general, a ***search*** is a governmental encroachment upon a location where a person has a reasonable expectation of privacy. And a ***seizure*** is a governmental exercise of control over a person or item. Determining the reasonableness of a search or seizure, however, can be a bit more complicated. In most cases, courts tend to conduct a balancing test, which considers the ***totality of the circumstances*** and measures the government's need for the evidence against the level of encroachment upon the individual's right to privacy.[3]

search and seizure clause
Fourth Amendment provision barring government from engaging in unreasonable searches and seizures of persons, houses, papers, and effects

warrant provision
Fourth Amendment requirement that government demonstrate probable cause before a warrant will be issued by a judge

search
a governmental encroachment upon a location where a person has a reasonable expectation of privacy

seizure
a governmental exercise of control over a person or item

totality of the circumstances
a legal standard used to measure the constitutionality of many searches and seizures; considers the overall context of the detention or search, including what actions and words the officer used, the location of the detention, and the length of the stop

Over time, the Supreme Court has adopted a number of specific tests to be used in particular types of searches and seizures (see below). Ultimately, however, even with these tests, assessing the reasonableness of a search or seizure can be a somewhat subjective and value-laden process. As a result, it is ultimately up to jurists to determine the meaning and scope of these terms based on the facts presented during a suppression hearing. What makes a search or an arrest unreasonable? How much evidence constitutes probable cause? These and other questions, left unanswered by the explicit text of the Fourth Amendment, ultimately require the application of values from beyond the text.

Law Line 11-1
Fourth Amendment Information

Additional Standards

Recall from Chapters 2 and 8 that the Fourth Amendment establishes the *minimum* standards for government conduct in performing searches and seizures of criminal evidence. But some states have additional standards and protections for searches and seizures that might exist within their own constitutions, statutes, and judicial opinions. Individual states can establish enhanced standards for their law enforcement officers. As a result, while the focus of this chapter is on the national standards for searches and seizures established under the Fourth Amendment, in state cases professionals need to assess whether their state offers additional standards that might apply to the particular facts present in those cases.

That does not mean that state standards will always prevail. In *Virginia v. Moore* (2008),[4] Virginia authorities stopped motorist David Lee Moore based on suspicion that he was driving with a suspended driver's license—a misdemeanor under state law. After confirming Moore's suspended license, police arrested him, which was contrary to a Virginia statute that only permitted police to issue Moore a summons for his traffic-related misdemeanor. In arresting Moore, officers found sixteen grams of crack cocaine in his pants and charged him with possession of cocaine with the intent to distribute. Moore moved to have the drug evidence suppressed, asserting that it was the product of an illegal arrest.

The Virginia Supreme Court agreed with Moore, finding that because authorities seized the drug evidence pursuant to an arrest that violated the state statute, it was the product of an illegal search under the Fourth Amendment. But the U.S. Supreme Court overturned this decision. In a unanimous ruling, the Court found that, although Moore's arrest may have violated Virginia statutory law, it did not constitute an unreasonable seizure of Moore's person under the Fourth Amendment. The Court suggested that, if the Virginia no-arrest policy had been a state *constitutional* standard, the outcome might have been different under the Fourth Amendment. But according to the Court, "the arrest rules that the officers violated were those of state law alone, and as we have just concluded, it is not the province of the Fourth Amendment to enforce state law. That Amendment does not require the exclusion of evidence obtained from a constitutionally permissible arrest."

Law Line 11-2
Virginia v. Moore (2008)

Nevertheless, in state and local cases, legal professionals need to consider all search and seizure standards that might exist under state law. And in these cases, motions from the defense side should ask the trial court to exclude evidence under both the Fourth Amendment *and* the applicable state legal standards. See Figure 11-1.

Evaluating Search and Seizure Issues

As addressed in Chapter 10, the propriety of searches and seizures in criminal cases is reviewed primarily through the defendant's filing of a motion to suppress and the trial court's review of evidence during a suppression hearing. During these proceedings, the central concern is the manner by which the government obtained

FIGURE 11-1 **Example of Opening Paragraph to Motion to Suppress Citing Both Federal and State Standards**

COURT OF COMMON PLEAS
HAMILTON COUNTY, OHIO

State of Ohio	:	CASE NO.: B-2011-55555
PLAINTIFF	:	JUDGE: Summers
-vs-	:	
Joseph Stanton	:	**MOTION TO SUPPRESS**
DEFENDANT	:	

Pursuant to Ohio Criminal Rule 12(B)(3), Defendant Joseph Stanton hereby moves this Court for an order suppressing any evidence which the state may seek to introduce at trial in the above captioned matter on the grounds that this evidence is the fruit of an unconstitutional search and seizure in violation of the rights guaranteed Mr. Stanton by the Fourth and Fourteenth Amendments to the United States Constitution and Article 1, Section 14 of the Ohio Constitution.

---

its evidence for trial. As a result, legal professionals must consider and review both the substance and the pedigree (source) for all pretrial evidence. This evidence can be found in a variety of sources.

The most obvious source is the material in the government's discovery response. At times, the evidence listed or provided by the prosecutor during the pretrial discovery phase will supply some insight into whether there may be search and seizure issues for a motion to suppress. Though typically prosecutors do not have to offer the source for their trial evidence identified in their discovery response, the evidence itself may reveal its probable source.

Police reports and witness statements can also offer details on the methods used to obtain the government's evidence. In many cases, law enforcement will write a narrative of what occurred during a defendant's arrest. And this might include discussion about how certain evidence was acquired. In cases where a search warrant was executed, authorities generally must supply the court with a return on the warrant (see below), which outlines how the warrant was executed and what evidence was obtained as a result.

In addition, the testimony and exhibits introduced during preliminary hearings may also suggest search and seize issues. Recall from Chapter 9 that these hearings usually include testimony from the arresting or investigating officer in the case. As a result, during these hearings, defense professionals can often obtain considerable insight into how the government obtained its evidence for trial.

And finally, for defense professionals, clients themselves can also provide considerable detail about law enforcement methods involving searches and seizures. Often clients can describe how they were arrested, how they were searched, and what law enforcement officers did to acquire evidence for trial. All of this information can then be considered and used to conduct legal research for a motion to suppress evidence.

Under the Fourth Amendment, there are three primary categories of constitutional review for searches and seizures. These involve evidence obtained through (1) the arrest or other detention of persons, (2) warrantless searches and seizures of places or things, and (3) warrant-based searches and seizures. Each category has its own set of constitutional standards.

FIGURE 11-2 **Primary Categories of Search and Seizure under the Fourth Amendment**

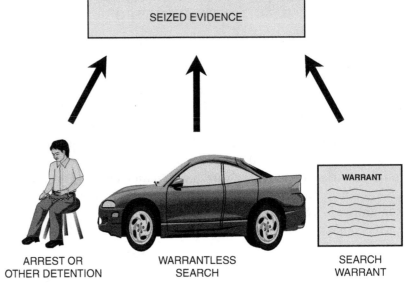

To determine which set of Fourth Amendment rules apply, legal professionals must identify the original source and method used by the government to acquire the challenged evidence. For example, in a drug case, the government may seek to introduce ten grams of cocaine as primary evidence against the defendant. The government could have obtained this evidence from (1) the seizure, arrest, or other detention of the defendant, (2) the execution of a search warrant, or (3) a warrantless search of a place or thing. See Figure 11-2. Once the source and methods for the search and seizure are identified, legal professionals can then begin to assess the constitutional validity of the government's conduct under the Fourth Amendment.

THE SEIZURE, ARREST, OR OTHER DETENTION OF PERSONS

The most serious form of search and seizure under the Fourth Amendment is the seizure, arrest, or other detention of persons. In many cases, governmental seizures of individuals will be obvious, particularly in cases where the person is arrested by police and taken into custody. In other cases, law enforcement may stop short of formally arresting someone, but their actions may still constitute a type of seizure or detention under the Fourth Amendment.

Seizure of Persons

seizure of a person
police use of force or the threat of force to detain a person, thereby causing the person to reasonably believe that he or she cannot freely leave

The Fourth Amendment may apply to police detentions that fall short of full-blown arrests. In other words, in some cases, police may seize persons without formally arresting them. A *seizure of a person* occurs when a law enforcement officer uses force or the threat of force to detain a person, thereby causing the person to reasonably believe that he or she cannot freely leave the presence of the official.[5] In these situations, a seizure will be determined based on the totality of the circumstances (the overall context of the detention, including what actions and words the officer used, the location of the detention, and the length of the stop) and an assessment of ***reasonableness*** (what a reasonable person would believe under the circumstances).

reasonableness
legal standard that considers what a reasonable person would believe under the circumstances

In *Michigan v. Chesternut* (1988), the Supreme Court unanimously ruled that police pursuits do not per se constitute a seizure under the Fourth Amendment. In *Chesternut*, the defendant saw a police car approaching and began to run. As police started to follow him "to see where he was going," the defendant discarded a number of packets containing illegal drugs. After his arrest, the defendant tried to suppress the drug evidence, asserting that it was obtained by police during an unconstitutional seizure of his person. The Court, however, held that the officers' pursuit of the defendant did not constitute a "seizure" under the Fourth Amendment. The Court reasoned that the appropriate test is whether a reasonable person, viewing the particular police conduct as a whole and within the setting of all of the surrounding circumstances, would have concluded that the police had in some way restrained his liberty so that he was not free to leave.

Similarly, in *California v. Hodari D.* (1991),[6] where a defendant fled and began discarding drug evidence after police told him to stop, the Court likewise concluded the defendant was not seized as he discarded the drug evidence. The Court ruled that, to constitute a seizure of the person, just as to constitute an arrest, there must be either the application of physical force, however slight, or, where that is absent, submission to an officer's "show of authority" to restrain the subject's liberty. The Court concluded that, even though the police may have displayed a "show of authority" by ordering Hodari to halt, the defendant was not seized by police at that time because he did not comply with the police order.

In addition, in *Florida v. Bostick* (1991),[7] the Court ruled that law enforcement authorities who boarded a transport bus, asked passengers for identification, and requested to search their luggage did not necessarily engage in a seizure of persons under the Fourth Amendment. After being questioned by two police officers on the bus, the defendant gave police officers permission to search his luggage, which resulted in the officers finding cocaine. The Court remanded the case to the lower court, instructing that the appropriate inquiry for Bostick's motion to suppress was whether a reasonable passenger would feel free to decline the officers' request or otherwise terminate the encounter.

Law Line 11-3
Florida v. Bostick (1991)

But in *Brendlin v. California* (2007) (see below),[8] the Court held that, when police officers make a traffic stop, a passenger in the car, like the driver, is seized for Fourth Amendment purposes. Applying the rationale from *Bostick*, the Court ruled that a person is seized and thus entitled to challenge the government's action when officers, by physical force or a show of authority, terminate or restrain the person's freedom of movement through means intentionally applied.

In sum, legal professionals should ask the following questions when assessing whether a person was seized for Fourth Amendment purposes:

- Was the person physically seized or restrained by police?
- Did the officer engage in some physical contact with the person?
- Did the person submit to an officer's show of legal authority?
- Did the officer display a threatening presence to the person?
- Did the officer display a weapon?
- Did the officer's language or demeanor suggest compliance was required?

Arrests

In many criminal cases, a law enforcement officer physically takes a person into custody against his or her will for purposes of initiating criminal prosecution or investigation. This is called an ***arrest***. There are two basic types of arrests—arrests made pursuant to an arrest warrant and warrantless arrests.

An ***arrest warrant*** is a judicial order authorizing law enforcement officers to arrest a person. In some cases, arrest warrants are procured immediately after a grand jury issues an indictment. But in other cases, an arrest warrant can be issued without any grand jury action. An arrest warrant must be based on probable cause (see below).

At common law, an arrest warrant was a more critical factor in determining the validity of an arrest. Under common law principles, officers could make warrantless arrests only in cases where they reasonably believed the suspect had committed a felony or where they actually witnessed the suspect committing a misdemeanor in their presence. Today, however, although the Fourth Amendment states that warrants must be supported by probable cause, it does not specifically require all arrests or arrestlike detentions be made pursuant to a warrant.

Home Arrests.   Under normal circumstances, the Court still requires police to obtain a warrant before arresting individuals within their homes.[9] These are known as ***home arrests***. And generally, unless police are operating under exigent circumstances (see below), a warrant is necessary to make a nonconsensual entry into a private residence to arrest someone inside. With a court-issued arrest warrant, police are authorized to enter a person's home and effectuate an arrest, although normally they must knock and announce their identity and purpose before making a forcible entry into the home.

In some cases, police may effectuate a warrantless arrest inside a person's home, if the officers are operating under ***exigent circumstances***. These might include situations where officers have received the consent of the home owner, or someone who has apparent authority over the home, to enter the home; cases where police are in hot pursuit of a suspect who runs into a home; and situations where an immediate danger exists, such as the possible escape of the suspect or the possible destruction of criminal evidence.

Other Warrantless Arrests.   The vast majority of arrests are made without a warrant. These are known as ***warrantless arrests***. In these cases, particularly in a public place, officers can make an arrest if they have probable cause to believe that a crime has occurred. Thus, to be constitutional, both arrest warrants and warrantless arrests must be based on probable cause.

For example, in *Atwater v. Lago Vista* (2001),[10] the Court held that the Fourth Amendment does not require police to have an arrest warrant to effectuate an arrest for a minor criminal offense, such as a misdemeanor seatbelt violation punishable only by a fine. In *Atwater*, police arrested Gail Atwater for violating a Texas seat belt law. The law made it a misdemeanor, punishable only by a fine, for failing to secure any small child riding in the front of a vehicle. A police officer pulled Atwater over, verbally berated her, handcuffed her, placed her in his squad car, and drove her to the local police station, where she was made to remove her shoes, jewelry, and eyeglasses, and empty her pockets. Officers also took her "mug shot" and placed her, alone, in a jail cell for about an hour, after which she was taken before a magistrate and released on bond. Atwater challenged her arrest, arguing that it was an unreasonable seizure of her person under the Fourth Amendment. But the Supreme Court disagreed, concluding that because the officer had probable cause to believe Atwater was

arrest
when a law enforcement officer takes a person into custody against his or her will for purposes of initiating criminal charges

arrest warrant
a judicial order based on probable cause authorizing a law enforcement officer to make an arrest

home arrests
arrests that occur within an individual's home; usually require a warrant

exigent circumstances
an exception to the warrant requirement that allows home arrests where pressing needs of the public outweigh the individual's right to privacy

warrantless arrests
arrests conducted without a warrant

committing a criminal offense, even though a minor offense, the arrest was not unreasonable under the Fourth Amendment.

The Need for Probable Cause. ***Probable cause*** is a legal standard requiring the warrant-issuing judge or warrantless-arrest-making law enforcement officer to have sufficient, articulable, and trustworthy information to reasonably believe that a person has committed a crime.[11] The Supreme Court has approached the probable cause standard as a degree of probability that cannot be easily defined out of context. Specifically, the Court has stated, "[t]he probable-cause standard is incapable of precise definition or quantification into percentages because it deals with probabilities and depends on the totality of the circumstances. We have stated, however, that the substance of all the definitions of probable cause is a reasonable ground for belief of guilt, and that the belief of guilt must be particularized with respect to the person to be searched or seized."[12] As a result, like many other constitutional concepts in criminal cases, determining whether an officer had probable cause to arrest is based on the totality of the circumstances and a reflection on what is reasonable under those circumstances.

Law Line 11-4
Atwater v. Lago Vista (2001)

probable cause
the legal standard for issuing a warrant; requires sufficient, articulable, and trustworthy information to reasonably believe that a person has committed a crime

IN THE FIELD

Keep in mind that an illegal arrest, in and of itself, may not affect whether the prosecution can move forward with criminal charges. But if authorities acquire evidence for trial as a result of an illegal arrest, this evidence may be deemed fruit of the poisonous tree and excluded from trial under the exclusionary rule. See Chapter 10. In assessing whether an arrest is based on probable cause and is otherwise lawful, legal professionals should ask the following questions:

- What was the totality of factual circumstances surrounding the arrest?
- What articulable observations and information did the officer provide as a basis for making the arrest?
- Would a reasonable person find these observations and information to be trustworthy?
- Based on the information identified by the officer, would a reasonably prudent person believe that the arrested person had committed or was committing a crime?

Use of Deadly Force

In some cases, police use ***deadly force***, which is perhaps the most severe form of governmental seizure, to apprehend criminal suspects. Under the Supreme Court's analysis, the use of deadly force to seize or stop individuals is unreasonable under the Fourth Amendment unless the officer has probable cause to believe that the person presents a substantial threat of death or serious physical harm to the officer or other persons.[13] In other words, the use of deadly force by police officers can be constitutional when the person or persons in question are believed to present an immediate life-threatening danger to people around them. For example, an armed man in a shopping mall shooting at random without regard to the safety of the people around him, and refusing or being unwilling to negotiate, would likely warrant the use of deadly force to prevent further danger to the community.

The leading case in this area is *Tennessee v. Garner* (1985), where the Supreme Court ruled that "deadly force . . . may not be used unless necessary to prevent the

deadly force
the use of potentially deadly methods by police to apprehend a suspect

Law Line 11-5
Tennessee v. Garner (1985)

reasonableness test
a legal standard used to judge whether use of deadly force by police was constitutional; force must be necessary to prevent the escape and the officer has probable cause to believe that the suspect poses a significant threat of death or serious physical injury to the officer or others

Law Line 11-6
Scott v. Harris (2007)

escape and the officer has probable cause to believe that the suspect poses a significant threat of death or serious physical injury to the officer or others." This is generally known as the **reasonableness test**.

More recently, in *Scott v. Harris* (2007),[14] the Court held that a police officer's attempt to terminate a dangerous high-speed car chase that threatens the lives of innocent bystanders does not violate the Fourth Amendment, even when it places the fleeing motorist at risk of serious injury or death. In *Harris*, a police officer in a high-speed chase of a suspect applied his cruiser's bumper to the rear of a suspect's car, which caused the suspect to wreck his car and sustain serious injuries. Applying the reasonableness test established in *Garner*, the Court found that because the car chase suspect posed a substantial and immediate risk of serious physical injury to others, the police officer's attempt to terminate the chase by forcing the suspect off the road was reasonable under the Fourth Amendment.

ETHICAL PRINCIPLES

CLIENT CONFIDENCES

National Association of Legal Assistants Code of Ethics and Professional Responsibility Canon 7

A paralegal must protect the confidences of a client and must not violate any rule or statute now in effect or hereafter enacted controlling the doctrine of privileged communications between a client and an attorney.

Courtesy of the National Association of Legal Assistants

Investigatory Detentions (*Terry* Stops)

investigatory detention or
***Terry* stop**
a brief detention of persons by a police officer for legitimate investigative purposes

Separate from situations involving an arrest, the Supreme Court also has interpreted the Fourth Amendment to allow officers to briefly detain persons for legitimate investigative purposes, even where the officer does not have probable cause to believe that a crime has occurred. This is known as an **investigatory detention** or a **Terry stop**. The term derives from the Supreme Court's landmark ruling in *Terry v. Ohio* (1968),[15] where the Court ruled that, during investigatory stops, if a reasonably prudent officer believes that his safety or that of others is endangered, he may make a reasonable search for weapons of the person believed by him to be armed and dangerous regardless of whether he has probable cause to arrest that individual for crime. In *Terry*, the Court upheld the pat-down search conducted by Cleveland police officers of three men who were stopped on suspicion of robbery. During the investigatory stop, an officer patted down a suspect's outside clothing and found a pistol in the suspect's overcoat pocket. The suspect was then charged with carrying a concealed weapon. The Court concluded that the officer's protective seizure and limited search were reasonable under the Fourth Amendment, both at their inception and as conducted.

Specifically, an investigatory detention or stop is a police officer's relatively brief stop of a person for purposes of conducting a reasonable investigation of possible criminal activity. An investigatory stop is different from an arrest. With a stop, police ostensibly are not making an arrest or arrestlike seizure of a person—at least initially. Rather they wish to briefly detain a person to investigate what might be criminal activity.

Law Line 11-7
Terry v. Ohio (1968)

Need for Reasonable Suspicion.   In order for investigatory detentions to be constitutional under the Fourth Amendment, an officer must have reasonable suspicion that the person being stopped is involved in criminal activity. **Reasonable suspicion** is a less stringent standard than probable cause. And although the Court has not specifically defined the concept, reasonable suspicion generally requires an officer to have articulable facts that would lead a reasonable person to suspect that criminal activity is afoot.[16] Reasonable suspicion is not as rigorous a standard as probable cause (above), but it does require the officer to have more than just a vague hunch or gut feeling about possible criminal activity. And like probable cause, determining whether an officer has reasonable suspicion to stop someone is based on the totality of the circumstances and the degree of reasonableness underlying the officer's judgment.

In *Illinois v. Wardlow* (2000), William Wardlow was walking in a Chicago neighborhood known for high levels of illegal drug trafficking. After seeing a group of police cars, Wardlow began running. Police caught up with Wardlow and stopped him. An officer then conducted a protective pat-down search for weapons (described below) because, in his experience, there were usually weapons in the vicinity of narcotics transactions. The officer found a handgun during the pat-down and arrested Wardlow for unlawful possession of a firearm.

The Supreme Court was asked to determine whether officers had reasonable suspicion to stop Wardlow for an investigatory detention. The Court found that Wardlow's presence in a high crime area, by itself, did not provide a reasonable, particularized suspicion of criminal activity, but that the neighborhood's characteristics were relevant to the officer's judgment to make the stop. The Court further found that Wardlow's unprovoked flight, when coupled with the neighborhood characteristics, provided the officers with the reasonable suspicion necessary to conduct an investigatory detention. According to the Court, the reasonable suspicion determination must be based on commonsense judgments and inferences about human behavior.

But in *Florida v. J.L.* (2000),[17] the Court ruled that an anonymous tip to police that a person is carrying a gun is not, without more, sufficient to justify a police officer's stop and frisk of that person. In *J.L.*, the Court observed that the officers' suspicion that the defendant was carrying a gun came not from their own observations, but from a call made by an unknown person from an unknown location. According to the Court, this anonymous tip lacked sufficient indicia of reliability to provide reasonable suspicion to make a *Terry* stop because it did not provide predictive information. As a result, it left the police without means to test the informant's knowledge or credibility.

Detention Must Be Relatively Brief.   Assuming that an officer's initial detention of a person is based on reasonable suspicion of criminal activity, a number of other conditions affect whether the stop will remain constitutional while it is being executed. For one, investigatory detentions must be relatively brief in duration. This means that the officer cannot detain a person any longer than is necessary to confirm or reject the officer's initial suspicion.

For example, if an officer stops a person believing her to be a parole violator, the officer can only detain her long enough to confirm or deny her parole status, unless the officer develops more suspicion or probable cause of additional criminal activity during the brief stop. If an officer unreasonably prolongs the investigatory detention to the point where the initially-brief stop actually develops into a seizure or arrestlike situation, the officer must have probable cause for such a detention.

Police Pat-Downs or Frisks.   One of the most critical events that occur during an investigatory stop is the frisking or patting down of the detained

reasonable suspicion
a legal standard used to judge investigatory detentions; requires an officer to have articulable facts that would lead a reasonable person to suspect that criminal activity is afoot

Law Line 11-8
Illinois v. Wardlow (2000)

Law Line 11-9
Florida v. J.L. (2000)

stop and frisk or *Terry* frisk
a police technique employed during investigatory detentions, whereby person detained is patted down for weapons

frisk
to pat the outer clothing of an individual

individual. This is sometimes called a ***stop and frisk*** or ***Terry frisk***. The Supreme Court has ruled that an officer is permitted to ***frisk*** a person (to pat the outer clothing) during an investigatory stop, if the officer has reasonable suspicion that the person is armed and dangerous. The purpose of this limited search is to ensure the officer's safety by ascertaining that the stopped person does not have any weapons on or about his person. As discussed below, the evidence seized by police during this frisking process often serves as the basis of criminal charges.

IN THE FIELD

Legal professionals are likely to see many criminal cases involving investigatory detentions and *Terry* searches. Remember there are two primary stages for these searches—the reason for the stop and the stop itself. First, the suspect must be lawfully detained during an investigative detention. This means that the detention must be based upon reasonable suspicion that criminal activity is afoot. In determining whether an officer had reasonable suspicion for an investigatory detention, legal professionals should ask these questions:

- Can the officer provide articulable, objective, and particularized reasons for making the stop?
- Do these reasons identify behavior that is different from what one might ordinarily expect from law-abiding citizens in the area?
- Do these reasons explain why the suspect's conduct suggested possible criminal activity?
- Based on these articulable reasons and observations, would a reasonable person suspect that the individual may be involved in criminal activity?

Second, during the investigatory detention, the officer's search, including length of time and the performance of any protective pat-down for weapons, must be reasonable. In assessing this second area, legal professionals should ask the following:

- What was the officer's original suspicion for the stop?
- How long did the detention last?
- What information did the officer receive that might confirm or reject the initial suspicion?
- Did the officer perform a *Terry* search? What articulable facts did the officer rely on to form the belief that the suspect might be armed?
- Was the scope of the officer's original pat-down consistent with a search for weapons?
- What evidence did the officer discover during the pat-down? What articulable facts led the officer to believe that the evidence seized was criminal contraband?
- Was the seizure of this evidence based on the officer's plain view or plain feel of an object that reasonably appeared or felt as though it was an item of criminality?
- What experience or knowledge did the officer possess that led to the conclusion that the seized item was criminal contraband?

---

stop and identify laws
statutes that require individuals properly detained by police to provide their identity to the investigating officer during the stop

Stop and Identify Laws

A number of states have adopted ***stop and identify laws***, which require individuals properly detained by police to provide their identity to the investigating officer during the stop.[18] The wording of these laws varies from state to state, but generally, they allow an officer to ask or require suspects to disclose their identity during an investigatory stop.

In some cases, the Supreme Court has found these laws to be unconstitutionally vague. For example, in *Kolender v. Lawson* (1983),[19] the Court invalidated a California law because its wording was too broad and imprecise. The law required persons who loiter or wander on the streets to identify themselves and to account for their presence when requested by a peace officer. The Court invalidated the statute, finding that it failed to clarify what is contemplated by the requirement that a suspect provide a "credible and reliable" identification.

But in *Hiibel v. Sixth Judicial District of Nevada* (2004),[20] the Court upheld a Nevada law requiring properly detained persons to provide their identity to law enforcement officers. The Nevada law read in relevant part:

> Any peace officer may detain any person whom the officer encounters under circumstances which reasonably indicate that the person has committed, is committing or is about to commit a crime.
>
> . . .
>
> The officer may detain the person pursuant to this section only to ascertain his identity and the suspicious circumstances surrounding his presence abroad. Any person so detained shall identify himself, but may not be compelled to answer any other inquiry of any peace officer.

The Court found that, in contrast to the "credible and reliable" identification requirement in *Kolender,* the Nevada Supreme Court has interpreted the Nevada law to require only that a suspect disclose his name. It apparently does not require him to produce a driver's license or any other document. As a result, the Court ruled that *Terry*-search principles (above) permit a State to require a suspect to disclose his name in the course of a *Terry* stop. According to the Court, the Nevada statute was consistent with Fourth Amendment prohibitions against unreasonable searches and seizures because it properly balanced the intrusion on the individual's interests against the promotion of legitimate government interests.

Law Line 11-10
Hiibel v. Sixth Judicial District of Nevada (2004)

Motor Vehicle Stops

One area of personal seizure that has presented unique constitutional challenges under the Fourth Amendment is the detention of persons operating motorized vehicles. Generally speaking, the Court has required that governmental stops of persons operating motorized vehicles be based on either probable cause (to make a full seizure or arrest of the person) or reasonable suspicion (to briefly investigate possible illegal activity, including the violation of traffic laws). Consistent with these standards, the Court has held that officers cannot randomly stop persons in automobiles, without sufficient cause or suspicion, just to check their driver's information.[21]

The Court, however, has ruled that police may engage in pretextual stops of motorists if the officers have probable cause to believe that the driver has committed a traffic violation or some other crime. In *Whren v. Brown* (1996),[22] police stopped a driver in a high-drug-crime neighborhood, after the driver failed to use his turn signal before making a turn. Although the underlying motive of police in making the stop may have been to investigate possible drug activity, for which they lacked reasonable suspicion or probable cause, the Court ruled that the officers were nonetheless justified in making the stop because they had probable cause to believe that a traffic violation occurred. According to the Court, since an actual traffic violation occurred, the ensuing search and seizure of the offending vehicle was reasonable, regardless of what other personal motivations the officers might have had for stopping the vehicle.

In some cases, officers engaging in traffic stops detain more than just the driver of the vehicle. Read the Court's opinion in *Brendlin v. California* (2007), where the Court considered whether passengers involved in a traffic stop are detained under the Fourth Amendment, thereby allowing them to challenge the legality of the traffic stop.

CAPSTONE CASE *Brendlin v. California*, 551 U.S. 249 (2007)

Justice Souter delivered the opinion of the Court.

Early in the morning of November 27, 2001, Deputy Sheriff Robert Brokenbrough and his partner saw a parked Buick with expired registration tags. In his ensuing conversation with the police dispatcher, Brokenbrough learned that an application for renewal of registration was being processed. The officers saw the car again on the road, and this time Brokenbrough noticed its display of a temporary operating permit with the number "11," indicating it was legal to drive the car through November. The officers decided to pull the Buick over to verify that the permit matched the vehicle, even though, as Brokenbrough admitted later, there was nothing unusual about the permit or the way it was affixed. Brokenbrough asked the driver, Karen Simeroth, for her license and saw a passenger in the front seat, petitioner Bruce Brendlin, whom he recognized as "one of the Brendlin brothers." He recalled that either Scott or Bruce Brendlin had dropped out of parole supervision and asked Brendlin to identify himself. Brokenbrough returned to his cruiser, called for backup, and verified that Brendlin was a parole violator with an outstanding no-bail warrant for his arrest. While he was in the patrol car, Brokenbrough saw Brendlin briefly open and then close the passenger door of the Buick. Once reinforcements arrived, Brokenbrough went to the passenger side of the Buick, ordered him out of the car at gunpoint, and declared him under arrest. When the police searched Brendlin incident to arrest, they found an orange syringe cap on his person. A pat-down search of Simeroth revealed syringes and a plastic bag of a green leafy substance, and she was also formally arrested. Officers then searched the car and found tubing, a scale, and other things used to produce methamphetamine.

Brendlin was charged with possession and manufacture of methamphetamine, and he moved to suppress the evidence obtained in the searches of his person and the car as fruits of an unconstitutional seizure, arguing that the officers lacked probable cause or reasonable suspicion to make the traffic stop. He did not assert that his Fourth Amendment rights were violated by the search of Simeroth's vehicle, but claimed only that the traffic stop was an unlawful seizure of his person. The trial court denied the suppression motion after finding that the stop was lawful and Brendlin was not seized until Brokenbrough ordered him out of the car and formally arrested him. Brendlin pleaded guilty, subject to appeal on the suppression issue, and was sentenced to four years in prison . . .

A person is seized by the police and thus entitled to challenge the government's action under the Fourth Amendment when the officer, "'by means of physical force or show of authority,'" terminates or restrains his freedom of movement, *Florida v. Bostick*, 501 U.S. 429, 434 (1991), "*through means intentionally applied.*" Thus, an "unintended person . . . [may be] the object of the detention," so long as the detention is "willful" and not merely the consequence of "an unknowing act." A police officer may make a seizure by a show of authority and without the use of physical force, but there is no seizure without actual submission; otherwise, there is at most an attempted seizure, so far as the Fourth Amendment is concerned.

When the actions of the police do not show an unambiguous intent to restrain or when an individual's submission to a show of governmental authority takes the form of passive acquiescence, there needs to be some test for telling when a seizure occurs in response to authority, and when it does not. The test was devised by Justice Stewart in *United States v. Mendenhall*, 446 U.S. 544 (1980), who wrote that a seizure occurs if "in view of all of the circumstances surrounding the incident, a reasonable person would have believed that he was not free to leave." Later on, the Court adopted Justice Stewart's touchstone, but added that when a person "has no desire to leave" for reasons unrelated to the police presence, the "coercive effect of the encounter" can be measured better by asking whether "a reasonable person would feel free to decline the officers' requests or otherwise terminate the encounter."

. . .

The State concedes that the police had no adequate justification to pull the car over, but argues that the passenger was not seized and thus cannot claim that the evidence was tainted by an unconstitutional stop. We resolve this question by asking whether a reasonable person in Brendlin's position when the car stopped would have believed himself free to "terminate the encounter" between the police and himself. We think that in these circumstances any reasonable passenger would have understood the police officers to be exercising control to the point that no one in the car was free to depart without police permission.

A traffic stop necessarily curtails the travel a passenger has chosen just as much as it halts the driver, diverting both from the stream of traffic to the side of the road, and the police activity that normally amounts to intrusion on "privacy and personal security" does not normally (and did not here) distinguish between passenger and driver. An officer who orders one particular car to pull over acts with an implicit claim of right based on fault of some sort, and a sensible person would not expect a police officer to allow people to come and go freely from the physical focal point of an investigation into faulty behavior or wrongdoing. . . .

It is also reasonable for passengers to expect that a police officer at the scene of a crime, arrest, or investigation will not let people move around in ways that could jeopardize his safety. . . .

Brendlin was seized from the moment Simeroth's car came to a halt on the side of the road, and it was error to deny his suppression motion on the ground that seizure occurred only at the formal arrest. It will be for the state courts to consider in the first instance whether suppression turns on any other issue. The judgment of the Supreme Court of California is vacated, and the case is remanded for further proceedings not inconsistent with this opinion.

It is so ordered.

WHAT DO *YOU* THINK?

1. Is it reasonable to conclude that all passengers involved in motor vehicle stops do not feel free to leave during a motor vehicle stop? What if the officer informs the passengers that they are free to leave, while the officer investigates the driver and the vehicle? Would that make a difference?
2. Would it make a difference if the stop were in a residential area with sidewalks?

Traffic Checkpoints. In some circumstances, however, the Court has permitted suspicionless stops to occur. For example, the Court has authorized the use of **sobriety checkpoints**, which typically involve the stopping of vehicles at a fixed checkpoint without any particularized suspicion in order to detect drunk driving. The Court has ruled that these checkpoints are permissible as long as

sobriety checkpoints
a police technique used to catch drunk drivers; involves stopping of vehicles at a fixed checkpoint without any particularized suspicion

officers stop cars based on some neutral and articulable standard (for example, every fifth car).

In *Michigan Department of State Police v. Sitz* (1988),[23] the Court upheld a Michigan program that established a sobriety checkpoint pilot program in early 1986. Under the program, police-operated checkpoints were to be set up at selected sites along state roads. All vehicles passing through a checkpoint would be stopped and their drivers briefly examined for signs of intoxication. In cases where a checkpoint officer detected signs of intoxication, the motorist would be directed to a location out of the traffic flow where an officer would check the motorist's driver's license and car registration and, if warranted, conduct further sobriety tests. All other drivers would be permitted to resume their journey immediately. The Court concluded that the public's interest in preventing drunk driving and maintaining safe roadways outweighs the limited burden on a driver being stopped.

Other Motor Vehicle Stops. The Supreme Court also has given law enforcement greater constitutional leeway to conduct international border stops, where usually every car is stopped to determine the occupants' citizenship. The Court has concluded that national security interests and the constitutional authority given to Congress under Article I to regulate immigration justify greater governmental intrusions during border stops.[24]

And in cases involving boats, the Court generally has not required the government to demonstrate probable cause or reasonable suspicion before stopping operators, given the difficulty in conducting fixed checkpoints in the sea and the compelling need to maintain safe waterways.[25]

Law Line 11-11
Michigan Department of State Police v. Sitz (1988)

EVIDENTIARY SEARCHES AND SEIZURES

Beyond the seizure of persons, the Fourth Amendment also applies to searches and seizures of places and things, but not all places and things. Rather, the Supreme Court has held that the Fourth Amendment search and seizure provision applies only to governmental conduct that interferes with an individual's reasonable expectation of privacy.[26] Thus, at the outset of all evidentiary searches and seizures, legal professionals must assess whether two primary conditions are met: (1) a search or seizure must involve some type of substantial governmental action, and (2) the search or seizure must interfere with a person's reasonable expectation of privacy.

Governmental Conduct

Governmental conduct involves law enforcement officers and their agents performing work that is funded or facilitated by public resources. Certainly, this includes state highway patrol officers, state detectives, local police officers, FBI agents, DEA agents, and other publicly paid authorities performing a law enforcement function. For example, in *Ferguson v. City of Charleston* (2001),[27] staff members at a state hospital conducted a diagnostic test on a nonconsenting pregnant patient to see if she was using cocaine. The Supreme Court invalidated this search, finding that, because the hospital was a state-run facility, its staff members were government actors subject to the Fourth Amendment's requirements.

In some cases, governmental conduct might include private citizens acting as informants at the behest and direction of law enforcement. For example, if public authorities instruct a jail inmate to elicit a confession from another inmate, this might involve sufficient government conduct to invoke the Fourth Amendment. But such conduct would not likely include conduct by mall security guards, bouncers, or other private security employees.[28]

In most cases, the presence of governmental conduct in the search and seizure will be obvious—a police officer or federal agent conducts a search. But in rare cases, this issue may be less obvious. For example, if a wife accesses her husband's computer files and finds evidence of criminal activity, whereupon she gives this evidence to police, the defendant/husband likely would not be able to assert a Fourth Amendment violation because government agents did not perform the search. As invasive of the defendant's privacy as this search may be, the Fourth Amendment targets unreasonable behavior by government, not private, citizens.

But if the wife calls police while accessing her husband's computer and asks for instructions on what to do, this may constitute sufficient government conduct for the defendant to invoke the Fourth Amendment. In these more-nuanced cases, legal professionals must first determine whether governmental conduct, as opposed to private action, was involved in the search.

Reasonable Expectation of Privacy

In addition, in order for the Fourth Amendment to be applicable, individuals asserting this right must show that they had a reasonable expectation of privacy in the place or property that was searched. A **reasonable expectation of privacy** is a reasonable person's legitimate expectation that certain property or places will not be involuntarily viewed or inspected by third parties. Such an expectation is determined based on the totality of the circumstances.

The leading case in this area is *Katz v. United States* (1967).[29] *Katz* involved a defendant whose phone conversation was seized by government authorities by means of an electronic listening device placed on the outside of a telephone booth. The Supreme Court ruled that the Fourth Amendment protected the defendant from the warrantless eavesdropping because he "justifiably relied" upon the privacy of the telephone booth. In a concurring opinion, Justice John Harlan observed that a Fourth Amendment search occurs when the government violates a subjective expectation of privacy that society recognizes as reasonable. Over the years, the Court has relied on this observation in holding that a Fourth Amendment search does *not* occur—even when the explicitly protected location of a *house* is concerned—unless "the individual manifested a subjective expectation of privacy in the object of the challenged search," and "society [is] willing to recognize that expectation as reasonable."[30] This is generally known as the ***Katz* test**. Under the *Katz* test, the Supreme Court has found that persons generally have a reasonable expectation of privacy in their own home and body.

For example, in *Kyllo v. United States* (2001),[31] the Court ruled that the warrantless governmental use of thermal imaging equipment to explore details of a private home was presumptively unreasonable. In *Kyllo*, authorities suspected the defendant was growing marijuana in his home and used a thermal imaging device to scan the house to determine if the amount of heat emanating from it was consistent with the high-intensity lamps typically used for indoor marijuana growth. The scan showed that the defendant's garage roof and a side wall were relatively hot compared to the rest of his home and substantially warmer than the neighboring units. Based in part on the thermal imaging, a federal magistrate judge issued a warrant to search Kyllo's home, where the agents found marijuana growing.

The Supreme Court, however, rejected this use of thermal imaging, stating, "[w]e have said that the Fourth Amendment draws 'a firm line at the entrance to the house.' That line, we think, must be not only firm but also bright—which requires clear specification of those methods of surveillance that require a warrant. . . .

reasonable expectation of privacy
a reasonable person's legitimate expectation that certain property or places will not be involuntarily viewed or inspected by third parties

Katz test
a legal standard used to assess reasonable expectation of privacy; supports notion that persons must manifest a subjective expectation of privacy in the object of the challenged search

Law Line 11-12
Katz v. United States (1967)

open fields doctrine
a legal theory that holds that places outside the curtilage of a home (the immediate, enclosed area surrounding a house or dwelling) are generally held out to the public; used to judge a person's reasonable expectation of privacy

Where, as here, the Government uses a device that is not in general public use, to explore details of the home that would previously have been unknowable without physical intrusion, the surveillance is a 'search' and is presumptively unreasonable without a warrant."

But in other cases, the Court has found no such reasonable expectation of privacy. The Court has approved governmental intrusions into areas held out to the public, such as one's handwriting and the scent coming from one's luggage at an airport.[32] The Court has reasoned that, because reasonable persons have little or no expectation of privacy in places or property that are readily available to the public or held out to the public, these items and locations are not entitled to Fourth Amendment protection. In particular, the Court has developed the **open fields doctrine**, which holds that places outside the curtilage of a home (the immediate, enclosed area surrounding a house or dwelling) are generally held out to the public. The Court has used the doctrine to approve searches involving a person's barn, airplane and helicopter flyovers, and discarded garbage left at a home's curbside.[33]

The Process for Evaluating Evidentiary Searches and Seizures

There are three basic steps in assessing the constitutionality of searches and seizures. At the outset, the court must determine whether the defendant had a Fourth Amendment right that was violated by governmental authorities during the search. This involves two questions: (1) Was there sufficient governmental conduct involved in the search? and (2) Did the defendant have a reasonable expectation of privacy in the place or thing that was searched? Each of these questions must be answered in the affirmative in order for the defendant to assert the Fourth Amendment against a search or seizure. If both of these questions are answered in the affirmative, the court must determine whether the search was conducted pursuant to a valid warrant. If not, it must determine whether there was a constitutionally recognized exception that allowed the authorities to conduct the search without a court-approved search warrant. See Figure 11-3.

WARRANT-BASED SEARCHES AND SEIZURES

The plain text of the Fourth Amendment includes the statement that "no warrants shall issue, but upon probable cause, supported by oath or affirmation, and particularly describing the place to be searched, and the persons or things to be seized." A **search warrant** is essentially written authorization from a court to perform a search. See Figures 11-4 and 11-5. The language of the Fourth Amendment suggests that the Constitution places great value on the use of warrants when police search places or seize property or persons. It also suggests that the underlying constitutional value to the Fourth Amendment is *reasonableness*, and that one measure of reasonableness is the presence of a search warrant. Because the Fourth Amendment stresses the importance of a warrant, and warrants are considered a strong measurement of the reasonableness of a search, searches and seizures performed without warrants are presumed unconstitutional.[34] Of course, this does not mean that all warrantless searches are unconstitutional. As will be discussed later in this chapter, the Supreme Court has identified several situations where a warrantless search can be deemed reasonable and therefore valid under the Fourth Amendment.

search warrant
written authorization from a court to perform a search

FIGURE 11-3 **Four Basic Steps for Evaluating Searches and Seizures**

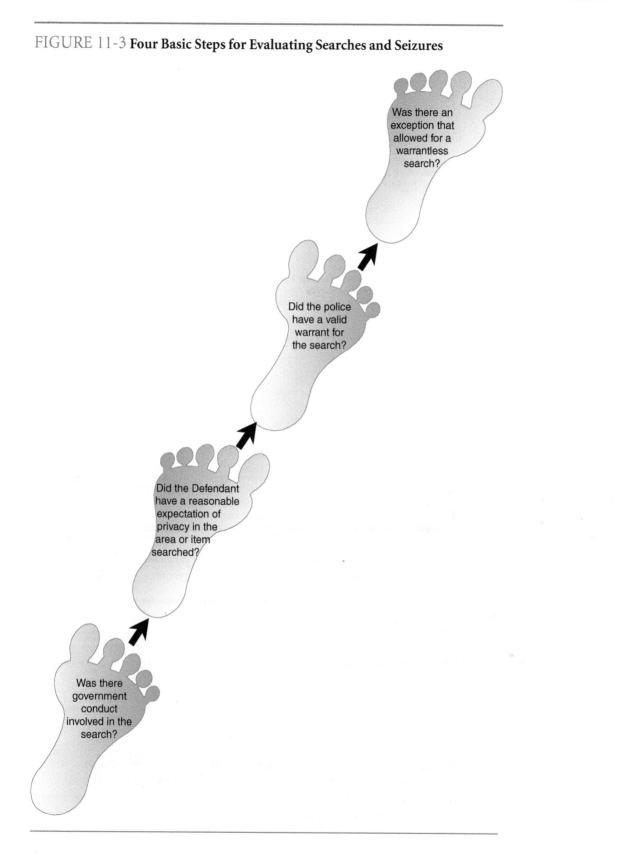

FIGURE 11-4 **Federal Search Warrant Form**

AO 93 (Rev. 12/09) Search and Seizure Warrant

UNITED STATES DISTRICT COURT

for the

In the Matter of the Search of)
(Briefly describe the property to be searched)
or identify the person by name and address)) Case No.
)
)
)

SEARCH AND SEIZURE WARRANT

To: Any authorized law enforcement officer

An application by a federal law enforcement officer or an attorney for the government requests the search of the following person or property located in the _____ District of _____
(identify the person or describe the property to be searched and give its location):

The person or property to be searched, described above, is believed to conceal *(identify the person or describe the property to be seized)*:

I find that the affidavit(s), or any recorded testimony, establish probable cause to search and seize the person or property.

YOU ARE COMMANDED to execute this warrant on or before _____
(not to exceed 14 days)

❑ in the daytime 6:00 a.m. to 10 p.m.   ❑ at any time in the day or night as I find reasonable cause has been established.

Unless delayed notice is authorized below, you must give a copy of the warrant and a receipt for the property taken to the person from whom, or from whose premises, the property was taken, or leave the copy and receipt at the place where the property was taken.

The officer executing this warrant, or an officer present during the execution of the warrant, must prepare an inventory as required by law and promptly return this warrant and inventory to United States Magistrate Judge

_____
(name)

❑ I find that immediate notification may have an adverse result listed in 18 U.S.C. § 2705 (except for delay of trial), and authorize the officer executing this warrant to delay notice to the person who, or whose property, will be searched or seized *(check the appropriate box)* ❑for _____ days *(not to exceed 30).*
❑until, the facts justifying, the later specific date of _____ .

Date and time issued: _____   _____
Judge's signature

City and state: _____   _____
Printed name and title

(continued)

Overall, if law enforcement properly executes a valid search warrant, generally the search will be deemed reasonable and therefore constitutional under the Fourth Amendment. But if the search warrant is invalid, or if it is executed in an unreasonable manner, the search may be declared unconstitutional.

Parts of a Warrant

application for a search warrant a document used by police to apply for a search warrant; must demonstrate probable cause

Four basic documents are involved in obtaining a search warrant. Initially, a law enforcement officer prepares an ***application for a search warrant***, which usually is a standard form that allows the officer to identify the places to be

FIGURE 11-4 **Continued**

AO 93 (Rev. 12/09) Search and Seizure Warrant (Page 2)

Return		
Case No.:	Date and time warrant executed:	Copy of warrant and inventory left with:

Inventory made in the presence of :

Inventory of the property taken and name of any person(s) seized:

Certification

     I declare under penalty of perjury that this inventory is correct and was returned along with the original warrant to the designated judge.

Date: _____

_____
Executing officer's signature

_____
Printed name and title

searched and the basis for requesting the warrant. See Figures 11-6 and 11-7. In most cases, the requesting officer attaches to a search warrant application a sworn **affidavit** (a written statement of facts made under oath by a witness), wherein the officer outlines the factual details that ostensibly provide the court with the probable cause necessary to issue the warrant. Assuming there is probable cause for the warrant, the judge or magistrate will issue an actual warrant, which again is the legal document that authorizes authorities to conduct a search. Then, once the search is executed, the officer performing the search must complete the **return on the warrant**, which is an accounting of when the search was conducted and what evidence was seized. See Figure 11-4. The return is filed with the trial court that issued the warrant. All together, these four documents compose the written foundation for search warrants.

affidavit
a written statement of facts made under oath by a witness

return on the warrant
the last section of a warrant, where an officer provides an accounting of when the search was conducted and what evidence was seized

FIGURE 11-5 **State Search Warrant**

SEARCH WARRANT   SUPP CRN 09-000672

STATE OF MISSOURI)
) ss
COUNTY OF CLAY)

In the Court of Clay County, Missouri

THE STATE OF MISSOURI TO ANY PEACE OFFICER IN THE STATE OF MISSOURI:

WHEREAS, on this 14th day of January, 2009 Application for Issuance of a Search Warrant and affidavit(s) in writing, duly verified by oath or affirmation, has been filed with the undersigned Judge of thi Court, stated that heretofore the following described property is subject to seizure and search, to-wit:

An Oral Swab Of The Mouth (Buccal Swab) For DNA; a full set of fingerprint impressions, including, but not limited to the palms, each individual finger, thumbs, and multiple fingers together for both the right and left hand.

And it further appears that there is PROBABLE CAUSE to believe that said property subject to seizure and search is being kept or held in this county and state on the following person, place or thing, to-wit:

The Body Of Shon Pernice, W/M, 12-23-72

NOW THEREFORE, IN THE NAME OF THE STATE OF MISSOURI, I Command that you seize and search the person, place or thing above described within 10 days after filing of the Application for issuance of this Warrant, by day or night, as soon as practicable, and to take with you, if need be, the power of your county, and, if said above described property, or any part thereof, be found on said person place or thing, that said property be seized, searched or photographed, or copied and returned, or the photograph or copy, be brought to the Judge, who issued the Warrant to be dealt with accordingly to law. That you make a complete and accurate inventory of the property so taken by you from whose possession the property was taken by you and to give to such person from whose possession the property was taken a Receipt for such property, together with a copy of the Warrant, or if no person can be found in possession of said property, leaving said Receipt and copy of said Warrant at the site of the search. After execution of the Search Warrant, the Warrant with a Return thereon, signed by the officer making the seizure and search, shall be delivered to the Judge who issued the Warrant.

WITNESS my hand and the SEAL of this Court on this
14th day of JANUARY, 2009 at the hour of 3:45 AM/PM

JUDGE
COUNTY OF CLAY COUNTY, STATE OF MISSOURI

Validity of a Search Warrant

As briefly discussed above, the Supreme Court generally has deemed searches performed with a valid warrant to be reasonable and therefore constitutional under the Fourth Amendment. The validity of a search warrant is assessed based on four primary factors: (1) whether the warrant was issued by a neutral and detached judicial authority, (2) whether the warrant was based on a 1finding of probable cause, (3) whether the warrant provides sufficiently detailed or particular instructions to the police officer about the person or places to be searched and the items to be seized, and (4) whether the warrant was properly executed.

FIGURE 11-6 **Federal Search Warrant Application**

UNITED STATES DISTRICT COURT
for the

In the Matter of the Search of
*(Briefly describe the property to be searched
or identify the person by name and address)*

))
))
))
))
))

Case No.

APPLICATION FOR A SEARCH WARRANT

I, a federal law enforcement officer or an attorney for the government, request a search warrant and state under penalty of perjury that I have reason to believe that on the following person or property *(identify the person or describe the property to be searched and give its location)*:

located in the _____ District of _____ , there is now concealed *(identify the person or describe the property to be seized)*:

The basis for the search under Fed. R. Crim. P. 41(c) is *(check one or more)*:
  ❏ evidence of a crime;
  ❏ contraband, fruits of crime, or other items illegally possessed;
  ❏ property designed for use, intended for use, or used in committing a crime;
  ❏ a person to be arrested or a person who is unlawfully restrained.

The search is related to a violation of:

Code Section   *Offense Description*

The application is based on these facts:

  ❏ Continued on the attached sheet.
  ❏ Delayed notice of _____ days (give exact ending date if more than 30 days: _____) is requested under 18 U.S.C. § 3103a, the basis of which is set forth on the attached sheet.

_____
Applicant's signature

_____
Printed name and title

Sworn to before me and signed in my presence.

Date: _____

_____
Judge's signature

City and state: _____

_____
Printed name and title

Judicial Neutrality and Detachment.   With respect to ***judicial neutrality and detachment***, generally, the judicial authority (typically a judge or magistrate) issuing the warrant must not have a conflict of interest in evaluating the request for the warrant or its execution. This requires the judicial authority to be sufficiently objective (neutral) regarding the persons or matters involved in the search warrant and not to have a personal stake in issuing the warrant. Individuals who are working in law enforcement, conducting the search, or receiving compensation based on the issuance of a warrant would not be regarded as neutral and detached.[35]

judicial neutrality and detachment
a requirement for judges when issuing search warrants; judge must be neutral and not have a conflict of interest in evaluating the request for the warrant or its execution

FIGURE 11-7 State Application for Search Warrant (abbreviated)

AFFIDAVIT / APPLICATION FOR SEARCH WARRANT   SUPP CRN 09-000672

STATE OF MISSOURI)
)   ss
COUNTY OF CLAY)

I, Detective Robert D. Blehm #4104 affiant and applicant herein, being duly sworn, appears now before the undersigned Judge authorized to issue Warrants in criminal cases and makes this Affidavit and Application in support of the issuance of a Search Warrant, to seize and Search the following described person, place or thing:

The Body Of Shon Pernice, W/M, 12-23-72

And to there seize and search, photograph or copy, and make return thereof, according to law, the following property or things:

An Oral Swab Of The Mouth (Buccal Swab) For DNA; a full set of fingerprint impressions, including, but not limited to the palms, each individual finger, thumbs, and multiple fingers together for both the right and left hand.

Affiant and Applicant being duly sworn deposes and states that he has Probable Cause to believe that the above listed property to be seized and searched, photographed or copied, is now located upon said described person place or thing based upon the following facts, to-wit: (and additional sheet(s) if needed)

On 01-03-09 at approximately 1230 hrs., officers of the Kansas City, Missouri Police Department were dispatched to 1105 NW 66th Ter., Kansas City, Clay County, Missouri on a reported Check The Welfare Call. When they arrived at the residence they knocked on the door and did not receive an answer. The officers were then contacted by multiple family members (FREDERICK PRETZ (father), LISA MOONEY(sister), JEFF MOONEY (Brother-in-law), NANCY PRETZ (step-mom)) of RENEE PERNICE at the North Patrol Division. The family members were extremely concerned for the safety of RENEE. Family members advised that RENEE and her husband SHON PERNICE had significant marital problems. Family members stated that SHON and RENEE were in the process of getting a divorce. They stated that SHON was scheduled to leave for military training on 01-02-09 at 1200 hrs., and be gone approximately three weeks. They further advised that both SHON and RENEE had agreed that when SHON returned from the military training he would not be living at the residence any longer.

[sections omitted]

Family members of RENEE told police officers that SHON PERNICE, RENEE PERNICE, JOSE PERNICE, and NICHOLAS PERNICE all resided in the residence located at 1105 NW 66th Ter., Kansas City, Clay County, Missouri.

It was also noted to be highly unlikely that RENEE ever left her residence at all due to the fact he work I.D., vehicle (Gray 2007 Toyota Matrix, four-door, Mo. Lic. # OAY-62W), personal belonging purse, and kids were not with her.

Furthermore family members stated that RENEE purchased and maintained the residence on he own and had done so prior to ever meeting SHON. This residence and the ability to provide for children were extremely important to RENEE. The idea she would leave all this to SHON a man was divorcing is so highly unlikely that it does not warrant thought.

_____   DET. ____ D. ____ #4104
Assistant Prosecutor   Affiant and Applicant

Subscribed and Sworn to me this ___14th___ Day of __January__ , __2009__.

at the hour of ___3:45___ (AM/PM)

_____
JUDGE

Probable Cause.   The warrant must also be supported by probable cause, which, as discussed above, is a legal standard requiring sufficient, articulable, and trustworthy information to reasonably believe that a person has committed a crime. In most cases, an officer appears before a judicial authority with an application for a search warrant and an attached affidavit asserting the basis for the requested warrant. Within the application and affidavit, the officer must supply the judicial authority with the requisite amount of facts to support a finding of probable cause.

Like many other evidentiary standards in criminal justice, the judge or magistrate reviews the totality of the circumstances within the application and affidavit to determine whether probable cause exists for the warrant. Under most circumstances, probable cause must be found within the four corners (within the page of paper) of the application and affidavit. This is known as the *four corners rule*. Under this standard, magistrates and judges cannot rely on verbal exchanges or other undocumented information provided by the applying officer to find probable cause for the warrant.

four corners rule
the requirement that, to be valid, a search warrant application must demonstrate probable cause within the four corners (within the page of paper) of the application and affidavit

Under Federal Rule of Criminal Procedure 41(d)(2), a magistrate or judge may find probable cause for a warrant based on an officer's sworn verbal testimony. But this testimony must be recorded by a court reporter or recording device, and the judge must file the transcript or recording with the clerk, along with any affidavit.

If there are insufficient facts within the application and affidavit to support probable cause, or if the officer seeking the warrant intentionally or recklessly provided materially false statements to the magistrate or judge, the warrant could be deemed invalid, thereby causing any subsequent search to be ruled unconstitutional. In *Franks v. Delaware* (1978),[36] the Supreme Court held that "where the defendant makes a substantial preliminary showing that a false statement knowingly and intentionally, or with reckless disregard for the truth, was included by the affiant in the warrant affidavit, and if the allegedly false statement is necessary to the finding of probable cause, the Fourth Amendment requires that a hearing be held at the defendant's request." This is called a *Franks hearing*. But because an affidavit supporting a search warrant is generally presumed to be valid under the law, a defendant has the burden of making a preliminary showing of deliberate falsehoods in that affidavit before becoming entitled to a *Franks* hearing. As the Supreme Court explained:

Franks **hearing**
a type of hearing to determine whether a search warrant was supported by probable cause or based on falsities or misrepresentations of the truth

> To mandate an evidentiary hearing, the challenger's attack must be more than conclusory and must be supported by more than a mere desire to cross-examine. There must be allegations of deliberate falsehood or of reckless disregard for the truth, and those allegations must be accompanied by an offer of proof. They should point out specifically the portion of the warrant affidavit that is claimed to be false; and they should be accompanied by a statement of supporting reasons. Affidavits or sworn or otherwise reliable statements of witnesses should be furnished, or their absence satisfactorily explained. Allegations of negligence or innocent mistake are insufficient.

When a challenge is made as to whether a search warrant affidavit is legally sufficient to show probable cause, the reviewing court is limited to the "four corners" of the affidavit. This is different from a challenge to the truthfulness of a warrant affidavit and whether the affiant made knowing misrepresentations to establish probable cause. When the defendant challenges the warrant affidavit on the ground that it contains known falsehoods, the reviewing court is not limited to the four corners of the affidavit.

Law Line 11-15
Franks v. Delaware (1978)

particularity requirement
requirement that the judge or magistrate be precise in describing the places to be searched and the things to be seized when issuing a warrant

no-knock warrant
a warrant that allows officers to execute a warrant without knocking on the door of the search premises

knock and announce rule
a requirement in some state jurisdictions that police knock and announce their presence before executing a warrant on a dwelling

Law Line 11-16
Hudson v. Michigan (2006)

Particularity Requirement. In addition to demonstrating probable cause, a warrant must also particularly describe the place to be searched and the items to be seized. In other words, the judge or magistrate must be sufficiently precise in the warrant so as to avoid a general or overreaching search by the executing officer. This is known as the ***particularity requirement***. For example, a warrant authorizing officers to search "any property owned by John Smith for any criminal contraband" likely would be too broad to satisfy the particularity requirement of the Fourth Amendment. But if a warrant authorized police to search "the residence at 704 Houser Street for illegal narcotics," this likely would be sufficiently particular.

Execution of Warrant. Once a warrant is issued by a judicial authority, it must be properly and fairly executed by law enforcement. This includes the requirement that a public police officer, as opposed to a private figure, execute the warrant within a reasonable time after it has been issued and that the search be conducted within the scope outlined in the warrant.

In some cases, police officers may request a ***no-knock warrant***, which if granted allows them to enter the place to be searched without knocking on the door or otherwise notifying the property occupants of the police presence. The purpose of no-knock warrants is to protect the safety of the officers in situations where occupants of a dwelling may respond violently upon hearing police officers at the door. According to the U.S. Department of Justice:

> Federal judges and magistrates may lawfully and constitutionally issue "no-knock" warrants where circumstances justify a no-knock entry, and federal law enforcement officers may lawfully apply for such warrants under such circumstances. Although officers need not take affirmative steps to make an independent re-verification of the circumstances already recognized by a magistrate in issuing a no-knock warrant, such a warrant does not entitle officers to disregard reliable information clearly negating the existence of exigent circumstances when they actually receive such information before execution of the warrant.

Until recently, the Supreme Court had held that police were required to knock and announce their presence before executing a warrant on a dwelling, unless they reasonably believed their safety would be jeopardized. This is known as the ***knock and announce rule***. But this requirement was relaxed in *Hudson v. Michigan* (2006).[37] In *Hudson*, police obtained a warrant authorizing a search for drugs and firearms at the home of Booker Hudson. When police executed the warrant, they announced their presence, but waited only a short time before entering Hudson's home. In a 5-4 ruling, the Court upheld the search, observing that "the social costs of applying the exclusionary rule to knock-and-announce violations are considerable." As a result, the Court concluded that "[r]esort to the massive remedy of suppressing evidence of guilt is unjustified." In short, the Court ruled that the failure of police officers to knock and announce their presence before executing a warrant will not result in evidence being suppressed under the exclusionary rule.

Despite this ruling, there still may be situations where the unreasonable execution of a perfectly valid warrant results in an unconstitutional search under the Fourth Amendment. Many states have their own constitutional or statutory standards for executing search warrants. And some specifically require police to engage in certain procedural actions, including in some cases knocking and announcing their presence, before making a warranted entry into a dwelling.

Good Faith Exception

Even in cases where a search warrant is deemed invalid, the fruits of a resulting search may not result in the suppression of evidence if the executing officer relied in good faith on the apparent validity of the warrant. This rather substantial exception to the valid warrant requirement is known as the ***good faith exception*** or ***Leon rule***. This exception was also discussed in Chapter 10 as an exception to the exclusionary rule.

In *United States v. Leon* (1984),[38] the Court ruled that an invalid warrant, which appears on its face to be valid, will not automatically result in an unconstitutional search if the officer executing the warrant reasonably relied on the facial validity of the warrant. In *Leon*, a police officer obtained a search warrant from a judge and believed it was valid. The officer then used the warrant to search a property where large quantities of drugs and other evidence were found. The district court, however, ruled that the affidavit used to procure the warrant did not establish probable cause for the warrant. The Supreme Court ruled that, despite the probable cause deficiency with the warrant, the Fourth Amendment exclusionary rule does not bar the use of the obtained evidence because the officer acted in reasonable reliance on the search warrant. As a result, even if a warrant is ultimately proven to be deficient because it is not supported by probable cause, a search executed based on the warrant nevertheless can be upheld, if the executing officer had no reason to believe the warrant was deficient.

The Court's reasoning behind this rule is that the Fourth Amendment was designed to punish police overreaching and misconduct, and therefore it should not apply to officers who, in good faith, rely on a seemingly valid warrant. This exception would not apply if (1) the officer executing the warrant makes misrepresentations to the judge or magistrate in order to obtain the warrant, (2) the warrant is so deficient on its face that any reasonable officer should know that it is unsupported by probable cause, or (3) the application and/or affidavit is so deficient in probable cause that no reasonable officer would have relied on it. Keep in mind too that some state jurisdictions have rejected the good faith exception and instead rely on state constitutional principles to exclude evidence procured through defective search warrants in state cases. See Chapters 8 and 10.

good faith exception or *Leon* rule
an exception to the exclusionary rule that allows the fruits of a search based on an invalid warrant to be admitted if the executing officer reasonably believed the warrant was valid

Law Line 11-17
United States v. Leon (1984)

IN THE FIELD

Legal professionals can work with search warrants in a variety of ways. For those working with prosecutors, this may include helping prosecutors evaluate warrant applications and affidavits prepared by police officers for presentation to judges or magistrates. In these types of projects, legal professionals will likely apply the probable cause and particularity requirements to ensure that the officer has enough detail and evidence to support the requested search warrant. In addition, legal professionals may assist prosecutors by reviewing search warrants and their applications as part of preparing a memorandum in response to defendant's motion to suppress evidence obtained during the execution of a search warrant. Under either scenario, keep in mind, evidence supporting probable cause must be found within the text of the application and affidavit.

For defense professionals, the work with search warrants typically occurs after a client's place or property is searched. In these cases, legal professionals must initially gather all four documents related to the warrant—application, affidavit, warrant, and return—and review them carefully to see whether they contain the

(continued)

requisite elements of probable cause and particularity. If these elements are lacking, or if there are material falsehoods or misrepresentations contained in the warrant application affidavit, a motion to suppress the fruits of the search should be prepared and a *Franks* hearing should be requested.

Realize, however, that even if the warrant turns out to be defective, the prosecutor is likely to assert the good faith exception. In these cases, defense professionals typically must show at the suppression hearing that the officer's reliance on the defective warrant was not reasonable and/or not in good faith. This can be a particularly challenging task. But in cases where material misrepresentations or falsehoods were used to obtain the warrant, and the officer who applied for the warrant also executed it, the claim of good faith or a *Leon* exception can be effectively challenged.

WARRANTLESS EVIDENTIARY SEARCHES AND SEIZURES

Perhaps the largest percentage of criminal searches and seizures involve warrantless searches of places or things. Again, because the Fourth Amendment stresses the importance of a warrant, searches and seizures performed without warrants are presumed unconstitutional.[39] There are exceptions to this presumption that allow law enforcement to engage in warrantless searches and still use the fruit from these searches during a criminal trial. But because of the constitutional presumption against warrantless searches, the government bears the burden of demonstrating that a valid exception excuses the lack of a warrant in a particular case.

Exceptions to the Warrant Requirement

Over the years, the Court has recognized a number of exceptions to the Fourth Amendment warrant requirement that allow law enforcement officers to perform warrantless searches and still comply with the Constitution. Arguably, these exceptions have become so numerous as to greatly overshadow the general presumption against warrantless searches.

Search Incident to a Lawful Arrest

search incident to a lawful arrest an exception to the warrant requirement; allows police to conduct a warrantless search when arresting someone

The first exception is a ***search incident to a lawful arrest***. Under this exception, if police are conducting a valid arrest of a person, they may conduct a warrantless search of the arrestee. This search may include inspections of the area within the "wingspan" of the suspect, a protective sweep of the larger area around the suspect if other criminal suspects are believed to be in the vicinity, and the passenger seat of the suspect's automobile.[40] Similarly, police may take a full inventory (the administrative equivalent of a search) of a suspect's possessions, including items within the suspect's automobile, when these items are held pursuant to an incarceration of the suspect.[41] The basic theory behind this exception is that arrests and incarcerations are often such dynamic and hostile situations, which may involve dangerous items or the threat of harm, as to make it impractical for police to obtain a search warrant prior to performing these procedures.

The leading case for this exception is *Chimel v. California* (1969),[42] where the Supreme Court held that when an arrest is made, it is reasonable for the officer to search the arrestee for weapons and evidence. According to the Court, such a search includes the area within the arrestee's immediate control—areas where defendants may gain access to a weapon or evidence. This is sometimes referred to as the **wingspan rule**. As a result, generally speaking, police can search the room in which the arrest is made. In addition, the Supreme Court generally has recognized that police officers can conduct a **protective sweep** of the location where the defendant is arrested, if authorities reasonably believe that accomplices may be in the area and threaten the safety of the officers. Essentially, a protective sweep is a larger search of a location whereby the officers assess other rooms or areas of a property to see if other persons or harmful devices are present.

But more recently, the Court held that police cannot search inside an arrested person's vehicle after the person is taken away from the car, unless police have reason to believe that there is criminal evidence inside the vehicle. In *Arizona v. Gant* (2009), the Court refused to apply the incident to a lawful arrest exception to car searches where the driver or arrested person no longer had access to the vehicle. Read the Court's opinion in *Gant* to appreciate the limitations on this exception to warrantless searches.

wingspan rule
a rule under the search incident to a lawful arrest exception; allows police to search the immediate area around an arrested person

protective sweep
a rule applicable during warrantless searches conducted pursuant to a lawful arrest; allows police to search the premises if authorities reasonably believe that accomplices may be in the area and threaten the safety of the officers

CAPSTONE CASE *Arizona v. Gant*, 129 S. Ct. 1710 (2009)

Justice Stevens delivered the opinion of the Court.

After Rodney Gant was arrested for driving with a suspended license, handcuffed, and locked in the back of a patrol car, police officers searched his car and discovered cocaine in the pocket of a jacket on the backseat. Because Gant could not have accessed his car to retrieve weapons or evidence at the time of the search, the Arizona Supreme Court held that the search-incident-to-arrest exception to the Fourth Amendment's warrant requirement, as defined in *Chimel v. California*, 395 U.S. 752 (1969), and applied to vehicle searches in *New York v. Belton*, 453 U.S. 454 (1981), did not justify the search in this case. We agree with that conclusion.

Under *Chimel*, police may search incident to arrest only the space within an arrestee's "immediate control," meaning "the area from within which he might gain possession of a weapon or destructible evidence." The safety and evidentiary justifications underlying *Chimel*'s reaching-distance rule determine *Belton*'s scope. Accordingly, we hold that *Belton* does not authorize a vehicle search incident to a recent occupant's arrest after the arrestee has been secured and cannot access the interior of the vehicle . . . [W]e also conclude that circumstances unique to the automobile context justify a search incident to arrest when it is reasonable to believe that evidence of the offense of arrest might be found in the vehicle.

. . .

Consistent with our precedent, our analysis begins, as it should in every case addressing the reasonableness of a warrantless search, with the basic rule that "searches conducted outside the judicial process, without prior approval by judge or magistrate, are *per se* unreasonable under the Fourth Amendment—subject only to a few specifically established and well-delineated exceptions." Among the exceptions to the warrant requirement is a search incident to a lawful arrest. The exception derives from interests in officer safety and evidence preservation that are typically implicated in arrest situations. . . .

The State does not seriously disagree with the Arizona Supreme Court's conclusion that Gant could not have accessed his vehicle at the time of the search, but it nevertheless asks us to uphold the search of his vehicle under the broad reading of *Belton* discussed above. The State argues that *Belton* searches are reasonable regardless of the possibility of access in a given case because that expansive rule correctly balances law enforcement interests, including the interest in a bright-line rule, with an arrestee's limited privacy interest in his vehicle.

(continued)

(continued)

For several reasons, we reject the State's argument. First, the State seriously undervalues the privacy interests at stake. Although we have recognized that a motorist's privacy interest in his vehicle is less substantial than in his home, the former interest is nevertheless important and deserving of constitutional protection. . . . A rule that gives police the power to conduct such a search whenever an individual is caught committing a traffic offense, when there is no basis for believing evidence of the offense might be found in the vehicle, creates a serious and recurring threat to the privacy of countless individuals. Indeed, the character of that threat implicates the central concern underlying the Fourth Amendment—the concern about giving police officers unbridled discretion to rummage at will among a person's private effects. . . .

Contrary to the State's suggestion, a broad reading of *Belton* is also unnecessary to protect law enforcement safety and evidentiary interests. Under our view, *Belton* and *Thornton* permit an officer to conduct a vehicle search when an arrestee is within reaching distance of the vehicle or it is reasonable to believe the vehicle contains evidence of the offense of arrest. Other established exceptions to the warrant requirement authorize a vehicle search under additional circumstances when safety or evidentiary concerns demand. . . .

These exceptions together ensure that officers may search a vehicle when genuine safety or evidentiary concerns encountered during the arrest of a vehicle's recent occupant justify a search. Construing *Belton* broadly to allow vehicle searches incident to any arrest would serve no purpose except to provide a police entitlement, and it is anathema to the Fourth Amendment to permit a warrantless search on that basis. . . .

Police may search a vehicle incident to a recent occupant's arrest only if the arrestee is within reaching distance of the passenger compartment at the time of the search or it is reasonable to believe the vehicle contains evidence of the offense of arrest. When these justifications are absent, a search of an arrestee's vehicle will be unreasonable unless police obtain a warrant or show that another exception to the warrant requirement applies. The Arizona Supreme Court correctly held that this case involved an unreasonable search. Accordingly, the judgment of the State Supreme Court is affirmed.

It is so ordered.

WHAT DO *YOU* THINK?

1. What implications does this opinion have for other types of searches where a suspect is placed in government custody?
2. What techniques might police employ to avoid the limitations implemented by this opinion?

Consent Searches

consent search
an exception to the warrant requirement for searches; allows police to conduct searches with the permission or consent of a person who has actual or apparent authority over the property being searched

Another exception to the warrant requirement is ***consent searches***. These are searches performed with the permission or consent of a person who is has actual or apparent authority over the property being searched. The Court has held that a person's consent to a search must be made voluntarily and intelligently, meaning that police cannot unreasonably coerce a person to consent or take advantage of a person who does not have sufficient mental ability to consent.[43] For example, police cannot falsely announce that they have a warrant to search a home in order to obtain consent from the home owner. Like many other standards in criminal procedure, the validity of a person's consent will be judged based on the totality of the circumstances. Factors such as the person's age, mental capacity, state of intoxication, and language barriers can be considered to assess whether a person voluntarily and intelligently consented to a search.

The Court has ruled that a consent search will be valid even if the consenting person did not really have authority to consent to the search, as long as the police had a reasonable belief that the person was authorized to give consent for the search.[44] This is known as the ***apparent authority rule*** and it generally recognizes that other people may have authority to give consent to search a home and that the focus should be on what the officers reasonably believed regarding the consenting person's authority over the home.

Sometimes consent-based searches can be complicated. For example, in *Georgia v. Randolph* (2006),[45] the defendant's estranged wife gave police permission to search the marital residence for items of drug use, after the defendant, who was also present, had clearly refused to give consent. Essentially, when the police asked for consent to search the home, the wife said yes, but the husband-defendant said no. Based on the subsequent search, the defendant was indicted for possession of cocaine. The Supreme Court, however, invalidated this search, finding that the physically present co-occupant's clear refusal to permit entry rendered the warrantless entry and search unreasonable and invalid as to him.

In addition, the scope of a person's consent can also be limited, thereby limiting the scope of the search performed. For example, if a person authorizes police to search the bathroom of her home, but police also search two bedrooms and a hall closet, the additional searches generally would be deemed beyond the scope of consent. As a result, any criminal contraband obtained in these additional searches would not qualify for the consent exception for warrantless searches.

Plain View Searches

Searches and seizures of property within plain view also provide an exception to the warrant requirement. Under the ***plain view doctrine***, if police are lawfully in a location where they plainly see evidence of criminal activity, they may search and seize the evidence without a warrant.[46] There are three basic requirements for this exception: (1) police must have legal authority to be in a location, (2) they must find an item in plain view, and (3) they must have probable cause to believe the item is evidence of a crime. As a result, if police are searching a home for illegal aliens pursuant to a valid warrant and they discover illegal narcotics in plain sight, they do not need an additional warrant to seize the narcotics. The Court has reasoned that, even without a warrant, the search and seizure of criminal contraband within plain view is not unreasonable.

In *Arizona v. Hicks* (1987),[47] police lawfully entered the defendant's apartment to search for a shooting suspect. Inside the apartment, an officer noticed two sets of expensive stereo components, which he suspected were stolen. The officer read and recorded the serial numbers from the components, moving some of them to do so. Based on these serial numbers, officers learned the components were stolen and charged the defendant with robbery. Upon review, however, the Supreme Court invalidated the search. The Court concluded that, while the mere recording of the serial numbers did not constitute a "seizure," the moving of the equipment was a "search" separate and apart from the search that was the lawful objective (related to the shooting) of entering the apartment. The Court refused to apply the plain view doctrine to the search because the serial numbers were not in the officer's plain view.

apparent authority rule
a rule used to judge some types of consent searches; allows police to rely on consent given by persons that police reasonably believed were authorized to give consent

Law Line 11-18
Georgia v. Randolph (2006)

plain view doctrine
an exception to the warrant requirement for searches; allows police to seize evidence if they are lawfully in a location where they plainly see evidence of criminal activity

Law Line 11-19
Arizona v. Hicks (1987)

Terry Searches (Stop and Frisk)

The Court also has interpreted stop and frisk situations (*Terry* stops) as an exception to the warrant requirement. Recall from the discussion above that officers are permitted to briefly detain and question individuals when they have reasonable suspicion that the individuals are engaged or about to engage in criminal activity. Police are also permitted to perform a frisk or pat-down of the person to assess whether the person is armed and/or dangerous. The Supreme Court has identified this frisking or patting down during a *Terry* stop as another type of permissible warrantless search. This is known as the **stop and frisk exception**. It maintains that officers conducting a brief investigation of a person based on reasonable suspicion may conduct a warrantless "pat-down" of the person's outer clothing in order to ensure that the person is not armed or dangerous.[48]

While conducting a *Terry*-based stop and frisk, police officers may discover criminal contraband, including illegal drugs and firearms. Such discoveries gathered during *Terry* searches can lead to an arrest or to a more invasive search based on probable cause. It is important to note, however, that the scope of the officer's initial frisking or pat-down must be for weapons, not other criminal contraband. But in the course of conducting a pat-down for weapons, officers may either see or feel items that they reasonably believe to be elements of criminality. This may include non-weapon forms of contraband (drugs, drug paraphernalia, and the like) that the officer reasonably detects as a part of a properly executed pat-down.

As discussed above, under the plain view doctrine, officers may seize items that they can patently observe during the course of an investigation. But in addition, the Supreme Court has also ruled that police may seize items that they reasonably discover through plain touch or feel during a properly conducted investigatory stop. This is known as the **plain feel exception** to the warrant requirement. In *Minnesota v. Dickerson* (1993),[49] the Court held that police may seize nonthreatening contraband detected through the sense of touch during a protective pat-down search of the sort permitted by *Terry*, so long as the search stays within the bounds marked by *Terry*.

For example, while conducting a protective pat-down for weapons, officers may feel something that they reasonably believe may be a crack pipe, bag of illegal narcotics, or other criminal contraband. Assuming the officer's suspicion is reasonable—which again is based on the totality of the circumstances, including the officer's experience and knowledge of articulable facts—the officer may conduct a more invasive search of the suspect item, including reaching into the suspect's pockets or pants, and this search generally will be deemed reasonable under the Fourth Amendment.

Exigent Circumstances

Another exception to the warrant requirement developed by the Court is the **exigent circumstances exception**, which generally allows law enforcement to conduct warrantless searches where there is a need to apprehend a dangerous person or prevent an imminent and serious threat to the police or public.[50] Although the Court has made it clear that this is not a general or catchall exception, it has approved some warrantless searches conducted under particular circumstances of exigency.

These include cases where the police are pursuing fleeing felons, who may run into a home or other place that is traditionally associated with a reasonable expectation of privacy. In such instances, police are permitted to continue the pursuit without the search becoming unreasonable under the Fourth Amendment. This is known as the **hot-pursuit rule**.

---

stop and frisk exception

an exception to the warrant requirement; allows officers to seize evidence obtained during a pat and frisk procedure of a *Terry* stop

plain feel exception

an exception to the warrant requirement; allows police to seize nonthreatening contraband detected through the sense of touch during a protective patdown search of a *Terry* stop

Law Line 11-20
Minnesota v. Dickerson (1993)

exigent circumstances exception

an exception to the warrant requirement; allows law enforcement to conduct warrantless searches where there is a need to apprehend a dangerous person or prevent an imminent and serious threat to the police or public

hot-pursuit rule

an exigent circumstances situation that allows police to pursue fleeing suspects into places without obtaining a warrant

The Court has also authorized police to perform warrantless seizures of evidence that may be destroyed or evaporate. This called the ***evanescent evidence exception***, and it generally recognizes situations where police cannot obtain a warrant before evidence may dissipate or otherwise disappear. For example, in *Cupp v. Murphy* (1973),[51] during a police station detention, police took samples from a murder suspect's fingernails over his protests and without a warrant. The Court ruled that this intrusion, which was undertaken to preserve highly evanescent evidence, did not violate the Fourth Amendment.

The Court also has sanctioned warrantless searches performed during circumstances that pose an imminent threat to public safety.[52] This is known as the ***public safety exception***. For example, if authorities view a home on fire or see children in trouble on private property, they can access and search the property within the scope of the emergency. The Court, however, has held that the exigent circumstances exception should not be applied to cases where the police would have a reasonable opportunity to obtain a warrant in time to address the perceived threat.[53]

Vehicle Searches

The Court also has applied a warrant exception to many automobile searches. Under the ***automobile exception***, police generally may search a vehicle without a warrant as long as they have probable cause that the vehicle or a part thereof contains evidence of criminality.[54] The Court has theorized that this exception is appropriate because vehicles can be readily moved, thereby making the acquisition of a warrant impractical. The Court also has suggested that people have a lesser expectation of privacy in their automobiles because they are used among the public and on public roads.

As a result, in addition to warrantless automobile searches conducted under the *Terry* stop or stop and frisk exception (see above), police may also search areas within vehicles and any containers therein if they have probable cause to believe that these areas or containers hold criminal contraband or the instruments of crime. Of course, if police believe the vehicle itself is evidence of a crime, they may seize the entire vehicle.

evanescent evidence exception
an exigent circumstances situation that allows police to perform warrantless seizures of evidence that may be destroyed or evaporate

public safety exception
an exception to the warrant requirement; allows warrantless searches performed during circumstances that pose an imminent threat to public safety

automobile exception
an exception to the warrant requirement; allows police to search vehicles without a warrant as long as they have probable cause that the vehicle or a part thereof contains evidence of criminality

In Texas, Department of Public Safety officers arrest a driver after finding allegedly stolen goods in his car.

Administrative and Border Searches

There are several other specialized settings for which the Court has approved warrantless searches. These include, but are not limited to, stops at international borders, where officials may stop vehicles at fixed checkpoints, even without reasonable suspicion, and search them for criminal contraband or persons unauthorized to enter the country. The Court has also authorized warrantless and suspicionless searches of airline passengers boarding planes and of businesses that are substantially regulated by the government, including gun and liquor stores.[55] And for similar reasons, the Court has upheld warrantless drug testing of employees involved in public safety occupations, such as railroad workers and customs officials. When conducted in a neutral and fair manner, the seizures of bodily fluids from some public safety professionals may be conducted, even without reasonable suspicion.[56]

In addition, the Court has ruled that prison officials can conduct warrantless searches of a prisoner's cell and personal property.[57] The Court reasoned that, given the circumstances surrounding incarceration, prisoners have no reasonable expectation of privacy within their prison cells or within the property found therein. As a result, the Court found that generally prisoners have no Fourth Amendment rights when officials search their prison cell or personal property.

And even after prisoners are released, they may have limited Fourth Amendment safeguards against warrantless searches. The Court has also approved warrantless stops and searches of persons on parole. In *Samson v. California* (2006), the Supreme Court upheld a police officer's warrantless and suspicionless search of a parolee, which was conducted pursuant to a California statute that required persons on parole to "agree in writing to be subject to search or seizure by a parole officer or other peace officer . . . with or without a search warrant and with or without cause." The Court upheld the search and the statute, finding that parolees have fewer expectations of privacy and that California's law was a reasonable measure designed to ensure public safety.

In each of these settings, the Court generally has found that the heightened interest in maintaining public safety outweighs the need for a warrant or probable cause in government searches.

School Searches

In addition, the Court has ruled that searches of public school property, including student lockers, may be performed if based on reasonable suspicion. In *New Jersey v. T.L.O.* (1985),[58] the Court recognized that public school children have legitimate expectations of privacy, but that these interests must be weighed against the school's need to maintain an effective learning environment. In balancing these two interests, the Court held that school officials need not obtain a warrant before searching students who are under their authority and that searches do not need to be based on probable cause. Instead, the legality of a student search depends simply on the reasonableness of the search, based on all the circumstances.

In *Safford Unified School District #1 v. Redding* (2009), the Court ruled that a school search will be permissible in scope when the measures adopted are reasonably related to the objectives of the search, and not excessively intrusive in light of the student's age and sex and the nature of the infraction. Read the Court's opinion in *Redding* (below), which involves a school administrator's strip search of a junior high school student. Notice how the Court applies the reasonable suspicion standard to searches performed in public school settings.

Savana Redding, age 19, is seen in front of the U.S. Supreme Court in an April 21, 2009 photo. The Supreme Court later ruled that a strip search performed on Redding at her Arizona school violated the Fourth Amendment ban on unreasonable searches. Another student accused Redding of giving out prescription-strength ibuprofen, the equivalent of two over-the-counter Advils, when she was in eighth grade. No pills were found.

CAPSTONE CASE *Safford Unified School District #1 v. Redding,* 129 S. Ct. 2633 (2009)

Justice Souter delivered the opinion of the Court.

The events immediately prior to the search in question began in 13-year-old Savana Redding's math class at Safford Middle School one October day in 2003. The assistant principal of the school, Kerry Wilson, came into the room and asked Savana to go to his office. . . .

Wilson then showed Savana four white prescription-strength ibuprofen 400-mg pills, and one over-the-counter blue naproxen 200-mg pill, all used for pain and inflammation but banned under school rules without advance permission. He asked Savana if she knew anything about the pills. Savana answered that she did not. . . . Helen Romero, an administrative assistant, came into the office, and together with Wilson they searched Savana's backpack, finding nothing.

At that point, Wilson instructed Romero to take Savana to the school nurse's office to search her clothes for pills. Romero and the nurse, Peggy Schwallier, asked Savana to remove her jacket, socks, and shoes, leaving her in stretch pants and a T-shirt (both without pockets), which she was then asked to remove. Finally, Savana was told to pull her bra out and to the side and shake it, and to pull out the elastic on her underpants, thus exposing her breasts and pelvic area to some degree. No pills were found.

. . .

The Fourth Amendment "right of the people to be secure in their persons . . . against unreasonable searches and seizures" generally requires a law enforcement officer to have probable cause for conducting a search. . . .

In [*New Jersey* v. *T. L. O.*, 469 U.S. 325 (1985)], we recognized that the school setting "requires some modification of the level of suspicion of illicit activity needed to justify a search," and held that for searches by school officials "a careful balancing of governmental and private interests suggests that the public interest is best served by a Fourth Amendment standard of reasonableness that stops short of

(continued)

(continued)

probable cause." We have thus applied a standard of reasonable suspicion to determine the legality of a school administrator's search of a student, and have held that a school search "will be permissible in its scope when the measures adopted are reasonably related to the objectives of the search and not excessively intrusive in light of the age and sex of the student and the nature of the infraction."

. . .

Perhaps the best that can be said generally about the required knowledge component of probable cause for a law enforcement officer's evidence search is that it raise a "fair probability," or a "substantial chance," of discovering evidence of criminal activity. The lesser standard for school searches could as readily be described as a moderate chance of finding evidence of wrongdoing. This suspicion of Wilson's was enough to justify a search of Savana's backpack and outer clothing. . . . And the look into Savana's bag, in her presence and in the relative privacy of Wilson's office, was not excessively intrusive, any more than Romero's subsequent search of her outer clothing.

Here it is that the parties part company, with Savana's claim that extending the search at Wilson's behest to the point of making her pull out her underwear was constitutionally unreasonable. The exact label for this final step in the intrusion is not important, though strip search is a fair way to speak of it. . . .

Savana's subjective expectation of privacy against such a search is inherent in her account of it as embarrassing, frightening, and humiliating. The reasonableness of her expectation (required by the Fourth Amendment standard) is indicated by the consistent experiences of other young people similarly searched, whose adolescent vulnerability intensifies the patent intrusiveness of the exposure. . . .

The indignity of the search does not, of course, outlaw it, but it does implicate the rule of reasonableness as stated in *T. L. O.*, that "the search as actually conducted [be] reasonably related in scope to the circumstances which justified the interference in the first place." The scope will be permissible, that is, when it is "not excessively intrusive in light of the age and sex of the student and the nature of the infraction."

Here, the content of the suspicion failed to match the degree of intrusion. Wilson knew beforehand that the pills were prescription-strength ibuprofen and over-the-counter naproxen, common pain relievers equivalent to two Advil, or one Aleve. He must have been aware of the nature and limited threat of the specific drugs he was searching for, and while just about anything can be taken in quantities that will do real harm, Wilson had no reason to suspect that large amounts of the drugs were being passed around, or that individual students were receiving great numbers of pills. . . .

In sum, what was missing from the suspected facts that pointed to Savana was any indication of danger to the students from the power of the drugs or their quantity, and any reason to suppose that Savana was carrying pills in her underwear. We think that the combination of these deficiencies was fatal to finding the search reasonable. . . .

The strip search of Savana Redding was unreasonable and a violation of the Fourth Amendment. . . .

It is so ordered.

WHAT DO *YOU* THINK?

1. Is the reasonable suspicion standard the appropriate level of scrutiny for school searches? Would probable cause be suitable for these searches?

2. What additional evidence or knowledge would have helped the school administrators satisfy the reasonable suspicion standard necessary for the strip search?

IN THE FIELD

For legal professionals, the review of warrantless searches and seizures has a basic legal framework. See Figure 11-8. At the outset, the defendants have the burden of proof to show that they had a Fourth Amendment interest in the place that was searched or the property that was seized. This requires two things:

- A showing that there was sufficient government conduct involved in the search.
- Proof that the defendant had a reasonable expectation of privacy in the place searched or item seized.

Once this is shown, the burden of proof shifts to the prosecutor, who must demonstrate that the warrantless search was conducted pursuant to a constitutionally recognized exception to the general rule requiring a warrant. This involves the following:

- A legal demonstration that there is a recognized exception to the warrant requirement that might apply to the current case.
- A factual showing that the officers who conducted the search met the legal standards set forth in the exception.

In most cases, this process involves a suppression hearing and testimony from the officer who executed the search. In many cases, defendants or their witnesses will also testify to refute the officer's testimony. For example, if the officer might claim that the defendant consented to the search, the defendant might deny this claim and offer a different set of facts. If so, the trial court will have to decide which account of the facts is more credible.

Thus, while the legal framework for warrantless searches and seizures may be easy to understand, the evidentiary challenges that go along with proving or refuting a government-asserted exception to the warrant requirement can be far more complicated. But at the outset, legal professionals should identify any and all possible exceptions that might be used to justify the warrantless search and be prepared to solicit or cross-examine the testimony from witnesses who seek to support or refute the exception(s).

FIGURE 11-8 **Framework for Evidentiary Searches and Seizures**

Was there sufficient government conduct involved in executing the search?

NO ⇨ No Fourth Amendment violation

YES ⇨ Did the person who owned or occupied the place being searched have a reasonable expectation of privacy?

NO ⇨ No Fourth Amendment violation

YES ⇨ Did police conduct the search pursuant to a valid search warrant? (neutral judicial authority, demonstration of probable cause, warrant sufficiently detailed the search, and officers reasonably executed the warrant)

YES ⇨ Search likely does not violate Fourth Amendment

NO ⇨ Is there a recognized exception to the warrant requirement that applies? (incident to lawful arrest, consent, plain view, *Terry* search, exigent circumstances, automobile search, administrative search, etc.)

YES ⇨ Search likely does not violate Fourth Amendment

NO ⇨ Search likely violates Fourth Amendment

CHAPTER **SUMMARY**

- The Fourth Amendment contains two primary provisions the search and seizure clause, which bars government from engaging in unreasonable searches and seizures of persons, houses, papers and effects, and the warrant provision, which provides that the government must demonstrate probable cause before a warrant will be issued by a judge.
- A search is a governmental encroachment upon a location where a person has a reasonable expectation of privacy, while a seizure is a governmental exercise of control over a person or item.
- There are three primary categories of constitutional review for searches and seizures: (1) the arrest or other detention of persons, (2) warrantless searches and seizures of places or things, and (3) warrant-based searches and seizures.
- The most serious form of search and seizure under the Fourth Amendment is the seizure, arrest, or other detention of persons.
- A seizure of a person occurs when a law enforcement officer uses force or the threat of force to detain a person, thereby causing the person to reasonably believe that he or she cannot freely leave the presence of the official.
- An arrest happens when a law enforcement officer physically takes a person into custody against his or her will for purposes of initiating criminal prosecution or investigation.
- In some cases, police may effectuate a warrantless arrest inside a person's home, if the officers are operating under exigent circumstances. In some cases, police may make other forms of warrantless arrests as long as they have probable cause to believe the suspect has committed a crime.
- To be constitutional, both arrest warrants and warrantless arrests must be based on probable cause.
- Probable cause is a legal standard requiring the warrant-issuing judge or warrantless-arrest-making law enforcement officer to have sufficient, articulable, and trustworthy information to reasonably believe that a person has committed a crime.
- In some cases, an officer may briefly detain persons for legitimate investigative purposes, even where the officer does not have probable cause to believe that a crime has occurred. This is known as an investigatory detention or a *Terry* stop.
- In order for investigatory detentions to be constitutional under the Fourth Amendment, an officer must have reasonable suspicion that the person being stopped is involved in criminal activity.
- Reasonable suspicion is a less stringent standard than probable cause, which generally requires an officer to have articulable facts that would lead a rea-

sonable person to suspect that criminal activity is afoot.
- During an investigatory stop, police may frisk the person stopped if they believe the person may have weapons on or about his person. This is a *Terry* search.
- In general, police may stop persons operating motorized vehicles, if they have probable cause (to make a full seizure or arrest of the person) or reasonable suspicion (to briefly investigate possible illegal activity, including the violation of traffic laws).
- Most police searches are performed without a warrant. These searches involve three questions: (1) is there sufficient governmental conduct involved in the search? (2) did the defendant have a reasonable expectation of privacy in the place or thing that was searched? and (3) is there a constitutionally recognized exception that would allow the authorities to conduct the search without a court-approved search warrant?
- Governmental conduct involves law enforcement officers and their agents performing work that is funded or facilitated by public resources.
- A reasonable expectation of privacy is a reasonable person's legitimate expectation that certain property or places will not be involuntarily viewed or inspected by third parties.
- The Court has recognized exceptions to the warrant requirement for searches. These exceptions include (1) searches incident to a lawful arrest, (2) consent searches, (3) plain view searches, (4) *Terry* searches, (5) searches performed under exigent circumstances, (6) vehicle searches, and (7) some administrative and border searches.
- A search warrant is essentially written authorization from a court to perform a search.
- There are four basic documents involved in obtaining a search warrant: application, affidavit, warrant, and return.
- The validity of a search warrant is assessed based on four primary factors: (1) whether the warrant was issued by a neutral and detached judicial authority; (2) whether the warrant was based on a finding of probable cause; (3) whether the warrant provides sufficiently detailed or particular instructions to the police officer about the person or places to be searched and the items to be seized; and (4) whether the warrant was properly executed.
- Even if a search warrant is deemed invalid, the fruits of a resulting search may not result in the suppression of evidence, if the executing officer relied in good faith on the apparent validity of the warrant. This is known as the good faith exception or *Leon* rule.

KEY **TERMS**

affidavit
apparent authority rule
application for a search warrant
arrest
arrest warrant
automobile exception
consent search
deadly force
evanescent evidence exception
exigent circumstances
exigent circumstances exception
four corners rule
Franks hearing
frisk
good faith exception or *Leon* rule
home arrests

hot-pursuit rule
investigatory detention or *Terry* stop
judicial neutrality and detachment
Katz test
knock and announce rule
no-knock warrant
open fields doctrine
particularity requirement
plain feel exception
plain view doctrine
probable cause
protective sweep
public safety exception
reasonable expectation of privacy
reasonable suspicion
reasonableness

reasonableness test
return on the warrant
search
search and seizure clause
search incident to a lawful arrest
search warrant
seizure
seizure of a person
sobriety checkpoints
stop and frisk exception
stop and frisk or *Terry* frisk
stop and identify laws
totality of the circumstances
warrant provision
warrantless arrests
wingspan rule

QUESTIONS FOR **DISCUSSION**

1. What is the difference between probable cause and reasonable suspicion?

2. What types of arrests, stops, and searches require probable cause? Which ones require reasonable suspicion?

3. What is the difference between a police detention, arrest, and investigatory stop?

4. Under what circumstances can police arrest someone without a warrant?

5. What does an officer need to do in order to get a search warrant?

6. What standards must defendants meet before they can assert a Fourth Amendment right against a search and seizure?

7. Under what circumstances can police conduct a warrantless search?

8. What standard of review applies to searches conducted on students and their property while in public schools?

9. What is a *Franks* hearing? How does a defendant go about getting one?

10. What is the *Leon* rule? How does it affect invalid warrants?

REFERENCES

1. See *Wolf v. Colorado*, 338 U.S. 25 (1949) and *Carroll v. United States*, 267 U.S. 132 (1925).

2. *Delaware v. Prouse*, 440 U.S. 648 (1979).

3. See *Winston v. Lee*, 470 U.S. 753 (1985).

4. 553 U.S. 164 (2008).

5. See *Florida v. Bostick*, 501 U.S. 429 (1991) (finding that officials boarding a transport bus and asking passengers for identification and request to search luggage did not result in a seizure under the Fourth Amendment).

6. 499 U.S. 621 (1991).

7. 501 U.S. 429 (1991).

8. 551 U.S. 249 (2007).

9. See *Payton v. New York*, 445 U.S. 573 (1980).

10. 532 U.S. 318 (2001).

11. See *Beck v. Ohio*, 379 U.S. 89 (1964).

12. *Maryland v. Pringle*, 540 U.S. 366, 371 (2003) (citations omitted).

13. See *Tennessee v. Garner*, 471 U.S. 1 (1985).

14. *Scott v. Harris*, 550 U.S. 372 (2007).

15. 392 U.S. 1 (1968).

16. See *United States v. Sokolow*, 490 U.S. 1 (1989) (finding that defendant's activity at an airport, which included traveling under a different name than that which matched his phone number, paying for a ticket with small bills, and appearing nervous, gave rise to reasonable suspicion of illegal activity).

17. 529 U.S. 266 (2000).

18. See Ala. Code §15-5-30 (West 2003); Ark. Code Ann. §5-71-213(a)(1) (2004); Colo. Rev. Stat. §16-3-103(1) (2003); Del. Code Ann., Tit. 11, §§1902(a), 1321(6)

(2003); Fla. Stat. §856.021(2) (2003); Ga. Code Ann. §16-11-36(b) (2003); Ill. Comp. Stat., ch. 725, §5/107-14 (2004); Kan. Stat. Ann. §22-2402(1) (2003); La. Code Crim. Proc. Ann., Art. 215.1(A) (West 2004); Mo. Rev. Stat. §84.710(2) (2003); Mont. Code Ann. §46-5-401(2)(a) (2003); Neb. Rev. Stat. §29-829 (2003); N. H. Rev. Stat. Ann. §§594:2 and 644:6 (Lexis 2003); N. M. Stat. Ann. §30-22-3 (2004); N. Y. Crim. Proc. Law §140.50(1) (West 2004); N. D. Cent. Code §29-29-21 (2003); R. I. Gen. Laws §12-7-1 (2003); Utah Code Ann. §77-7-15 (2003); Vt. Stat. Ann., Tit. 24, §1983 (Supp. 2003); Wis. Stat. §968.24 (2003).

19. 461 U.S. 352 (1983).

20. 542 U.S. 177 (2004).

21. See *Delaware v. Prouse*, 440 U.S. 468 (1979).

22. 517 U.S. 806 (1996).

23. 496 U.S. 444 (1990).

24. See *Martinez v. Fuerte*, 428 U.S. 543 (1976).

25. See *United States v. Villamonte-Marquez*, 462 U.S. 579 (1983).

26. See *Rakas v. Illinois*, 439 U.S. 128 (1978).

27. 532 U.S. 67 (2001).

28. See *United States v. Jacobsen*, 466 U.S. 109 (1984) (finding insufficient governmental conduct in search of package opened by a private freight operator).

29. 389 U.S. 347 (1967).

30. *California v. Ciraolo*, 476 U.S. 207 (1986).

31. 533 U.S. 27 (2001).

32. See *United States v. Mara*, 410 U.S. 19 (1973) (handwriting); *United States v. Place*, 462 U.S. 696 (1983) (luggage sniffed by drug dogs); *California v. Greenwood*, 486 U.S. 35 (1988) (curbside garbage); *California v. Ciraolo*, 476 U.S. 207 (1986) (police flying over a person's home).

33. See *Florida v. Riley*, 488 U.S. 445 (1989) (flyover); *United States v. Dunn*, 480 U.S. 294 (1987) (search of barn); *California v. Greenwood*, 486 U.S. 35 (1988).

34. See *Dow Chemical Co. v. United States*, 476 U.S. 227 (1986).

35. See *Coolidge v. New Hampshire*, 403 U.S. 443 (1971) (state attorney general not neutral); *Lo-Ji Sales, Inc. v. New York*, 442 U.S. 319 (1979) (magistrate participating in execution of warrant); *Connally v. Georgia*, 429 U.S. 245 (1977) (magistrate got paid for issuing warrant).

36. 438 U.S. 154 (1978).

37. 126 S. Ct. 1836 (2006).

38. 468 U.S. 897 (1984).

39. See *Dow Chemical Co. v. United States*, 476 U.S. 227 (1986).

40. See *Chimel v. California*, 395 U.S. 752 (1969) (wingspan rule allowing police to inspect areas where suspect might obtain weapons or other items); *Maryland v. Buie*, 494 U.S. 325 (1990) (allowing protective sweeps of premises); *New York v. Belton*, 453 U.S. 454 (1981) (permitting search of passenger seat area upon arresting driver).

41. See *Illinois v. Lafayette*, 459 U.S. 986 (1983) (search pursuant to incarceration); *Colorado v. Bertine*, 479 U.S. 367 (1987) (allowing inspection of contents of impounded vehicle).

42. 395 U.S. 752 (1969).

43. See *Bumper v. North Carolina*, 391 U.S. 543 (1968) (officers cannot induce consent by falsely claiming they have a search warrant).

44. See *Illinois v. Rodriguez*, 497 U.S. 177 (1990) (apparent authority is sufficient); but see *Georgia v. Randolph*, 547 U.S. 103, 126 S. Ct. 1515 (2006).

45. 547 U.S. 103 (2006).

46. See *Arizona v. Hicks*, 480 U.S. 321 (1987).

47. 480 U.S. 321 (1987).

48. See *Terry v. Ohio*, 392 U.S. 1 (1968).

49. See *Minnesota v. Dickerson*, 508 U.S. 366 (1993).

50. See *Minnesota v. Olson*, 495 U.S. 91 (1990).

51. 414 U.S. 291 (1973).

52. See *United States v. Santana*, 427 U.S. 38 (1976) (pursuit of suspect into private home); *Schmerber v. California*, 384 U.S. 757 (1966) (warrantless seizure of blood sample suspected to contain alcohol); *North American Cold Storage v. City of Chicago*, 211 U.S. 306 (1908) (emergency search of contaminated food); *Michigan v. Tyler*, 436 U.S. 499 (1978) (search conducted during burning fire).

53. See *Mincey v. Arizona*, 437 U.S. 385 (1978) (search of a murder scene).

54. See *Carroll v. United States*, 267 U.S. 132 (1925) (addressing theory behind exception); *California v. Acevedo*, 500 U.S. 565 (1991) (searches of containers within vehicles).

55. See *United States v. Martinez-Fuerte*, 428 U.S. 543 (1976) (border checkpoints); *Colonnade Catering Corp. v. United States*, 397 U.S. 72 (1970) (liquor-related business); *United States v. Biswell*, 406 U.S. 311 (1972) (gun-related business).

56. See *Skinner v. Railway Labor Executive's Assoc.*, 489 U.S. 602 (1989); *National Treasury Employees Union v. Von Raab*, 489 U.S. 656 (1989) (both involving employee drug testing).

57. See *Hudson v. Palmer*, 468 U.S. 517 (1984).

58. 469 U.S. 325 (1985).

APPENDIX

DEVELOPING YOUR LEGAL ANALYSIS

A. THE LAW WHERE YOU LIVE

Assume that you are working for a public defender's office and that one of the attorneys in the office has been assigned to represent Tiffany Jones in *State v. Jones*, Case No. 2011-0655. The prosecutor in your local jurisdiction has charged Ms. Jones with two criminal offenses—contributing to the delinquency of a minor and supplying a minor with alcohol.

Tiffany, who is twenty-five years old, was staying at her parents' house while they were away on vacation. She was watching the home along with her sister, Sheila Jones, who is seventeen and still in high school. After working an eight-hour shift at her job, Tiffany arrived at her parents' home, entered through the front door, and went upstairs to change out of her work clothes. When she arrived at the house, Tiffany heard loud music coming from the backyard and assumed that her sister might be having some friends over. While Tiffany was upstairs changing, a police officer walked into the bedroom and began questioning her about the people in the backyard and the presence of beer. Although Tiffany explained that she had just got home, the officer arrested her and initiated the two criminal charges outlined above.

According to the officer's report, police received a phone call from one of the neighbors complaining about loud music coming from the Jones's home. When police arrived at the house, they heard the loud music and noticed several young-looking individuals in the backyard. One officer went immediately to the backyard and began asking for identification from the individuals. The other officer went to the front door, opened it, and went upstairs, where he found Tiffany, who was the only adult on the premises.

Tiffany's attorney would like to file a motion to suppress the police findings within the home, particularly the discovery of Tiffany in the bedroom. The attorney's position is that the officer's entrance into the home was unconstitutional under the Fourth Amendment, and but for this illegal entry, the officer would not have found Tiffany.

Based on the materials in this chapter, along with those addressing the exclusionary rule in Chapter 10, prepare a legal memorandum for the attorney wherein you outline the legal issues for a motion to suppress. Specifically, address whether the officer's search of the Jones home was constitutional and whether the officer's observations made within the home should be excluded from evidence during trial.

B. INSIDE THE FEDERAL COURTS

Assume that you are a legal assistant working in a U.S. Attorney's office. One of your responsibilities is to advise federal agents on search warrant applications. Assume further that a new agent, Special Agent Robert Fisk, has come to you seeking assistance in applying for a search warrant for a home at 704 Houser Street. The agent believes the home owner is growing marijuana in the garage.

Using facts that you might imagine to be present in a case of this type, read Federal Rule of Criminal Procedure 41, and then prepare a search warrant application and affidavit for Special Agent Fisk, so that he may go to the federal magistrate and request a search warrant.

If you need help finding the requisite forms or understanding the rules, consult

http://www.law.cornell.edu/rules/frcrmp/Rule41.htm or http://www.uscourts.gov/forms/AO106.pdf.

C. CYBER SOURCES

Assume that you have just been hired as a legal assistant in the legal division of Boogle—a start-up company that provides Internet and search engine services. The attorneys in your office expect that one of the regular legal issues they will face as a young company is the receipt of search warrants and other court orders from federal agents seeking access to customers' computer accounts. The attorneys would like to be prepared when these anticipated warrants and other orders start arriving. Accordingly, they have asked you to prepare an overview—either in standard memorandum form or in an electronic presentation medium—where you outline the particular legal parameters for federal searches of computer records.

In particular, the attorneys want to know the impact of the federal Electronic Communications Privacy Act and the PATRIOT Act on such searches. Using the resources offered by the Department of Justice at http://www.justice.gov/criminal/cybercrime/searching.html#searchlaws1, as well as any other resources you find insightful, prepare the overview requested by your new employer.

D. ETHICS AND PROFESSIONALISM

Assume that you are working as a legal assistant in a state prosecutor's office. You have been assigned to the case of *State v. Tom Zink*, a felonious assault and domestic violence case involving a man who allegedly beat his wife. Although the case is in its early stages, you have worked closely with the prosecutor and Sally Zink, the victim in the case, to obtain necessary information for trial. The trial judge has issued a protective order against the defendant, ordering him not to have any contact with his wife during the pendency of the case. Sally is quite afraid of her husband and has gone to a protected location out of fear that her husband will try to find her.

You are preparing discovery materials to be sent to Mr. Zink's attorney. The prosecutor assigned to the case asked you to send several discovery documents via facsimile to Mr. Zink's attorney. After you completed this task, you discover that you accidently included in the faxed discovery materials three pages of your notes, which contain the phone number, address, and whereabouts for Sally.

The assistant prosecutor is in court at the moment, but is reachable via text message. Consider the following resources, as well as any ethical standards for preserving confidential materials within your home jurisdiction. Then write a text message to the assistant prosecutor in which you identify the ethical problems and possible solutions associated with your situation.

American Bar Association

http://www.abanet.org/legalservices/paralegals/downloads/modelguidelines.pdf

The American Alliance of Paralegals, Inc.

http://www.aapipara.org/Ethicalstandards.htm

National Association of Legal Assistants

http://www.nala.org/code.aspx

chapter **twelve**

EVIDENCE FROM INTERROGATIONS, IDENTIFICATIONS, AND LINEUPS

The Fifth Amendment is an old friend and a good friend. It is one of the great landmarks in men's struggle to be free of tyranny, to be decent and civilized.

—Justice William O. Douglas, *An Almanac of Liberty* (1954)

All confessions are Odysseys.

—Raymond Queneau French poet and novelist

Because interrogations are intended to coerce confessions, interrogators feel themselves justified in using their coercive means. Consistency regarding the technique is not important; inducing anxiety and fear is the point.

—Aldrich Ames Convicted spy and former CIA agent

LEARNING OBJECTIVES

After reading this chapter, you should be able to

- Understand the basic constitutional protections afforded criminal defendants under the Fifth Amendment right against self-incrimination.

- Explain the process for evaluating the constitutionality of police-led interrogations of criminal suspects.

- Recognize different forms of police conduct that might violate a defendant's constitutional rights to remain silent.

- Appreciate the importance of *Miranda* warnings in processing criminal defendants.

- Prepare a motion to suppress a defendant's statement given to police during custodial interrogation.

- Understand the requirements for a valid waiver of the Fifth Amendment right against self-incrimination.

- Identify the stages of a criminal case during which a defendant or suspect has the right to an attorney under either the Fifth or Sixth Amendments.

- Identify the legal and constitutional defects that are associated with conducting pretrial identifications.

INTRODUCTION

In additional to gathering criminal evidence from searches and seizures, law enforcement can also gain information by (1) interrogating or questioning suspects, (2) securing identifying evidence from suspects, such as handwriting, fingerprints, and voice samples, and (3) placing suspects in lineups or showups for a witness to review. This evidence, like that obtained from a search and seizure, is often the subject of pretrial challenges brought in the form of motions to suppress. In such cases, defendants assert that the methods employed by law enforcement in obtaining a defendant's statements, confession, or other identifying information were unconstitutional, and therefore the evidence obtained must be excluded from trial.

Challenges to evidence gained through custodial interrogation, identification samples, and lineups can be based on a number of constitutional foundations. Defendants sometimes assert the right to the due process of law as a check on unduly coercive police tactics that yield incriminating information.[1] More notably, defendants often cite the Fifth Amendment protection against compulsory self-incrimination as a limitation on government interrogating or otherwise interfacing with criminal suspects. And finally, defendants sometimes rely on the Sixth Amendment right to counsel to challenge statements, confessions, and other identifying information obtained by authorities *after* adversarial proceedings are initiated. See Figure 12-1.

RIGHT TO DUE PROCESS: THE NEED FOR VOLUNTARINESS

As with most interactions between government and individuals, criminal interrogations and other criminal inquiries often involve matters of due process of law. Recall that the Constitution has two due process clauses—one found in the Fifth Amendment, which applies to federal cases, and one in the Fourteenth Amendment, which is relevant to state cases. Regardless of the jurisdiction, these

FIGURE 12-1 **Constitutional Sources for Reviewing Government Acquisition of Defendant's Statements and Confessions**

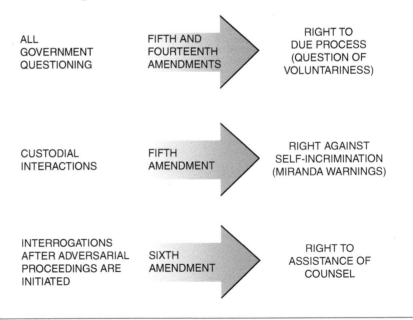

provisions require government to ensure that suspects and defendants are treated fairly during interrogations and other governmental inquiries.

For most criminal cases, the due process of interrogations is determined based on whether the suspect's statements, admissions, or confessions were provided to authorities voluntarily. This is known as the **voluntariness requirement**. According to the Supreme Court, "coercive police activity is a necessary predicate to finding that a confession is not 'voluntary' within the meaning of the Due Process Clause."[2] In other words, to comply with due process standards, law enforcement cannot engage in coercive tactics that produce involuntary testimonial statements by suspects. According to the Court, "certain interrogation techniques, either in isolation or as applied to the unique characteristics of a particular suspect, are so offensive to a civilized system of justice that they must be condemned."[3]

There is no precise formula or test to determine the voluntariness of a suspect's statements. Instead, like other evidentiary standards, this standard is evaluated under the **totality of the circumstances**. Relevant factors might include the suspect's mental capacity, age, education, and physical condition, as well as the type, severity, duration, and reasonableness of tactics used by authorities to procure the suspect's statements.

In some cases, the involuntary nature of a suspect's statements might be obvious. For example, in *Brown v. Mississippi* (1936), the Supreme Court ruled that a confession procured after police physically beat the suspect was made involuntarily and therefore was inadmissible under the Due Process Clause. Similarly, in cases where police falsely promise suspects a more lenient charge or lesser sentence in exchange for their confessions, resulting confessions or statements may be deemed involuntary.

In other cases, like those where police use deceptive tactics to induce a statement or confession, the question of voluntariness may be less obvious. For example, in *Leyra v. Denno* (1954),[4] an interrogating officer told a suspect that he (the officer) would lose his job and his family would suffer if he did not obtain a confession from the suspect. In response, the suspect confessed. The Supreme Court, however, invalidated this confession, concluding that, under the totality of the circumstances, the confession was not made voluntarily. But in *Colorado v. Connelly* (1986),[5] where a mentally challenged suspect provided police with several details and a confession about a murder case, the Court ruled that, absent coercive police conduct, the suspect's statements were not involuntary, despite his mental condition.

voluntariness requirement
a legal standard used to assess whether a suspect's statements to police were elicited according to due process requirements; determined based on the totality of the circumstances

totality of the circumstances
a legal standard that takes into account all relevant factors relating to the voluntariness of a suspect's statements to police

Law Line 12-1
False Confessions

IN THE FIELD

Overall, to determine whether a suspect's statements to police are voluntary, legal professionals must assemble all of the facts surrounding the statements. Based on these facts, legal professionals should ask these questions:

- What were the defendant's age, mental state, and physical condition when the statements were made?
- Were police aware of defendant's age, mental state, and physical condition?
- Did police engage in coercive tactics that took advantage of defendant's condition?
- Under what conditions were the statements procured by police?
  - What was the location and time of day of the interrogation?
  - How long was the interrogation?
  - Was suspect deprived of anything—food, water, and so on?
  - Did police promise suspect anything in exchange for the statements?
  - Did police use deceptive tactics or ploys to obtain the statements?
  - Did police engage in any physical or mental abuse of suspect?

FIFTH AMENDMENT RIGHT AGAINST SELF-INCRIMINATION

right against self-incrimination
the Fifth Amendment right of individuals not to offer statements or other testimony-like evidence to police

privilege
a phrase used to describe the Fifth Amendment right against self-incrimination

The Fifth Amendment provides a more particular provision affecting a suspect's statements and confessions, which is called ***the right against self-incrimination***. Specifically, the Fifth Amendment provides, "No person . . . shall be compelled in any criminal case to be a witness against himself." This basically means that government cannot coerce or force persons to provide incriminating statements against themselves, including confessions, within a criminal context. In some settings, people refer to this right as *pleading the Fifth* or *taking the Fifth*. In other settings, some refer to this as a ***privilege*** (as in *he asserted the privilege*) because it affords individuals the privilege (a special legal status) of not having to testify.

Of course, the Fifth Amendment does not preclude individuals from knowingly, intelligently, and voluntarily providing statements to government. Nor does it prevent persons from being compelled to provide nonincriminating statements or to testify in situations where they do not face criminal liability. It essentially is designed to bar the government from employing unreasonable tactics against suspects during custodial criminal investigations.

At the outset, appreciate that the Fifth Amendment applies to testimony-like evidence obtained by government sources during a custodial interrogation. This assessment involves four basic factors. First, the evidence obtained by police must be testimonial in nature, as opposed to being merely a physical characteristic or observable fact. Second, the evidence must be obtained through sufficient government conduct, as opposed to private coercion or voluntary production. Third, persons from whom the evidence is obtained must be in governmental custody or reasonably believe they cannot leave police presence. And fourth, the evidence must be obtained through police interrogation or intentional questioning designed to elicit incriminating responses.

Assuming these four factors are present, legal professionals must then inquire as to whether law enforcement authorities properly notified the suspects of their Fifth Amendment rights (gave *Miranda* warnings) before the interrogation; whether these rights were asserted or waived by the suspect; whether the suspect's rights were honored by the officers; and if not, whether there is a recognized legal exception that would still allow the evidence to be used by the prosecutor. See Figure 12-2.

Testimonial Evidence

testimonial information
an incriminating form of communication that provides a factual assertion or an affirmation of substantive information

The Supreme Court has ruled that the Fifth Amendment right against self-incrimination applies to a suspect's testimony, statements, or other testimonial information, but not to physical evidence. Generally speaking, ***testimonial information*** is an incriminating form of communication that provides a factual assertion or an affirmation of substantive information. In other words, the Fifth Amendment applies to evidence that is the equivalent of a person verbally testifying about incriminating and factual claims.

In most situations, the testimonial quality of a person's communications will be obvious. Suspects often provide confessions or other verbal disclosures revealing incriminating information. Similarly, a person's testimony at trial or other proceedings would also be testimonial. In addition, silence, nodding, head shaking, or thumbs-up approval, while in custody, may also be considered testimonial in nature because they communicate, either implicitly or explicitly, a factual claim, which is the equivalent of formal testimony.[6] As a result, prosecutors typically cannot

FIGURE 12-2 **Analysis for Fifth Amendment Right Against Self-Incrimination**

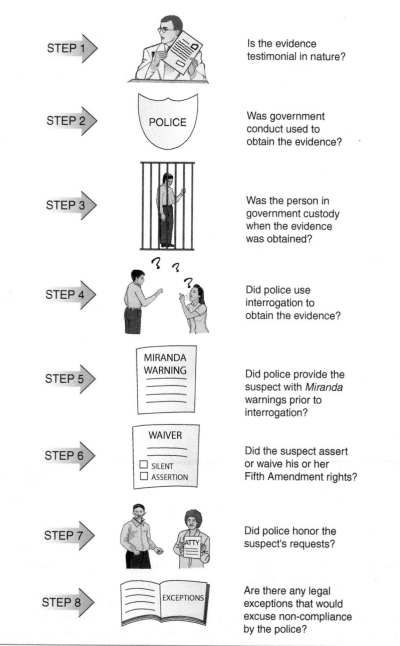

STEP 1 — Is the evidence testimonial in nature?

STEP 2 — POLICE — Was government conduct used to obtain the evidence?

STEP 3 — Was the person in government custody when the evidence was obtained?

STEP 4 — Did police use interrogation to obtain the evidence?

STEP 5 — MIRANDA WARNING — Did police provide the suspect with *Miranda* warnings prior to interrogation?

STEP 6 — WAIVER — SILENT — ASSERTION — Did the suspect assert or waive his or her Fifth Amendment rights?

STEP 7 — ATTY — Did police honor the suspect's requests?

STEP 8 — EXCEPTIONS — Are there any legal exceptions that would excuse non-compliance by the police?

compel defendants to testify against themselves at trial, nor can they comment on defendants' silence during interrogations or their failure to testify at trial.

The Supreme Court, however, has ruled that police can require a suspect to provide other forms of nontestimonial evidence that may contain incriminating information. For example, if authorities issue a subpoena or search warrant seeking certain documents or records, the person receiving it likely must comply with these orders, even though the contents of the materials may incriminate the person. Generally, courts find that requiring the production of physical evidence is not the equivalent of compelling persons to testify against themselves. Similarly, courts have found that the compelled production of a person's blood sample, saliva sample, voice exemplars (a recorded recitation of certain words or expressions), participation in lineups (see below), and handwriting samples is not testimonial evidence subject to the Fifth Amendment.[7]

Government Conduct

government conduct requirement
a condition necessary for the Fifth Amendment right against self-incrimination to apply; requires the presence of sufficient law enforcement influence in extracting a statement from a suspect

First, an authorized law enforcement officer must be involved in extracting information from the person. This is the **government conduct requirement**. Private security guards or other nongovernmental persons who are not working in conjunction with police are not bound by the Fifth Amendment, and thus they are not constitutionally restricted in obtaining confessions from individuals. But if police direct or cause a nongovernmental person to interrogate another person who is in custody, this delegation of task may constitute government conduct.

In *United States v. Henry* (1980),[8] the defendant Henry was arrested and indicted for bank robbery. Henry obtained an appointed attorney and was held in jail pending trial. Another inmate in the jail, who was working as a paid FBI informant, told authorities that he was housed in Henry's cellblock. Federal authorities told the informant to pay attention to Henry's statements, but not to initiate any conversations with or question Henry about the bank robbery. Henry and the informant later engaged in conversations, where Henry discussed the robbery. These statements were then used to convict Henry at trial. The Supreme Court, however, reversed the conviction, finding that federal authorities had "deliberately elicited" incriminating statements from Henry. Authorities claimed that they should not be held responsible for the informant's conduct, because they had told him not to question Henry. But the Court rejected this claim, finding that, under the circumstances, agents must have known that the informant would take affirmative steps to secure incriminating information. In the end, the Court held that "[b]y intentionally creating a situation likely to induce Henry to make incriminating statements without the assistance of counsel, the Government violated [his] Sixth Amendment right to counsel."

Law Line 12-2
Interrogation of former U.S. Senator Larry Craig

In *Kuhlmann v. Wilson* (1986),[9] however, the Court upheld the use of a defendant's statements, which were obtained by authorities through an informant-cellmate. The Court found that confessions are not obtained unconstitutionally where an informant, either through prior arrangement or voluntarily, reports a defendant's incriminating statements to the police. Instead, a defendant must demonstrate that the police and their informant took some action, beyond merely listening, that was designed deliberately to elicit incriminating remarks.

In the vast majority of cases, the presence of government involvement will be quite obvious. Most interrogations are conducted openly and directly by police officers and other law enforcement agents. But in select cases, questions may arise over whether the statements obtained by authorities were derived through government-led interrogations. In these rare situations, legal professionals must assess the extent and nature of the government's acts in procuring the subject statements from the defendant.

Custody Requirement

custodial requirement
a condition necessary for the Fifth Amendment right against self-incrimination to apply; means that the police must have physically apprehended someone and restrained the person's ability to leave

In addition to government involvement, a person must be within governmental custody before Fifth Amendment protections will apply. This is known as the **custodial requirement** and generally means that the police must have physically apprehended someone and restrained the person's ability to leave. In many cases, this means that a suspect has been arrested or otherwise involuntarily taken into a police station or jail setting. In this scenario, custody is determined based on whether a person's ability to move is restricted in a substantial manner.

In other contexts, however, the government may stop short of arresting or substantially detaining a person, but nonetheless create a situation where the person reasonably believes he is in custody. In this situation, the Supreme Court has held that custody is assessed based on whether a reasonable person (not the actual suspect) placed in similar circumstances would feel free to leave the presence of police.[10]

For example, in *Orozco v. Texas* (1969),[11] the Supreme Court found that a suspect was in custody when he was interviewed by four police officers at 4 A.M. in his bedroom because he was under arrest and not free to leave during the questioning. But in *Beckwith v. United States* (1976),[12] the Court found that a suspect questioned by police in his private home was not in custody for Fifth Amendment purposes because he did not reasonably believe that he was prohibited from leaving. Likewise, in *Berkemer v. McCarty* (1984),[13] the Court concluded that a suspect questioned by police during a roadside traffic stop was not in custody because the officer never communicated his intention to arrest the motorist during the roadside questioning.

Overall, the Court has rejected the notion that the custody requirement is satisfied simply because a suspect being interviewed is the focus of a criminal investigation. Instead, the Court has concluded that "the only relevant inquiry is how a reasonable [person] in the suspect's position would have understood his situation."[14] As a result, questions regarding whether the defendant was actually in police custody during an interrogation typically involve fine fact-intensive inquiries. Legal professionals must consider (1) the location of the interrogation, including whether it occurred in a government facility, a confined space, a place with locked doors, or another area where a reasonable person would feel confined and limited in the ability to leave; (2) the presence of government agents, including who was present, how many agents there were, what they were wearing, and whether they demonstrated any sign, symbol, or use of authority; (3) the conditions under which the interrogation occurred, such as the length of the confinement and whether the suspect was denied food, water, or other basic necessities; (4) the mindset of the suspect, including what the officers told the suspect, the age and mental condition of the suspect, and other knowledge the suspect had during the interrogation; and (5) how the suspect arrived at the location of the interrogation, including whether the suspect was taken to the location by authorities or arrived at the police station voluntarily. The totality of these and other circumstances will indicate whether a reasonable person in the suspect's situation would reasonably believe she was in police custody.

Interrogation Requirement

Finally, the Fifth Amendment protection applies where governmental authorities are actually interrogating an individual. *Interrogation* includes questions asked by police in an effort to obtain incriminating information, as well as other forms of police conduct that are designed or likely to elicit an incriminating response from a person in custody. Under *Miranda*, an interrogation includes not only express questioning but also any words or actions on the part of the police (other than those normally attendant to arrest and custody) that the police should know are reasonably likely to elicit an incriminating response from the suspect. But if a person held in police custody voluntarily offers information without being asked or provoked by police, the Fifth Amendment would not prevent such information from being used against the individual because it is not the product of a police-led interrogation.

interrogation
a technique used by police in an effort to obtain incriminating information from suspects

For example, in *Rhode Island v. Innis* (1980),[15] police arrested a man who was suspected of wielding a sawed-off shotgun. But at the time of arrest, officers could not find the suspected shotgun. Officers gave the suspect his *Miranda* warnings and placed him in a police car for transport to the central police station. While driving to the station, two officers began talking between themselves about the missing shotgun. One officer stated that there were "a lot of handicapped children running around in this area" because a school for such children was located nearby, and "God forbid one of them might find a weapon with shells and they might hurt themselves." Upon hearing this exchange, the suspect interrupted the officers to say that he would show them where the gun was located. The suspect then led the officers to the gun, stating "he wanted to get the gun out of the way because of the kids in the area in the school." Under these circumstances, the Supreme Court ruled that the police did not interrogate the suspect in the police car. In a 6-3 opinion, the Court reasoned that the conversation between the two officers was, at least in form, nothing more than a dialogue between them to which no response from respondent was invited. The Court also found that the suspect was not subjected to the "functional equivalent" of questioning because the officers did not know that their conversation was reasonably likely to elicit an incriminating response.

Law Line 12-3
Rhode Island v. Innis (1980)

In most cases, the presence of an interrogation will be obvious. Law enforcement agents will directly question a suspect in an effort to obtain incriminating and other useful information to assist with a criminal investigation. But in some cases, it will not be clear whether the interactions between police and a suspect constitute a form of interrogation. In these situations, legal professionals must assess whether the words and actions of the police were designed or reasonably likely to elicit an incriminating response from the suspect. In making this inquiry, legal professionals must pay particular attention to the perceptions of the suspect, rather than the intent of the police. Factors such as the suspect's age, mental state, background, philosophical or religious beliefs, and other particular vulnerabilities are important in assessing whether the actions or words of the police might reasonably trigger an incriminating response from a suspect.

Normally, basic questions asked by police during the "booking" process regarding a suspect's name, address, age, or other identity-related questions are not deemed to be a form of interrogation because they are not likely to elicit incriminating responses. Instead, they are designed to obtain some basic personal characteristics to enable the suspect's identification. In addition, generally, police can also give alcohol and drug tests, but the individuals being tested may refuse to answer questions.

Constitutional Standards

Miranda Warnings.   Once it is determined that police are engaging in a custodial interrogation, the question becomes, what do the police need to do in order to comply with the Fifth Amendment in performing this task? The Supreme Court has ruled that, prior to engaging in custodial interrogation, police must inform suspects of their Fifth Amendment rights if they wish to use evidence gathered during such interrogations.

Law Line 12-4
Miranda v. Arizona (1966)

The constitutionality of many custodial interrogations is largely controlled by the Court's famous ruling in *Miranda v. Arizona* (1966).[16] The Court observed that "there can be no doubt that the Fifth Amendment privilege is available outside of criminal court proceedings, and serves to protect persons in all settings in which their freedom of action is curtailed in any significant way from being compelled to incriminate themselves." The Court further recognized that, in order to ensure that this right is protected, certain procedural safeguards must be installed to provide suspects with the full opportunity to exercise the privilege against self-incrimination. Specifically, the Court stated:

> [T]he following measures are required. He must be warned prior to any questioning that he has the right to remain silent, that anything he says can be used against him in a court of law, that he has the right to the presence of an attorney, and that, if he cannot afford an attorney one will be appointed for him prior to any questioning if he so desires. Opportunity to exercise these rights must be afforded to him throughout the interrogation. After such warnings have been given, and such opportunity afforded him, the individual may knowingly and intelligently waive these rights and agree to answer questions or make a statement. But unless and until such warnings and waiver are demonstrated by the prosecution at trial, no evidence obtained as a result of interrogation can be used against him.

Under the Court's *Miranda* ruling, police must inform suspects that (1) they have the right to remain silent; (2) anything they say can and will be used against them in court; (3) they have the right to the presence of an attorney; and (4) if they cannot afford an attorney, one will be provided for them. These **Miranda warnings** are designed to ensure that, prior to police questioning, individuals are informed of two basic rights under the Constitution—the right to be silent and the right to an attorney. See Figure 12-3.

Miranda warnings
words of advice given by police to suspects prior to custodial interrogation, including admonitions of the right to remain silent and the right to counsel

FIGURE 12-3 **Sample *Miranda* Warnings and Waiver Form**

Miranda Rights

1. You have the right to remain silent.
2. If you decide to say anything, anything you do say can and will be used against you in a court of law.
3. You have the right to talk to a lawyer and to have the lawyer present with you while you are being questioned.
4. If you cannot afford to hire a lawyer, one will be appointed to represent you before any questioning, if you wish.
5. You can decide at any time to exercise these rights and not answer any questions or make any statements.

Waiver of Miranda Rights

Before being asked any questions, I have been told of my right to remain silent, that anything I say can and will be used against me in court, and that I have the right to talk with a lawyer and to have the lawyer with me during questioning. I have also been told that if I cannot afford a lawyer, one will be appointed for me, at no cost to me, before I am questioned. I have also been told that I can stop talking at anytime. I understand all of these rights and I am willing to talk to you.

_____   _____
(Signature)   (Date Signed)

_____   _____
(Witness Signature)   (Date Signed)

_____   _____
(Witness Signature)   (Date Signed)

Wording of the Warnings.   Given the depiction of *Miranda* warnings on television and other media, many citizens can recite the requisite warnings verbatim from the Court's opinion. But generally, police do not have to read *Miranda* warnings precisely as they were announced by the Court. Instead, if police provide suspects with the basic substance of their Fifth Amendment rights, this will often satisfy the *Miranda* requirements. For example, in *Duckworth v. Eagan* (1989),[17] the police advised a suspect that "[w]e have no way of giving you a lawyer, but one will be appointed for you, if you wish, if and when you go to court." The Supreme Court found that these words sufficiently provided the suspect with his *Miranda* warnings.

Read the Supreme Court's opinion in *Florida v. Powell* (2010), where a 7-2 majority opinion upheld the constitutional validity of preinterrogation warnings provided by Florida police. At issue was whether the warnings adequately notified the suspect of his right to an attorney during custodial interrogation.

CAPSTONE CASE   *Florida v. Powell,* 559 U.S. ___ (2010)

Justice Ginsburg delivered the opinion of the Court.

On August 10, 2004, law enforcement officers in Tampa, Florida, seeking to apprehend respondent Kevin Dewayne Powell in connection with a robbery investigation, entered an apartment rented by Powell's girlfriend. After spotting Powell coming from a bedroom, the officers searched the room and discovered a loaded nine-millimeter handgun under the bed.

The officers arrested Powell and transported him to the Tampa Police headquarters. Once there, and before asking Powell any questions, the officers read Powell the standard Tampa Police Department Consent and Release Form 310. The form states:

"You have the right to remain silent. If you give up the right to remain silent, anything you say can be used against you in court. You have the right to talk to a lawyer before answering any of our questions. If you cannot afford to hire a lawyer, one will be appointed for you without cost and before any questioning. You have the right to use any of these rights at any time you want during this interview."

Acknowledging that he had been informed of his rights, that he "underst[oo]d them," and that he was "willing to talk" to the officers, Powell signed the form. He then admitted that he owned the handgun found in the apartment. Powell knew he was prohibited from possessing a gun because he had previously been convicted of a felony, but said he had nevertheless purchased and carried the firearm for his protection.

Powell was charged in state court with possession of a weapon by a prohibited possessor. . . . Contending that the *Miranda* warnings were deficient because they did not adequately convey his right to the presence of an attorney during questioning, he moved to suppress his inculpatory statements. . . .

To give force to the Constitution's protection against compelled self-incrimination, the Court established in *Miranda* [*v. Arizona* (1966)] "certain procedural safeguards that require police to advise criminal suspects of their rights under the Fifth and Fourteenth Amendments before commencing custodial interrogation." Intent on "giv[ing] concrete constitutional guidelines for law enforcement agencies and courts to follow," *Miranda* prescribed the following four now-familiar warnings:

> "[A suspect] must be warned prior to any questioning [1] that he has the right to remain silent, [2] that anything he says can be used against him in a court of law, [3] that he has the right to the presence of an attorney, and [4] that if he cannot afford an attorney one will be appointed for him prior to any questioning if he so desires."

Miranda's third warning—the only one at issue here—addresses our particular concern that "[t]he circumstances surrounding in-custody interrogation can operate very quickly to overbear the will of one merely made aware of his privilege [to remain silent] by his interrogators." . . . The question before us is whether the warnings Powell received satisfied this requirement.

The four warnings *Miranda* requires are invariable, but this Court has not dictated the words in which the essential information must be conveyed. . . . In determining whether police officers adequately conveyed the four warnings, we have said, reviewing courts are not required to examine the words employed "as if construing a will or defining the terms of an easement. The inquiry is simply whether the warnings reasonably 'conve[y] to [a suspect] his rights as required by *Miranda*.'" . . .

[Here] [t]he Tampa officers did not "entirely omi[t]," any information *Miranda* required them to impart. They informed Powell that he had "the right to talk to a lawyer before answering any of [their] questions" and "the right to use any of [his] rights at any time [he] want[ed] during th[e] interview." The first statement communicated that Powell could consult with a lawyer before answering any particular question, and the second statement confirmed that he could exercise that right while the interrogation was underway. In combination, the two warnings reasonably conveyed Powell's right to have an attorney present, not only at the outset of interrogation, but at all times. . . .

For these reasons, "all . . . federal law enforcement agencies explicitly advise . . . suspect[s] of the full contours of each *[Miranda]* right, including the right to the presence of counsel during questioning." The standard warnings used by the Federal Bureau of Investigation are exemplary. They provide, in relevant part: "You have the right to talk to a lawyer for advice before we ask you any questions. You have the right to have a lawyer with you during questioning." This advice is admirably informative, but we decline to declare its precise formulation necessary to meet *Miranda*'s requirements. Different words were used in the advice Powell received, but they communicated the same essential message.

For the reasons stated, the judgment of the Supreme Court of Florida is reversed, and the case is remanded for further proceedings not inconsistent with this opinion.

It is so ordered.

WHAT DO *YOU* THINK?

1. Did the words offered by the Florida police satisfy the standards of the Fifth Amendment?
2. Does this opinion invite more variation by police officers in providing suspects with *Miranda* warnings?
3. Would it have been more effective for the Court to simply maintain bright-line standards for *Miranda* warnings?

Application to Federal and State Proceedings.   Two years after the 1966 *Miranda* ruling, Congress passed the Omnibus Crime Control Act of 1968, a portion of which was designed to negate the *Miranda* requirements in federal criminal cases. Specifically, under 18 U.S.C. § 3501, Congress declared that pretrial admissions by defendants should not be evaluated based on *Miranda,* but rather should be decided solely on whether they were made voluntarily.

For years, federal courts generally enforced the rigors of *Miranda,* despite the federal law allowing them to disregard it. But in *Dickerson v. United States* (2000),[18] the Supreme Court confronted a lower court ruling that essentially held that the federal law trumped the *Miranda* decision in federal criminal cases. In *Dickerson,* the Supreme Court rejected the lower court's ruling and reaffirmed *Miranda*'s application to federal cases, holding that its requirements were based on the Constitution and therefore prevailed against the federal statute. As a result, the Court ruled that *Miranda* and its progeny govern the admissibility of statements made during custodial interrogation in both state and federal courts.

Timing of *Miranda* Warnings.   Law enforcement authorities must provide Miranda warnings to suspects in custody *prior to* conducting an interrogation. In *Missouri v. Seibert* (2004),[19] police obtained a confession from an arson and homicide suspect without providing *Miranda* warnings. After the confession, police gave the suspect a twenty-minute break before they returned, gave her *Miranda* warnings, and obtained a signed waiver. Police then resumed questioning by confronting the suspect with her pre-*Miranda* statements and getting her to repeat the information. The suspect moved to suppress both her pre-*Miranda* and post-*Miranda* statements. In a 5-4 opinion, the Supreme Court ruled that the suspect's statements were inadmissible. The Court concluded that, under the circumstances, the postinterrogation *Miranda* warnings given could not function "effectively" as *Miranda* requires. According to the Court, "it is likely that if the interrogators employ the technique of withholding warnings until after interrogation succeeds in eliciting a confession, the warnings will be ineffective in preparing the suspect for successive interrogations, close in time and similar in content."

Law Line 12-5
Missouri v. Seibert (2004)

Waiver of Rights

When law enforcement provides *Miranda* warnings, suspects may waive these rights and agree to talk to police. A **waiver** essentially forfeits the rights held by a suspect. If this occurs, the government has the burden of proving that any waiver made by a suspect was made knowingly, intelligently, and voluntarily.[20] Authorities cannot coerce a suspect into waiving Fifth Amendment protections.

In general, in cases where defendants allege that their waiver was coerced, trial courts must consider two primary factors. First, the court must assess whether the defendant's actions were voluntary, which means that they were the product of a free and deliberate choice, as opposed to intimidation, coercion, or deception. And second, the defendant's waiver must have been made with a full awareness both of the nature of the right being abandoned and the consequences of the decision to abandon it. Reviewing the totality of the circumstances, a court must find both an uncoerced choice and a sufficient level of understanding to conclude that that a defendant waived *Miranda* rights.

In addition, more particularized standards for a valid waiver may apply, depending on the situation and jurisdiction. This is particularly true when juveniles are interrogated. Some states provide greater protection for juveniles during custodial interrogations, requiring in some cases that the child's parent, guardian,

waiver
a forfeiture of known rights; must be made knowingly and voluntarily

or attorney be notified prior to an interrogation. For example, the Indiana Code provides the following with respect to waivers provided by children:

IC 31-32-5-1 Waiver of rights guaranteed to child

Sec. 1. Any rights guaranteed to a child under the Constitution of the United States, the Constitution of the State of Indiana, or any other law may be waived only:

1. by counsel retained or appointed to represent the child if the child knowingly and voluntarily joins with the waiver;
2. by the child's custodial parent, guardian, custodian, or guardian ad litem if:
   A. that person knowingly and voluntarily waives the right;
   B. that person has no interest adverse to the child;
   C. meaningful consultation has occurred between that person and the child; and
   D. the child knowingly and voluntarily joins with the waiver; or
3. by the child, without the presence of a custodial parent, guardian, or guardian ad litem, if:
   A. the child knowingly and voluntarily consents to the waiver; and
   B. the child has been emancipated under IC 31-34-20-6 or IC 31-37-19-27, by virtue of having married, or in accordance with the laws of another state or jurisdiction.

The Indiana law and others like it are significant because they provide statutory factors for determining whether juvenile suspects have legally waived their Fifth Amendment rights. In jurisdictions that do not provide statutory protections for juveniles during interrogations, the same factors identified in the Indiana law may still prove to be insightful concerning whether, under the totality of circumstances, juvenile suspects knowingly and intelligently waived their rights. In these circumstances, factors such as the age of the juvenile, the length of detention, the nature and content of any police communications with the juvenile, including whether the juvenile was promised or threatened with anything if she did not cooperate with police, and other indicators of the juvenile's mental state will be important in assessing whether the person executed a legal waiver before talking with police.

In short, in state cases involving waivers, it is important to consider any standards or requirements provided by the state's constitution or statutes. There may be provisions that afford custodial suspects even greater rights than those protected under the Fifth Amendment.

Right to Remain Silent. In cases where a suspect asserts a right to remain silent, prior to or during an interrogation, the police must immediately stop questioning the defendant regarding the particular offense for which he is being interrogated. Suspects may assert this right at any time prior to or during an interrogation. And the Supreme Court has ruled that police cannot restart questioning unless (1) the defendant initiates such questioning on his own; (2) the police seek to ask questions about another offense; or (3) the police "scrupulously honor" the suspect's request not to talk, wait a sufficient amount of time before trying to continue the questioning, and do not coerce the suspect into resuming the questioning.[21]

For example, in *Michigan v. Mosely* (1975),[22] police arrested a suspect in connection with certain robberies and gave him his *Miranda* warnings. In response, the suspect asserted his Fifth Amendment right to remain silent and declined to discuss the robberies. As a result, the detective ceased the interrogation. More than two hours later, another detective seeking to investigate an unrelated murder case met with the suspect and issued a separate set of *Miranda* warnings. This time, the suspect did not assert his right to remain silent and offered an inculpatory statement to the detective regarding the homicide case. This statement was later used to convict the suspect of murder. The Supreme Court upheld the use of the suspect's statement, finding that it did not violate his Fifth Amendment rights under *Miranda*. The Court observed that the suspect's right to stop police questioning was scrupulously honored, the police immediately ceased the robbery interrogation after the suspect asserted his right to remain silent, and the police questioning about the homicide case occurred after a significant lapse of time and after a fresh set of warnings were issued.

Overall, it is important to remember that a suspect's right to remain silent under *Miranda* is generally offense specific. This means that suspects who assert the right to remain silent for one criminal investigation must make another assertion of this right if they are later questioned about a separate and unrelated offense.

Request for Counsel.   In cases where a suspect invokes a right to an attorney, the rule is more clear and strict: police must cease all questioning—even that related to other offenses—until an attorney is provided or until the suspect initiates, on his own accord, additional conversation. According to the Supreme Court in *Edwards v. Arizona* (1981),[23] where a suspect initially asserts the right to have counsel present, any subsequent waiver of this right requires "additional safeguards." Specifically, the Court stated, "a valid waiver of that right cannot be established by showing only that he responded to further police-initiated custodial interrogation even if he has been advised of his rights. . . . [He] is not subject to further interrogation by the authorities until counsel has been made available to him, unless the accused himself initiates further communication, exchanges, or conversations with the police."

But in *Maryland v. Shatzer* (2010), the Court found that, after a suspect has asserted the right to counsel and authorities have stopped all questioning, authorities may seek to reinterrogate the suspect, if they allow the suspect a two-week break between government attempts. This is known as the ***two-week break standard***. Read the Court's opinion in *Shatzer* and consider whether a two-week break between interrogation attempts sufficiently protects a suspect's Fifth Amendment rights.

Law Line 12-6
Edwards v. Arizona (1981)

two-week break standard
a legal standard holding that, after a suspect has asserted the right to counsel and authorities have stopped questioning, they may try to reinterrogate the suspect after a break of two weeks

CAPSTONE CASE *Maryland v. Shatzer,* 559 U.S. ___ (2010).

Justice Scalia delivered the opinion of the Court.

We consider whether a break in custody ends the presumption of involuntariness established in *Edwards v. Arizona*, 451 U.S. 477 (1981).

In August 2003 . . . [Michael] Shatzer was incarcerated at the Maryland Correctional Institution–Hagerstown, serving a sentence for an unrelated child-sexual-abuse offense. Detective Shane Blankenship . . . interviewed Shatzer at the correctional institution on August 7, 2003. Before asking any questions, Blankenship reviewed Shatzer's *Miranda* rights with him, [but] Shatzer declined to speak without an attorney. Accordingly, Blankenship ended the interview, and Shatzer was released back into the general prison population. . . .

On March 2, 2006, [detectives] went to the Roxbury Correctional Institute, to which Shatzer had since been transferred, and interviewed Shatzer in a maintenance room outfitted with a desk and three chairs. . . . [An investigator] then read Shatzer his *Miranda* rights and obtained a written waiver on a standard department form. . . .

At no point during the interrogation did Shatzer request to speak with an attorney or refer to his prior refusal to answer questions without one.

Five days later . . . [a]fter reading Shatzer his *Miranda* rights and obtaining a written waiver, [another] detective administered [a polygraph] test and concluded that Shatzer had failed. When the detectives then questioned Shatzer, he became upset, started to cry, and incriminated himself by saying, "'I didn't force him.

I didn't force him.'" After making this inculpatory statement, Shatzer requested an attorney, and [the detective] promptly ended the interrogation.

[After being charged with child-related sex offenses], Shatzer moved to suppress his March 2006 statements pursuant to *Edwards*. . . .

To counteract the coercive pressure, *Miranda* announced that police officers must warn a suspect prior to questioning that he has a right to remain silent, and a right to the presence of an attorney. After the warnings are given, if the suspect indicates that he wishes to remain silent, the interrogation must cease. Similarly, if the suspect states that he wants an attorney, the interrogation must cease until an attorney is present. . . .

In *Edwards*, the Court determined that [the] traditional standard for waiver was not sufficient to protect a suspect's right to have counsel present at a subsequent interrogation if he had previously requested counsel; "additional safeguards" were necessary. The Court therefore superimposed a "second layer of prophylaxis." . . .

The rationale of *Edwards* is that once a suspect indicates that "he is not capable of undergoing [custodial] questioning without advice of counsel," "any subsequent waiver that has come at the authorities' behest, and not at the suspect's own instigation, is itself the product of the 'inherently compelling pressures' and not the purely voluntary choice of the suspect." . . .

When . . . a suspect has been released from his pretrial custody and has returned to his normal life for some time before the later attempted interrogation, there is little reason to think that his change of heart regarding interrogation without counsel has been coerced. He has no longer been isolated. He has likely been able to seek advice from an attorney, family members, and friends. And he knows from his earlier experience that he need only demand counsel to bring the interrogation to a halt; and that investigative custody does not last indefinitely. In these circumstances, it is far fetched to think that a police officer's asking the suspect whether he would like to waive his *Miranda* rights will any more "wear down the accused," than did the first such request at the original attempted interrogation—which is of course not deemed coercive. . . . Uncritical extension of *Edwards* to this situation would not significantly increase the number of genuinely coerced confessions excluded. . . .

We conclude that such an extension of *Edwards* is not justified; we have opened its "protective umbrella" far enough. The protections offered by *Miranda*, which we have deemed sufficient to ensure that the police respect the suspect's desire to have an attorney present the first time police interrogate him, adequately ensure that result when a suspect who initially requested counsel is reinterrogated after a break in custody that is of sufficient duration to dissipate its coercive effects. . . .

We think it appropriate to specify a period of time to avoid the consequence that continuation of the *Edwards* presumption "will not reach the correct result most of the time." It seems to us that period is 14 days. That provides plenty of time for the suspect to get reacclimated to his normal life, to consult with friends and counsel, and to shake off any residual coercive effects of his prior custody. . . .

Because Shatzer experienced a break in *Miranda* custody lasting more than two weeks between the first and second attempts at interrogation, *Edwards* does not mandate suppression of his March 2006 statements. . . .

It is so ordered.

WHAT DO *YOU* THINK?

1. Is fourteen days a long enough break between interrogations for the underlying purposes of *Miranda* to be satisfied?
2. Was Shatzer really ever released to "normal life" in between interrogations, if he was in prison the whole time?

Exceptions to the Rule

As with many other doctrines of criminal procedure, the Supreme Court has carved out exceptions to the *Miranda* rule and its companion doctrine, the exclusionary rule. These include exceptions involving (1) independent source, (2) inevitable discovery, (3) public safety, (4) harmless error, (5) immunized testimony, (6) grand jury testimony, and (7) impeachment evidence.

Independent Source.   As outlined in Chapter 10, the Court has ruled that, if police can show that the evidence was obtained from a source that was separate or independent from an illegal interrogation, they can still use the evidence. This is called the **independent source rule**. As a result, if police unconstitutionally coerce a suspect into providing incriminating evidence, this evidence may still be used at trial if authorities can demonstrate that the same evidence was also acquired from a proper search of the defendant's home or from another source unrelated to the defendant's statement.[24]

Inevitable Discovery.   Also recall from Chapter 10 that the Court has adopted the **inevitable discovery exception** to the exclusionary rule. This exception allows illegally obtained evidence to be admitted if the government can show that it eventually would have been discovered through proper and constitutional means.[25] Thus, in some cases, evidence gained through an unconstitutional interrogation may still be used at trial if authorities can demonstrate that they would have discovered the evidence eventually without the defendant's statement.[26]

Public Safety.   The Court also has identified a **public safety exception** to the *Miranda* requirement. The details and scope of this exception remain somewhat undefined. But in at least one case, the Court used this exception to allow police to question a suspect in custody without supplying the requisite warnings when the questions were designed to address an imminent matter of public safety.

In *New York v. Quarles* (1984),[27] police pursued an armed suspect into a supermarket and ordered him to stop. Upon frisking the suspect, police discovered that he no longer had the gun he was carrying. Without providing *Miranda* warnings, police then asked the suspect where he put the gun. The suspect nodded toward some empty cartons and responded that "the gun is over there." During pretrial proceedings, the suspect asserted that his pre-*Miranda* statements, as well as all fruits of evidence derived therefrom, should be suppressed. The Supreme Court, however, ruled that the suspect's statements were admissible even though they were provided without *Miranda* warnings. The majority opinion stated, "we do not believe that the doctrinal underpinnings of *Miranda* require that it be applied in all its rigor to a situation in which police officers ask questions reasonably prompted by a concern for the public safety . . . the need for answers to questions in a situation posing a threat to the public safety outweighs the need for the prophylactic rule protecting the Fifth Amendment's privilege against self-incrimination."

More recently, federal authorities cited the public safety exception as justification for their *Miranda*-less interrogation of Faisal Shahzad in relation to a 2010 bombing attempt in New York City's Times Square. In May 2010, federal officials arrested Shahzad under suspicion that he parked a bomb-loaded vehicle in Times Square in an attempt to commit an act of terrorism. The bomb did not explode and no one was injured in the incident. Nonetheless, when authorities took Shahzad into custody, they immediately began to interrogate him without providing any *Miranda* warnings. Department of Justice officials claimed that these warnings were not required because authorities believed that there was an ongoing and immediate threat of terrorism acts related to Shahzad's alleged conduct.

---

independent source rule

an exception to the exclusionary rule in self-incrimination cases; allows testimonial evidence to be admitted without proper *Miranda* warnings, if police can show that the evidence was obtained by a source that was separate or independent from the illegal interrogation

inevitable discovery exception

an exception to the exclusionary rule in self-incrimination cases; allows testimonial evidence to be admitted without proper *Miranda* warnings, if the government can show that it eventually would have been discovered through proper and constitutional means

public safety exception

an exception to the exclusionary rule in self-incrimination cases; allows testimonial evidence to be admitted without proper *Miranda* warnings, if police questions were designed to address an imminent matter of public safety

---

Law Line 12-7
New York v. Quarles (1984)

Officials asserted that this situation qualified as a public safety exception to the *Miranda* rule. After a period of *Miranda*-less questioning, authorities became confident that there were no imminent acts of terrorism planned. At that point, officials purportedly read Shahzad his *Miranda* warnings. According to authorities, Shahzad waived his *Miranda* rights and continued to talk to investigators.

Law Line 12-8
Faisal Shahzad Case

In the end, the scope and substance of the public safety exception is largely unknown. Investigators and courts continue to debate how far and under what circumstances this exception should be applied.

Harmless Error.   The doctrine of harmless error may be relevant when *Miranda*-related issues are argued on appeal or during postconviction proceedings. The **harmless error doctrine** holds that a legal error made during a criminal trial, that did not likely change the outcome of the case, will not result in a reversal of the trial court's judgment. A harmless error is contrasted with a **reversible error**, which is a legal defect that materially altered the outcome of the case. Under the harmless error doctrine, if a reviewing court finds that the defendant still would have been convicted for the same offense(s), even if an incriminating statement or evidence derived therefrom had been excluded, the conviction likely will be sustained.[28]

harmless error doctrine
the principle that a legal error made during a criminal trial that did not likely change the outcome of the case will not result in a reversal of the trial court's judgment

reversible error
a legal defect in a criminal case that materially altered the outcome of the case

As a result, legal professionals generally must show not only that a *Miranda* violation occurred but that the introduction of evidence acquired through this violation had a material impact on the outcome of the criminal case. In some cases, this can easily be shown. For example, in cases where the defendant's statement or confession to police was a critical part of the prosecution's case, the admission of this statement or confession would not likely be found to be harmless. But if the defendant's statements to authorities were only a small part of a large volume of evidence demonstrating the defendant's guilt, the admission of these statements could be found to be harmless. In other words, determining harmless error often depends on a comparative analysis, where the trial court's admission of the defendant's statement is considered in relation to the other evidence of guilt presented by the prosecutor.

Grants of Immunity.   The Fifth Amendment, as well as companion protections under *Miranda* and the exclusionary rule, do not apply to situations where the government has granted immunity to witnesses in exchange for their testimony. As addressed in Chapter 9, **immunity** is a form of legal absolution that ensures witnesses cannot face criminal sanctions based on their testimony. The most common form of immunity is called **use and derivative use immunity**, which is a governmental guarantee that a person's testimony, as well as all evidence derived therefrom, will not be used against the person in a criminal case. If granted immunity from prosecution, a witness can be compelled to provide testimony during a trial or other official proceedings. The theory is that, because immunity removes the possibility of self-incrimination, Fifth Amendment protections are no longer applicable.

immunity
a form of legal absolution that ensures witnesses cannot face criminal sanctions based on their testimony

use and derivative use immunity
a type of immunity where the government guarantees that a person's testimony, as well as all evidence derived therefrom, will not be used against the person in a criminal case

Grand Jury Proceedings.   The Supreme Court has held that *Miranda* warnings are not required prior to a person's grand jury testimony.[29] This is the **grand jury exception** to the *Miranda* rule. Of course, witnesses appearing before grand juries can still assert Fifth Amendment protections against self-incrimination (the right to remain silent), just as they can in civil cases and other official proceedings (see photo of Kenneth Lay). But they are not entitled to have *Miranda* warnings read to them in advance of their testimony, nor are they entitled to have an attorney with them inside the grand jury room. See Chapter 9 (grand juries). Some witnesses, however, have an attorney just outside the grand jury

grand jury exception
an exception that allows statements made without *Miranda* warnings to be introduced to the grand jury

Former Enron Chairman Kenneth Lay raises his right hand as he is sworn in before the Senate Committee on Commerce Science and Transportation February 12, 2002 in Washington, DC. Lay executed his Fifth Amendment right and refused to testify before the Senate Committee that was investigating the collapse of the Enron Corporation.

impeachment exception
an exception that allows statements made without *Miranda* warnings to be used by prosecutors to impeach the defendant's testimony if the defendant testifies during trial

room, and generally, they are permitted to excuse themselves from the grand jury proceedings in order to consult with their counsel.

Impeachment Evidence.   In addition, voluntary (as opposed to involuntary) statements made without a *Miranda* warning can also be used to impeach the defendant's testimony during trial, if he chooses to testify.[30] To impeach a witness is to undermine or challenge the truth or reliability of his testimony. Under the ***impeachment exception*** to the *Miranda* rule, a prosecutor can introduce a defendant's pretrial statement (obtained in violation of *Miranda*) to challenge, undermine, or contradict the defendant's trial testimony. For example, if during a pretrial interrogation a defendant acknowledged knowing the crime victim, but later during trial testimony the defendant denies knowing the victim, the prosecutor can introduce the prior inconsistent statement in order to undermine the credibility of the defendant's testimony.

IN THE FIELD

One of the great challenges for legal professionals in preparing and defending against motions to suppress and custodial interrogations is establishing the facts surrounding the interrogation. See Figure 12-4. As with many situations in criminal cases, the events leading up to a suspect's statements are often a matter of he-said/she-said, where the suspect and the interrogators disagree on what was said and done during the interrogation. Essentially, this is an evidentiary problem. But given this reality, legal professionals should be prepared to address all possible factual scenarios that a trial judge may find in considering a defendant's motion to suppress. In general, this means that you should consider your legal argument under both the best-case and worst-case scenarios of the facts.

But regardless of the facts, the basic outline for reviewing the constitutionality of a defendant's statements, confessions, and other incriminating information is the same. As illustrated in Figure 12-5, legal professionals must ask a series of questions to determine whether a defendant's statements were voluntarily offered and whether law enforcement officials complied with the Fifth Amendment in obtaining these statements.

UNITED STATES DISTRICT COURT
FOR THE DISTRICT OF HAWAII

UNITED STATES OF AMERICA,	)	CASE NO. 2011-1234
	)	
Plaintiff,	)	**MOTION TO SUPPRESS**
v.	)	**STATEMENTS**
	)	
FRANCIS M. JOHNSON,	)	
	)	
Defendant.	)	

Francis Johnson, by and through counsel, moves this Court for an order suppressing all statements taken from her in violation of the Fifth and Sixth Amendments. Ms. Johnson's statements must be suppressed because they were involuntary and because they were obtained in violation of *Miranda v. Arizona*, 384 U.S. 436 (1966). This motion is submitted pursuant to Fed.R.Crim.p. 12(b), and is based upon the Memorandum of Law and the Affidavit of Ms. Johnson filed herewith.

MEMORANDUM OF LAW IN SUPPORT OF MOTION

I. Statement of the Facts

On June 4, 2010, at approximately 8:00 p.m., Special Agents Bob Thomas and Susan James went to the Sixth Avenue Jail to interview Francis Johnson, a suspect in a bank robbery case and the defendant in this matter. Ms. Johnson was taken from her cell and placed in an interview room with the two agents. The agents explained that they knew that she was the woman who robbed the First National Bank back in June and that they wanted to question her. Because Ms. Johnson was in custody, the agents advised her of the rights contained on an FD-395 Interrogation - Advise of Rights Form. Ms. Johnson began to cry and became very emotional. She signed this form, but requested the opportunity to speak with an attorney.

Notwithstanding her request for counsel, the agents remained in the room and obtained biographical information regarding her family, her education, her substance abuse, and her past criminal activities. During the course of the interrogation, Ms. Johnson acknowledged that she robbed the bank on June 1, 2010.

II. Ms. Johnson's Statements Were Obtained By Coercive, Police-Dominated Activity.

Whenever the government seeks to introduce an admission by the accused, it has the burden of proving by a preponderance of the evidence that the statement was voluntarily given. *Lego v. Twomey*, 404 U.S. 477 (1972). The Court must "determine whether, under the totality of the circumstances, the challenged confession was obtained in a manner compatible with the requirements of the Constitution[.]" *Collazo v. Estelle*, 940 F.2d 411, 415 (9th Cir. 1991). An admission is involuntary if it is extracted by any sort of threats or violence or by the exertion of any other improper influence. The test is whether, considering the totality of the circumstances, the government obtained the admission by physical or psychological coercion such that the suspect's will is overborne. *Derrick v. Peterson*, 924 F.2d 813, 817 (9th Cir. 1991).

An evidentiary hearing in this case will demonstrate that the statements at issue resulted from unconstitutional police coercion. Because police agents overbore Ms. Johnson's will to resist, the statement at issue was involuntary and must be suppressed.

III. Ms. Johnson's Statement Was Obtained In Violation Of Her Fifth And Sixth Amendment Rights To Counsel.

Since 1966, law enforcement officers engaged in custodial interrogation of a suspect have been required to recite a prophylactic warning designed to alert the suspect to his or her Sixth Amendment rights. Prior to any questioning, the person must be warned that he has a right to remain silent, that any statement he does make may be used as evidence against him, and that he

(continued)

FIGURE 12-4 **Continued**

has the right to the presence of an attorney, either retained or appointed. *Miranda v. Arizona*, 384 U.S. 436, 344-45 (1966). Whenever custodial interrogation proceeds, the government must demonstrate that the accused "knowingly and voluntarily waived his or her privilege against self-incrimination and his or her right to retained or appointed counsel." *Id.* at 475.

In the instant case, Ms. Johnson was clearly in custody when questioned by the law enforcement officers in this case. She found herself in a "police dominated" environment, far from public view that clearly implicated the coercion associated with custodial interrogation. She also unequivocally expressed the desire to deal with the authorities in this matter through counsel. Notwithstanding her invocation of her Fifth and Sixth Amendment rights to counsel, the agents engaged in the functional equivalent of interrogation in violation of *Rhode Island v. Innis*, 456 U.S. 942 (1982).

IV. Conclusion

For these reasons, Ms. Johnson's statements to the special agents must be suppressed.

Respectfully submitted,

_____

J.Q. ATTORNEY

UNITED STATES DISTRICT COURT
FOR THE DISTRICT OF HAWAII

UNITED STATES OF AMERICA,	)	CASE NO. 2011-1234
	)	
Plaintiff,	)	**AFFIDAVIT OF**
v.	)	**FRANCIS JOHNSON**
	)	
FRANCIS M. JOHNSON,	)	
	)	
Defendant.	)	
	)	

FRANCIS M. JOHNSON, being first duly sworn upon oath, deposes and says as follows:

1. I am the citizen accused in the above styled matter.
2. I remember when the two F.B.I. agents came to see me at the Sixth Avenue Jail.
3. I did not know that they were coming and I was surprised when I was brought to the interview room to speak with them.
4. I remember them telling me that they knew I was the woman that robbed a bank in June 2010.
5. I remember them telling me that they were there to talk with me about the robbery and I remember them advising me of my rights.
6. I remember that I was very upset and that I began to cry. I also remember that I told them that I wanted an attorney.
7. I remember them asking me a lot of questions about my family background and about my criminal history.
8. I remember that I did not want to talk to them without an attorney and I remember that I told them that.

FURTHER YOUR AFFIANT SAYETH NAUGHT.

_____

FRANCIS JOHNSON

Subscribed and sworn to before me this ___ day of February, 2011.

_____

Notary Public in and for Hawaii
My Commission Expires: _____

FIGURE 12-5 **Framework for Evaluating Defendant's Statements**

Is the evidence testimonial in nature (as opposed to physical evidence)?

NO ⇨ No Fifth Amendment violation

YES ⇨ Was statement made voluntarily to police?

    NO ⇨ Unconstitutional interrogation

    YES ⇨ Was statement made while suspect was in law enforcement custody?

        NO ⇨ No Fifth Amendment violation

        YES ⇨ Was statement made during government-led interrogation?

            NO ⇨ No Fifth Amendment violation

            YES ⇨ Did did police provide suspect with *Miranda* warnings?

                NO ⇨ Does the public safety exception apply?

                NO ⇨ Fifth Amendment violation

                    YES ⇨ No Fifth Amendment violation

                    YES ⇨ Did suspect waive these rights knowingly and intelligently?

                        YES ⇨ No Fifth Amendment violation

                        NO ⇨ Fifth Amendment violation

PRETRIAL RIGHT TO COUNSEL

As outlined above, the Fifth Amendment provides protection against self-incrimination even before a person is formally charged with a crime. This includes the right to the assistance of counsel during custodial interrogations. But it is important to note that the Sixth Amendment also contains a right to counsel, which provides additional protections against compulsory statements once adversarial proceedings (usually the filing of a criminal charge) have started. Specifically, the Sixth Amendment states that "[i]n all criminal prosecutions, the accused shall . . . have the assistance of counsel for his defence."

The right to an attorney under the Fifth Amendment and *Miranda* is fundamentally distinct from the right to counsel under the Sixth Amendment. The Supreme Court has interpreted the Sixth Amendment to apply *after* formal charges have been filed against a defendant. The Fifth Amendment right to counsel, however, exists during custodial interrogations that occur before charges have been filed. As a result, in cases where a person provides police with information *after* being charged with a crime, the right to counsel under the Sixth Amendment should also be assessed.

Fifth Amendment Approach

In *Escobedo v. Illinois* (1964),[31] law enforcement officials took the defendant into custody and interrogated him in a police station for the purpose of obtaining a confession. The police did not effectively advise him of his right to remain silent or of his right to consult with his attorney. Rather, they confronted him with an alleged accomplice who accused him of having perpetrated a murder. When the defendant denied the accusation and said, "I didn't shoot Manuel, you did it," they handcuffed him and took him to an interrogation room. There, while handcuffed and standing, he was questioned for four hours until he confessed. During this interrogation, the police denied his request to speak to his attorney, and they prevented his retained attorney, who had come to the police station, from consulting with him.

Law Line 12-9

Escobedo v. Illinois (1964)

The Supreme Court ruled that the statements were constitutionally inadmissible. The Court specifically held that where an investigation is "no longer a general inquiry into an unsolved crime but has begun to focus on a particular suspect," the suspect is effectively in custody and has the right to consult a lawyer. Accordingly, when a suspect requests an attorney, police must comply with the request, even if formal charges have not been filed.

ETHICAL PRINCIPLES

CONFLICTS OF INTEREST
RULE 1.6

National Federation of Paralegal Associations Model Code of Ethics and Professional Responsibility

A PARALEGAL SHALL AVOID CONFLICTS OF INTEREST AND SHALL DISCLOSE ANY POSSIBLE CONFLICT TO THE EMPLOYER OR CLIENT, AS WELL AS TO THE PROSPECTIVE EMPLOYERS OR CLIENTS.

ETHICAL CONSIDERATIONS

1.6(a). A paralegal shall act within the bounds of the law, solely for the benefit of the client, and shall be free of compromising influences and loyalties. Neither the paralegal's personal or business interest, nor those of other clients or third persons, should compromise the paralegal's professional judgment and loyalty to the client.

1.6(b). A paralegal shall avoid conflicts of interest that may arise from previous assignments, whether for a present or past employer or client.

1.6(c). A paralegal shall avoid conflicts of interest that may arise from family relationships and from personal and business interests.

1.6(d). In order to be able to determine whether an actual or potential conflict of interest exists a paralegal shall create and maintain an effective record-keeping system that identifies clients, matters, and parties with which the paralegal has worked.

1.6(e). A paralegal shall reveal sufficient non-confidential information about a client or former client to reasonably ascertain if an actual or potential conflict of interest exists.

1.6(f). A paralegal shall not participate in or conduct work on any matter where a conflict of interest has been identified.

1.6(g). In matters where a conflict of interest has been identified and the client consents to continued representation, a paralegal shall comply fully with the implementation and maintenance of an Ethical Wall.

Courtesy of The National Federation of Paralegal Associations, http://www.paralegals.org

Sixth Amendment Approach

The Court also has ruled that, *after* charges have been filed against a defendant, the Sixth Amendment right to counsel applies. Once the right to counsel has attached and been asserted, the State must honor it. In particular, under the Sixth Amendment law enforcement has an affirmative obligation to respect and preserve the defendant's decision to ask for the assistance of counsel. According to the

Court, this right to counsel attaches at earlier, critical stages of the criminal justice process "where the results might well settle the accused's fate and reduce the trial itself to a mere formality."[32]

In *Massiah v. United States* (1964),[33] the defendant was indicted, along with a codefendant, for conspiracy to possess and to distribute cocaine. The defendant hired an attorney, pleaded not guilty, and was released on bail. The codefendant, however, reached a cooperation agreement with the government and allowed authorities to install a radio transmitter under the front seat of his car. Later, the codefendant had a long conversation with the defendant in the car, while authorities listened over the radio. The defendant's statements during this conversation were later used against him at trial. The Supreme Court, however, reversed this conviction, concluding that the incriminating statements were obtained in violation of the defendant's right to counsel under the Sixth Amendment. The Court emphasized that the interview occurred after the defendant's indictment, a point where he was clearly entitled to the assistance of counsel.

Overall, legal professionals should appreciate that a suspect's right to counsel under the Sixth Amendment can be different from the right to counsel during interrogations, which is protected by the Fifth Amendment. While each right involves the assistance of an attorney, questions about when and whether a person has such a right often depend on the type of proceeding and the nature of the government's conduct.

Critical Stages

Keep in mind that defendants do not enjoy a Sixth Amendment right to be represented by counsel during every phase of litigation that follows the initiation of formal adversarial proceedings. Rather, defendants may only assert this right during **critical stages** of the proceedings. Specifically, the Sixth Amendment right to counsel exists during critical stages of the prosecution "where substantial rights of a criminal accused may be affected."[34]

critical stages
proceedings during a criminal case when the defendant has the right to counsel; includes postindictment lineups, arraignments, and other important stages of the criminal process

The Court's critical stage demarcation has resulted in a long and detailed case analysis to determine which of the many criminal proceedings are considered "critical," thereby resulting in the Sixth Amendment right to counsel, and which are deemed noncritical, resulting in no right to counsel. But generally, a critical stage of prosecution includes every instance in which the advice of counsel is necessary to ensure a defendant's right to a fair trial or in which the absence of counsel might impair the preparation or presentation of a defense. Figure 12-6 outlines the pretrial stages during which a defendant has the right to the presence of counsel, as well as those pretrial stages where such right is not absolute.

Right Is Offense Specific

The Sixth Amendment right to counsel during pretrial critical stages is offense specific. This means that, if the defendant asserts the right to counsel after being charged with one particular offense, police may still question the defendant about a separate and unrelated offense. Of course, in questioning a suspect about another offense, police must issue another set of *Miranda* warnings and the suspect may again assert the right to counsel during this second interrogation.

In *Texas v. Cobb* (2001),[35] state authorities initially charged the defendant with burglary and assigned him an attorney. Later, police questioned the defendant without his attorney present about some murder offenses related to the originally charged burglary offense. The defendant confessed to these murders and the state used this confession to convict the defendant of capital murder. On appeal, the defendant asserted that his confession should have been suppressed because it was

FIGURE 12-6 **Sixth Amendment Right to Counsel During Pretrial Proceedings**

Critical Stages

Preliminary Hearings
  Coleman v. Alabama, 399 U.S. 1 (1970)

Postindictment lineups where the accused is exhibited to a witness
  United States v. Wade, 388 U.S. 218 (1967)

Court-ordered psychiatric exams of defendant
  Estelle v. Smith, 451 U.S. 454 (1981)

Plea hearings where defendant pleads guilty
  Iowa v. Tovar, 541 U.S. 77 (2004)

Postarrest interrogation
  Brewer v. Williams, 430 U.S. 387 (1977)

One-person showup identification procedures
  Moore v. Illinois, 434 U.S. 220 (1977)

Arraignments
  Hamilton v. Alabama, 368 U.S. 52 (1961)

Plea negotiations
  McMann v. Richardson, 397 U.S. 759 (1970)

Noncritical Stages

Taking of blood sample from defendant
  Schmerber v. California, 384 U.S. 757 (1966)

Lineups before the formal charge of a suspect
  Kirby v. Illinois, 406 U.S. 682 (1972)

Postindictment photographic array
  United States v. Ash, 413 U.S. 300 (1973)

Postindictment taking of handwriting exemplars
  Gilbert v. California, 388 U.S. 263 (1967)

Scientific analysis of defendant's fingerprints, clothing, hair, and the like
  United States v. Wade, 388 U.S. 218 (1967)

---

obtained in violation of his Sixth Amendment right to counsel, which he claimed attached when counsel was appointed in the burglary case.

But the Supreme Court disagreed, holding that the Sixth Amendment right to counsel is "offense specific," and therefore it attaches only to charged offenses. The Court ruled that the right to pretrial counsel does not necessarily extend to offenses that are "factually related" to those that have actually been charged. According to the Court, the test to determine whether there are two different offenses or only one is whether each provision requires proof of a fact that the other does not. See Chapter 13 (*Blockburger* test). In *Cobb*, the Court found that, at the time the defendant confessed to the murders, he had been indicted for burglary but had not been charged in the murders. And as defined by Texas law, these crimes were not the same offenses. As a result, the Court concluded that the Sixth Amendment right to counsel did not bar police from interrogating the defendant about the murders.

In cases where counsel is denied to an individual during a critical *pretrial* stage, any evidence gathered by the government as a result of such denial can be excluded from evidence (see below). The other major dimension of the Sixth Amendment right to counsel involves trial-related proceedings, which will be addressed in Chapter 13.

PRETRIAL IDENTIFICATIONS

As specified above, a number of other pretrial identification procedures do not rise to the level of custodial interrogations. These include ***in-person lineups***, where a number of individuals are placed in a line for witnesses to view and identify; one-person ***showups***, where an individual is asked to appear at a particular location for identification purposes; ***photo arrays***, where authorities present a number of photographs to a witness; blood, hair, or tissue samples, where police obtain bodily samples from suspects; ***handwriting exemplars***, where suspects are compelled to provide nontestimonial samples of their handwriting; and ***voice exemplars***, where suspects provide nontestimonial samples of their voice.

     If performed properly, these methods do not compel individuals to provide testimonial forms of evidence, and therefore they ordinarily do not present Fifth Amendment challenges. Nevertheless, pretrial identification procedures can present a number of other legal concerns, as a substantial body of research has questioned the reliability of eyewitness identifications.[36] Indeed, the Supreme Court has recognized that issue:

> [D]espite its inherent unreliability, much eyewitness identification evidence has a powerful impact on juries. . . . All the evidence points rather strikingly to the conclusion that there is almost nothing more convincing than a live human being who takes the stand, points a finger at the defendant, and says, "That's the one!"[37]

As a result, pretrial methods of identification may involve two other constitutional issues—the Sixth Amendment right to counsel and the right to due process of law.

Sixth Amendment

The Sixth Amendment right to counsel during pretrial identification proceedings essentially requires three conditions: (1) the identification must occur after the defendant is charged, (2) the identification must require the defendant's physical presence, and (3) the identification method must involve a trial-like confrontation between the defendant and witness.[38] Thus, generally speaking, the Sixth Amendment right to counsel does not apply to precharge showups or other identification proceedings because the defendant has not been charged. The right does not exist for photo arrays or photographic lineups because the defendant's presence is not required.[39] And the right is not involved where the government is securing blood, DNA, handwriting, or voice samples because these identification methods do not involve trial-like confrontations between the defendant and a witness.

     Defendants, however, have a Sixth Amendment right to counsel during postcharge lineups and showups, which require the defendant's presence and can involve trial-like confrontations. An attorney can observe any suggestive parts of the lineup or showup and use them to challenge the procedure or cross-examine the identifying witness at trial.

State Standards

Some states provide additional protections and procedures for investigators when conducting criminal identifications. For example, in April 2010, the State of Ohio enacted several reforms to the way police conduct custodial interrogations and lineups. The Ohio Justice Reform Act encourages police to electronically record custodial interrogations in cases involving serious offenses. Specifically, the law

in-person lineups
an identification procedure where a number of individuals are placed in a line for witnesses to view and identify

showups
an identification procedure where one person is asked to appear at a particular location for identification purposes

photo arrays
an identification procedure where authorities present a number of photographs to a witness

handwriting exemplar
an identification procedure where suspects are compelled to provide nontestimonial samples of their handwriting

voice exemplars
an identification procedure where suspects provide nontestimonial samples of their voice

provides that all statements made by a person suspected of murder and other homicide offenses, rape, or sexual battery during a custodial interrogation in a place of detention must be "electronically recorded." There is no penalty for police who fail to make such recordings. In fact, the law specifically states that the failure to electronically record a statement, as required under the law, does not provide the basis to exclude or suppress the statement in any criminal proceeding. See O.R.C. 2933.81(C).

In addition, the Justice Reform Act provides that, unless impractical, police lineups must be "double blind." A double-blind lineup is a photo or live lineup that is conducted by someone other than the lead investigator on the case. The notion is that both the officer conducting the lineup and the witness reviewing the lineup will be "blind" as to which person the police believe to be the main suspect. This method is designed to avoid situations where an officer conducting a lineup may send inadvertent body gestures or cues to witnesses, signaling which person the police believe to be the perpetrator of the crime.

The new Ohio law also imposes certain recordkeeping requirements on police who conduct lineups, including the recording of (1) all identification and nonidentification results obtained during the lineup, signed by the eyewitnesses, including the eyewitnesses' confidence statements made immediately at the time of the identification, (2) the names of all persons present at the lineup, (3) the date and time of the lineup, (4) any eyewitness identification of one or more other individuals in the lineup, (5) the names of the lineup members and other relevant identifying information, and (6) the sources of all photographs or persons used in the lineup. And in cases where blind administrators are conducting the live lineup or the photo lineup, they must inform the witness that the suspect may or may not be in the lineup and that the administrator does not know who the suspect is.[40]

Overall, legal professionals should be mindful that there may be additional constitutional and statutory protections and procedures under state law that may inform the constitutionality of pretrial techniques used in state criminal cases.

Due Process

Regardless of whether the Sixth Amendment right to counsel applies, defendants may still challenge pretrial identification procedures if they undermine the right to due process of law. This involves a showing that the manner of identification (1) was unnecessarily suggestive, and (2) produced an unreliable identification (created a substantial likelihood of misidentification).[41] Both factors must be present in order for the identification to be invalid under due process standards. This can be a difficult task for most defendants.

Unnecessary Suggestiveness.   Overly suggestive identifications typically involve three factors. First, the place where a lineup, showup, or other identification is conducted can unfairly taint the impression a witness has of the person being presented for identification. As a result, in *State v. Dubose* (2005),[42] the Wisconsin Supreme Court cautioned that "it is important that showups are not conducted in locations, or in a manner, that implicitly conveys to the witness that the suspect is guilty. Showups conducted in police stations, squad cars, or with the suspect in handcuffs that are visible to any witness, all carry with them inferences of guilt, and thus should be considered suggestive. . . ."

Second, the **prefatory remarks** offered by police to witnesses prior to conducting identifications might also be suggestive. For example, an officer could say to a witness, "We found the person who stole your purse and need you to identify him." Or police might tell a witness, "We found this guy with your wallet,

prefatory remarks
comments offered by police to witnesses prior to conducting identifications

is he the person who took your purse?" These prefatory remarks could function as "a cue for the witness to confirm the suspect as the perpetrator, much like the cue of 'get set' for runners at a track meet to concentrate on and perceive the split second firing of the starting gun."[43]

And third, the person's appearance (particularly clothing) during lineups, showups, or other identifications can also create unfair impressions for witnesses. If a person is shown with handcuffs or in a jail uniform, this may be unduly suggestive, particularly if the other persons presented are not wearing these items. For example, in *Commonwealth v. Johnson* (1995),[44] a Massachusetts court found that a showup procedure was "unnecessarily suggestive" where the suspect was displayed in clothes similar to those allegedly worn by the perpetrator. Similarly, in *State v. Mitchell* (2003),[45] an Ohio court noted that the witness admitted that the suspect's wearing of white shoes played a crucial role in identifying him, where no other person in the lineup was wearing white shoes.

Unreliability.   Where identification procedures are unduly suggestive, they can produce unreliable identifications. As a result, the Supreme Court has found that "reliability is the linchpin in determining the admissibility of identification testimony." In *Neil v. Biggers* (1972),[46] the Supreme Court held that the factors to be considered in evaluating the likelihood of misidentification include (1) the opportunity of the witness to view the suspect at the time of the crime, (2) the witness's degree of attention, (3) the accuracy of the witness's prior description of the suspect, (4) the level of certainty demonstrated by the witness at the confrontation, and (5) the length of time between the crime and the confrontation.

IN THE FIELD

In cases where pretrial identifications have produced evidence that can be used against the defendant at trial, legal professionals likely will be involved with motions to suppress this evidence. See Figure 12-7. This motion is much like other suppression motions and will often lead to the trial court conducting an evidentiary hearing on the matter.

Legal professionals preparing or responding to motions to suppress pretrial identification evidence should ask the following questions:

- When did the identification occur—precharge or postcharge?
- Was the defendant present during the identification?
- What type of identification method was used—lineup, showup, blood test, or other?
- Did the identification method involve a trial-like confrontation between the defendant and the identifying witness?
- Was the defendant's attorney present during the identification?
- Was the identification method unnecessarily suggestive?
- Where did the identification occur?
- What did the police say to the witness before the identification?
- What was the defendant wearing?
- Was the identification reliable?
- Did the witness see the suspect at the time of the crime?
- How attentive was the witness during the crime and identification?
- How certain and accurate was the witness's description of the suspect?
- How much time had passed between the crime and the identification?

FIGURE 12-7 **Sample Motion to Suppress Pretrial Identification (Abbreviated)**

IN THE UNITED STATES DISTRICT COURT
FOR THE DISTRICT OF COLUMBIA

UNITED STATES)	
)	
Plaintiff)	
v.)	**Criminal No. 97-019-01 (EGS)**
)	**(Evidentiary Hearing Requested)**
MICHAEL THOMAS,)	
)	
Defendant.)	

MOTION TO SUPPRESS IDENTIFICATION EVIDENCE

Defendant Michael Thomas, through undersigned counsel, respectfully moves the Court for an Order suppressing as evidence against him at trial testimony about out-of-court and in-court identifications, on the ground that law enforcement officers used identification procedures that were unnecessarily suggestive. The resulting identifications of Mr. Thomas are unreliable and testimony about them should not be permitted at trial.

MEMORANDUM IN SUPPORT

Defendant Thomas has moved the Court for an Order suppressing identification evidence. As set forth below, law enforcement officers used identification procedures in this case that were unnecessarily suggestive and the resulting identification evidence is unreliable. As a result, testimony about out-of-court and in-court identifications should be excluded at trial.

BACKGROUND

According to discovery provided by the prosecution, on December 18, 2009, one (or possibly two) civilian witnesses told Officer Creamer that they had seen a man, wearing all black, who had a gun. At a later point, police conducted a "show-up" identification, and identified Mr. Thomas as a man whom they had seen earlier with a gun.

ARGUMENT

I. LEGAL PRINCIPLES.

Identification evidence must be excluded at trial when police use a pretrial identification procedure so impermissibly suggestive that it gives rise to a "substantial likelihood of irreparable misidentification" in violation of the Due Process Clause. *Manson v. Braithwaite*, 432 U.S. 98, 107 (1977). When a pretrial identification procedure is unnecessarily suggestive, the court must weigh "the corrupting effect of the suggestive identification" against the criteria for a reliable identification, including the opportunity of the witness to view the criminal at the time of the crime, the witness' degree of attention, the accuracy of his prior description of the criminal, the degree of certainty demonstrated at the confrontation, and the time between the crime and the confrontation. *Id*. at 114.

After an out-of-court identification that was unduly suggestive, the prosecution can elicit an in-court identification only after demonstrating that any in-court identification by the witness rests on a source independent of the tainted pretrial identification. *See United States v. Wade*, 388 U.S. 218, 241 (1967). If an out-of-court identification is unreliable and hence inadmissible, any subsequent in-court identification almost always will be inadmissible.

II. APPLICATION OF LEGAL PRINCIPLES.

In this case, police used unnecessarily suggestive identification procedures giving rise to a "substantial likelihood of irreparable misidentification" of Mr. Thomas. Evidence of both the out-of-court and any in-court identifications of Mr. Thomas because the "show up" identification was conducted while Mr. Thomas was in custody, handcuffed, and surrounded by police officers. This procedure itself was tainted, unnecessarily suggestive and unreliable. This scenario

(continued)

FIGURE 12-7 **Continued**

indicates that police used identification procedures that were impermissibly suggestive, giving rise to a "substantial likelihood of irreparable misidentification" of Mr. Thomas. *See Braithwaite*, 432 U.S. at 107.

Mr. Thomas requests an evidentiary hearing on this motion, so that he can demonstrate the unnecessarily suggestive nature of the procedures and the unreliability of the resulting identifications.

CONCLUSION

For the foregoing reasons, and any others which may appear to the Court following a hearing, Mr. Thomas requests that the Court grant a hearing and suppress the identification evidence.

Respectfully submitted,

_____

J.Q. ATTORNEY

CHAPTER **SUMMARY**

- Law enforcement can gain evidence for criminal trials by (1) interrogating suspects, (2) securing identifying evidence from suspects, such as handwriting, fingerprints, and voice samples, and (3) placing suspects in lineups or showups for review by witnesses or victims.
- Defendants sometimes assert the right to the due process of law, as a check on unduly coercive police tactics that yield incriminating information. The due process of interrogations is determined based on whether the suspect's statements, admissions, or confessions were provided to authorities voluntarily.
- Defendants also cite the Fifth Amendment protection against compulsory self-incrimination as a limitation on government interrogations. This right applies to testimony-like evidence obtained by government sources during a custodial interrogation.
- For the right against self-incrimination to apply, (1) the evidence obtained by police must be testimonial in nature, (2) the evidence must be obtained through sufficient government conduct, (3) the person must be in government custody, and (4) the evidence must be obtained through police interrogation.
- If these four factors are present, legal professionals must ask whether *Miranda* warnings were provided before the interrogation; whether these rights were asserted or waived; whether the suspect's rights were honored by the officers; and if not, whether there is a legal exception to the general rule.
- Prior to custodial interrogations, police must inform suspects of their *Miranda* rights, which are the following: (1) they have the right to remain silent; (2) anything they say can and will be used against

them in court; (3) they have the right to the presence of an attorney; and (4) if they cannot afford an attorney, one will be provided for them.
- If a suspect asserts a right to remain silent, prior to or during an interrogation, the police must immediately stop questioning the defendant regarding the particular offense for which he is being interrogated. Police cannot restart questioning unless (1) the defendant initiates such questioning on his own; (2) the police seek to ask questions about another offense; or (3) the police "scrupulously honor" the suspect's request not to talk, wait a sufficient amount of time before trying to continue the questioning, and do not coerce the suspect into resuming the questioning.
- If a suspect invokes a right to an attorney, the rule is more clear and strict: police must cease all questioning— even that related to other offenses—until an attorney is provided or until the suspect initiates, of his own accord, additional conversation. But authorities may seek to reinterrogate the suspect if they allow the suspect a two-week break between government attempts.
- There are a number of exceptions to the *Miranda* rule. These include exceptions involving (1) independent source, (2) inevitable discovery, (3) public safety, (4) harmless error, (5) immunized testimony, (6) grand jury testimony, and (7) impeachment evidence.
- The Sixth Amendment also contains a right to counsel, which provides additional protections against compulsory statements after charges are filed.
- The Sixth Amendment right to counsel exists during critical stages of the prosecution "where substantial rights of a criminal accused may be affected." This

includes preliminary hearings, postindictment lineups, postarrest interrogations, and postcharge showups. But they do not include the taking of blood, voice, or handwriting samples or photo arrays.

- The Sixth Amendment right to counsel during pretrial identification proceedings essentially requires three conditions: (1) the identification must occur after the defendant is charged, (2) the identification must require the defendant's physical presence, and (3) the identification method must involve a trial-like confrontation between the defendant and witness.

- Defendants may still challenge pretrial identification procedures if they undermine the right to due process of law. This involves a showing that the manner of identification (1) was unnecessarily suggestive and (2) produced an unreliable identification.

KEY **TERMS**

critical stages
custodial requirement
government conduct requirement
grand jury exception
handwriting exemplar
harmless error doctrine
immunity
impeachment exception
independent source rule

inevitable discovery exception
in-person lineups
interrogation
Miranda warnings
photo arrays
prefatory remarks
privilege
public safety exception
reversible error

right against self-incrimination
showups
testimonial information
totality of the circumstances
two-week break standard
use and derivative use immunity
voice exemplars
voluntariness requirement
waiver

QUESTIONS FOR **DISCUSSION**

1. What provisions found within the Fifth, Sixth, and Fourteenth Amendments might be involved in assessing the constitutionality of custodial interrogations and other government-led methods of identification?

2. What standards are used to determine whether an interrogation complies with the Due Process Clause?

3. Identify the steps in reviewing police questioning of suspects under the Fifth Amendment.

4. Under what circumstances must police provide suspects with *Miranda* warnings?

5. What is necessary for suspects to properly waive their Fifth Amendment rights?

6. Should there be separate constitutional and statutory standards for judging police interrogations of juveniles?

7. Identify all of the exceptions to the *Miranda* and exclusionary rules under the Fifth Amendment.

8. Under what circumstances might the public safety exception apply?

9. Consider the case of Faisal Shahzad (the Times Square bombing suspect discussed above). Do you find that federal authorities were justified in withholding *Miranda* warnings during the early stages of their interrogation of Shahzad?

10. What is the difference between the right to counsel under the Fifth and the Sixth Amendments?

11. What is a critical stage of pretrial proceedings? Identify four of them.

12. Would it be more effective and easier for the defendant to simply have the right to counsel in any forum where there is government interaction?

13. What constitutional standards are involved in reviewing police lineups, showups, handwriting samples, and voice exemplars?

14. What must a defendant demonstrate to prove that a pretrial method of police identification violated due process protections?

REFERENCES

1. See *Brown v. Mississippi*, 297 U.S. 278 (1936) (police beat defendant to get confession).

2. *Colorado v. Connelly*, 479 U.S. 157 (1986).

3. *Miller v. Fenton*, 474 U.S. 104 (1985).

4. 347 U.S. 556 (1954).

5. 479 U.S. 157 (1986).

6. See *Greer v. Miller*, 483 U.S. 756 (1987) (prosecutor cannot comment on silence after arrest and *Miranda* warnings).

7. See *Gilbert v. California*, 388 U.S. 263 (1967) (handwriting and voice samples); *Schmerber v. California*, 384 U.S. 757 (1966) (blood samples).

8. 447 U.S. 264 (1980).

9. 477 U.S. 436 (1986).

10. See *Orozco v. Texas*, 394 U.S. 324 (1969) (suspect questioned in his bedroom).

11. 394 U.S. 324 (1969).

12. 425 U.S. 341 (1976).

13. 468 U.S. 420 (1984).

14. *Id.* at 442.

15. 446 U.S. 291 (1980).

16. 384 U.S. 436 (1966).

17. 492 U.S. 195 (1989).

18. 530 U.S. 428 (2000).

19. 542 U.S. 600 (2004).

20. See *Colorado v. Spring*, 479 U.S. 564 (1987) (discussing waiver requirements).

21. See *Michigan v. Mosely*, 423 U.S. 96 (1975).

22. *Id.*

23. 451 U.S. 477 (1981).

24. See *Segura v. United States*, 468 U.S. 796 (1984).

25. See *Nix v. Williams*, 467 U.S. 431 (1984).

26. *Id.*

27. 467 U.S. 649 (1984).

28. See *Greer v. Miller*, 483 U.S. 756 (1987); *Arizona v. Fulminante*, 499 U.S. 279 (1991).

29. See *United States v. Wong*, 431 U.S. 174 (1977).

30. See *Mincey v. Arizona*, 437 U.S. 385 (1978).

31. 378 U.S. 478 (1964).

32. *United States v. Wade*, 388 U.S. 218, 224 (1967).

33. 377 U.S. 201 (1964).

34. *Mempa v. Rhay*, 389 U.S. 128, 134 (1967).

35. 532 U.S. 162 (2001).

36. See Patrick M. Wall, *Eye-Witness Identification in Criminal Cases* (Springfield, IL: C.C. Thomas, 1965), pp. 31–33; Brian L. Cutler et al., "Juror Sensitivity to Eyewitness Identification Evidence," *Law and Human Behavior* 14 (1990): 185; Samuel R. Gross et al., "Exonerations in the United States 1989 Through 2003," *Journal of Criminal Law and Criminology* 95 (2005): 523, 542.

37. *Watkins v. Sowders*, 449 U.S. 341, 352 (1981) (Brennan, J., dissenting) (quoting E. Loftus, *Eyewitness Testimony* 19 (1979)).

38. See *Moore v. Illinois*, 434 U.S. 220 (1977); *United States v. Wade*, 388 U.S. 218 (1967).

39. See *United States v. Ash*, 413 U.S. 300 (1973).

40. See http://www.lsc.state.oh.us/analyses128/s0077-ps-128.pdf

41. *Stovall v. Denno*, 388 U.S. 293 (1967).

42. 699 N.W.2d 582, 594 (Wis. 2005).

43. Barbara H. Agricola, "The Psychology of Pretrial Identification Procedures: The Showup Is Showing Out and Undermining the Criminal Justice System," Law and Psychology Review, (Annual 2009).

44. 650 N.E.2d 1257, 1259 (Mass. 1995).

45. No. 21413, 2003 WL 22399720, at *2 (Ohio Ct. App. Oct. 22, 2003).

46. 409 U.S. 188, 199–200 (1972).

APPENDIX
DEVELOPING YOUR LEGAL ANALYSIS

A. THE LAW WHERE YOU LIVE

Assume you are working for a law firm that has been retained to represent Ima Yung, a juvenile facing homicide charges. The state in which you live has charged Ima, who is fifteen years old, with one count of voluntary manslaughter. The state claims that, during a neighborhood fight, Ima took a knife from her parents' kitchen and stabbed the victim to death. Authorities say that, while they were questioning Ima at the police station, she confessed to the crime and told police where to find the knife. Prosecutors plan to introduce Ima's confession, the knife, fingerprints taken from the knife, and blood samples from the knife as evidence during the criminal trial.

Upon review, you learn that Ima's statements to police occurred after she was taken to the police station in a patrol car and placed in a locked room with two police detectives. According to Ima, she was not allowed to call her parents and was denied food and water. Ima says that she initially denied having any involvement with the stabbing incident and asked authorities if she could speak with her parents. Authorities refused to allow Ima to see or talk with her parents. According to Ima, after four hours of being questioned by police, she reluctantly signed a *Miranda* form, thereby waiving her Fifth Amendment rights, and gave police the information they requested.

Your assignment is to examine Ima's case under Fifth Amendment standards, along with any additional legal protections provided by your state for juveniles, custodial interrogations, or waivers, and then prepare a motion to suppress Ima's statements to police and other evidence derived therefrom. Be sure to identify whether your state has special legal procedures for interrogating juveniles and how these procedures might apply to Ima's case.

B. INSIDE THE FEDERAL COURTS

Assume you are working in a U.S. Attorney's office in the criminal division. You are working with an Assistant U.S. Attorney (AUSA) who is assigned to the grand jury room. As a part of your job, you help to coordinate witnesses and exhibits to be presented before grand juries. In one case, the grand jury has subpoenaed Luke Atmee to testify. Mr. Atmee is a witness to a purported federal bank robbery offense, but he fears that he may also be a suspect in the case. As a result, he does not wish to offer any incriminating statements to the grand jury in violation of his Fifth Amendment rights.

During Mr. Atmee's testimony before the grand jury, he has asserted a Fifth Amendment right not to respond to several questions posed by the prosecutor. Specifically, Mr. Atmee has refused to answer the following questions, based on his claim that his responses might tend to incriminate him:

What is your name?
Do your friends call you by any other name?
How tall are you?
How much do you weigh?
How old are you?
Please state the following in a normal tone of voice: "Give me cash; I have a gun."
Print the following in your normal handwriting: "Put the money in this bag; I have a gun."
Do you know the person in this photo?
Where were you on October 22, 2011?

After refusing to answer these questions, the AUSA working with the grand jury wants to seek an order from the magistrate judge assigned to the grand jury compelling Mr. Atmee to answer the questions listed above. But before doing this, the AUSA wants to make sure that he is entitled to gain answers to each of these questions. Accordingly, you are asked to review each question to determine whether Mr. Atmee has a Fifth Amendment right not to answer the individual questions. Prepare a memorandum for the AUSA wherein you outline whether Mr. Atmee has a testimonial privilege to remain silent in the face of these questions or whether the district court can compel him to respond.

C. CYBER SOURCES

Assume you working as an intern for a large police department. The department conducts a lot of lineups, showups, photo arrays, and other identification procedures designed to get eyewitnesses to identify suspects in criminal cases. The department wants to make sure that its procedures for its lineups and other identification methods are reliable and produce the most accurate information for charging individuals with crime. Specifically, the detectives in the department are concerned, after obtaining information from the Innocence Project indicating, that mistaken identifications are a leading cause for wrongful convictions.

The Innocence Project is a national litigation and public policy organization dedicated to exonerating the wrongly convicted through DNA testing and reforming the criminal justice system. It was founded in 1992 at the Benjamin N. Cardozo School of Law at Yeshiva University. To date, 265 people in the United States have been exonerated by DNA testing, including seventeen who served time on death row. Many of the cases where a person was wrongly convicted were based on mistaken identifications of the defendant as a perpetrator of crime.

Accordingly, you are asked to review several of the wrongful conviction cases identified on the Innocence Project's website (below) to determine the causes for misidentifications in criminal cases. Then based on the information you compile, prepare a memorandum wherein you outline the shortcomings associated with police lineups and other identification procedures and make recommendations for addressing these common problems.

Innocence Project Case Profiles, http://www.innocence-project.org/know/Browse-Profiles.php (last visited January 1, 2011).

D. ETHICS AND PROFESSIONALISM

Assume that you are working with Linda Chavez, a well-known and highly-respected criminal defense attorney. You have just received a call from your sister about her fiance, Bill Novak. According to your sister, Bill was arrested last night for driving under the influence of alcohol and needs an attorney. You make arrangements for Bill to meet with Linda the next day. Linda asks you to attend the meeting, so that

you can begin preparing the case. During the meeting, you learn that Bill not only has a DUI charge, but that he also has an outstanding warrant for failing to make child support payments to his former wife. You are quite sure that your sister does not know that Bill had been married or that he has a child. Your sister and Bill are scheduled to be married in three weeks and you believe that your sister would want to know about Bill's former wife and current child. Prepare a two-page memorandum addressing whether you are at liberty to give your sister this information. Also address whether you should have attended the initial meeting between Linda and Bill. In addition to the sections on conflicts of interest and client confidences contained in the following sources, be sure to consider any particular rules that apply in your home jurisdiction.

American Bar Association

http://www.abanet.org/legalservices/paralegals/downloads/modelguidelines.pdf

The American Alliance of Paralegals, Inc.

http://www.aapipara.org/Ethicalstandards.htm

National Federation of Paralegal Associations

http://www.paralegals.org/displaycommon.cfm?an=1&sub articlenbr=133

chapter **thirteen**

RIGHTS TO A FAIR TRIAL: DUE PROCESS, SPEEDY TRIAL, JURIES, COUNSEL, AND DOUBLE JEOPARDY

LEARNING OBJECTIVES

After reading this chapter, you should be able to

- Recognize the many different rights that are associated with affording defendants "the right to a fair trial."

- Identify different forms of prosecutorial and juror misconduct.

- Prepare a basic set of jury instructions for a criminal case.

- Understand the legal standards for speedy trial rights under the Sixth Amendment, the federal Speedy Trial Act, and your local state standards for a speedy trial.

- Understand the nature and scope of a defendant's right to a jury trial.

- Appreciate the factors that might lead defendants to waive their right to a jury trial.

- Recognize the extent of a defendant's rights under the Confrontation Clause.

- Understand the importance of a defendant's right to the effective assistance of counsel and the impact of ineffective assistance of counsel issues during the appeal process.

- Identify the limitations of the right against double jeopardy, including the many exceptions to the double jeopardy rule.

The purpose of a jury is to guard against the exercise of arbitrary power—to make available the commonsense judgment of the community as a hedge against the over- zealous or mistaken prosecutor and in preference to the professional or perhaps overconditioned or biased response of a judge.
—Justice Byron White, *Taylor v. Louisiana* (1965)

All sides in a trial want to hide at least some of the truth.
—Alan Dershowitz

We have a criminal jury system which is superior to any in the world; and its efficiency is only marred by the difficulty of finding twelve men every day who don't know anything and can't read.
—Mark Twain

INTRODUCTION

As noted in Chapter 10, most criminal cases are not resolved through trial. In fact, less than 5 percent of all criminal cases actually go to trial.[1] The rest are resolved during pretrial proceedings, usually in the form of a plea agreement. And when it comes to jury trials in criminal cases, the percentage drops to at or below 1 percent.[2] Thus, despite the hype and attention paid by popular culture to the drama of criminal trials, particularly jury trials, the reality for most legal professionals is that the experience of an actual criminal trial will be the exception, not the rule.

But just because the odds are against a criminal case going to trial does not mean that the rights and procedures associated with trials are insignificant. This is true for at least three reasons. First, in most cases, legal professionals cannot tell at the outset of a case whether it will go to trial. As a result, they need to prepare each case as if it is going to trial. Second, preparing a case for trial, including interviewing all witnesses, examining all evidence, and considering all appropriate legal options, helps to ensure that the defendant and government receive the justice that the system advertises will be given to the parties in a court of law. Even in the vast majority of cases resolved through plea agreement, defense attorneys and prosecutors can instill more confidence in their clients and other affected persons when a case is prepared for trial. Finally, and perhaps most importantly, the strength and success of the parties in plea bargaining often depends on the level and quality of their trial preparation. Legal professionals who are prepared for trial can negotiate plea agreements from a position of strength and achieve better results for their clients when the opposing party believes that a trial is a very real possibility.

RIGHTS TO A FAIR TRIAL

Although people often refer to a defendant's right to a fair trial, this right is not explicitly mentioned in the Constitution. Instead, a defendant's right to a fair trial is composed of many other specific rights and protections found in the Fifth, Sixth, and Fourteenth Amendments.

In the Fifth Amendment, three basic provisions protect defendants during trial. This amendment provides in relevant part:

> No person shall . . . be subject for the same offence to be twice put in jeopardy of life or limb; nor shall be compelled in any criminal case to be a witness against himself, nor be deprived of life, liberty, or property, without due process of law. . . .

The **Self-Incrimination Clause** ensures that defendants are not forced to testify against themselves in a criminal trial, as discussed in Chapter 12. The **Double Jeopardy Clause** provides that government may not punish a person twice for the same offense.[3] And the **Due Process Clause** provides that the federal government may not deprive a person of life, liberty, or property without due process of law. This clause, which is repeated in the Fourteenth Amendment (below), requires, among other things, that government treat individuals fairly during criminal trials. This includes the right to be free from outrageous conduct by prosecutors and judges.[4]

The Sixth Amendment provides several standards for criminal trials. This Amendment states:

> In all criminal prosecutions, the accused shall enjoy the right to a speedy and public trial, by an impartial jury of the State and district wherein the crime

Self-Incrimination Clause
a Fifth Amendment right of defendants not to be forced to testify against themselves in a criminal trial or otherwise give incriminating statements

Double Jeopardy Clause
a Fifth Amendment right providing that government may not try a person twice for the same offense

Due Process Clause
a right, found in both Fifth and Fourteenth Amendments, providing that the government may not deprive a person of life, liberty, or property without due process of law

Speedy Trial Clause
a Sixth Amendment right of individuals to have a speedy trial

Public Trial Clause
a Sixth Amendment right that ensures public criminal trials

Jury Trial Clause
a Sixth Amendment right of individuals to have their criminal cases decided by an impartial jury (as opposed to a judge) within the jurisdiction where the crime was allegedly committed

Information Clause
a Sixth Amendment provision that requires government to notify defendants of the nature and cause of the criminal charges

Confrontation Clause
a Sixth Amendment right of the accused to confront (generally interpreted as to view and cross-examine) any witnesses providing testimony against them

Compulsory Process Clause
a Sixth Amendment right that allows defendants to compel witnesses to appear and testify on their behalf during trial

Assistance of Counsel Clause
a Sixth Amendment right of defendants to have an attorney assist them during criminal trial proceedings

Equal Protection Clause
a right found explicitly in Fourteenth Amendment and implicitly in the Fifth Amendment that serves to protect defendants from unlawful discrimination by judges and prosecutors

harmless error
an error during trial that did not change the outcome of the case

mistrial
the termination of the trial before verdict due to error or surprise

shall have been committed, which district shall have been previously ascertained by law, and to be informed of the nature and cause of the accusation; to be confronted with the witnesses against him; to have compulsory process for obtaining witnesses in his favor, and to have the Assistance of Counsel for his defence.

The **Speedy Trial Clause** provides individuals with a right to a speedy trial.[5] Similarly, the **Public Trial Clause** states that individuals are also entitled to a public trial.[6] The **Jury Trial Clause** provides that individuals have a right to have their criminal cases decided by an impartial jury (as opposed to a judge) within the jurisdiction where the crime was allegedly committed.[7] The **Information Clause** requires government to notify defendants of the nature and cause of the criminal charges. The **Confrontation Clause** provides the accused with the right to confront (generally interpreted as to view and cross-examine) any witnesses testifying against them.[8] The **Compulsory Process Clause** allows defendants to compel witnesses to appear and testify on their behalf during trial.[9] And the **Assistance of Counsel Clause** provides that defendants have the right to an attorney during criminal trial proceedings.[10]

And finally, the Fourteenth Amendment contains two primary protections for criminal defendants during state trials. This amendment states in relevant part:

> [N]or shall any State deprive any person of life, liberty, or property, without due process of law; nor deny to any person within its jurisdiction the equal protection of the laws.

As noted above, the Due Process Clause ensures that defendants are treated fairly by judges, juries, and prosecutors during state trials. And the **Equal Protection Clause** serves to protect defendants from unlawful discrimination by judges and prosecutors.

DUE PROCESS

Many things that occur during trial can deny the defendant the due process of law. Prosecutors can engage in misconduct. Judges can make erroneous rulings on evidence or jury instructions. And jurors can misbehave. There are hundreds, if not thousands, of events that might occur during trial to undermine a defendant's right to due process. But regardless of the type of misconduct or error, the basic constitutional analysis is the same.

First, the behavior, ruling, or event must be unfair or improper. In other words, the identified conduct or event during trial has to fall below some objective standard for legal propriety. This can range from the judge incorrectly applying a rule of law to a juror disregarding instructions for deciding a case. And second, where improper, the conduct or event complained of must also cause the defendant substantial prejudice or harm to the point where it interfered with the ability to receive a fair trial. In other words, the trial error or impropriety must actually cause harm to the defendant's case. If it does not, the error or misconduct might be deemed **harmless error**. See Chapter 12. But where error or misconduct causes prejudice to the defendant's case, it denies this defendant the right to due process of law.

If such a violation occurs during trial and is recognized by the trial court, the judge must declare a **mistrial** (the termination of the trial) or impose some other remedy designed to cure the misconduct and the prejudice (e.g., provide jurors with curative jury instructions). But where the due process violation is recognized by an appellate court, the appropriate remedy is usually the reversal of the defendant's conviction.

Prosecutorial Misconduct

Obviously, in criminal cases, the prosecutor is an adversary to the defendant and typically seeks to secure a conviction. But prosecutors are also public officials who have ethical obligations to pursue broader interests of justice. In addition, like all attorneys, prosecutors are officers of the court, with ethical duties to act within the bounds of professional standards. Given these sometimes competing roles, the Supreme Court has cautioned that a prosecutor may "strike hard blows, [but] he is not at liberty to strike foul ones."[11]

Where prosecutors exceed the bounds of fairness, ethical propriety, or courtroom professionalism, thereby causing prejudice to a criminal defendant, principles of due process are breached. This is identified as *prosecutorial misconduct*. The test for prosecutorial misconduct is whether the prosecutor's actions or remarks are improper and, if so, whether they prejudicially affect the defendant's substantial rights, particularly the right to a fair trial.

According to the Center for Public Integrity,[12] prosecutorial misconduct falls into several categories, including the following:

1. Courtroom misconduct
   - Making inappropriate or inflammatory comments in front of the jury
   - Introducing or attempting to introduce inadmissible, inappropriate, or inflammatory evidence
   - Mischaracterizing the evidence or the facts to the court or jury
   - Using improper methods of jury selection, such as excluding jurors based on race, ethnicity, gender, or some other discriminatory grounds
   - Making improper closing arguments
2. Mishandling of physical evidence
   - Hiding, destroying, or tampering with evidence, case files, or court records
3. Failing to disclose exculpatory evidence
4. Threatening, badgering, or tampering with witnesses
5. Using false or misleading evidence
6. Harassing, displaying bias toward, or having a vendetta against the defendant or defendant's counsel
   - Selective or vindictive prosecution
   - Denial of a speedy trial

One of the more publicized examples of prosecutorial misconduct occurred in 2006, when Michael Nifong, the elected county prosecutor for Durham, North Carolina, initiated sexual assault charges against members of the Duke University lacrosse team. These charges were based on the allegations of a stripper who was hired by members of the Duke men's lacrosse team to perform at a team party. Nifong filed criminal charges despite numerous inconsistencies in the accuser's story, a lack of DNA evidence connecting the players to the alleged sexual assault, and credible alibis for at least two of the accused players. Nifong also made several inflammatory statements to the media. Eventually, the case against the players fell apart and all charges were dropped. Later, the North Carolina State Bar disbarred Nifong for his misconduct during this case.

In cases of prosecutorial misconduct, trial judges have a number of options. In jury trials, judges can admonish the prosecutor and provide instructions to the jury in an attempt to remedy the prejudice caused by the prosecutor's actions. These are known as *curative instructions*. In more severe situations, where the prosecutor's conduct has caused irreparable harm to the defendant, the trial judge can order a mistrial, which terminates the trial proceedings and dismisses the jury.

prosecutorial misconduct
the situation where prosecutors exceed the bounds of fairness, ethical propriety, or courtroom professionalism, thereby causing prejudice to a criminal defendant, contrary to principles of due process

curative instructions
instructions given to the jury in an attempt to remedy prejudice caused by the prosecutor's actions or some other event

Reporters shout questions at Durham County District Attorney Mike Nifong, right, after a community forum to discuss the rape allegations against the Duke lacrosse team in Durham, N.C., April 11, 2006. Later, due to Nifong's unfair and prejudicial actions against defendants in the case, the criminal cases were dismissed and Nifong was disbarred by North Carolina.

In extreme cases, particularly those where the trial judge concludes that the prosecutor's actions were designed to provoke a mistrial or otherwise designed to interfere with the defendant's right to a fair trial, the trial court can dismiss the criminal charges altogether. The difference between a mistrial and a dismissal is that a mistrial stops the trial proceedings but does not end the criminal charges against the defendant, whereas a dismissal eliminates the current indictment or criminal complaint. Of course, the trial judge's failure to take sufficient action to correct the prejudice caused by prosecutorial misconduct may form the basis of an appeal, should the defendant be convicted.

Juror Misconduct

In criminal cases, defendants are entitled to a jury that is unbiased, that rationally decides the facts based on the evidence, and that follows the judge's instructions. Where jurors engage in conduct that undermines these rights, a defendant's right to due process can be compromised. This is known as *juror misconduct*.

juror misconduct
jurors' conduct that undermines a defendant's right to due process and a fair trial

Types of Juror Misconduct. According to the American Judicature Society,[13] there are many types of juror misconduct that can unfairly impact a defendant's criminal trial. These include the following:

1. During jury selection:
   - Giving mistaken answers to voir dire questions or questionnaires
   - Lying in response to voir dire questions or questionnaires
2. Improper contacts:
   - With participants in the case—witnesses, parties, attorneys, the judge, the bailiff or discussing the case with other jurors before deliberations
   - With non-participants in the case—for example, discussing the case with friends or relatives, talking with relatives of a party or witness, or with reporters
3. Misbehavior that interferes with thought processes:
   - Drinking during trial recesses; using illegal drugs during trial
   - Sleeping in court
4. Receiving information not presented as evidence in the case:
   - Visiting the scene of the crime
   - Conducting experiments related to the evidence

- Conducting legal or factual research on the case
- Reading news reports about the case
5. During deliberations:
   - Refusing to participate at all
   - Coercing other jurors
   - Making statements indicating racial or other kinds of prejudice
6. Improper mechanisms for arriving at a verdict:
   - Using a game of chance, such as a coin flip
   - Agreeing to ignore the law
7. Corrupt conduct:
   - Taking a bribe
   - Establishing a close personal relationship with one of the participants in the trial[14]

Time of Discovery.   If juror misconduct is identified before jury deliberations begin, a trial court can often remedy the misconduct by excusing the misbehaving juror and replacing the person with an alternate juror and/or by providing the jury with corrective jury instructions. Where the juror misconduct has tainted the entire jury, the judge can also declare a mistrial. But in cases where jury misconduct is discovered after a guilty verdict is rendered, the typical remedy is to order a **new trial** for the defendant. See Chapter 14. And just like prosecutorial misconduct, if the trial judge fails to take sufficient curative action to address the prejudice caused by juror misconduct, this may form the basis of an appeal from any verdict of conviction.

new trial
a remedy provided in some cases to correct an error during an initial trial

Limits on Jury Misconduct Evidence.   In most jurisdictions, there are evidentiary rules that limit or preclude testimony or other evidence from jurors regarding what occurred during jury deliberations. For example, Federal Rule of Evidence 606(b) states:

(b) Inquiry into validity of verdict or indictment. Upon an inquiry into the validity of a verdict or indictment, a juror may not testify as to any matter or statement occurring during the course of the jury's deliberations or to the effect of anything upon that or any other juror's mind or emotions as influencing the juror to assent to or dissent from the verdict or indictment or concerning the juror's mental processes in connection therewith, except that a juror may testify on the question whether extraneous prejudicial information was improperly brought to the jury's attention or whether any outside influence was improperly brought to bear upon any juror. Nor may a juror's affidavit or evidence of any statement by the juror concerning a matter about which the juror would be precluded from testifying be received for these purposes.

In many cases, courts have applied Rule 606(b) or similar rules to preclude defendants from using posttrial juror statements, affidavits, or testimony to challenge the legal propriety of a jury verdict. But in other cases, courts have found that this statutory evidentiary standard is trumped by the defendant's constitutional right to a fair trial, including the right to an impartial jury that decides cases according to the law.

For example, in *Ohio v. Widmer* (2009), a Warren County, Ohio, jury convicted Ryan Widmer of murdering his wife by drowning her in a bathtub. The case centered on evidence relating to the bathtub and the amount of water found at the scene. The trial court instructed jurors not to engage in any form of independent investigation, and to base their verdict on the evidence introduced during the trial. But days after the jury found the defendant guilty, defense attorneys produced an affidavit from a juror indicating that the jury had considered "home experiments" performed by some of the jurors. See Figure 13-1. Based on this revelation, the trial judge granted the defendant a new trial, finding that his right to a fair trial superseded Ohio's evidentiary rule barring postverdict juror affidavits from being used to challenge a jury verdict.

Jury Instructions

It is certainly no surprise that jurors must decide criminal cases based on the law. Their job is to review all of the evidence presented during trial and evaluate it under the applicable legal standards. But these legal standards are often far from

---

FIGURE 13-1 **Juror Affidavit Used to Successfully Challenge Murder Conviction Based on Juror Misconduct in *State of Ohio v. Widmer***

AFFIDAVIT

State of Ohio   )

) SS:

Warren County   )

        Jon W. Campbell, being first duly cautioned and sworn, deposes and says:

        1.   I served as a juror during the Widmer trial that took place in Warren County beginning March 23, 2009.

        2.   During the first day of jury deliberations, one of the jurors told the rest of us that she did a home experiment by air drying after showering and she told us that it took her 12 minutes to dry.

        3.   On the second day of deliberations another juror indicated that she had done a home experiment air drying and actually laying on the bedroom carpet. She indicated that she was not even dry after 15 minutes.

        4.   Shortly after the second juror talked about the experiment, another juror said she tried to also air dry and that it took her eight minutes and, at the end of eight minutes, her body was substantially dry and her hair was kind of wet.

        5.   Sometime after the disclosure by the jurors of the outside experiments, another juror talked about bathing his child in a tub and lifting him out of the tub. He indicated that there was water on the tub's edge and on the floor and that he decided to return several hours later and everything was still wet.

(continued)

FIGURE 13-1 **Continued**

6.   Based on the experiments as they were related to the rest of us, I believe several of the jurors were influenced and it helped them decide their vote.

7.   After reflection, I felt I had a moral duty to come forth with this information.

Further affiant sayeth naught.

Jon W. Campbell
Jon W. Campbell

Sworn to before me and subscribed in my presence this 9th day of April, 2009.

Kathy Haag Edwards
Notary Public

KATHY HAAG EDWARDS
Notary Public
In and for the State of Ohio
My Commission Expires
September 29, 2012

clear or simple. Instead, the trial court must give the jury the necessary and appropriate legal standards for deciding the case. These are known as ***jury instructions.***

Most jurisdictions have standard jury instructions for all types of criminal cases. These are often called ***pattern jury instructions.*** Judges can simply use these pattern instructions to write the particular instructions for a given case. But in many cases, the parties may ask the judge to read more individualized instructions to the jury to inform them of a certain legal standard or to account for more current interpretations of the law. In these situations, a prosecutor or defense attorney will file a set of ***proposed jury instructions*** with the trial court. See Figure 13-2. This document provides the court with specific instructions, as well as the legal authority supporting them, and asks the court to read these instructions to the jury. In cases where the trial judge refuses to include a defendant's proposed jury instruction or erroneously includes a prosecutor's proposed instruction (often over the defense attorney's objection), and the trial court's actions cause material prejudice to the defendant, such actions can deny defendants the due process of law and may serve as a basis for reversing a jury's verdict of conviction.

One of the most frequently debated jury instructions is that defining the government's burden of proof in criminal cases—beyond a reasonable doubt.

jury instructions
directions and explanations about law and fact given by the trial judge to the jury; they provide the standards to be used to evaluate the evidence against the defendant.

pattern jury instructions
standard jury instructions within a given jurisdiction for all types of criminal cases

proposed jury instructions
requested instructions for the jury submitted by the prosecutor or defense attorney

Obviously, there are many different ways this legal standard can be defined. In the highly publicized 1995 murder trial of O. J. Simpson, Judge Lance Ito instructed the jury:

> Reasonable doubt is defined as follows. It is not a mere possible doubt, because everything relating to human affairs is open to some possible or imaginary doubt. It is that state of the case which, after the entire comparison and consideration of all the evidence, leaves the minds of the jurors in that condition that they cannot say they feel an abiding conviction of the truth of the charge.

FIGURE 13-2 **Example of Defendant's Proposed Jury Instructions**

**IN THE UNITED STATES DISTRICT COURT
FOR THE DISTRICT OF COLUMBIA**

UNITED STATES	)	
	)	
Plaintiff,	)	
	)	
v.	)	**Criminal No. 2011-025(PCD)**
	)	
ROBERT SMITH,	)	
	)	
Defendant.	)	

DEFENDANT'S PROPOSED JURY INSTRUCTIONS

Defendant Robert Smith, through undersigned counsel, respectfully proposes the following jury instructions. Unless otherwise identified, the numeric references are taken from *Criminal Jury Instructions for the District of Columbia* (4th ed. 1993).

I. GENERAL INSTRUCTIONS
1.08 Expert Testimony
1.10 Evaluation of Prior Inconsistent Statement
2.05 Statements of Counsel
2.06 Indictment Not Evidence
2.08 Burden of Proof - Presumption of Innocence

Additional Requested Instruction regarding burden of proof:

The government has the burden of proving the defendant guilty beyond a reasonable doubt. In civil cases, it is only necessary to prove that a fact is more likely true than not, or, in some cases, that its truth is highly probably. In criminal cases such as this one, the government's proof must be more powerful than that. It must be beyond a reasonable doubt. Reasonable doubt, as the name implies, is a doubt based upon a reason -a doubt for which you have a reason based upon the evidence or lack of evidence in the case. If, after careful, honest, and impartial consideration of all the evidence, you cannot say that you are firmly convinced of the defendant's guilt then you have a reasonable doubt.

Reasonable doubt is the kind of doubt that would cause a reasonable person, after careful and thoughtful reflection, to hesitate to act in the graver or more important matters in life. However, it is not an imaginary doubt, nor a doubt based on speculation or guess work; it is a doubt based upon reason. The government is not required to prove guilt beyond all doubt, or to a mathematical or scientific certainty. Its burden is to prove guilt beyond a reasonable doubt. *Smith v. United States,* 709 A.2d 78, 82 (D.C. 1998) (en banc)

(continued)

FIGURE 13-2 **Continued**

II. INSTRUCTIONS ON CHARGED OFFENSE (18 U.S.C. § 922(g)(1))

4.79 Possession of Firearm

Additional requested instruction regarding Mr. Smith's prior conviction:

The only relevance of Mr. Smith's prior conviction is for purposes of determining whether Mr. Smith falls into the category of individuals who are covered by the statute. This prior conviction should <u>not</u> in any way be considered by you for purposes of determining whether it is more likely or less likely that Mr. Smith possessed a handgun on February 25th. Rather, you may only consider the prior conviction in determining whether the government has met its burden of establishing this specific element of the offense.

III. CLOSING INSTRUCTIONS

2.72 Unanimity
2.73 Exhibits During Deliberations
2.75 Communications Between Court and Jury During Jury's Deliberations

Respectfully submitted,

J.A. Attorney

J.A. Attorney
555 Iowa Avenue, N.W., Suite 555
Washington, D.C. 20004
(555) 555-5555

But in other cases and jurisdictions, reasonable doubt has been defined differently. For example, in *Cage v. Louisiana* (1990),[15] jurors were told:

> [A reasonable doubt] is one that is founded upon a real tangible substantial basis and not upon mere caprice and conjecture. *It must be such doubt as would give rise to a grave uncertainty*, raised in your mind by reasons of the unsatisfactory character of the evidence or lack thereof. A reasonable doubt is not a mere possible doubt. *It is an actual substantial doubt*. It is a doubt that a reasonable man can seriously entertain. What is required is not an absolute or mathematical certainty, but a *moral certainty* (emphasis added).

The Supreme Court found that these instructions violated the defendant's right to due process because the words *substantial* and *grave*, especially when used in conjunction with moral certainty, suggest a higher degree of doubt than is required for acquittal under the reasonable doubt standard. According to the Court, the use of these instructions could cause a reasonable juror to find guilt based on a degree of proof below that required by the Due Process Clause.

Legal professionals working on jury trials must pay close attention to the instructions given by the trial court to jurors. In many cases, legal professionals must prepare a list of proposed jury instructions with supporting legal authorities and provide this list to the court in advance of trial. These proposed instructions should describe the legal standards for the case in a way that is most favorable to the client. And where the instructions ultimately adopted by the court appear misleading, unfair, or incomplete, objections must be raised so that this issue can be preserved for possible appellate review. The bottom line with jury instructions is that words matter. And where there is a "reasonable likelihood" that a particular jury instruction caused a jury to misapply the law, the defendant's rights to due process may be violated.[16]

Unfair Surprise or Undue Influence

In rare cases, situations may develop during trial that are simply unexpected, and as a result, they cause unfair prejudice to the defendant's case. Witnesses may disclose embarrassing or prejudicial facts previously ruled inadmissible by the trial judge; there may be outbursts from courtroom observers; or the parties may discover new and material information in the middle of trial. Where these surprises unfairly prejudice the defendant's case, they can deny them due process of law.[17]

In *Estelle v. Williams* (1976),[18] the Court ruled that, under the Due Process Clause, authorities cannot compel any defendant to stand trial before a jury while dressed in identifiable prison clothes. But in *Holbrook v. Flynn* (1986),[19] the Court held that the presence of four uniformed state troopers sitting immediately behind the defendant during a jury trial was not so inherently prejudicial that it denied the defendant a fair trial. In both cases, the Court stated that the question in these trial situations is whether there is "an unacceptable risk" that "impermissible factors" will influence the jury. Similarly, in *Carey v. Musladin* (2006), the Court refused to reverse the murder conviction of a defendant on the ground that the courtroom spectators, including three family members of the murder victim, wore buttons visually depicting the victim.

On a more local level, during the vehicular homicide trial in *Ohio v. Kortum* (2000),[20] the defense attorney used information provided by the prosecutor to tell the jury that the legal speed limit for the road where the fatal accident occurred was 45 miles per hour. Later during the trial, the prosecutor informed the court that he had just learned that the speed limit was actually 55 miles per hour. Based on this revelation, the defense attorney moved for a mistrial, which the court denied. The jury convicted the defendant of vehicular homicide, but the appeals court reversed, finding that the defendant was denied a fair trial when the prosecution changed an important fact during the middle of the case. According to the appellate court, the surprise discovery undermined the credibility of the defendant's attorney before the jury because he could no longer support his original assertion to jurors that the speed limit was 45 miles per hour.

Excessive Publicity

The Sixth Amendment generally ensures that as a part of the basic *right to a public trial*, most trial proceedings will be open to the public. But in extremely rare occasions, trials or pretrial proceedings may be closed to the public if such closure is necessary to ensure the defendant receives a fair trial. For example, in *Sheppard v. Maxell* (1966),[21] the Supreme Court ruled that a murder defendant was denied a fair trial because the trial court failed to protect him from the massive, pervasive, and prejudicial publicity surrounding his trial. In most cases, however, where defendants may want to close or limit public access to their criminal proceedings, two competing constitutional rights—the First Amendment freedom of the press and the Sixth Amendment guarantee to a public trial—usually dissuade trial judges from closing the proceedings.[22]

Where extreme forms of publicity might influence criminal proceedings, trial judges have a number of options. First, in nearly all criminal trials, judges instruct jurors not to read or otherwise avail themselves of media accounts of the trial. In fact, this is a standard jury instruction.

Second, in state cases, the trial judge can limit the number of cameras in the courtroom, allowing a single camera to be positioned in the courtroom, with multiple connections for media outside the room. Of course, in most federal trial courts, cameras are prohibited altogether. Instead, sketch artists are permitted to make visual renderings of the proceedings.

Third, in rare cases, the trial judge may change the venue (location) of the trial. A ***change of venue*** moves the trial to another geographic location, where the residents summoned for jury duty are not as likely to have been subjected to the level of pretrial publicity as those in the original venue. Federal Rule of Criminal Procedure 21 provides:

change of venue
a trial court's order to move the trial to another geographic location

---

(a) For Prejudice.

Upon the defendant's motion, the court must transfer the proceeding against that defendant to another district if the court is satisfied that so great a prejudice against the defendant exists in the transferring district that the defendant cannot obtain a fair and impartial trial there.

(b) For Convenience.

Upon the defendant's motion, the court may transfer the proceeding, or one or more counts, against that defendant to another district for the convenience of the parties and witnesses and in the interest of justice.

In cases where defendants file motions for a change of venue (see Law Line 13-3), trial judges often wait until after voir dire (the initial questioning of the jury) to determine whether pretrial publicity has unduly influenced the jury pool.

And finally, in extreme cases, trial judges can sequester the jury during the proceedings. ***Jury sequestration*** involves isolating jurors in a controlled location (hotel), where their access to media and other influences can be removed. This procedure is rarely employed. But in particularly high-profile jury trials, where media attention will be overwhelming, jury sequestration can be an effective way of maintaining the integrity of the trial process.

jury sequestration
an order by the trial court to isolate jurors during a criminal trial

Law Line 13-3
Motion for Change of Venue Filed by Timothy McVeigh

IN THE FIELD

Keep in mind that a defendant's right to due process during trial proceedings can be affected by many and events. For legal professionals working with defendants, it is important to identify any and all forms of potentially prejudicial and unfair forms of courtroom behavior and bring them to the attention of the trial court through an objection or motion for a mistrial. In many situations, a defendant's right to assert these due process violations on appeal can be compromised or, in some cases, waived, if counsel does not timely and properly notify the trial court of the problem.

For professionals working with prosecutors, it is important to respond to any and all defense claims of misconduct or due process violations. Where these claims may have merit, prosecutors can try to mitigate any prejudice to the defendant by encouraging the trial judge to issue curative instructions to the jury or take other corrective action that does not rise to the level of a mistrial or dismissal of the case.

SPEEDY TRIAL

The *right to a speedy trial* is designed to ensure that defendants are not held in custody for unreasonable periods of time before their trial. Under the Sixth Amendment, the right to a speedy trial usually begins when the defendant is arrested or charged with a criminal offense.[23] The Supreme Court, however, has not provided a clear definition of what constitutes a speedy trial. In fact, in *Barker v. Wingo* (1972),[24] the Court has stated that a defendant's constitutional right to a speedy trial cannot be established by any inflexible rule, but can be determined only on an ad hoc balancing basis in which the conduct of the prosecution and that of the defendant are weighed. More specifically, under the *Wingo* analysis, the Court evaluates pretrial delays based on the totality of the circumstances, which includes an assessment of the length of and reason for the delay, whether the defendant asserted his rights, and the nature and extent of prejudice to the defendant caused by the delay.

For example, in *Doggett v. United States* (1992),[25] the Court held that federal authorities violated a defendant's speedy trial rights when they failed to make reasonable efforts to apprehend the defendant after he was indicted. The Court applied the *Wingo* test and found (1) the government's delay was excessively long—eight and one-half years between the defendant's indictment and his trial; (2) the government was to blame for the delay because it failed to pursue the defendant after indictment; (3) the defendant asserted his right to a speedy trial in due course; and (4) the pretrial delay prejudiced the defendant's ability to prepare an adequate defense.

But in *Vermont v. Brillon* (2010),[26] the Court found that trial delays caused by a public defender did not violate a defendant's right to a speedy trial. In *Brillon*, the defendant's trial was held three years after he was charged. During this time, the defendant was held in pretrial custody. Much of the delay was caused by the fact that the court-appointed attorneys representing the defendant were unprepared for trial, were fired, or failed to move the case to trial. In a 7-2 ruling, the Supreme Court concluded that court-appointed attorneys representing defendants should not be treated as state actors for speedy trial considerations. According to the Court, "[a]ssigned counsel, just as retained counsel, act on behalf of their clients, and delays sought by counsel are ordinarily attributable to the defendants they represent."

Like most other rights, a defendant's right to a speedy trial—under both constitutional and any statutory protections—can be waived, and in many cases, defendants agree to waive their speedy trial rights in order to afford their attorneys more time to prepare for trial. A ***speedy trial waiver*** is valid if the defendant voluntarily and intelligently agrees to waive the right to a speedy trial. In most criminal cases, particularly those involving serious offenses, the trial court requires the defendant to sign a written waiver form and the judge will make sure the defendant understands this waiver before it will be accepted.

speedy trial waiver
a defendant's abdication of the right to a speedy trial

Speedy Trial Act

It is important to note that the federal government and many states have enacted more specific statutes that govern a defendant's speedy trial rights. These statutes establish more detailed standards and timetables for bringing a defendant to trial. At the federal level, the ***Speedy Trial Act of 1974***[27] generally requires a federal criminal trial to begin within seventy days after a defendant is charged or makes an

Speedy Trial Act of 1974
a federal statute that generally requires a federal criminal trial to begin within seventy days after a defendant is charged or makes an initial appearance, whichever is later

initial appearance, whichever is later. If this timetable is not met, the district court must dismiss the case, although the court may choose whether to do so with or without prejudice to the government. A ***dismissal with prejudice*** means that the prosecutor cannot indict the defendant again on the same charges. A ***dismissal without prejudice*** allows the prosecutor to seek another indictment against the defendant on the same charges.

There are, however, several types of delays that are not counted toward this seventy-day time period. Under the act, some delays automatically do not count toward the seventy-day limitation. These include delays "resulting from any proceeding, including any examinations, to determine the mental competency or physical capacity of the defendant" and delays resulting from any interlocutory appeal. But other delays, such as those caused by a request for a continuance or a request for additional time to file pretrial motions, will count toward the seventy-day time period, unless the district court specifically finds that "the ends of justice served by taking such action outweigh the best interest of the public and the defendant in a speedy trial." These findings must be placed on the record of the case, either orally or in writing.

In *Zedner v. United States* (2006),[28] the defendant's trial did not start within seventy days of the indictment. In fact, the trial did not begin until more than *seven years* after the indictment. But during pretrial proceedings, the defendant, at the suggestion of the trial judge, signed a blanket, prospective waiver of his rights under the act. This document purportedly waived defendant's speedy trial rights "for all time" during the case. After the waiver was signed, the trial court granted continuances in the case, but because of the prospective waiver, the court did not make specific findings on the record to support the granting of these continuances. The trial court found that this waiver tolled the time requirements of the Speedy Trial Act. The Supreme Court, however, ruled that the defendant's prospective waiver did not operate to stop the speedy trial clock for all future delays. Instead, pursuant to the statutory requirements of the Speedy Trial Act, the trial judge was required to make specific findings before granting continuances in the case.

Similarly, in *Bloate v. United States* (2010), under the Speedy Trial Act the defendant's indictment on federal firearm and drug possession charges started the seventy-day clock on August 24, 2006. After the defendant's arraignment, the district court ordered the parties to file pretrial motions by September 13. On September 7, the court granted the defendant's motion to extend that deadline. But on the new due date (September 25), the defendant waived his right to file pretrial motions. On October 4, the district court found this waiver to be voluntary and intelligent. During the next three months, the trial was delayed several times, often at the defendant's request. On February 19, 2007 (179 days after the defendant was indicted), he moved to dismiss the indictment, claiming that the act's seventy-day limit had elapsed.

On appeal, the government claimed that the Speedy Trial Act automatically excludes from the seventy-day period "delay resulting from . . . proceedings concerning the defendant" and that the defendant's request for time to file pretrial motions should be classified under this automatic tolling section. But the Supreme Court held that the time granted to *prepare* pretrial motions is not automatically excludable from the seventy-day limit under subsection (h)(1). Instead, such time may be excluded only when a district court grants a continuance based on appropriate findings under § 3161(h)(7), which was not done in this case. As a result, the Court found that the defendant's speedy trial rights were violated.

dismissal with prejudice
the trial court's dismissal of criminal charges in such a way that the prosecutor cannot recharge the defendant on the same offenses

dismissal without prejudice
the trial court's dismissal of criminal charges in a way that allows the prosecutor to seek another indictment or charge against the defendant on the same offenses

Law Line 13-4
Speedy Trial Act

For legal professionals, it is important to realize that most speedy trial issues will be governed by the statutory requirements of speedy trial legislation within the governing jurisdiction of the criminal court. These statutory standards can be quite detailed and lengthy. To assist in calculating how much "countable" time has elapsed under a speedy trial law, it is often helpful to prepare a chart outlining the amount of time that has passed since the defendant was charged or made an initial appearance before the court, the reasons for any delays in the case, and the findings made by the trial court in issuing any orders of continuance or extension.

In some settings, practitioners have created computer applications that allow them to calculate a defendant's speedy trial status. For example, in Florida, lawyers have constructed a speedy trial calculator, which is an "app" for certain electronic devices and is designed to help attorneys with speedy trial calculations. This app uses statutory requirements to assess both misdemeanor and felony speedy trial calculations for Florida criminal cases.

RIGHT TO JURY TRIAL

The text of the Sixth Amendment states that "[i]n all criminal prosecutions, the accused shall enjoy the right to a speedy and public trial, by an impartial jury. . . ." In addition, Article III, section 3 of the Constitution provides, "[t]he Trial of all Crimes, except in Cases of Impeachment, shall be by Jury; and such Trial shall be held in the State where the said Crimes shall have been committed. . . ." The Sixth Amendment right to a jury trial has been incorporated through the Fourteenth Amendment.[29] It therefore applies to both state and federal criminal cases. But despite the textual language of the Sixth Amendment suggesting that the right to a jury trial exists in *all* criminal cases, there are a number of important caveats with regard to this right.

Serious versus Petty Offenses

First, the Sixth Amendment right to a jury does not exist in all criminal cases. Instead, this right depends on the nature of the offense with which the defendant is charged. The Supreme Court has ruled that the Sixth Amendment right to a jury trial exists only with regard to criminal cases involving ***serious offenses***, which are offenses for which a defendant could receive more than six months of imprisonment. If a person faces six months or less of incarceration, the offense is referred to as a ***petty offense***, and there is no constitutional right to a jury trial.[30] To determine whether an offense is petty, legal professionals must consider the maximum penalty attached to the offense within the statute. According to the Supreme Court, this criterion is the most relevant factor for judging the character of an offense because it reveals the legislature's judgment about the offense's severity.

And even where a defendant is charged with multiple petty offenses in the same case, the Sixth Amendment right to a jury trial does not apply, even though the total amount of imprisonment might exceed six months. In *Lewis v. United States* (1996),[31] the Supreme Court ruled that there is no constitutional right to a jury trial where a defendant is prosecuted for multiple petty offenses. In *Lewis*, the defendant was charged with two petty offenses, each carrying the possibility of a six-month jail term, thereby presenting the possibility of a twelve-month sentence. Given the possible total jail time, the defendant asserted that he was entitled to a jury trial. But the Supreme Court disagreed, finding that because the Sixth Amendment right to a jury

serious offenses
offenses for which a defendant could receive more than six months of imprisonment

petty offense
a criminal charge where the defendant faces six months or less of incarceration

trial does not extend to petty offenses, its scope does not change where a defendant faces a potential aggregate prison term in excess of six months for petty offenses charged.

Realize, however, that under many state constitutional and statutory standards, defendants are eligible for jury trials if they can be sentenced to *any* jail time. In other words, many states afford defendants a jury trial in all criminal cases, except those involving minor misdemeanors where defendants typically are not incarcerated. As a result, in state cases, defendants often receive greater access to jury trial under their state law than under the Sixth Amendment.

Jury Size and Unanimity

Second, while twelve-member juries are the norm in American criminal cases, the Supreme Court has ruled that the Sixth Amendment does not entitle defendants to a jury of this size. Instead, the Court has ruled that there must be at least six jurors to decide a case. But again, many state constitutions and statutes have supplemented the Court's standards by requiring larger jury memberships—typically twelve jurors in felony cases.

The Supreme Court has permitted states to adopt jury standards that deviate from the traditional federal jury standard of twelve members who must reach a unanimous verdict. Specifically, in *Williams v. Florida* (1970),[32] the Court found a six-member jury constitutional. But in *Ballew v. Georgia* (1978), the Court found that a Georgia law allowing criminal juries of just five persons violated the Sixth Amendment rights of defendants.

In reality, however, all federal criminal courts use a twelve-person jury, and only a handful of states allow juries of less than twelve for felony trials. In misdemeanor cases, roughly half of all states allow juries with fewer than twelve members. In these jurisdictions, misdemeanor cases are often decided by six-member juries.

With regard to the unanimity of criminal juries, the Supreme Court has held that a guilty verdict from a twelve-person jury need not be unanimous. Instead, a nine-vote guilty verdict is constitutionally permissible. In two cases heard together—*Apodaca v. Oregon* (1972)[33] and *Johnson v. Louisiana* (1972)[34]—the Court reviewed two laws allowing guilty verdicts based on nonunanimous jury verdicts. In 5-4 rulings, the Court upheld an Oregon law allowing convictions based on 10-2 verdicts, and a Louisiana law permitting convictions based on verdicts of 9-3. But in *Burch v. Louisiana* (1979),[35] the Court found that another Louisiana law, which authorized criminal convictions based on 5-1 verdicts, violated the Sixth Amendment right to a jury trial. As a result, if a court uses a six-person jury in a criminal case, a guilty verdict must be unanimous.

Despite the Court's Sixth Amendment standards, federal statutes and most state laws require a unanimous verdict in both felony and misdemeanor cases. All states except Louisiana and Oregon require unanimous verdicts in felony cases, while only a few states permit nonunanimous verdicts in misdemeanor cases.

Waiver

And finally, in most state jurisdictions, a defendant can unilaterally waive the right to a jury trial and have the case decided by a judge. In other words, the decision to have a jury trial belongs exclusively to the defendant. A waiver is typically exercised in two instances—where the defendant wishes to proceed with a **bench trial** (have the judge decide the case) and where the defendant wishes to enter a plea of guilty or no contest with the court.

Law Line 13-5
"Trial Juries: Size and Verdict Rules"

bench trial
a trial before a judge, as opposed to a jury

FIGURE 13-3 **Sample Waiver of Right to Jury Trial**

FORM 32 - WAIVER OF JURY TRIAL PURSUANT TO RULE 26.01, SUBD. 1(2)(a)

STATE OF MINNESOTA   DISTRICT COURT
COUNTY OF _____   _____ JUDICIAL DISTRICT

_____,   WAIVER OF JURY TRIAL
                 Plaintiff,   PURSUANT TO RULE 26.01,
                                          SUBD. 1(2)(a)

vs.

_____,
                 Defendant.   District Court File No. ____

   Having been advised by the Court of my right to trial by jury and having had an opportunity to consult with counsel, I do hereby, with the approval of this Court, waive my right to trial by jury.

Dated: _____   _____
                                                   (Defendant)

                             APPROVED BY:

                             _____
                             Judge of District Court

But in federal cases, the defendant, the prosecutor, and the trial court must consent to a nonjury trial. Under Federal Rule of Criminal Procedure 23(a), a defendant is entitled to a jury trial and the trial must be by jury unless (1) the defendant waives a jury trial in writing, (2) the government consents, and (3) the court approves. As a result, there are very few bench trials in the federal system. Of course, a defendant wishing to enter a guilty plea before a federal court can waive the right to a jury trial and proceed with the trial court's adjudication of guilt. See Figure 13-3.

To make a valid waiver, defendants must understand their right to a jury trial and voluntarily agree to waive this right. Some jurisdictions impose additional requirements. For example, Ohio Revised Code Section 2945.05 provides that a waiver of a jury trial must be in writing, signed by the defendant, and filed with the court record in order to be effective. This provision also requires that all waivers of jury trials "be made in open court after the defendant has been arraigned and has had opportunity to consult with counsel."

Legal professionals should be mindful that waivers of jury trials are often strictly scrutinized by trial and appellate courts. For example, in *State v. Burnside* (2010),[36] an Ohio court of appeals reversed a defendant's bench trial conviction because his jury waiver was performed in the trial judge's chambers and not in open court, as required under Ohio law. According to the court, the requirements for jury waivers under Ohio law must be followed strictly in order to be valid. And because the trial court did not have the defendant acknowledge the jury waiver in open court before conducting the bench trial, it did not comply with Ohio law.

Related Sentencing Issues

In recent years, the Supreme Court has used the Sixth Amendment right to a jury trial to strike down some sentencing laws at the state and federal levels. During the 1980s and 1990s, many states and the federal government passed sentencing regulations that allowed judges to enhance a defendant's sentence beyond the statutory maximum penalty if aggravating factors, such as the use of a gun or the infliction of extreme cruelty, were present in the case. Under a typical scenario, a defendant would be convicted of an offense during trial and then, during sentencing, a judge would make a number of additional factual findings that were not found by the jury and use them to increase the defendant's sentence.

The Supreme Court, however, has ruled that allowing judges to enhance a defendant's sentence based on facts that are not decided by a jury or admitted by the defendant (typically within a plea agreement) violates a defendant's Sixth Amendment right to have a jury decide all relevant facts used for assessing criminal culpability. In *Blakely v. Washington* (2004),[37] the Court struck down state sentencing practices that allowed judges to increase a defendant's sentence based on facts not found by a jury or admitted to by the defendant. And in the combined cases of *United States v. Booker* and *United States v. Fanfan* (2005),[38] the Court invalidated similar judicial fact-finding practices under the federal sentencing guidelines. A more thorough discussion of these cases is provided in Chapter 14.

Law Line 13-6
United States v. Booker and *United States v. Fanfan* (2005)

EQUAL PROTECTION

The constitutional right to equal protection, as protected by the Fifth Amendment's Due Process Clause in federal cases, and by the Fourteenth Amendment's Equal Protection Clause in state cases, provides criminal defendants with certain procedural safeguards at trial. In general, equal protection standards ensure that the government does not unfairly discriminate against defendants based on arbitrary and prohibited classifications, such as race, sex, ethnicity, or religion. Equal protection claims arise in two primary contexts—the decision to charge individuals with a criminal offense and the government's method for selecting juries.

Selective Prosecution

Constitutional equal protection standards dictate that police and prosecutorial decisions on whether to prosecute an individual may not be based on an arbitrary classification such as race, sex, religion, or another arbitrary classification. When such decisions are based on these or other prohibited criteria, this is referred to as selective prosecution.[39] To prove a selective prosecution claim under federal equal protection standards, a defendant must demonstrate that the prosecutorial policy had a discriminatory effect and was motivated by a discriminatory purpose. For example, to establish a discriminatory effect in a race case, the claimant must show that similarly situated individuals of a different race were not prosecuted.

In many cases, a defendant may suspect selective prosecution but not have the evidence to back it up. After all, much of the evidence needed to support such a claim, if it exists, is often held by the government, and the defendant would need to obtain it through discovery (see Chapter 10). In *United States v. Armstrong* (1996),[40] the Supreme Court ruled that, in order for defendants to establish a right to such discovery, they must produce credible evidence that similarly situated defendants of other races (or other prohibited criteria) could have been prosecuted but were not. This is a difficult evidentiary burden for most defendants.

For example, in *United States v. Bass* (2002),[41] the defendant asserted that the government chose to seek the death penalty against him based on his race. The District Court and Sixth Circuit Court of Appeals found that the defendant was entitled to discovery on this claim and ordered the government to supply the defendant with the appropriate materials. The Sixth Circuit concluded that the defendant had shown, based on nationwide statistics, that the government charges blacks with death-eligible offenses more than twice as often as it charges whites and that it enters into plea bargains more frequently with whites than with blacks. On review, however, the Supreme Court reversed the lower court's ruling, finding that the defendant's nationwide statistics did not constitute a credible showing that similarly situated individuals of a different race were not prosecuted with death penalty charges. According to the Court, "[e]ven assuming that a nationwide showing can satisfy the *Armstrong* requirement, raw statistics regarding overall charges say nothing about charges brought against similarly situated defendants. And the plea bargain statistics are even less relevant, since respondent declined the plea bargain offered him."

Jury Selection

Equal protection guarantees also ensure that fair and impartial juries are selected in criminal cases. Jury selection typically involves court administrators issuing a summons (see Chapter 9) to residents living within the court's jurisdiction, requiring them to appear in court for jury duty. Once convened in the trial court and assigned to a particular courtroom, these residents responding to the summons constitute the jury pool or **venire** from which the trial court will select the trial jury. Members of the venire are questioned by the trial judge and/or attorneys about their backgrounds and their abilities to serve on the jury. This process is known as **voir dire** (to speak the truth).

During voir dire, the prosecutor and defense attorney can challenge members of the venire, which may lead to their exclusion from the jury. These challenges come in two forms—for cause and peremptory. **Challenges for cause** assert that there is good reason for excluding a person from the jury. Cause might be based on an assertion that the person is biased or prejudiced against parties involved in the case or may demonstrate other inabilities to serve as a fair and impartial member of the jury. When attorneys raise a challenge for cause, they must offer a reason for seeking to exclude the targeted juror. **Peremptory challenges**, however, allow attorneys to remove jurors without giving the court or opposing counsel a reason for the dismissal. Typically, an attorney exercising a peremptory challenge will simply say, "we would like to thank and excuse juror number five." Under normal circumstances, an attorney making a peremptory challenge does not have to provide a reason for excluding a juror. But if evidence exists that a prosecutor might be using peremptory challenges to systematically exclude jurors based on their race or sex, the defendant can object to such use on equal protection grounds. This is generally referred to as a **Batson challenge**.

In *Batson v. Kentucky* (1986),[42] the Supreme Court ruled that, under the Equal Protection Clause, prosecutors cannot exclude potential jurors from serving on a jury solely based on their race or based on "the assumption that black jurors as a group will be unable impartially to consider the State's case against a black defendant." In *Batson*, the prosecutor used his peremptory challenges to strike all four black persons on the venire, and a jury composed only of white persons was selected. Although the defendant objected to the prosecutor's actions, the trial court did not investigate the matter by requiring the prosecutor to justify his exclusion based on race-neutral criteria. The Supreme Court reversed and remanded the case for such an inquiry. The Court stated, "[w]hile the peremptory challenge occupies an important position in trial procedures, the above-stated principles will not undermine the contribution that the challenge generally makes to the administration of justice." Later, in *J.E.B. v. Alabama ex rel. T.B.*, (1994),[43] the Court imposed the same restriction with regard to the exclusion of jurors based on sex.

venire

the jury pool or group of citizens from which a jury is selected

voir dire

the process by which members of a jury venire are questioned by the trial judge and/or attorneys about their backgrounds and their abilities to serve on the jury; means "to speak the truth"

challenge for cause

the removal of a potential juror for good reason

peremptory challenge

the removal of a potential juror without providing a reason or cause

Batson challenge

an attorney's challenge of an opposing party's peremptory challenge, asserting that it is based on race or sex

When defense attorneys assert a *Batson* challenge, they must first show the trial court that the prosecutor used peremptory challenges to exclude jurors who have the same race or sex. Upon making this showing, the trial court will require prosecutors to provide a race-neutral or gender-neutral reason (depending on the nature of the *Batson* challenge) for excluding the identified group of jurors. The prosecutor may not rebut the defendant's assertions by claiming that the excluded group would be partial to the defendant because of their shared race or sex. If the prosecutor is able to demonstrate credible and neutral reasons for the peremptory challenges, the trial court will allow the exclusions and the jury selection typically will continue. But if the prosecutor is unable to make the requisite showings, the trial judge will find an equal protection violation. As a remedy, trial judges may have to declare a mistrial and dismiss the rest of the members of the venire. Where *Batson* violations are not recognized until an appeal, the conviction will be overturned.

Read the Supreme Court's opinion in *Snyder v. Louisiana* (2008), where the Court conducted a *Batson* analysis of the prosecutor's exclusion of African-American jurors in a death penalty case. Notice how challenging it is to determine whether a prosecutor is actually using race as a factor in excluding potential jurors.

Law Line 13-7
Batson v. Kentucky (1986)

CAPSTONE CASE *Snyder v. Louisiana*, 552 U.S. 472 (2008)

Justice Alito delivered the opinion of the Court.

Petitioner Allen Snyder was convicted of first-degree murder in a Louisiana court and was sentenced to death. He asks us to review a decision of the Louisiana Supreme Court rejecting his claim that the prosecution exercised some of its peremptory jury challenges based on race, in violation of *Batson v. Kentucky*, 476 U. S. 79 (1986) . We hold that the trial court committed clear error in its ruling on a *Batson* objection, and we therefore reverse. . . .

Voir dire began on Tuesday, August 27, 1996. . . . [After different phases of this process were complete], [e]ighty-five prospective jurors were questioned as members of a panel. Thirty-six of these survived challenges for cause; 5 of the 36 were black; and all 5 of the prospective black jurors were eliminated by the prosecution through the use of peremptory strikes. The jury found petitioner guilty of first-degree murder and determined that he should receive the death penalty. . . .

Batson provides a three-step process for a trial court to use in adjudicating a claim that a peremptory challenge was based on race: "'First, a defendant must make a prima facie showing that a peremptory challenge has been exercised on the basis of race[; s]econd, if that showing has been made, the prosecution must offer a race-neutral basis for striking the juror in question[; and t]hird, in light of the parties' submissions, the trial court must determine whether the defendant has shown purposeful discrimination.'" . . .

Petitioner centers his *Batson* claim on the prosecution's strikes of two black jurors, Jeffrey Brooks and Elaine Scott. Because we find that the trial court committed clear error in overruling petitioner's *Batson* objection with respect to Mr. Brooks, we have no need to consider petitioner's claim regarding Ms. Scott. . . .

When defense counsel made a *Batson* objection concerning the strike of Mr. Brooks, a college senior who was attempting to fulfill his student-teaching obligation, the prosecution offered two race-neutral reasons for the strike. The prosecutor explained:

"I thought about it last night. Number 1, the main reason is that he looked very nervous to me throughout the questioning. Number 2, he's one of the fellows that came up at the beginning [of *voir dire*] and said he was going to miss class. He's a student teacher. My main concern is for that reason, that

(continued)

(*continued*)

being that he might, to go home quickly, come back with guilty of a lesser verdict so there wouldn't be a penalty phase. Those are my two reasons."...

With respect to the first reason, the Louisiana Supreme Court was correct that "nervousness cannot be shown from a cold transcript, which is why ... the [trial] judge's evaluation must be given much deference."... Here, however, the record does not show that the trial judge actually made a determination concerning Mr. Brooks' demeanor....

The second reason proffered for the strike of Mr. Brooks—his student-teaching obligation—fails even under the highly deferential standard of review that is applicable here. At the beginning of *voir dire*, when the trial court asked the members of the venire whether jury service or sequestration would pose an extreme hardship, Mr. Brooks was 1 of more than 50 members of the venire who expressed concern that jury service or sequestration would interfere with work, school, family, or other obligations....

A comparison between Mr. Brooks and Roland Laws, a white juror, is particularly striking. During the initial stage of *voir dire*, Mr. Laws approached the court and offered strong reasons why serving on the sequestered jury would cause him hardship. Mr. Laws stated that he was "a self-employed general contractor," with "two houses that are nearing completion, one [with the occupants] ... moving in this weekend." He explained that, if he served on the jury, "the people won't [be able to] move in." Mr. Laws also had demanding family obligations....

If the prosecution had been sincerely concerned that Mr. Brooks would favor a lesser verdict than first-degree murder in order to shorten the trial, it is hard to see why the prosecution would not have had at least as much concern regarding Mr. Laws....

[I]n light of the circumstances here—including absence of anything in the record showing that the trial judge credited the claim that Mr. Brooks was nervous, the prosecution's description of both of its proffered explanations as "main concern[s]," and the adverse inference noted above—the record does not show that the prosecution would have pre-emptively challenged Mr. Brooks based on his nervousness alone....

We therefore reverse the judgment of the Louisiana Supreme Court and remand the case for further proceedings not inconsistent with this opinion.

It is so ordered.

WHAT DO *YOU* THINK?

1. Absent a clearly inconsistent statement or excuse offered by a prosecutor for excluding minorities from the jury, how might a defendant demonstrate that prosecutors used race to exclude jurors?

2. Should it matter whether minorities were intentionally excluded by the prosecutor or whether, as a matter of demographics, a jury lacks members from a particular segment of the population? In other words, should both intentional and unintentional forms of racial exclusion from juries be deemed unconstitutional?

Juries Drawn from Fair Cross Section of Community

One right that promotes equal protection and fairness in criminal cases is the Sixth Amendment right of criminal defendants to an impartial jury drawn from a fair cross section of the community. Essentially, this constitutional protection ensures that government does not seek to systematically exclude members of distinctive groups when establishing jury pools for criminal cases.

In *Duren v. Missouri* (1979),[44] the Supreme Court outlined the requirements for proving prima facie violation of the Sixth Amendment's requirement of a fair cross section. The defendant must show "(1) that the group alleged to be excluded is a 'distinctive' group in the community; (2) that the representation of this group in venires from which juries are selected is not fair and reasonable in relation to the number of such persons in the community; and (3) that this underrepresentation is due to systematic exclusion of the group in the jury-selection process." This is known as the **Duren test**. In most cases, the first requirement is often easily shown, but the second and third standards are often more challenging.

In *Duren*, the defendant met all three requirements. He identified women as being underrepresented in the county's jury pool used for his trial. He established that women were 54 percent of the jury-eligible population but accounted for only 26.7 percent of the persons summoned for jury service. And he identified a Missouri law exempting women from jury service, as well as the manner in which the trial court administered this exemption, as the form of systematic government exclusion. As a result, the Court held that the county's method for identifying jurors violated the defendant's Sixth Amendment right to a jury drawn from a fair cross section of the community.

But in *Berghuis v. Smith* (2010), the Court ruled that a murder defendant failed to support his assertion that there were too few African-Americans in a state court's jury pool. The defendant claimed that there were only three African-Americans in the pool of sixty to one hundred prospective jurors, and none of them made it into the final thirty-seven considered for his trial's panel. To support the third prong of the *Duren* test, the defendant, in part, claimed that the county's assignment procedure for prospective jurors systematically excluded African-Americans by assigning prospective jurors first to local district courts and, only after filling local needs, making remaining persons available to the countywide Circuit Court, which heard felony cases like the defendant's. The defendant called this a "siphoning" procedure. But the Court rejected this argument under federal habeas corpus rules, finding that, because the Supreme Court had never identified this form of systematic exclusion, the state court's ruling rejecting the defendant's claim must be upheld, as it did not violate a clearly established principle of the Supreme Court. In addition, the Court found that absolute disparity and comparative disparity measurements can be misleading when, as here, "members of the distinctive group comp[ose] [only] a small percentage of those eligible for jury service." According to the Court, "[n]o court . . . has accepted [a standard deviation analysis] alone as determinative in Sixth Amendment challenges to jury selection systems."

Duren test
the standard used to judge whether the defendant's Sixth Amendment right to a jury composed of a fair cross section of the community is violated

Law Line 13-8
Berghuis v. Smith (2010)

CONFRONTATION CLAUSE

The Sixth Amendment provides that "[i]n all criminal prosecutions, the accused shall enjoy the right . . . to be confronted with the witnesses against him." This is known as the Confrontation Clause and it generally allows defendants the opportunity to cross-examine the prosecutor's witnesses and examine and challenge any other testimonial evidence presented by the government during trial. In short, this right allows defendants to confront those who "bear testimony" against them.

In most cases, this right is easily and readily afforded to defendants by allowing their defense attorneys to cross-examine the prosecutor's witnesses. But in some cases, confrontation issues can be a bit more complicated. For example, in *Giles v. California* (2008),[45] a defendant was convicted of murder during a trial in which prosecutors introduced the victim's statements made during a domestic violence call. The defendant objected to the admission of these statements, claiming that his rights of confrontation were violated because he could not confront the victim-witness at trial. The prosecutor, however, countered that the defendant had essentially forfeited his rights of confrontation by killing the victim. The State further argued that the admission of statements by a dying victim was a recognized exception to the hearsay rule under California's Rules of Evidence. The Supreme Court rejected those claims, finding that the Sixth Amendment right of defendants to confront adverse witnesses superseded any state rule on evidence. The Court also ruled that the State's theory of forfeiture was not an exception to the Confrontation Clause because it was not recognized at the time of the adoption of the Sixth Amendment.

Similarly, in *Melendez-Diaz v. Massachusetts* (2009),[46] a state prosecutor introduced a drug laboratory chemist's written analysis to demonstrate the weight and nature of drug evidence in a drug case. The prosecutor asserted that the state's rules of evidence allowed the admission of the report without the testimony of the chemist because it was a certified and notarized document produced by a state official. The defendant, however, objected, asserting that he had a right to confront the "testimony" of the lab technician who produced the report. On review, the Supreme Court agreed with the defendant, ruling that admitting the lab chemist's written analysis into evidence, without having him testify, violated the Confrontation Clause. In a 5-4 ruling, the Court identified the information in the lab technician's report as being testimonial in nature and held that it could be introduced only if the defendant had the opportunity to cross-examine the lab technician who conducted the testing.

Overall, for legal professionals who face these types of unique and challenging confrontation issues during trial, two important factors must be evaluated. First, the Confrontation Clause applies to testimony-like information. As a result, it will apply to any documents or other tangible evidence that contains information akin to that offered as testimony by a witness during trial. And second, if prosecutors wish to assert an exception to the right of confrontation, they must demonstrate that the exception was recognized by the founders who adopted the Sixth Amendment.

Law Line 13-9
Melendez-Diaz v. Massachusetts
(2009)

THE RIGHT TO COUNSEL

The Sixth Amendment provides that "[i]n all criminal prosecutions, the accused shall . . . have the assistance of counsel for his defence." As addressed in Chapter 12, the right to counsel is also protected under the Fifth Amendment as a part of the right against self-incrimination. The primary difference is that the Supreme Court has interpreted the Sixth Amendment to apply after formal charges have been filed against a defendant, while the Fifth Amendment right to counsel during custodial interrogation can be present even before charges have been filed. But the Court also has ruled that, even after a defendant has been charged, the Sixth Amendment right to counsel applies only to "critical stages" of the prosecution "where substantial rights of a criminal accused may be affected."[47] Trial-related proceedings are generally deemed to be critical stages under the Sixth Amendment.

Nature of the Right

The right to counsel under the Sixth Amendment is grounded in the Supreme Court's landmark ruling in *Gideon v. Wainwright* (1963).[48] In that case, Clarence Gideon was charged by Florida authorities with breaking and entering a pool hall—a noncapital felony. Gideon, however, did not have the money to retain an attorney for the case and asked the Florida trial court to appoint counsel for him. The judge, however, denied this request, finding that the state law permitted appointment of counsel for indigent defendants only in capital cases. Gideon later went to trial representing himself. He was convicted and sentenced to a term of imprisonment. But the Supreme Court reversed Gideon's conviction, ruling that the right of an indigent defendant in a criminal trial to have the assistance of counsel is a fundamental right essential to a fair trial, and Gideon's trial and conviction without the assistance of counsel violated the Sixth Amendment right to counsel and the Fourteenth Amendment right to due process. In short, *Gideon* established that criminal defendants have a constitutional right to an attorney during state criminal proceedings and that, if they cannot afford an attorney, the court is required to appoint one.

Later in *Argersinger v. Hamlin* (1972),[49] the Supreme Court held that the Sixth Amendment right of an indigent criminal defendant to the assistance of counsel is not limited to cases involving felony or nonpetty offenses. In that case, a Florida court denied an indigent defendant the right to appointed counsel in a misdemeanor case, where the defendant faced up to six months in jail and received a ninety-day jail sentence, finding that the right to counsel applies only to nonpetty offenses. But the Supreme Court reversed this judgment, ruling that no defendant may be deprived of his liberty as the result of any criminal prosecution, whether felony or misdemeanor, in which he was denied the assistance of counsel.

But in *Scott v. Illinois* (1979),[50] the Court ruled that, in misdemeanor cases, the Sixth Amendment right to counsel applies only where defendants actually receive a term of incarceration as a part of their criminal sentence. In *Scott*, an Illinois trial court denied the right to appointed counsel to an indigent defendant charged with shoplifting, an offense that carried a maximum penalty of one year in jail. The trial court convicted the defendant and imposed a $50 fine as the sentence. The defendant appealed this conviction, claiming that he was entitled to the appointment of counsel because his offense carried the possibility of imprisonment. The Supreme Court, however, rejected this argument, ruling that the Sixth and Fourteenth Amendments do not require trial courts in misdemeanor cases to appoint counsel for criminal defendants charged with offenses for which imprisonment is authorized but not imposed.

Thus, as a matter of constitutional law, the Sixth Amendment right to counsel during trial proceedings applies to all felony trials and in those misdemeanor cases where imprisonment is actually imposed (as opposed to cases where jail time is a possibility).[51] Keep in mind too that in state criminal cases, there may be state constitutional or statutory rights to counsel that provide greater protections to criminal defendants than those afforded under the Sixth Amendment.

In the end, however, the reality is that most trial courts in misdemeanor cases cannot predict whether a defendant charged with a jail-eligible offense will actually receive a sentence of incarceration. Thus, as a matter of administrative practicality, judges in misdemeanor cases typically appoint attorneys to represent indigent defendants if there is a possibly the defendants could eventually be imprisoned or jailed—regardless of whether the defendant actually receives jail time or the length of the sentence.[52] In cases where the government wrongly denies a defendant the right to be represented by counsel during eligible court proceedings, or the defendant receives ineffective assistance of counsel (see below) during such proceedings, adverse rulings or conviction by the trial court can be reversed.

Law Line 13-10
Gideon v. Wainwright (1963)

Law Line 13-11
Scott v. Illinois (1979)

An unidentified ten-year-old boy (L) listens as his public defender explains his right to counsel while being questioned by police during an appearance in a Milwaukee County Children's courtroom in Wauwatosa, Wisconsin, October 3, 2002.

Appointment of Counsel

public defenders

government attorneys who represent indigent defendants in criminal cases

In many jurisdictions, indigent defendants are represented by government attorneys known as ***public defenders***. These individuals are defense attorneys who work for a public defender's office. Generally, they are government employees who get paid a regular salary, regardless of the number or nature of cases they handle. In other jurisdictions, the task of representing indigent defendants is handled or shared by appointed counsel—typically attorneys in private practice who agree to be appointed by the trial court as the assigned counsel for an indigent defendant. ***Appointed attorneys*** are paid by the court for the work they do on a particular case.

appointed attorneys

private attorneys who are appointed by courts to represent indigent clients in criminal cases

For many legal professionals working for defendants or as court administrators, the Sixth Amendment right to counsel involves preparing, reviewing, and processing payment claims filed by appointed attorneys. See Figure 13-4. In most cases, court payments for appointed attorneys are capped or limited by the jurisdiction based on the type and nature of the case. In most jurisdictions, appointed counsel must submit a reimbursement form to the court in order to get paid. To complete these forms, legal professionals must properly account for the time and nature of the work spent on a case.

Waiver

pro se

representing oneself during court proceedings; means "for yourself"

Of course, the right to counsel, like other constitutional rights, can be waived by defendants if their decision to represent themselves is made knowingly and intelligently. This is known as ***pro se*** (for yourself) counsel or representation. Defendants

FIGURE 13-4 **Sample Reimbursement Form for Appointed Counsel**

MOTION, ENTRY, AND CERTIFICATION FOR APPOINTED COUNSEL FEES

In the _____ Court of _____, Ohio

Plaintiff: _____

Case No. _____

Appellate Case No. (if app.) _____

v.

☐ Capital Offense Case (*check if Capital Offense case*)
☐ Guardian Ad Litem (*check if appointed as GAL*)

Defendant/Party Represented

In re: _____ Judge: _____

MOTION FOR APPROVAL OF PAYMENT OF APPOINTED COUNSEL FEES AND EXPENSES

The undersigned having been appointed counsel for the party represented moves this Court for an order approving payment of fees and expenses as indicated in the itemized statement herein. I certify that I have received no compensation in connection with providing representation in this case other than that described in this motion or which has been approved by the Court in a previous motion, nor have any fees and expenses in this motion been duplicated on any other motion. I, or an attorney under my supervision, have performed all legal services itemized in this motion.

☐ Periodic Billing (*check if this is a periodic bill*)

As attorney/guardian ad litem of record, I was appointed on _____, _____. This case terminated and/or was

disposed of on _____,_____. I am submitting this application on _____, _____.

Name_____ Signature_____

Address_____ SSN/Tax ID_____
　　　No. and Street　　　　　　　　*City*　　　*State*　*Zip*　OSC Reg. No. _____

SUMMARY OF CHARGES, HOURS, EXPENSES, AND BILLING

OFFENSE/CHARGE/MATTER	ORC/CITY CODE	DEGREE	DISPOSITION
1.)			
2.)			
3.)			

List only the three most serious charges beginning with the one of greatest severity and continuing in descending order.

		IN-COURT			
Grand Total Hours From Other Side:	OUT-OF-COURT	PRE-TRIAL HEARINGS	ALL OTHER IN-COURT	IN-COURT TOTAL	GRAND TOTAL

☐ Flat Fee　Hrs:In _____ X Rate _____ = $_____ Tot. Fees $_____

☐ Min Fee　Hrs:Out _____ X Rate _____ = $_____ Expenses $_____ Total $_____

JUDGMENT ENTRY

The Court finds that counsel performed the legal services set forth on the itemized statement on the reverse hereof, and that the fees and expenses set forth on this statement are reasonable, and are in accordance with the resolution of the Board of County Commissioners of _____ County, Ohio relating to payment of appointed counsel, that all rules and standards of the Ohio Public Defender Commission and State Public Defender have been met.

IT IS THEREFORE ORDERED that counsel fees and expenses be, and are hereby approved, in the amount of $_____.
It is further ordered that the said amount be, and hereby is, certified by the Court to the County Auditor for payment.

☐ *Extraordinary fees granted (copy of journal entry attached)*　Judge _____
　　　　　　　　　　　　　　　　　　　　　　　　　　　　Signature　　　　　　　　　*Date*

CERTIFICATION

The County Auditor, in executing this certification, attests to the accuracy of the figures contained herein. A subsequent audit by the Ohio Public Defender Commission and/or Auditor of the State which reveals unallowable or excessive costs may result in future adjustments against reimbursement or repayment of audit exceptions to the Ohio Public Defender Commission.

County Number _____ Warrant Number _____ Warrant Date _____

County Auditor _____

(continued)

do not need to show that they are competent in the law or even capable of representing themselves. They only need to show that they are sufficiently competent to make of valid waiver of their rights. This course of action, however, generally is not recommended and has led to the expression "the person who represents himself has a fool for a client."

Ineffective Assistance of Counsel

One of the most dynamic questions under the Sixth Amendment right to counsel is whether a person who had counsel during criminal proceedings actually received sufficient and competent service from the defense attorney. Under the Sixth

FIGURE 13-4 **Continued**

CASE NUMBER _____   ATTORNEY/GAL _____

IF CAPITAL OFFENSE CASE, LIST CO-COUNSEL'S NAME HERE: _____

ITEMIZED FEE STATEMENT

I hereby certify that the following time was expended in representation of the defendant/party represented:

DATE OF SERVICE	OUT-OF-COURT TOTAL	IN-COURT		IN-COURT TOTAL	DAILY TOTAL	DATE OF SERVICE (continued)	OUT-OF-COURT TOTAL	IN-COURT		IN-COURT TOTAL	DAILY TOTAL
		PRE-TRIAL HEARINGS	ALL OTHER IN-COURT					PRE-TRIAL HEARINGS	ALL OTHER IN-COURT		
							GRAND TOTAL				

Continue at top of next column.   Time is to be reported in tenth of an hour (6 minute) increments.

I hereby certify that the following expenses were incurred:

Use the following categories for Type: (1) Experts   (2) Postage/Phone   (3) Records/Reports   (4) Transcripts   (5) Travel   (6) Other

TYPE	PAYEE	AMOUNT
	TOTAL	

Clearly identify each expense and include a receipt for any expense over $1.00. See Section (P)(1)(c) for privileged information.

Amendment, persons are not just entitled to an attorney during trial proceedings, they are entitled to the effective assistance of counsel. As a result, if a person has an attorney during criminal proceedings, but the attorney's services are deficient, thereby causing prejudice to the defendant, it may be a violation of the right to counsel. This is called ***ineffective assistance of counsel*** *or* ***IAC***. Claims regarding IAC are one of the most frequently litigated issues in appellate courts, particularly cases involving habeas corpus petitions and death penalty sentences. See Chapter 14.

In *Strickland v. Washington* (1984),[53] the Supreme Court held that defendants seeking to prove a violation of the right to counsel based on a claim that their attorney was ineffective must demonstrate two things: (1) the attorney's

ineffective assistance of counsel or IAC
an attorney's services that are deficient, thereby causing prejudice to a criminal defendant in violation of the Sixth Amendment right to counsel

representation fell below objective standards of reasonableness (it was deficient), and (2) there is a reasonable probability that the outcome of the criminal proceedings would have been different but for counsel's deficient performance. Later, in *Lockhart v. Fretwell* (1993),[54] the Court suggested that a defendant in some cases may also be required to prove that counsel's deficiency caused the result to be fundamentally unfair or unreliable. In cases where counsel is proved to be ineffective during trial or appellate proceedings, the trial court's conviction and/or sentence can be reversed.

Deficient Performance.   A defense attorney's performance is deficient if it falls below an objective standard of reasonableness. According to the Supreme Court, this standard is defined in terms of prevailing professional norms. The Court thus conducts an objective review of a defense attorney's performance, measured for reasonableness under prevailing professional norms, including a context-dependent consideration of the challenged conduct as seen from counsel's perspective at the time of that conduct. In *Wiggins v. Smith* (2003),[55] the Court found that counsel's failure to investigate the defendant's background or provide mitigating evidence during a sentencing hearing was deficient, thereby warranting reversal of the death sentence. The Court further suggested that the legal professional standards established by the American Bar Association (ABA) for trial attorneys and death penalty causes can be used as a standard for evaluating counsel's performance.

Law Line 13-12
ABA Guidelines for Defense
Counsel in Capital Cases

But the Court has not made the establishment of deficient attorney performance an easy task. Instead, the Court has stated that "[j]udicial scrutiny of counsel's performance must be highly deferential." More emphatically, the Court has stated:

> [S]trategic choices made after thorough investigation of law and facts relevant to plausible options are virtually unchallengeable; and strategic choices made after less than complete investigation are reasonable precisely to the extent that reasonable professional judgments support the limitations on investigation. In other words, counsel has a duty to make reasonable investigations or to make a reasonable decision that makes particular investigations unnecessary. In any ineffectiveness case, a particular decision not to investigate must be directly assessed for reasonableness in all the circumstances, applying a heavy measure of deference to counsel's judgments.[56]

In *Strickland*, the Court found that the defendant was unable to demonstrate that his attorney was constitutionally deficient. The defense attorney had chosen not to present evidence during a capital sentencing hearing regarding the defendant's character and psychological condition. According to the attorney, he wanted to limit the prosecutor's ability to offer potentially harmful evidence regarding the defendant's criminal history, which might be admitted into evidence to counter the defendant's character and psychological evidence. On review, the Supreme Court found this decision to be "the result of reasonable professional judgment." As a result, the defendant's IAC claim was denied.

Resulting Prejudice.   To prove a Sixth Amendment violation, defendants must demonstrate that their attorney's deficient performance prejudiced the defense. In *Strickland,* the Court announced that, to establish prejudice, a "defendant must show that there is a reasonable probability that, but for counsel's unprofessional errors, the result of the proceeding would have been different. A reasonable probability is a probability sufficient to undermine confidence in the outcome."

In some cases, the Court has indicated a willingness to presume a prejudicial impact on the defendant. Presumed prejudice might be found in cases where the defendant was denied the right to counsel, where the government has affirmatively interfered with the right to counsel, or where the defense attorney has a conflict of interest in representing a defendant. But cases of presumed prejudice are rare. For example, in *Burger v. Kemp* (1987),[57] the Court refused to presume prejudice to a capital murder defendant, even though his attorney worked for a law firm that represented another defendant charged with the same murder, and the defense strategy of each defendant was to point the finger at the other defendant in order to avoid a death sentence.

And in cases involving plea agreements, the Court has established an even higher standard for a showing of prejudice. In *Hill v. Lockhart* (1986),[58] the Court held that in order to satisfy the prejudice prong in cases where a defendant pleads guilty, the defendant must show that there is a reasonable probability that, but for counsel's errors, the defendant would not have pleaded guilty and would have insisted on going to trial. This standard of proof essentially renders it quite challenging for defendants to prove ineffectiveness of counsel during the plea bargaining process. With deficient counsel, many defendants simply would insist on more favorable terms for their plea bargains, not necessarily insist on going to trial. But for these defendants, under the Court's standards, prejudice will not be found under the Sixth Amendment.

ETHICAL PRINCIPLES

BILLING FOR CLIENT SERVICES

National Federation of Paralegal Associations Model Code of Ethics and Professional Responsibility

Rule 1.2

A PARALEGAL SHALL MAINTAIN A HIGH LEVEL OF PERSONAL AND PROFESSIONAL INTEGRITY.

ETHICAL CONSIDERATIONS

1.2(c). A paralegal shall ensure that all timekeeping and billing records prepared by the paralegal are thorough, accurate, honest, and complete.

1.2(d). A paralegal shall not knowingly engage in fraudulent billing practices. Such practices may include, but are not limited to: inflation of hours billed to a client or employer; misrepresentation of the nature of tasks performed; and/or submission of fraudulent expense and disbursement documentation.

1.2(e). A paralegal shall be scrupulous, thorough and honest in the identification and maintenance of all funds, securities, and other assets of a client and shall provide accurate accounting as appropriate.

1.2(f). A paralegal shall advise the proper authority of non-confidential knowledge of any dishonest or fraudulent acts by any person pertaining to the handling of the funds, securities or other assets of a client. The authority to whom the report is made shall depend on the nature and circumstances of the possible misconduct, (e.g., ethics committees of law firms, corporations and/or paralegal associations, local or state bar associations, local prosecutors, administrative agencies, etc.). Failure to report such knowledge is in itself misconduct and shall be treated as such under these rules.

Courtesy of The National Federation of Paralegal Associations http://www.paralegals.org

Practical Realities of IAC Cases.   A wide range of attorney behavior can be asserted as the basis of an IAC claim. Some involve trial performance issues, such as a defense counsel's conflict of interest or the failure to object during proceedings, file necessary motions, investigate evidence, or call witnesses. Others involve an attorney's advice regarding a plea agreement, such as the failure to notify a client that he may be deported if he agrees to a proposed plea agreement, presented in *Padilla v. Kentucky* (2010) (See below). Many involve the defense attorney's performance during sentencing hearings, particularly those in capital cases, where defense counsel's role in presenting mitigating evidence to a jury in order to avoid a death sentence can be critical. For example, in *Williams v. Taylor*, (2000),[59] a defense attorney's failure to discover and present certain mitigation evidence in a capital sentencing hearing failed the *Strickland* test and was ineffective. And in *Wiggins v. Smith* (2003),[60] an attorney's failure to look beyond the presentence report and department of social services records to discover mitigation evidence—in a capital case that showed years of abuse, homelessness, foster care, and physical torment—was deemed ineffective.

But proving the ineffective assistance of counsel is not an easy task. And in most cases, courts find that IAC claims fall short of meeting the two-part *Strickland* standard. This occurs for two primary reasons. First, as illustrated above, in most cases, defendants are presumed to have received the effective assistance of counsel, and to overcome this presumption, the *Strickland* test imposes relatively high evidentiary burdens upon defendants. And second, many IAC claims are presented to courts in the form of federal habeas corpus petitions, which are governed by federal statutes, including the Antiterrorism and Effective Death Penalty Act of 1996. The statutory requirements of this act, as well as those imposed by associated Supreme Court rulings, which have restricted federal court access for state defendants seeking to challenge their convictions for sentences, have made it particularly difficult for defendants to successfully assert IAC claims in federal courts. See Chapter 14.

To better understand how the *Strickland* test is applied to IAC claims, read the Supreme Court's ruling in *Padilla v. Kentucky* (2010). In *Padilla*, the Court ruled 7-2 that the Sixth Amendment guarantee of effective assistance of counsel requires a criminal defense lawyer to advise a noncitizen client that pleading guilty to an aggravated felony will trigger mandatory, automatic deportation.

CAPSTONE CASE   *Padilla v. Kentucky*, 559 U.S. ___ (2010)

Justice Stevens delivered the opinion of the Court.

Petitioner Jose Padilla, a native of Honduras, has been a lawful permanent resident of the United States for more than 40 years. Padilla served this Nation with honor as a member of the U.S. Armed Forces during the Vietnam War. He now faces deportation after pleading guilty to the transportation of a large amount of marijuana in his tractor-trailer in the Commonwealth of Kentucky.

In this postconviction proceeding, Padilla claims that his counsel not only failed to advise him of this consequence prior to his entering the plea, but also told him that he "'did not have to worry about immigration status since he had been in the country so long.'" Padilla relied on his counsel's erroneous advice when he pleaded guilty to the drug charges that made his deportation virtually mandatory. He alleges that he would have insisted on going to trial if he had not received incorrect advice from his attorney. . . .

(continued)

(continued)

Under *Strickland* [*v. Washington*], we first determine whether counsel's representation "fell below an objective standard of reasonableness." Then we ask whether "there is a reasonable probability that, but for counsel's unprofessional errors, the result of the proceeding would have been different.". . .

The weight of prevailing professional norms supports the view that counsel must advise her client regarding the risk of deportation. "[A]uthorities of every stripe—including the American Bar Association, criminal defense and public defender organizations, authoritative treatises, and state and city bar publications—universally require defense attorneys to advise as to the risk of deportation consequences for non-citizen clients. . . ." . . .

In the instant case, the terms of the relevant immigration statute are succinct, clear, and explicit in defining the removal consequence for Padilla's conviction. Padilla's counsel could have easily determined that his plea would make him eligible for deportation simply from reading the text of the statute, which addresses not some broad classification of crimes but specifically commands removal for all controlled substances convictions except for the most trivial of marijuana possession offenses. Instead, Padilla's counsel provided him false assurance that his conviction would not result in his removal from this country. This is not a hard case in which to find deficiency: The consequences of Padilla's plea could easily be determined from reading the removal statute, his deportation was presumptively mandatory, and his counsel's advice was incorrect. . . .

Accepting his allegations as true, Padilla has sufficiently alleged constitutional deficiency to satisfy the first prong of *Strickland*. Whether Padilla is entitled to relief on his claim will depend on whether he can satisfy *Strickland*'s second prong, prejudice, a matter we leave to the Kentucky courts to consider in the first instance. . . .

It is our responsibility under the Constitution to ensure that no criminal defendant—whether a citizen or not—is left to the "mercies of incompetent counsel." To satisfy this responsibility, we now hold that counsel must inform her client whether his plea carries a risk of deportation. Our longstanding Sixth Amendment precedents, the seriousness of deportation as a consequence of a criminal plea, and the concomitant impact of deportation on families living lawfully in this country demand no less. . . .

The judgment of the Supreme Court of Kentucky is reversed, and the case is remanded for further proceedings not inconsistent with this opinion.

It is so ordered.

WHAT DO *YOU* THINK?

1. Did the defense attorney's advice to Padilla fall short of Sixth Amendment standards for the effective assistance of counsel?

2. What role should the trial court play in guaranteeing a defendant fully understands the consequences of a plea agreement and that defense attorneys have satisfied their professional obligations to their clients?

IN THE FIELD

Most legal professionals working in the criminal justice system will face issues involving the ineffective assistance of counsel. These issues are normally raised on appeal, during state postconviction proceedings, or in federal habeas corpus filings (see Chapter 14). But they can also be presented in trial court proceedings. For example, if a defense attorney fails to file pretrial motions in a timely manner, thereby undermining the defendant's rights, judges often have to decide between enforcing the court's administrative rules regarding motion deadlines and the defendant's constitutional right to the effective assistance of counsel.

As identified above, there are two basic issues for IAC claims. The first is identifying whether the defense attorney's actions fell below an objective standard of reasonableness. There are several sources that can be used to make this assessment, including the ABA's standards for attorneys (cited above), the state or federal rules for attorney professionalism, and even testimony or affidavits provided by other attorneys. These sources may provide a benchmark for reasonable attorney behavior. In many cases, prosecutors will assert that the attorney's conduct was part of a reasonable trial strategy, which while ineffective in retrospect was a reasonable decision at the time it was made.

The second prong of an IAC analysis can be particularly challenging in some cases because it essentially asks, "What would have happened if the defense attorney had not made the error?" In some cases, the answer may be clear-cut. For example, if the attorney fails to object to clearly inadmissible critical evidence introduced by the prosecutor, the prejudice to the defendant may be apparent. But where the attorney error occurred as a part of many other factors that could have led to a particular verdict or ruling, the ability to show prejudice is more challenging. In these situations, the parties likely will debate whether the attorney's mistake was harmless error.

DOUBLE JEOPARDY

One of the most misunderstood rights in criminal procedure is the right against double jeopardy. The Fifth Amendment provides in relevant part that "[no person shall] be subject for the same offence to be twice put in jeopardy of life or limb." The basic concept of double jeopardy is that when the government has tried a person (placed the person in jeopardy) once, it cannot do it again for that offense. As the Supreme Court explained in *Green v. United States* (1958),[61] the Double Jeopardy Clause protects two important interests of the criminal defendant: (1) the right to have guilt or innocence determined by the particular jury then empanelled, and (2) the right to be free from harassing multiple prosecutions for the same offense. The basic notion is that the government "with all its resources and power should not be allowed to make repeated attempts to convict an individual for an alleged offense, thereby subjecting him to embarrassment, expense and ordeal and compelling him to live in a continuing state of anxiety and insecurity, as well as enhancing the possibility that even though innocent he may be found guilty."[62]

But while the Double Jeopardy Clause may appear self-explanatory to some, the Court has interpreted the terms "jeopardy" and "same offence" in ways that preclude a strict application of this right.

Civil (Remedial) versus Criminal (Punitive) Proceedings

The Court has interpreted jeopardy to mean a form of punitive sanction or punishment, as opposed to civil or remedial measures, imposed by government against an individual. A ***punitive sanction*** is designed to achieve the objectives of punishing a person through societal forms of deterrence and retribution. The classic form of a punitive sanction is a criminal sentence. But at times government seeks to impose other measures upon individuals that are more remedial or civil in nature. A ***remedial measure*** or civil sanction, in theory, is not designed to punish someone, but rather seeks to correct a social problem or to compensate someone

punitive sanction
a court-imposed remedy that seeks to achieve the objectives of punishing a person through societal forms of deterrence and retribution

remedial measure
a type of civil sanction that is not designed to punish someone, but rather seeks to correct a social problem or to compensate someone for a harm or loss

for a harm or loss. For example, a lawsuit for personal injury is a civil proceeding that seeks to compensate injured persons for any losses they incurred. Because punitive sanctions and remedial measures fulfill different objectives, a government may pursue both for the same offense without violating the Double Jeopardy Clause.

The distinction between punitive sanctions and remedial measures means that, based on the same act, a person may be tried as a defendant in a criminal case and then later tried in civil proceedings or vice versa. The classic example of this principle is O. J. Simpson, who was initially acquitted of homicide charges in a state criminal case, but was later found liable for the same homicides in a civil case. The logic behind allowing these double trials is that a person is not truly in jeopardy of life or limb (instead usually risks only monetary loss) in a civil case.

But there are times when the distinction between punitive sanctions and remedial measures is not always clear. For example, in *United States v. Ursery* (1996),[63] the defendant argued that the government could not prosecute him for criminal drug offenses and then, based on the same offenses, pursue civil forfeiture proceedings against him, where the government sought to acquire the defendant's private property used in the commission of the drug offenses. The Supreme Court, however, rejected this argument, finding that the government's civil forfeiture proceedings were not a form of punishment under the Fifth Amendment. The Court applied a two-part analysis asking (1) whether Congress intended the particular forfeiture action to be a remedial civil sanction or a criminal penalty, and (2) whether the forfeiture proceedings are so punitive in fact as to establish that they may not legitimately be viewed as civil in nature. The Court concluded that Congress intended forfeiture laws to be remedial and that their application to the defendant was not so punitive in nature as to constitute a second form of criminal jeopardy. As a result, the Court concluded that the defendant was not placed twice in criminal jeopardy by the subsequent forfeiture proceedings.

To determine whether a government sanction is punitive in nature, the Court looks to several factors, including whether (1) the sanction involves an affirmative disability or restraint upon an individual, (2) the sanction has historically been regarded as a punishment, (3) the sanction comes into play only on a finding of scienter, (4) its operation will promote the traditional aims of punishment—retribution and deterrence, (5) the behavior to which it applies is already a crime, (6) an alternative purpose to which it may rationally be connected is assignable for it, and (7) it appears excessive in relation to the alternative purpose assigned.[64]

Many convicted sex offenders have asserted double jeopardy challenges to state and federal laws requiring them to register as sex offenders and abide by restrictive residency conditions after they have completed their criminal sentences. In most of these cases, courts have found these registry and residency laws not to violate the Fifth Amendment because they do not impose sanctions that are excessively punitive in nature. For example, in *Kansas v. Hendricks* (1997),[65] the Supreme Court upheld the Kansas Sexually Violent Predator Act, which allowed the state to hold sexual offenders in indefinite civil confinement after their criminal sentences if there was evidence that they would likely engage in predatory acts of sexual violence. The Court concluded that the law did not violate double jeopardy standards because it did not establish new criminal proceedings or impose a second form of punishment, but rather was designed to remedy a potential harm to the community.

More recently, however, some courts have ruled that state sexual offender registration laws passed pursuant to the federal Adam Walsh Child Protection and Safety Act (2006) violate double jeopardy principles. The Adam Walsh Act established a national sex offender registry law that, among other things, created financial incentives for states to increase their registration and residency requirements for sexual offenders. These new and enhanced state laws reclassify many sexual offenders and increase their original registration requirements. In some cases, courts have ruled these measures are substantively more punitive in nature than earlier forms of sexual offender registration and notification laws and, therefore, constitute a second form of punishment.[66]

Law Line 13-13
Double Jeopardy

Attachment of Jeopardy

The Court has ruled that a defendant is placed in jeopardy (jeopardy attaches) at different times depending on the nature of the proceeding. In a jury trial, jeopardy attaches when the jury is sworn to duty. In a bench trial, where a judge is the trier of fact, jeopardy is initiated when the first witness is sworn for testimony. And even though juvenile proceedings normally are not regarded as criminal in nature, jeopardy nonetheless still attaches in juvenile proceedings when they commence.[67]

It is also important to note that, once jeopardy attaches for a particular offense, it also attaches for all lesser-included offenses and most higher-level offenses that could be charged for the same act.[68] For example, if a person is charged with a single count of robbery, and jeopardy attaches to this case, the government normally cannot charge the defendant with theft (a lesser included offense) or aggravated robbery (a higher-level offense) based on the same act. The principle underlying this rule is that the prosecution should not be able to get a second or third attempt to convict a person by merely adjusting the level of charge in order to gain another trial. The one primary exception to this limitation is homicide charges, where a defendant charged with assaulting another person may be charged with homicide (a higher-level offense) if the victim later dies as a result and within a specified time period after the assault.

Exceptions

Even where it appears that the government is seeking a second form of punitive sanctions upon a person for the same act, the Court has carved out a number of exceptions to the Double Jeopardy Clause.

Dual Sovereigns. First, the right against double jeopardy does not bar multiple prosecutions by different sovereign governments. Under the **dual sovereignty doctrine**, federal and state governments may try a person for the same act, just as two or more states may try a person for the same act because they are separate sovereigns. But two municipalities within the same state may not impose multiple punishments because they are technically part of the same sovereign (agents of the same state).

dual sovereignty doctrine
an exception to the double jeopardy clause wherein different governments may try a person for the same act

Mistrials. Second, a person may be tried multiple times if the prior trial ended due to **manifest necessity** (a compelling need to stop the trial prior to a verdict being reached), which may include a **hung jury** (a jury that cannot reach a decision after sufficient deliberations) or the declaration of a *mistrial* (the termination of a trial prior to a verdict) where the prosecution did not intentionally seek to cause the mistrial. Generally, a jury's inability to reach a decision is the kind of manifest necessity that permits the declaration of a mistrial and the continuation of the initial jeopardy that commenced when the jury was first impaneled. As a result, the Supreme Court has found that the interest in giving the prosecution one complete opportunity to convict those who have violated its laws justifies treating the jury's inability to reach a verdict as a nonevent that does not bar retrial.

manifest necessity
a compelling need to stop the trial prior to a verdict being reached and declare a mistrial

hung jury
a jury that cannot reach a decision after sufficient deliberations

But if a trial court declares a mistrial based on prosecutorial misconduct, which involves gross negligence or intentional misconduct, the government likely will be barred from reprosecuting the defendant. The principle is that prosecutors should not be able to intentionally create a mistrial in order to restart a criminal case.

Reversals on Appeal.   Third, individuals may be tried again in cases where their initial conviction is reversed on appeal. The theory behind this exception is that "[i]t would be a high price indeed for society to pay were every accused granted immunity from punishment because of any defect sufficient to constitute reversible error in the proceedings leading to conviction."[69] If, however, a person's conviction is reversed due to insufficient evidence being offered during the first trial, the prosecution will be barred from initiating a second trial.

Breach of Plea Agreement.   And finally, prosecutors may sometimes reinstate criminal charges against criminal defendants after a case has concluded where defendants breach the terms of their plea agreement with the government.[70] In these situations, where defendants agree to assist the government with an ongoing investigation, pay restitution, or provide some other benefit to the government, in exchange for a reduced criminal charge or sentence, the termination of jeopardy (the original case) is conditioned on the defendant's fulfillment of the terms of the plea agreement. Where a condition of the agreement is not met, the government may be able to reinstate the criminal case (jeopardy).

Same Offenses — *Blockburger* Test

Perhaps the most challenging aspect of the Double Jeopardy Clause is determining when two offenses are actually the "same offense." For example, if a person is convicted of speeding, reckless driving, and driving under the influence, all based on the same act of driving, it may seem as though the driver is being punished in multiple ways for the same offense. But the Supreme Court has ruled that two or more criminal charges will not be deemed to be the same offense if each charge requires proof of an additional criminal element (another form of intent or an additional act). This is known as the ***Blockburger*** or ***same-elements test***.[71] Essentially, this test asks whether each offense contains an element not contained in the other. In cases where they do not, they are considered the same offense, and double jeopardy bars subsequent punishment or prosecution.

Blockburger or same-elements test
the Supreme Court standard for determining whether two offenses constitute the "same offense" under the Double Jeopardy Clause

For example, under the *Blockburger* test, the government would be able to proceed against the above-referenced driver for speeding, reckless driving, and DUI because each offense likely contains a unique or additional element different from the other charges. Similarly, a prosecutor could proceed with each of the following pairs of companion charges: vehicular manslaughter and leaving the scene of an accident; mail fraud and uttering a forged check; and armed robbery and unauthorized use of a firearm. In each set of cases, the prosecutor would have to prove at least one different element to secure a conviction for the second offense.

lesser included offense
criminal offense for which all of the elements for conviction are also elements for a more serious crime

In some cases, however, one criminal charge may be considered a lesser included offense of another criminal charge and, therefore, considered the same offense for double jeopardy purposes. A ***lesser included offense*** is a criminal offense for which all of the elements for conviction are also elements for a more serious crime. For example, in some criminal codes, the offenses of assault and theft may be lesser included offenses of robbery. So if a defendant is acquitted of robbery (use of a weapon to commit a theft offense), the prosecutor cannot use the same factual scenario from the robbery case to charge the defendant with theft and/or assault because these subsequent charges were essentially lesser included parts of the robbery charge.

Similarly, in most cases, prosecutors cannot charge defendants with greater offenses after their case on a lesser included offense is resolved. For example, if a defendant is acquitted of robbery, a prosecutor cannot use the same factual basis from this case to indict the defendant for aggravated robbery. One exception to this principle is often found in homicide cases, where a defendant convicted of an assault or battery offense may, in some cases, be indicted for a homicide offense if the victim later dies as a proximate cause of the assault or battery.[72]

Read the majority opinion in *Yeager v. United States* (2009), where the Supreme Court ruled 6-3 that the Double Jeopardy Clause bars the government from retrying a defendant who was acquitted of some charges on factually related counts on which the jury failed to reach a verdict.

CAPSTONE CASE   *Yeager v. United States*, 557 U.S. __ (2009)

Justice Stevens delivered the opinion of the Court.

The question presented in this case is whether an apparent inconsistency between a jury's verdict of acquittal on some counts and its failure to return a verdict on other counts affects the preclusive force of the acquittals under the Double Jeopardy Clause of the Fifth Amendment. We hold that it does not.

In 1997, Enron Corporation (Enron) acquired a telecommunications business that it expanded and ultimately renamed Enron Broadband Services (EBS). Petitioner F. Scott Yeager served as Senior Vice President of Strategic Development for EBS from October 1, 1998, until his employment was terminated a few months before Enron filed for bankruptcy on December 2, 2001....

On November 5, 2004, a grand jury returned a "Fifth Superseding Indictment" charging petitioner with 126 counts of five federal offenses: (1) conspiracy to commit securities and wire fraud; (2) securities fraud; (3) wire fraud; (4) insider trading; and (5) money laundering. The Government's theory of prosecution was that petitioner—acting in concert with other Enron executives—purposefully deceived the public about the EIN project in order to inflate the value of Enron's stock and, ultimately, to enrich himself.

The trial lasted 13 weeks. After four days of deliberations, the jury notified the court that it had reached agreement on some counts but had deadlocked on others.... The jury acquitted petitioner on the fraud counts but failed to reach a verdict on the insider trading counts. The court entered judgment on the acquittals and declared a mistrial on the hung counts.

On November 9, 2005, the Government obtained a new indictment against petitioner. This "Eighth Superseding Indictment" recharged petitioner with some, but not all, of the insider trading counts on which the jury had previously hung....

Petitioner moved to dismiss all counts in the new indictment on the ground that the acquittals on the fraud counts precluded the Government from retrying him on the insider trading counts. He argued that the jury's acquittals had necessarily decided that he did not possess material, nonpublic information about the performance of the EIN project and its value to Enron. In petitioner's view, because reprosecution for insider trading would require the Government to prove that critical fact, the issue-preclusion component of the Double Jeopardy Clause barred a second trial of that issue and mandated dismissal of all of the insider trading counts....

The Double Jeopardy Clause of the Fifth Amendment provides: "[N]or shall any person be subject for the same offence to be twice put in jeopardy of life or limb."...

Our cases have recognized that the Clause embodies two vitally important interests. The first is the "deeply ingrained" principle that "the State with all its resources and power should not be allowed to make repeated attempts to convict

(continued)

(continued)

an individual for an alleged offense, thereby subjecting him to embarrassment, expense and ordeal and compelling him to live in a continuing state of anxiety and insecurity, as well as enhancing the possibility that even though innocent he may be found guilty." The second interest is the preservation of "the finality of judgments." . . .

We must determine whether the interest in preserving the finality of the jury's judgment on the fraud counts, including the jury's finding that petitioner did not possess insider information, bars a retrial on the insider trading counts . . . The proper question, under the Clause's text, is whether it is appropriate to treat the insider trading charges as the "same offence" as the fraud charges. Our opinion in *Ashe v. Swenson*, 397 U. S. 436 (1970), provides the basis for our answer.

In *Ashe*, we squarely held that the Double Jeopardy Clause precludes the Government from relitigating any issue that was necessarily decided by a jury's acquittal in a prior trial. . . . We explained that "when an issue of ultimate fact has once been determined by a valid and final judgment" of acquittal, it "cannot again be litigated" in a second trial for a separate offense. . . .

The reasoning in *Ashe* is . . . controlling because, for double jeopardy purposes, the jury's inability to reach a verdict on the insider trading counts was a nonevent and the acquittals on the fraud counts are entitled to the same effect as Ashe's acquittal. . . .

Accordingly, we hold that the consideration of hung counts has no place in the issue-preclusion analysis. . . . A jury's verdict of acquittal represents the community's collective judgment regarding all the evidence and arguments presented to it. Even if the verdict is "based upon an egregiously erroneous foundation," its finality is unassailable. Thus, if the possession of insider information was a critical issue of ultimate fact in all of the charges against petitioner, a jury verdict that necessarily decided that issue in his favor protects him from prosecution for any charge for which that is an essential element. . . .

The judgment is reversed, and the case is remanded to the Court of Appeals for further proceedings consistent with this opinion.

It is so ordered.

WHAT DO *YOU* THINK?

1. Does the Court's ruling fulfill the basic purpose of the Double Jeopardy Clause?
2. How does the Court's inquiry regarding the jury's decision compare with the rules and standards for reviewing juror misconduct?

IN THE FIELD

For most legal professionals, double jeopardy issues are not that common. But to the extent they arise, they are usually found in two scenarios. The first occurs when a trial court declares a mistrial in a case and the prosecutor subsequently attempts to retry the defendant. In these situations, legal professionals must closely examine the trial judge's reason for declaring a mistrial to determine whether it involved an act of intentional prosecutorial misconduct or gross negligence. In most cases, a mistrial will not bar a second trial. But where the prosecutor's actions were intended to provoke a mistrial or were intentionally designed to undermine the defendant's right to a fair trial, double jeopardy standards may preclude this second trial. As a result, legal professionals may find themselves debating the nature and intention behind a prosecutor's conduct if it leads to the declaration of a mistrial.

The second scenario involving double jeopardy issues involves cases where the prosecutor seeks to impose "administrative" sanctions against the defendant following a criminal conviction. For example, if a state modifies its sexual offender registration and notification requirements by imposing increased obligations on sex offenders, these enhanced requirements need to be examined under double jeopardy standards. The question in these cases is whether these additional administrative conditions amount to the imposition of a second form of punishment. In other words, in cases where the additional conditions impose unusually harsh or restrictive conditions on the defendant, legal professionals may want to consider whether these conditions are truly administrative or remedial in nature or whether they have crossed the line into a second set of punitive sanctions. Where they appear more punitive in nature, there may be double jeopardy issues to raise before the trial court.

CHAPTER **SUMMARY**

- The rights of defendants at trial are primarily contained in the Fifth and Sixth Amendments, with more general protections of due process and equal protection found in the Fifth and Fourteenth Amendments.
- The Supreme Court generally has refused to apply these provisions literally, but instead has developed a series of tests, doctrines, and exceptions to effectuate these constitutional protections. Many of these standards have changed over time based on the makeup of the Court and their constitutional values.
- Due process protections ensure that prosecutors treat defendants fairly during trial by giving them sufficient notice and providing them with exculpatory evidence and materials, where available, to impeach the government's witnesses.
- The right to equal protection guards against selective prosecution and prohibits the prosecutor's use of race or sex to exclude potential members from the jury.
- In jury trials, where is appears that the prosecutor is using peremptory challenges to systematically exclude jurors based on their race or sex, defendants can assert a *Batson* challenge in an effort to correct this misconduct.
- The defendant's right to due process at trial involves many particular rights, including protections against prosecutorial misconduct, jury misconduct, and improper or misleading jury instructions.
- The Sixth Amendment protects the right to counsel after criminal charges are filed. This right exists at all critical stages of the prosecution, which includes arraignment, guilty pleas, trials, and sentencing.
- The right to counsel includes the right to the effective assistance of counsel. To prove a case of ineffective

assistance, defendants must show that their attorney was deficient and that, but for the deficiency, the result of the proceeding would have been different.
- The right against double jeopardy generally precludes the government from placing a person in criminal jeopardy more than once. This right applies to cases where the same sovereign seeks to prosecute a person for a second time after a final judgment on the merits of the case is issued.
- The right to a fair trial encompasses the Sixth Amendment right to a public, speedy trial by jury, as well as more general rights of due process and equal protection.
- In most cases, the right to a public trial is absolute except where trial publicity may infringe upon the right to a fair trial.
- The right to confront witnesses allows defendants to cross-examine persons who offer testimony-like evidence against them during trial.
- The right to a speedy trial is determined based on the totality of the circumstances, requiring the court to consider the length of and reason for the delay and the resulting prejudice to the defendant.
- In federal cases, the right to a speedy trial is also assessed under the Speedy Trial Act, which sets a seventy-day time period within which a criminal case must be tried. This limit, however, has many exceptions and also can be waived by the defendant.
- The right to a jury trial exists for all serious offenses, which typically means offenses for which a person faces more than six months of incarceration. In most states, each of these rights is supplemented with state constitutional or statutory protections.

KEY **TERMS**

appointed attorneys
Assistance of Counsel Clause
Batson challenge
bench trial
Blockburger or same-elements
   test
challenge for cause
change of venue
Compulsory Process Clause
Confrontation Clause
curative instructions
dismissal with prejudice
dismissal without prejudice
Double Jeopardy Clause
dual sovereignty doctrine
Due Process Clause

Duren test
Equal Protection Clause
harmless error
hung jury
ineffective assistance of counsel
   or IAC
Information Clause
juror misconduct
jury instructions
jury sequestration
Jury Trial Clause
lesser included offense
manifest necessity
mistrial
new trial
pattern jury instructions

peremptory challenge
petty offense
pro se
proposed jury instructions
prosecutorial misconduct
public defenders
Public Trial Clause
punitive sanction
remedial measure
Self-Incrimination Clause
serious offenses
Speedy Trial Act of 1974
Speedy Trial Clause
speedy trial waiver
venire
voir dire

QUESTIONS FOR **DISCUSSION**

1. What basic protections of criminal procedure do the Fifth, Sixth, and Fourteenth Amendments provide to criminal defendants during trial?

2. What particular rights are involved in affording defendants the right to a fair trial? Is the government entitled to receive a fair trial as well?

3. What must defendants prove in order to show that they were denied the effective assistance of counsel?

4. How can jury instructions undermine a defendant's right to a fair trial?

5. What types of behavior might be identified as prosecutorial misconduct?

6. How is the right to confrontation involved when a prosecutor seeks to introduce an official report, such as a death certificate or toxicology report, into evidence?

7. Do sexual offender registration and notification laws violate the right against double jeopardy?

8. If a defendant's conviction is reversed on appeal, can a prosecutor try the defendant a second time under the Double Jeopardy Clause?

9. During jury selection, what is the difference between challenges for cause and peremptory challenges? How do these challenges relate to a *Batson* challenge?

10. What constitutional protections are designed to ensure a person a fair trial?

REFERENCES

1. See Robert Burns, *The Death of the American Trial* (Chicago: University of Chicago Press, 2009).

2. Marc Galanter, "The Vanishing Trial: An Examination of Trials and Related Matters in Federal and State Courts," *Journal of Empirical Legal Studies* 1 (2004): 459.

3. See *Benton v. Maryland*, 395 U.S. 784 (1969).

4. See *Ward v. City of Monroeville*, 409 U.S. 57 (1972) (barring mayor from presiding over trial because of city's financial interest in imposing fines); *Batson v. Kentucky*, 476 U.S. 79

(1989) (precluding prosecutor's use of race to exclude jurors during voir dire).

5. See *Klopfer v. North Carolina*, 386 U.S. 213 (1967).

6. See *In re Oliver*, 333 U.S. 257 (1948).

7. See *Duncan v. Louisiana*, 391 U.S. 145 (1968).

8. See *Pointer v. Texas*, 380 U.S. 400 (1965).

9. See *Washington v. Texas*, 388 U.S. 14 (1967).

10. See *Gideon v. Wainwright*, 372 U.S. 335 (1963) (applicable to felony cases); *Argersinger v. Hamlin*, 407 U.S. 25

(1972) (applicable to misdemeanor cases if sentence includes imprisonment).

11. *Berger v. United States*, 295 U.S. 78, 88 (1935).

12. Steve Weinberg, "Breaking the Rules: Who suffers when a prosecutor is cited for misconduct?" Center for Public Integrity, http://projects.publicintegrity.org/pm/default.aspx?act=main.

13. See http://www.ajs.org/jc/juries/jc_decision_misconduct_kinds.asp.

14. See *id.*

15. 498 U.S. 39 (1990).

16. *Victor v. Nebraksa*, 511 U.S. 1 (1994).

17. *Estelle v. Williams*, 425 U. S. 501, 503–6 (1976); *Holbrook v. Flynn*, 475 U. S. 560, 568 (1986).

18. 425 U. S. 501, 503–6 (1976).

19. 475 U. S. 560, 568 (1986).

20. CA2000-02-016, 2000 Ohio App. LEXIS 4540, October 2, 2000.

21. 384 U.S. 333 (1966).

22. See *Press-Enterprise Co. v. Superior Court*, 478 U.S. 1 (1986) (competing interest of the press in public trials).

23. See *Barker v. Wingo*, 407 U.S. 514 (1972); *Doggett v. United States*, 505 U.S. 647 (1992).

24. 407 U.S. 514, 530 (1972).

25. 505 U.S. 647 (1992).

26. 556 U.S. ___ (2009).

27. 18 U.S.C. §§3161–74.

28. 547 U.S. 489 (2006).

29. *Duncan* V. *Louisiana*, 391 U.S. 145, 159 (1968).

30. See *Blanton v. City of North Las Vegas*, 489 U.S. 538 (1989).

31. 518 U.S. 322 (1996).

32. 399 U.S. 78 (1970).

33. 406 U.S. 404 (1972).

34. 406 U.S. 356 (1972).

35. 441 U.S. 130 (1979).

36. *State v. Burnside*, 2010-Ohio-1235.

37. 542 U.S. 296 (2004).

38. 543 U.S. 220 (2005).

39. See David Cole, *No Equal Justice:Race and Class in the American Criminal Justice System* (New York: New Press. 2000); Angela Davis, *Arbitrary Justice: The Power of the American Prosecutor* (New York: Oxford University Press, 2007).

40. 517 U.S. 456 (1996).

41. 536 U.S. 862 (2002).

42. 476 U.S. 79 (1986).

43. 511 U.S. 127 (1994).

44. 439 U.S. 357 (1979).

45. 554 U.S.___, 128 S. Ct. 2678 (2008).

46. 557 U.S. ___, 129 S. Ct. 2527 (2009).

47. *Mempa v. Rhay*, 389 U.S. 128, 134 (1967).

48. 372 U.S. 335 (1963).

49. 407 U. S. 25 (1972).

50. 440 U.S. 367 (1979).

51. See *Gideon v. Wainwright*, 372 U.S. 335 (1963 (felonies); *Hamilton v. Alabama*, 368 U.S. 52 (1961) (arraignments); *Moore v. Illinois*, 434 U.S. 220 (1977) (postcharge lineups); *Massiah v. United States*, 377 U.S. 201 (1964) (postcharge interrogations); *Douglas v. California*, 372 U.S. 353 (1963) (appeals as a matter of right).

52. See *Gilbert v. California*, 388 U.S. 263 (1967) (handwriting and voice exemplars); *United States v. Ash*, 413 U.S. 300 (1973) (photo identifications); *Ross v. Moffitt*, 417 U.S. 600 (1974) (discretionary appeals); *Gagnon v. Scarpelli*, 411 U.S. 778 (1973) (parole hearings); *Pennsylvania v. Finely*, 481 U.S. 55 (1987) (habeas proceedings).

53. 466 U.S. 668 (1984).

54. 506 U.S. 364 (1993).

55. 539 U.S. 510 (2003).

56. *Id.*

57. 483 U.S. 776 (1987).

58. 474 U.S. 52 (1986).

59. 529 U.S. 362 (2000).

60. 539 U.S. 510 (2003).

61. 355 U.S. 184, 187-88 (1958).

62. *Yeager v. United States*, 557 U.S. ___ (2009).

63. 518 U.S. 267 (1996).

64. *Hudson v. United States*, 522 U.S. 93 (1997).

65. 521 U.S. 346 (1997).

66. *Doe v. Alaska*, 189 P.3d 999 (2008).

67. See *Crist v. Bretz*, 437 U.S. 28 (1978) (jury trials); *Breed v. Jones*, 421 U.S. 519 (1975) (juvenile proceedings).

68. See *Harris v. Oklahoma*, 433 U.S. 682 (1977) (lesser included offenses); *Brown v. Ohio*, 432 U.S. 161 (1977) (high-level offenses); *Diaz v. United States*, 223 U.S. 442 (1912) (exception to rule in homicide cases).

69. *United States v. Tateo*, 377 U.S. 463, 466 (1964).

70. See *Heath v. Alabama*, 474 U.S. 82 (1986) (separate sovereigns); *Illinois v. Somerville*, 410 U.S. 458 (1973) (manifest necessity); *Burks v. United States*, 437 U.S. 1 (1978) (retrial after appeal).

71. The name of this test comes from the Court's opinion in *Blockburger v. United States*, 284 U.S. 299 (1932); see also *Missouri v. Hunter*, 459 U.S. 359 (1983) (successive punishments for same crime).

72. *Diaz v. United States*, 223 U.S. 442 (1912).

APPENDIX
DEVELOPING YOUR LEGAL ANALYSIS

A. THE LAW WHERE YOU LIVE

Assume that you are assisting an attorney who is preparing a criminal case for trial. The case is *State v. Morgan*, where the defendant is charged with soliciting a minor for sex over the Internet. In some jurisdictions, this is called sexual solicitation, while in others, it is referred to as importuning.

The indictment alleges that Steve Morgan used his home computer to enter an electronic chat room and sent messages to a person whom he believed to be a minor wherein he requested forms of sexual activity, including sexual intercourse. No one actually saw the defendant use his computer. Rather, investigators have used forensic evidence to trace the electronic messages to the defendant's home computer and assert that circumstantial evidence demonstrates that the defendant would be the only person to use this computer. Assume that the defendant is not going to testify at trial.

Initially, assume you are working for the defendant. Using the model jury instructions from your home state jurisdiction, draft a memorandum of proposed jury instructions for the trial court. Be sure to identify instructions that (1) define the basic elements of the charged offense—sexual solicitation or importuning, (2) provide a definition of beyond a reasonable doubt, (3) address the fact that the defendant did not testify during trial, and (4) inform the jury how to evaluate circumstantial and direct evidence.

Next, assume you are assisting the prosecutor in the case. Using the same model jury instructions for your home state, determine whether you would propose any different or additional instructions for the trial court for the four areas addressed above. In this second memorandum, explain why your proposed instructions for the prosecutor differ from or are the same as those filed on behalf of the defendant.

B. INSIDE THE FEDERAL COURTS

Assume you are assisting an attorney who is assigned to represent a convicted capital defendant in his federal habeas corpus petition. The defendant was sentenced to death by a state court after a jury convicted him for the aggravated murder of his girlfriend.

One of the issues your attorney has identified for the defendant-petitioner's habeas corpus petition is the claim of ineffective assistance of counsel. In particular, the attorney has determined that the client's trial attorney failed to call any witnesses during the defendant's sentencing hearing who could have offered mitigating evidence on the defendant's behalf. Your attorney has located several family members and friends of the defendant, as well as the defendant's former physician, who all indicate that the defendant suffered from serious posttraumatic stress disorder related to combat duty with the U.S. military. Your attorney believes that, had the jury been presented with this evidence during the sentencing hearing, it may have recommended life in prison, rather than the death penalty, as the defendant's sentence.

Your attorney would like for you to prepare a memorandum wherein you outline cases that would support the claim of ineffective assistance of counsel. Using the summaries of ineffective assistance found at the following website, identify, review, and summarize ten federal cases that best support the claim of IAC in your case.

http://www.capdefnet.org/hat/contents/constitutional_issues/ineffective_assist/ineffective_assistance_of_counsel.htm

C. CYBER SOURCES

Assume that you are asked to assist in preparing a presentation for a Continuing Legal Education course on prosecutorial misconduct. The course is sponsored by a group of prosecutors and defense attorneys who wish to assist young prosecutors and defense attorneys with identifying and avoiding prosecutorial misconduct and other due process violations in the courtroom.

Using the materials provided by the Center for Public Integrity on prosecutorial misconduct at the following website, as well as any other reliable source material you find, prepare a PowerPoint or other electronic presentation wherein you illustrate some of the most common and egregious forms of prosecutorial misconduct, as identified through case law. Explain what occurred and how it might be avoided. In addition, be sure to explain the difference between harmless error and prejudicial error as they relate to prosecutorial misconduct issues.

Center for Public Integrity—http://projects.publicintegrity.org/pm/

D. ETHICS AND PROFESSIONALISM

Assume you are working for a Jay Simon, a criminal defense attorney who handles a lot of Driving While Intoxicated (DWI) cases. In many of these cases, the local trial court appoints Mr. Simon to represent indigent clients. In these cases, you are responsible for tracking the time spent on each case and submitting the form for reimbursement of legal fees from the court. A few months ago, Mr. Simon represented Steve Tinker, an indigent DWI defendant, in a case involving a pretrial motion to suppress the blood alcohol test results. Mr. Simon put a lot of time and expense into the case, including the time you spent preparing several large charts to use during the suppression hearing. These charts were used to explain to the trial judge the science of BAC testing and the fact that the instrument used by police was legally deficient, thereby warranting the suppression of the test results. Mr. Simon was successful in getting the BAC results suppressed in that case. But because the trial court limits the amount of legal fees an attorney can receive in an appointed case, Mr. Simon was not fully reimbursed for his time and expenses in preparing the motion to suppress. Instead, Mr. Simon received $2,500 in reimbursement fees, the maximum allowed for a misdemeanor DWI case.

Last week, Mr. Simon represented Candice Jones, another indigent DWI defendant in another case before another judge. In that case, Mr. Simon filed a motion to suppress the BAC results, based on the same legal theories and strategies that he used in the Tinker case. In fact, the motions were virtually identical. And during the suppression hearing, Mr. Simon used the same charts that were used during the Tinker hearing. Because the work on the motion and exhibits was already done, Mr. Simon and you put very little time into preparing Ms. Jones's case. Nonetheless, Mr. Simon achieved the same success for Ms. Jones as he did for Mr. Tinker.

You are now preparing the forms for court reimbursement in the Jones case. Mr. Simon would like for you to submit time and costs for the motion and exhibits, so that the court will reimburse him at the maximum rate of $2,500. Mr. Simon's theory is that Jones benefited from his time and costs in the Tinker case and the court has not yet fully compensated him for this work. The question is, on the court reimbursement form, can you ethically include time and costs for preparing the Jones motion and exhibits, if they were already prepared for the Tinker case? Prepare a two-page memorandum in which you offer your assessment to the managing partner of your law firm. In addition to considering any local standards that might apply, be sure to consider the following sources:

National Federation of Paralegal Associations

http://www.paralegals.org/displaycommon.cfm?an=1&subarticlenbr=133

Missouri v. Jenkins, 491 U.S. 274 (1989)

chapter **fourteen**

POSTCONVICTION PROCEDURES: MOTIONS, SENTENCES, APPEALS, AND HABEAS CORPUS

LEARNING OBJECTIVES

After reading this chapter, you should be able to

- Recognize the many different stages and procedures that can occur after a defendant is convicted of a criminal offense.

- Appreciate the dynamics of a sentencing hearing, including the factors used to set a defendant's sentence, the constitutional and legal requirements of a sentencing hearing, the possibility of sentencing enhancements, the availability of sentencing enhancements, and the role of the U.S. Sentencing Guidelines in federal cases.

- Explain the availability and use of post-conviction motions, including a motion to withdraw a plea, a motion for a new trial, and a motion for judgment of acquittal.

- Prepare a basic motion for a new trial and a motion to withdraw a defendant's plea.

- Understand the nature and procedures associated with a forfeiture hearing.

- Prepare a notice of appeal.

- Understand the appellate process within your state's court system and the federal judiciary.

- Appreciate the process for filing a petition for a writ of habeas corpus in the federal courts.

We will not punish a man because he hath offended, but that he may offend no more; nor does punishment ever look to the past, but to the future; for it is not the result of passion, but that the same thing be guarded against in time to come.

—Seneca (3 B.C.–A.D. 65)

Punishment, that is justice for the unjust.

—Saint Augustine (A.D. 354–430)

An appeal . . . is when you ask one court to show its contempt for another court.

—Finley Peter Dunne (1867–1936)

INTRODUCTION

This chapter examines the procedural and legal issues facing professionals after a defendant is convicted. Several possible proceedings can occur after a conviction, including postconviction motions, sentencing hearings, appeals, and habeas corpus petitions. Among other things, this chapter addresses withdrawing pleas, motions for acquittal and new trial, the purposes of sentencing, the unique features of the U.S. Sentencing Guidelines, the process of appellate brief writing, and the procedures for seeking a writ of habeas corpus.

POSTCONVICTION TRIAL MOTIONS

As previously noted, the overwhelming majority of criminal convictions in the United States come through a plea agreement, where a defendant agrees to plead guilty or *nolo contendere* (no contest) to a criminal charge or charges. But in approximately 5 percent of criminal cases, convictions come by way of trial verdict, where a judge or jury finds the defendant guilty of a charged criminal offense or offenses. In both scenarios, there is a period between the conviction and the sentencing hearing where defendants may seek to undo their convictions by filing motions with the trial court. In most jurisdictions, these include a motion to withdraw the plea, motion for judgment of acquittal, and motion for new trial.

Motion to Withdraw Plea

Some defendants convicted through plea agreements have second thoughts about their pleas before they are sentenced. And in some instances, these defendants may wish to withdraw their plea agreement and proceed to trial. In these cases, legal professionals may be assisting attorneys in filing or defending against a ***motion to withdraw the plea***. Under the Federal Rule of Criminal Procedure 11(d), a motion to withdraw a plea can be filed anytime before a defendant is sentenced. But if the motion is filed after the district court has accepted the plea, but before sentencing, the defendant must show "a fair and just reason for requesting the withdrawal." Rule 11(d) provides:

motion to withdraw the plea
a legal petition asking the court to allow the defendant to undo a previously entered plea to a criminal charge

---

(d) Withdrawing a Guilty or *Nolo Contendere* Plea.

A defendant may withdraw a plea of guilty or nolo contendere:

    (1) before the court accepts the plea, for any reason or no reason; or

    (2) after the court accepts the plea, but before it imposes sentence if:

        (A) the court rejects a plea agreement under Rule 11(c)(5); or

        (B) the defendant can show a fair and just reason for requesting the withdrawal.

The task for legal professionals representing defendants is to find and support a "fair and just reason" for withdrawing the plea. Such reasons might include the defendant's misunderstanding of the plea agreement's content, undue pressure placed on the defendant to enter a plea, or ignorance of the plea agreement's possible consequences. Typically, this is not an easy task, and defense professionals will need to provide the court with specific and credible evidence for the motion. See Figure 14-1. This might include an affidavit from the defendant and anyone else (family member, physician, attorney, and so on) who may have insight into what the defendant was thinking at the time the original plea was entered.

FIGURE 14-1 **Motion to Withdraw Plea Agreement Filed by Convicted 9/11 Conspirator Zacarias Moussaoui**

THE UNITED STATES DISTRICT COURT
FOR THE EASTERN DISTRICT OF VIRGINIA
Alexandria Division

UNITED STATES OF AMERICA	)	
	)	
v.	)	Criminal No. 01-455-A
	)	Hon. Leonie M. Brinkema
ZACARIAS MOUSSAOUI	)	

DEFENDANT'S MOTION TO WITHDRAW GUILTY PLEA

Defendant Zacarias Moussaoui ("Moussaoui"), through counsel, pursuant to Rule 11(d) of the Federal Rules of Criminal Procedure,[1] respectfully moves the Court to allow him to withdraw his guilty plea and have a new trial on the question of his guilt to the charges in the Indictment. In support of this motion, Moussaoui states as follows:

1. On April 22, 2005, Moussaoui entered a guilty plea to all of the charges contained in the Indictment. The Court accepted that plea and thereafter, proceeded to conduct a sentencing trial to determine whether Moussaoui should receive the penalty of death.

2. On May 3, 2006, the jury impaneled to determine Moussaoui's sentence rejected imposition of the death penalty for him. The following day, on May 4, 2006, the Court sentenced Moussaoui to consecutive life counts.

3. On May 5, 2006, Moussaoui informed his counsel that he wished to withdraw his guilty plea.

4. As stated in the attached notarized affidavit from Moussaoui dated May 6, 2006, Moussaoui wishes to withdraw his guilt plea because when he entered the plea, his "understanding of the American legal system was completely flawed." Affidavit at ¶ 8. "Because I now see that it is possible that I can receive a fair trial," the Affidavit states, "even with Americans as jurors and that I can have the opportunity to prove that I did not have any knowledge of and was not a member of the plot to hijack planes and crash them into buildings on September 11, 2001, I wish to withdraw my guilty plea and ask the Court for a new trial to prove my innocence of the September 11 plot." *Id.* at ¶ 18.

CONCLUSION

For the foregoing reasons, Defendant Zacarias Moussaoui respectfully requests that the Court permit him to withdraw his guilty plea and have a new trial so that he may contest his guilt to the charges contained in the Indictment.

---

[1] Defense counsel are aware that Rule 11(e) prohibits a defendant from withdrawing a guilty plea after imposition of sentence. Notwithstanding this prohibition, counsel is filing this motion given their problematic relationship with Moussaoui, of which the Court is well aware.

(continued)

FIGURE 14-1 **Continued**

Respectfully Submitted,

Zacarias Moussaoui
By Counsel

/s/

Gerald T. Zerkin
Sr. Assistant Federal Public Defender
Kenneth P. Troccoli
Anne M. Chapman
Assistant Federal Public Defenders
Eastern District of Virginia
1650 King Street, Suite 500
Alexandria, VA 22314
(703) 600-0800

/s/

Edward B. MacMahon, Jr.
107 East Washington Street
P.O. Box 903
Middleburg, VA 20117
(540) 687-3902

/s/

Alan H. Yamamoto
643 South Washington Street
Alexandria, VA 22314
(703) 684-4700

For prosecutorial professionals, the task is to show that the defendant properly understood the terms and consequences of the plea agreement and otherwise entered into the agreement voluntarily. Prosecutors typically rely on the transcript from the plea hearing, where the trial court asked the defendant several questions about the defendant's understanding of the plea agreement prior to accepting the defendant's plea. The defendant's answers provided during this prior hearing are then used to rebut the defendant's current claims of misunderstandings about the terms or consequences of the plea agreement.

Again, it is important to note that, under Federal Rule 11(e), "[a]fter the court imposes sentence, the defendant may not withdraw a plea of guilty or *nolo contendere*, and the plea may be set aside only on direct appeal or collateral attack." As a result, in these situations, a different motion must be used to set aside the plea agreement.

Motion for Judgment of Acquittal

In cases where defendants are convicted by a judge or jury, they often ask the trial court to nonetheless issue a judgment of acquittal, asserting that the evidence presented during trial was insufficient to meet the elements of the charged offense. The argument is presented through a ***motion for judgment of acquittal***. Typically, this motion can be filed, either orally or in writing, at three points during the trial process—after the prosecution rests its case, after both sides have rested their case, and following the verdict. With regard to the first two stages where a motion for acquittal can be filed, Federal Rule of Criminal Procedure 29(a) provides:

motion for judgment of acquittal a defendant's legal petition to the court to find him not guilty

(a) Before Submission to the Jury.

After the government closes its evidence or after the close of all the evidence, the court on the defendant's motion must enter a judgment of acquittal of any offense for which the evidence is insufficient to sustain a conviction. The court may on its own consider whether the evidence is insufficient to sustain a conviction. If the court denies a motion for a judgment of acquittal at the close of the government's evidence, the defendant may offer evidence without having reserved the right to do so.

In cases where defendants are convicted by a judge or jury, they may file a motion for judgment of acquittal before they are sentenced, arguing that the evidence in the trial record does not support the conviction. Federal Rule of Criminal Procedure 29(c) provides:

(c) After Jury Verdict or Discharge.

(1) Time for a Motion.

A defendant may move for a judgment of acquittal, or renew such a motion, within 14 days after a guilty verdict or after the court discharges the jury, whichever is later.

(2) Ruling on the Motion.

If the jury has returned a guilty verdict, the court may set aside the verdict and enter an acquittal. If the jury has failed to return a verdict, the court may enter a judgment of acquittal.

In most postconviction motions for judgment of acquittal, the job of the defense professional is to demonstrate that there is not enough evidence in the record to prove all elements of the charged criminal offense. Typically, this is done by comparing the evidence reflected in the trial transcript to the elements of the charged offense. By breaking down each element of the offense and matching it to the evidence (or lack thereof) in the transcript, defendants can show that the prosecutor failed to meet the burden of proof in the case.

For prosecutorial professionals, the task is very much the same. In responding to a defendant's motion for judgment of acquittal, prosecutors demonstrate points of evidence found in the trial record that sufficiently support each element of the criminal charge. Oftentimes, this involves a formal review of the trial transcript and a written response to the defendant's motion. But in other cases, this procedure is more informal, using an oral argument before the court based on a general recollection of the evidence presented during trial.

Law Line 14-1
Motion for Judgment of Acquittal

Motion for New Trial

In some cases where defendants are convicted through trial, they may seek a new trial based on extenuating circumstances that they believe affected the verdict. A defendant's request for a new trial is made through a ***motion for a new trial***. This motion asks the trial court to vacate the defendant's earlier conviction and allow a second trial to proceed. Typically, to support a motion for a new trial, defendants must show that "the interest of justice" warrants a new trial. Such interest might include evidence of misconduct by the jury, prosecutor, or trial court, unfair surprise during trial, or newly discovered evidence obtained after the verdict. Federal Rule of Criminal Procedure 33 outlines the procedure for requesting a new trial in federal courts:

motion for a new trial
a legal petition by a defendant to a court seeking a new criminal trial; often based on newly discovered evidence

---

(a) Defendant's Motion.

Upon the defendant's motion, the court may vacate any judgment and grant a new trial if the interest of justice so requires. If the case was tried without a jury, the court may take additional testimony and enter a new judgment.

(b) Time to File.

(1) Newly Discovered Evidence.

Any motion for a new trial grounded on newly discovered evidence must be filed within 3 years after the verdict or finding of guilty. If an appeal is pending, the court may not grant a motion for a new trial until the appellate court remands the case.

(2) Other Grounds.

Any motion for a new trial grounded on any reason other than newly discovered evidence must be filed within 14 days after the verdict or finding of guilty.

Defense professionals seeking to support a motion for a new trial must provide the trial court with specific evidence demonstrating that the "interest of justice" requires a new trial. Unlike a motion for judgment of acquittal, where the question is whether there is sufficient evidence to support the criminal charges, a motion for new trial assesses whether extraordinary factors or circumstances unduly and unfairly influenced the trial process. In some cases, this may include new evidence—a previously unknown witness, document, or forensic item, which is favorable to the defendant but discovered after the verdict. In other cases, it might include jury misconduct, prosecutorial misconduct, purportedly incorrect and prejudicial court rulings, or other unusual and unfair events that likely impacted the guilty verdict. See Figure 14-2.

FIGURE 14-2 **Motion for New Trial**

**IN THE CIRCUIT COURT OF GREENE COUNTY, MISSOURI
THIRTY-FIRST JUDICIAL DISTRICT**

CITY OF SPRINGFIELD,

Plaintiff,   Case No. 398MU0065

Vs.

Robin C. McDermott,

Defendant)

<u>MOTION FOR NEW TRIAL</u>

COMES NOW Robin C. McDermott, defendant, pursuant to Missouri Supreme Court Rule 29.11 (d) requesting this honorable court grant defendant a new trial in the above style case. In support of her request defendant offers the following:

1. The trial court erred in allowing prosecutor to proceed against defendant in charging a non-existent and spurious offense under Springfield City Code 26-17. What the defendant was convicted of is not a crime, but rather constitutionally protected free speech.
2. The trial court erred in failing to instruct the jury in writing as to what Springfield City Code 26-17 says and erred again when the jury requested to see 26-17 and was denied, and erred again when the defendant requested the jury read 26-17, in contradiction to Missouri Supreme Court Rule 27.03. The text of 26-17 had been admitted into evidence and the jury should have had access to that evidence. Had the jury read the City Code, the defendant would have been found to be not guilty.
3. The trial court erred in refusing to allow defendant's offering of the written United States Supreme Court case of <u>City of Houston v. Hill</u> with regard to its holding concerning "verbal aggression" and city ordinances, but rather allowed itself to be persuaded by plaintiff rattling off cases he claimed had ruling authority over the holding in the Hill case but which when asked by the court could not tell the court the holdings of any of his cited cases and in so doing the defendant's right to present a viable defense was prevented by the court.
4. The trial court erred in holding instruction conference prior to the close of all evidence. Missouri Supreme Court Rule 28.03 (e) states in relevant part, "at the **close** of evidence the court shall call a conference of counsel for the purpose of considering instruction and verdict forms." As the court well knows, defendant was not permitted to finish presenting her case or to be fully apprised of the testimony of plaintiff's rebuttal witness before the court held the instruction conference and thereby significantly prejudiced defendant's opportunity to request appropriate instructions. Had the instruction conference been held at the correct time, the defendant would have offered additional or different instructions.

(continued)

FIGURE 14-2 **Continued**

5. The trial court erred in denying the defendant's jury instruction informing the jury that cussing a cop is constitutionally protected free speech and that the standard of "fighting words" is what constitutes a crime. The defendant was denied the opportunity to give the jury a definition of "fighting words".

6. The trial court erred in that the instruction does not comport the offense charged and there is a significant variance between the information and the verdict director. The verdict director enlarges the presumption of guilt beyond an already spurious offense charged in the information in that the information specifies "obstructed officer Royal by verbal aggression" and the verdict director specified "interfered with officers" and equates interference as meaning obstruction and lessens the burden of proof the plaintiff is required to carry.

7. The trial court erred in allowing the jury to remain during sidebar argument over the ambush of defendant by plaintiff with an inadmissible, misrepresented, and ancient past history of defendant that the plaintiff had no right to introduce. It prejudiced the jury in that it caused the jury to assume that the defendant was hiding a criminal history. The court should have declared a mistrial.

8. The trial court erred in prohibiting note taking by jurors stating that the case was not complex enough and then subsequently stating that the court did not know what the case was about. The two statements are not compatible. The fact that at least one juror felt it necessary to take notes in order to keep the facts of the case correctly before him contraindicates the court's pronouncement.

9. The trial court erred in allowing the plaintiff to question defendant concerning irrelevant, immaterial and inflammatory matters concerning the status of defendant's employer's lawsuits. This line of questioning prejudiced the rights of the defendant by creating a negative association with the defendant's employer's lawsuit history without establishing any evidentiary grounds to support its relevancy.

10. A new trial should be granted because the prosecutor's attempted assassination of defendant's character through plaintiff's innuendo that she is a doper and all her friends are dopers during the last five minutes of his closing arguments when the defendant had no opportunity to rebut these allegations.

11. The totality of the plaintiff's case shows an insufficiency of evidence to convict defendant of obstructing officer Royal by verbal aggression in that the state offered no evidence or argument that the defendants language rose to the level of "fighting words". Had the jury been given the language of the information, the language of Springfield City Code 26-17 alongside of the improper jury instruction #7, and in light of the evidence presented by plaintiff, the defendant would have been acquitted.

WHEREFORE defendant prays the court find that defendant was not given a fair trial on 19 and 20 April 99 in this case and is entitled to a new trial and that the court enter its order for same.

Respectfully submitted,

_____
Robin C. McDermott

Prosecutors generally respond to motions for a new trial by evaluating the credibility of the claims asserted by the defendant and assessing whether, if reliable, these claimed irregularities made a difference in the trial verdict. In most cases, prosecutors will argue that the "interest of justice" does not merit a new trial because the defendant's claims are not reliable and/or not sufficient to warrant a new trial. In circumstances involving claims of newly discovered evidence, prosecutors may claim that the evidence would not have made a difference in the first trial or that the defendants had access to or should have reasonably discovered the evidence prior to the first trial.

Legal professionals in the criminal justice system regularly work with presentence motions for plea withdrawals, judgments of acquittal, and new trials. Obviously, professionals should become familiar with the format and procedural requirements for these motions, as dictated by the applicable court rules. Legal professionals also need to hone their observation skills and learn to closely monitor the events surrounding a defendant's plea or trial. With regard to pleas, pay attention to the defendant's demeanor and any circumstances that occur between the plea hearing and the sentencing hearing. For trial settings, professionals must outline the elements of the charged offense prior to trial and compare them to the evidence being introduced. If there is insufficient evidence to support even one element of the offense, this assertion should be addressed in a motion for judgment of acquittal. Also monitor any unusual events—including problems with the jury members, court rulings, or prosecutorial behavior. These items may form the basis of a postconviction motion. In addition, if these items are asserted in a motion but denied by the trial court, they may also form the basis for an appeal (see below).

SENTENCING

In criminal cases, **sentencing** is typically the last proceeding before a trial court. Sentencing can be defined as the process through which a sentencing authority imposes a lawful punishment or other sanction on a person convicted of violating the criminal law. One fundamental way of distinguishing crimes from violations of the civil law, or torts, is to recognize that crimes are subject to punishment. As one legal scholar notes, "[t]he best candidate for a conceptual proposition about the criminal law is that the infliction of 'punishment' is sufficient to render a legal process criminal in nature."[1] Thus, it is important to realize that punishment, as a mechanism of the criminal law, can be distinguished from other attempts to discourage undesirable conduct, such as taxes, licensing requirements, civil liability, and administrative regulations.

sentencing
the process through which a sentencing authority imposes a lawful punishment or other sanction on a person convicted of violating the criminal law

Purposes of Punishment

Punishment is not the only goal of sentencing. There are five primary sentencing rationales that operate in American criminal justice today: (1) retribution, (2) deterrence, (3) rehabilitation, (4) restoration, and (5) incapacitation. See Figure 14-3.

Retribution is the most punishment-oriented of all sentencing goals and underlies the just deserts philosophy. The basic purpose of retribution is to "get back" at the offender by meting out a punishment that is in some primal way satisfying to the social group and to the victim or his or her survivors. Still, retribution may call for even harsher punishments than those that are merely "deserved." As a result, some legal philosophers have suggested that punishment should never be based solely on retributive sentiments. Jeremy Bentham, for example, whose writings have substantially influenced American jurisprudence, suggested that "punishment ought not be inflicted . . . where it must be inefficacious: where it cannot act so as to prevent the mischief."[2]

Criminal sentencing also has **deterrence** as one of its goals. Deterrence, like retribution, also depends on the imposition of punishment—although for a different purpose. With deterrence, punishment is seen as a powerful inhibitor, capable of keeping behavior in line. There are two types of deterrence—specific and general. **Specific deterrence** is intended to deter the individual sentenced to punishment from

retribution
the act of taking revenge on a criminal perpetrator; the most punishment-oriented of all sentencing goals, claiming that we are justified in punishing offenders because they deserve it

deterrence
a goal of criminal sentencing that seeks to prevent persons from committing crimes similar to the one for which an offender is being sentenced

specific deterrence
a goal of criminal sentencing that seeks to prevent a particular offender from engaging in repeat criminality

FIGURE 14-3 **Objectives of Sentencing**

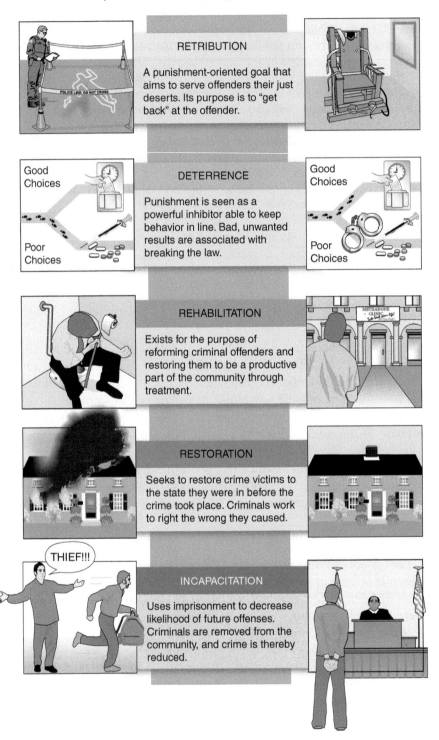

general deterrence
a goal of criminal sentencing that seeks to prevent others from committing crimes similar to the one for which a particular offender is being sentenced by making an example of the person sentenced

committing future offenses. A burglar sentenced to a number of years in prison, for example, may find the lack of freedom such a painful experience that he refrains from committing any new crimes once released. *General deterrence*, on the other hand, uses punishment as an example to others who may be contemplating breaking the law. As a result, the burglar sentenced to prison stands as an example to associates that they, too, may face a similar fate if they choose the same course of action.

Rehabilitation is a third goal of criminal sentencing. The purpose of rehabilitation is to reform criminal offenders, restoring them to productive lives within the community. Rehabilitation programs may include a punishment component but may also include job or skills training, educational course work leading to high school completion, counseling, and psychological treatment. From the point of view of rehabilitation, the nature of the criminal offense is of less significance than the supposed likelihood of reforming the offender—except insofar as the offense committed provides a clue to the need for specific rehabilitative strategies.

Another goal of criminal sentencing can be ***restoration*** or restitution. This objective emphasizes the emotional and financial cost of crime to its victims and seeks to restore crime victims to their position in life before victimization. This is sometimes called "making the victim whole." This sentencing objective seeks to make victims and the community whole again. It frequently builds on the use of fines, restitution, and community service—forms of punishment that may be imposed on offenders by a sentencing judge.

A final sentencing purpose can be ***incapacitation***, which typically uses imprisonment or another form of confinement to protect the community from additional harm. Essentially, incapacitation is based on the notion that "those who are removed from a community, particularly through incarceration, cannot victimize society during a time of physical separation."[3] For example, the federal sentencing guidelines allow defendants to be designated as ***career offenders*** if "(1) the defendant was at least eighteen years old at the time of the . . . offense, (2) the . . . offense is a crime of violence or trafficking in a controlled substance, and (3) the defendant has at least two prior felony convictions of either a crime of violence or a controlled substance offense."[4] Similarly, as discussed in greater detail below, some states have adopted three-strikes legislation, which mandates long prison sentences for offenders convicted of a third felony offense.

Sentencing Hearings

The procedures followed during sentencing hearings can vary depending on the jurisdiction and the nature of the criminal case.

State Misdemeanor Cases. In many state and local courts, sentencing hearings for misdemeanor cases can be fairly quick and informal. In some cases, when a defendant stands before a judge and pleads guilty or no contest to a criminal charge, the court will immediately impose the sentence. But even in these informal proceedings, judges must afford defendants the ***right of allocution***, which is the opportunity to speak to the court prior to being sentenced. This is a fundamental right of all criminal defendants and, if not offered, can lead to the reversal of the sentence on appeal. In many cases, the court satisfies this right by turning to the defendant or the defense attorney and asking, "Anything in mitigation?" This allows defendants or their attorneys to provide the court with information about the defendant or the circumstances of the crime.

In some cases, defendants want to offer the court some personal information, such as the defendant's family, employment, or health circumstances. In other cases, defendants want to apologize to the court and/or the victim(s) and assure the court that they will not commit future offenses. In still other cases, defendants might say nothing, especially when advised by their attorneys that any admissions during a sentencing hearing might undermine an anticipated appeal of the case. In some jurisdictions, in order for some issues to be preserved for appeal, defendants must maintain their innocence throughout the trial court proceedings. Thus, defendants who admit fault or apologize to victims may compromise their ability to present some issues on appeal.

rehabilitation

the attempt to reform a criminal offender; also, the state in which a reformed offender is said to be

restoration

a sentencing goal that seeks to make victims and the community "whole again"

incapacitation

the use of imprisonment or other means to reduce the likelihood that an offender will be capable of committing future offenses

career offender

under federal sentencing guidelines, a person who (1) is at least eighteen years old at the time of the most recent offense, (2) is convicted of a felony that is either a crime of violence or a controlled substance offense, and (3) has at least two prior felony convictions of either a crime of violence or a controlled substance offense

right of allocution

the right of a criminal defendant to speak to the trial court before a sentence is imposed

Law Line 14-2

National Alliance of Sentencing Advocates and Mitigation Specialists

presentence investigation report (PSR or PSI)
a written report prepared for a trial judge containing information and factors about the defendant and the offense; used to help the judge make a sentencing decision

State Felony Cases.   In more serious state criminal cases, including many felony cases, the judge will order the probation department to prepare a ***presentence investigation report*** (**PSR or PSI**). A probation officer is then assigned to compile information in a report for the judge. The length and detail of these reports can vary. But generally, the PSR or PSI is designed to provide the sentencing judge with some background information on the defendant and the circumstances of the offense. PSRs are particularly instructive in cases where defendants are convicted through a plea, where judges are not given the same depth of detail regarding the offense as they would receive during a full trial. Accordingly, defendants, their attorneys, and prosecutors must work closely with the probation officer to ensure that relevant and accurate information is supplied in the PSR. In addition, where defendants plan to file an appeal on guilt-based issues, defendants and their counsel must be careful not to admit guilt or responsibility to probation officers, as this may undermine these issues for appeal.

During felony sentencing hearings, defendants must still be afforded the right of allocution. And in some cases, defendants or their attorneys may wish to provide the court with witnesses or other evidence supporting the defendant's good character. In other cases, defendants want the court to know they have family members or employers who need them and who would suffer if they are incarcerated. Overall, the basic purpose of this evidence is to provide the court with mitigating factors (see below) surrounding the defendant and/or the crime.

victim impact statements
statements made to the trial court by victims during a sentencing hearing

Conversely, prosecutors may call victims, their family members, or investigating officers to testify about the aggravating factors (see below) surrounding the defendant or the crime. This evidence often comes in the form of ***victim impact statements***, which are statements provided by victims and designed to show the court the full impact of the defendant's criminal conduct. In addition, the sentencing court needs to know the defendant's criminal history—the nature and scope of the defendant's prior convictions. As such, prosecutors and defense attorneys must carefully review the defendant's criminal record to ensure its accuracy.

Federal Cases.   In federal cases, sentencing hearings tend to be more formal and lengthy than in state courts. Once a federal defendant is convicted, either through plea agreement or trial, the district court judge refers the case to the U.S. probation department, where a probation officer is assigned to the case. The probation officer then prepares a PSR or PSI for the judge's review. The PSR in federal cases is similar to that used in some state cases, but generally federal PSRs are far more detailed and lengthy than most state reports. A federal PSR contains a substantial amount of information about the background of the defendant and the facts and circumstances of the criminal offense(s).

One of the primary purposes of the PSR is to provide the judge with an initial calculation of the federal sentencing guidelines (see below) as they apply to the facts of the case. To complete this task, the probation officer makes certain factual and legal judgments about the defendant's conduct and criminal history, as well as the applicability of the sentencing guidelines. To this end, both the Assistant U.S. Attorney (AUSA) and the defense attorney (possibly along with the defendant) meet with the probation officer to discuss the details of the case, as they view them. The probation officer may also contact other individuals associated with the case in order to gather sufficient information for the PSR. This process can take several weeks.

Once completed, the PSR is submitted to the district court. The AUSA and defense attorney are permitted to file objections to the PSR's findings based on legal and/or factual disputes. The district court then conducts a sentencing hearing where the judge—who is free to adopt, modify, or reject the findings in the PSR—will address and rule upon the parties' objections to the PSR. At the hearing, the parties can present additional evidence or argument regarding the applicability of the sentencing guidelines to the case. At the end of the hearing, the judge announces the defendant's sentence from the bench and later produces a written sentencing order that is filed with the clerk of court. Generally, this order constitutes the district court's final judgment in the case.

Sentencing Factors

In cases not involving mandatory minimum sentencing, judges must decide the appropriate sentence for the defendant. Generally, judges consider both aggravating and mitigating circumstances underlying the case. *Aggravating factors* are "circumstances relating to the commission of a crime which cause its gravity to be greater than that of the average instance of the given type of offense."[5] Conversely, *mitigating factors* are "circumstances surrounding the commission of a crime which do not in law justify or excuse the act, but which in fairness may be considered as reducing the blameworthiness of the defendant."[6] some typical aggravating and mitigating factors considered by judges are listed in Figure 14-4.

aggravating factor
a circumstance surrounding a crime that makes the offense appear to be more serious than the average offense of this type

mitigating factor
a circumstance surrounding a crime that makes the offense appear to be less serious than the average offense of this type

---

FIGURE 14-4 **Aggravating and Mitigating Factors**

AGGRAVATING FACTORS

- The defendant induced others to participate in the commission of the offense.
- The offense was especially heinous, atrocious, or cruel.
- The defendant was armed with or used a deadly weapon at the time of the crime.
- The offense was committed for the purpose of avoiding or preventing a lawful arrest or effecting an escape from custody.
- The offense was committed for hire.
- The offense was committed against a present or former law enforcement officer or correctional officer while engaged in the performance of official duties or because of the past exercise of official duties.
- The defendant took advantage of a position of trust or confidence to commit the offense.

MITIGATING FACTORS

- The defendant has no record of criminal convictions punishable by more than 60 days of imprisonment.
- The defendant has made substantial or full restitution.
- The defendant has been a person of good character or has had a good reputation in the community.
- The defendant aided in the apprehension of another felon or testified truthfully on behalf of the prosecution.
- The defendant acted under strong provocation, or the victim was a voluntary participant in the criminal activity or otherwise consented to it.
- The offense was committed under duress, coercion, threat, or compulsion, which was insufficient to constitute a defense but significantly reduced the defendant's culpability.
- The defendant was suffering from a mental or physical condition that was insufficient to constitute a defense but significantly reduced culpability for the offense.

Legal professionals working on sentencing matters must use the aggravating or mitigating factors to persuade the judge for a higher or lower sentence than that given to the average defendant in a similar case. For defense professionals, the focus is typically on the mitigating factors, such as a first-time offender, limited loss, extreme remorse, or other factors sympathetic to the defendant. For prosecutorial professionals, the focus is often on the aggravating factors, such as the defendant's criminal history, the scope of the damages, or the defendant's lack of remorse.

Judges may use a checklist to assess the appropriateness of a criminal sentence. In some jurisdictions, these lists outline the possible aggravating and mitigating factors surrounding a criminal offense, as established under the criminal law, thereby allowing the judge to simply check a box or two of factors to justify the court's sentencing order. In other jurisdictions, the checklist focuses on the severity of the offense and the likelihood of the defendant's *recidivism* (committing additional crimes in the future). For example, in Ohio felony cases, judges are instructed to evaluate (1) the seriousness of the defendant's offense(s), using factors that might indicate that it was either more serious or less serious than the average type of offense, and (2) the likelihood of the defendant's recidivism, using factors that indicate a greater or lesser likelihood of future criminal activity by the defendant. See Figure 14-5. These charts can also assist legal professionals in tailoring the facts of their case to the relevant standards for sentencing.

Law Line 14-3
Mitigating Circumstances

recidivism
repeated criminal activity

FIGURE 14-5 **Ohio's Judicial Reference Sheet for Felony Sentencing**

FELONY SENTENCING QUICK REFERENCE GUIDE
May, 2002
Ohio Criminal Sentencing Commission-Chief Justice Thomas Moyer, Chairman-David Diroll, Director prepared with support from the Ohio Judicial Conference

PURPOSES AND PRINCIPLES The sentence must comply with these purposes and principles—$2929.11:
☐ **Overriding Purposes:** Punish the offender and protect the public from future crime by the offender and others
☐ **Principles:** Always consider the need for incapacitation, deterrence, rehabilitation, and restitution
    ☐ Sentence should be commensurate with, and not demeaning to, the seriousness of offender's conduct and restitution impact on the victim and consistent with sentences for similar crimes by similar offenders
    ☐ Do not sentence based on the offender's race, ethnicity, gender, or religion

FACTORS TO CONSIDER IN EVERY CASE Weight these factors, if present:
More Serious—$2929.12(B):
    ☐ Injury exacerbated by victim's physical or mental condition or age
    ☐ Victim suffered serious physical, psychological, or economic harm
    ☐ Offender held public office or position of trust and the offense related to the office or position
    ☐ Offender's occupation obliged the offender to prevent the offense or to bring those committing it to justice
    ☐ Offender's reputation, occupation, or office used to facilitate offense or likely to influence other's conduct

(continued)

FIGURE 14-5 **Continued**

- □ Offender's relationship with the victim facilitated the offense
- □ Offender acted for hire or as part of organized criminal activity
- □ Offender's was motivated by prejudice based on race, ethnicity, gender, sexual orientation, or religion
- □ Offender is a parent or other custodian and the offense was domestic violence or an assault involving a family or household member committed in the vicinity of one or more children other than the victim
- □ Any other relevant factor(s) indicating the conduct is more serious

Less Serious—$2929.12(C):

- □ Victim induced or facilitated the Offense
- □ Offender acted under strong provocation
- □ Offender did not cause or expect to cause harm to person or property
- □ There are substantial grounds to mitigate the offender's conduct
- □ Any other relevant factor(s) indicating the conduct is less serious

Recidivism More Likely—2929.12(D):

- □ Offense while on bail, awaiting sentencing, on community control, PRC, etc, or after unfavorable PRC
- □ Offender has a history of criminal convictions or juvenile delinquency adjudications
- □ Offender has not responded favorably to sanctions previously imposed in adult or juvenile court
- □ Offender has pattern of alcohol/drug use related to offense & does not acknowledge it or refuses treatment
- □ Offender shows no genuine remorse
- □ Any other relevant factor(s) indicating recidivism is more likely

Recidivism Less Likely—2929.12(E):

- □ Offender has no prior juvenile delinquency adjudication
- □ Offender has no prior adult conviction
- □ Offender has led a law-abiding life for a significant number of years
- □ Offense was committed under circumstances unlikely to recur
- □ Offender shows genuine remorse
- □ Any other relevant factors(s) indicating recidivism is less likely

MANDATORY PRISON TERMS A prison term must be imposed in these cases—$2929.13(F):

- □ Aggravated murder when a death sentence is not imposed, or murder
- □ **Certain sex offenses:** Any rape; attempted rape with victim under 13; gross sexual imposition or sexual battery if with prior conviction for rape, FSP, GSI, or sexual battery involving victim under 13; and anyone convicted of a sexually violent predator specification
- □ Felony vehicular homicides/assaults and felony OVI when specfied by statute as mandatory
- □ F-1, F-2, and F-3 drug offenses when specified by statute as mandatory
- □ Agg. murder, murder, or any F-1, F-2, or F-3 offense of violence in a school safety zone
- □ Any repeat violent offender (RVO) as defined in $2929.01(DD)
- □ Any other F-1 orF-2 when the offender has a prior agg. murder, murder, F-1, or F-2

(continued)

FIGURE 14-5 **Continued**

☐ Anyone convicted of a gun specificatiojn (gun spec time is mandatory; the underlying offense may not be)
☐ Anyone convicted of wearing or carrying body armor in committing a felony offense of violence
☐ Corrupt activity (racketeering) when the mose serious predicate offense is an F-1
    ☐ Any felony offense of violence involving criminal gang activity
    ☐ Any prison employee convicted of illegally conveying improper items into the prison

---

Federal Sentencing Guidelines

United States Sentencing Guidelines (USSG)
federal standards used to assess sentences in criminal cases

In federal criminal cases, judges used the ***United States Sentencing Guidelines*** (USSG) when imposing criminal sentences. In 1984, Congress passed the Sentencing Reform Act,[7] which established the U.S. Sentencing Commission and authorized this agency to establish determinate sentencing guidelines for federal cases. The sentencing guidelines adopted by the Sentencing Commission became effective on November 1, 1987.

The federal sentencing guidelines use two primary factors to compute a range for a defendant's sentence—the seriousness of the defendant's offense and the defendant's criminal history. The sentencing guidelines are built around a table containing forty-three rows and six columns. Each row corresponds to a separate offense level, reflective of the seriousness of the crime. And each column corresponds to a different criminal history category. The federal sentencing table is reproduced in Figure 14-6.

In terms of the offense level, the sentencing guidelines manual outlines a multitude of factors that are used to calculate the severity of the offense. Generally speaking, defendants who cause more harm receive more points than those causing less harm. For example, defendants involved with larger drug quantities in narcotics cases or who cause greater financial loss in fraud cases generally will receive more points based on their conduct. In addition, points can be subtracted as well, if there are mitigating factors surrounding the defendant's conduct. For example, if a defendant accepts responsibility for the offense or provides substantial assistance to law enforcement officers, the point total may be reduced. After all factors are considered under the sentencing guidelines, a resulting point total will indicate the defendant's offense level.

federal question
constitutional doctrine that requires litigants seeking jurisdiction before a federal judicial body to present a question (issue of law) involving a federal constitutional provision, a U.S. treaty or statute, or an action by federal authorities

With regard to a defendant's criminal history, the appropriate criminal history category (column) is determined based the number and nature of the defendant's prior convictions. Generally, each prior sentence of imprisonment for more than one year and one month counts as three points. Two points are assigned for each prior prison sentence over six months or if the defendant committed the offense while on probation, parole, or work release. The system also assigns points for other types of previous convictions and for offenses committed less than two years after release from imprisonment. Points are added to determine the criminal history category into which an offender falls.

Then using the defendant's calculated criminal history category and offense level, a recommended range for sentencing is identified. These ranges are identified in terms of months. For example, a judge reviewing a defendant with a criminal

FIGURE 14-6 **U.S. Sentencing Guidelines Chart**

Months of Imprisonment
Criminal History Category (Criminal History Points)

	Offense Level	I (0 or 1)	II (2 or 3)	III (4, 5, 6)	IV (7, 8, 9)	V (10, 11, 12)	VI (13 or More)
Zone A	1	0–6	0–6	0–6	0–6	0–6	0–6
	2	0–6	0–6	0–6	0–6	0–6	1–7
	3	0–6	0–6	0–6	0–6	2–8	3–9
	4	0–6	0–6	0–6	2–8	4–10	6–12
	5	0–6	0–6	1–7	4–10	6–12	9–15
	6	0–6	1–7	2–8	6–12	9–15	12–18
	7	0–6	2–8	4–10	8–14	12–18	15–21
	8	0–6	4–10	6–12	10–16	15–21	18–24
Zone B	9	4–10	6–12	8–14	12–18	18–24	21–27
	10	6–12	8–14	10–16	15–21	21–27	24–30
	11	8–14	10–16	12–18	18–24	24–30	27–33
Zone C	12	10–16	12–18	15–21	21–27	27–33	30–37
	13	12–18	15–21	18–24	24–30	30–37	33–41
	14	15–21	18–24	21–27	27–33	33–41	37–46
	15	18–24	21–27	24–30	30–37	37–46	41–51
	16	21–27	24–30	27–33	33–41	41–51	46–57
	17	24–30	27–33	30–37	37–46	46–57	51–63
	18	27–33	30–37	33–41	41–51	51–63	57–71
	19	30–37	33–41	37–46	46–57	57–71	63–78
	20	33–41	37–46	41–51	51–63	63–78	70–87
	21	37–46	41–51	46–57	57–71	70–87	77–96
	22	41–51	46–57	51–63	63–78	77–96	84–105
	23	46–57	51–63	57–71	70–87	84–105	92–115
	24	51–63	57–71	63–78	77–96	92–115	100–125
	25	57–71	63–78	70–87	84–105	100–125	110–137
	26	63–78	70–87	78–97	92–115	110–137	120–150
Zone D	27	70–87	78–97	87–108	100–125	120–150	130–162
	28	78–97	87–108	97–121	110–137	130–162	140–175
	29	87–108	97–121	108–135	121–151	140–175	151–188
	30	97–121	108–135	121–151	135–168	151–188	168–210
	31	108–135	121–151	135–168	151–188	168–210	188–235
	32	121–151	135–168	151–188	168–210	188–235	210–262
	33	135–168	151–188	168–210	188–235	210–262	235–293
	34	151–188	168–210	188–235	210–262	235–293	262–327
	35	168–210	188–235	210–262	235–293	262–327	292–365
	36	188–235	210–262	235–293	262–327	292–365	324–405
	37	210–262	235–293	262–327	292–365	324–405	360–life
	38	235–293	262–327	292–365	324–405	360–life	360–life
	39	262–327	292–365	324–405	360–life	360–life	360–life
	40	292–365	324–405	360–life	360–life	360–life	360–life
	41	324–405	360–life	360–life	360–life	360–life	360–life
	42	360–life	360–life	360–life	360–life	360–life	360–life
	43	Life	Life	Life	Life	Life	Life

Source: U.S. Sentencing Commission.

history category of II and an offense level of 16 would find that the sentencing guidelines recommend a sentence of twenty-four to thirty months.

As you can see, the sentencing guidelines table is also divided into four zones, which are organized by the three staircase lines running through the chart. These zones indicate the type of incarceration for defendants. Judges imposing sentences within Zone A can place the defendant on probation in lieu of incarceration. Zone B sentences allow judges to order defendants to serve their time in a "jail-like setting," which may include home incarceration, a treatment program, or some other nonprison setting. Under Zone C, judges can allow defendants to serve the second half of their sentence in a jail-like setting, after the first half is served in prison. And for Zone D, a defendant's full sentence must be served in prison. In addition, in most cases, defendants are eligible to receive fifty-four days per year of "good time" credit against their time, if they behave while in prison.

In *Mistretta v. United States* (1989),[8] the U.S. Supreme Court upheld the constitutionality of federal sentencing guidelines, after a federal prisoner argued that Congress had exceeded its constitutional authority in creating the U.S. Sentencing Commission and delegating legislative power to write federal sentencing practices. The Court concluded that, in a complex society, "Congress cannot do its job absent an ability to delegate power under broad general directives."

Law Line 14-4
United States Sentencing
Commission

Judicial Discretion in Sentencing

Generally, judges have considerable discretion in sentencing defendants. In most cases not involving mandatory minimum sentences, judges are free to sentence defendants to any sanction within those authorized under the criminal statute. And as long as judges do not abuse their discretion and can provide an identifiable and reasonable basis for their sentence under the relevant statute, their sentencing orders will likely be upheld as valid. But in recent years, there has been increased scrutiny given to judicial discretion and criminal sentences. And in a series of U.S. Supreme Court rulings, the Court has both enhanced this discretion and limited it.

In *Apprendi v. New Jersey* (2000),[9] the Supreme Court questioned the fact-finding authority of judges in making sentencing decisions, ruling that other than the fact of a prior conviction, any fact that increases the penalty for a crime beyond the prescribed statutory maximum is, in effect, an element of the crime that must be submitted to a jury and proved beyond a reasonable doubt. The Court held that "under the Due Process Clause of the Fifth Amendment and the notice and jury trial guarantees of the Sixth Amendment, any fact (other than prior conviction) that increases the maximum penalty for a crime must be charged in an indictment, submitted to a jury, and proven beyond a reasonable doubt." The *Apprendi* case raised the question of whether judges can deviate from established sentencing guidelines or apply sentence enhancements based on judicial determinations—as opposed to jury findings or defendant admissions—of aggravating factors that deviate from those guidelines.

Similarly, in *Ring v. Arizona* (2002),[10] the Supreme Court held that Arizona's capital sentencing law, which allowed judge-determined facts to serve as the basis of a death sentence, violated the Sixth Amendment right to a trial by jury. The *Ring* decision effectively overturned death penalty sentencing practices in as many as nine states. Essentially, *Ring* established that juries, not judges, must decide the facts that lead to a death sentence.

In *Blakely v. Washington* (2004),[11] the U.S. Supreme Court extended *Apprendi* and *Ring* by effectively invalidating sentencing schemes that allow judges rather than juries to determine any factor that imposes a mandatory increase in a defendant's criminal sentence, except for prior convictions. The Court found that because the facts supporting Blakely's increased sentence (a determination that he had acted with deliberate cruelty in kidnapping his estranged wife) were neither admitted by Blakely nor found by a jury, the sentence violated Blakely's Sixth Amendment right to trial by jury. The *Blakely* decision required that the sentencing laws of several jurisdictions be rewritten.

Law Line 14-5
Blakely v. Washington (2004)

Finally, in two 2005 cases, the U.S. Supreme Court further expanded the influence of *Apprendi*, *Ring*, and *Blakely* by applying their rationale to the federal sentencing guidelines. In *United States v. Booker*,[12] a Wisconsin federal jury convicted Freddie Booker of possessing and distributing crack cocaine and also determined that Booker had 92.5 grams of crack in his possession. Under federal sentencing guidelines, that amount of the drug would have limited Booker's maximum prison sentence to twenty-one years and ten months. During sentencing, however, the trial judge determined that Booker had distributed an additional 566 grams of crack cocaine, had perjured himself at trial, and had twenty-three prior convictions. As a result, the judge sentenced Booker to thirty years in prison. In other words, the judge-determined facts were used to enhance Booker's sentence beyond what the federal sentencing guidelines called for based on the jury-determined facts. Accordingly, Booker argued that the use of judge-determined facts to enhance his sentence violated his Sixth Amendment right to a trial by jury.

In *Booker*, and its companion case, *United States v. Fanfan* (2005),[13] the Supreme Court held that, to the extent that the federal sentencing guidelines required the judge to enhance a defendant's sentence based on facts not found by juries or admitted to by defendants, they violated the Sixth Amendment right to trial by jury. In other words, the Court found that federal sentencing guidelines unconstitutionally forced judges to increase sentences based on their own factual findings rather than on those of a jury. The Court further declared that the federal guidelines are "effectively advisory" in nature and do not impose mandatory requirements upon federal judges. In effect, the Court's ruling now allows federal judges to consider federal guideline ranges for sentencing but does not require them to tailor the sentence to the confines of the guideline factors. For some, the Court's decision essentially restored judicial discretion in federal sentencing.[14] Read the Court's opinion in *United States v. Booker* and *United States v. Fanfan* (2008) to assess its potential impact on judicial decisions in sentencing hearings.

CAPSTONE CASE   *United States v. Booker* and *United States v. Fanfan*, 543 U.S. 220 (2005)

Justice Stevens delivered the opinion of the Court in part.

The question presented in each of these cases is whether an application of the Federal Sentencing Guidelines violated the Sixth Amendment. In each case, the courts below held that binding rules set forth in the Guidelines limited the severity of the sentence that the judge could lawfully impose on the defendant based on the facts found by the jury at his trial. . . . We hold that both courts correctly concluded that the Sixth Amendment as construed in *Blakely* does apply to the Sentencing Guidelines. In a separate opinion authored by Justice Breyer, the Court concludes that in light of this holding, two provisions of the Sentencing Reform Act of 1984 (SRA) that have the effect of making the Guidelines mandatory must be invalidated in order to allow the statute to operate in a manner consistent with congressional intent.

(continued)

(continued)

Respondent Booker was charged with possession with intent to distribute at least 50 grams of cocaine base (crack). Having heard evidence that he had 92.5 grams in his duffel bag, the jury found him guilty of violating 21 U.S.C. § 841(a)(1). That statute prescribes a minimum sentence of 10 years in prison and a maximum sentence of life for that offense. §841(b)(1)(A)(iii).

Based upon Booker's criminal history and the quantity of drugs found by the jury, the Sentencing Guidelines required the District Court Judge to select a "base" sentence of not less than 210 nor more than 262 months in prison. The judge, however, held a post-trial sentencing proceeding and concluded by a preponderance of the evidence that Booker had possessed an additional 566 grams of crack and that he was guilty of obstructing justice. Those findings mandated that the judge select a sentence between 360 months and life imprisonment; the judge imposed a sentence at the low end of the range. Thus, instead of the sentence of 21 years and 10 months that the judge could have imposed on the basis of the facts proved to the jury beyond a reasonable doubt, Booker received a 30-year sentence. . . .

It has been settled throughout our history that the Constitution protects every criminal defendant "against conviction except upon proof beyond a reasonable doubt of every fact necessary to constitute the crime with which he is charged." It is equally clear that the "Constitution gives a criminal defendant the right to demand that a jury find him guilty of all the elements of the crime with which he is charged." These basic precepts, firmly rooted in the common law, have provided the basis for recent decisions interpreting modern criminal statutes and sentencing procedures. . . .

In *Jones v. United States* (1999) . . . we noted . . . a "rule requiring jury determination of facts that raise a sentencing ceiling" in state and federal sentencing guidelines systems.

In *Apprendi v. New Jersey* (2000), the defendant pleaded guilty to second-degree possession of a firearm for an unlawful purpose, which carried a prison term of 5-to-10 years. Thereafter, the trial court found that his conduct had violated New Jersey's "hate crime" law because it was racially motivated, and imposed a 12-year sentence. This Court set aside the enhanced sentence. We held: "Other than the fact of a prior conviction, any fact that increases the penalty for a crime beyond the prescribed statutory maximum must be submitted to a jury, and proved beyond a reasonable doubt."

. . .

In *Ring v. Arizona* (2002), we reaffirmed our conclusion that the characterization of critical facts is constitutionally irrelevant. There, we held that it was impermissible for "the trial judge, sitting alone" to determine the presence or absence of the aggravating factors required by Arizona law for imposition of the death penalty. "If a State makes an increase in a defendant's authorized punishment contingent on the finding of a fact, that fact—no matter how the State labels it—must be found by a jury beyond a reasonable doubt.". . . .

In *Blakely v. Washington* (2004), we dealt with a determinate sentencing scheme similar to the Federal Sentencing Guidelines. There the defendant pleaded guilty to kidnaping, a class B felony punishable by a term of not more than 10 years. Other provisions of Washington law, comparable to the Federal Sentencing Guidelines, mandated a "standard" sentence of 49-to-53 months, unless the judge found aggravating facts justifying an exceptional sentence. Although the prosecutor recommended a sentence in the standard range, the judge found that the defendant had acted with "'deliberate cruelty'" and sentenced him to 90 months.

For reasons explained in *Jones, Apprendi,* and *Ring,* the requirements of the Sixth Amendment were clear. The application of Washington's sentencing scheme violated the defendant's right to have the jury find the existence of "'any particular fact'" that the law makes essential to his punishment. That right is implicated whenever a judge seeks to impose a sentence that is not solely based on "facts reflected in the jury verdict or admitted by the defendant." . . . The determination that the defendant acted with deliberate cruelty, like the determination in *Apprendi* that the defendant acted with racial malice, increased the sentence that the defendant could have otherwise received. Since this fact was found by a judge using a preponderance of the evidence standard, the sentence violated Blakely's Sixth Amendment rights. . . .

If the Guidelines as currently written could be read as merely advisory provisions that recommended, rather than required, the selection of particular sentences in response to differing sets of facts, their use would not implicate the Sixth Amendment. We have never doubted the authority of a judge to exercise broad discretion in imposing a sentence within a statutory range. . . .

All of the foregoing support our conclusion that our holding in *Blakely* applies to the Sentencing Guidelines. We recognize, as we did in *Jones, Apprendi,* and *Blakely,* that in some cases jury factfinding may impair the most expedient and efficient sentencing of defendants. But the interest in fairness and reliability protected by the right to a jury trial—a common-law right that defendants enjoyed for centuries and that is now enshrined in the Sixth Amendment—has always outweighed the interest in concluding trials swiftly. . . .

Accordingly, we reaffirm our holding in *Apprendi:* Any fact (other than a prior conviction) which is necessary to support a sentence exceeding the maximum authorized by the facts established by a plea of guilty or a jury verdict must be admitted by the defendant or proved to a jury beyond a reasonable doubt.

WHAT DO *YOU* THINK?

1. What impact does this case have on the rights of defendants during sentencing? Will this ruling ultimately result in trial courts imposing higher, lower, or about the same level of criminal punishment in criminal cases?

2. To what extent did the law prior to this case serve to limit the role of judges as persons who exercise "judgment?"

SENTENCING OPTIONS

Sentencing is fundamentally a risk-management strategy designed to protect the public while serving the ends of rehabilitation, deterrence, retribution, and restoration. Criminal sentences, just like the goals of sentencing, are often disputed. Lengthy prison terms do little for rehabilitation, while community release programs can hardly protect the innocent from offenders bent on continuing criminality. Each state has its own sentencing laws, and frequent revisions of these statutes are not uncommon. Due to considerable variations among the states, sentencing has been called "the most diversified part of the Nation's criminal justice process."[15] Many different instruments can be used as a part of a criminal sentence, including incarceration, probation, community service, fines, restitution, and alternative programs.

Incarceration

When imposing a sentence of incarceration, judges generally must abide by the parameters established by the applicable criminal statute. In most cases, this means that a judge cannot exceed the maximum term of incarceration allowed by the law. But criminal statutes can provide judges with different forms of incarceration sentencing authority.

indeterminate sentence

a relatively unspecific term of incarceration stated as a minimum and maximum time to be served (such as a term of imprisonment of "from one to ten years")

determinate sentence

a fixed term of incarceration specified by law; also called presumptive or fixed sentence

truth in sentencing

a theory behind some modern-day criminal sentencing laws that maintains that the sentence a judge imposes is the sentence a defendant should serve; used to undermine types of parole, shock probation, or other postsentencing methods of reducing a person's sentence

An ***indeterminate sentence*** is "a type of sentence to imprisonment in which the commitment, instead of being for a specified single time quantity, such as three years, is for a range of time, such as two to five years, or five years maximum and zero minimum."[16] Indeterminate sentences generally allow defendants to petition for an earlier release date, through either a parole board hearing, judicial petition, or another administrative review, based on good behavior, proof of rehabilitation, or other factors (see below). As such, indeterminate sentences, at least in theory, offer prison inmates an incentive to behave themselves and/or become rehabilitated while in custody.

Indeterminate sentences were the rule throughout most of the United States for well over a hundred years. But in the 1970s and 1980s, legislators in many jurisdictions grew frustrated with this form of sentencing and started to move to determinate sentencing methods. A ***determinate sentence*** sets a more definite "time quantity"[17] of imprisonment. Under this method, judges impose fixed times of incarceration, with little, if any, opportunity to reduce this time through good behavior, parole, shock probation, or other methods for reducing the sentence.

There are two primary forms of determinate sentencing—real-time sentencing and mandatory minimum sentencing. Under real-time sentencing or ***truth in sentencing*** approaches, criminal statutes require judges to impose fixed terms of incarceration or other finite forms of punishment. With indeterminate sentences, a ten-year prison term might have meant only a few years actually spent behind bars before the offender was released. And on average, good-time credits and parole reduced time served to about one-third of actual sentences.[18] See Figure 14-7. But under real-time sentencing and the theory "what you get is what you serve," a defendant

FIGURE 14-7 **Impact of Truth-in-Sentencing Laws**

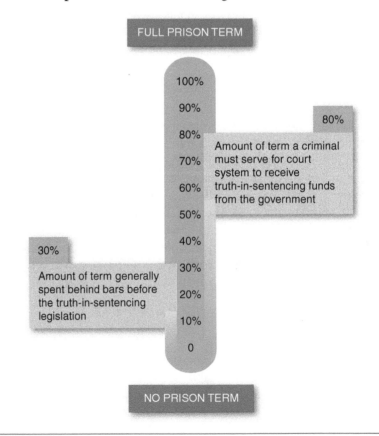

sentenced to ten years in prison actually serves ten years, with little or no opportunity to petition the trial court for parole, a reduction in sentence, or early release.

Truth in sentencing has become an important policy focus of many state legislatures and the federal Congress.[19] For example, in 1984, Congress passed the Federal Comprehensive Crime Control Act, which implemented determinate sentencing for nearly all federal offenders. Congress claimed that fixed prison terms were a more honest approach to sentencing.

Another form of determinate sentencing comes in the form of ***mandatory minimum sentences*** or ***mandatory time***. In many statutory schemes, legislators have written mandatory minimum sentences into the law, requiring the judge to impose at least the specified amount of prison time found in the statute. In some cases, the judge can impose a longer sentence but not a shorter term than that required by law. As a result, mandatory minimum sentencing removes a substantial amount of judicial discretion in sentencing, rendering judges more administrators than jurists. Offenses involving gun charges, sexual assaults, and high quantities of narcotics often carry mandatory minimum sentences.

In cases where defendants are convicted of multiple offenses, the judge must decide how to arrange the separate sentences for each offense. Multiple sentences can be imposed either concurrently or consecutively. A ***consecutive sentence*** is "one of two or more sentences imposed at the same time, after conviction for more than one offense, and which is served in sequence with the other sentences,"[20] that is, consecutive sentences are served one after the other. A ***concurrent sentence*** is one that is served at the same time another sentence is being served. See Figure 14-8.

Boot camp or ***shock incarceration*** is a modified form of incarceration that allows inmates to participate in a prison program modeled after military basic training. These programs are highly regimented and make use of strict discipline, rigorous physical training, and hard labor as a means of rehabilitating offenders. Under some programs, offenders can earn credits toward an earlier release date if they complete a prison boot camp program. Although most jurisdictions allow judges to place offenders into these programs, some delegate this authority to corrections officials.[21]

Home confinement or ***home incarceration*** requires that offenders be confined in their homes and sometimes makes use of electronic monitoring to ensure that they do not leave during the hours of confinement. Home confinement programs generally permit those so sentenced to travel to and from work, medical appointments, or treatment programs. Participants sometimes wear electronic ankle or arm bracelets, which track their location. House arrest can be an effective response to the rising cost of imprisonment.[22] Advocates of house arrest argue that it is also socially cost-effective[23] because it provides no opportunity for the kinds of negative socialization that occur in prison.

Probation

Probation, or ***community control*** as it is called in some jurisdictions, is actually a sentence of imprisonment that is suspended in lieu of good behavior. Judges impose a sentence of incarceration but suspend the imposition of this sentence, or at least a portion of it, on the condition that defendants meet certain behavioral requirements, such as avoiding future criminal violations. Often, the conditions of probation are used to restore the offender to the community and to accomplish other rehabilitative purposes. For example, alcohol and drug offenders may be required to enroll in substance-abuse counseling and to report for periodic substance-abuse testing.

mandatory minimum sentences or mandatory time
statutory sentencing conditions requiring a judge to impose a specific sentence

concurrent sentence
one of two or more sentences imposed at the same time, after conviction for more than one offense, and served simultaneously with the other sentences

consecutive sentence
one of two or more sentences imposed at the same time, after conviction for more than one offense, and served in sequence with the other sentences

shock incarceration
a sentencing option that makes use of "boot camp"–type prisons in order to impress on convicted offenders the realities of prison life

home confinement
a form of punishment in which individuals are confined to their home and may be monitored electronically to be sure they do not leave during the hours of confinement

probation
a sentence of imprisonment that is suspended; also, the conditional freedom granted by a judicial officer to an adjudicated or adjudged adult or juvenile offender, as long as the person meets certain conditions on behavior

FIGURE 14-8 **Types of Sentences**

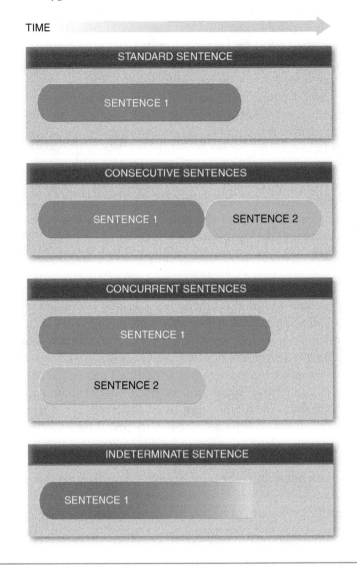

Different levels of scrutiny can be applied to probation periods. *Intensive supervised probation*—or similarly named forms of probation—imposes especially strict requirements on offenders. These requirements may include frequent reporting to probation officers, mandatory curfews, required employment, routine and unannounced alcohol and drug testing, and community service requirements. On the other end of the spectrum, *nonreporting probation* normally requires defendants to stay out of trouble during their probationary period. Under this form, defendants do not have to report to a probation officer, and as long as they avoid additional criminal charges and otherwise behave themselves, they will be in compliance with the terms of their probation. This form of probation is often assigned to first-time offenders and defendants convicted of misdemeanors or low-level felonies.

In cases where offenders fail to follow the terms of probation, the probation officer assigned to the case can file a notice of probation violation with the trial court. A probation officer's assertion of a *probation violation* or *PV*, as it is called

intensive supervision
a form of probation supervision involving frequent face-to-face contacts between the probationary client and probation officers

nonreporting probation
a type of suspended criminal sentence where the defendant must stay out of trouble during the probationary period, but does not require the defendant to report to the probation department

probation violation or PV
a defendant's breach of the terms of a probation order

in some circles, requires defendants to appear before the sentencing court and explain why they have not complied with the conditions of probation. If defendants do not provide a sufficient explanation for their noncompliance, the judge can terminate the defendant's probation and impose the term of incarceration that was originally suspended, or allow the defendant to remain on probation with the same or modified conditions.

Probation can be used in conjunction with an actual term of incarceration. This is typically done in the form of a ***split sentence***, in which the judge requires a defendant to serve a term of incarceration, followed by a term of probation. For example, a judge might order "ninety days in jail, to be followed by a probationary term of two years."

Shock probation is similar to a split sentence in that the offender serves a relatively short period of time in correctional custody and is then released by court order. But under shock probation programs, offenders must *apply* for release after entering confinement and are not guaranteed that this request will be granted. If it is, release may come as something of a shock to an offender, who might otherwise be anticipating a relatively long prison term. Shock parole is similar in purpose and design to shock probation. The main difference is that release decisions made under shock probation programs are made by a judge, while release decisions under shock parole programs are made by a paroling authority, such as a state parole board.

split sentence
a sentence explicitly requiring the convicted person to serve a period of confinement in a local, state, or federal facility, followed by a period of probation

shock probation
the practice of sentencing offenders to prison, allowing them to apply for probationary release, and granting release in surprise fashion

Law Line 14-6
Sentencing Project

Community Service

Community service is a sentencing alternative that requires an offender to spend time doing volunteer work that benefits the community. This work can range from picking up trash along roadways to volunteering at a homeless shelter. In some cases, community service is imposed along with another type of sentence, such as probation or incarceration. This is known as a ***mixed sentence***. Often, judges condition a defendant's term of probation on the completion of a certain number of community service hours within a particular time period. For example, a judge may order a defendant to complete one hundred hours of community service within six months. If the defendant fails to complete this task, the probation officer supervising the case can file a notice of probation violation with the trial court.

This type of sentence may require offenders to be incarcerated during certain periods of the day or week but allows them to be released for a period of time to perform employment or community service duties. In cases where the defendant is employed, this arrangement is sometimes known as ***work release***, because it allows defendants to maintain employment and still serve out a sentence of incarceration. Offenders with special skills, such as nurses, physicians, or accountants, may be ordered to serve the community in a capacity in keeping with their abilities.

community service
a sentencing alternative that requires offenders to spend at least part of their time working for a community agency

mixed sentence
a sentence that combines different forms of sentencing; for example, community service could be imposed along with another type of sentence, such as probation or incarceration.

work release
a condition of a criminal sentence that allows the defendant to be released from confinement for employment purposes

Fines, Court Costs, and Restitution

Trial judges may also impose financial sentences, including fines, court costs, and restitution. A ***fine*** is a form of punishment whereby a defendant must pay the court a certain amount of money. The range of this fine is stated within the penalty section of the relevant criminal statute. For example, a statute may read, "A person convicted of this offense can receive up to two years in prison, a one-thousand-dollar fine, or both." Generally, as long as a sentencing judge stays within the statutory limitations for imposing a fine and orders an amount that is proportional to the underlying harm caused by the defendant, the fine will be deemed reasonable. (See Cruel and Unusual punishment and excessive fines below).

fine
form of punishment whereby a defendant must pay the court a certain amount of money

court costs
costs associated with processing the case, including the use of the court's time and administrative fees

restitution
a financial payment from the defendant to the victims as a means of compensating them for their injuries

Trial judges also order court costs as a part of a criminal sentence. *Court costs* are the costs associated with processing the case, including the use of the court's time and administrative fees associated with subpoenas, jury summonses, and other filings. Court costs are normally based on standardized rates established by the court. Generally, court administrators calculate court costs based on nature and extent of the proceedings.

Unlike fines and court costs, which are paid to the trial court, restitution is paid to the victim(s) in a criminal case. *Restitution* is a financial payment from the defendant to the victims as a means of compensating them for their injuries. This may include the payment of medical bills or the return of stolen property. Although defendants typically pay court-ordered restitution through an agency of the court, such as the clerk of court's office, the money ultimately is given to the victim. Restitution payments, like fines, may be collected on an installment basis, as arranged by the court. At the federal level, the Victim and Witness Protection Act (1982) authorizes (and in many cases requires) federal courts to impose restitution as a part of criminal sentences.

Alternative Programs

Beyond traditional sentencing options, many jurisdictions have adopted other sentencing tools using innovative approaches. Many of these tools involve treatment programs that either substitute for or supplement more traditional forms of sentencing, including incarceration. Many of these programs are designed to address the underlying problem or condition that led to the criminal offense. For example, if a defendant's drug or alcohol addiction led or contributed to the commission of the crime, a court may order the defendant to complete an appropriate treatment program for the underlying addiction.

diversion programs
court-sponsored programs that allow defendants to avoid a conviction if they complete the program

treatment in lieu of conviction
a type of diversion program that allows defendants to get the drug treatment they need, and if successful, avoid being convicted of a crime

These alternative programs are implemented in a variety of ways. In some jurisdictions, there are specialized courts or programs that attempt to address the underlying circumstance of the charged offense. These are often called *diversion programs* because they divert certain cases from the standard criminal docket to another more-specialized court or program. For example, some states use drug courts that allow defendants with drug addictions to get treatment for their addiction instead of being convicted. In some courts, this is known as *treatment in lieu of conviction*. The details for these programs can vary, but the basic idea is that defendants can get the drug treatment they need and, if successful, avoid being convicted of a crime.

Other jurisdictions have specialized courts or programs to handle administrative-related driving issues, such as driving with a suspended license. In these cases, defendants charged with driving without a valid license or similar offenses can opt to have their criminal/traffic case diverted to a license intervention program—or another similarly named program—where defendants can fix the underlying problem with their license. In most cases, if defendants successfully complete the diversion program, they can return to the criminal/traffic court and their case will be dismissed.

In other cases and jurisdictions, alternative programs do not necessarily eliminate a criminal conviction, but rather serve as a substitute for jail time. For example, a number of jurisdictions use alcohol treatment programs as an alternative form of sentencing in driving under the influence (DUI) cases. Under most state laws, defendants convicted of drunk driving must serve a mandatory minimum amount of jail time—typically three days for an average first-time offender. But many jurisdictions allow defendants to complete an alcohol treatment program in lieu of serving time in an actual jail.

SENTENCING ENHANCEMENTS

Many states and the federal government provide for statutory enhancements that can increase a sentence beyond the general sentencing range for the convicted offense. For example, as mentioned earlier, some laws require increased sentences for **habitual offenders**, such as California's three-strikes legislation. Other sentencing enhancements include evidence of deliberate cruelty, the use of a gun, or, under the federal sentencing guidelines, the commission of a criminal act as a form of terrorism.[24]

In addition, some hate crime statutes also provide enhancements for sentencing. *Hate crimes* are criminal offenses in which the defendant's conduct was motivated by an identified form of hatred, bias, or prejudice.[25] For example, the California Penal Code defines a hate crime as "any act of intimidation, harassment, physical force, or the threat of physical force directed against any person, or family, or their property or advocate, motivated either in whole or in part by the hostility to the real or perceived ethnic background, national origin, religious belief, gender, age, disability, or sexual orientation, with the intention of causing fear and intimidation."[26]

In many statutory schemes, hate crimes are not separate offenses, but rather serve as a type of sentencing enhancement that, if proven, can be used to increase the sentence of a convicted offender. For example, Wisconsin enhances the possible penalty for most crimes when the offender "[i]ntentionally selects the person against whom the crime . . . is committed or selects the property that is damaged or otherwise affected by the crime . . . in whole or in part because of the actor's belief or perception regarding the race, religion, color, disability, sexual orientation, national origin or ancestry of that person or the owner or occupant of that property, whether or not the actor's belief or perception was correct."[27] In *Wisconsin v. Mitchell* (1993),[28] the U.S. Supreme Court upheld this law, finding that "[because] the statute has no 'chilling effect' on free speech, it is not unconstitutionally overbroad."

At the federal level, the Hate Crimes Sentencing Enhancement Act of 1994[29] provides for enhanced sentences when a federal offense is determined to be a hate crime. In 2009, Congress enacted the Matthew Shepard Hate Crimes Act, which extended provisions of federal hate crime laws that made it a federal crime to target individuals because of their race, religion, or national origin. Under the new law, judges can impose harsher penalties for crimes that are motivated by animus based on gender, sexual orientation, gender identity, or disability. The law was named for Matthew Shepard, a gay Wyoming college student who was murdered by a group of boys.

habitual offender
a person sentenced under a statute declaring that those who are convicted of a given offense and are shown to have previously been convicted of other specified offense(s) shall receive a more severe penalty than that for the current offense alone

hate crime
a criminal offense in which the defendant's conduct was motivated by hatred, bias, or prejudice, based on the actual or perceived race, color, religion, national origin, ethnicity, gender, or sexual orientation of another individual or group of individuals

Law Line 14-7
Center for the Study of Hate and Extremism

Law Line 14-8
Southern Poverty Law Center

IN THE FIELD

In most criminal sentencing hearings, the goals of defense professionals differ from those of their prosecutorial counterparts. For defense professionals, the basic objective is to present the court with mitigating evidence designed to minimize the severity of the sentence. In all federal cases, and in some state matters, this process will involve working closely with the probation officer who is assigned to prepare the presentence investigation report (PSR or PSI) for the sentencing judge.

Generally, defense professionals should provide the probation officer with favorable information so that it can be included in the PSR and be considered by the judge before the sentencing hearing. In addition, defense professionals in some cases may wish to prepare their own assessment of the crime and the defendant. For some, comparing the defendant's actions to the more harmful conduct of other defendants in similar cases may be a form of mitigating evidence. In addition, in some cases, it may be helpful to provide background information about the defendant so that the judge can see the totality of the defendant as a person. Some professionals use "day in the life" videos, computer slide presentations, or photo spreads that detail the life of the defendant and/or show the adverse impact a severe sentence will have on others, including the defendant's children, parents, employer, and so forth.

For prosecutorial professionals, the task in many sentencing hearings is to demonstrate the aggravating circumstances surrounding the defendant and the crime. This can be done by presenting evidence of the defendant's criminal history (where applicable) or the severity of the defendant's conduct in the instant case. Prosecutorial professionals also should work closely with the probation officer preparing the presentence report for the judge, providing relevant evidence of the aggravating factors in the case. During the sentencing hearing, prosecutors also might present testimony from the victim or victim's family to demonstrate the consequences of the defendant's criminal actions.

CAPITAL PUNISHMENT AND OTHER EIGHTH AMENDMENT ISSUES

capital punishment
the imposition of a sentence of death

Another form of punishment available in many jurisdictions—although by far the least commonly used—is *capital punishment*, or a sentence of death. A death sentence is, of course, the most extreme sentencing option available in the United States today. In 1995, the State of New York reinstated the death penalty after a thirty-year hiatus, and today, thirty-eight states and the federal government make capital punishment an option when serious crimes are committed. See Figure 14-9.

FIGURE 14-9 **Map of Death Penalty State Statutes in the United States**

Approximately, 3,800 death row inmates are housed in the nation's prisons, while around 100 executions are carried out yearly. The number of annual executions has been steadily rising as changes in the law and recent Supreme Court decisions have facilitated an increasing rate of legal death.

Capital punishment, as a sentencing possibility, was absent from federal law for a number of years before its reestablishment under the 1988 Anti-Drug Abuse Act, which included the possibility of capital punishment for drug-related murders. The 1994 Federal Violent Crime Control and Law Enforcement Act dramatically raised the number of crimes punishable by death under federal jurisdiction to around sixty distinct offenses. Candidates for death under the 1994 act are those who commit first-degree murder, espionage, kidnapping in which death results, murder of a foreign official, bank robbery in which death results, hostage taking resulting in death, murder for hire, genocide, carjacking that leads to death, "civil rights murders," the murder of federal law enforcement officials, foreign murder of U.S. nationals, sexual abuse resulting in death, sexual exploitation of children resulting in death, the murder of state or local officials (including state and local law enforcement officers and state correctional officers), murder by an escaped prisoner, the murder of federal witnesses or of court officers or jurors, and shipboard violence or violence at international airports resulting in death.

But the use of the death penalty is regularly challenged on at least two fronts. In many cases, the death penalty is confronted as being a form of cruel and unusual punishment under the Eighth Amendment. As a part of these challenges, defendants often allege procedural defects in the manner by which they were sentenced to death. And one analysis of capital convictions found serious reversible errors in nearly seven out of every ten capital cases.[30] The Eighth Amendment issues affecting the death penalty are addressed in the next section.

In addition, in some death penalty cases, defendants assert that they are actually innocent of the capital offense for which they were convicted. Since 1972, at least 130 people in twenty-six states have been released from U.S. death rows after proof of their innocence was substantiated.[31] Today, forensic technologies, like DNA testing, make it possible to demonstrate actual innocence in many cases. At the federal level, the Innocence Protection Act (2004)[32] provides federal funds to eliminate the backlog of unanalyzed DNA samples in the nation's crime laboratories[33] and sets aside money to improve the capacity of federal, state, and local crime laboratories to conduct DNA analyses.[34] The act also ensures access to postconviction DNA testing for those serving time in prison or on death row and sets forth conditions under which a federal prisoner asserting innocence may obtain postconviction DNA testing of specific evidence. The law mandates that a new trial or resentencing must be conducted "if the DNA test results, when considered with all other evidence in the case (regardless of whether such evidence was introduced at trial), establish by compelling evidence that a new trial would result in an acquittal."[35] Similarly, the legislation requires the preservation of biological evidence by federal law enforcement agencies for any defendant under a sentence of imprisonment or death.

The Eighth Amendment

Perhaps no other provision within criminal procedure invites more debate over constitutional values than the Eighth Amendment ban on cruel and unusual punishment. The ***Cruel and Unusual Punishment Clause*** provides that government may not inflict cruel and unusual punishment upon individuals. But the terms "cruel" and "unusual" are not defined in the Constitution. As a result, the Court and many advocates have waged an ongoing debate over the practical meaning and effect of this provision.

Cruel and Unusual Punishment Clause
Eighth Amendment right that guards against excessive punishments in criminal cases

The Supreme Court first incorporated the cruel and unusual punishment ban, thereby making it applicable to the states, in *Robinson v. California* (1962).[36] This is significant because the vast majority of punishments (criminal sentences)—including those in the form of the death penalty—occur at the state, not federal, level. As a result, the Court's incorporation of the cruel and unusual punishment provision in 1962 made it possible for many issues to be presented to the Court under the Eighth Amendment. There are four primary areas where cruel and unusual punishment challenges are raised—death penalty cases, cases involving allegedly disproportionate sentences, criminal statutes that create "status" crimes, and cases where inmates allege that their confinement conditions are unreasonable.

Death Penalty

The most frequently discussed issue under the Eighth Amendment involves the death penalty or capital punishment. Since 1976, the Court has ruled that the death penalty does not inherently violate the Eighth Amendment. The Court initially had struck down the death penalty in *Furman v. Georgia* (1972)[37] because some states had allowed triers of fact (usually juries) to impose death as a punishment without giving them sufficient standards or guidance when making their decisions.

But after the Court's 1972 ruling, many states revised their death penalty laws consistent with the Court's ruling and the Court upheld the new form in *Gregg v. Georgia* (1976).[38] In *Gregg*, the Court ruled that the death penalty is constitutionally permitted if implemented under a statutory scheme that provides triers of fact with reasonable discretion, sufficient information about the defendant, and legal standards for rendering their decision. In other words, the Court found that the death penalty can be constitutionally imposed if the law provides clear and fair standards for imposing this sentence. Under most statutory schemes, this involves specifying aggravating and mitigating factors to be used to assess whether the death penalty is appropriate.

The Court also observed that additional concerns about the arbitrary and capricious enforcement of the death penalty can be further addressed by using bifurcated proceedings in death penalty cases. A ***bifurcated proceeding*** separates the trial hearing, which decides the defendant's guilt or innocence, from the sentencing hearing, where the death penalty is considered. The theory is that, by separating these two proceedings, capital defendants will receive greater due process by allowing juries or judges to focus on the appropriateness of the defendant's sentence, as opposed to the question of guilt or innocence.

Since *Gregg*, the Court has ruled that the death penalty can be constitutionally applied to adults who are convicted of directly committing murder. Recently, in *Kennedy v. Louisiana* (2008), the Court, in a 5-4 ruling, held that states cannot impose capital punishment for the crime of child rape, when the sexual offense does not involve homicide. Read the excerpt from the majority opinion and assess whether there are any nonhomicide criminal offenses that should be eligible for the death penalty.

bifurcated proceeding
a legal mechanism that separates the trial hearing, which decides the defendant's guilt or innocence, from the sentencing hearing, where the death penalty is considered

---

Law Line 14-9
Death Penalty Information Center

CAPSTONE CASE *Kennedy v. Louisiana,* 554 U.S. 407 (2008)

Justice Kennedy delivered the opinion of the Court.

The National Government and, beyond it, the separate States are bound by the proscriptive mandates of the Eighth Amendment to the Constitution of the United States, and all persons within those respective jurisdictions may invoke its protection. Patrick Kennedy, the petitioner here, seeks to set aside his death sentence under the

Eighth Amendment. He was charged by the respondent, the State of Louisiana, with the aggravated rape of his then-8-year-old stepdaughter. After a jury trial petitioner was convicted and sentenced to death under a state statute authorizing capital punishment for the rape of a child under 12 years of age. This case presents the question whether the Constitution bars respondent from imposing the death penalty for the rape of a child where the crime did not result, and was not intended to result, in death of the victim. We hold the Eighth Amendment prohibits the death penalty for this offense. The Louisiana statute is unconstitutional. . . .

The Eighth Amendment, applicable to the States through the Fourteenth Amendment, provides that "[e]xcessive bail shall not be required, nor excessive fines imposed, nor cruel and unusual punishments inflicted." The Amendment proscribes "all excessive punishments, as well as cruel and unusual punishments that may or may not be excessive." The Court explained . . . that the Eighth Amendment's protection against excessive or cruel and unusual punishments flows from the basic "precept of justice that punishment for [a] crime should be graduated and proportioned to [the] offense." Whether this requirement has been fulfilled is determined not by the standards that prevailed when the Eighth Amendment was adopted in 1791 but by the norms that "currently prevail." The Amendment "draw[s] its meaning from the evolving standards of decency that mark the progress of a maturing society." This is because "[t]he standard of extreme cruelty is not merely descriptive, but necessarily embodies a moral judgment. The standard itself remains the same, but its applicability must change as the basic mores of society change."

Evolving standards of decency must embrace and express respect for the dignity of the person, and the punishment of criminals must conform to that rule. See *Trop, supra,* at 100 (plurality opinion). As we shall discuss, punishment is justified under one or more of three principal rationales: rehabilitation, deterrence, and retribution. It is the last of these, retribution, that most often can contradict the law's own ends. This is of particular concern when the Court interprets the meaning of the Eighth Amendment in capital cases. When the law punishes by death, it risks its own sudden descent into brutality, transgressing the constitutional commitment to decency and restraint.

For these reasons we have explained that capital punishment must "be limited to those offenders who commit 'a narrow category of the most serious crimes' and whose extreme culpability makes them 'the most deserving of execution.'" Though the death penalty is not invariably unconstitutional, the Court insists upon confining the instances in which the punishment can be imposed.

Applying this principle, we held . . . that the execution of juveniles and mentally retarded persons are punishments violative of the Eighth Amendment because the offender had a diminished personal responsibility for the crime. The Court further has held that the death penalty can be disproportionate to the crime itself where the crime did not result, or was not intended to result, in death of the victim. . . .

In these cases the Court has been guided by "objective indicia of society's standards, as expressed in legislative enactments and state practice with respect to executions." The inquiry does not end there, however. Consensus is not dispositive. Whether the death penalty is disproportionate to the crime committed depends as well upon the standards elaborated by controlling precedents and by the Court's own understanding and interpretation of the Eighth Amendment's text, history, meaning, and purpose.

Based both on consensus and our own independent judgment, our holding is that a death sentence for one who raped but did not kill a child, and who did not intend to assist another in killing the child, is unconstitutional under the Eighth and Fourteenth Amendments. . . .

(continued)

(continued)

Louisiana is the only State since 1964 that has sentenced an individual to death for the crime of child rape; and petitioner and Richard Davis, who was convicted and sentenced to death for the aggravated rape of a 5-year-old child by a Louisiana jury in December 2007, are the only two individuals now on death row in the United States for a nonhomicide offense.

After reviewing the authorities informed by contemporary norms, including the history of the death penalty for this and other nonhomicide crimes, current state statutes and new enactments, and the number of executions since 1964, we conclude there is a national consensus against capital punishment for the crime of child rape....

The judgment of the Supreme Court of Louisiana upholding the capital sentence is reversed. This case is remanded for further proceedings not inconsistent with this opinion.

It is so ordered.

WHAT DO *YOU* THINK?

1. Do you agree with the Court that, in terms of crimes against individuals, only the taking of a life is serious enough to impose death on the perpetrator?
2. The Court looks to "objective evidence" as guidance. Do you see flaws in this reasoning? Don't legislators make decisions that do not necessarily reflect the values of their constituents?
3. Can you speculate as to why so few states have lacked statutes imposing death on child rapists?

The Court has limited the application of capital punishment in other cases as well. In *Atkins v. Virginia* (2002),[39] the Court held that the death penalty could not be imposed on individuals with mental retardation. This ruling reversed a 1989 decision that had allowed such executions to occur. And in *Roper v. Simmons* (2005),[40] the Court ruled that the Eighth Amendment bars the execution of juveniles (persons who were under eighteen years of age at the time of their offense). This ruling reversed another 1989 opinion, which had allowed persons sixteen years of age and older to be executed. Both of these recent rulings acknowledged that the constitutional standards of what is "cruel and unusual" are not fixed or finite but can change over time.

In *Atkins*, the Court asserted, "[a] claim that punishment is excessive is judged not by the standards that prevailed in 1685 when Lord Jeffreys presided over the 'Bloody Assizes' or when the Bill of Rights was adopted, but rather by those that currently prevail." And in both *Atkins* and *Roper*, a majority of the Court recognized that public and legislative values regarding the execution of mentally retarded and underage persons had changed since 1989, thereby warranting a change in the constitutional standard of what is cruel and unusual. Note too that in both cases some justices also considered international or "world community" standards regarding the death penalty as a part of their opinion.

Proportionality Doctrine

proportionality doctrine theory under the Eighth Amendment that courts cannot impose punishments that are grossly disproportionate to the committed offense

Under the Eighth Amendment, courts also cannot impose punishments that are grossly disproportionate to the committed offense. This is called the ***proportionality doctrine***. As an example, in *Coker v. Georgia* (1977),[41] the Court ruled that a state cannot impose the death penalty for a rape conviction if the crime does not involve the death of another. The Court has indicated that the **proportionality** of a punishment should be evaluated by looking at (1) the seriousness of the offense and the severity of the imposed punishment, (2) the types of sentences given to other defendants for the same offense in the same jurisdiction, and (3) the types of sentences given in similar cases in other jurisdictions.

Currently, some so-called *three-strikes laws*—statutes passed in some jurisdictions that impose life sentences for repeat (usually third) offenses, regardless of the seriousness of the offense—are being challenged under this dimension of the Eighth Amendment. For example, California has one of the nation's toughest three-strikes laws, requiring life sentences for "three-time losers."[42] In 1998, the U.S. Supreme Court upheld a provision of the statute that doubles prison sentences for a second strike, saying that the sentencing requirement does not violate double jeopardy provisions of the Constitution.[43] Supporters of three-strikes laws argue that they lower crime rates by ensuring that those convicted under them are denied the opportunity to continue their criminal careers.

In 2003, in two separate cases,[44] the U.S. Supreme Court lent considerable support to California's three-strikes sentencing scheme when it upheld the three-strikes convictions of Gary Ewing and Leandro Andrade. Ewing, sentenced to twenty-five years to life in prison following conviction for felony grand theft of three golf clubs, had four prior felony convictions at the time he was convicted. Andrade, who had a long prison record, was sentenced to fifty years in prison (two twenty-five-year terms to be served consecutively) for two petty-theft convictions. Under California law, a person who commits petty theft can be charged with a felony if he or she has prior felony convictions. The charge is known as "petty theft with prior convictions." The Court noted that states should be able to decide when repeat offenders "must be isolated from society . . . to protect the public safety," even when nonserious crimes trigger the lengthy sentence. The Court also found that it is not cruel and unusual punishment to impose a possible life term for a nonviolent felony when a defendant has a history of serious or violent convictions.

Status Crimes

Second, the Eighth Amendment bars government from imposing punishment for *status crimes* or personal characteristic offenses—attempts to punish individuals based on their reputation or propensity for certain behavior. For example, in *Powell v. Texas* (1968),[45] the Court struck down a state law making it a crime to be a "common drunkard" because this crime was based largely on a person's status or reputation in a community, as opposed to specific and empirical forms of harmful conduct. Under the Court's ruling, government can punish persons for being under the influence of alcohol in public or while driving, but it cannot punish them based solely on their reputation for such activity. Thus, while the criminal offenses of public drunkenness and driving while intoxicated might be classified as status crimes in a generic sense, the statutory elements for these offenses are not based on the defendant's status or reputation in the community.

Unreasonable Confinement Conditions

Finally, the Court, at times, has applied the Eighth Amendment to redress unreasonable prison and other confinement conditions that inmates have faced after being sentenced. The Court, however, appears divided on whether the Eighth Amendment should apply to treatment imposed outside of criminal

proportionality
a sentencing principle that holds that the severity of sanctions should bear a direct relationship to the seriousness of the crime committed

three-strikes laws
statutory provisions that mandate lengthy prison terms for criminal offenders convicted of a third violent crime or felony

status crimes
a type of criminal statute prohibited under the Eighth Amendment; attempts to punish individuals based on their reputation or propensity for certain behavior

sentencing. In *Wilson v. Seiter* (1991),[46] the Court denied the claim of a prison inmate subjected to rat-infested and overcrowded conditions in an Ohio prison. The Court ruled that in cases where prison inmates are using the general conditions of their surroundings to assert their Eighth Amendment claim, they must demonstrate that prison officials engaged in "deliberate indifference" in responding to unreasonably harsh conditions. But in *Hudson v. McMillian* (1992),[47] the Court found that a prison inmate's Eighth Amendment right was violated when a prison guard used excessive force against him. The Court indicated that in "excessive force" cases, the Eight Amendment will apply if prison officials "maliciously and sadistically used force to cause harm." Interestingly, in both of these cases, Justice Thomas asserted that the Eighth Amendment should be limited to punishment imposed as a part of a court's sentencing and not to conditions that arise in prisons after sentencing.

Excessive Bail and Fines

The Eighth Amendment contains two other provisions—the **excessive bail** provision, which provides that the amount of bail (the collateral imposed by a court as a condition for pretrial release of the defendant) cannot be excessive, and the **excessive fines** provision, which provides that fines (a postconviction punishment in the form of monetary payment) cannot be excessive. But the Supreme Court has yet to formally apply these provisions to the states through the Fourteenth Amendment's Due Process Clause. But the imposition of unreasonable punishments through fines, particularly when the defendant is indigent, may run afoul of other constitutional standards, including equal protection.[48]

excessive bail
an excessive amount of bail (the collateral imposed by a court as a condition for pretrial release of the defendant) that is prohibited under the Eighth Amendment

excessive fines
an excessive amount of fines (postconviction punishment in the form of monetary payment) that is prohibited under the Eighth Amendment

---

IN THE FIELD

Death penalty cases and other matters involving cruel and unusual punishment are fact-intensive matters. Legal professionals working on these issues often find themselves working more as a criminal investigator than as a legal analyst. Without precise definition, the constitutional phrase *cruel and unusual* invites comparative factual analysis, where the contextual circumstances of other cases are considered in light of the case *sub judice* (under consideration). What is deemed cruel and unusual often depends on what has occurred or is occurring in other cases or other jurisdictions. In other words, legal professionals must provide the courts with a measuring stick or benchmark of cases or examples, so that they can compare the current case to what was or was not found to be cruel and unusual in other cases.

---

forfeiture
a court procedure by which the government obtains legal title to the defendant's property because it was involved in criminal activity

relation-back doctrine
a theory in criminal forfeiture cases that assumes that because the government's right to illicit proceeds relates back to the time they are generated, anything acquired through the expenditure of those proceeds also belongs to the government

FORFEITURE PROCEEDINGS

Forfeiture is an enforcement strategy that federal statutes and some state laws support—and one that bears special mention. Antidrug forfeiture statutes at both the state and federal levels provide a special category of forfeiture laws. Such statutes authorize judges to seize "all monies, negotiable instruments, securities, or other things of value furnished or intended to be furnished by any person in exchange for a controlled substance . . . [and] all proceeds traceable to such an exchange."[49] Forfeiture statutes find a legal basis in the relation-back doctrine. The **relation-back doctrine** assumes that because the government's right to illicit proceeds relates back

ETHICAL PRINCIPLES

PROFESSIONAL CONDUCT

NATIONAL FEDERATION OF PARALEGAL ASSOCIATIONS MODEL CODE OF ETHICS AND PROFESSIONAL RESPONSIBILITY

Rule 1.3

A PARALEGAL SHALL MAINTAIN
A HIGH STANDARD OF PROFESSIONAL CONDUCT.

ETHICAL CONSIDERATIONS

1.3(c) Should a paralegal's fitness to practice be compromised by physical or mental illness, causing that paralegal to commit an act that is in direct violation of the Model Code/Model Rules and/or the rules and/or laws governing the jurisdiction in which the paralegal practices, that paralegal may be protected from sanction upon review of the nature and circumstances of that illness.

1.3(d) A paralegal shall advise the proper authority of non-confidential knowledge of any action of another legal professional that clearly demonstrates fraud, deceit, dishonesty, or misrepresentation. The authority to whom the report is made shall depend on the nature and circumstances of the possible misconduct, (e.g., ethics committees of law firms, corporations and/or paralegal associations, local or state bar associations, local prosecutors, administrative agencies, etc.). Failure to report such knowledge is in itself misconduct and shall be treated as such under these rules.

1.3(e) A paralegal shall not knowingly assist any individual with the commission of an act that is in direct violation of the Model Code/Model Rules and/or the rules and/or laws governing the jurisdiction in which the paralegal practices.

1.3(f) If a paralegal possesses knowledge of future criminal activity, that knowledge must be reported to the appropriate authority immediately.

Courtesy of The National Federation of Paralegal Associations http://www.paralegals.org

---

to the time they are generated, anything acquired through the expenditure of those proceeds also belongs to the government.[50]

The first federal laws to authorize forfeiture as a criminal sanction were both passed in 1970. They are the Continuing Criminal Enterprise (CCE) statute and the Organized Crime Control Act. A section of the Organized Crime Control Act, known as the **RICO statute** (for Racketeer Influenced and Corrupt Organizations), was designed to prevent criminal infiltration of legitimate businesses and has since been extensively applied in federal drug-smuggling cases. In 1978, Congress authorized civil forfeiture of any assets acquired through narcotics trafficking in violation of federal law. Many states modeled their own legislation after federal law and now have similar statutes. See Figure 14-10.

Forfeiture statutes have provided considerable grist for the judicial mill. For example, in *United States v. 92 Buena Vista Ave.* (1993),[51] the Supreme Court established an "innocent owner defense" in forfeiture cases, whereby federal authorities were forbidden from seizing drug transaction assets that were later

RICO statute

Racketeer Influenced and Corrupt Organizations Act; federal law designed to prevent criminal infiltration of legitimate businesses

FIGURE 14-10 **Forfeiture Actions**

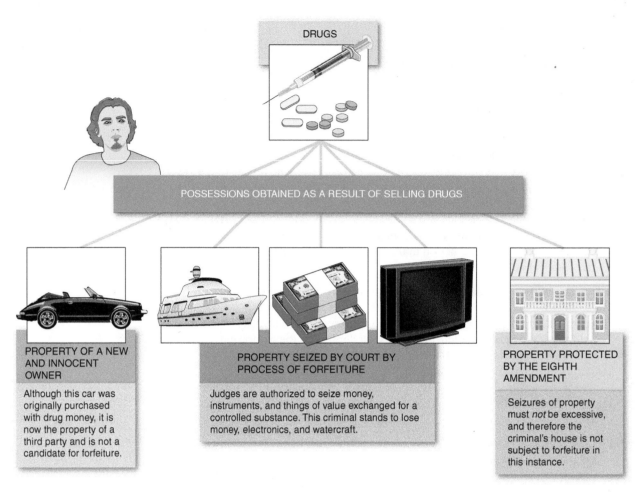

acquired by a new and innocent owner. In the same year, in the case of *Austin v. United States* (1993),[52] the Court placed limits on the government's authority to use forfeiture laws against drug criminals, finding that seizures of property must not be excessive when compared to the seriousness of the offense charged. Otherwise, the Court wrote, the Eighth Amendment's ban on excessive fines could be contravened. The Court, however, refused to establish a rule by which excessive fines could be judged, saying that "[t]he Court declines to establish a test for determining whether a forfeiture is constitutionally 'excessive,' since prudence dictates that the lower courts be allowed to consider that question." The *Austin* ruling was supported by two other 1993 cases, *Alexander v. United States*, 509 U.S. 544 (1993) and *United States v. James Daniel Good Real Property*, 510 U.S. 43 (1993). In *Alexander,* the Court found that forfeitures under the RICO statute must be limited according to the rules established in *Austin,* while in the second case, the Court held that "[a]bsent exigent circumstances, the Due Process Clause requires the Government to afford notice and a meaningful opportunity to be heard before seizing real property subject to civil forfeiture."

In *Bennis v. Michigan* (1996),[53] however, the Supreme Court upheld the seizure of private property used in the commission of a crime, even though the property belonged to an innocent owner not involved in the crime. In *Bennis,* the government seized a car that had been used by the owner's husband in procuring the services of a prostitute. In effect, the Court ruled that an innocent owner is not protected from forfeiture of property related to criminal convictions.

Also, in *United States v. Ursery* (1996),[54] the Supreme Court rejected claims that civil forfeiture laws constitute a form of double jeopardy. In *Ursery*, the defendant's house had been seized by federal officials who claimed that it had been used to facilitate drug transactions. The government later seized other personal items owned by Ursery, saying that they had been purchased with the proceeds of drug sales and that Ursery had engaged in money-laundering activities to hide the source of his illegal income. The court of appeals reversed Ursery's drug conviction and the forfeiture judgment, holding that the Double Jeopardy Clause of the U.S. Constitution prohibits the government from both punishing a defendant for a criminal offense and forfeiting his property for that same offense in a separate civil proceeding. In reaffirming Ursery's conviction, however, the Court ruled that "a forfeiture [is] not barred by a prior criminal proceeding after applying a two-part test asking, first, whether Congress intended the particular forfeiture to be a remedial civil sanction or a criminal penalty, and second, whether the forfeiture proceedings are so punitive in fact as to establish that they may not legitimately be viewed as civil in nature, despite any congressional intent to establish a civil remedial mechanism." The Court concluded that "civil forfeitures are neither 'punishment' nor criminal for purposes of the Double Jeopardy clause." In distinguishing civil forfeitures and criminal punishments, the majority opinion held that "Congress has long authorized the Government to bring parallel criminal actions and . . . civil forfeiture proceedings based upon the same underlying events . . . , and this Court consistently has concluded that the Double Jeopardy Clause does not apply to such forfeitures because they do not impose punishment."

CRIMINAL APPEALS

Once a criminal case is complete at the trial court, defendants can ask an appellate court to review the lower court proceedings. This is called an ***appeal***. Recall from Chapter 2 that the basic judicial process in America involves two separate systems—a federal judiciary and state judiciaries. Each of these systems is structured in a three-layer hierarchy, with the trial courts at the bottom, the courts of appeals in the middle, and a supreme court (or other high court) at the top. Most appeals begin when a party asks an intermediate court (court of appeals) to review the judgment of a lower trial court.

In order to begin an appeal, defendants (or in rare cases, prosecutors) must file a ***notice of appeal*** with the trial court and/or appellate court, notifying these bodies that they wish to have a secondary review of the trial court proceedings. A notice of appeal is a basic document, often only one page in length, that provides a statement about the judgment from which the party is appealing, as shown in Figure 14-11. In addition, many courts of appeals require the appealing party to complete an ***appeal information form*** (or similar document), which is often a checklist form that solicits more details about the nature of the appeal, the parties, and their attorneys.

Direct, Interlocutory, and Collateral Appeals

Most appeals are initiated by defendants after they are convicted and sentenced by the trial court. This is known as a ***direct appeal*** and, in most cases, defendants must wait until the trial court enters a ***final judgment*** before an appeal can be

Law Line 14-10
Forfeiture Laws

appeal
a stage of court proceedings where a party asks an appellate court to review the lower court proceedings

notice of appeal
a legal pleading that is filed with the trial court and/or appellate court, notifying these bodies that a party wishes to have an appellate review of the lower court proceedings

appeal information form
a standardized form seeking background information about the parties and issues in a case; must be completed in order to perfect an appeal

direct appeal
an appeal directly from a lower court's ruling; occurs after the trial court enters a final judgment in the case; distinguished from collateral appeal

final judgment
the judgment of a court that concludes a case

FIGURE 14-11 **Sample Notice of Appeal**

STATE OF VERMONT
_____ COUNTY, SS.

_____   VERMONT DISTRICT/SUPERIOR COURT
Plaintiff

v.

_____   DOCKET N O. _____
Defendant

NOTICE OF APPEAL

    Notice is hereby given that _____, plaintiff/defendant above named,
hereby appeals to the Supreme Court (from the final judgment),_____ (from
the order (describing it)) entered in this _____ (action) _____(proceeding)
on the _____ day of _____, 200___.

(Signed) _____
(Mailing address)   _____
                                 _____

9/06 SML

---

filed. Normally, a final judgment is the judgment of conviction and sentencing order issued by the trial court. Once the lower court proceedings are completed, the defendant can then file a notice of appeal and proceed with a direct appeal to the appellate court.

But in rare cases, and depending on the rules of the local appellate court, defendants and prosecutors can sometimes appeal a criminal case before a defendant's conviction and sentence. These are known as ***interlocutory appeals*** because they allow the trial court to received guidance (an opinion) from an appellate court before a final verdict is rendered. In some instances, defendants may assert that moving forward with trial without appellate review of a particular issue will cause them irreparable harm. In other cases, prosecutors may claim that a trial court's ruling barring the admission of critical evidence against the defendant has made it impossible to properly proceed to trial against the defendant. But again, these circumstances are generally rare, and appellate courts prohibit most issues in criminal cases from being raised in the form of an interlocutory appeal.

A direct appeal is also different from a collateral appeal. A ***collateral appeal*** is an additional round of review of a defendant's conviction that can occur after the direct appeal process has concluded. For example, habeas corpus cases (discussed below) are a type of collateral appeal. Most collateral appeals begin back at the original trial court, with a convicted person filed a petition for a writ of habeas corpus or some other form of postconviction relief. Collateral appeals may appear like another round of direct appeals, but the nature of the proceedings and the rules by which they are reviewed are much different (see below).

interlocutory appeal
an appeal that occurs while a case is still pending in a lower court (prior to final judgment)

collateral appeal
an additional round of review of a defendant's conviction that can occur after the direct appeal process has concluded; for example, habeas corpus review

Right of Appeal versus Discretionary Appeal

After a trial court has entered final judgment against a defendant, the defendant is entitled to at least one review of the lower court's judgment by a court of appeals. This is known as the *right of appeal* or *an appeal as a matter of right*. As long as defendants file a timely notice of appeal and otherwise comply with the court's rules for an appeal, they are entitled to have their conviction and/or sentence reviewed by an appellate court. This is designed to ensure that defendants receive due process and other elements of fairness in the criminal justice system. Of course, defendants are not required to seek appellate review of their convictions and sentences and are free to accept the trial court's judgment.

In most cases, the appellate review provided by an intermediate court of appeals is the only appeal that is afforded as a matter of right. Generally, if parties wish to seek review by a higher tribunal, they must petition the higher court for review. This is known as *discretionary review*. At the state level, most high courts have the discretion to accept or decline criminal appeals, unless the cases involve some extraordinary circumstances, such as a death sentence. When a high court has discretionary review, a party must convince the court to accept the appeal, usually by filing a *petition for jurisdiction* or some other form of request, and this petition must be granted before the case will receive full review by the high court.

After a state criminal case is reviewed by the state's highest court or is denied such review, it is possible that it may be reviewed by U.S. Supreme Court. The odds of gaining such review by the high court are not good. But if a state case involves a `—a dispute over the application of a provision of the U.S. Constitution, a federal statute, treaty, or administrative regulation, or some other federal action—and the Court issues a writ of certiorari to hear the case, the Court has jurisdiction to hear the case. See Chapter 2. Parties seeking review by the U.S. Supreme Court must file a petition for a writ of certiorari with Court and have the writ granted in order to gain further appellate review by the Court.

In federal cases, the direct appeal begins at the circuit court of appeals, which has jurisdiction over the district court that issued the final judgment. As in state appeals, defendants who file a timely notice of appeal have a right to at least one level of appellate review, which is normally performed by a three-judge panel of the circuit court of appeals. Once this panel renders its opinion, the losing party has two options for continuing the direct appeal process. The nonprevailing party can petition the Supreme Court for a writ of certiorari, much like the process used to appeal state cases. Or the nonprevailing party can petition the full circuit court for en banc review of the case. *En banc* review is an appellate review by all members of the circuit court—not just the three-judge panel. The number of judges in the circuit courts ranges from six (First Circuit) to twenty-nine (Ninth Circuit), with most of the other circuits having between eleven and seventeen judges. If the circuit court grants en banc review, the opinion from the three-judge panel is vacated and the en banc panel will rehear the case. Once the en banc opinion is rendered, the nonprevailing party has the option of seeking a writ of certiorari from the Supreme Court.

Appellate Parties and Procedures

In appellate cases, the party who filed the notice of appeal is called the *appellant*, and the party responding to the appeal is called the *appellee*. In most criminal appeals, the defendant is the appellant and the government is the appellee. When cases go to the highest court within a jurisdiction (often the supreme court), the party initiating the high court's review is called the *petitioner*, while the opposing party is called the *respondent*. See Figure 14-12.

right of appeal or an appeal as a matter of right
an appeal to which a defendant has an absolute right, as opposed to a discretionary appeal

discretionary review
an appeal allowed through the discretion of the higher court, distinguished from an appeal as a matter of right

Law Line 14-11
U.S. Supreme Court Merit Briefs

petition for jurisdiction
a pleading used to seek discretionary appellate review from a higher court

en banc
a type of intermediate court appellate review where the entire panel (bank) of appellate judges hears the appeal

appellant
the party who files an appeal

appellee
the party responding to an appeal

petitioner
the party initiating appellate review from the highest court in the state or federal judiciary

respondent
the party responding to appellate review by the highest court in the state or federal judiciary

FIGURE 14-12 **Common Titles Given to Parties in the Appellate Process**

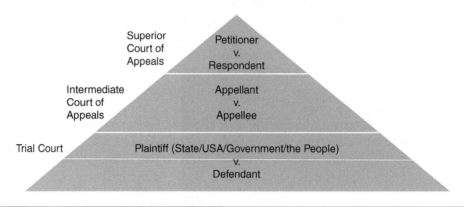

Prosecutors are limited in their ability to file an appeal. In fact, in cases where a defendant is acquitted by a judge or jury based on conclusions of fact, the prosecutor is barred under principles of double jeopardy from appealing the factual acquittal. But there are limited situations where a prosecutor can appeal a criminal case, including trial court rulings on the law. For example, if the trial court dismisses an indictment based on a finding that the criminal statute is unconstitutional, a prosecutor can file an appeal of that ruling. Similarly, if a trial court grants the defendant's motion to exclude evidence, thereby eliminating essential evidence for the prosecutor's case, the prosecutor can appeal the trial court's ruling by certifying that the government cannot proceed with the prosecution without the excluded evidence. Finally, a prosecutor can also appeal trial court conclusions regarding a defendant's sentence. If the prosecutor believes the trial court erroneously applied the sentencing law or abused its discretion in making factual conclusions regarding the defendant's sentence, the government can file an appeal.

It should come as no surprise to learn that an appellate case is much different from trial proceedings. For starters, there are no witnesses, testimony, or evidence being introduced at the court of appeals. Instead, typically a three-judge panel reviews the trial court record to determine whether matters were handled properly. The **trial court record** consists of a transcript (a typed narrative) of all proceedings before the trial court, the motions, opinions, and other filings with the trial court, and all exhibits and other tangible evidence presented to the trial court. The court of appeals then reviews this record to determine whether the relevant legal standards were properly applied when the trial court entered its judgment in the case. The appellate court is assisted by the parties in this review, with both sides filing **legal briefs** with the court and, in many cases, appearing in front of the court for **oral argument**.

Initially, the tasks of legal professionals in appellate cases are to gather the record, make it available to the court of appeals, and begin reviewing it for possible error. This includes ordering a copy of the transcript from the court reporter and requesting the court reporter to file the complete trial court record with the court of appeals. Once the transcript is received, legal professionals must review it carefully and thoroughly to assess whether there is evidence of reversible error. In criminal cases, there are essentially two types of error that can occur at the trial court level—reversible error and harmless error. **Reversible error** or **prejudicial error** is a mistake made by the trial court or another participant in the lower court proceedings that likely affected the final judgment in the case, thereby causing

---

trial court record
a compilation of trial court materials, including the transcript (a typed narrative) of all proceedings before the trial court, the motions, opinions, and other filings with the trial court, and all exhibits and other tangible evidence presented to the trial court

legal briefs
typed legal arguments filed with an appellate court

oral argument
verbal presentations before an appellate court

Law Line 14-12
Oral Arguments

---

reversible error or prejudicial error
a mistake made by the trial court or another participant in the lower court proceedings that likely affected the final judgment in the case

prejudice to the appellant. This can be an error affecting the defendant's conviction or an error affecting the defendant's sentence. ***Harmless error*** is a mistake at the trial court level that likely did not affect the defendant's conviction or sentence. In most cases, an appellate court will reverse the judgment of the lower court only upon finding reversible error.

Once legal professionals have reviewed the trial court record, they must begin researching the legal standards for the identified issues (errors) and then start organizing the legal brief to be submitted to the court of appeals. A legal brief is simply a typewritten argument in which parties identify the factual and legal points of their appeal. Initially, appellants file their brief with the court and serve a copy on the appellee. This is called the ***appellant's brief*** or ***merit brief***. Then, based on the arguments raised in the appellant's brief, the appellee will file an ***appellee's brief or response brief***, wherein the appellee tries to counter the appellant's arguments. In some jurisdictions and in some cases, these two briefs constitute the written legal argument before the court of appeals. But in other jurisdictions and cases, appellants are allowed to reply to the arguments raised in the appellee's brief by filing a ***reply brief***. See Figure 14-13 for issues commonly raised on appeal.

harmless error
a mistake at the trial court level that likely did not affect the defendant's conviction or sentence

appellant's brief or merit brief
the brief filed by the appellant in an appeal

appellee's brief or response brief
the brief filed by an appellee to counter the appellant's arguments

reply brief
a brief filed by an appellant in reply to an appellee's brief

---

FIGURE 14-13 **Common Issues Raised on Appeal**

By Defendants
Defects in indictment
 Criminal statute used to charged defendant is unconstitutional
 Grand jury process was flawed
 Statute of limitations has expired
 Speedy trial rights were violated
 Court lacks jurisdiction over charges
Adverse rulings on pretrial motions
 Motions to suppress evidence denied
 Motion in *limine* denied
 Requests for discovery or the testing of evidence denied
 Motions regarding defendant's competency denied
 Prosecutor's motions limiting defendant's evidence granted
Jury selection flawed
Inadmissible evidence admitted during trial
 Irrelevant, unreliable, unfairly prejudicial, improperly, or illegally obtained
 evidence was used to convict defendant
Irregularities with jurors' conduct
Prejudicial prosecutorial misconduct
Legal defects in sentencing
 Trial court wrongly applied sentencing standards
Trial court abused its discretion in sentencing
Verdict is against manifest weight of evidence presented during trial
Verdict is not supported by sufficient evidence
Defendant received ineffective assistance of trial counsel

By Prosecutors
Indictment wrongly dismissed
 Criminal statute used to charge defendant is constitutional
 Grand jury process not flawed

(continued)

FIGURE 14-13 **Continued**

Indictment filed within statute of limitations
Defendant's speedy trial rights were satisfied
Jurisdiction properly with the trial court
Evidence wrongly suppressed prior to trial
Exclusion of evidence precluded government from going to trial
Trial court abused its discretion in sentencing
Trial court made legal errors in sentencing

---

rules of appellate procedure
legislative rules for processing an appeal within a given jurisdiction

Courts of appeal have requirements for briefs, including page limitations, citation requirements, and timetables for filing. These requirements are typically found in the ***rules of appellate procedure*** for the subject court. Once filed, the briefs serve as the primary communication of argument between the parties and the court of appeals. In many jurisdictions and cases, the parties are permitted or, in some cases, required to present an oral argument to the court of appeals. Typically, at the intermediate level, each side is given fifteen minutes to present its arguments before a three-judge panel. During this time, the judges can ask the attorneys questions and otherwise inquire about the merits of their case. Again, appellate oral arguments do not involve trial-like procedures, such as the introduction of witnesses and evidence. They are simply verbal exchanges of ideas and claims about the propriety of the trial court proceedings. Attorneys typically offer their interpretations of the trial court record, case law, statutory provisions, and other legal doctrines in an effort to persuade the court of appeals to rule in their client's favor. Following oral arguments, the case is submitted to the court of appeals, and the court will decide the case and write an opinion. Often the parties do not receive this opinion for a few or even several months after oral argument.

After a court of appeals or high court issues its opinion in a case, the nonprevailing party must decide whether to seek additional forms of appellate review, if they are available. The direct appeal process concludes after the parties have exhausted all forms of direct appeal. Once the direct appeal process has concluded, defendants may seek additional review through a collateral appeal, in the form of either a petition for a writ of habeas corpus or some other form of postconviction remedy made available as a part of a new round of review.

Attorney Laurence Tribe (R), representing the American Civil Liberties Union (ACLU), argues his case in front of judges of the 9th U.S. Circuit Court of Appeals, in a San Francisco courtroom.

Legal professionals working on criminal appeals will be working with detailed documents and procedures. In most cases, the trial record provides the entire parameter for the appellate court's review. Legal professionals have to carefully review the trial record to identify the errors (or lack thereof) for the appellate briefs. This can be tedious work, particularly for those professionals who did not participate in the trial proceedings, and therefore are not readily familiar with the notable events before the trial court. For example, some trial transcripts can be several hundred pages in length, and each page must be carefully reviewed to determine whether it contains an issue for appeal. In addition, all other filings, exhibits, and motions presented to the trial court must be carefully inspected. Finally, legal professionals are advised to thoroughly review and outline the rules of appellate procedure that apply to the particular court of appeals. Professionals should identify the page limitations, formatting requirements, and filing deadlines for all briefs and note all other formal requirements for perfecting an appeal, submitting briefs, and presenting an oral argument.

HABEAS CORPUS PETITIONS AND OTHER COLLATERAL APPEALS

Beyond the direct appeal process, there are other forms of court review that can be sought collaterally. These are known as collateral appeals. A **_collateral appeal_** is a proceeding filed separately from (and frequently after) the direct appeal, based on an allegation that a person is being unlawfully held in government custody. This is different from a direct appeal, which proceeds directly from a judgment of conviction and is based on the assertion that the conviction and/or sentence should be reversed.

For example, in the criminal case of _State v. Jones_, the direct appeal would involve the prosecution-appellee (State) and the defendant-appellant (Jones). But in a collateral proceeding, such as a habeas corpus petition, Jones would file an action against the person or persons he alleges are unlawfully holding him in custody. In many collateral proceedings, petitioners identify prison wardens as the respondents because the petitioner is being held in prison. Thus, in a collateral proceeding, the case might be captioned _Jones v. Warden_.

In most collateral appeals, the legal arguments presented are the same as or similar to those argued in the direct appeal. But the nature of the proceedings is technically different. In direct appeals, defendants seek the reversal of their convictions and/or sentences. But in most collateral appeals, the petitioners (former defendants) seek their release from government custody. In addition, while direct appeals remain criminal cases throughout the direct appeal process, most collateral appeals are treated as civil cases. There are two primary sources of law for filing a collateral appeal—state and federal.

Collateral Review by State Courts

After completing their direct appeals, persons held in state custody often pursue collateral review by the state courts. In some states, this is called a state **_habeas corpus_** proceeding. Habeas corpus is a Latin term that literally means "you have the body." And a writ of habeas corpus is an order requiring that a prisoner be brought before a court for the purpose of determining the legality of the

collateral appeal
an additional round of review of a defendant's conviction that can occur after the direct appeal process has concluded; for example, habeas corpus review

habeas corpus
a writ challenging the legality of incarceration, or a writ ordering a prisoner to be brought before a court to determine the legality of the prisoner's detention; means "you have the body"

postconviction relief
a name given to proceedings like habeas corpus in some state courts

prisoner's detention. In other states, collateral review of state criminal convictions is called ***postconviction relief***.

Regardless of the name, the basic process is the same. A person being held in state custody asks the state courts to review whether the person is being held lawfully. In most instances, the requirement of custody is interpreted broadly and includes incarceration, forms of probation, pretrial bond, home detention, and other restrictions on a person's movement as being forms of custody. A petition for a state writ of habeas corpus or postconviction relief is normally filed in the state trial court. Again, typically this involves the person held in custody filing an action against the custodian (the person or entity holding the person in custody) and claiming that the detention is unlawful.

For example, Ohio refers to its collateral proceedings as a petition for postconviction relief and allows petitioners to assert both state and federal claims that their detention is unlawful. Section 2953.21 of the Ohio Revised Code provides:

2953.21 Post conviction relief petition.

(A)(1)(a) Any person who has been convicted of a criminal offense or adjudicated a delinquent child and who claims that there was such a denial or infringement of the person's rights as to render the judgment void or voidable under the Ohio Constitution or the Constitution of the United States, and any person who has been convicted of a criminal offense that is a felony, who is an inmate, and for whom DNA testing that was performed . . . and analyzed . . . provided results that establish, by clear and convincing evidence, actual innocence of that felony offense or, if the person was sentenced to death, establish, by clear and convincing evidence, actual innocence of the aggravating circumstance or circumstances the person was found guilty of committing and that is or are the basis of that sentence of death, may file a petition in the court that imposed sentence, stating the grounds for relief relied upon, and asking the court to vacate or set aside the judgment or sentence or to grant other appropriate relief. The petitioner may file a supporting affidavit and other documentary evidence in support of the claim for relief.

In most instances, petitioners attach affidavits or other supporting documentation to their petitions, in an effort to demonstrate the unlawfulness of their custody. Claims for relief can be either record-based (based on evidence found within the original criminal trial court record) or extra-record (based on evidence introduced outside of the trial court record). For extra-record claims, petitioners can request an evidentiary hearing before the trial court, where they can supply additional evidence or offer oral argument in support of their petition. For example, a petitioner may wish to demonstrate evidence of ineffective assistance of trial counsel or jury misconduct, which is not found in the original record. But generally, petitioners are not automatically entitled to an evidentiary hearing. Remember that, in most settings, these proceedings are civil matters, not criminal, and thus, most due process rights normally afforded to criminal defendants do not apply. Moreover, after the trial court rules on the petition, the losing party—either petitioner or respondent-custodian—can appeal the trial court's verdict to the court of appeals. Unlike in direct appeals, where the state's ability to appeal is limited, state parties are generally not so limited in appealing collateral rulings by the trial court regarding petitions for habeas corpus or postconviction relief.

In most instances, persons seeking to file federal collateral petitions must first complete the state-provided collateral appeal process. This is known as the ***exhaustion of remedies doctrine***. Under this doctrine, petitioners held in state custody must give the state courts an opportunity to remedy the alleged problem

exhaustion of remedies doctrine
a legal theory in federal habeas corpus proceedings that requires persons to first complete the state-provided collateral appeal procedures

before turning to the federal courts for intervention. Thus, persons who have very little hope of getting a state court to grant their release from custody may nevertheless file collateral petitions in the state courts in order to establish their right to file a petition for a writ of habeas corpus in the federal courts.

Law Line 14-13
Filing a Habeas Corpus Petition

Federal Habeas Corpus Proceedings

The U.S. Constitution allows people who are in custody to challenge the legality of their confinement by seeking a writ of **habeas corpus**. Article I, Section 9 provides, "[t]he privilege of the writ of habeas corpus shall not be suspended, unless when in cases of rebellion or invasion, the public safety may require it." The Supreme Court has held that, while Congress may not "suspend" the federal habeas corpus relief, except for those reasons provided in the Constitution, it may nonetheless implement reasonable restrictions on judicial authority in reviewing habeas petitions, such as limiting the number of petitions a person may file.

The right to petition for habeas corpus relief, also known as the *Great Writ*, is generally regarded as a right to petition federal courts for relief from unlawful detention by either state or federal authorities. There are three primary categories of federal habeas corpus filings—2241 petitions, 2254 petitions, and 2255 petitions.

Section 2241 Petitions.   Under 28 U.S.C. § 2241, a person in either state or federal custody who is not seeking to challenge the validity of his or her conviction or sentence can petition federal courts for a writ of habeas corpus in any of the following situations:

1. He is in custody under or by color of the authority of the United States or is committed for trial before some court thereof; or
2. He is in custody for an act done or omitted in pursuance of an Act of Congress, or an order, process, judgment or decree of a court or judge of the United States; or
3. He is in custody in violation of the Constitution or laws or treaties of the United States; or
4. He, being a citizen of a foreign state and domiciled therein is in custody for an act done or omitted under any alleged right, title, authority, privilege, protection, or exemption claimed under the commission, order or sanction of any foreign state, or under color thereof, the validity and effect of which depend upon the law of nations; or
5. It is necessary to bring him into court to testify or for trial.

For persons in pretrial custody, 28 U.S.C. § 2241 generally allows state or federal defendants to file habeas corpus petitions in federal court, if they are asserting pretrial double jeopardy claims or, in some cases, where they are asserting excessive or unreasonable amounts of pretrial bail. Federal defendants in custody after conviction may file habeas corpus petitions under 28 U.S.C. § 2241 if (1) they are not challenging the validity of their conviction or sentence, but rather are claiming that the judgment is being improperly executed by administrative authorities, or (2) in rare situations, if they are in custody and can demonstrate that other postconviction remedies are not sufficient to bring about entitled relief.

In most cases, petitioners must be in custody in order to file a § 2241 petition. The concept of custody, however, is broadly interpreted, and normally includes cases of persons released on bond pending trial, probation, and parole. In addition, § 2241 petitions must be filed in the federal district court with jurisdiction over the location where the petitioner is being held.

Section 2254 Petitions. Under 28 U.S.C. §2254, persons convicted in state proceedings may file a petition for a writ of habeas corpus in federal courts in order to challenge their conviction and/or sentence based on constitutional grounds. In these petitions, federal courts are asked to review state proceedings to determine whether the petitioner is in custody in violation of the U.S. Constitution or federal laws and treaties. Section 2254(a) provides:

> The Supreme Court, a Justice thereof, a circuit judge, or a district court shall entertain an application for a writ of habeas corpus in behalf of a person in custody pursuant to the judgment of a State court only on the ground that he is in custody in violation of the Constitution or laws or treaties of the United States.

Persons held in state custody may file § 2254 petitions in either the federal district where they are incarcerated or the district where they were convicted. As with state habeas procedures and §2241 petitions, custody is broadly construed to include incarceration, parole, probation, and other forms of detention.

Section 2255 Petitions. Under 28 U.S.C. § 2255, persons convicted in federal court proceedings may file a petition for a writ of habeas corpus in federal courts in order to challenge their conviction and/or sentence on constitutional grounds. Essentially, § 2255 is the federal custody counterpart to § 2254. In these petitions, federal courts are asked to consider whether a federal conviction or sentence was imposed in violation of federal legal standards or is otherwise excessive. Section 2255(a) provides:

> A prisoner in custody under sentence of a court established by Act of Congress claiming the right to be released upon the ground that the sentence was imposed in violation of the Constitution or laws of the United States, or that the court was without jurisdiction to impose such sentence, or that the sentence was in excess of the maximum authorized by law, or is otherwise subject to collateral attack, may move the court which imposed the sentence to vacate, set aside or correct the sentence.

Normally, petitioners in federal custody must file their § 2255 claim in the district court where they were convicted. Section 2255(e) further requires petitioners to give the original sentencing court an opportunity to correct the errors identified as claims in the habeas petition. Section 2255(e) provides:

> An application for a writ of habeas corpus in behalf of a prisoner who is authorized to apply for relief by motion pursuant to this section, shall not be entertained if it appears that the applicant has failed to apply for relief, by motion, to the court which sentenced him, or that such court has denied him relief, unless it also appears that the remedy by motion is inadequate or ineffective to test the legality of his detention.

Like other the other forms of habeas review, the custody requirement is interpreted broadly for § 2255 petitions.

Procedural Restrictions on Federal Habeas Petitions

A number of procedural restrictions are placed on petitioners filing federal habeas corpus applications. These restrictions come from both federal statutes and Supreme Court rulings.

In 1996, Congress passed the ***Antiterrorism and Effective Death Penalty Act (AEDPA)***, which implemented several strict procedures for federal habeas corpus petitioners. Under the AEDPA, most habeas petitioners must file their petitions within one year after convictions became final. A conviction becomes final when

Antiterrorism and Effective Death Penalty Act (AEDPA) a federal law that imposes several strict procedures for federal habeas corpus petitioners

the U.S. Supreme Court denies review on direct appeal or when a defendant terminates discretionary appeals on direct appeal. In cases where the defendant fails to file an appeal, the one-year time period starts from the deadline date for filing the notice of appeal.

In § 2254 cases, the AEDPA also requires federal courts to give substantial deference to the factual findings made by the state courts. To overcome this deference, petitioners must show that the state court findings were "objectively unreasonable." And with respect to conclusions of law, petitioners must demonstrate that state courts engaged in clear legal error. Section 2254(d) provides that the state court adjudication of the petitioner's claims must have "(1) resulted in a decision that was contrary to, or involved an unreasonable application of, clearly established Federal law, as determined by the Supreme Court of the United States; or (2) resulted in a decision that was based on an unreasonable determination of the facts in light of the evidence presented in the State court proceeding."

The AEDPA also mandates that § 2254 petitioners exhaust all state-provided remedies before pursuing a federal writ, under the exhaustion of remedies requirement. Section 2254(b) provides that "[a]n application for a writ of habeas corpus on behalf of a person in custody pursuant to the judgment of a State court shall not be granted unless it appears that— (A) the applicant has exhausted the remedies available in the courts of the State; or (B) (i) there is an absence of available State corrective process; or (ii) circumstances exist that render such process ineffective to protect the rights of the applicant." To exhaust state remedies, a petitioner must have "fairly presented" to the state courts both the legal and factual bases of all claims that are presented on federal habeas corpus review.

Moreover, under the AEDPA, federal courts may not consider claims that were procedurally defaulted in the trial court or direct appeal proceedings. Generally, the rule of **procedural default** applies when defendants fail to object to a violation of their rights in the trial court or fail to present an issue on direct appeal. There are some exceptions to this rule, but generally speaking, when a claim is procedurally defaulted, federal courts cannot provide habeas corpus relief, even though the substance of the claim may have merit.

> **procedural default**
> a legal theory in habeas corpus cases that maintains that, when defendants fail to object to a violation of their rights in the trial court or present an issue on direct appeal, they may lose the right to present this issue later in appellate or habeas corpus proceedings

The AEDPA further requires federal courts to dismiss claims presented in second or successive federal habeas applications if the claims were presented in a prior application. This requirement reinforces the Supreme Court's decision in *McCleskey v. Zandt* (1991),[55] holding that repeatedly filing petitions for the sole purpose of delay promotes "disrespect for the finality of convictions" and "disparages the entire criminal justice system." According to *McCleskey*, in any petition in federal court beyond the first, capital defendants must demonstrate (1) good cause why the claim now being made was not included in the first filing and (2) how the absence of that claim may have harmed the petitioner's ability to mount an effective defense.

The AEDPA also restricts the ability of petitioners to obtain an evidentiary hearing to supplement the record of the state court proceedings. If an applicant failed to develop the factual record for a claim in state court proceedings, the federal court cannot hold an evidentiary hearing on the claim unless "(1) the claim relies on (a) a new rule of constitutional law, made retroactive to cases on collateral review by the Supreme Court, that was previously unavailable, or (b) a factual predicate that could not have been previously discovered through the exercise of due diligence; *and* (2) the facts underlying the claim would be sufficient to show by clear and convincing evidence that but for constitutional error, no reasonable fact finder would have found the applicant guilty of the underlying offense." In short, under the AEDPA, a habeas petitioner's failure to develop facts in the state court bars a federal evidentiary hearing, unless the petitioner makes a strong showing of actual innocence or relies on a "new rule" made applicable to cases on collateral review.

In addition, the Supreme Court ruled in *Stone v. Powell* (1976)[56] that federal courts may not grant federal habeas relief based on Fourth Amendment exclusionary rule claims involving searches and seizures, where the petitioner had a "full and fair opportunity" to litigate the claim at trial and on direct appeal.

Finally, in order to appeal a federal court's denial of habeas relief, the petitioner must obtain a ***certificate of appealability*** (**COA**) from the district court. To obtain a COA, a petitioner must make a "substantial showing" of a denial of a constitutional right regarding each claim sought to be appealed. If a COA is denied by the district court, a petitioner may seek a COA from the circuit court of appeals. And if denied there, a petitioner may request a COA from the Supreme Court justice assigned to the circuit. But a petitioner must have a COA in order to proceed with an appeal under federal habeas corpus requirements.

certificate of appealability (COA) a document needed by habeas corpus petitioners in order to appeal an adverse ruling from the district court to a circuit court

---

IN THE FIELD

For legal professionals working on habeas corpus cases, the tasks can be quite labor intensive and are strictly controlled by detailed rules. At the outset, legal professionals must become intimately familiar with the applicable rules for their particular type of habeas matter. Filing deadlines, procedural requirements, claim restrictions, and other rules are extremely important in these cases. In addition, legal professionals must be prepared to review a substantial amount of material before preparing or responding to a habeas petition. All transcripts, motions, and appellate briefs must be carefully reviewed and compared. And given the importance of federal exhaustion of remedies requirements and procedural default rules, legal professionals must be able to track the consistency of all potential habeas claims to ensure that they were properly presented to the trial and appellate courts during the direct appeal process and, where applicable, during the state collateral appeal process. If some habeas claims were not presented or were inconsistently presented during other stages of the case, legal professionals must assess whether there is a statutory or judicial exception that will excuse such a defect.

CHAPTER **SUMMARY**

- After defendants are convicted but before they are sentenced, a number of motions can be filed with the trial court. These include a motion to withdraw the plea, a motion for judgment of acquittal, and a motion for a new trial.
- Sentencing is the process through which a sentencing authority imposes a lawful punishment or other sanction on a person convicted of violating the criminal law.
- There are several possible goals of sentencing, including retribution, deterrence, rehabilitation, restoration, and incapacitation.
- Two major approaches to sentencing are found in the indeterminate and determinate models. An indeterminate sentence is a type of sentence to imprisonment in which the commitment, instead of being for a specified single time quantity, such as three years, is for a range of time, such as two to five years or five

years maximum and zero minimum. A determinate sentence sets a single standard time quantity of imprisonment.
- Sentencing schemes typically take into consideration both aggravating and mitigating factors in reaching sentencing decisions. Aggravating factors are circumstances relating to the commission of a crime that cause its gravity to be greater than that of the average instance of the given type of offense. Conversely, mitigating factors are circumstances surrounding the commission of a crime that do not in law justify or excuse the act but which in fairness may be considered as reducing the blameworthiness of the defendant.
- A recent movement toward truth in sentencing at both the state and federal levels has tended to ensure that the time inmates actually serve in prison closely matches the sentences that were imposed.

- Several traditional sentencing orders can be imposed as a part of a criminal sentence, including incarceration, probation, community service, fines, court costs, and restitution.
- In addition, many alternative programs are also used in some cases. These include treatment programs and diversion programs.
- Under many criminal statutes, the judge can increase the severity of a defendant's sentence if certain factors are found, such as the use of a gun, abuse of a child, or extreme cruelty. These statutory factors are known as sentencing enhancements.
- In some jurisdictions, defendants convicted of capital murder or other capital offenses can be sentenced to death, or capital punishment.
- The Eighth Amendment bars cruel and unusual punishment. This provision is often discussed in five different areas of criminal procedure: the death penalty, disproportionate sentences, status crimes, unreasonable confinement conditions, and excessive bail and fines.
- In most cases, a criminal appeal can occur after the trial court has entered final judgment in a criminal case. This is known as a direct appeal. In most cases, defendants have the right to have their conviction and/or sentence reviewed by at least one appellate court. After that, many appeals to superior or supreme courts are discretionary.
- There are different types of appeals. The most common is a direct appeal, which occurs after a trial court enters final judgment in a case and the defendant appeals the judgment of conviction and/or sentence to an intermediate court of appeals. An interlocutory appeal, which is rare, occurs when a party appeals an issue while the case is still pending before the trial court. A collateral appeal is an appeal that occurs after the direct appeal has concluded.
- Collateral appeals can occur after the direct appeal process is over. At the state level, a collateral appeal is known as a state habeas corpus petition or a petition for postconviction relief.
- At the federal level, collateral appeals are conducted primarily through the habeas corpus process, whereby persons held in custody petition the federal courts for release or some other form of relief based on the claim that their custody violates their rights under the U.S. Constitution.
- In federal habeas corpus cases, Congress and the Supreme Court have imposed several procedural requirements, including those mandated by the Antiterrorism and Effective Death Penalty Act of 1996.

KEY **TERMS**

aggravating factor
Antiterrorism and Effective Death
 Penalty Act (AEDPA)
appeal
appeal information form
appellant
appellant's brief or merit brief
appellee
appellee's brief or response brief
bifurcated proceeding
capital punishment
career offender
certificate of appealability (COA)
collateral appeal
community service
concurrent sentence
consecutive sentence
court costs
Cruel and Unusual Punishment Clause
determinate sentence
deterrence
direct appeal
discretionary review
diversion programs
en banc

excessive bail
excessive fines
exhaustion of remedies doctrine
final judgment
fine
forfeiture
general deterrence
habeas corpus
habitual offender
harmless error
hate crime
home confinement
incapacitation
indeterminate sentence
intensive supervision
interlocutory appeal
legal briefs
mandatory minimum sentences or
 mandatory time
mitigating factor
mixed sentence
motion for a new trial
motion for judgment of acquittal
motion to withdraw the plea
nonreporting probation

notice of appeal
oral argument
petition for jurisdiction
petitioner
postconviction relief
presentence investigation report
 (PSR or PSI)
probation
probation violation or PV
procedural default
proportionality
proportionality doctrine
recidivism
rehabilitation
relation-back doctrine
reply brief
respondent
restitution
restoration
retribution
reversible error or prejudicial error
RICO statute
right of allocution
right of appeal or an appeal as a matter
 of right

rules of appellate procedure
sentencing
shock incarceration
shock probation
specific deterrence

split sentence
status crimes
three-strikes laws
treatment in lieu of conviction
trial court record

truth in sentencing
United States Sentencing Guidelines
 (USSG)
victim impact statements
work release

QUESTIONS FOR **DISCUSSION**

1. Identify the different motions that might be filed in a criminal case after defendants are convicted but before they are sentenced. What standards must be met before a judge will grant these motions?

2. What are the purposes of criminal sentencing? What sentencing strategies are most closely associated with each sentencing purpose?

3. How is each purpose of criminal sentencing served by indeterminate sentencing? By determinate sentencing? Which sentencing model (determinate or indeterminate) is more appropriate today? Why?

4. What is the right of allocution? What is a victim impact statement? How do these items affect sentencing hearings?

5. What are the U.S. Sentencing Guidelines? In general, how do they work?

6. What governmental practices have been prohibited or limited under the Eighth Amendment ban on cruel and unusual punishment?

7. What is the difference between a direct appeal, an interlocutory appeal, and a collateral appeal?

8. Identify the names or titles given to the parties during a criminal appeal. In general, explain how the names or titles might change as the appeal progresses.

9. Explain how briefing and oral argument is conducted in most criminal appeals.

10. Identify and explain the different types of federal habeas corpus applications that can be filed.

11. What procedural limitations have Congress and the Supreme Court imposed on federal habeas corpus petitions?

REFERENCES

1. George P. Fletcher, *Rethinking Criminal Law* (Boston: Little, Brown, 1978), p. 408.

2. Jeremy Bentham, *An Introduction to the Principles of Morals and Legislation* (1789; repr., Oxford: Clarendon Press, 1996).

3. John S. Baker, Jr., et al., *Hall's Criminal Law: Cases and Materials*, 5th ed. (Charlottesville, VA: Michie, 1993), p. 842.

4. U.S. Sentencing Commission, *Federal Sentencing Guidelines Manual* (Washington, DC: U.S. Government Printing Office, 1987), p. 207.

5. *Id.* at 15.

6. *Id.* at 16.

7. Public Law 98-473 (1984).

8. *Mistretta v. United States*, 488 U.S. 361, 371 (1989).

9. *Apprendi v. New Jersey*, 530 U.S. 466 (2000).

10. *Ring v. Arizona*, 536 U.S. 584 (2002).

11. *Blakely v. Washington*, 542 U.S. 296 (2004).

12. *United States v. Booker*, 543 U.S. 220 (2005).

13. *United States v. Fanfan*, 543 U.S. 220 (2005).

14. Tony Mauro, "Supreme Court: Sentencing Guidelines Advisory, Not Mandatory," Law.com, January 1, 2005 (accessed July 4, 2009).

15. *Report to the Nation on Crime and Justice*, 2d ed. (Washington, DC: U.S. Department of Justice, 1988), p. 90.

16. Bureau of Justice Statistics, *Dictionary of Criminal Justice Data Terminology*, 2d ed. (Washington, DC: U.S. Department of Justice, 1981), p. 107.

17. *Id.* at 107.

18. U.S. Sentencing Commission, *Federal Sentencing Guidelines Manual*, p. 2.

19. Lawrence A. Greenfeld, "Prison Sentences and Time Served for Violence," Bureau of Justice Statistics, *Selected Findings*, no. 4 (April 1995).

20. *Id.* at 46.

21. *Multisite Evaluation of Shock Incarceration* (Washington, DC: National Institute of Justice, 1995).

22. Joan Petersilia, "House Arrest," *Crime File Study Guide* (Washington, DC: National Institute of Justice, 1988).

23. *BI Home Escort: Electronic Monitoring System*, advertising brochure, BI Incorporated, Boulder, CO (no date).

24. See U.S. Sentencing Commission, *Federal Sentencing Guidelines Manual*, Section 3A1.4.

25. H.R. 4797, 102d Cong., 2d Sess. (1992).

26. California Penal Code, Section 13519.6.

27. Wisconsin Statutes, Chapter 939, Section 645(1)(b).

28. *Wisconsin v. Mitchell*, 508 U.S. 47 (1993).

29. Violent Crime Control and Law Enforcement Act of 1994, Section 280003.

30. James S. Liebman, Jeffrey Fagan, and Valerie West, "A Broken System: Error Rates in Capital Cases, 1973–1995," *Texas Law Review* (October 2000): i, 4–5.

31. Death Penalty Information Center, "Innocence and the Death Penalty." http://www.deathpenaltyinfo.org/innocence-and-death-penalty (accessed January 4, 2011).

32. Title IV of the Justice for All Act of 2004.

33. At the time the legislation was enacted, Congress estimated that 300,000 rape kits remained unanalyzed in police department evidence lockers across the country.

34. The act also provides funding for the DNA Sexual Assault Justice Act (Title III of the Justice for All Act of 2004) and the Rape Kits and DNA Evidence Backlog Elimination Act of 2000 (42 U.S.C. § 14135), authorizing more than $500 million for programs to improve the capacity of crime labs to conduct DNA analysis, reduce non-DNA backlogs, train evidence examiners, support sexual assault forensic examiner programs, and promote the use of DNA to identify missing persons.

35. *Id.*

36. 370 U.S. 660 (1962).

37. 408 U.S. 238 (1972).

38. 428 U.S. 153 (1976).

39. 536 U.S. 304 (2002).

40. 543 U.S. 551 (2005).

41. 433 U.S. 584 (1977).

42. *People v. Superior Court of San Diego (Romero)*, 13 Cal. 4th 497 (1996).

43. *Monge v. California*, 118 S. Ct. 2246 (1998).

44. *Ewing v. California*, 123 S. Ct. 1179, 155 L. Ed. 2d 108 (2003); and *Lockyer v. Andrade*, 123 S. Ct. 1166, 155 L. Ed. 2d 144 (2003).

45. 392 U.S. 514 (1968).

46. 501 U.S. 294 (1992).

47. 503 U.S. 1 (1992).

48. See *Williams v. Illinois*, 399 U.S. 235 (1970) (nonpayment of fine); *Tate v. Short*, 401 U.S. 395 (1971) (restrictive fines).

49. 21 U.S.C. § 881(a)(6).

50. Michael Goldsmith, *Civil Forfeiture: Tracing the Proceeds of Narcotics Trafficking* (Washington, DC: Police Executive Research Forum, 1988), p.3.

51. *United States v. 92 Buena Vista Ave.*, 113 S. Ct. 1126, 122 L. Ed. 2d 469 (1993).

52. *Austin v. United States*, 113 S. Ct. 2801, 15 L. Ed. 2d 448 (1993).

53. *Bennis v. Michigan*, 116 S. Ct. 1560, 134 L. Ed. 2d 661 (1996).

54. *United States v. Ursery*, 116 S. Ct. 2135, 135 L. Ed. 2d 549 (1996).

55. *McCleskey v. Zandt*, 499 U.S. 467, 493–94 (1991).

56. 428 U.S. 465 (1976).

APPENDIX
DEVELOPING YOUR LEGAL ANALYSIS

A. THE LAW WHERE YOU LIVE

Assume that a partner in your law firm has been retained to handle a criminal appeal arising out of *State v. Timothy Jenkins*, Case No. 2011-0655, a felony assault case tried before Judge Susan Thomas in your local state district court. It seems the client, Mr. Jenkins, was convicted by a jury on October 1, 2011, and sentenced by Judge Thomas to three years in prison. The trial court entered its final judgment of conviction on December 20, 2011.

In preparation for the appeal, your supervising attorney has asked you to review the Rules for Appellate Procedure used by your local court of appeals and to identify the following items: (1) the deadline for filing a notice of appeal in Mr. Jenkins's case, (2) the court in which the notice must be filed, (3) the procedure for ordering the trial court transcript and record, (4) the process for filing briefs (deadlines and other conditions), and (5) the technical requirements for filing an appellate brief in Mr. Jenkins's case, including page length, format, and any court rules for citation. In addition, you are asked to draft a notice of appeal to be filed in the appropriate court.

B. INSIDE THE FEDERAL COURTS

Assume you are working in a federal public defender's office. The office represents three defendants in unrelated cases that are all scheduled for sentencing before the district court. The federal probation officers assigned to each case have supplied the office with the presentence investigation reports (PSR) in each case. In *United States v. Williams*, the PSR recommends an offense level of 5 and a criminal history category of II. In *United States v. Stevens*, the PSR recommends an offense level of 11 and a criminal history category of I. And in *United States v. Moore*, the PSR recommends an offense level of 36 and a criminal history category of V. Each of the clients is anxiously awaiting word on the probation officer's recommendations and what they mean for him or her. Using classmates as "clients," you are asked to consider the recommendations under the U.S. Sentencing Guidelines and then explain them to each client or the client's family members. In particular, the clients want to know how much prison time, if any, they face if the district court follows the PSR's recommendations. They also want to know if they are eligible for probation or home incarceration.

If you need assistance in finding the sentencing guidelines chart or understanding it, you may consult: www.ussc.gov or http://www.jailguide.com/federalsentencing.php.

C. CYBER SOURCES

Assume you are working for an attorney who has asked for your assistance with two clients in criminal cases. Shelly Bond was convicted in federal district court of bank fraud and is currently awaiting sentencing. Your supervising attorney expects that Ms. Bond will receive some prison time as a part of her sentence and would like to ask the district court judge to recommend that Ms. Bond be imprisoned at a penal facility close to her hometown (which is also your hometown), so that family and friends can visit her. Accordingly, you are asked to consult the website for the federal Bureau of Prisons (http://www.bop.gov/) and identify the federal prison closest to your hometown that is capable of housing a nonviolent female inmate.

In addition, your supervising attorney needs to visit Antonio Smith, another client who is currently serving federal prison time for drug trafficking offenses. Your firm is representing Mr. Smith in his appeal and your supervising attorney needs to meet with him to discuss the case. To that end, you are asked to use the website for the Federal Bureau of Prisons (http://www.bop.gov/) and locate the facility where Mr. Smith is imprisoned (select a medium security facility for male inmates near your hometown). Then identify and outline the policies and procedures for attorney visitation at the facility. Provide this information in a memorandum to your supervising attorney, along with all requisite forms and supporting documentation required by the Bureau of Prisons.

D. ETHICS AND PROFESSIONALISM

Assume you are assisting Dora Smith, a criminal defense attorney. You are in a local trial court with Ms. Smith, who is representing Tom Davis in a case involving three charges—driving while intoxicated (DWI), possessing drug paraphernalia, and speeding. Ms. Smith has just worked out a plea agreement with the prosecutor, whereby Davis will plead guilty to the DWI charge, and in exchange, the prosecutor will dismiss the other two charges. You are sitting in the courtroom watching the plea and sentencing hearing. You hear the judge say, "Now, Mr. Davis, because this is your first DWI offense, I'm going to sentence you to 180 days in jail. I will suspend 177 of those days, and allow you to complete a three-day alcohol awareness program in lieu of a three-day jail sentence." The judge then imposes this sentence and the parties leave the courtroom.

You are troubled by these events because Davis previously confided in you that he had another DWI conviction two years ago in another state. During your initial meeting with Davis, he told you about this prior conviction. And you know that if the trial court knew about this prior conviction, Davis would not have been eligible for the three-day sentence. Instead, under your state's mandatory minimum sentence law in DWI cases, he would have to do at least six days in jail because this case involved a repeat offense.

You immediately notify Ms. Smith about this situation outside the courtroom. In response, Ms. Smith tells you, "Don't worry about it. The judge did not ask us about any prior convictions, so we did not misrepresent anything to the court." Despite Ms. Smith's words, you remain concerned about this situation. Prepare a two-page memorandum to your office manager where you address your ethical responsibilities in this case. Be sure to address (1) whether you can reveal the client's information to the trial court without violating your ethical duties to maintain the client's confidences, and (2) whether the court's failure to affirmatively inquire about the defendant's prior convictions makes a difference with regard to your ethical obligations. In addition to consulting any standards for your home jurisdiction, review the following standards as well:

National Federation of Paralegal Associations

http://www.paralegals.org/displaycommon.cfm?an=1&sub articlenbr=133

American Bar Association

http://www.abanet.org/legalservices/paralegals/downloads/ modelguidelines.pdf

The American Alliance of Paralegals, Inc.

http://www.aapipara.org/Ethicalstandards.htm

Appendix **A**

LEGAL RESEARCH AND BRIEFING

A. DOING LEGAL RESEARCH

Legal research involves the ability to fully and authoritatively explore all aspects of a question of law. It includes ascertaining the current status of relevant law in the proper jurisdiction, finding all cross-references and parallel case citations necessary to properly analyze a question as well as to analyze the arguments of the opposing side, finding relevant law in the proper format and context—including annotations and history, and verifying that the law the researcher has uncovered is still valid and has not been replaced or overruled. Proprietary electronic databases, which are available either online or as stand-alone software tools, offer fantastic and complete resources for legal research. Primary among such databases are LexisNexis™ and Westlaw®, both of which are available on a fee-paid basis. For anyone undertaking serious legal research, a subscription to one or both of those services (or others like them) is probably mandatory.

The Web offers a limited ability to perform some aspects of legal research—although the quality and availability of free materials on the Web may never be a replacement for proprietary legal databases. This is so because most free Web-based materials are not subject to peer review and may contain gaps and delays in the availability of crucial subject matter. Similarly, few free materials allow for easy cross-referencing and comprehensive analysis.

Nonetheless, a number of readily available Web-based resources in the legal area can give students of the law a sense of the issues involved in legal research, and they permit anyone with the requisite computer equipment and necessary skills to access a wealth of potentially useful information. A variety of Web-based legal resources and law-related services are highlighted in the chapters, and issues pertaining to Web-based legal resources are discussed. A number of legal research links that you may find useful as starting points in any research effort include the following:

Cornell University's Legal Information Institute

http://www.law.cornell.edu

An excellent starting point for online legal research.

FindLaw.com

http://www.findlaw.com

Extensive collection of legal information. Ranges from links to state and federal court cases and statutes, to analysis of the U.S. Constitution and Bill of Rights with case law annotations.

Georgetown University Law Center

http://www.ll.georgetown.edu/guides/history_crime_punish.cfm

> The Georgetown Law Library's History of Crime and Punishment Research Guide.

Legal Research Using the Internet

http://www.lib.uchicago.edu/~llou/mpoctalk.html

> Overview of Internet legal research with links to useful sites.

Lexis One

http://law.lexisnexis.com/webcenters/lexisone/

> A free resource from the Lexis-Nexis Group. Lexis One provides free case law research, free legal forms, the Legal Internet Guide, and more.

Rule of Law Resource Center

http://law.lexisnexis.com/webcenters/RuleoflawResourceCenter

> Provides advocates engaged in the rule of law access to critical information such as applicable law, news, and expert analysis.

B. LEGAL BRIEFS

Throughout this textbook, the authors cite a number of important cases. The full-text court opinions for many of these cases can be found online at the Law Line website that supports this book. Your instructor may ask that you prepare a brief of some of these cases or that you brief other cases that may be assigned.

Generally speaking, two types of briefs are used in the legal profession. The first is extensive and summarizes cases, statutes, regulations, and related legal materials that are pertinent to a legal issue that is under consideration. This is often referred to as an appellate brief or merit brief. See Chapter 14. It is usually offered to a judge or a court in support of the position of the submitting party.

A second type of brief—the kind with which we are concerned here—is simply a concise summary of the relevant facts of a single case. A brief of this sort is prepared in order to analyze a case and to present needed information in an abbreviated format that is convenient for use in class or as part of legal research. To prepare a brief for use in class, you need to read the court's written opinion and take notes on the case, being careful to arrange them in a specific format. A case brief, which may be only one or two pages in length, generally includes seven parts: (1) the case citation, (2) a short statement of the facts of the case, (3) a brief procedural history of the case, (4) a summation of the issue or issues involved, (5) the court's decision, (6) an overview of the rationale provided by the court for its decision, and (7) notes to yourself about the case. Each of these parts is briefly discussed below.

C. CASE CITATION

The citation includes the name of the case (usually found italicized or underlined at the top of the page in a case reporter or in large boldface type at the beginning of an opinion published online), conventional information needed to find the case through legal research, a reference to the court that issued the opinion, and the date the case was decided. A typical citation might look like this:

> *State v. Smith*, 58 So. 2d 853 (Ala. Crim. App. 1997)

In this instance, *58* refers to the volume number of the reporter in which the case has been published, while *So. 2d* is the name of the reporter—in this case, the second series of the *Southern Reporter*. The number *853* refers to the page number in the reporter where the decision begins; *Ala. Crim. App.* references the court issuing the decision (in this case, the Alabama Court of Criminal Appeals); and *1997* is the year in which the case was decided. Often court names are not given, since one familiar with legal citation can deduce the court from the name of the reporter. In that case, a citation may look like this:

People v. Versaggi, 83 N.Y.2d 123 (1994)

Practiced legal researchers will probably understand that *N.Y.* in this citation refers to the New York Court of Appeals. Anyone who is not sure can check the reporter referenced by the citation, in which the court's entire name is given.

The citation format used in this book follows the convention of italicizing the names of the plaintiff (in these examples, the State or the "People") and the defendant. Note that the *v.*, which appears between the names of the parties (and stands for *versus*) is italicized. Other formats may differ. To learn more about legal citations, you might want to consult a printed guide, such as *A Uniform System of Citation*,[1] known in the legal profession as the *Bluebook*.[2] The *Bluebook* is the result of the collaborative efforts of the Columbia Law Review Association, the Harvard Law Review Association, the University of Pennsylvania Law Review, and the Yale Law Review. As an alternative, you might also survey the appropriate format for legal citations through an online service, such as Boston College's Law Library (www.bc.edu/schools/law/library).

Relational electronic databases now under development will soon allow rapid online retrieval of case opinions by employing technologically advanced computerized search capabilities. Newly emerging citation styles, needed to take full advantage of the capabilities of such electronic case databases, may augment the standard citation format in years to come.

In recognition of just such a possibility, the seventeenth edition of the *Bluebook* addresses citability of opinions found on the Internet. It suggests, "When citing the materials found on the Internet, provide . . . the title or top level heading of the material being cited, and the Uniform Resource Locator (URL). The URL is the electronic Internet address of the material and should be given in brackets. . . . Point citations should refer to the paragraph number if available."[3] An example might be:

LLR No. 9405161.PA, P10 [http://www.versuslaw.com]

In this example, from the Versus Law website, *LLR* refers to Lawyer's Legal Research, an electronic citation format created by the Versus Law staff. The number after the *LLR* designator refers to a specific case (in this instance, a 1994 Pennsylvania Supreme Court case, *Commonwealth* v. *Berkowitz*), and the letters after the period reference the jurisdiction (Pennsylvania). *P10* identifies the tenth paragraph in the case, and the URL for Versus Law is provided in brackets.

On August 6, 1996, in an effort to further standardize case citations, the ABA's House of Delegates passed a motion to recommend a universal citation system to the courts. The resolution recommends that courts adopt a universal citation system using sequential decision numbers for each year and internal paragraph numbers within the decision. The numbers should be assigned by the court and included in the decision at the time it is made publicly available by the court. The standard form of citation, shown for a decision in a federal court of appeals, would be as follows:

Smith v. Jones, 1996 5Cir 15, ¶ 18, 22 F.3d 955

In this example, *1996* is the year of the decision; *5Cir* refers to the U.S. Court of Appeals for the Fifth Circuit; *15* indicates that this citation is to the fifteenth decision released by the court in the year; *18* is the paragraph number where the material referred to is located; and the remainder is the parallel citation to the volume and page in the printed case report, where the decision may also be found.

Many jurisdictions do not follow the Bluebook or ABA recommended form of citation. Instead, they have their own preferred methods for citing cases and other legal authorities. Before beginning any legal writing project, legal professionals should identify and understand the preferred or required methods for citing and formatting legal briefs, memoranda, and other pleadings that are used by the court hearing the case.

D. HOW TO BRIEF A CASE

There are a number of steps you should follow when briefing an individual case, either for yourself or to assist another legal professional.

1. READ THE OPINION written by the Court, including any concurring and/or dissenting opinions. As you read the opinion, make a note of any legal terms or factual matters that you do not understand. Now you are prepared to brief (which is a not-so-fancy word for "summarize") the opinion. This brief or summary should follow the following format:

2. FACTS—In a paragraph or two, describe the relevant facts of the case. In essence, describe who did what to whom when and how. In this section, try to identify the parties to the case, how they came to interact, and the critical events or items of information that are primarily relevant to the Court's decision. In some cases, it may be relevant and important to describe how the parties got to the Supreme Court or other tribunal. In other words, the procedure of the case (the initial filing of the case and the lower courts' rulings) may be important to the Court's ruling, and thus, should be included in the factual portion of your brief. In other cases, the process used to get to the Supreme Court will not be relevant to the Court's opinion. In these cases, you will not need to devote as much attention to the judicial procedures that occurred prior to the Supreme Court. At first, it may be difficult to determine which facts to leave out and which ones to include. But as you do more briefs, this process should become easier.

3. ISSUE—In a sentence or two, identify the constitutional or legal question(s) being addressed by the Court. This sentence (or two) should be written in the form of a question and include the relevant constitutional, statutory, or other legal provision that is under consideration (free speech, free exercise, Commerce Clause, Americans with Disabilities Act, etc.) as well as the relevant facts under consideration. For example, in *Texas v. Johnson*, 491 U.S. 397 (1989), the issue could be written as "Did the State of Texas violate Greg Johnson's First Amendment right to freedom of expression by arresting him for burning an American flag during a political protest?"

4. JUDGMENT (HOLDING) of the Court—Next, in a sentence or two, explain how the Court answered the constitutional question(s) that you identified in section 3. In other words, describe what the Court decided when it answered the constitutional or legal issue. For example, in response to the issue presented in the *Johnson* case, you could write: "Yes, the State of Texas violated Johnson's right to free expression when it arrested him for burning the flag." This section should include a numeric breakdown of the vote and an accounting of how each justice voted. Was the opinion unanimous (9-0)? Was the Court divided 5-4, with five justices writing a majority opinion and four justices writing a dissenting opinion? Was there a plurality opinion (e.g., three writing the primary opinion and two writing a concurring opinion with four writing dissenting opinions)?

5. RATIONALE—In a few paragraphs, explain how the majority (if there is one) of the Court reached its judgment by explaining the rationale used by the Court to justify its decision. This should include an explanation of how the Court interpreted the relevant constitutional or legal standards at issue in the case. In other words, explain the logic used by the Court to justify its judgment/holding. Typically, this should be the bulk of your brief.

6. OTHER OPINIONS—Also, be sure to identify any concurring opinions (opinions that agree with the judgment of the Court but disagree with its rationale) and any dissenting opinions (opinions that disagree with the judgment and most likely with the rationale as well). Briefly identify the justices writing these other opinions and explain their rationale.

7. YOUR ASSESSMENT—Finally, in a paragraph or two, explain how you view the Court's opinion. Explain your basis for agreeing or disagreeing with the Court's ruling. In addition, address the implications for the Court's decision. What impact do you expect this case will have on the Constitution and the political process?

Overall, briefs will be approximately two pages in length, although longer briefs may be necessary, particularly when there are multiple opinions and/or complicated facts within the decision. Conversely, briefs may be shorter if the Court's opinion is unanimous and is decided on narrow and clear legal grounds.

REFERENCES

1. A Uniform System of Citation, 17th ed. (Cambridge, MA: Harvard Law Review Association, 2001).

2. *Bluebook* format requires that the *v.* between parties be italicized.

3. *A Uniform System of Citation*, Section 17.3.3.

Appendix **B**

THE CONSTITUTION OF THE UNITED STATES OF AMERICA

WE THE PEOPLE of the United States, in Order to form a more perfect Union, establish Justice, insure domestic Tranquility, provide for the common defence, promote the general Welfare, and secure the Blessings of Liberty to ourselves and our Posterity, do ordain and establish this CONSTITUTION for the United States of America.

ARTICLE I

Section 1

All legislative Powers herein granted shall be vested in a Congress of the United States, which shall consist of a Senate and House of Representatives.

Section 2

The House of Representatives shall be composed of Members chosen every second Year by the People of the several States, and the Electors in each State shall have the Qualifications requisite for Electors of the most numerous Branch of the State Legislature.

No Person shall be a Representative who shall not have attained to the Age of twenty-five Years, and been seven Years a Citizen of the United States, and who shall not, when elected, be an Inhabitant of that State in which he shall be chosen.

Representatives and direct Taxes shall be apportioned among the several States which may be included within this Union, according to their respective Numbers, which shall be determined by adding to the whole Number of free Persons, including those bound to Service for a Term of Years, and excluding Indians not taxed, three fifths of all other Persons. The actual Enumeration shall be made within three Years after the first Meeting of the Congress of the United States, and within every subsequent Term of ten Years, in such Manner as they shall by Law direct. The Number of Representatives shall not exceed one for every thirty Thousand, but each State shall have at Least one Representative; and until such enumeration shall be made, the State of New Hampshire shall be entitled to chuse three, Massachusetts eight, Rhode-Island and Providence Plantations one, Connecticut five, New York six, New Jersey four, Pennsylvania eight, Delaware one, Maryland six, Virginia ten, North Carolina five, South Carolina five, and Georgia three.

When vacancies happen in the representation from any State, the Executive Authority thereof shall issue Writs of Election to fill such Vacancies.

The House of Representatives shall chuse their Speaker and other Officers; and shall have the sole Power of Impeachment.

Section 3

The Senate of the United States shall be composed of two Senators from each State, chosen by the Legislature thereof for six Years; and each Senator shall have one Vote.

Immediately after they shall be assembled in Consequence of the first Election, they shall be divided as equally as may be into three Classes. The Seats of the Senators of the first Class shall be vacated at the Expiration of the second Year, of the second Class at the Expiration of the fourth Year, and of the third Class at the Expiration of the sixth Year, so that one third may be chosen every second Year; and if Vacancies happen by Resignation, or otherwise, during the recess of the Legislature of any State, the Executive thereof may make temporary Appointments until the next Meeting of the Legislature, which shall then fill such Vacancies.

No Person shall be Senator who shall not have attained to the Age of thirty Years, and been nine Years a Citizen of the United States, and who shall not, when elected, be an Inhabitant of that State for which he shall be chosen.

The Vice President of the United States shall be President of the Senate, but shall have no Vote, unless they be equally divided.

The Senate shall chuse their other Officers, and also a President pro tempore, in the absence of the Vice President, or when he shall exercise the Office of President of the United States.

The Senate shall have the sole Power to try all Impeachments. When sitting for that Purpose, they shall be on Oath or Affirmation. When the President of the United States is tried, the Chief Justice shall preside: And no Person shall be convicted without the Concurrence of two thirds of the Members present.

Judgment in Cases of Impeachment shall not extend further than to removal from Office, and disqualification to hold and enjoy any Office of honor, Trust, or Profit under the United States: but the Party convicted shall nevertheless be liable and subject to Indictment, Trial, Judgment and Punishment, according to Law.

Section 4

The Times, Places and Manner of holding Elections for Senators and Representatives, shall be prescribed in each State by the Legislature thereof; but the Congress may at any time by Law make or alter such Regulations, except as to the Place of chusing Senators.

The Congress shall assemble at least once in every Year, and such Meeting shall be on the first Monday in December, unless they shall by law appoint a different Day.

Section 5

Each House shall be the Judge of the Elections, Returns and Qualifications of its own Members, and a Majority of each shall constitute a Quorum to do Business; but a smaller Number may adjourn from day to day, and may be authorized to compel the Attendance of absent Members, in such Manner, and under such Penalties as each House may provide.

Each House may determine the Rules of its Proceedings, punish its Members for disorderly Behaviour, and, with the Concurrence of two thirds, expel a Member.

Each House shall keep a Journal of its Proceedings, and from time to time publish the same, excepting such Parts as may in their Judgment require Secrecy; and the Yeas and Nays of the Members of either House on any question shall, at the Desire of one fifth of those Present, be entered on the journal.

Neither House, during the Session of Congress, shall, without the Consent of the other, adjourn for more than three days, nor to any other Place than that in which the two Houses shall be sitting.

Section 6

The Senators and Representatives shall receive a Compensation for their Services, to be ascertained by Law, and paid out of the Treasury of the United States. They shall in all Cases, except Treason, Felony and Breach of the Peace, be privileged from Arrest during their Attendance at the Session of their respective Houses, and in going to and returning from the same; and for any Speech or Debate in either House, they shall not be questioned in any other Place.

No Senator or Representative shall, during the Time for which he was elected, be appointed to any civil Office under the Authority of the United States, which shall have been created, or the Emoluments whereof shall have been encreased during such time; and no Person holding any Office under the United States, shall be a Member of either House during his Continuance in Office.

Section 7

All Bills for raising Revenue shall originate in the House of Representatives; but the Senate may propose or concur with Amendments as on other Bills.

Every Bill which shall have passed the House of Representatives and the Senate, shall, before it become a Law, be presented to the President of the United States; If he approve he shall sign it, but if not he shall return it, with his Objections to that House in which it shall have originated, who shall enter the Objections at large on their Journal, and proceed to reconsider it. If after such Reconsideration two thirds of that House shall agree to pass the Bill, it shall be sent, together with the Objections, to the other House, by which it shall likewise be reconsidered, and if approved by two thirds of that House, it shall become a Law. But in all such Cases the Votes of both Houses shall be determined by Yeas and Nays, and the Names of the Persons voting for and against the Bill shall be entered on the Journal of each House respectively. If any Bill shall not be returned by the President within ten Days (Sundays excepted) after it shall have been presented to him, the Same shall be a Law, in like Manner as if he had signed it, unless the Congress by their Adjournment prevent its Return, in which Case it shall not be a Law.

Every Order, Resolution, or Vote to which the Concurrence of the Senate and House of Representatives may be necessary (except on a question of Adjournment) shall be presented to the President of the United States; and before the Same shall take Effect, shall be approved by him, or being disapproved by him, shall be repassed by two thirds of the Senate and House of Representatives, according to the Rules and Limitations prescribed in the Case of a Bill.

Section 8

The Congress shall have Power to lay and collect Taxes, Duties, Imposts and Excises, to pay the Debts and provide for the common Defence and general Welfare of the United States; but all Duties, Imposts and Excises shall be uniform throughout the United States;

To borrow Money on the credit of the United States;

To regulate Commerce with foreign Nations, and among the several States, and with the Indian Tribes;

To establish an uniform Rule of Naturalization, and uniform Laws on the subject of Bankruptcies throughout the United States;

To coin Money, regulate the Value thereof, and of foreign Coin, and fix the Standard of Weights and Measures;

To provide for the Punishment of counterfeiting the Securities and current Coin of the United States;

To establish Post Offices and post Roads;

To promote the Progress of Science and useful Arts, by securing for limited times to Authors and Inventors the exclusive Right to their respective Writings and Discoveries;

To constitute Tribunals inferior to the supreme Court;

To define and punish Piracies and Felonies committed on the high Seas, and Offences against the Law of Nations;

To declare War, grant Letters of Marque and Reprisal, and make Rules concerning Captures on Land and Water;

To raise and support Armies, but no Appropriation of Money to that Use shall be for a longer Term than two Years;

To provide and maintain a Navy;

To make Rules for the Government and Regulation of the land and naval Forces;

To provide for calling forth the Militia to execute the Laws of the Union, suppress Insurrections and repel Invasions;

To provide for organizing, arming, and disciplining the Militia, and for governing such Part of them as may be employed in the Service of the United States, reserving to the States respectively, the Appointment of the Officers, and the Authority of training the Militia according to the discipline prescribed by Congress;

To exercise exclusive Legislation in all Cases whatsoever, over such District (not exceeding ten Miles square) as may, by Cession of particular States, and the Acceptance of Congress, become the Seat of the Government of the United States, and to exercise like Authority over all Places purchased by the Consent of the Legislature of the State in which the Same shall be, for the Erection of Forts, Magazines, and Arsenals, dock-Yards, and other needful Buildings;—And

To make all Laws which shall be necessary and proper for carrying into Execution the foregoing Powers, and all other Powers vested by this Constitution in the Government of the United States, or in any Department or Officer thereof.

Section 9

The Migration or Importation of such Persons as any of the States now existing shall think proper to admit, shall not be prohibited by the Congress prior to the Year one thousand eight hundred and eight, but a Tax or duty may be imposed on such Importation, not exceeding ten dollars for each Person.

The privilege of the Writ of Habeas Corpus shall not be suspended, unless when in Cases of Rebellion or Invasion the public Safety may require it.

No Bill of Attainder or ex post facto Law shall be passed.

No Capitation, or other direct, Tax shall be laid, unless in Proportion to the Census or Enumeration herein before directed to be taken.

No Tax or Duty shall be laid on Articles exported from any State.

No Preference shall be given by any Regulation of Commerce or Revenue to the Ports of one State over those of another: nor shall Vessels bound to, or from, one State, be obliged to enter, clear, or pay Duties in another.

No Money shall be drawn from the Treasury, but in Consequence of Appropriations made by Law; and a regular Statement and Account of the Receipts and Expenditures of all public Money shall be published from time to time.

No Title of Nobility shall be granted by the United States: And no Person holding any Office of Profit or Trust under them, shall, without the Consent of the Congress, accept of any present, Emolument, Office, or Title, of any kind whatever, from any King, Prince, or foreign State.

Section 10

No State shall enter into any Treaty, Alliance, or Confederation; grant Letters of Marque and Reprisal; coin Money; emit Bills of Credit; make any Thing but gold and silver Coin a Tender in Payment of Debts; pass any Bill of Attainder, ex post facto Law, or Law impairing the Obligation of Contracts, or grant any Title of Nobility.

No State shall, without the consent of the Congress, lay any Imposts or Duties on Imports or Exports, except what may be absolutely necessary for executing its inspection Laws: and the net Produce of all Duties and Imposts, laid by any State on Imports or Exports, shall be for the Use of the Treasury of the United States; and all such Laws shall be subject to the Revision and Control of the Congress.

No State shall, without the Consent of Congress, lay any Duty of Tonnage, keep Troops, or Ships of War in time of Peace, enter into any Agreement or Compact with another State, or with a foreign Power, or engage in War, unless actually invaded, or in such imminent Danger as will not admit of delay.

ARTICLE II

Section 1

The executive Power shall be vested in a President of the United States of America. He shall hold his Office during the Term of four Years, and, together with the Vice President, chosen for the same Term, be elected, as follows.

Each State shall appoint, in such Manner as the Legislature thereof may direct, a Number of Electors, equal to the whole Number of Senators and Representatives to which the State may be entitled in the Congress: but no Senator or Representative, or Person holding an Office of Trust or Profit under the United States, shall be appointed an Elector.

The Electors shall meet in their respective States, and vote by Ballot for two persons, of whom one at least shall not be an Inhabitant of the same State with themselves. And they shall make a List of all the Persons voted for, and of the Number of Votes for each; which List they shall sign and certify, and transmit sealed to the Seat of the Government of the United States, directed to the President of the Senate. The President of the Senate shall, in the Presence of the Senate and House of Representatives, open all the Certificates, and the Votes shall then be counted. The Person having the greatest Number of Votes shall be the President, if such Number be a Majority of the whole Number of Electors appointed; and if there be more than one who have such Majority, and have an equal Number of Votes, then the House of Representatives shall immediately chuse by Ballot one of them for President; and if no Person have a Majority, then from the five highest on the List the said House shall in like Manner chuse the President. But in choosing the President, the Votes shall be taken by States, the Representation from each State having one Vote; A quorum for this Purpose shall consist of a Member or Members from two thirds of the States, and a Majority of all the States shall be necessary to a Choice. In every Case, after the Choice of the President, the Person having the greatest Number of Votes of the Electors shall be the Vice President. But if there should remain two or more who have equal Votes, the Senate shall chuse from them by Ballot the Vice President.

The Congress may determine the Time of chusing the Electors, and the Day on which they shall give their Votes; which Day shall be the same throughout the United States.

No person except a natural born Citizen, or a Citizen of the United States, at the time of Adoption of this Constitution, shall be eligible to the Office of President; neither shall any Person be eligible to that Office who shall not have attained to the Age of thirty five Years, and been fourteen Years a Resident within the United States.

In Case of the Removal of the President from Office, or of his Death, Resignation, or Inability to discharge the Powers and Duties of the said Office, the same shall devolve on the Vice President, and the Congress may by Law provide for the Case of Removal, Death, Resignation or Inability, both of the President and Vice President, declaring what Officer shall then act as President, and such Officer shall act accordingly, until the Disability be removed, or a President shall be elected.

The President shall, at stated Times, receive for his Services, a Compensation, which shall neither be increased nor diminished during the Period for which he shall have been elected, and he shall not receive within that Period any other Emolument from the United States, or any of them.

Before he enter on the Execution of his Office, he shall take the following Oath or Affirmation:—"I do solemnly swear (or affirm) that I will faithfully execute the Office of President of the United States, and will to the best of my Ability, preserve, protect and defend the Constitution of the United States."

Section 2

The President shall be Commander in Chief of the Army and Navy of the United States, and of the Militia of the several States, when called into the actual Service of the United States; he may require the Opinion in writing, of the principal Officer in each of the executive Departments, upon any subject relating to the Duties of their respective Offices, and he shall have Power to grant Reprieves and Pardons for Offenses against the United States, except in Cases of Impeachment.

He shall have Power, by and with the Advice and Consent of the Senate, to make Treaties, provided two thirds of the Senators present concur; and he shall nominate, and by and with the Advice and Consent of the Senate, shall appoint Ambassadors, other public Ministers and Consuls, Judges of the supreme Court, and all other Officers of the United States, whose Appointments are not herein otherwise provided for, and which shall be established by Law: but the Congress may by Law vest the Appointment of such inferior Officers, as they think proper, in the President alone, in the courts of Law, and in the Heads of Departments.

The President shall have Power to fill up all Vacancies that may happen during the Recess of the Senate, by granting Commissions which shall expire at the End of their next Session.

Section 3

He shall from time to time give to the Congress Information of the State of the Union, and recommend to their Consideration such Measures as he shall judge necessary and expedient; he may, on extraordinary Occasions, convene both Houses, or either of them, and in Case of Disagreement between them, with Respect to the Time of Adjournment, he may adjourn them to such Time as he shall think proper; he shall receive Ambassadors and other public Ministers; he shall take Care that the Laws be faithfully executed, and Shall Commission all the Officers of the United States.

Section 4

The President, Vice President and all civil Officers of the United States, shall be removed from Office on Impeachment for, and Conviction of, Treason, Bribery, or other high Crimes and Misdemeanors.

ARTICLE III

Section 1

The judicial Power of the United States, shall be vested in one supreme Court, and in such inferior Courts as the Congress may from time to time ordain and establish. The Judges, both of the supreme and inferior Courts, shall hold their Offices during good Behavior, and shall, at stated Times, receive for their Services, a Compensation, which shall not be diminished during their Continuance in Office.

Section 2

The judicial Power shall extend to all Cases, in Law and Equity, arising under this Constitution, the Laws of the United States, and Treaties made, or which shall be made, under their Authority;—to all Cases affecting Ambassadors, other public Ministers and Consuls;—to all Cases of admiralty and maritime Jurisdiction;—to Controversies to which the United States shall be a Party;—to Controversies between two or more States;—between a State and Citizens of another State;—between citizens of different States;—between Citizens of the same State claiming Lands under Grants of different States, and between a State, or the Citizens thereof, and foreign States, Citizens or Subjects.

In all Cases affecting Ambassadors, other public Ministers and Consuls, and those in which a State shall be Party, the supreme Court shall have original Jurisdiction. In all the other Cases before mentioned, the supreme Court shall have appellate Jurisdiction, both as to Law and Fact, with such exceptions, and under such Regulations as the Congress shall make.

The Trial of all Crimes, except in Cases of Impeachment, shall be by Jury; and such Trial shall be held in the State where the said Crimes shall have been committed; but when not committed within any State, the Trial shall be at such Place or Places as the Congress may by Law have directed.

Section 3

Treason against the United States, shall consist only in levying War against them, or in adhering to their Enemies, giving them Aid and Comfort. No Person shall be convicted of Treason unless on the Testimony of two Witnesses to the same overt Act, or on Confession in open Court.

The Congress shall have Power to declare the Punishment of Treason, but no Attainder of Treason shall work Corruption of Blood, or Forfeiture except during the Life of the Person attainted.

ARTICLE IV

Section 1

Full Faith and Credit shall be given in each State to the public Acts, Records, and judicial Proceedings of every other State. And the Congress may by general Laws prescribe the Manner in which such Acts, Records and Proceedings shall be proved, and the Effect thereof.

Section 2

The Citizens of each State shall be entitled to all Privileges and Immunities of Citizens in the several States.

A Person charged in any State with Treason, Felony, or other Crime, who shall flee from Justice, and be found in another State, shall on Demand of the executive Authority of the State from which he fled, be delivered up, to be removed to the State having Jurisdiction of the Crime.

No Person held to Service or Labour in one State, under the Laws thereof, escaping into another, shall, in Consequence of any Law or Regulation therein, be discharged from such Service or Labour, but shall be delivered up on Claim of the Party to whom such Service or Labour may be due.

Section 3

New States may be admitted by the Congress into this Union; but no new State shall be formed or erected within the Jurisdiction of any other State; nor any State be formed by the Junction of two or more States, or parts of States, without the Consent of the Legislatures of the States concerned as well as of the Congress.

The Congress shall have Power to dispose of and make all needful Rules and Regulations respecting the Territory or other Property belonging to the United States; and nothing in this Constitution shall be so construed as to Prejudice any Claims of the United States, or of any particular State.

Section 4

The United States shall guarantee to every State in this Union a Republican Form of Government, and shall protect each of them against Invasion; and on Application of the Legislature, or of the Executive (when the Legislature cannot be convened) against domestic Violence.

ARTICLE V

The Congress, whenever two thirds of both Houses shall deem it necessary, shall propose Amendments to this Constitution, or, on the Application of the Legislatures of two thirds of the several States, shall call a Convention for proposing Amendments, which, in either

Case, shall be valid to all Intents and Purposes, as Part of this Constitution, when ratified by the Legislatures of three fourths of the several States, or by Conventions in three fourths thereof, as the one or the other Mode of Ratification may be proposed by the Congress; Provided that no Amendment which may be made prior to the Year One thousand eight hundred and eight shall in any Manner affect the first and fourth Clauses in the Ninth Section of the first Article; and that no State, without its Consent, shall be deprived of its equal Suffrage in the Senate.

ARTICLE VI

All Debts contracted and Engagements entered into, before the Adoption of this Constitution, shall be as valid against the United States under this Constitution, as under the Confederation.

This Constitution, and the Laws of the United States which shall be made in Pursuance thereof; and all Treaties made, or which shall be made, under the Authority of the United States, shall be the supreme Law of the Land; and the Judges in every State shall be bound thereby; any Thing in the Constitution or Laws of any State to the Contrary notwithstanding.

The Senators and Representatives before mentioned, and the Members of the several State Legislatures, and all executive and judicial Officers, both of the United States and of the several States, shall be bound by Oath or Affirmation, to support this Constitution; but no religious Test shall ever be required as a Qualification to any Office or public Trust under the United States.

ARTICLE VII

The Ratification of the Conventions of nine States shall be sufficient for the Establishment of this Constitution between the States so ratifying the Same.

AMENDMENTS

AMENDMENT I. (1791)

Congress shall make no law respecting an establishment of religion, or prohibiting the free exercise thereof; or abridging the freedom of speech, or of the press; or the right of the people peaceably to assemble, and to petition the Government for a redress of grievances.

AMENDMENT II. (1791)

A well regulated Militia, being necessary to the security of a free State, the right of the people to keep and bear Arms, shall not be infringed.

AMENDMENT III. (1791)

No Soldier shall, in time of peace be quartered in any house, without the consent of the Owner, nor in time of war, but in a manner to be prescribed by law.

AMENDMENT IV. (1791)

The right of the people to be secure in their persons, houses, papers, and effects, against unreasonable searches and seizures, shall not be violated, and no Warrants shall issue, but upon probable cause, supported by Oath or affirmation, and particularly describing the place to be searched, and the persons or things to be seized.

AMENDMENT V. (1791)

No person shall be held to answer for a capital, or otherwise infamous crime, unless on a presentment or indictment of a Grand Jury, except in cases arising in the land or naval forces, or in the Militia, when in actual service in time of War or public danger; nor shall any person be subject for the same offence to be twice put in jeopardy of life or limb; nor shall be compelled in any criminal case to be a witness against himself, nor be deprived of life, liberty, or property, without due process of law; nor shall private property be taken for public use, without just compensation.

AMENDMENT VI. (1791)

In all criminal prosecutions, the accused shall enjoy the right to a speedy and public trial, by an impartial jury of the State and district wherein the crime shall have been committed, which district shall have been previously ascertained by law, and to be informed of the nature and cause of the accusation; to be confronted with the witnesses against him; to have compulsory process for obtaining Witnesses in his favor, and to have the Assistance of Counsel for his defence.

AMENDMENT VII. (1791)

In Suits at common law, where the value in controversy shall exceed twenty dollars, the right of trial by jury shall be preserved, and no fact tried by a jury, shall be otherwise reexamined in any Court of the United States, than according to the rules of the common law.

AMENDMENT VIII. (1791)

Excessive bail shall not be required, nor excessive fines imposed, nor cruel and unusual punishments inflicted.

AMENDMENT IX. (1791)

The enumeration of the Constitution, of certain rights, shall not be construed to deny or disparage others retained by the people.

AMENDMENT X. (1791)

The powers not delegated to the United States by the Constitution, nor prohibited by it to the States, are reserved to the States respectively, or to the people.

AMENDMENT XI. (1798)

The Judicial power of the United States shall not be construed to extend to any suit in law or equity, commenced or prosecuted against one of the United States by Citizens of another State, or by Citizens or Subjects of any Foreign State.

AMENDMENT XII. (1804)

The Electors shall meet in their respective states and vote by ballot for President and Vice-President, one of whom, at least, shall not be an inhabitant of the same state with themselves; they shall name in their ballots the person voted for as President, and in distinct ballots the person voted for as Vice-President, and they shall make distinct lists of all persons voted for as President, and of all persons voted for as Vice-President, and of the number of votes for each, which lists they shall sign and certify, and transmit sealed to the seat of the government of the United States, directed to the President of the Senate;—The President of the Senate shall, in the presence of the Senate and House of Representatives, open all the certificates and the votes shall then be counted;—The person having the greatest number of votes for President, shall be the President, if such number be a majority of the whole number of Electors appointed; and if no person have such majority, then from the persons having the highest numbers not exceeding three on the list of those voted for as President, the House of Representatives shall choose immediately, by ballot, the President. But in choosing the President, the votes shall be taken by states, the representation from each state having one vote; a quorum for this purpose shall consist of a member or members from two-thirds of the states, and a majority of all the states shall be necessary to a choice. And if the House of Representatives shall not choose a President whenever the right of choice shall devolve upon them, before the fourth day of March next following, then the Vice-President shall act as President, as in the case of the death or other constitutional disability of the President. The person having the greatest number of votes as Vice-President, shall be the Vice-President, if such number be a majority of the whole number of Electors appointed, and if no person have a majority, then from the two highest numbers on the list, the Senate shall choose the Vice-President; a quorum for the purpose shall consist of two-thirds of the whole number of Senators, and a majority of the whole number shall be necessary to a choice. But no person constitutionally ineligible to the office of President shall be eligible to that of Vice-President of the United States.

AMENDMENT XIII. (1865)

Section 1

Neither slavery nor involuntary servitude, except as a punishment for crime whereof the party shall have been duly convicted, shall exist within the United States, or any place subject to their jurisdiction.

Section 2

Congress shall have power to enforce this article by appropriate legislation.

AMENDMENT XIV. (1868)

Section 1

All persons born or naturalized in the United States, and subject to the jurisdiction thereof, are citizens of the United States and of the State wherein they reside. No State shall make or enforce any law which shall abridge the privileges or immunities of citizens of the United States; nor shall any State deprive any person of life, liberty, or property, without due process of law; nor deny to any person within its jurisdiction the equal protection of the law.

Section 2

Representatives shall be apportioned among the several States according to their respective numbers, counting the whole number of persons in each State, excluding Indians not taxed. But when the right to vote at any election for the choice of electors for President and Vice-President of the United States, Representatives in Congress, the Executive and Judicial officers of a State, or the members of the Legislature thereof, is denied to any of the male inhabitants of such State, being twenty-one years of age, and citizens of the United States, or in any way abridged, except for participation in rebellion, or other crime, the basis of representation therein shall be reduced in the proportion which the number of such male citizens shall bear to the whole number of male citizens twenty-one years of age in such State.

Section 3

No person shall be a Senator or Representative in Congress, or elector of President and Vice-President, or hold any office, civil or military, under the United States, or under any State, who, having previously taken an oath, as a member of Congress, or as an officer of the United States, or as a member of any State legislature, or as an executive or judicial officer of any State, to support the Constitution of the United States, shall have engaged in insurrection or rebellion against the same, or given aid or comfort to the enemies thereof. But Congress may by a vote of two-thirds of each House, remove such disability.

Section 4

The validity of the public debt of the United States, authorized by law, including debts incurred for payment of pensions and bounties for services in suppressing insurrection or rebellion, shall not be questioned. But neither the United States nor any State shall assume or pay any debt or obligation incurred in aid of insurrection or rebellion against the United States, or any claim for the loss or emancipation of any slave; but all such debts, obligations and claims shall be held illegal and void.

Section 5

The Congress shall have power to enforce, by appropriate legislation, the provisions of this article.

AMENDMENT XV. (1870)

Section 1

The right of citizens of the United States to vote shall not be denied or abridged by the United States or by any State on account of race, color, or previous condition of servitude.

Section 2

The Congress shall have power to enforce this article by appropriate legislation.

AMENDMENT XVI. (1913)

The Congress shall have power to lay and collect taxes on incomes, from whatever source derived, without apportionment among the several States, and without regard to any census or enumeration.

AMENDMENT XVII. (1913)

The Senate of the United States shall be composed of two Senators from each State, elected by the people thereof, for six years; and each Senator shall have one vote. The electors in each State shall have the qualifications requisite for electors of the most numerous branch of the State legislatures.

When vacancies happen in the representation of any State in the Senate, the executive authority of such State shall issue writs of election to fill such vacancies: *Provided,* That the legislature of any State may empower the executive thereof to make temporary appointments until the people fill the vacancies by election as the legislature may direct.

This amendment shall not be so construed as to affect the election or term of any Senator chosen before it becomes valid as part of the Constitution.

AMENDMENT XVIII. (1919)

Section 1

After one year from the ratification of this article the manufacture, sale, or transportation of intoxicating liquors within, the importation thereof into, or the exportation thereof from the United States and all territory subject to the jurisdiction thereof for beverage purposes is hereby prohibited.

Section 2

The Congress and the several States shall have concurrent power to enforce this article by appropriate legislation.

Section 3

This article shall be inoperative unless it shall have been ratified as an amendment to the Constitution by the legislatures of the several States, as provided in the Constitution, within seven years from the date of the submission hereof to the States by the Congress.

AMENDMENT XIX. (1920)

The right of citizens of the United States to vote shall not be denied or abridged by the United States or by any State on account of sex.

Congress shall have power to enforce this article by appropriate legislation.

AMENDMENT XX. (1933)

Section 1

The terms of the President and Vice President shall end at noon on the 20th day of January, and the terms of Senators and representatives at noon on the 3d day of January, of the years in which such terms would have ended if this article had not been ratified; and the terms of their successors shall then begin.

Section 2

The Congress shall assemble at least once in every year, and such meeting shall begin at noon on the 3d day of January, unless they shall by law appoint a different day.

Section 3

If, at the time fixed for the beginning of the term of the President, the President elect shall have died, the Vice President elect shall become President. If a President shall not have been chosen before the time fixed for the beginning of his term, or if the President elect shall have failed to qualify, then the Vice President elect shall act as President until a President shall have qualified; and the Congress may by law provide for the case wherein neither a President elect nor a Vice President elect shall have qualified, declaring who shall then act as President, or the manner in which one who is to act shall be selected, and such person shall act accordingly until a President or Vice President shall have qualified.

Section 4

The Congress may by law provide for the case of the death of any of the persons from whom the House of Representatives may choose a President whenever the right of choice shall have devolved upon them, and for the case of the death of any of the persons from whom the Senate may choose a Vice President whenever the right of choice shall have devolved upon them.

Section 5

Sections 1 and 2 shall take effect on the 15th day of October following the ratification of this article.

Section 6

This article shall be inoperative unless it shall have been ratified as an amendment to the Constitution by the legislatures of three-fourths of the several States within seven years from the date of submission.

AMENDMENT XXI. (1933)

Section 1

The eighteenth article of amendment to the Constitution of the United States is hereby repealed.

Section 2

The transportation or importation into any State, Territory, or possession of the United States for delivery or use therein of intoxicating liquors, in violation of the laws thereof, is hereby prohibited.

Section 3

This article shall be inoperative unless it shall have been ratified as an amendment to the Constitution by conventions in the several States, as provided in the Constitution, within seven years from the date of the submission hereof to the States by the Congress.

AMENDMENT XXII. (1951)

Section 1

No person shall be elected to the office of the President more than twice, and no person who has held the office of President, or acted as President, for more than two years of a term to which some other person was elected president shall be elected to the office of the President more than once. But this Article shall not apply to any person holding office of President when this Article was proposed by the Congress, and shall not prevent any person who may be holding the office of President, or acting as President, during the term within which this Article becomes operative from holding the office of President or acting as President during the remainder of such term.

Section 2

The article shall be inoperative unless it shall have been ratified as an amendment to the Constitution by the legislatures of three-fourths of the several States within seven years from the date of its submission to the States by the Congress.

AMENDMENT XXIII. (1961)

Section 1

The District constituting the seat of Government of the United States shall appoint in such manner as the Congress may direct:

A number of electors of President and Vice President equal to the whole number of Senators and Representatives in Congress to which the District would be entitled if it were a State, but in no event more than the least populous State; they shall be in addition to those appointed by the States, but they shall be considered, for the purposes of the election of President and Vice President, to be electors appointed by a State; and they shall meet in the District and perform such duties as provided by the twelfth article of amendment.

Section 2

The Congress shall have power to enforce this article by appropriate legislation.

AMENDMENT XXIV. (1964)

Section 1

The right of citizens of the United States to vote in any primary or other election for President or Vice President, for electors for President or Vice President, or for Senator or Representative in Congress, shall not be denied or abridged by the United States or any State by reason of failing to pay any poll tax or other tax.

Section 2

The Congress shall have power to enforce this article by appropriate legislation.

AMENDMENT XXV. (1967)

Section 1

In case of the removal of the President from office or of his death or resignation, the Vice President shall become President.

Section 2

Whenever there is a vacancy in the office of the Vice President, the President shall nominate a Vice President who shall take office upon confirmation by a majority vote of both Houses of Congress.

Section 3

Whenever the President transmits to the President pro tempore of the Senate and the Speaker of the House of Representatives his written declaration that he is unable to discharge the powers and duties of his office, and until he transmits to them a written declaration to the contrary, such powers and duties shall be discharged by the Vice President as Acting President.

Section 4

Whenever the Vice President and a majority of either the principal officers of the executive departments or of such other body as Congress may by law provide, transmit to the President pro tempore of the Senate and the Speaker of the House of Representatives their written declaration that the President is unable to discharge the powers and duties of his office, the Vice President shall immediately assume the powers and duties of the office as Acting President.

Thereafter, when the President transmits to the President pro tempore of the Senate and the Speaker of the House of Representatives his written declaration that no inability exists, he shall resume the powers and duties of his office unless the Vice President and a majority of either the principal officers of the executive department or of such other body as Congress may by law provide, transmit within four days to the President pro tempore of the Senate and the Speaker of the House of Representatives their written declaration that the President is unable to discharge the powers and duties of his office. Thereupon Congress shall decide the issue, assembling within forty-eight hours for that purpose if not in session. If the Congress, within twenty-one days after receipt of the latter written declaration, or, if Congress is not in session, within twenty-one days after Congress is required to assemble, determines by two-thirds vote of both Houses that the President is unable to discharge the powers and duties of his office, the Vice President shall continue to discharge the same as Acting President; otherwise, the President shall resume the powers and duties of his office.

AMENDMENT XXVI. (1971)

Section 1

The right of citizens of the United States, who are eighteen years of age or older, to vote shall not be denied or abridged by the United States or by any State on account of age.

Section 2

The Congress shall have power to enforce this article by appropriate legislation.

AMENDMENT XXVII. (1992)

No law, varying the compensation for the services of the Senators and Representatives, shall take effect, until an election of Representatives shall have intervened.

Photo Credits

Index